D1069317

PRACTICAL
CHRISTIAN
THEOLOGY

PRACTICAL CHRISTIAN THEOLOGY

Floyd H. Barackman

kregel
PUBLICATIONS

Grand Rapids, MI 49501

Practical Christian Theology, by Floyd H. Barackman.
© 1981, 1984, 1990, 1992 and published in 1992 by
Kregel Publications, a division of Kregel, Inc.
P. O. Box 2607, Grand Rapids, MI 49501. All rights
reserved.

Cover Design: Al Hartman

Library of Congress Cataloging-in-Publication Data

Barackman, Floyd H. (Floyd Hays)
    Practical Christian theology / Floyd Hays Barackman
        p.   cm.
    Includes bibliographical references and indexes.
    1. Theology, Doctrinal. I. Title.

BT75.2.B33   1992   230—dc20   92-21651
                                                                    CIP
ISBN   0-8254-2281-7 (pbk.)

                2 3 4 5 Printing/Year 96 95 94

Printed in the United States of America

To
my children
Ruth and Philip,
their spouses
Wilmer and Deborah,
and their posterity
this book is
affectionately dedicated.

CONTENTS

PREFACE

The Lord Jesus regards us who are saved through faith in His atoning work to be His friends (Jn. 15:15). Hence, He has made known to us through the Scriptures what the Father has revealed to Him (cp. 16:15). Ordinarily, a slaveholder would not feel obligated to tell his slaves the reasons for his instructions or to reveal to them his plans, but he might share these with a friend. Although we are the Lord's slaves by redemption, we are also His friends, particularly when we obey Him (15:14). Because of this, He has made known to us divine truth, which remains hidden from the world's understanding (I Cor. 2:7), so that we might live obedient, fruitful lives (Jn. 15:16; cp. Deut. 29:29).

The following pages present my understanding of the great doctrines of the Christian faith. Having been forged during more than two decades of classroom discussion, this understanding continues to grow as the Holy Spirit gives further insight into His truth. Although our understanding of divine things is incomplete, we who are saved can say that we know God's truth. Contrary to the epistemology of the world, spiritual understanding follows the acquisition of spiritual knowledge, which is received through faith in the canonical Scriptures (I Cor. 2:12; Heb. 11:3). For instance, from the Scriptures we know that the Lord Jesus was virgin born, yet we do not fully understand this unique event. Contrariwise, the world must understand a matter in order to know it, for their knowledge is acquired by the scientific method and requires empirical verification. For this reason, the world regards believers to be naive and unscientific when we claim infallible knowledge of divine things, based on inerrant divine revelation.

Beginners are surprised that there is no textbook that satisfactorily answers all theological questions and that good men differ in their understanding of spiritual truth. While all believers agree on what doctrines are Christian, they do not all have the same understanding of these teachings. Their differences of understanding spring from the fact that one's insight into divine truth is relative, being formed by his overall grasp of the Scriptures, religious training and conditioning, and other elements of life experience that affect one's understanding. Thus, I do not offer this work as being complete or final, but I trust that it will be used of God to give fresh insight into His truth and to stimulate its study. Theologically, its slant is toward a modified Calvinism that rejects limited atonement as well as Universalism — the doctrine that all people will finally be saved. Also, it recognizes the various dispensations that God has given to mankind.

It is impossible to give credit to all who have contributed toward my understanding of these doctrines. If the reader should come upon the thoughts of others, with or without new garb, he should give credit to whom it is due. Ultimately, all praise must be given to our God—the living and true God—who has been pleased to teach His people His self-revelation.

While many have encouraged me in this work, I wish to acknowledge two colleagues who are now with the Lord: Professor Urban F. Cline, who read the manuscript of the first edition, and Professor John L. Benson, who appraised many insights that are expressed in this third edition. Also, I wish to recognize my wife, Ella, whose constant support has done much to make this possible.

This work rests upon the staunch conviction that the Bible, consisting of the sixty-six canonical books, is the inerrant Word of God, that it was given in verbal form within the history of earthly place and time, and that its truth can be understood only as the student stands in a right relationship with God and as he is taught by the Holy Spirit. May it be the purpose of both author and reader not only to gain a greater understanding of God's unchanging truth but also to submit to its authority and allow it to govern our lives for His glory. Then, we shall show to the Lord Jesus that we are His friends (Jn. 15:14).

F.H.B.
Practical Bible Training School
Bible School Park, N.Y. 13737

Introduction

INTRODUCTION

Before beginning our study of the content of Christian systematic theology, we must consider the answers to several basic questions that are relevant to this subject: What are the requirements of this study? What is the meaning of Christian theology? Into what divisions is Christian theology usually divided? Why do we systematize Christian theology? What are the major parts of Christian systematic theology? What are the main beliefs of the major Protestant theological systems?

BASIC REQUIREMENTS TO STUDY CHRISTIAN THEOLOGY
- **We must be born again (Jn. 3:6-7).**

The new birth brings us the renewal of our inner human nature, including our mind, and the spiritual equipment that enable us to comprehend God's truth (cp. Eph. 4:17-21; I Cor. 2:12; I Jn. 2:20, 27; Heb. 11:3).

- **We must accept the divine authority and inerrancy of the Bible and the infallibility of its teachings (Jn. 17:17; II Tim. 3:15-16; Ps. 119:105).**

It is the creature's duty to receive God's Word and to align his thinking with what God says (Ps. 36:9; Rom. 3:4; cp. 1:18).

- **We must follow the inductive method of reasoning.**

This starts with the Scriptures and formulates doctrinal statements from them. By this method we consider the truths given in the Bible and derive from them specific theological principles and teachings (cp. Acts 17:11; II Tim. 3:16). This objective approach allows God to instruct us through His Word. Observe that the mind, renewed by the Holy Spirit and taught from the Word, is the doorway to spiritual understanding and experience (Rom. 12:2; Eph. 4:17-24; Ps. 1:1-3).

- **We must rely on the ministry of the Holy Spirit.**

He alone can give us right direction in theological study and clear understanding of God's truth (I Cor. 2:10-12). This requires our being yielded to Him and our responding favorably to this truth (Ps. 119:18; Lk. 8:18; Jn. 7:17; I Tim. 4:13-16; I Jn. 2:27).

- **We must seek to understand all that the Bible teaches about a subject and all the subjects that it teaches.**

It is our duty to learn and to minister the whole counsel of God (Acts 20:27).

THE MEANING OF THEOLOGY
- **Its Etymology**

The word *theology* is derived from the Greek words *theos* (meaning

"God") and *logos* (meaning "word," "discourse," or "doctrine"). Theology is a discourse or teaching about God and the things of God. It is the science of God.

• Its Definition

Christian theology may be defined in two ways: in a broad sense it is the whole scope of Christian doctrine, revealed in the Scriptures; in a narrow sense it is the Christian doctrine of God—Theology Proper.

Sometimes Christian theology is identified as *revealed theology*, based on truth that is revealed in the Bible. On the contrary, *natural theology* is a science of God that is based solely on what is revealed about Him in nature. The primary fault of natural theology is that it does not recognize any divine explanation of the things that make up nature or any revelation of the divine will for man.

THE DIVISIONS OF CHRISTIAN THEOLOGY

• Exegetical Theology

Being based on biblical interpretation, this theology concerns the study of the Scripture text. This division includes the study of biblical languages, biblical archaeology, biblical introduction, biblical theology, and Bible hermeneutics. Biblical theology seeks to arrange systematically the truth revealed within the various periods of the Old Testament (such as the Mosaic period, the monarchal period) and in the writings of the New Testament authors (such as the writings of John, the writings of Paul).

• Historical Theology

Being based on the history of doctrinal thought, this theology traces the origin, development, and spread of true Christian religion together with its doctrines, institutions, and practices. It covers biblical history, church history, the history of missions, the history of doctrine, and the history of creeds and confessions.

• Systematic Theology

Being derived from exegetical and historical theology, this arranges the Bible's teachings and man's explanation of them in logical order under the heads of theological study. In addition to the systematic arrangement of doctrine, this division also includes Christian apologetics, polemics and ethics.

• Practical Theology

Consisting of the practical application of theology, this seeks to use that which is contributed by the other divisions of Christian theology in the salvation, sanctification, edification, education, and service of the gospel believer. This division comprises homiletics, church organization and administration, worship, Christian education, the work of missions, and pastoral theology.

THE NEED FOR CHRISTIAN SYSTEMATIC THEOLOGY

Our need for a systematic form of Christian theology not only points to the practicality of theology but also motivates us in its study. This need is indicated by the following:

• **It is required by our minds.**

Our minds are not contented with an accumulation of facts. They seek to unify and systematize these facts by looking for the relation between them and arranging them in logical order. In our study of God, we not only learn what the Bible reveals about Him but we also organize this truth into a system. In this sense, theology is a science.

• **It is required by the organization of the Bible.**

The Bible is not formally organized into a systematic theology. It consists of a variety of literary forms, including history, poetry, prophetic utterances, biographical notes, and letters. The theological truth scattered throughout this literature must be gathered and assembled into a logical system. Although there are Scripture passages that extensively treat certain doctrines, none treats any doctrine completely. In this logical construction, we must take care that our deductions do not exceed what God has revealed.

• **It is required by life's questions and problems.**

The world must be shown that the Bible has the answers to basic questions about the universe which man's philosophy does not have, such as those about origin (Where did man come from?), meaning (What is man?), purpose (Why does man exist?), relation (How is man related to everything else that comprises the universe?) and destination (Where is man going?). Moreover, the Bible offers better solutions to human problems than what the world proposes. The Scriptures present a rational, full, consistent world view that agrees with man's essential nature. Meeting this need requires a systematic grasp and presentation of Christian theology (cp. I Pet. 3:15; II Tim. 3:15; I Cor. 1:18-25).

• **It is required for spiritual living.**

The concept that theology has a deadening effect upon our spiritual life is wrong. Right belief rightly influences behavior (Prov. 23:7; Mt. 7:15-20). Christian theology teaches us the kind of life we are to live (II Tim. 3:16-17) motivates us to live this way (cp. Eph. 4:1 ff. with chs. 1-3; Col. 3:1 ff. with chs. 1, 2; Rom. 12:1 ff. with chs. 5-8), and shows us how to live it (Phil. 4:13).

• **It is required for Christian service.**

The Lord Jesus and His apostles taught doctrine (Mk. 4:2; Acts 2:42; II Tim. 3:10), and His people are exhorted to do the same (Mt. 28:19-20; Tit. 1:9; II Tim. 2:2; 4:2). Christian theology teaches us the nature, resources, and operation of Christian services as well as the need to which we are to minister.

THE MAJOR PARTS OF CHRISTIAN SYSTEMATIC THEOLOGY

Bibliology .... the doctrine of the Scriptures
Theology Proper .... the doctrine of God
Paterology .... the doctrine of God the Father
Christology .... the doctrine of God the Son
Pneumatology .... the doctrine of God the Holy Spirit
Angelology .... the doctrine of angels
Anthropology .... the doctrine of man
Hamartiology .... the doctrine of sin
Soteriology .... the doctrine of salvation
Ecclesiology .... the doctrine of church
Eschatology .... the doctrine of future, prophetic events

MAJOR PROTESTANT THEOLOGICAL SYSTEMS

While it is primarily important for us to seek to understand what the Bible teaches about various theological subjects, we cannot ignore the theological systems which were developed during and after the Reformation era and upon which much systematic theology rests. A summary of these systems follows:

• Calvinism

Calvinism is that system of theology which grew out of the study and writings of the Genevan reformer, John Calvin (1509-1564). Essentially, this is the development and Protestant form of the teachings of Augustine (353-430).

Holding the Bible to be the Word of God, Calvinism seeks to build its system on the Scriptures. Its basic doctrine is the total sovereignty of God. Recognizing human responsibility, it associates this with the comprehensive plan of God. Obedience to God is man's supreme duty. While this was possible before the fall, it can now be only by God's sovereign grace. In Christ God redeems only the elect. The church, the ordinances of baptism and the Lord's Supper, and civil government are divine institutions. This is the theology of the Reformed, Congregational, and Presbyterian churches.

• Arminianism

Arminianism is that system of theology which grew out of the study and writings of the Dutch theologian, Jacob Arminius, the Latin form of James Harmensen (1560-1609). He protested against the extreme form of Calvinism that prevailed at the close of the 16th century and which was defended by Theodore Beza (1519-1605). Arminius saw what he believed were two great errors in Calvinism: one, it made God the author of sin; and two, it did away with genuine human freedom.

In their discussions with their opponents, the Arminians rejected five points of the Calvinist's theological system, for they believed that these points were not taught in the Scriptures. They set forth their own position in the five articles of their "Remonstrance" of 1610.

The two positions are contrasted in the following:

Calvinism	Arminianism
(1) Total depravity as to ability and merit to gain salvation.	(1) By divine grace all men have the capacity for good and the energy of free will.
(2) Unconditional election. God's choice of whom He would save was not determined by anything in man.	(2) Election and condemnation were conditioned upon foreseen faith or unbelief of men.
(3) Limited atonement. Christ's atoning death applies only to the elect.	(3) Atonement for all, but only believers enjoy its benefits.
(4) Irresistible grace. The elect cannot successfully resist being drawn to God in salvation.	(4) Resistible grace. Divine grace can be resisted to one's damnation.
(5) Perseverance of the saints. Because they persist in faith, they cannot lose salvation.	(5) Perseverance is open to inquiry.

Regarding the fifth point, Philip Schaff adds, "On this point the disciples of Arminius went further and taught the possibility of a total and final fall of believers from grace...They moreover denied, with the Roman Catholics, that anybody can have a certainty of salvation except by special revelation."[1]

The student must beware of the logic of Calvinism which sometimes leads to conclusions that go beyond what God has revealed in His Word. Also, he must beware of the reasonableness of Arminianism which sometimes seeks to establish doctrine on purely human concepts contrary to what God has revealed.

With a note of moderation, Philip Schaff (German Reformed) writes, "Calvinism emphasizes divine sovereignty and free grace; Arminianism emphasizes human responsibility. The one restricts the saving grace to the elect; the other extends it to all men on the condition of faith. Both are right in what they assert; both are wrong in what they deny. If one important truth is pressed to the exclusion of another truth of equal importance, it becomes an error, and loses its hold upon the conscience. The Bible gives us a theology which is more human than Calvinism and more divine than Arminianism, and more Christian than either of them."[2]

---

[1] Philip Schaff, *The Creeds of Christendom* (Grand Rapids: Baker Bookhouse, n.d.), I, 519. See pp. 509-23 for a fuller discussion.

In our theological studies it is impossible to avoid a position that is to some degree either Calvinistic or Arminian. But as I see it, our purpose should be to strive for a position that is as objectively biblical as possible rather than to conform to some theological system.

• Lutheranism

While accepting the three ancient ecumenical creeds (the Apostles', the Nicene, and the Athanasian), Lutheranism differs from Calvinism in that it teaches the necessity of water baptism for salvation, the real presence of Christ's body and blood "in, with, and under" the bread and cup of the Lord's Supper, and the qualities of Christ's divine nature as belonging to His human nature. It differs from Arminianism further in that it teaches total depravity, the bondage of the will to sin, and an unconditional predestination of the elect unto everlasting life.[3]

• Anglicanism

While neither Roman Catholic nor Calvinistic, Anglicanism continues to preserve old English catholicism, rejecting the peculiar errors and abuses of Rome and holding royal supremacy in ecclesiastical as well as civil matters.[4] Calvinistic elements persist in the evangelical section of the Church of England.

Observe that the doctrinal position of large segments of the Protestant church is stated in their historical creeds: Lutheranism in the Augsburg Confession (1530), Anglicanism in the Thirty-nine Articles (1571), Presbyterianism and early Congregationalism in the Westminster Confession of Faith (1646), and Methodism in the Twenty-five Articles of Religion (1784). Historically, Baptists have not had a common doctrinal creed, but they have universally adhered to certain principles that make them distinctive (see Appendix P) and have been willing to express their doctrinal convictions in regional confessions of faith (cp. The Philadelphia Confession of Faith, 1742; The New Hampshire Confession, 1833).

---

[2] Philip Schaff, *History of the Christian Church* (New York: Charles Scribner's Son, 1910) VIII, 815 f.
[3] Philip Schaff, "Lutheran Church," in *Schaff-Herzog Encyclopaedia of Religious Knowledge* (New York: Funk & Wagnalls Company, 1891), II, 1370 f.
[4] Philip Schaff, *The Creeds of Christendom*, I, 622 f.

A Review of the Introduction

1. What are the basic requirements for the study of Christian theology?
2. Why must we rely on the Holy Spirit for an understanding of Christian theology?
3. Define Christian theology in its broad and narrow senses.
4. Briefly explain exegetical, historical, systematic, and practical theologies.
5. Why is Christian systematic theology required by our minds, the organization of the Bible, and life's questions and problems?
6. How does Christian systematic theology relate to spiritual living and Christian service?
7. List the major parts of Christian systematic theology.
8. List the five points of Calvinism to which the Arminians objected.
9. What was the Arminian position on these points?
10. Of what should the student beware regarding Calvinism and Arminianism?
11. How does Lutheranism differ from Calvinism and Arminianism?
12. In what way is the Baptist denomination different from others?
13. List the Baptist distinctives.
14. Have you been born again?

Bibliology

BIBLIOLOGY
The Doctrine of the Bible

Although the doctrine of the holy Scriptures—the sixty-six canonical books of the Bible—belongs with that of God's special revelation, it seems better to look at this before Theology Proper. The importance of this study is indicated by the Bible's being the basis of Christian belief and conduct and the special means by which God makes Himself and His will known to mankind. One's belief about the Bible fashions his view of God and the Christian faith.

THE CONTENT OF THE BIBLE

Being His special revelation (in contrast to His general revelation through nature), the Bible is God's message to man. It is His speaking (Heb. 1:1-2); it is His Word, formed by His breath (II Tim. 3:16). By the Scriptures God tells all that He thinks is necessary for mankind to know about Himself. Also, by the Scriptures He gives us information about the universe—its origin, meaning, purpose, unity, and destiny—which man cannot discover in any other way (see Heb. 11:3; I Cor. 2:7-13).

The dominant theme of the Scriptures is the Lord Jesus Christ, God's promised Saviour (Lk. 24:27, 44; Jn. 1:45, 5:39; Mt. 1:21; Gen. 3:15). The Lord's atoning work was anticipated in the Old Testament by prophecy (Isa. 52:13-53:12) and types (the Levitical offerings), was accomplished in the Gospels by His death and resurrection, was applied to them who received Him in the Acts, was explained in the Epistles, and was consummated in the Revelation, which deals with His second coming, millennial rule, and the beginning of the eternal state.

THE MAJOR DIVISIONS OF THE BIBLE

These divisions are the Old Testament and the New Testament. A better word for "testament" is "covenant." God's covenants are His solemn declarations to certain people of what He promises to do.

THE OLD TESTAMENT
- **Its Meaning**
The Old Testament derived its name from the covenant that God made with Israel at Mt. Sinai (Ex. 19:1-8; 24:8). Early Christians gave to this part of the Bible this title because the statement of this covenant and the history of Israel's relation to God under this covenant make up almost all of this section of the Bible (Exodus ch. 19 through Malachi ch. 4). These thirty-nine books were written during the period 1446-430 B.C.

- **Its Arrangement**

In our English Bible the arrangement of the thirty-nine books follows that of the Greek *Septuagint* and the Latin *Vulgate*. This appears to have been governed by content.

A helpful analysis follows:[1]

History		Teaching		Prophecy	
Legislative[2]	Executive[2]	Poetry	Wisdom	Major[2]	Minor[2]
Genesis	Joshua	Job	Proverbs	Isaiah	Hosea
through	through	Psalms	Ecclesiastes	Jeremiah	through
Deuteronomy	Esther	Song of		Ezekiel	Malachi
		Solomon		Daniel	
		Lamentations			

- **Its Value**

The Old Testament's value is indicated by the following:

1. It was the Bible of our Lord and His apostles (Mt. 5:17-18; Lk. 24:27; Acts 17:2).

2. It is the foundation of the New Testament:

a. Regarding its basic teachings such as the unity and holiness of God (Deut. 6:4; Isa. 6:1-5; 57:15), the creation of the universe (Gen. ch. 1), the fall of man (Gen. ch. 3), and justification by faith (Gen. 15:6).

b. Regarding prophecies about the Lord Jesus Christ that are fulfilled in the New Testament (cp. Mt. 1:22-23).

c. Regarding God's program for the world, which comes to a climax in Christ's work as described in the New Testament (Ps. 2; Isa. 2:1-5; Rev. 19:11 — 20:15).

3. It contains a wealth of material that promotes devotional and spiritual growth, such as the Psalms, the biographical portions, and the wisdom passages (Rom. 15:4; I Cor. 10:11).

4. It presents many details of Christ's earthly, millennial rule which are not repeated in the New Testament (cp. Isa. 11:1-9). However, there is nothing revealed in the Old Testament about His present work of building the church (Eph. 3:1-11).

5. It presents the history of God's dealings with Israel, the reasons for their existence, and their future restoration to God and to their land.[3]

---

[1] W. G. Scroggie, *The Unfolding Drama of Redemption* (London: Pickering & Inglis Ltd., 1953), I, 27. Mr. Scroggie places Job with the wisdom books, but later he says that it is "a poetical treatment of historical facts" (p. 93).

[2] "Legislative" refers to the giving of the Mosaic Law; "executive" to carrying out the law in the life of Israel. The "major" and "minor" prophetic books are described as such for their length. For instance, Daniel has 357 verses in the KJV and Zechariah has 211 verses.

[3] Some reasons for Israel's existence are these: to bear witness to God's reality and unity, to demonstrate the blessing of serving the true God, to be the writers and guardians of the Old Testament, to give birth to the Saviour, and in time to be the channel of divine blessing to the world (Rom. 3:2; 9:4, 5; 11:13-18; Jn. 4:22).

THE NEW TESTAMENT

• Its Meaning

The New Testament received its name from the New Covenant, which replaced the old Covenant of the Mosaic Law (Heb. 10:9; 8:6-13; II Cor. 3:6-14). The New Covenant was predicted in Jeremiah 31:31-34 and was brought into force by Christ's death and resurrection (Lk. 22:20; Heb. 9:15). This section of the Bible not only tells us about Jesus' atoning work which made the New Covenant effective, but it also elaborates on the covenant's promises and states God's will (the Dispensation of Grace) for them who are its recipients. The twenty-seven New Testament books were written during the period A.D. 45-95.

• Its Arrangement

Again, the arrangement of the twenty-seven books of the New Testament in our English Bible follows the order of the Greek and Latin versions, which also appears to have been governed by content. The four Gospels were brought together into a collection, called "The Gospels." Also, the writings of Paul were gathered under the title, "The Apostle." In time "The Acts of the Apostles" became the link between the two collections, and there were added the writings of other apostles and apostolic men (men closely associated with the apostles), which were recognized as having divine authority.[4]

The arrangement of the New Testament is similar to that of the Old Testament:[1]

History		Teaching		Prophecy[5]
Of Christ	Of Church	Pauline	General	Apocalyptic
The Gospel according to —	The Acts of the Apostles	The Epistle of Paul to — churches	The Epistle to — Hebrews	Revelation
Matthew		Romans	The	
Mark		Corinthians (2)	Epistles	
Luke		Galatians	of —	
John		Ephesians	James	
		Philippians	Peter (2)	
		Colossians	John (3)	
		Thessalonians (2)	Jude	
		friends		
		Timothy (2)		
		Titus		
		Philemon		

---

4 See F. F. Bruce, *The Books and the Parchments* (London: Pickering & Inglis Ltd., 1963) pp. 107-13.
5 There are two kinds of divine prophecy: one, any communication from God by words through a divinely inspired person; two, any divine prediction or vision of future events.

- **Its Value**

The value of the New Testament is indicated by the following:

1. It fulfills or anticipates the fulfillment of all that was foreshadowed by Old Testament types and predicted in Old Testament prophecies (Mt. 5:17-18; Lk. 18:31; 21:22; Rom. 16:25-26).

2. It presents the Founder and content of real Christianity (Lk. 1:1-4; John 14:6; 16:12-15; Eph. 4:20-21; II Thess. 2:15; II Pet. 3:1-2).

3. It tells how sinners may be saved and come into a right relation with God (Jn. 3:16-18, 36; Rom. 3:9-26; Eph. 2:1-10).

4. It presents God's will for His people who are living in the present Church Age (cp. Gal. 6:2). This divine will for Christians is called the Dispensation of Grace.

5. It presents Christ's program for the present age (the building of His church; Mt. 16:18; Acts) and the events associated with His second coming to earth (Mt. ch. 24; Rev. chs. 4-20; II Thess. ch. 2).

THE INSPIRATION OF THE BIBLE

We shall now look at how the Word of God was produced. As we do, there are three theological terms that we must distinguish. These are revelation, illumination, and inspiration. *Revelation* refers either to God's activity of making known His truth (Gal. 1:12; Eph. 3:3; I Cor. 2:9-10) or to the truth that He has revealed (Rev. 1:1). On the other hand, *illumination* concerns God's activity of giving to us understanding of His truth (I Cor. 2:11-12; I Jn. 2:20, 27; Eph. 1:17-18). In contrast to these terms, *inspiration* has to do with the production of God's truth in human words, whether spoken or written (I Cor. 2:13; II Pet. 1:21; II Tim. 3:16). It is to this last divine work that we direct our attention.

FALSE THEORIES OF INSPIRATION

It will help us to understand the doctrine of the divine inspiration of the Scriptures if we first examine several theories that are untrue. These show us what divine inspiration is not.

- **Natural Inspiration**

This states that the Bible was written by men who had a high order of genius or creativity, as that which belongs to poets, musicians, and others with creative ability.

My objection to this theory is that it would make the Scriptures the product of men and subject to human error. *The true view* of inspiration is that it is the work of God the Holy Spirit in and through men (II Pet. 1:21).

- **Universal or Mystical Inspiration**

This holds that the Bible writers were inspired in the same way, though to a fuller degree, as Holy Spirit filled men today are inspired when they prepare a message or preach a sermon.

My objection to this theory is that it fails to distinguish between the *prophet* who under inspiration spoke the Word of God and the *preacher* who proclaims the Word of God by interpreting it and applying it to the needs of his listeners. Involving human understanding, this theory would make the Scriptures subject to human error. *The true view* of inspiration is that it was a particular work of the Holy Spirit in and through certain men whom He filled (II Pet. 1:21; I Pet. 1:10, 11). His inspiring men is not the same as His filling them or illuminating them.

- **Inspired Concept Inspiration**

This teaches that God gave His spokesmen and Bible writers thoughts or ideas of divine truth and allowed them to express these in their own words as they remembered and understood them.

I object to this theory, for it would make the Bible a human product and subject to human error. *The true view* holds that divine inspiration is verbal, extending to each word of Scripture and to the grammatical form of each word (II Pet. 1:20; I Cor. 2:13; cp. Jn. 10:34-36; Gal. 3:16; Mt. 5:18).

- **Variable Inspiration**

This theory says that some parts of the Bible are more inspired than other inspired parts, whereas other parts are not inspired at all.

I object to this theory on two counts: One, the nature of divine inspiration is such that it does not admit degrees; it is absolute—either a text is inspired or it is not. Two, unaided man is not capable of judging whether or not a text is inspired. *The true view* teaches that divine inspiration is plenary, extending to every part of the Bible to an equal degree (II Tim. 3:16). While some parts of the Bible are more "inspiring" (exerting an animating influence upon the reader), all parts are uniformly inspired to the same degree.

- **Dictation Inspiration**

This theory holds that every word of Scripture was dictated by God and that the writers recorded these words as a stenographer would do.

My objections to this theory are that it does not account for the characteristic style of the writers and that dictation does not protect from error in the hearing and recording of words. *The true view* of divine inspiration is that the Holy Spirit incorporated the writer's literary style, vocabulary, individuality, intelligence, and temperament and produced through him the very words of God. When portions of the Bible were dictated in their production, divine inspiration governed both speaker and writer (cp. Jer. 36:4; Rom. 16:22).

THE TRUE VIEW OF INSPIRATION

Although this has been briefly stated under false theories of inspiration, the true doctrine of divine inspiration may be summarized as follows: The *Scriptures* are inspired in the sense that they are the product of God's breath, that is, a special work of the Holy Spirit (II Tim. 3:16). The *speakers and writers* of God's words were inspired in the sense that they were acted upon by the Holy Spirit to produce God's truth in human language (II Pet. 1:21). Let us look more closely at what the inspiration of the Scriptures really is.

- **Definitions**

Divine inspiration is the activity of the Holy Spirit whereby He enabled certain humans to receive God's special revelation and to speak it or write it in their language and style, without error or omission, as the very words of God (II Pet. 1:21).

Plenary inspiration means that every part of the sixty-six canonical books of the Bible is the product of divine inspiration to an equal degree (II Tim. 3:16).

Verbal inspiration means that divine inspiration extends to every word of the Scriptures and to its grammatical form (cp. Gal. 3:16).

- **Observations**

1. Inspiration concerns God's spokesmen only when they spoke or wrote His Word. It does not relate to their other actions and words (cp. II Sam. 7:3).

2. Under divine inspiration the speakers and writers of God's Word not only were kept from every error of communication but also from any omission. Their utterances and writings were complete and accurate within their divinely determined limits. Moreover, they did not say or write more than what God intended for them to do.

3. While God did not approve every action or statement of angels and humans recorded in the Scriptures, divine inspiration secured an inerrant biblical record of their actions and utterances.

4. Our inability to understand how the Holy Spirit used fallible men to produce an inerrant record is not sufficient reason to deny His ability to do this and the fact that He did do this. Indeed, we do not fully understand any work of the Holy Spirit, such as the new birth.

5. Divine inspiration relates only to the original utterances and writings of God's spokesmen and writers. Our translations and copies of the Scriptures have both real and apparent errors. *Real errors* are mistakes that entered the text when it was copied (cp. II Chron. 36:9 with II Kings 24:8, "eight" for "eighteen"), translated (S. of Sol. 3:5, "he" for "she"), or printed (Mt. 23:24, "at" for "out"). Also, there are recited errors which God included in His Word for our learning (cp. Gen. 3:4). The science of textual criticism has discovered most scribal errors. *Apparent errors* are not real errors but difficulties that rise from our present lack of knowledge regarding the

---

[6] For a discussion of the inerrancy and infallibility of the Scriptures, see Appendix S.

languages of the original text or the cultural and historical background of the text.

The Holy Spirit has so overruled the transmission of the Scriptures that present copies are virtually infallible in their teachings. Although they are not actually inspired, good copies of the inspired original writings and good translations of these copies are virtually inspired and are adequate for the divine purpose for which they have been preserved. For all practical purposes, we can unhesitatingly say that we have the inspired Word of God, which is infallible in its teachings, insofar as these translations convey the truth of the original writings.

6. Because of the sufficiency of the Bible for belief and conduct and the suggestion of such references as Proverbs 30:5-6; I Corinthians 13:8 and Revelation 22:18, 19, it appears that no special revelation has been given since the close of the New Testament Canon at the end of the first century. Consisting of sixty-six canonical books, the Bible is the complete written revelation of God. It is noteworthy that the world's religions and cults are doctrinally based on alleged extra revelation, in addition to or in place of the Bible.

7. The Bible teaches that divine special revelation had its source in God the Father (Rev. 1:1), was clothed in human language by the Holy Spirit's work in men (I Cor. 2:13; II Pet. 1:21), and was transmitted through God's spokesmen as the very words of God (Deut. 18:18; Heb. 1:1-2). Being the Revelator of the Father (Mt. 11:27), the Lord Jesus not only spoke the Father's words but also manifested by His earthly life the Father's character and works (Jn. 12:49-50; 1:14; 14:9-11). Furthermore, having received the New Testament revelation from the Father, He conveyed it to His apostles and their associates by the Holy Spirit (Jn. 16:13-15; I Cor. 2:13; Eph. 4:20-21; Rev. 1:1).

8. God rarely spoke through unsaved people (II Chron. 35:21-22; Jn. 11:49-51).

THE BIBLE'S TESTIMONY TO ITS OWN INSPIRATION

In addition to such supporting evidence as the confirmation of Christian experience and the verification of logic in the law of contradiction (the Scriptures cannot be inspired and not inspired at the same time), there is the witness of the Scriptures to their own inspiration (II Tim. 3:16).

• The Inspiration of the Old Testament

Although not every book in the Old Testament bears specific witness to its own inspiration, each one belongs to a section which does give this testimony. Following the arrangement of the Hebrew Old Testament, there are three of these sections (Lk. 24:44): *the Law* (Torah), consisting of the five books of Moses (the Pentateuch); *the Prophets* (Nebhiim), consisting of the "Early Prophets" (Joshua, Judges, I and II Samuel, I and II Kings), and the "Latter Prophets" (Isaiah, Jeremiah, Ezekiel, the Twelve); and *the Writings* (Kethubhim), consisting of the poetical books—*Psalms, Proverbs, and Job; the*

"Rolls"—Song of Solomon, Ruth, Lamentations, Ecclesiastes, and Esther; and the historical books—Daniel, Ezra-Nehemiah, I and II Chronicles.

This arrangement appears to be based on the prophetic rank of the writer. First, there are the writings of Moses, the greatest of the prophets, with whom the LORD spoke face to face (Ex. 33:11; Num. 12:7-8; Deut. 34:10). Next there are the writings of those who were professional prophets, such as Isaiah and Jonah. Finally, there are the writings of those who had the prophetic gift but who followed other vocations, such as David and Daniel.

1. *THE TESTIMONY OF THE OLD TESTAMENT WRITERS*

Certain writers of each section of the Hebrew Old Testament bear witness to their own inspiration: Moses (Ex. 20:1; 32:16; Lev. 27:34; Num. 36:13), the Prophets (Josh. 24:26-27; I Sam. 3:18-19; Isa. 1:1-2; Jer. 1:1-2; Ezek. 1:3), and the Writings (Ps. 45:1; Eccles. 1:16; 12:9). They also regarded other portions of the Old Testament as being inspired: the Law (I Kings 2:3), the Prophets (Neh. 9:20; Dan. 9:2, 10), and the Writings (II Sam. 23:1-2; I Kings 4:29-32).

2. *THE TESTIMONY OF JESUS*

The Lord's regard for the Old Testament is a powerful witness to its inspiration.

a. He recognized the whole Old Testament (Jn. 5:39; Lk. 24:44-46) as well as its three sections (Mk. 7:8-13; Mt. 13:13-14; Jn. 10:34-35) as Scripture.

b. In His recorded utterances there are references to fourteen Old Testament books: Genesis (Mk. 10:6-8), Exodus (Lk. 18:20), Numbers (Jn. 3:14), Deuteronomy and Leviticus (Lk. 10:26-28), I Samuel (Mk. 2:25), I Kings (Mt. 12:42), Psalms (Mk. 12:10), Isaiah (Lk. 4:17-21), Daniel (Mt. 24:15), Hosea (Mt. 9:13), Jonah (Mt. 12:40), Zechariah (Mt. 26:31), and Malachi (Mt. 11:10).

c. He believed the historicity of such persons and events as Abel (Lk. 11:51), Noah and the flood (Mt. 24:37-39), Moses (Jn. 3:14), David (Lk. 20:41), Jonah and the fish (Mt. 12:40), man's creation and the divine institution of marriage (Mt. 19:4-7), and Daniel (Mt. 24:15).

d. He readily submitted Himself to the authority of the Old Testament (Mt. 5:17; 26:54; Lk. 18:31). Although He broke Jewish traditional law when it conflicted with the Father's will (cp. Jn. 9:16), He never violated God's law as given in the Old Testament (Mt. 3:17; 5:17; 17:5; Jn. 8:29).

e. He had complete trust in the teachings of the Old Testament. This is indicated by His appealing to God's will when He was tempted (Mt. 4:4, 7, 10), His referring to God's statement regarding marriage (Mt. 19:4-6), and His reference to the doctrine of the resurrection (Mt. 22:29-32).

f. He declared that Scripture cannot be broken (Jn. 10:35). In context, the Lord said that the Scripture, which He identified as the Word of God, cannot be annulled as though its declarations were untrue.

3. *THE TESTIMONY OF NEW TESTAMENT WRITERS*

In addition to the witness of Jesus in the Gospels, several New Testament writers give evidence for the inspiration of the Old Testament.

a. They quote from or allude to all of the Old Testament books except the Song of Solomon.[7]

b. They call the Old Testament "Scripture" (Lk. 24:27, 44-45; Acts 17:11; 18:24; Rom. 1:2), even declaring that it is "God-breathed" (II Tim. 3:16).

c. They refer to each section of the Hebrew Old Testament as being God's Word: the Law (Rom. 10:5-7, 17), the Prophets (Rom. 9:25; Heb. 10:15), and the Writings (Acts 1:15-16; 4:24-26).

- **The Inspiration of the New Testament**
  The inspiration of the New Testament books rests upon the authority of Christ and that which He delegated to His apostles (John 3:34-35; 12:49-50; Rom. 12:3; 15:15, 16; I Cor. 14:37; II Cor. 5:20; 13:10; Gal. 1:1, 11-12; I Thess. 5:27; II Pet. 3:1-2).[8] Our Lord testified to His own prophetic ministry (Jn. 3:11, 34; 7:15-17; 8:28; 12:49-50; 14:10, 24). The apostles regarded their message as being from God (Gal. 1:11, 12; Acts 1:2-3), as being the Word of God (I Pet. 1:25; I Thess. 2:13), and as being equal to that of the Old Testament prophets (II Pet. 3:1-2). With this in view, let us examine the testimonies of Jesus and the apostles regarding the New Testament writings.

  1. *THE TESTIMONY OF THE LORD JESUS*

  Jesus anticipated His giving the New Testament revelation when He spoke to His apostles about His later communicating to them "many things" which they could not then bear (Jn. 16:12-15). He indicated that He would do this by the Holy Spirit, to whom He would give the truth which He himself would receive from the Father. That the New Testament had its origin in our Lord's prophetic ministry is further suggested by Acts 1:1; Ephesians 4:20-21; and Revelation 1:1-2. Upon His return to Heaven, Jesus received it from the Father and communicated it to His apostles and apostolic men by inspiration of the Holy Spirit.

  2. *THE TESTIMONY OF NEW TESTAMENT WRITERS*

  John testifies to the inspiration of his writings in John 21:24, I John 5:6-13; Revelation 1:1-2; 21:5; 22:9. Paul bears witness to his own writings in I Thessalonians 4:2, 15; I Corinthians 2:13; 14:37; II Corinthians 2:17, and to Luke's writings in I Timothy 5:18 (cp. Lk. 10:7 with Deut. 25:4). Also, Peter speaks of the inspiration of his writings in II Peter 3:1-2 and of Paul's in II Peter 3:15-16. Finally, Jude bears witness to Peter's writings in verses 17 and 18 (cp. II Pet. 3:5).

  This witness to the inspiration of the Bible may not be convincing to the unsaved, whose understanding is affected by their sinful state and their bent toward protecting their autonomy (cp. Rom. 1:18; 8:7; Jn. 5:40; 3:19-

---

[7] Kurt Aland, Matthew Black, Bruce M. Metzger, and Allen Wikgren, eds., *The Greek New Testament* (London: United Bible Societies, 1966), p. 897 ff.

[8] Clark H. Pinnock, *Biblical Revelation — The Foundation of Christian Theology* (Chicago: Moody Press, 1971), pp. 63-66.

20; I Cor. 2:14). But to us who are saved it is sufficient for our belief and conduct (Ps. 119:105; II Tim. 3:15-17).

THE AUTHORITY OF THE BIBLE

Springing from the truth of the inspiration of the Bible is that of its authority. These truths go hand in hand. If the Scriptures are not God's Word, then they do not bear His authority in matters of faith and behavior. But since they are His Word, they inherently possess His authority as His speaking.

ITS DEFINITION

The authority of the Bible has been described as that property by which the Scriptures demand faith in and obedience to all of their declarations.[9] Being God's Word, the Scriptures inherently possess the right to command and to enforce obedience to their revelation of His will for mankind, both the lost and the saved. This right is the Bible's authority.

ITS EVIDENCE

The fact of the Bible's authority is manifest in the following:

* **The Character of the Bible**

Being God's Word, the Bible possesses many divine attributes (cp. Ps. 19:7-9; 119:39, 43, 62, 86, 89; Jn. 17:17; Heb. 4:12; I Pet. 1:25) and is involved in the works of God (Heb. 4:12; Jn. 5:45; 12:48; II Tim. 3:15; I Pet. 1:23).

* **The Inspiration of the Bible**

Being the inspired Word of God, the Bible is God's authoritative communication to man (II Tim. 3:16; Heb. 1:1-2). This authority is manifest in the Old Testament by the recurring phrase, "Thus saith the LORD." It is also manifest in the New Testament by the authority expressed by Christ's utterances (Mt. 11:27; 7:28-29; Jn. 12:49-50) and by His apostles, who spoke as His official representatives (Jn. 20:21-23; Mt. 28:18-20; I Thess. 2:13; II Pet. 3:2; Rev. 21:5).

* **The Submission of Jesus to the Scriptures**

Although the Lord possessed all authority (Mt. 28:18), exercised authority (Lk. 4:33-36), and taught with authority (Mt. 7:28-29), He appealed to the authority of the Old Testament Scriptures (Jn. 5:45-47; Mt. 23:23). He also submitted Himself to their authority in His life and work (cp. Mt. 5:17; 26:52-56; Lk. 18:31-33).

---

[9] D. Martyn Lloyd-Jones, "The Authority of the Scriptures," *Eternity Magazine*, Vol. 8, No. 4 (1957), 39.

- **The Recognition of the Apostles**

  The apostles recognized the authority of the Scriptures, both the Old Testament (II Tim. 3:16; Acts 2:14-36; Rom. 3:9-22) and the New Testament (I Thess. 2:13; II Pet. 3:2).

ITS APPLICATION

This authority applies to all the areas of which the Bible speaks. It is the final authority in matters of history and science as well as belief and conduct. Since the Scriptures express God's truth and will with His authority, then it is the duty of all people to submit themselves to these by receiving and obeying His Word. This response to His Word exhibits our love for Him (Jn. 14:15, 21, 23).

THE CANONICITY OF THE BIBLE

Canonicity concerns the right of any literature to be accepted as the Word of God. *Canon*, derived from the Hebrew word for reed and often used for measuring distance, refers to the *standard* that a literary work must pass before it is recognized by believers as Scripture and to the *collection* of books that meet this standard. Let us consider, in reverse order, these two ideas associated with canon.

THE FORMATION OF THE CANON OF SCRIPTURE

Here we are thinking of canon as a collection of books — the sixty- six books which comprise the Bible. The formation of the canons of the Old and New Testaments followed their production under divine inspiration and their being recognized by the Lord's people as His Word.

- **The Old Testament Canon**

  As these books were written, they were immediately recognized as being inspired of God and were deposited at the side of the ark of the covenant, first in the tabernacle and later in the temple, along with the accumulative store of holy writings (Deut. 17:18; 31:9, 24-26; I Sam. 10:25; II Kings 22:8; II Chron. 34:14). The priests of Israel cared for these sacred writings and made new copies when they were needed (Deut. 17:18).

  When the temple in Jerusalem was destroyed in 587 B.C., the holy writings were carried to Babylon (cp. Dan. 9:2). Later, they were restored to their place in the second temple (cp. Ezra 7:6; Neh. 8:1; Jer. 27:21-22). The Old Testament Canon was completed about 430 B.C., with Nehemiah and Malachi being the last to write. There was no further prophetic voice heard in Israel until that of John the Baptist, about A.D. 26 (Lk. 3:1-2).

- **The New Testament Canon**

  Since there was no central place where these books were kept, the extent of their collection varied in different localities. The New Testament Canon closed with the writings of the apostle John at the end of the first century, but it was not until the fifth century that the whole New Testament Canon was universally received by the churches. This was due, in part, to the slow circulation of these books and to the wide distribution of Christian churches. In the West the canonicity of *Hebrews* was debated because of its uncertain authorship. In the East there was opposition to *Revelation* because its authorship was questioned and its millennialism was challenged. In the West the Synods of Hippo (393) and of Carthage (397) recognized the canonicity of the twenty-seven books of the New Testament. The matter was settled in the East later.

Several factors helped to form the New Testament Canon: one, the influence of the incomplete canon of the heretic Marcion, a native of Asia Minor who went to Rome in A.D. 140; two, the appearance of a number of non-canonical writings (see Appendix T), which were held by many to be canonical; and three, the edict of the Roman emperor Diocletian (303) that the Scriptures be destroyed. This led to the sifting of the books that were to be preserved. Influenced by these factors, the early believers were motivated to judge what literature was truly inspired of God.

THE TESTS OF CANONICITY

Throughout the time when the canonical books of the Bible were written and afterward, other literature was produced which was asserted to be the word of God (cp. Lk. 1:1-3; II Thess. 2:1-5; see Appendix T). This led godly believers to develop certain tests, based on the canonical books of the Bible, by which to judge the validity of these claims. The application of these tests does not impart canonicity, for the canonicity of any literature is determined by God. However, these tests enable us to recognize whether or not any literature is canonical. They follow in question form.

- **The Test of Divine Inspiration**
  Does the book claim to be divinely inspired? Is it inspired?

- **The Test of Human Authorship**
  Is the book written, edited, or endorsed by an accredited agent of God, such as a prophet, the Lord Jesus Christ, or one of His apostles? If not, did the writer have the gift of prophecy (David, Daniel) or a relation to a prophet or an apostle (Mark, Luke) that would raise his book to the level of their writings?

- **The Test of Genuineness**
  Can the book be traced back to the time and/or the writer from whom it professes to have come? This concerns the manuscript evidence of the book.

Can the book be shown to have content that agrees with the time of which it speaks or in which it was written? This concerns the book's historicity. Archaeological discovery has revealed much about the history and culture of biblical times and has repeatedly shown the agreement of these features with the Bible.

• The Test of Authenticity

Is the book factually true? It is noteworthy that Bible authors did not use the false philosophical and scientific opinions of their times. But they sometimes used popular expressions that are universally understood (cp. Isa. 11:12).

• The Test of Testimony

Was the book universally recognized by the Jews and/or by the Christian church as being God's Word? Does the Holy Spirit bear witness to the regenerated reader that the book is His Word?

• The Test of Authority

Does the book authoritatively demand faith in and obedience to its declarations? "Thus saith the LORD" and the like occur about 3,800 times in the Old Testament.

• The Test of Agreement

Does the book agree doctrinally with the teachings of known canonical books? While there is progression in the Bible's revelation of doctrine, there is no contradiction.

• The Test of Fulfillment

Is there any evidence in history or in the known canonical books of the fulfillment of this book's promises or predictions?

• The Test of Endurance

Does the book convey God's message to each generation of God's people in a living, fresh way (cp. I Pet. 1:23-25)?

• The Test of Spirituality

Is the content of the book of such spiritual character that it is in harmony with the dignity and majesty of God?

May I repeat again that these tests are based on what is known of the sixty-six canonical books of the Bible. When these tests are applied to ancient or current non-canonical literature that claims to be divine revelation, they readily show the falseness of this claim. They reveal that non-canonical literature does not meet the standard that is set by the Bible. Any literature that does not meet this standard is not God's Word.

We praise God for His self-revelation by the written Word. As the psalmist of old, let us strive to meditate on it day and night (Ps. 1:1-3). They who do are blessed of God and lead happy and productive lives.

The liberal's charge that we who believe the Bible to be God's Word are bibliolaters (ones who worship the Bible) is not true. We worship the God who has spoken this Word. Bibliolatry is not the problem with believers that they who reject the God of the Bible and His Word imagine. The greater problem lies with them who call God a liar (I Jn. 5:10).

A Review of Bibliology

1. Essentially, what is the Bible, or the Scriptures?
2. What is the main theme of the Scriptures? Why is this?
3. Give the two major divisions of the Bible.
4. Why are these divisions named as they are?
5. Give the arrangement of these two divisions.
6. What determined this arrangement?
7. Give the place of any book of the Bible according to the Bible's major divisions and the arrangement of each division.
8. Give the values of the Old Testament.
9. Give the values of the New Testament.
10. Why is the New Testament so important to us Christians?
11. Briefly explain the terms *revelation, illumination,* and *inspiration.*
12. Briefly explain the false theories of inspiration and give one objection to each theory.
13. Explain the divine inspiration of the Scriptures as indicated by II Timothy 3:16.
14. Explain the divine inspiration of the speakers and writers of God's Word as indicated by II Peter 1:21.
15. Define verbal inspiration and plenary inspiration.
16. To what extent are present-day translations and copies of the Scriptures the inspired Word of God?
17. Explain the terms *inerrancy* and *infallibility* as they relate to the Bible (see Appendix S).
18. What leads us to believe that God is not giving us more special revelation in the form of Scripture today?
19. In whom does all divine revelation have its source?
20. What is meant by the term *Bible authority?*
21. What makes the Bible to be authoritative?
22. In what ways did Jesus express His recognition of the Scriptures' authority?
23. What should be our response to the Bible's authority?
24. What is the meaning of *canonicity* and *canon?*
25. Give the steps in the formation of the Old Testament canon.
26. During what time span were the Old Testament books written?
27. Where were these books kept during this time?
28. Give the steps in the formation of the New Testament canon.

29. During what time span were the New Testament books written?

30. Why did it take so long for the church to agree upon the books of the New Testament canon?

31. Give the tests of canonicity.

32. How were these tests devised?

33. If men did not impart canonicity to the Scriptures, what is its source?

34. Give the classes of books (canonical and noncanonical) that relate to the Old Testament period (see Appendix T).

35. Give the classes of books (canonical and noncanonical) that relate to the New Testament period (see Appendix T).

36. What is the value of this noncanonical literature?

37. Which of these noncanonical books are included in some versions of the Bible?

38. Why do we not accept this noncanonical literature as being God's Word?

Theology Proper

THEOLOGY PROPER
The Doctrine of God

We who are saved have the blessed privilege of knowing the one true and living God, who exists as three, eternal, simultaneous Persons. However, our knowing Him does not mean that we automatically understand Him. Since He has been pleased to reveal some things about Himself in the Scriptures, it is our duty to search these out and to learn from them all that we can about Him.[1] Before looking at the doctrine about each Person of the Godhead, let us examine the truth that belongs to them in common.

THE FACT OF GOD

We who believe in the existence of God are *theists*, in contrast to *atheists*, who do not believe that any God (true or false) exists. *Christian theism* is belief in the true God, who has revealed Himself to mankind and who exists as three simultaneous Persons — the Father, the Son, and the Holy Spirit.

THE DEFINITION OF GOD

If by definition we mean a complete explanation of God, then He cannot be defined, for we who are finite cannot wholly explain the infinite One. On the other hand, God may be partly defined in so far as He has been pleased to reveal Himself.

When we define something, we may identify its *genus* (the kind of things to which it belongs) and describe its *differentiae* (its essential qualities that distinguish it from all other members of its kind). For example, we may say that a stool belongs to the genus of seat and has qualities that distinguish it from the other members of this kind, such as chair, bench, and chaise lounge. While God is uniquely different from all the personal creatures whom He made, we may say that, having personhood, His genus is personal being and that He is distinguished from all other personal beings by those essential qualities that He has revealed about Himself (see "The Attributes of God" below).

THE EXISTENCE OF GOD

How do we know that God exists? We cannot know by the evidence that is required by the scientific method and that is demanded by the unsaved (I Cor. 2:9). The tools of science are not capable of detecting Him or other spiritual realities like Heaven and angels. This knowledge rests upon His self-revelation, both special and general. (vs. 10).

---

[1] When referring to God, the Scriptures often use the singular pronoun although the Godhead consists of three Persons: the Father, the Son, and the Holy Spirit (Gen. 1:10; Ps. 150; Rom. 1:20).

- **God's Special Revelation**

Today, His special revelation is the Scriptures, which declare His existence. Assuming God's existence to be true, the Bible does not attempt to prove this by rational argument (Gen. 1:1). Actually, rational proof is not necessary, for the Bible is His Word (Heb. 1:1-2) and His creatures intuitively recognize His voice (Gen. 3:8; Rom. 1:18).

- **God's General Revelation**

This revelation is manifest by the universe which God made and now governs. There are several aspects of this witness of general revelation to mankind as seen in Romans 1:18-20.

1. *GOD'S WITNESS OF HIS EXISTENCE TO MAN'S EXPERIENCE (Rom. 1:18)*

God's dealings with unsaved people show His existence. He deals with them in judgment (Rom. 1:18) as well as in benevolence (Acts 14:17). Throughout history people everywhere have acknowledged God's hand upon them, thus, His existence (Ex. 12:31-33; Josh. 2:1-11; Dan. 4:34-37).

God's dealings with saved people also show His existence (cp. Jn. 9:25). These dealings include His changing them (II Cor. 5:17; Col. 3:9-10), answering their prayers (Jn. 14:13; Mt. 7:11), disciplining them (Heb. 12:6), caring for them (Mt. 10:29-31), and producing His fruit in them (Gal. 5:22-23).

2. *GOD'S WITNESS OF HIS EXISTENCE TO MAN'S INNATE AWARENESS (Rom. 1:19a).*

Man intuitively knows of God's existence, for "that which may be known of God is manifest in them." Being made in God's image, man universally has innate awareness of the Creator's existence. This means that humans, apart from reason or sense perception, have immediate, nonrational knowledge of God's existence. Still, they do not know the Creator personally, unless they have been born again (Jn. 17:3). That people universally have this awareness is seen in their impulse to worship a supreme being (Acts 17:22-23).

3. *GOD'S WITNESS OF HIS EXISTENCE TO MAN'S SENSES (Rom. 1:19b-20a)*

Paul also declares that which may be known of God has been shown to man (vs. 19b). Although God is invisible, the qualities of His nature "are clearly seen" (20a). Everything in the universe that people can perceive with their senses has the impress of God upon it and bears witness to His creatorhood as well as to His power and deity.

4. *GOD'S WITNESS OF HIS EXISTENCE TO MAN'S REASON (Rom. 1:20b).*

The things that God has made not only bear witness of His existence to man's senses but also to his reason (the process and conclusion of logical thinking). The apostle declares that the invisible things of God are understood by the things that are made. Consider how this occurs in the following rational arguments for God's existence.

First, there is the *cosmological argument* which points to an adequate Cause of all things. The existence of the universe requires a Creator (Heb. 3:4). Everything that makes up the universe is the result of a Cause that was sufficient to produce it. A product points to a producer.

Some say that the weakness of this argument is that the cause need not be omnipotent if the universe is finite. In reply, we observe that God's creating the universe instantly by command was an expression of infinite power. Opponents who reject God as the originating Cause of the universe say that matter is eternal and that the universe is a closed, self-contained, self-maintained, eternal system.

To the saved person the cosmological argument points to the conclusion that there is a Cause that is sufficiently great to bring the universe into existence and to sustain it. This Cause is God. Declaring that the universe, excepting sin, was made by God, the Bible supports this conclusion (Gen. 1:1; Ps. 90:2).

Second, there is the *teleological argument* which points to an intelligent Cause. This argues from the the the design, order, and purpose that are manifest in the universe. These point to an intelligent Creator who planned and constructed the universe.

Some say that the weakness of this argument is that the designer may be impersonal. Opponents to Christianity hold that design and order are the products of evolutionary forces such as chance mutation and natural selection. But the question remains, How can impersonal, chance forces produce a product that exhibits intelligence, order, and purpose, which these forces themselves do not have? Everyone knows that these qualities belong to personal beings and are exhibited in their works.

To the saved person the teleological argument points to the conclusion that the originating Cause of the universe possesses sufficient intelligence and will not only to devise but also to carry out His plan of creation. The Bible declares that this intelligent Cause is God (Ps. 19:1; 139:13-17).

Third, there is the *anthropological argument* that points to a personal Cause. This argues that man's having self-awareness and moral self-determination points to a personal Creator who has these qualities.

Some say that the weakness of this argument is that this does not require a primary, personal cause but a personality producing force that need not be personal in itself. Opponents to the Bible believe that man's make-up is the product of chance, evolutionary development and that his idea of god is the projection of his personality into infinity. Again, we assert that it is yet to be demonstrated that chance, impersonal forces can create personal beings. That personal beings produce personal beings is a daily occurrence on earth.

To the saved person the anthropological argument points to the conclusion that the originating Cause of the universe is a personal, self-determining Being, who is similar to mankind in His having personhood, or self. The Bible supports this view with the revelation that this personal Cause exists as three Persons: the Father, the Son, and the Holy Spirit (Mt. 28:19).

Finally, there is the *ontological argument* which reasons that since we have a concept of a perfect Being, this Being must exist. If He did not exist, then He would not be perfect since existence is a quality of perfection.[2]

The weakness of this argument is that we cannot deduce real existence from abstract thought. The idea of God does not prove that He exists any more than the idea of Martians proves that some kind of beings live on Mars. Opponents say that man cannot form a true conception of God.

To the saved person the ontological argument shows what God must be if He does exist. It shows that He is infinite and perfect, not because we can prove this but our mentality will not allow us to think otherwise.[3]

Observe that these four arguments do not prove with mathematical certainty the existence of God. But they do point to a superhuman Being whom Christians believe is the true God — the God of the Bible. While these arguments do not compel belief, they do give a rational explanation of our belief in God's existence (I Pet. 3:15; cp. Acts 14:15-17; 17:23-28).

God's self-revelation by means of His works is clear and efficient to the degree that all people who do not respond to it in an appropriate manner are without excuse (Rom. 1:20c; Acts 17:27). The problem is not man's ignorance of the Creator's existence but his unwillingness to accept this fact (Jn. 3:19-20; 5:40; Rom. 3:11). Deceived by satanic philosophy and directed by rebellious hearts, the unsaved prefer to deny or to ignore God's existence than to acknowledge any responsibility to Him. Their rebelliousness is manifest in their attributing all things to chance. But their course will bring them to divine judgment (Acts 17:30-31; Rev. 20:11-15).

NON-CHRISTIAN VIEWS OF GOD

- **Atheism**
  This denies the existence of any God or gods.

- **Agnosticism**
  This holds that the existence and nature of God are unknown and unknowable.

---

[2] The first three arguments for God's existence are called *posteriori* arguments, by which reasoning leads from particulars to principles. This kind of reasoning considers the facts and draws from them certain principles or conclusions. In contrast to this kind of argument, the ontological argument is called an *a priori* argument, which is based on principles that are recognized as being true apart from observation or experience. This kind of reasoning leads from principles to particulars. It argues from abstract, but necessary, ideas.

[3] Augustus Hopkins Strong, *Systematic Theology* (Philadelphia: American Baptist Publication Society, 1907), p. 87.

- **Polytheism**
  This holds that there are many gods.

- **Zoroastrianism**
  This assumes that there are two distinct, eternal, irreducible realities (one good and the other evil) which oppose each other.

- **Pantheism**
  This believes that all things are merely aspects, modifications, or parts of the one eternal self-existing being or principle; that god is everything and everything is god.

- **Deism**
  This holds the existence of God but rejects His having any relation to the world or self-revelation. As pantheism accepts the immanence of God to the exclusion of His transcendence, so deism accepts the transcendence of God to the exclusion of His immanence. For deism God is an absentee landlord who, having made the universe like a vast machine, allows it to operate on its own by inherent natural law without His personal supervision. It claims that all truths are discoverable by reason and that the Bible is merely a book on the principles of natural religion, which are discernible by the light of nature.

- **Theism**
  This is the view that people have of any god other than that of the Bible.
  Needless to say, we who hold Christian theism reject these false views. In the following sections, we shall examine what God has revealed about Himself and His relation to the universe.

THE REVELATION OF GOD

If God had not revealed Himself to mankind, there would be nothing that we would know or could say of Him. But in His grace He condescended to communicate truth about Himself by His works and words.

ITS DEFINITION

God's self-revelation has both active and passive aspects. Actively, it is His communicating to mankind truth about Himself (cp. I Cor. 2:9-12). Passively, it is the truth that He communicates (cp. Rev. 1:1).

God's self-revelation also contains truth about the universe and ourselves that could not be known in any other way. James Packer writes, "Revelation is a divine activity: not, therefore, a human achievement. Revelation is not the same thing as discovery or the dawning of insight, or the emerging of a bright idea. Revelation does not mean man finding God, but God finding man, God sharing His secrets with us, God showing us Himself."[4]

---

[4] James I. Packer, "God Speaks to Man," in *Christian Foundations* (Philadelphia: The Westminster Press, 1965), II, 29.

ITS NECESSITY

God's self-revelation is necessary, for His transcendence makes Him inaccessible to His creatures unless He reveals Himself to them (Ps. 97:9; 113:4-6). Furthermore, the nature and state of man requires God to take the initiative in His self-revelation if man is to know and worship Him. Let us look at man's need for divine revelation.

• Man's Nature

By nature man is a creature, in marked contrast to the Creator who is infinitely greater and higher than he. Because of this, unaided man cannot see God (I Tim. 6:16), find Him by searching (Job 23:3-9), or read His thoughts (Isa. 55:8). Even unfallen man required revelation of the divine will for his obedience to God (Gen. 2:16-17).

• Man's State

Man's fall and subsequent sinful condition intensified his need for divine revelation (especially for that which concerns salvation, II Tim. 3:15) and for God to take the initiative in revealing Himself (cp. Lk. 19:10; Gen. 3:8-9). Fallen man's powers of spiritual perception have been blinded by Satan (II Cor. 4:3-4) and sin (I Cor. 2:14; Eph. 4:17-19). Moreover, the unsaved person's mind is possessed by fanciful ideas that are nourished by Satan's lies and protected by humanistic assumptions (Rom. 1:21-25, 28; I Cor. 1:21). In fact, unsaved people suppress God's truth (Rom. 1:18), for being in a state of rebellion against God, they do not want Him (Jn. 3:19-20; 5:40; 12:37). But this spiritual state does not keep God from doing His sovereign work in the hearts of the elect (II Cor. 4:3-6).

We who are saved have the desire and the ability to receive God's revelation and to profit from it (I Cor. 2:9-12; Eph. 1:17-18; 4:23; Phil. 2:13). Therefore, we should strive to learn all we can about our God and to respond to this truth in a manner which glorifies Him.

ITS KINDS

There are two kinds or forms of divine revelation: general and special. B. B. Warfield observes that these two kinds constitute a whole, each being incomplete without the other (cp. Ps. 19:1, 4 with 7). He writes, "Without special revelation, general revelation would be for sinful men incomplete and ineffective, and could issue...only in leaving them without excuse (Rom. 1:20). Without general revelation special revelation would lack that basis in the fundamental knowledge of God as mighty and wise, righteous and good, maker and ruler of all things, apart from which the further revelation of this great God's interventions in the world for the salvation of sinners could not be either intelligible, credible or operative."[5]

---

[5] Benjamin Breckinridge Warfield, *The Inspiration and Authority of the Bible* (Philadelphia: The Presbyterian and Reformed Publishing Company, 1948), p. 75.

- **General Revelation**

General revelation is that which God makes continuously to all people by His works or actions. This kind of revelation points to the existence of God and the creaturehood of man. Because of this revelation, the world is without excuse for its failure to acknowledge the true God, to seek Him, and to render Him basic honors and service (Rom. 1:20; Acts 17:23-29).

1. *ITS MEANS*

God's general revelation is given by His works or actions in His creating and governing the universe. His creating the universe manifests His eternality, power, divinity (Rom. 1:20), glory (Ps. 19:1), purpose (Rev. 4:11), wisdom (Ps. 136:5), and immensity (Isa. 66:1). God's government of the universe reveals His goodness in providing for man and beast (Acts 14:17; Rom. 2:4; Ps. 104), His sovereignty in controlling nature (Job chs. 38-41) and the affairs of men (Dan. 4:17), His holiness in expressing wrath against wickedness (Rom. 1:18; 9:22; Ps. 9:16), and His mercy in dealing with His people (Rom. 9:15, 23; Ps. 103:13).

2. *ITS INSUFFICIENCY*

Contrary to the teaching of natural religion, general revelation is not in itself adequate to meet man's spiritual needs. It does not reveal God's will for man, particularly how man may become rightly related to his Creator and please Him. This does not imply that general revelation is defective, for it fulfills God's purpose in making His existence known to man and showing man's need to seek after the Creator, who visits sinners with awful judgments. But general revelation does not show man everything that he should know about God and the universe; it says nothing about salvation. Special revelation supplies this truth.

3. *ITS EFFECTIVENESS*

The effectiveness of general revelation is seen in that all people are without excuse for refusing to respond to God's clear manifestation of Himself by the things He has made (Rom. 1:18-20).

- **Special Revelation**

Special revelation is that which God makes known to people by words. This completes general revelation by providing additional information about God and the universe, by making known God's will for man, and by revealing salvation through the Lord Jesus Christ. While only the elect receive and understand God's special revelation of words such as given in the gospel, God still has something to say to the nonelect through His gospel appeals (Lk. 24:47; Acts 17:30) and warnings of coming judgment (Acts 17:31; Rom. 2:3-9).

1. *ITS MEANS*

God has given special revelation in various ways throughout human history.

a. During the Old Testament period

During the early part of man's history, God spoke to people directly by voice alone (Gen. 3:8-9; 13:14), theophany (a visible manifestation of God's presence) and voice (Gen. 17:1; ch. 18), dreams (Gen. 28:12-13), and visions (occurring while the recipient is awake, Gen. 46:1-4).

Later on, God spoke indirectly through angels (Dan. 9:21) and human agents (Jer. 18:18). Man's deteriorating spiritual condition may have required this. These agents were the holy prophets (II Pet. 1:21; Heb. 1:1), the high priests of Israel (Num. 27:21), and certain wise men (Dan. 5:11; I Kings 3:5-12). It appears that the high priests received yes and no answers by the Urim and Thummim, which were carried in a pouch in their breastplate (Ex. 28:30; I Sam. 28:6). Such wise men as Daniel and Solomon had the prophetic gift, but they were not officially prophets. In any case, all humans whom God used to make known His special revelation did so under divine inspiration (II Pet. 1:21).

b. During the New Testament period

During this time God revealed Himself uniquely through the Lord Jesus Christ (Heb. 1:1-2; Jn. 1:18; I Tim. 3:16). Unlike a temporary theophany, this special revelation was a permanent incarnation of God the Son. The Lord Jesus revealed the Father by His holy character and moral excellence (Jn. 1:14), His actions (Jn. 14:8-10), His words (Heb. 1:2; Jn. 3:34; 7:16-17; 8:26, 28, 38, 40; 12:49-50; 14:10, 24; 15:15; 17:8, 14), and His emotions (Mk. 3:5; 10:21; Mt. 9:36). Personwise, Jesus was distinct from the Father. Still, His life so manifested the Father that, for all practical purposes, to see Him was to see the Father (Jn. 14:9). Indeed, He was (and is) the Revelator of the Father (Mt. 11:27).

God also revealed Himself directly by dreams and visions (Mt. 1:20; 2:12, 22; Acts 9:4; 10:10-16; 22:17-18). Furthermore, He revealed Himself indirectly through His servants, particularly by their teaching (I Thess. 2:13; Eph. 4:20-21) and in their writing the New Testament (Jn. 16:12-15; I Cor. 2:10-13; Rev. 1:1-2).

c. Today

God is still revealing Himself in a special way in and through the sixty-six canonical books of the Bible. But is He giving additional special revelation? Some hold that He is through unusual events, dreams, visions, and indescribable encounters. As I see it, I do not think that He is using these or any other means to give new special revelation today. I do not believe that He has given any additional special revelation since the closing of the New Testament canon. There does not seem to be any need for more revelation since the Bible provides us with sufficient truth for our belief and conduct during the present dispensation (II Tim. 3:16-17; see the warnings of Rev. 22:18-19; Deut. 4:2; Prov. 30:5-6; I Jn. 4:1). More revelation will be given during the time when the Lord rules on earth (Isa. 2:3; Joel 2:28).

It must be remembered that all religious or spiritual experience must be tested by the Scriptures to determine its spirituality and genuineness. It is Christian only so far as it conforms to what the Bible teaches about its nature and results (see Mt. 5:16; Jn. 3:21; 8:12; 15:5; Rom. 14:17; Eph. 5:8; Phil. 1:20-21; I Jn. 1:7). Also, all literature that professes to be God's revelation must be tried by the tests of canonicity, which are determined by the sixty-six canonical books of the Bible. With the Bible in hand and the Holy Spirit filling our hearts, we who are saved can examine any alleged divine special revelation and know whether or not it is from God.

2. ITS SUFFICIENCY

Complementing general revelation, special revelation completes God's self-disclosure by providing the truth that He would have people know and that general revelation does not give. Special revelation makes known God's gracious provision of salvation through Jesus (II Tim. 3:15). It also provides the truth that believers need for their faith and conduct (II Tim. 3:16-17). Furthermore, it explains God's being and works as well as man's existence and world. God has not told us everything, but He has revealed what we need to know for our present life and our anticipation of the future (cp. Deut. 29:29; Jn. 15:15; I Cor. 2:9-10).

3. ITS EFFECTIVENESS

The effectiveness of special revelation is seen in the salvation of the elect (II Tim. 3:15), their instruction in the things of God (vss. 16-17), and their sanctification in daily life (Jn. 15:3; Eph. 5:25-26).

4. ITS REALITY

The followers of religious liberalism deny the possibility of divine revelation in words (propositional revelation). They hold that God's revelation cannot be expressed in human words or be inerrantly recorded by fallible men. They hold that God's revelation is nonverbal and existential, that divine revelation consists of what one experiences in a personal, indescribable encounter with God.

In reply James I. Packer writes, "Indeed, the Biblical position is that the mighty acts of God are not revelation to man at all, except so far as they are accompanied by the words of God to explain them. Leave man to guess God's mind and purpose, and he will guess wrong; he can know it only by being told it. Moreover, the whole purpose of God's mighty acts is to bring man to know Him by faith; and Scripture knows no foundation for faith but the spoken word of God, inviting our trust in Him on the basis of what He has done for us. Where there is no word from God, faith cannot be...The need for verbal revelation appears most clearly when we consider the Person and work of Christ. His life and death were the clearest and fullest revelation of God that ever was or could be made. Yet it could never have been understood without explanation."[6]

Religious liberals and their theology ignore the work of God the Holy Spirit in inspiration — His control in securing an inerrant, verbal record of God's special revelation through fallible men (II Pet. 1:21). They also ignore Hebrews 1:1-2 which describes God as speaking! God's special revelation is real, as the lives of countless numbers of people show.

THE NATURE OF GOD

Remembering our creaturehood, let us reverently seek to understand what God is and of what substance He consists. Only the Holy Spirit can illuminate our hearts through the Scriptures regarding this deep truth, yet whatever He is pleased to teach us will be only a small part of what God is. If God were understood easily and fully, then He would be nothing more than what we are. But because He is limitless, we shall be learning about Him throughout eternity, as the experience of the holy angels indicates (Eph. 3:10; I Pet. 1:10-12). However, it is important to our lives to learn now all that the Scriptures reveal about Him.

GOD'S CONSTITUTION

As incomprehensible as God's makeup is, it seems to consist of personhood with the divine nature.

- **God is a person.**

Although God exists as three distinct, simultaneous Persons, each of whom is wholly Deity, our present concern is to see God as a personal Being. Having personhood, God is a divine Person (actually, three Persons). Because personhood is, in my opinion, the divine image in man, we have some concept of what this is and what some of its features are.

God's personhood is indicated by His having personal features such as we find in ourselves, including a unique selfhood with its self-awareness (Ex. 3:13-14; Lev. 11:44-45; Isa. 44:6; 45:22; 46:9) and self-determination (the ability to choose and direct one's affairs in a responsible way) (Isa. 46:9-10; Rom. 11:33-34; Eph. 1:11), a sense of morality with its awareness of good and evil (Prov. 15:3; Rom. 2:5-6; II Tim. 2:13), and perpetuity (Ps. 102:12). Other features that often are attributed to personhood, such as intelligence or reason (Isa. 1:18; 55:9), emotion (Jn. 3:16; Ps. 5:5), and communication (Heb. 1:1-2), really are not indicative of personhood since they belong to higher forms of animals as well as to personal beings.

- **God has the divine nature.**

The divine nature is that substance or essence, with its qualities and powers, that makes the three Persons of the Godhead to be God.[7] The pos-

---

[6] James I. Packer, *Fundamentalism and the Word of God* (London: Inter-Varsity Fellowship, 1958), p. 92.
[7] I regularly use the words *nature, substance,* and *essence* to represent the same thing.

session of the divine nature distinguishes God from other persons, such as angels and humans. We shall examine the qualities of God's substance when we study His attributes.

God's divine nature, which is uncreated and which underlies all of His outward manifestations, is spirit (Jn. 4:24). Being without material body or substance, this essential spirit is invisible (Jn. 1:18; Col. 1:15; Heb. 11:27). We must distinguish between the spirit of which the divine nature consists and the Holy Spirit. Excepting John 4:24, all references to the divine Spirit in the Scriptures refer to the Holy Spirit, the Third Person of the divine Trinity. Moreover, this substance differs from that of angels, who are created spirits, and from the created human spirit, which is an essential part of man's make-up.

The Bible distinguishes between God's personhood and His nature. It teaches that the Godhead consists of three Persons, each of whom possesses in common with the others the one, undivided divine nature and His own separate personhood. (cp. Jn. 10:15, 30; "one" is neuter gender).

GOD'S ATTRIBUTES

• Their Definition

God's *attributes* are those essential qualities that belong to His nature and that outwardly reveal this substance. Perhaps the word *perfections* would be a better term, since the word *attributes* conveys the idea of assigning something to one; but because of its general usage we employ the word *attributes*.

Regarding the relation between God's substance and its attributes, W. G. T. Shedd writes, "The attributes are not parts of the essence, of which the latter is composed. The whole essence is in each attribute, and the attribute in the essence. We must not conceive of the essence as existing by itself, and prior to the attributes, and of the attributes as an addition to it. God is not essence *and* attributes, but *in* attributes. The attributes are essential qualities of God."[8]

For example, we must not think of God's substance as existing apart from His love or His love as something which is independent of Him and to which He must conform. Being a quality which is determined by His nature, divine love is what God is (I Jn. 4:8). On the other hand, He is much more than love, for no one attribute makes up the sum of what He is. He is many other qualities as well (I Jn. 1:5).

Each attribute has its own sphere of expression within His nature and does not modify or eclipse the other qualities that are present. Each one expresses itself freely and harmoniously with the others that belong to His nature. For example, in love the Lord Jesus wept over

---

[8] William G. T. Shedd, *Dogmatic Theology* (Grand Rapids: Zondervan Publishing House, 1969), I, 334.

Jerusalem when He foresaw the reaction of His holiness against the city's sins (Lk. 19:41-44). His love did not stifle the judicial expression of His holiness, as later events have shown.

• Their Classifications

Theologians have made various classifications of God's attributes: that based upon moral qualities (non-moral and moral), that based on God's relation to the universe (absolute or intransitive and relative or transitive), and that based upon similar qualities found in personal creatures (incommunicable and communicable). In this survey of God's attributes, we shall not attempt to classify them.

It appears that God shares with His creatures only His moral attributes such as righteousness, ethical holiness, and love. These were displayed in our Lord's human life (Jn. 1:14) and are now reproduced in His people by the Holy Spirit (Gal. 5:22-23; Rom. 14:17; Heb. 12:10). The display of these qualities in our lives is Christlikeness. This participation in these moral attributes does not make us God. We shall always be finite human beings, made in the image of Jesus' glorified humanity, morally and physically (Phil. 3:21).

• Their Description

When listing the divine attributes, some teachers include personality and spirituality. But I do not regard these features to be attributes of the divine nature. *Personality* is usually associated with personhood, which is not a part of the divine nature. To my mind, personality is the expression of one's personhood as it is affected by his nature. *Spirituality* here is not an attribute of the divine nature as are love and holiness. It describes God's nature as being spirit in substance. It has to do with the "stuff" of which the divine nature consists. Contrariwise, the divine nature does not consist of love or holiness although it possesses these qualities.

Having the one divine nature, all Three Persons of the Godhead have the same essential qualities to the same degree. As we reflect upon these divine attributes, may God give us understanding and blessing.

1. LIFE

(the quality of being alive)

a. Function

This quality makes God uniquely alive. Life itself is undefinable. We can describe what it does, but we cannot explain what it is.

b. Comment

(1) God is alive (Jer. 10:10; I Thess. 1:9).

He is alive in a way that nothing or no one else is. He is eternally self-existent. This means that the ground of His existence is wholly within Himself (Jn. 5:26). He does not have need of or depend on anything outside of Himself for His existence (Acts 17:25). He is the eternal "I Am" (Ex. 3:14).

(2) God is the source of all creatural life.

(a) As the Creator of physical life

All physical life has its source in God (Acts 17:25). It is also maintained by God (Job 34:14-15). Thus God as the Creator has an impersonal, metaphysical relationship with all of His creatures.

All physical life was initially imparted by God at creation (Gen. 1:21, 25-27; 2:7); with earthly creatures, it is now transmitted through propagation (1:22, 28). Upon death physical life, which has its seat in the spirit (and soul) of humans and animals (Jas. 2:26), returns to God (Eccles. 12:7; Job 34:14). We humans continue to exist beyond physical death (Heb. 12:22-23; Rev. 6:9-11) because of the perpetuity of our personhood (self). In time, God the Holy Spirit will reanimate the bodies of humans with a new kind of life, which they will possess in the eternal state (Rom. 8:11; I Cor. 15:44).

(b) As the Father of spiritual life

God the Father is the source of spiritual life (I Pet. 1:3). This is a new kind of life that is imparted to all who receive the Saviour (I Jn. 5:11-12). Because of this, God has a personal, spiritual relationship with His people as their heavenly Father (Mt. 6:32; Gal. 3:26; 4:6). He is Father in the sense that He has given to born again people this new kind of life. He is not Father in the sense that He has transmitted to us His own inherent, divine life by propagation, as human life is propagated.

Spiritual life, or "eternal life," is more than everlasting existence. It brings to all who possess it new power (Phil. 4:13), new direction (II Tim. 3:16-17), new purpose (I Cor. 10:31), new knowledge (2:12), new associations (I Jn. 1:3), new character (Gal. 5:22-23), new desire (Phil. 2:13), new activity (Eph. 2:10; 5:17), new interests (Col. 3:1), new hope (Tit. 2:13), and new destination (Phil. 3:20-21).

While God the Father is the Source of this new life (Rom. 6:23), the Lord Jesus is the Expression of this new life (Jn. 14:6). Also, the Holy Spirit is the Imparter and Energy of this new life (Jn. 3:6; Gal. 5:25).

Having this new life, we who are saved should allow its expression in our daily experience (Gal. 4:19). We do this by abiding in Christ (Jn. 15:4-5) and by cooperating with the Holy Spirit (Gal. 5:25). The expression of this new life in us is called Christlikeness.

2. UNITY
   (the quality of being one in number and parts)
   a. Function

(1) This quality makes God to be one in singularity.

This means that God is one in number. Having the one divine nature, the three Persons of the Godhead are one God, not three Gods (Deut. 6:4; I Tim. 2:5).

(2) This quality makes God to be one in simplicity.

Being only spirit (Jn. 4:24) and having no essential parts, the divine nature is simple rather than complex. Also, it is undivided and indivisible.

b. Comment

(1) God's singularity

Israel worshiped the one, true God (Deut. 6:4). This was in striking contrast to their neighbors, the Canaanites, who honored ten gods. Unlike Israel, these pagans did not have a god who was big enough to look after all the needs of the universe. See Psalm 146:5-10.

(2) God's simplicity

Having the divine nature which is spirit, the true God does not have parts as our human nature does. The parts of God, about which we read in the Bible (eyes, hands, soul, etc.), are figurative expressions called anthropomorphisms, which attribute to God human parts, actions, and characteristics that He neither has nor needs (Prov. 15:3; Jer. 9:20; 27:5; Isa. 42:1). They graphically convey truth about God with which we can identify and which we can understand.

This singleness of the divine nature assures the unity and the equality of the three Persons of the Godhead in their attributes and will (Jn. 10:30). Because They have the same qualities, powers, and purpose, what essentially is true of One is also true of the Others.

For example, while it is said that the Lord Jesus loves us (Jn. 13:1), the Father and the Holy Spirit also love us (Jn. 14:21; Rom. 15:30). However, in Their dealings with the universe, these three Persons have different roles, or functions, as we shall see later.

3. IMMUTABILITY
(the quality of being unchanging)

a. Function

This quality makes God to be forever the same (Ps. 102:25-27).

b. Comment

Because of its immutability, God's nature never changes by development or degeneration as ours does. The qualities of God's nature are constant and eternal (Jas. 1:17).

Consequently, God is unchanging...

(1) In His purpose (Isa. 46:10)

He will complete what He has planned to do. Also, He will never change His plan. This fact seems to be challenged by God's repenting (an apparent change in mind or attitude leading to a change of action) on certain occasions (Num. 23:19 with Gen. 6:6-7; Ex. 32:14; Amos 7:3). As

Jonah 3:5-10 shows, when He repents, God responds differently toward people according to their change of attitude or behavior. Actually, this change in the divine response is not an essential change at all. Beneath this apparent change God's nature and purpose always remain the same. It is man who actually changes in his attitudes and actions. God's responses to man, whether in His acts of judgment or mercy, always conform to His unchanging holiness and justice and follow a righteous course (cp. Rom. 9:14-18).

(2) In His Word (Ps. 119:89)

God does not lie (Num. 23:19). He freely fulfills His conditional promises when their requirements are met; He also fulfills His unconditional promises according to His purpose. This truth provides a basis for our faith in Him, for His unchanging promises give us something to believe.

It is important to distinguish between those promises that are unconditional in their fulfillment and those that are conditional. His keeping His conditional promises depends upon our meeting the stated conditions. If we fail to do this, we shall not experience what He conditionally promises to do. His immutability is seen by His abiding by the conditions of His promises.

(3) In His attributes (Mal. 3:6)

The qualities of His unchanging nature are always the same. Because of this, God never changes.

When God the Son assumed a created human nature, there was no change in His uncreated divine nature. He continues to possess all of the unchanging attributes of Deity. United in Him, the divine and human natures remain distinct, separate, and unmodified in every way.

God's immutability contributes to our stability (Ps. 102:28). He is always the same in loving His people and being with them, regardless of their circumstances (Jn. 13:1; Isa. 41:10). Moreover, because He always hates sin and loves righteousness (Ps. 45:7), we can be assured that He will punish evil doers and will reward those who do His will (Rev. 22:12).

4. *INFINITY*
(the quality of being without limits)

a. *Function*

This quality makes God to be without bounds in His nature and its attributes.

b. *Comment*

God's limitlessness is manifest qualitatively as perfection and quantitatively as fullness.

(1) Qualitatively, God is without limit in perfection, or excellence (Mt. 5:48).

His qualities of nature are perfect in their character and expression (Ps. 18:30). They are free of any defect such as a blemish or a lack of completeness.

(2) Quantitatively, God is without limit in fullness (Ps. 145:3).

There is never any consumption or shortage of any of His attributes. He always has a full, unlimited supply of each of these qualities.

Because of this truth, God never tires or is in need of replenishing (Isa. 40:25-31). He is more than able to provide for our needs (Jn. 7:37-39; Jas. 1:17).

5. *TRUTHFULNESS*
(the quality of being real and reliable)

a. *Function*

This quality makes God to be true in His nature (I Jn. 5:20) and with reference to His Word (Jn. 17:17).

b. *Comment*

(1) God is true in His nature in the sense that He is real, or genuine.

He is everything that He has revealed Himself to be (Jer. 10:10). This is in contrast to false gods that differ from what they are alleged to be (Ps. 115:2-8).

(2) God is true with reference to His Word.

(a) He is true in His Word in the sense that all that He says or that He inspires men to speak or to write is without error. His Word is absolutely trustworthy (Ps. 19:7-11).

(b) He is true to His Word in the sense that He does what He says He will do (Heb. 10:23; cp. I Cor. 1:9; 10:13; I Thess. 5:24). He keeps His Word, fulfilling His unconditional promises to those to whom they are made and His conditional promises to those who meet His requirements. He cannot lie (Tit. 1:2; Num. 23:19).

Daily, we should thank God for the privilege of knowing and belonging to Him — the true and living God. The true God deserves from His people more devotion, loyalty, and service than that which false gods receive from their followers (Jn. 8:12). He is worthy of our complete trust (Gal. 2:20).

6. *ETERNALITY*
(the quality of being infinite in duration)

a. *Function*

This quality makes God to be without beginning and without ending (Deut. 33:27; Isa. 57:15; Jer. 10:10).

b. *Comment*

Time results from a succession of events. It began with the creation of the universe (Gen. 1:1) and will continue forever (Eph. 2:7, "ages").

(1) From the divine standpoint, God is timeless as His name "I Am" suggests (Ex. 3:14).

The whole of God's existence is one indivisible present (Ps. 90:4; II Pet. 3:8). There is no succession of events among the Persons of the Godhead in their internal relationships. On the other hand, God observes time in His dealings with the universe and in carrying out His plan for it (Dan. 9:2, 24; Gal. 4:4; Acts 1:7). Being creatures who shall always experience succession of events, humans will always be aware of time. We who are saved will be involved with the Father's future Messianic programs for His Son. These will consume time as the word "ages" suggests (Eph. 2:7).

(2) From our time-conscious standpoint, we see God as having no beginning or ending (Ps. 90:2; Isa. 44:6; Rev. 1:8).

Existing from everlasting to everlasting, God is endless in His duration.

God is sensitive to our restriction by time. He allows us enough time to do His will. What crowds us for time are those things that we take on and that are in addition to His will (Mt. 6:34; Eph. 5:17; Rom. 13:11-14).

7. IMMENSITY
(the quality of being spatially limitless)

a. Function

This quality makes God to be without measurable dimensions (I Kings 8:27).

b. Comment

God's nature is immeasurable. He cannot be contained in a box or even the universe, regardless of its size (Isa. 66:1; Acts 7:48-49). This truth emphasizes God's *transcendence*, which speaks of His being above, outside, separate from, and something other than the universe He created (Ps. 113:4-6).

Although He cannot be confined to our bodies, God is within us who are saved (I Cor. 6:19). Our body is His temple. Should this truth affect the way that you treat your body?

8. OMNIPRESENCE
(the quality of being everywhere present)

a. Function

This quality enables God to be wholly present everywhere at once (Ps. 139:7-10).

b. Comment

Although he transcends all spatial limitations, God is wholly present at the same time at every point in the universe, sustaining its existence. This truth emphasizes God's *immanence*, which speaks of His being everywhere present in the universe, but not a part of it or limited by it (Jer. 23:23-24). Unlike anything in this world, God's omnipresence does not occur by extension, multiplication, or division of the divine nature.

As a man the Lord Jesus is seated in Heaven at the right hand of the Father (Heb. 1:3); as God He is present everywhere (Mt. 28:20). Although He dwells in Heaven (Mt. 6:9), God is everywhere present, even in Hades, or Sheol (Ps. 139:8). By His presence and power He sustains the existence of all things, even Hell itself (Heb. 1:3; Col. 1:16-17).

While He is with all people metaphysically, God has a personal relationship with each of His regenerated people (Mt. 28:20; I Jn. 1:7). We can be aware of His personal, paternal presence intuitively as we walk with Him in obedience (Jn. 14:21) and rationally as we claim the promise of His presence (Ps. 16:8; Isa. 41:10; Heb. 13:5-6).

9. OMNISCIENCE
(the quality of knowing everything)

a. Function

This quality makes God fully aware of all things and gives Him complete understanding of everything.

b. Comment

Because of this quality God knows everything...

Comprehensively, in that His knowledge embraces all knowable things, both actual and possible (Job. 37:16).

Regarding the *actual,* God knows all existing things in the past (Prov. 24:12), the present (Jer. 32:19; Prov. 15:3), and the future (Isa. 46:10). Regarding the *possible,* God knows all that is capable of existing or occurring but never does (I Sam. 23:12; Mt. 11:21, 23).

Completely, in that He fully knows all that can be known about everything such as its nature, condition, place, and activity (Ps. 147:5).

Independently, in that He never needs or receives information as from an instructor or informer (Isa. 40:13-14).

Simultaneously, in that He is aware of all things at once in their totality and detail (Acts 15:18).

Innately, in that His knowledge is inherent in His nature. It is not acquired by observation or reasoning (Isa. 65:24).

Knowing all that can be known, God knows all about us — our condition and circumstances, our thoughts and actions (Ps. 139:1-6). While He wants us to pray about everything, He does not depend upon this for information (Mt. 6:8).

In the light of His omniscience, God's *foreknowledge* is really an anthropomorphism, for there is no before or after in His awareness. The concept of an advance divine knowledge, or foresight, is really looking at God's knowledge from the creature's point of view. In fact, there was nothing to foresee if it had not been made certain by the divine decree. God's foreknowledge is equated with His counsel (His plan or decree) in Acts 2:23, where the Granville Sharp rule applies and "counsel" comes first in order.[9]

As suggested by Romans 8:28-29, with God's "purpose" representing His decree and preceding His "foreknowledge," the logical order of the components of God's knowledge follows:

His Necessary—▶ Knowledge	His Decree—▶	His Free Knowledge—▶	Reality
Knowledge determined by His nature and causing Him to know all *possible* things.	His plan embracing all *actual* things that He chose from all possible things.	His foreknowledge of all actual things, determined by His decree freely without outside influence.	The actual things He brings to pass or allows to come to pass as decreed.

10. WISDOM
     (the quality of know-how)

     a. Function

     This quality gives to God the ability to use His knowledge in a manner that will best accomplish His purpose.

     b. Comment

     Wisdom is the ability to apply knowledge in a practical way. It is knowing best what to do, how to do it, and when to do it. Being all-wise (I Tim. 1:17), God knows how best to carry out His own plan as well as to give the best direction to His personal creatures (I Cor. 1:21-25; Eph. 3:10; Rom. 12:2).

     We may rely on God's knowing what is best for us (Mt. 7:11) and may confidently follow His direction for our lives (Ps. 1:1-3; 16:11; Rom. 12:2; Jn. 8:12).

11. OMNIPOTENCE
     (the quality of being all-powerful)

     a. Function

     This quality gives to God all power, including the ability to carry out His plan. He is the Almighty God (Gen. 17:1)

     b. Comment

     (1) God has the skill and the strength to do all that He wishes (Isa. 40:26).

     Some people have the skill but not the strength to do a certain

---

[9] The Granville Sharp rule applies here: "When the copulative *kai* connect two nouns of the same case, if the article *o* or any of its cases precedes the first of the said nouns or participles, and is not repeated before the second noun or participle, the latter always relates to the same person that is expressed or described by the first noun or participle." Quoted from H. E. Dana and J. R. Mantey, *A Manual Grammar of the Greek New Testament* (New York: The Macmillan Company, 1941), p. 147.

work; others have the strength but not the skill. God has both. Nothing that He does baffles Him or tires Him (Isa. 40:28). Think of the immense power that He exercised in creating the universe instantly (Gen. 1:1; Ps. 33:6, 9).

(2) There are some things that God has chosen not to do.

He has chosen not to save everyone (II Thess. 2:13).

(3) There are some things that He cannot do.

Morally, He cannot sin or look with approval upon sin (Hab. 1:13). He cannot lie (Tit. 1:2; Heb. 6:18), be tempted with evil (Jas. 1:13), or do anything that is contrary to His perfections (II Tim. 2:13).

Logically, He cannot do what is irrational such as make a square triangle. W.G.T. Shedd observes that logical impossibilities are absurdities and, therefore, nonentities. God's power is involved in creating what is real.[10]

Being all-powerful, God is greater than our circumstances and needs and is able to help us as we look to Him in submission and faith (Eph. 3:20; Phil. 4:13; Heb. 13:5-6; II Chron. 14:11-12). See Luke 1:37; 18:27.

12. HOLINESS
(the quality of being set apart)

a. Function

Since the basic idea of holiness is the condition of being set apart, this quality makes God to be distinctive from the universe and separate from sin.

b. Comment

(1) Being holy, God is set apart from the universe.

This means that He is transcendent and exalted above all things (Isa. 57:15; Ps. 113:4-6) and is different from them (I Sam. 2:2). Because He is holy, all personal creatures must look up to Him (Isa. 6:1).

(2) Being holy, God is set apart from sin and from what is sinful (Hab. 1:12-13; Isa. 6:1-5; I Jn. 1:5).

Being omnipresent, God is in every place where sin is; being holy, He has no personal involvement with sin. Being without sin, He is absolutely morally pure. Because of His moral purity and intrinsic goodness, God, together with His law or Word, is the standard by which all moral evaluations are to be made (Rom. 3:20, 23).

Because God is holy, we who are saved are also to live holy lives (I Pet. 1:14-16), separating ourselves from that which is sinful (II Cor. 6:14-7:1) and living unto Him by doing His will (Rom. 6:11-13; 12:2). We can now experience periods of moral holiness as we abide in Jesus and walk in the power of the Holy Spirit (Rom. 6:15-22; Gal. 5:16).

---

[10] Shedd, *Dogmatic Theology,* I, 359 f.

13. RIGHTEOUSNESS AND JUSTICE

Since both of these qualities are translations of the same words in the original, biblical languages, we shall consider them together. Their meaning is determined by the subject matter of the texts in which they occur and by their contexts.

a. RIGHTEOUSNESS
(the quality of being or doing right)

(1) Function
This quality requires God to be always morally consistent by His acting in conformity to His nature and His laws (Ps. 145:7, 17).

(2) Comment
God always does what is right in conformity to His laws, as given in His Word. For example, He was right in forgiving the O.T. saints their sins because of the coming sacrifice of the Lord Jesus (Rom. 3:25-26).

We are to live righteous lives, that is, lives that are in conformity to God's will (Ps. 11:7; Acts 10:35; Phil. 1:11; I Jn. 2:29).

b. JUSTICE
(The quality of being fair)

(1) Function
This quality requires God to do what is right in dealing with His personal creatures (Isa. 45:21). In all His dealings He is fair.

(2) Comment
Being *righteous,* God requires of His personal creatures obedience to His laws, or will; being *just,* He gives to people what is due them according to their response to His laws. He exacts penalties from the disobedient and gives rewards and blessings to the obedient (Neh. 9:32-35; Acts 17:31; Rom. 2:6, 11; II Tim. 4:8).

We are to treat others fairly regardless of their station in life. This means that we are not to be partial toward those of high rank or to ignore others of low rank (Jas. 2:2-9).

14. GOODNESS
(the quality of being and doing good)

a. Function
This quality makes God to be morally excellent and to deal well with His creatures (Nahum 1:7).

b. Comment
God is good both qualitatively and dynamically (Ps. 119:68).

(1) God is good qualitatively in that He is morally excellent (Mk. 10:18, Ps. 25:8).

God is good. While *holiness* emphasizes God's sinlessness, or moral purity, *goodness* emphasizes His moral excellence and essential perfection.

(2) God is good dynamically in that He deals well with His creatures.

God does good. He bountifully bestows His gifts (Ps. 103:1-5; Mt. 7:11) and lavishly extends His mercy (Ps. 145:9). He calls sinners to repentance (Rom. 2:4). He also prescribes for His people His good will (Rom. 12:2), which is called "good works" when done by the power of the Holy Spirit (Heb. 13:21). His dynamic goodness is an outward expression of His love.

We not only should praise God for His goodness to us (I Tim. 6:17) but we should also seek to do good (vs. 18; Eph. 2:10). This consists of our doing God's will (Eph. 5:17; Rom. 12:2), which includes ministering to the needs of others (Tit. 3:1; Gal. 6:9-10). We can do these things only as we are empowered by the Holy Spirit (Gal. 5:22-23).

15. LOVE
(the quality of caring)

a. Function

God's love is an affection that moves Him to provide for the well-being of His personal creatures, regardless of their personal merit, worth, or spiritual state (Jn. 3:16; I Jn. 3:16-18).

b. Comment

God's love must be distinguished from human love, which is often spontaneous and which rises from pleasure in its object. In spite of His hostility toward us when we were sinners, God graciously chose to love us and to provide a way by which to deliver us from our sins and to bring us into a right relation with Himself (Rom. 5:7-8). Because of our sin-ruined condition and hostility toward God, there was nothing in us that attracted His love. He did not spontaneously love us or like us in our sinful state. He loved us because He chose to do so, not because He was compelled by anything in us.

John 3:16 reveals several qualities of God's love. It is *universal:* He loved the whole human race. It is *sacrificial:* Its great cost is seen in that the Father gave His Son, and the Son gave Himself in atonement for our sins. It is *gracious:* He loved us when, as guilty, ruined sinners and enemies, we were undeserving of this love. And it is *beneficent:* Because of this love He is ready to bring about the greatest good in the lives of all who trust the Saviour.

God's love is also transient toward the unsaved: His love for the world was expressed in the giving of His Son. They who reject this love have left to them only God's wrath (Jn. 3:36). On the other hand, God's love for His people is everlasting (Jn. 13:1; Rev. 1:5).

In the O.T. there is found a special covenant-love (Heb. chesed) that God has for His people. This is most often represented in the KJV by "kindness" (Neh. 9:17; Isa. 54:8, 10), "lovingkindness" (Ps. 69:16; 92:2; Jer. 9:24), and "mercy" (Ps. 100:5; 103:8, 11, 17). This love emphasizes God's faithfulness toward His covenant people. It is a steadfast love, committed to His fulfilling the promises of His gracious covenants.

We who are saved are commanded to express God's love to others, to saved and unsaved alike, to friend and foe (Jn. 13:34; Mt. 5:44). The expression of this love is our caring for others, especially undeserving people, and our seeking to provide for their well-being, even at personal cost (I Jn. 3:16-18). The expression of this love is the badge of true discipleship (Jn. 13:35). We can do this only with the help of the Holy Spirit (Gal. 5:22).

16. HATRED
(The quality of reacting against sin and sinners)

a. Function

This quality gives to God an extreme dislike for, and opposition toward, sinners and their sins (Ps. 5:5; 11:5; Hos. 9:15; Mal. 1:2-3).

b. Comment

This hatred is not the sinful kind that we humans feel toward our enemies. Human hatred lacks justice and desires ill toward the offender rather than seeking his good. For this reason, we are not allowed to avenge our wrongs (Rom. 12:17-21). Divine hatred is the stern, spontaneous reaction of God's holiness against sinners and their sins. While holiness emphasizes God's character as being separate from sin, hatred emphasizes His reaction to sin.

(1) *Passively,* this hatred expresses itself as an attitude of hostility and a resolution to punish sinners (Rom. 1:18; Jn. 3:36).

(2) *Actively,* this hatred expresses itself as destructive judgment, or punishment (Ps. 5:5-6; Rev. 14:19; 15:1; 19:15).

In spite of this hatred, God deliberately chose to love sinners and to provide for them salvation. However, this love for unrepentant sinners is not everlasting. When sinners reject God's Son and His atoning work (the greatest expression of divine love for humans), there remains for them only divine wrath (Jn. 3:36). In all of His expressions of hatred, God is always just, dealing out to sinners what they deserve (Rom. 2:2-12).

In our gospel ministry to sinners, we need to emphasize God's displeasure with them before speaking of His love for them, which if presented alone may be misunderstood as an indulgent sentimentality. While we are to love sinners, as God does through the gospel and its ministry to them, we must hate sin (Rom. 12:9). Moreover, we must accept God's attitude toward sin and fear Him with a wholesome respect (Heb. 12:28-29).

17. *GRACE*
    (The quality of exercising unmerited favor)
    a. *Function*

This quality enables God to deal favorably with undeserving people according to His sovereign purpose (Gen. 6:8; Jonah 4:2; Eph. 2:8; Heb. 2:9; Rom. 11:5).

b. *Comment*

(1) Grace does not recognize human merit, worth, or works (Rom. 3:24).

Because of this, God graciously gives to gospel believers salvational blessings which they do not deserve.

(2) Grace is the only principle by which God can save sinners (Gal. 2:16).

Grace is the only principle of divine dealing whereby God can deliver sinners from the penalty, ruin, and power of sin (Eph. 2:8). The principle of works requires Him to deal with people as they deserve (cp. Rom. 11:5-6). Deserving Hell, sinners cannot be saved by their human merit, worth, or good works (Eph. 2:9).

The same grace that saves also keeps people saved in spite of their spiritual lapses (Rom. 5:2). Compare the Corinthians believers (I Cor. 1:4-9).

(3) In grace God enables His people to do His will (II Cor. 1:12) and to endure their circumstances (12:7-10).

Divine grace portrays God in action, doing for us what we cannot do for ourselves. With the help of this grace, we can be the kind of people He wants us to be and do the things He wants us to do (I Cor. 15:10). Moreover, by God's grace we can make the best of our circumstances (Phil. 4:10-13; II Cor. ch. 4).

(4) This grace responds to faith (Eph. 2:8).

This is that faith which God gives and which we must exercise for salvation, daily life, and ministry (Rom. 1:17; 12:3, 6; Gal. 2:20). As we believe God's promises, we become the recipients of divine grace and its operation in our life.

We not only are saved by divine grace (Eph. 2:8) but we also are to live our Christian life and serve the Lord by this grace (II Cor. 1:12; I Cor. 15:10; Rom. 12:3-8). God's grace is more than sufficient for every demand (II Cor. 9:8; 12:9-10).

18. *MERCY*
    (The quality of showing compassion)
    a. *Function*

This quality enables God to show a benevolent compassion toward the guilty and the distressed (Deut. 4:31).

b. Comment

(1) In mercy God shows compassion toward the guilty.

He does this by withholding the punishment they deserve (Neh. 9:17; Jer. 33:23-26; Rom. 11:30-32; Eph. 2:4; Tit. 3:5). However, His mercy is not endless toward the wicked. He will deal out judgment to those who reject His salvation in Christ (Rom. 2:8-9).

(2) In mercy God shows compassion toward those who suffer or who are in distress.

He does this by granting them relief (Ps. 103:8-18; Isa. 49:13; Heb. 4:16; Jas. 5:11).

Not only should we be grateful to God for His mercy to us but we should also show this mercy to others (Mt. 5:7; Col. 3:12).

19. LONGSUFFERING

(The quality of being patient)

a. Function

This quality enables God to bear long with those who annoy or provoke Him (Rom. 15:5).

b. Comment

(1) God is patient with His people (Ps. 86:14-17).

He is patient in that He puts up with their frailties, including their immaturity, dullness, ignorance, and obstinacy.

(2) He is patient with the unsaved (Rom. 2:4; 9:22).

In spite of their sins against Him, He gives many of them opportunity to repent and believe the gospel. However, His patience with the lost is not endless. Having graciously given them opportunity to repent, He will judge those who reject Him and the gospel (II Pet. 3:9-10).

We, too, are to be longsuffering toward others who try us and provoke us (Eph. 4:2). This forbearance is a fruit of the Holy Spirit (Gal. 5:22).

20. SOVEREIGNTY

(The quality of being supreme)

a. Function

This quality makes God to be the highest in position and authority.

b. Comment

(1) God is supreme in position.

He is above all persons, things, and places (Deut. 10:14; Isa. 40:15-17; Ps. 24:1).

(2) God is supreme in authority.

He commands all personal creatures and things (Ps. 119:91; 103:19; 47:2-3). Nothing exists that is not ultimately under His direction and control (Job 1:15; 2:6).

It is our duty to recognize God's sovereignty over our life and to submit daily to His will (Rom. 14:6-9; II Cor. 5:14-15). He also gives to some people positions of authority in civil government (Rom. 13:1-5), the church (Heb. 13:7, 17), and the home (Eph. 5:22-23; 6:1), for which they are accountable to Him.

Again, observe that some of these qualities of God's nature, at least to some extent, are transferable to His people as they are reproduced in us by God the Holy Spirit (Gal. 5:22-23; Rom. 14:17). These include holiness (I Pet. 1:15), righteousness (I Jn. 2:29), justice (Jas. 2:1-9), goodness (III Jn. 11), faithfulness (I Cor. 4:2), love (Jn. 13:34-35; Mt. 5:44), hatred (Rom. 12:9), grace (Col. 4:6; II Cor. 6:1), mercy (Col. 3:12), longsuffering (Eph. 4:2), and authority (I Cor. 12:28). To express these, we must submit to the Holy Spirit and look to Him in faith to reproduce these in us. Then it can be said that we are godly people.

How wonderful our God is! Let us meditate upon these perfections and consider their many applications to our lives. Also, let us allow Him to fill us with the fulness of Himself and to express Himself through us in this world's darkness (Eph. 5:1-21). In our worship, we can praise God for these qualities of His nature and thank Him for all that He is doing for us.

HUMAN AND ANIMAL FEATURES ATTRIBUTED TO GOD

In the Bible it is said that God has human forms (anthropomorphisms) and animal forms (zoomorphisms) and that He expresses human feelings (anthropopathisms), all of which are not attributable to His divine nature. Since God does not have parts as we do, the purpose of these figurative expressions is to reveal truth about God in an impressive way, to which we humans can relate.

W.H. Griffith Thomas explains, "In revealing Himself God has to descend to our capacities and use language which can be understood. But this can never fully reveal Him since that which is finite could never explain the Infinite. So that God must necessarily speak of Himself as a Man, for so only could we comprehend anything about Him. Hence, both as to Person and actions, everything is spoken after the manner of men. But all these are only figures of speech, by which alone we can obtain any ideas of reality."[11]

We must keep before us the purpose of God's self-revelation in the following ways lest we have distorted views of Him. On the other hand, having permanently taken to himself a complete human nature, God the Son experiences all that His glorified, sinless humanity contributes to Him. In other words, the Second Person of the divine Trinity does have eyes, hands, mouth, and the like, because He is man as well God.

---

[11] W.H. Griffith Thomas, *The Principles of Theology* (London: Church Book Room Press Ltd., 1963), p. 15).

- **Human Features (anthropomorphisms)**

This is any human part, action, or characteristic that is attributed to God. For example, God is said to have a soul (Isa. 1:14), eyes (Prov. 15:3), feet (Nahum 1:3), ears (Num. 11:18), hand (Amos 9:2), arm (Jer. 27:5), face (Num. 6:25), head (Ps. 60:7), and mouth (Jer. 9:20). It is also said that He remembered (Gen. 8:1), smelled (vs. 21), saw (6:5), went down (11:5), and heard (21:17).

- **Human Feelings (anthropopathisms)**

This is any human emotion that is attributed to God. For example, God is said to be weary (Isa. 1:14). Also, He is said to be jealous (Ex. 20:5; 34:14). This means that He will not tolerate any compromise of His people's love for Him. This jealousy is based on His relationship with His people. He alone has exclusive claim to their devotion; and He is zealous to maintain the purity of this relation. Incidentally, God's love for us is not an anthropopathism. It is a quality of His divine nature.

- **Animal Features (zoomorphisms)**

This is any animal part, action, or characteristic that is attributed to God. He is said to have feathers and wings (Ps. 91:4) and to roar like a lion (Hos. 11:10).

When you come across these graphic, figurative expressions in the Scriptures, consider what truth they convey about God.

GOD'S UNITY AND TRIUNITY

Earlier, when we considered the divine attribute of unity, we noted God's singularity — that God is one God. It is also the teaching of the Bible that God exists as three eternal, simultaneous Persons (I Jn. 5:7).[12] Regarding these truths we can say that God is one in nature and three in person. Let us look at this more closely.

- **The Unity of God's Essence**

The singularity of God (His being one God) is taught in Deuteronomy 4:35, 39; 6:4; I Kings 8:60; II Kings 19:15; Psalm 86:10; Isaiah 45:5-6; Zechariah 14:9; Mark 12:28-29; John 17:3; Romans 3:30; Ephesians 4:6; and I Timothy 2:5.

God is one God because there is only one divine nature (essence, substance) which is undivided and indivisible. Although there are three Persons (Selves) in the Godhead, They possess in common the one nature, which constitutes Them as one God.

The reason for the Old Testament's emphasis on the unity of God seems to be the fact of mankind's falling into idolatry and their worshiping false

---

[12] Though not found in the Vatican and Alexandrian Greek MSS, the authenticity and integrity of I John 5:7 are maintained by its agreement with the teaching of the Bible, its contribution to the unity and flow of the passage, and its being favorably quoted by Jerome, Augustine, Cyprian and Tertullian.

gods and their images (Rom. 1:21-25). Even the nation of Israel fell into idolatry during their sojourn in Egypt (Josh. 24:14) and lapsed into this sin at Mt. Sinai (Ex. 32:1-6) and in Canaan (Judg. 2:11-13; II Kings 17:7-23). Because of their role in God's redemptive program, Israel needed to be reminded of God's unity while they lived in the midst of pagan idolatry. Their worship of the one, true God was a witness to His unity and was essential to their place in His program (Deut. 6:4-15; Isa. 43:10).

- **The Triunity of God's Person**

While unity emphasizes the oneness of God, triunity speaks of there being three Persons, or Selves, simultaneously possessing the one divine nature. Generally, we speak of this truth as the doctrine of the divine Trinity. The Trinity consists of three simultaneous, coexistent, eternal Persons — the Father, the Son, and the Holy Spirit (Mt. 28:19; I Jn. 5:7). Let us examine this doctrine in greater detail.

1. FALSE VIEWS OF THE TRINITY

The early Christian thinkers of the post-New Testament period did not have a clear conception of the doctrine of the Trinity. During the third and fourth centuries there arose heretical views which prodded the church to define this doctrine. The chief false views of the Trinity follow:

a. Sabellianism

Sometimes called "modal monarchianism," this view was taught by Sabellius, a teacher at Rome (c. 215). It holds that God is a Monad (an ultimate unit of being) that expressed itself in three consecutive operational manifestations: the Father as essence, and the Son and the Spirit as His modes of self-expression. Thus, by a process of development, the Father projected Himself first as the Son and then as the Spirit.[13]

Essentially, this view holds that the Persons of the Godhead are simply different, temporary (but not simultaneous) forms by which the Monad expressed itself. Compare the erroneous illustration of the Trinity, which people often use, that expresses this false view: water as a solid (ice) becoming a liquid and turning to steam.

Contrariwise, the Bible teaches that the Members of the Godhead are distinct, eternal, coexistent Persons.

b. Arianism

This takes the name from Arius, a presbyter of Alexandria (4th c.), who held that there is only one God, God the Father; that the Son is a personal creature whom the Father formed out of nothing by command; and that the Spirit is an impersonal essence, unlike that of the Father. Later Arians regarded the Holy Spirit to be the noblest of the creatures produced by the Son at the Father's bidding.[14]

---

[13] J. N. D. Kelley, *Early Christian Doctrines* (New York: Harper & Row Publishers, 1960), p. 121 f.
[14] J. N. D. Kelley, pp. 226-31, 255.

Contrariwise, the Bible teaches that the Son and the Holy Spirit are each God and are equal to the Father in their essential qualities.

c. Tritheism

This holds that the Trinity consists of three separate divine essences; thus, there are three gods rather than one God.

Contrariwise, the Scriptures teach that there is only one God, existing as three distinct, eternal Persons, each of whom is God. Their possessing in common the one divine nature makes Them to be one God.

With these false views of the Trinity in mind, we must be on the alert for so-called Christian movements that are heretical in their teachings of the Trinity. Some (cp. The United Pentecostal Movement) hold the deity of the Father, the Son, and the Holy Spirit but deny their being distinct, coexistent Persons. This is Sabellianism. Others (cp. the Jehovah's Witnesses) deny the deity of the Lord Jesus Christ and the deity and personality of the Holy Spirit. This is Arianism. Any religious organization that denies the biblical teaching of the Trinity is not truly Christian. Let us consider the biblical teaching of this doctrine.

2. THE TRUE DOCTRINE OF THE TRINITY

The biblical doctrine of the Trinity may be summarized as follows: There is one God; the Godhead consists of three Persons; the Father, the Son, and the Holy Spirit are distinct, coexistent, eternal Persons; and the Father, the Son, and the Holy Spirit are each God.

a. The New Testament teaching of the Trinity

The New Testament gives us more detail of this doctrine because it describes the incarnation of God the Son and the various ministries of God the Holy Spirit relating to the Lord Jesus and to His people.

(1) There is one God.

This is stated in I Corinthians 8:4; Galatians 3:20; I Timothy 2:5 and is implied in Matthew 28:19, where the singular noun "Name" is used in the baptismal formula. Regarding this verse B.B. Warfield observed,

> It does not say, "In the names (plural) of the Father and of the Son and of the Holy Ghost"; nor yet (what might be taken to be equivalent to that), "In the name of the Father, and in the name of the Son, and in the name of the Holy Ghost," as if we had to deal with three separate Beings. Nor, on the other hand, does it say, "In the name of the Father, Son, and Holy Ghost," as if "the Father, Son and Holy Ghost" might be taken as merely three designations of a single person. With stately impressiveness it asserts the unity of the three by combining them all within the bounds of the single Name; and then throws up into emphasis the distinctness of each by introducing them in turn with the repeated article...these three, the Father, and the Son, and the Holy Ghost, all unite in some profound sense in the

common participation of the one Name.[15]

Jesus also said that He and His Father were one (Jn. 10:30). Being neuter gender, "one" means one thing (God), not one person.

(2) The Godhead consists of three Persons.

That the Godhead consists of three, coexistent Persons, or a Trinity, is seen in the following references: Matthew 28:19 and II Corinthians 13:14 (the word "God" occurring with the names of other Members of the Godhead refers to the Father).

(3) Each Member of the Godhead is a distinct, coexistent Person.

This is seen in such passages as John 14:16-17 where Jesus speaks about asking the Father to send another Helper, who is the Holy Spirit. These words indicate that Jesus did not think of Himself as being the Father or the Holy Spirit. Including Himself, He refers to three distinct Persons.

(4) Each Member of the Godhead is God.

The Father is God (Jn. 6:27; Rom 1:7; I Pet. 1:2); the Son is God (Jn. 1:1, 14; Rom. 9:5; Heb. 1:8; I Jn. 5:20); and the Holy Spirit is God (I Cor. 3:16; Acts 5:3-4).

b. The Old Testament teaching of the Trinity

B. B. Warfield writes, "The Old Testament may be likened to a chamber richly furnished but dimly lighted. The introduction of light brings into it nothing which was not in it before, but it brings into clearer view much of what is in it but was dimly or even not at all perceived before. The mystery of the Trinity is not revealed in the Old Testament, but the mystery of the Trinity underlies the Old Testament revelation, and here and there almost comes into view."[16]

(1) There is one God.

This is stated in Deuteronomy 6:4 and implied in Isaiah 45:5, 6, 18, 22.

(2) The Godhead consists of three Persons.

That the Godhead consists of more than two Persons is indicated by the plural noun "God" ("Elohim" in Gen. 1:1) and the plural pronoun "us" (Gen. 1:26; 3:22; 11:7; Isa. 6:8). The three Persons of the Godhead are given in Isaiah 48:16 and 61:1, with the Son (Messiah) speaking in both references (cp. Isa. 49:8-9 with Lk. 4:16-21).

(3) Each Member of the Godhead is a distinct, coexistent Person.

The Members of the Godhead are distinguished in various passages. "LORD" is distinguished from "Lord" (Gen. 19:24; Hos. 1:4). "The Lord" has a "Son" (Ps. 2:7, 12; cp. Prov. 30:2-4). "Spirit" is distinguished from "LORD" (Num. 27:18) and from "God" (Ps. 51:10-12). "God" the Son is

---

[15] "Trinity," *The International Standard Bible Encyclopaedia* (1949), V, 3017.
[16] Op. cit., V, 3014.

distinguished from "God" the Father (Ps. 45:6-7; Heb. 1:8-9).

    (4) Each Member of the Godhead is God.

    The *Father* is called "LORD," God's personal name ["Yahweh" in Ps. 110:1]. The Father and the Son are called "God" (Ps. 45:6-7; Heb. 1:8-9). The *Son* is called God [Isa. 7:14 ("Immanuel" meaning "God with us"); 9:6 ("Everlasting Father" probably means "Father of eternity")]. As the speaker of the words of Jeremiah 31:33-34, the *Holy Spirit* is identified as LORD (Heb. 10:15-16).

This biblical evidence demonstrates the fact of the divine Trinity. Our God — the true and the living God — is one God, consisting of three simultaneous Persons: God the Father, God the Son, and God the Holy Spirit. We can readily grasp the truth that each Member of the Godhead is God and that each One is a Person. But it is incomprehensible how these three Persons possess the single divine nature in such a manner so as to be one God, yet each wholly God, without confounding the Persons or dividing the essence. This aspect of the doctrine has no analogy in nature and must be received by faith in God's Word.

3. THE RELATION OF THE PERSONS WITHIN THE GODHEAD

    We shall now try to understand these unfathomable, eternal processes that are involved in the internal, constitutional relationships of the Trinity. Let us first examine these relations and then the subordinations that rise from them.

    a. *Their relation to One Another*

      (1) In constitution

    This has to do with the manner in which They possess the one divine nature so that They are one God. The designations "Father" and "only begotten Son" indicate that the Father eternally generates the Son (Jn. 5:26; Ps. 2:7).[17] In our human experience generation is a single act of a human father, initiating the divine creation of personhood and the natural propagation of human nature. However with reference to God, generation is neither a single act in time nor the creation of someone or something. By an eternal process the Father's generative action makes the divine nature common to Himself and to the Son. There is no creation of the Son's personhood or of new divine nature. By this continuing process, the eternally existing divine nature is communicated to the Son in such a way that it remains undivided, yet wholly possessed by the Father and by the Son individually. By this perpetual, generative action the Son is wholly God as the Father is wholly God.

---

[17] It appears that the Father's words in Psalm 2:7 refer to the eternal generation of the Son, for this declaration concerning the Son is made in the day of God's decree, which itself is eternal. The decree itself is not about the generation of the Son (an eternal, internal relationship that is not determined by divine decree), but it concerns the incarnation and Messianic work of the Son, as shown by the context and by Paul in Acts 13:33 (cp. vs. 22). The external relationship of the Members of the Godhead to the universe and their interpersonal relationships required by this are determined by divine decree. In other words, the generation of the Son is not determined by divine decree, but His Messiahship is.

Possessing the one divine nature, They are one God but not one and the same Person. Theologians call this process of communicating the divine nature "generation" and its result "filiation."

In a similar way the divine nature, possessed in common by the Father and the Son, is communicated by Them to the Holy Spirit. This, too, is done in such a way that it remains undivided, yet wholly possessed by the Holy Spirit as well as by the other Members of the Godhead. The designation "Spirit" means "breath" or "wind." This suggests that unlike the Son who is generated, the Holy Spirit possesses the divine essence by an eternal breathing action of the Father through the Son, as reflected in Their roles relating to Their dealings with the universe.[18] This process is called "spiration" and its result "procession."

(2) In activity

What did these divine Persons do from all eternity before Their creating the universe? The only thing that is revealed is Their having perpetual, intimate fellowship wih One Another (Jn. 1:1, 18; 17:5).

b. *Their subordination to One Another*

(1) *Their subordination in order*

The Scriptures show a subordination among the Members of the Godhead. This subordination is represented by an arrangement of the names and activities of the Persons in a dependent series in respect to Their order and work.

Their subordination in order is expressed by the arrangement of Their names and the internal relationships suggested by these names — the Father, the Son, and the Holy Spirit (Mt. 28:19). This subordination rises from the eternal, internal relationship which exists between these Persons. Being the Unbegotten, the Father is first in order; being the only Begotten, the Son is second; and proceeding from the Father through the Son, the Holy Spirit is third. Theologians call this subordination in order, position, or rank "ontological subordination," for this concerns the Trinity's being, or essential make-up. This order of first, second, and third is not to be understood as representing qualitative differences between the Persons of the Godhead, for each One possesses the same divine essence, wholly and simultaneously, with the other two Persons. Consequently, They have equal qualities and powers.

(2) Their subordination in activity

There is also a subordination of the Members of the Trinity in Their works, as expressed by Their external relation to and dealings with the universe. This subordination is sometimes called "economical subordination"

---

[18] See Augustus Hopkins Strong, *Systematic Theology*, p. 323.

and is presented by the formula that all things (outside the Trinity) originate with (ek) the Father, are effected through (dia) the Son, and brought about in or by means of (en) the Holy Spirit. This subordination is manifest in the separate, yet harmonious, roles that the Persons of the Godhead have in Their relationships to people and things outside of Themselves.

The Father is the Originating Cause, or the Ultimate Source, of the universe (I Cor. 8:6; Rev. 4:11), divine revelation (Rev. 1:1), salvation (Jn. 3:16-17), and Jesus' Messianic (human) works (Jn. 5:17; 14:10). Thus the Father initiates and does all of these things.

The Son is the Instrumental Cause, or the Personal Agent, through whom the Father works to bring about these divine activities: the creation and maintenance of the universe (I Cor. 8:6; Jn. 1:3; Col. 1:16-17), divine revelation (Jn. 1:1; Mt. 11:27; Jn. 16:12-15; Rev. 1:1), salvation (II Cor. 5:19; Mt. 1:21; Jn. 4:42), and his Messianic works (Jn. 5:17, 19; 6:38; 8:29; 17:4). Thus the Father does all of these things through the Son, who functions as his Agent.

The Holy Spirit is the Dynamic Cause, by means of whom the Father brings about these divine activities: the creation and maintenance of the universe (Gen. 1:2; Job 26:13; Ps. 104:30), divine revelation (Jn. 16:12-15; Eph. 3:5; II Pet. 1:21), salvation (Jn. 3:6; Tit. 3:5; I Pet. 1:2), and Jesus' Messianic works (Isa. 61:1; Acts 10:38). Thus the Father does all of these things by means of the Holy Spirit who provides the operational power for these works.

In summary, all divine activities toward and dealings with the universe are done by the Father through the Son by means of the Holy Spirit.

One cannot reflect upon the nature and uniqueness of our God without being filled with awe and praise. We shall forever ponder these sacred mysteries and learn of this infinite Being. Meanwhile, it is our joy to fellowship with the Members of the Trinity and to express our love for Them by our trust and obedience (Mk. 12:30; Jn. 14:15, 21, 23).

THE NAMES OF GOD

While we use proper names for labels of identification, in the Bible they serve additional roles. Proper names are sometimes descriptive of people's character, as Nabal meaning "fool" (I Sam. 25:25), and of people's appearance, as Esau meaning "red" (Gen. 25:25); commemorative of some event, as Ichabod meaning "inglorious" (I Sam. 4:21); expressive of the faith or hope of parents, as Noah meaning "comfort" (Gen. 5:29); or a witness to prophecy, as Shearjashub meaning "a remnant shall return" (Isa. 7:3). Likewise, the names of God are a part of the self-revelation of His nature, character and works.

As we survey God's names that are given in the Scriptures, we must keep in mind the various kinds of designations: *generic names,* representing kind of being; *titles,* representing function, office or rank; and *personal names,* representing personal identification. Using "the man, President Abraham Lincoln" as an example, "man" is his generic name, "President" is his title, and "Abraham Lincoln" is his personal name.

GOD'S NAMES IN THE OLD TESTAMENT

• God's Basic Hebrew Names

1. ELOHIM

This plural form occurs about 2,300 times with reference to the true God. Its singular forms are *El, Eloah* (a poetic form often found in Job), and *Elah* (found in Ezra and Daniel).

This is the generic name of Deity and is translated in KJV "God" (Gen. 1:1) or "gods" (Ex. 20:3). With reference to the true God, it is translated in the singular, and with few exceptions (cp. Gen. 3:5; Deut. 5:26) it imposes the singular on those parts of the sentence that are grammatically related to it. This shows that the plural form does not speak of more than one God.

Some believe that the plural form, *Elohim*, is the abstract plural of greatness, majesty or rank, denoting God's unlimited greatness and power. We Trinitarians hold that it is a numerical plural, indicating the plurality of Persons within the Godhead. This plurality represents more than two Persons since *Elohim* has a plural ending rather than a dual one (Elohayim).

Elohim derives from a Hebrew root word which means "strength" or "might" (cp. "power" in Gen. 31:29; Prov. 3:27). This generic name of Deity signifies the putter forth of power.[19] The true God is the absolute Being to whom all power belongs (Gen. 1:1; 24:3; Ps. 91:2; Isa. 46:9).

2. ADONAI

This is the primary title of God in the Old Testament. Meaning "my lords," this title is translated "Lord" in the KJV about 450 times with reference to God. *Adonai* is the plural form of *Adon*, which means "lord" or "master" (Ps. 12:4). Like *Elohim*, the plural form indicates the plurality of Persons within the Godhead. The significance of this title is seen in the following: the lord or master of slaves (Gen. 24:9), a wife (Gen. 18:12), a people (I Kings 22:17), a country (Gen. 42:30), and a household (Gen. 45:8). This title expresses a personal relationship—one of authority on the one hand, and of allegiance and love on the other.[20] It was a title that a subordinate addressed to his superior.[21]

Adon, with its forms, means "the Lord as ruler" (Ps. 105:21), while *Baal means "the Lord as possessor or owner"; thus, God is the ruling Lord.*[22] *Baal was the title that the people of Canaan gave to their gods, with Bel as the* supreme deity. For this reason, God never called Himself Baal, nor did the

---

[19] Herbert F. Stevenson, *The Titles of the Triune God* (London: Marshall, Morgan & Scott, 1955), p. 16.
[20] Herbert F. Stevenson, p. 25.
[21] Edmond Jacob, *Theology of the Old Testament* (New York: Harper & Row Publishers, 1958), p. 59.
[22] Ludwig Koehler, *Old Testament Theology* (London: Lutterworth Press, 1957), p. 30.

Israelites often use this title for Him (cp. Hos. 2:16), although He is the owner of the universe (Ps. 24:1; 50:10-12).

With the meaning of *Adonai* ("my Lords") in view, it is profitable to reflect upon its significance in Genesis 15:2, 8; Joshua 7:7; Judges 6:13, 15; Psalm 35:23; 110:1; 114:7; Isaiah 6:1, 8; and Malachi 1:6.

3. YAHWEH

This is the personal name of God in the Old Testament (Jer. 33:2). In the KJV this personal name is translated "LORD" (Ps. 110:1), "JEHOVAH" (Ps. 83:18), and "GOD" (when following "Lord," Gen. 15:2). It occurs about 6,700 times.

In the KJV, "LORD" is not a translation of the Hebrew word for God's personal name but an arbitrary substitute. In post-New Testament times *Yahweh* ceased to be pronounced aloud by Jews in the public reading of the Scriptures and was replaced orally by the word *Adonai*. Later, when the Masoretes added vowels to the Hebrew consonants in the text of the Scriptures, they added the vowel points of *Adonai* to the consonants of the tetragrammaton (a word of four letters) *YHWH*. This created the word *YaHoWaH* or *Jehovah*. Scholars believe that *Yahweh* or *Jahveh* is nearer to the original pronunciation of *YHWH*, but this is not certain.

That *Yahweh* is the personal name of God is shown by the following: He says that it is His name (Isa. 42:8). It is not a title as *Adon* (Ruler, Master) or *Baal* (Owner, Possessor). It never occurs with the genitive as "Yahweh of Israel," but as "Yahweh, God of Israel" (Josh. 24:2). Also, it never occurs as "the Yahweh," "my Yahweh," or "the living Yahweh."

The name seems to come from the Hebrew root word "to be" (*hawah*) with a consonantal prefix (Y). The meaning is indicated in Exodus 3:13-14, where in answer to Moses' question about His name, God reveals Himself as "I AM THAT I AM." The name was not a new revelation (Gen. 4:1; 14:22; 24:3; Job 12:9), but it was now important to Israel that God renew the revelation and reveal its meaning, which may have been lost during the nation's sojourn in Egypt (Ezek. 20:6-8; Josh. 24:14; cp. Ex. 6:2-3).[23]

When *Yahweh* declares Himself to be "I AM THAT I AM," He may be saying that He is the eternal, unchanging One. When He says that He is "I AM," He may be saying that He is ultimate Reality. The root word, translated "to be," suggests continuous, absolute, self-determining existence. The truth was vital to Israel that their God was the ultimate, continuing Reality and that He was with them to work on their behalf (Ex. 3:12, 17). Hence, as always, He is all that is necessary when a need arises.

Yahweh is God's covenant name (see Gen. 15:1, 4, 18; Ex. 3:15-17; 20:1; II Sam. 7:4-16; Jer. 31:31-37). The name contained the pledge of all that He had promised to do for Israel and be to them. Knowing Him in a personal,

---

[23] See J. Barton Payne, *The Theology of the Older Testament* (Grand Rapids: Zondervan Publishing House, 1962), p. 145.

covenant relationship, they were to be His people and He their God.[24]

In addition to representing the Trinity (Deut. 6:4) Yahweh sometimes represents certain Persons of the Godhead: God the Father in Psalm 110:1; Isaiah 48:16; 61:1; God the Son in Isaiah 2:2-5; 33:21-22; 40:10; Jeremiah 23:6; and perhaps God the Holy Spirit in Jeremiah 31:31-34 (see Heb. 10:15-18).

- ## God's Compound Hebrew Names

In addition to the basic Hebrew names of Deity, there are several compound forms that include the name of El, Elohim, or Yahweh. To understand their significance more fully, these names should be studied in their context, and a concordance should be used to locate other passages where they occur.

1. THE EL FORMS

    a. El Shaddai—"the almighty God" (Gen. 17:1)
    With shad possibly meaning "breast," El Shaddai suggests
    that God is the sufficient supply and comfort of His people.

    b. El Olam—"the everlasting God" (Gen. 21:33)

    c. El Elyon—"the most high God" (Gen. 14:18-20)

    d. El Qodash—"God the holy One" (Josh. 24:19)

    e. El Qanno—"the jealous God" (Josh. 24:19)

    f. El Elohe Israel—"God, the God of Israel" (Gen. 33:20)

    g. El Roi—"the God who sees" (Gen. 16:13)

    h. El Gadol waw Nora—"the great and terrible God" (Deut. 7:21)
    The fear God incites is terror in His enemies and reverence
    in His people.

    i. El Chanun waw Rachum—"the gracious and merciful God" (Jonah 4:2)

    j. El Neeman—"the faithful God" (Deut. 7:9)

    k. El Chai—"the living God" (Josh. 3:10)

2. THE ELOHIM FORMS

    a. Elohim Chayim—"the living God" (Deut. 5:26)

    b. Elohim Sabaoth—"the God of hosts (armies)" (Amos 3:13)

3. THE YAHWEH FORMS

    a. Yahweh Sabaoth—"The LORD of hosts (armies)" (I Sam. 17:45)

    b. Yahweh Jireh—"the LORD who sees" (Gen. 22:14)
    Therefore, He provides for His people.

    c. Yahweh Rapha—"the LORD who heals" (Ex. 15:26)

    d. Yahweh Nissi—"the LORD my banner" (Ex. 17:15)
    A banner is a standard or flag around which people rally.

    e. Yahweh Qadash—"the LORD who sanctifies" (Lev. 20:8)

    f. Yahweh Rohi—"the LORD my shepherd" (Ps. 23:1)

---

[24] Herbert F. Stevenson, *The Titles of the Triune God*, p. 22.

g. *Yahweh Tsidkenu*—"the LORD our righteousness" (Jer. 23:6)

h. *Yahweh Shalom*—"the LORD (is) peace" (Judg. 6:24)

i. *Yahweh Shammah*—"the LORD (is) there" (Ezek. 48:35; cp. Zech. 8:22; 14:16-17)

• Some Other Names

Other names of God are "Rock" (Deut. 32:4; Ps. 18:1), "Fortress" (II Sam. 22:2; Ps. 18:1), "Maker" (Job 36:3), "King" (I Sam. 12:12), "Redeemer" (Ps. 19:14), "Saviour" (II Sam. 22:3), "Judge" (Gen. 18:25), "Shield" and "Buckler" (Ps. 18:2; Gen. 15:1), "Strength" (I Sam. 15:29), and "Portion" (Jer. 10:16).

In certain passages "the angel of the LORD" seems to refer to God (Gen. 16:7-13; 21:17-18; 22:11-12; 31:11-13; Ex. 3:2-4; Judg. 6:11-16). In others this refers to a holy angel (II Kings 19:35; II Sam. 24:16; Ps. 34:7).

GOD'S NAMES IN THE NEW TESTAMENT

The New Testament lacks the variety of names which are found in the Old Testament. The full name of Deity is stated in the phrase, "in the name of the Father, and of the Son, and of the Holy Spirit" (Mt. 28:19). The names of the individual Persons of the Godhead are given under Paterology, Christology, and Pneumatology.

• Their Generic Name

Occurring more than 1,000 times, this is "God" (Gk. *Theos*) as in Romans 1:1. When it occurs alone, "God" may refer to the Trinity if the context does not restrict the designation to a certain Person of the Godhead (Jas. 1:13). In passages that also refer to the Son, "God" represents the Father (Jn. 3:16; Rom. 1:8-9; I Cor. 1:3-4). In other passages "God" represents the Son (I Jn. 5:20) or the Holy Spirit (Acts 5:3-4; I Cor. 3:16), as determined by the context.

• Their Functional Names

Occurring about 600 times, Their primary title is "Lord" (Gk. *Kurios*), as in Ephesians 4:5. In quotations from the Old Testament, "Lord" represents either *Yahweh* or *Adonai*, as determined by their original references (cp. Mt. 3:3 with Isa. 40:3). When it is used in other passages, "Lord" seems to have a meaning similar to *Adonai*, for its Greek root, meaning "One who has power or authority," suggests this. Also, the ancient translators of the Old Testament into Greek (the Septuagint) used *Kurios* for *Adonai*. Generally, this title refers to God the Son (Acts 2:36; Eph. 4:5; I Cor. 8:6), rarely to God the Father (Acts 4:24; Rev. 4:11; 11:15), and very rarely to God the Holy Spirit (II Cor. 3:17; Heb. 10:15-16).

• Their Personal Names

There are no divine personal names revealed in the New Testament for the Persons of the Godhead. The titles "Father," "Son," and "Holy Spirit," are used as divine personal names.

"Jesus" is the human personal name of God the Son as in Matthew 1:21. It means "the LORD is salvation." He did not have this name before His incarnation.

THE DECREE OF GOD

In this area of our study, we probe beyond our understanding. Because of this, we must avoid hasty conclusions that present a distorted, unbiblical concept of God and man. We must also avoid, as much as possible, looking at the doctrine from only a human point of view. We must try to understand it from God's point of view as well. It is best to withhold final judgment until we have examined all of this doctrine. Whatever our final judgment may be, the truth lies in what the Bible says about God and man and allows God to be God and man to be man.

ITS DEFINITION

God's decree is His plan by means of which He has determined all things that relate to the universe, including His own actions toward it and all that comes to pass in it. In the Scriptures God's decree, or plan, is represented by His "counsel" (Isa. 46:10; Ps. 33:11; Acts 2:23; Eph. 1:11; Heb. 6:17), "purpose" (Isa. 14:24-27; Acts 4:28; Rom. 8:28; Eph. 1:11; 3:11), and "will" (Eph. 1:1, 5, 9, 11). The decree of Psalm 2:7 seems to refer to the Son's incarnation and Messianic work (cp. Acts 13:33; Mt. 3:17).

ITS CHARACTERISTICS

- **God's decree is one (Eph. 1:11; 3:11).**

This is indicated by the singular words, "purpose" and "counsel." W. G. T. Shedd writes, "The Divine decree is formed in eternity, but executed in time. There are sequences in the execution, but not in the formation of God's eternal purpose...For God there is no series of decrees each separated from the others by an interval of time. God is omniscient, possessing the whole of His plans and purposes simultaneously."[25]

- **It is eternal (Eph. 3:11).**

Although all the parts of God's plan come to pass in their divinely appointed time, the plan itself is eternal. From our point of view, the decree was formulated before the foundation of the world (II Tim. 1:9; Rev. 13:8; Tit. 1:2; Eph. 1:4); from God's point of view, it always existed in His mind.

- **It is immutable (Heb. 6:17).**

God never changes or alters His decree; it always remains the same (Ps. 33:11). His plan is never affected by mistake, ignorance, or inability on His

---

[25] W. G. T. Shedd, *Dogmatic Theology*, I, 394 f.

part or by anything outside of Himself, such as evil or the activities of angels or humans.

- **It is universal (Eph. 1:11; Rom. 11:36).**

God's decree includes everything that exists or comes to pass in the universe. This includes the decisions, actions, and conditions of all personal creatures (angels and humans), whether good or evil (II Chron. 10:15; 36:22). It also includes the actions and conditions of all living and non-living things (Ps. 119:90-91). Moreover, God appoints such things as "chance" events (Prov. 16:33; I Kings 22:34), the duration of life (Job 14:5), and man's sphere of habitation (Acts 17:26) and direction (Prov. 16:9).

Furthermore, this plan includes all of God's actions relating to the universe, such as His creating it, sustaining it, governing it, and using it to accomplish His objectives (Rev. 4:11). The decree does not determine the essential qualities of God's nature or the internal relationships of the Trinity.

- **It is certain (Prov. 19:21; Isa. 46:10).**

All that God has decreed will certainly come to pass without fail. Nothing can thwart His purpose (Prov. 21:30), for all that exists is determined by His decree. His decree renders certain the actions of all creatures and created things, but God (as we shall see) does not produce these actions or accept the responsibility of them such as the crucifixion of Jesus (Lk. 22:22; Acts 2:23; 4:27-28).

- **It is absolute (Acts 4:27-28).**

God not only has determined what should be but also how it should come to pass. The fulfillment of His decree in all of its particulars is not dependent upon anything that is not part of the decree itself. For instance, God not only planned that His Son should die as the substitute for sinners (I Pet. 1:19-20; Rev. 13:8) but also under what circumstances (Acts 4:27-28) and by what means He should die (Jn. 10:18). God left nothing to chance. He absolutely determined every detail of every event that comes to pass in the universe.

- **It is free (Eph. 1:5, 9, 11).**

God freely determined what His plan should be and what details it should include. He was not influenced by anyone or anything outside of Himself. Being alone when He (the Godhead) made the decree, God decreed freely, voluntarily, according to His own pleasure and will (Ps. 135:6; Isa. 40:13, 14; Rom. 11:33-36). At that time nothing had been made certain by any previous decree, so there was nothing to be foreseen which would influence the making of His plan.

- **It is hidden (Eph. 3:9-11).**

Being hidden within Himself, God's decree is secret except for that part which He has revealed in His Word and that which has come to pass (see

Deut. 29:29; I Cor. 2:6-12; Rom. 16:25-26; Amos 3:7; Jn. 15:15).

- **It is Christocentric (Eph. 3:11).**

God's decree centers in Christ in the sense that its composition (Eph. 1:4) and fulfillment are related to His divine activities as the Father's Agent (I Cor. 8:6) and to His human, Messianic works as the Father's Servant (Jn. 6:38; Eph. 1:10; II Tim. 1:9; Rev. 1:8).

The foregoing qualities demonstrate that God's decree is not controlled by or synonymous with fate (a system of undetermined, impersonal causes and effects). God's decree is personal; fate is impersonal. His decree is wisely planned for specific ends; fate is the action of chance, producing random, uncertain results.

ITS RELATIONS

The fact of God's decree raises inquiry about its relation to God and His creatures.

- **Its Relation to God**

In our study of God's omniscience we noted that His decree is the basis of His free knowledge (foreknowledge) of all actual things. This view is supported by the following: the order of Romans 8:28-29, where God's purpose precedes His foreknowledge; the truth that His election is one of divine grace, not foreseen human works or merit (Rom. 9:11; 11:5-6; II Tim. 1:9); the fact that foreknowledge is grammatically equated with His counsel in Acts 2:23; and the absolute sovereignty of God (Isa. 46:10), which precludes any rival or equal that would influence His actions. The fact remains that nothing can be foreseen until it has been made certain by the divine decree. That which is not decreed remains in the realm of possibility, but it never becomes a reality that can be foreseen.

With reference to His activities, God's decree concerns only His transitive acts — His works with reference to things outside of Himself, such as His creation of the universe, His dealings with creation, and His atonement for sins. His decree does not pertain to His essential Being, in the sense that He decreed to be holy or to exist as three Persons. Also, it does not relate to immanent activities within the Godhead, in the sense that the Father decreed to love the Son.

- **Its Relation to Creatures**

While God's decree makes certain the actions of all creatures, including angels and humans, these are not all brought to pass in the same manner. God brings some things to pass directly such as the creation of the universe (Gen. 1:1). He brings other things to pass indirectly through an intermediate agency such as natural law (Acts 14:17) or the activities of humans (Dan. 1:9; I Cor. 15:10). This is known as the *efficient aspect* of His decree, for which He assumes the responsibility for what comes to pass.

On the other hand, God allows other things to come to pass, which are made certain by His decree, but which He does not Himself bring to pass, and for which He does not assume the responsibility. This is the *permissive aspect* of His decree. This aspect concerns the sinful actions of angels and humans and their perdition (cp. Rom 9:22-23; see Appendix J). This is not to suggest that God passively allows evil to occur as though He could not prevent or control it. It means that He actively and freely chose evil to be a part of His decree and allowed it to express itself within divinely determined limits, so that by it He might attain certain ends (cp. the crucifixion of Jesus, Acts 2:23; Lk. 22:22). However, He is not the efficient Cause, or Producer, of evil.

ITS DISSIMILARITY

In our thinking about God's decree, we sometimes overlook the fact that His decree is not synonymous with the actions of His personal creatures or with His revealed desire for them. Let us look at this more closely.

- **The decree is not synonymous with the creature's action.**

For instance, while the decree included Adam's sin and made it certain, this part of the decree was not the act itself. The decree did not produce the sin, nor is God guilty of this sin. He did not by decree command Adam to sin. We are reminded that the decree is not addressed to man and is not to be regarded as law, imposing obligation on man's will.[26]

- **The decree is not synonymous with God's revealed desire.**

As strange as it appears, God's decree is not identical to His revealed will, or desire, for His creatures. Actually, being two different things, these truths are not contradictory. God's decree (decretive will, Eph. 1:5, 9, 11) is His secret plan while His commands (preceptive will, Eph. 5:17; I Thess. 4:3) are His revealed desire for His personal creatures.

For example, His desire for His people is that they not sin (cp. I Jn. 2:1), yet in our experience we often deviate from God's preceptive will. This deviation falls within the permissive aspect of the divine decree, but it is not God's preceptive will for us. Moreover, we are responsible for our sinning and for the penalty it incurs. Again, God's revealed desire for the unsaved is that they might be saved (I Tim. 2:4; II Pet. 3:9), but His decree is that only they whom He has chosen will be saved (II Thess. 2:13; Eph. 1:4-5). Whether elected or not, the unsaved person is responsible for his lost condition (Lk. 22:22; Rom. 1:18-32; 9:22-23). In the light of this distinction, it is our duty to be more concerned about God's revealed preceptive will for us than about His decree, which is secret.

Failure to recognize the distinction between God's decretive will and His preceptive will has led Arminian theologians, such as Richard Watson, to

---

[26] L. Berkhof, *Systematic Theology,* p. 103.

reject the absolute, free character of God's decree and to make it dependent upon events that He did not desire for His creatures.[27]

ITS OBJECTIVE (Eph. 1:3-6, 11-12)

The ultimate goal of God's decree is to bring glory to Himself (Isa. 42:8; 43:7; Rom. 9:17, 22; Eph. 3:21; Rev. 4:11). The glory of God consists of some manifestation of His Being (Ps. 19:1; Jn. 2:11) and of the praise which this manifestation evokes from His creatures (Mt. 5:16; 9:8; Rev. 5:11-14).

Although this goal may appear to express pride and selfishness, this is not the case. It is the Creator's right to exalt Himself and to receive from His creation all praise, for it is the creature's duty, whose very existence depends upon the Creator, to glorify his Maker. Actually, God has no equal, and there is nothing that can claim equal praise. Our highest duty is to glorify the Creator in all that we do (I Cor. 10:31; 6:20). This means that we are to live in a manner that will bring Him credit and praise. While sin in our lives makes us unlike Him and discredits Him, our obedience in His strength manifests Him and brings Him praise (Mt. 5:16; cp. Jn. 17:4). We exist for this purpose (Eph. 1:12).

ITS PROBLEMS

Surpassing the limits of our finite minds, the doctrine of God's decree poses two problems that we cannot wholly resolve.

• The Problem of Man's Moral Freedom

At first sight it would appear that God's decree, which renders all things contained therein certain, denies to angels and humans the freedom of choice and the responsibility of their actions. It would appear, at first sight, that people's actions are not free or (as the Arminians hold) occur outside of God's decree. But the crucifixion of Christ shows that God has decreed men's actions and that they are personally responsible for them (Lk. 22:22; Acts 2:23; 3:15; 4:27-28).

Our problem of understanding lies in our conception of freedom. We generally think of it as being absolute, unrestrained self-determination, but we creatures do not have such freedom (Jer. 10:23). Various factors influence our self-determination, such as inner conditioning governing our judgments, inclinations, subconscious motivations, and psychological states (cp. Paul's moral conditioning by the law, Rom. 7:7-9); physical states (cp. Gal. 4:13); external environment (cp. room temperature, people); the forces of evil (Rom. 7:15-23; Eph. 6:11-13; Rom. 12:2); and God (Ezra 6:22; 7:27-28; Prov. 21:1; Dan. 1:9; Jn. 6:44; Phil. 2:13; Rev. 17:17). By the same token, we are not mechanically determined or controlled like puppets. As relatively free agents, we have the capacity to determine and start action. It is in the realm of our

---

[27] Richard Watson, *Theological Institutes* (New York: Hunt & Eaton, 1889), II, 423-29.

consciousness that we freely choose our courses of action without any sense of divine necessity (I Cor. 7:37).[28] Having moral awareness and the power of conscious self-determination, we are accountable for our actions (Rom. 14:12). But beneath the level of our awareness, God acts upon our will in such a way as to accomplish His purpose and still preserve the integrity of our conscious freedom and responsibility. This is the heart of the problem and is beyond our ability to resolve. Since God's absolute sovereignty and man's responsibility are teachings of God's Word, these unresolvable truths must be accepted by faith.

- ## The Problem of God's Relation to Sin

It would appear that God's decree, which renders all things contained therein certain, makes Him to be the efficient Cause or Producer of sin. But this concept of God contradicts what He has revealed about His character (Ps. 92:15; Jas. 1:13; I Jn. 1:5) and ability (Jas. 1:13; Tit. 1:2). Neither is He sinful nor can He sin.

God knew the possibility of sin and for good reasons included it in His decree, but He himself did not bring it to pass. Giving angels and humans the ability to make moral choices, God created them with the ability to make the wrong choice and, thus, to sin. Lucifer chose to admire himself and his beauty rather than God and the beauty of divine holiness. This wrong choice to exalt himself led to pride and to his refusal to remain in his God-given place (I Tim. 3:6; Ezek. 28:13-17; Jn. 8:44).

In His permissive decree God chose to allow sin to come into existence, but He does not accept any responsibility for it. L. Berkhof explains, "The decree merely makes God the author of free, moral beings, who are themselves the authors of sin. God decrees to sustain their free agency, to regulate the circumstances of their life, and to permit that free agency to exert itself in a multitude of acts, of which some are sinful. For good and holy reasons He renders these sinful acts certain, but He does not decree to work evil desires or choices efficiently in man. The decree respecting sin is not an efficient but a permissive decree, or a decree to permit in distinction from a decree to produce sin by divine efficiency."[29]

ITS PRACTICALITY

This doctrine has practical application to life, as A. H. Strong observes:[30]

- It inspires humility by its representation of God's unsearchable counsels and absolute sovereignty.

---

[28] Lewis Sperry Chafer, *Systematic Theology* (Dallas: Dallas Seminary Press, 1947), I, 240.
[29] L. Berkhof, *Systematic Theology*, p. 108.
[30] A. H. Strong, *Systematic Theology*, I, 368.

- It teaches confidence in Him who has wisely ordered our birth, our death, our surroundings, even to the minutest particulars, and has made all things work together for the triumph of His kingdom and the good of those who love Him.

- It shows the enemies of God that, as their sins have been foreseen and provided for in God's plan, so they can never, while remaining in their sins, hope to escape their decreed and threatened penalty.

- It urges the sinner to avail himself of the appointed means of grace if he would be saved.

SOME OBSERVATIONS

- In no way does this doctrine stand in the way of anyone who wants to be saved. All who receive the Saviour are promised salvation (Jn. 1:12; 3:16; 6:37). In fact, all are commanded to receive Him (Acts 17:30, "repent" is a figurative word (synecdoche) for salvational faith; cp. 2:38; 26:20).

- In all of our thoughts about God, we must grant Him the highest honor. We must beware of Satan's attempts to lead us to hold wrong thoughts about God because of our lack of understanding (Rom. 3:4; 9:20; 11:33-36).

- We must be alert to people's reasoning which would lead us to embrace conclusions that are not supported by the clear teaching of Scripture or that conflict with the Scriptures.

- We who are saved should be concerned with God's preceptive will, or desire, for us rather than with what He has decreed. What He has decreed is His concern; what He desires for us should be our concern.

- God's sovereignty and human freedom with its responsibility cannot be reconciled in human thinking. To hold to one and to reject or diminish the other results in our having a distorted view of biblical truth. What we cannot understand by reason must be accepted by faith, for God has spoken and His Word is true.

THE WORKS OF GOD

In this section we shall study the major transitive acts of God that relate to the present universe. The psalmist described God's works to be great, majestic, glorious, wondrous, faithful, and right (Ps. 111:2-4, 7, Berkeley Ver.). This contemplation led him to exclaim, "Holy and awe- inspiring is His name" (vs. 9). As we examine these works, may our hearts be filled with similar praise.

THE CREATION OF THE UNIVERSE

True, reliable knowledge of God's creative work is only found in the Scriptures (Gen. chs. 1, 2), and it is to be received by faith (Heb. 11:3). Any opinion or theory that ignores this, and that does not make this truth its premise, is mere speculation.

- **Its Definition**

Creation may be defined as the work of God in bringing all things comprising the universe into existence. This did not include sin, which was generated later by some of His personal creatures.

- **Its Nature**

An analysis of God's creative work, as presented in the Scriptures, shows the following:

1. IT IS THE JOINT WORK OF THE TRINITY.

It is the work of the Father (I Cor. 8:6), the Son (Jn. 1:3; I Cor. 8:6; Col. 1:13-17), and the Holy Spirit (Gen. 1:2; Job 26:13; 33:4; Ps. 104:30; Isa. 40:12-13). While the work of creation is attributed to each Person, all things originated with the Father, were effected through the Son, and were brought about by means of the Holy Spirit (I Cor. 8:6; Jn. 1:3; Job 26:13). Thus the Father is the Originating Cause of the universe, the Son is its Instrumental Cause, and the Holy Spirit is its Dynamic Cause.

2. IT IS THE FREE ACT OF GOD.

God was not compelled by some force or necessity outside of Himself to create. It was something that He did freely, according to the counsel of His will (Eph. 1:11; Rev. 4:11).

3. IT CONSISTED OF TWO STEPS.

The first step was God's initial creative work. This was His creating the universe without using preexistent material, of which there was none (Gen. 1:1; Ps. 148:2-5; Heb. 11:3). Sometimes this is described as *ex nihilo* creation, that is, "out of nothing" creation. People who ignore this biblical truth speculate that the universe consists of eternal matter, is an emanation of the divine substance, or is some phenomenal appearance of Deity.

The second step was God's subsequent creative work by which He prepared the earth for man's habitation (Gen. 1:3, 6, 9, 14). God also made Adam and Eve as well as vegetation and animal life (11, 20, 24, 26-27; 2:7, 21-22). He used the existing created elements of water and soil to make their physical structures. He imparted to these structures physical life, which in animals and man has its seat in the soul and spirit (Gen. 1:20, 24; 2:7; 6:17; 7:21-22; Eccles. 3:19-20).

4. IT GIVES THE UNIVERSE DISTINCT, DEPENDENT EXISTENCE.

This means that the universe is not God or a part of Him, but it is wholly derived and distinct from Him (Acts 17:24-25). While God is not in any way dependent upon the universe for His existence (Jn. 5:26; Acts 17:25), the universe is wholly dependent upon Him (Heb. 1:3; Col. 1:17).

God's relation to the universe is both transcendent and immanent. Being transcendent, He is separate from, above, and other than the universe. Being immanent, He is everywhere in, with, and throughout the universe, but He is not a part of it or limited by it. This truth indicates that the universe is neither a part of God nor isolated from Him. Yet, it is distinct from Him and is wholly dependent upon Him for its existence.

5. ITS PRIMARY PURPOSE IS TO GLORIFY GOD.

God uses the universe to glorify Himself by manifesting some of His perfections through it (Ps. 19:1; Rom. 1:20), accomplishing His purpose for it (Rev. 4:11; Eph. 1:11-12), and evoking praise from His creatures (Ps. 148; Rev. 5:13; Rom. 11:33-36).

• Its Content

By content I mean all that God created (Col. 1:16; Neh. 9:6; Jn. 1:3) regarding being and place. "Being" refers to what He made — material and immaterial, animate and inanimate, personal and nonpersonal, visible and invisible. "Place" refers to where these persons and things exist. He created all persons and things in the heavens, on earth, and under the earth (Phil. 2:10; Rev. 5:13), which seems to refer to Hades (the contemporary prison of some fallen angels and all dead, unsaved humans).

Did God create evil? In those instances where evil means adversity, He does create this by intermediate causes (Isa. 45:7; cp. Amos 3:6; Isa. 10:5-6). On the other hand, where evil means sin, He is not its efficient Cause. Angels and humans were the generators of sin. Sin was not a part of the original creation. It was produced by personal creatures, who were created sinless and who chose to rebel against their Creator.

• Its Account

The only reliable information that man has of God's creative activity is that which the Creator has been pleased to give in the Scriptures (cp. Gen. 1:1-2:25). Under divine inspiration Moses accurately recorded this information for all future generations. But since this is God's Word, this revelation must be received by faith (regardless of the prevailing scientific opinion) if we are correctly to understand the origin of the universe and the world in which we live (Heb. 11:3). Jesus himself acknowledged the historicity and authenticity of the biblical account (Mt. 19:4-5). It is noteworthy that this account does not include any of the false ideas which were held in Moses' time.[31]

God's creative activity during the six days of creation week is indicated

---

[31] See "The Creation Epic" *Ancient Near Eastern Texts*, ed. James B. Pritchard (Princeton: Princeton University Press, 1955), pp. 60 ff.

by His creative command, "Let..," which does not allow a self-existent universe, intermediary creative agencies, or random chance start and development. His creative activity includes the following:

On the first day (Gen. 1:1-5) He created the heavens and the earth, including time, space, matter, energy, and gravity. The heavens included created angels and the physical celestial bodies, with their environment (Neh. 9:6; Ps. 136:5-6; 146:6; Ex. 20:11). The angels were present when God created the earth (Job 38:4-7). He ordered a temporary light to illuminate the earth until the fourth day, when sunlight shone upon the earth (vs. 17). He also set in motion the diurnal rotation of the earth, which was yet unprepared for man.

On the second day (vss. 6-8) He created the earth's atmosphere ("firmament," an expanse) which lay between the water on earth and the Noachian flood water suspended above the earth in vapor form.[32]

On the third day (vss. 9-13) He separated the sea and the land into individual masses and created vegetation.[33]

On the fourth day (vss. 14-19) He directed the lunar, solar, and stellar bodies to give their light simultaneously upon the earth. Verse 16 is to be understood either as God's making these bodies on this day from existing matter created on the first day or as a flashback to the first day when He created these bodies. In any case, on the fourth day He set them in place and caused their light to shine instantaneously upon the earth although they were millions of light years away.

On the fifth day (vss. 20-23) He created marine life and flying creatures, described as "living souls."[34]

On the sixth day (vss. 24-31) He created land animals, creeping forms of life, and man. Man is distinguished from animals by being made in the image of God. This image is that of similarity ("likeness"), not identicalness, and consists of personhood. God gave to newly created man a stewardship to fulfill.

That this creative activity was limited to six days is indicated in Genesis 2:1 and is declared in Exodus 20:11. On the seventh day (Gen. 2:1-3) God ceased from His creative activity regarding material creation. His resting was not because of exhaustion (Isa. 40:28) but because of His completing His creation purpose.

The second account of creation (Gen. 2:4-25) gives more details about the creation of Adam and Eve and their duties. (Verse 19a is a flashback to 1:21-25).

---

[32] Joseph C. Dillow, *The Waters Above: Earth's Pre-Flood Vapor Canopy* (Chicago: Moody Press, 1981).

[33] "After its kind" (Gen. 1:11-12, 21, 24-25) implies that the various kinds of life (flora and fauna) were at creation fixed to the extent that each would produce essentially the same as itself. Room was allowed in these kinds for the development of varieties.

[34] Like the creation of man (Gen. 2:7), God made the bodies of animals from existing matter (water or earth) and animated them with soul and spirit ("creature" literally is "soul"); animals also have a spirit (Eccles. 3:21; cp. Gen. 7:15, 22).

This information completes what is given in the first creation account (Gen. 1:1-2:3). It also provides information that is essential to a right understanding of man's fall, recorded in Genesis, chapter three.

How should we interpret the creation account? Religious liberals regard it as an unreliable redaction of earlier pagan traditions or a fallible statement of truth in the form of myth. On the other hand, people who believe in the divine inspiration of the account interpret it literally or accommodatively. Let us examine this more closely.

1. LITERAL INTERPRETATION OF CREATION

This understands the account to be a simple, straightforward statement of God's creative activity in normal language. This also holds that this activity occurred during the time of six days, all of which are to be regarded as twenty-four-hour days.[35] It understands the first verse of Genesis chapter one to be a broad, general declaration of God's creation of the heavens and the earth. What follows (vss. 2-31) is a detailed account of how God prepared the original, uninhabitable earth for man. It is noteworthy that verse two does not grammatically contain action but, having three circumstantial clauses, describes the earth's original condition. Grammatically, these descriptive clauses modify the main verb "said" in verse three.[36] Creating the earth a desolate mass, enveloped in darkness and covered with water, the Holy Spirit is seen hovering over the face of the waters, sustaining what had been done and being ready to carry out the remaining creative activity.

In answer to the protest that the description in verse two is one of an imperfect state, it may be said that the creation was not "perfect," in the sense that it was finished, until the end of the six days, but each step was perfect according to God's purpose.[37] According to E. J. Young, the words "without form" (meaning "desolation," "emptiness") and "void" (meaning "wasteness") "do not affirm that it was a confused mass, in the sense of being disordered or jumbled, but simply that it was not habitable, not ready for man...All was well-ordered and precisely as God desired it to be."[38] Thus, although the earth was incomplete (not yet ready for man), it was perfect for God's immediate purpose and its condition was in keeping with the divine will. (Isaiah 45:18 does not refer to Genesis 1:2 but to the fact that God did not fail to accomplish His purpose in providing inhabitants for the earth, rather than leaving it empty.)

Furthermore, the "darkness" of verse two is to be understood as literal

---

[35] Some hold that the first three days were not solar, twenty-four-hour days because the sun did not shine upon the earth. Others respond by pointing out that a twenty-four-hour day is determined by the rotation of the earth, which presumably began when it was created on the first day.

[36] E. J. Young. This may be paraphrased, "At the time when God said, 'Let there be light,' the three-fold condition recorded in verse two already existed." See Edward J. Young, Studies in Genesis One (Philadelphia: Presbyterian and Reformed Publishing Co., 1964), pp. 8 f.

[37] Henry Morris, Studies in the Bible and Science (Philadelphia: Presbyterian and Reformed Publishing Co., 1966), p. 32.

[38] Edward J. Young, op. cit., pp. 13, 38.

darkness, for God had not yet commanded light to appear. It is not to be interpreted as a figurative expression for sin or its results. It is noteworthy that God himself being light has eternally dwelt in the absence of any other kind of light (II Chron. 6:1; Ps. 97:2). He created darkness as well as light for the benefit of the universe (Isa. 45:7; Ps. 104:19-20).

The literal interpretation of the creation account holds that God's creative activities are fiat in nature, that is, by divine command. When He said, "Let there be....," it was done immediately, uniquely, apart from natural law, wholly by divine power (Ps. 33:6, 9). Being infinite in power, God did His creative work instantaneously. For example, if ten men can do a piece of work in one hundred days, then (disregarding logistics and the like) a hundred could do the same work in ten days and a thousand could do the work in one day. Thus the use of infinite power requires no time at all.

2. ACCOMMODATIVE INTERPRETATIONS OF CREATION

These interpretations are attempts to harmonize the biblical account of creation with scientific opinion about the universe. However, I believe that these should be rejected, for any attempt to harmonize God's inerrant account with changing scientific opinion not only requires an unnatural explanation of the creation record but also subjects God's authoritative Word to man's reasoning. The thinking which underlies scientific opinion is governed by the limitations of the scientific method, which cannot deal with such questions as origins, and by the presuppositions of the scientist, which often are unscriptural. To my mind, it seems very unlikely that God would reveal such important truth, of primary interest to all generations, in a form that could not be correctly understood until modern times. Some accommodative interpretations follow:

a. The day-age theory

This holds that the days of Genesis chapter one were six periods of time which represent geological history and that the creative events were carried out by God through natural processes within nature over vast periods of time.[39]

b. The progressive creation theory

This holds that on each day of geological history God started the creative activity by command and brought it to completion through the processes of natural law.[40]

c. The gap or reconstruction theory

While holding that the earth was prepared for man's habitation in six days, this theory believes that preceding this reconstruction, there was an interval of time, during which a perfect earth suffered divine judgment and

---

[39] See Walter J. Beasley, *Creation's Amazing Architect* (London: Marshall, Morgan, & Scott, 1955).
[40] See Bernard Ramm, *The Christian View of Science and Scripture* (London: The Paternoster Press, 1955), pp. 76-79.

experienced geological upheaval. Some believe that this gap was before Genesis 1:1.[41] This means that the initial creation (Jn. 1:3; Col. 1:16; Heb. 11:3) and Satan's rebellion (Ezek. 28:12-15) took place before Genesis 1:1. According to this view, Genesis 1:1-2 describes a later refashioning of a judgment-ridden earth in preparation for man's creation and habitation.

Popularized by *The Scofield Reference Bible,* a more commonly held view of the gap theory is that Genesis 1:1 refers to the original creation of the universe in perfect, finished form, with the earth under Lucifer's (Satan's name before his fall) supervision. But his revolt against God brought divine judgment upon the earth, resulting in the desolation described in verse two. After an unrecorded gap of geological ages, verse three marks the beginning of the earth's reconstruction for man.

d. The theistic evolution theory

This allegorizes the creation account as being a poetic expression of spiritual truth. This theory holds that God used an evolutionary process to create forms of life and to bring them to their present stage of development.

Accommodative interpretations of Genesis one generally assume that modern understanding of geological data is correct, that God initially created the earth in finished form, that the revolt of Lucifer took place before Genesis 1:3, that the linking verb "was" means "became" (vs. 2), that other biblical references describe the "chaos" of verse two as a divine judgment, and that death was the universal experience of creatures before man's fall. However, these assumptions are not necessarily biblical ones. Geological data may be the result of creative processes, the Noachic flood, and other natural disturbances of the earth's crust.[42] In the light of Genesis 1:31 and 1:26 with 9:2, it appears that Satan's revolt did not take place until after the creative week. After the Flood man did not have the same authority over the earth that Adam had. I believe that when he sinned, Adam lost this to Satan. Grammatically, the translation "was" is the right one in this context.[43] The contexts of Isaiah 24:1 and Jeremiah 4:23-26 show that these references speak of the prophetic future rather than of Genesis 1:2. It appears that creatures with soul (nephesh, Gen. 1:20-21, 24; 2:7) did not die until man's sin and the divine "vanity" was imposed upon them (Gen. 3:17-19, 21; 4:8; Rom. 5:12; 8:20-22). It is noteworthy that land animals and air-borne creatures were herbivorous before man's fall (Gen. 1:29-30).

That the six days of creation week were twenty-four-hour days is supported by the following considerations: This is the primary, ordinary meaning of "day" in the Bible. The phrase, "evening and morning," points to

---

[41] Merrill F. Unger, "Rethinking the Genesis Account of Creation," *Bibliotheca Sacra,* Vol. 115, No. 457 (1958), p. 28.

[42] John C. Whitcomb and Henry M. Morris, *The Genesis Flood* (Philadelphia: The Presbyterian and Reformed Publishing Company, 1962), ch. VI.

[43] Weston W. Fields, *Unformed and Unfilled* (Phillipsburg, N.J.: Presbyterian and Reformed Publishing Co., 1978), ch. 4.

the diurnal rotation of the earth upon its axis (a day of twenty- four hours is determined by the time consumed by a complete rotation of the earth, whether or not solar light reaches it). This view is supported by Exodus 20:9-11, where literal days are mentioned regarding the workweek and the Sabbath. In biblical usage whenever the word "day" is preceded by a numerical adjective or occurs in plural form, it means literal days (cp. Gen. 7:10-12). Adam was created on the sixth day, yet he was only 130 years old when Seth was born (Gen. 5:3). It may be that vegetation (created on the third day) needed the warmth and light of the sun (reaching earth on the fourth day) and the pollination of insects (created on the fifth day) for their survival. On the other hand, whenever the word "day" is used in the Scriptures for daytime or a period of more than twenty-four hours, it is indicated in the context (cp. Gen. 1:5; 2:4).

• Its Date

Many scientists believe that the earth is from three to five billion years old. This estimate is ultimately based on the principle of uniformitarianism,[44] which is applied to the interpretation of geological data and to the evaluation of radioactive dating materials. On the other hand, a number of Christian scholars and scientists prefer the view that the earth is about 10,000 years old,[45] although Bible chronology points to a younger age of some 6,000 years. Since nothing can be verified before the beginning of recorded history (c. 3,500 B.C.), all estimates of age are only guesses. The most reliable record, I believe, is given in the Bible, which gives a complete genealogy from Adam to Christ.[46]

• Its Antagonists

The antagonists of biblical revelation regarding the origin of the universe are scientism and its associate, evolutionism. Scientism is the philosophy that exalts the scientific method above God's Word and that says that where this method does not apply nothing exists. While the scientific method has legitimate application to material things such as their content and function, it is incapable of making any authoritative pronouncements about metaphysical matters, including the origin of the universe. Such questions as origins, meaning, and purpose can be answered only by divine revelation.

When unsaved people reject God's revelation of His creative activity, their alternative is to embrace the erroneous view that the universe is the product of impersonal chance. Having no explanation for the origin of matter, these

---

[44] Uniformitarianism is the theory that existing processes, observable in nature, have always operated essentially as they do now. While uniformity is manifest in nature, this theory ignores divine interventions in the past which have interrupted or altered these processes to the extent that they cannot be projected backward over long periods of time with accuracy.

[45] See Henry M. Morris, The Biblical Basis for Modern Science: (Grand Rapids: Baker Book House, 1984) pp. 260 ff.

[46] Philip Mauro, The Chronology of the Bible (Boston: Scripture Truth Dept., 1922), p. 17.

people regard it to be eternal and to have arrived at its present form by random evolutionary process.

The Columbia Encyclopedia defines organic evolution as "the belief that existing animals and plants developed by a process of gradual, continuous change from previously existing forms."[47] Evolutionists attribute this development to certain mechanics of change, now observable in nature, namely, adaptation, mutation, and natural selection.

We who accept God's account of His creative activity in the Scriptures hold the view of creationism — the belief that various basic forms of life were created by God apart from any evolutionary process. God may have used mechanics of change to bring about variety within definite boundaries, determined by the original "kind" of vegetation, marine life, flying creatures, and land animals (Gen. 1:11-12, 21, 24-25), such as the various strains of dogs. This may also account for the racial distinctions of man. William J. Tinkle offers the view that living organisms were created heterozygous, that is, with mixed genes which produced more, but not higher, types.[48]

1. EVOLUTION'S OPPOSITION TO THE SCRIPTURES

This opposition is expressed by the following comparisons:

Evolution attributes the present existence and form of the universe to impersonal chance — a view that is wholly mechanistic and materialistic. Contrariwise, the Scriptures reveal that the universe is the creation of the personal Creator God. Philosophically, the concept of theistic evolution is absurd, for it says that God worked together with chance in creating the universe.[49]

Evolution holds that all present life arose from a few simple forms. Contrariwise, the Bible teaches that God created life "after its kind" (Gen. 1:1-12, 21, 24-25). This does not say that all creatures living today appear exactly as their original "kinds" were created, since there was a development of variety within the limits of their orders. But this development is not to be regarded as evolutionary since higher types did not develop.

Evolution teaches that man is experiencing a moral improvement and that sins are traits of animal ancestry, which will gradually disappear with the continuation of man's development. Contrariwise, the Bible reveals that man is a responsible creature, who has sinned against his Creator and has incurred to himself awful penalties by this action.

Regarding the universe as a closed system (a vast machine that operates wholly on its own), evolution rejects the fact of the transcendent God who rules over the affairs of the universe. According to evolution any god there

---

[47] "Evolution," The Columbia Encyclopedia, the third edition, p. 685.

[48] William J. Tinkle, Heredity (Grand Rapids: Zondervan Publishing House, 1970), pp. 88-92.

[49] Chance, or fate, is a system of random, undetermined, impersonal causes and effects. This has no place in a universe over which God has sovereign control.

may be is a part of the machine and consists of the same substance as the universe. Contrariwise, the Bible teaches that God is a Reality other than the universe and that He governs its affairs to achieve His own purpose.

2. EVOLUTION'S OPPOSITION TO NATURAL LAW

Christian scholars and scientists point out that those natural processes that evolutionists believe account for evolutionary development really contradict two basic principles within the framework of which all natural processes must operate. These basic laws are known as the first and second laws of thermodynamics — the laws of the conservation and the deterioration of matter.

The first law (conservation) states that although energy or matter changes form, the total quantity is conserved, that matter is neither created nor destroyed. This principle contradicts the evolutionary view of spontaneous creation of energy, which accounts for increasing organization, integration, and development. The Bible supports this law of conservation (Gen. 2:1-3; Heb. 4:3-4, 10; II Pet. 3:10).

The second law (deterioration) states that all physical systems, if left to themselves, tend to become less ordered and useful. While the total amount of energy in the universe remains the same, the amount available for work becomes less (cp. a match burns only once). Thus, processes run down, and things wear out or become disorganized. Any temporary increase in an order requires an input of energy from outside the system itself (cp. Heb. 1:3). This principle contradicts the evolutionary view that a perpetual increase of organization and development is taking place in the universe according to natural processes.[50] Psalm 102:25-27 teaches otherwise.

The theory of evolution also opposes the principle of biogenesis. This principle states that life derives only from life. This contradicts the evolutionary view that life spontaneously arose from inanimate material. With the teaching that the living Creator is the source of all life, the Bible supports the principle of biogenesis (Acts 17:24-25).

Although the evolutionary theory contradicts these basic universal laws and rests upon the absurdity of random chance, brilliant people of the world prefer to accept this rather than the truth of the personal Creator. To accept the latter requires them to admit their creaturehood and their accountability to the Creator and their duty to pay honors to Him. Because they are in rebellion against God, unsaved people prefer Satan's lie above God's truth (cp. Rom. 1:18-25).

• Its Continuation

The present physical universe will continue until the close of Christ's millennial reign. At this time God will dissolve the present universe (II Pet.

---

[50] Henry M. Morris, *The Twilight of Evolution* (Grand Rapids: Baker Book House, 1963), ch. II. Henry M. Morris, *Biblical Cosmology and Modern Science* (Grand Rapids: Baker Book House, 1970), ch. VIII.

3:10-13; Rev. 20:11) and will create a new one, which will continue forever (Rev. 21:1-3). Between the dissolution of the universe and the creation of a new one, there will take place the judgment of the lost (Rev. 20:11-15).

Meanwhile, during the present age the Lord is building His church, which is called "one new man" (Mt. 16:18; Eph. 2:15). All who receive the Saviour are made new creatures in Christ (II Cor. 5:17; Eph. 2:10).

GOD'S SOVEREIGN RULE

The Scriptures teach that God exercises sovereign, absolute rule over the universe to do what He wills (I Chron. 29:11-12; Ps. 103:19; Eph. 1:11). J. I. Packer observes,

> This view of God's relation to the world must be distinguished from: (a) *pantheism,* which absorbs the world into God; (b) *deism,* which cuts it off from Him; (c) *dualism,* which divides control of it between God and another power; (d) *indeterminism,* which holds that it is under no control at all; (e) *determinism,* which posits a control of a kind that destroys man's moral responsibility; (f) the doctrine of *chance,* which denies the controlling power to be rational; and (g) the doctrine of *fate,* which denies it to be benevolent.[51]

God's sovereign rule is set forth in the biblical teaching of preservation and providence.

• His Preservation

Preservation concerns God's maintaining the existence of what He has made and His benevolent care of these things (Neh. 9:6; Col. 1:17; Heb. 1:3). He faithfully provides for the needs of the universe according to His purpose for these creatures and things. He cares for inanimate creation (Isa. 40:26), His creatures (Ps. 104:10-28), all people (Acts 14:17; 17:25, 28), and His elect people (Ps. 37:23-29; Isa. 41:10; Mt. 6:25-34; Jn. 6:39; 10:28).

• His Providence

Providence concerns God's directing everything to its divinely appointed goal. By His providence God works out His decree for all actual things. This is seen in His fulfilling His sovereign purpose throughout the universe (Dan. 4:35), His ruling all natural forces (Ps. 104; Job 38:4-38) and animals (Job 38:39-39:20; 40:15-41:34), His controlling the affairs of nations (Dan. 4:25; Isa. 10:5-6; II Chron. 10:12-16) and individuals (Isa. 44:28; Jer. 1:5; Prov. 16:9; 20:24; 21:1), and His overruling people's misfortunes (Gen. 39:1-2, 21-23; 45:7).

As we look at the truth of God's providence, several problems come into view. One of these is the material, temporal prosperity of the wicked (cp. Ps. 73:3). When the psalmist went into God's sanctuary, he learned that this prosperity was only temporary. He saw the awful end of the wicked (vss. 17-19) and reflected on his own blessings (vss. 23-28). In the New Testament we learn that God is patient with the wicked to give them opportunity to repent

---

[51] J. I. Packer, "Providence," *The New Bible Dictionary,* p. 1051.

(Rom. 2:4; II Pet. 3:9). The only prosperity they will ever enjoy will be in this present life (cp. Mt. 25:41, 46).

Another problem that comes into view is the suffering of godly people. God uses suffering for beneficial purposes (Prov. 3:11-12; Ps. 119:67, 71). He uses it to promote the practical sanctification and spiritual growth of His people (Jas. 1:2-4), to correct us when we fail to deal with known sins in our lives (Rev. 3:19; I Cor. 11:30-32), to bring us into subordination to His will, to instruct us and to cause us to be fruitful (Heb. 12:5-11). In spite of Satan's doubts and lies, God has our spiritual well-being in view in all of our suffering. We need to remember that He is more concerned about our spiritual state than our physical comfort. If necessary, He will deprive us of the physical in order to promote our spiritual growth and well-being. Faithfully borne suffering glorifies God as well as brings us personal blessing (Job 1:21; 42:1-6; Jn. 9:1-3; Jas. 1:2-4).

The godly also suffer because of the hostility of the world (Jn. 15:18-20). Jesus declared that the world hates His people because of their association with Him and their severance from it. This hatred is largely impersonal and constitutional (due to the essential differences between unsaved and saved people,) rising from the world's hostility toward God and the conflict of their depraved hearts with those who are saved (cp. Phil. 1:29; II Tim. 3:12; I Pet. 4:12-16; I Jn. 3:13).

Closely related to this problem is the suffering of "undeserving" people, including infants and children. These suffer because they are a part of a sinful world. H. E. Guillebaud writes, "Hard as it is for the individual who suffers through another's wickedness, it is in the best interests of mankind that the ugliness of sin should not be hidden, and nothing does more to show it in its true light than the misery which it brings to the innocent...A sinful world cannot be a world free of suffering."[52] Believing that children who die before reaching accountability are saved at death, I see something worse than their death. It is their experiencing the rigors of this life and in the end their going to Hell for not having received the Saviour.

Suffering of all kinds is an inevitable result of sin's entrance into the human family. It will be acutely experienced by the lost forever (Mt. 25:46), but we who are saved will one day be forever delivered from it (Rev. 21:3-5).

A last problem relating to God's providence is His involvement in the actions of personal, accountable creatures. The Bible shows that He permits some sins (Ps. 81:12-13; II Thess. 2:7-12), He prevents certain sins (Gen. 20:6; I Sam. 25:39), and He limits certain evil actions (Job 1:12; 2:6; II Thess. 2:7) according to His sovereign purpose. God not only allows unsaved people to do what they prefer (Rom. 9:22), but He also prompts His people to desire and do His good pleasure (Phil. 2:13).

---

[52] H. E. Guillebaud, *Some Moral Difficulties of the Bible* (London: Inter-Varsity Fellowship, 1949), p. 35.

This relation between God's sovereign influence upon personal creatures and their responsible actions is called "concurrence" (a running together), as seen in Deuteronomy 30:15-20; Proverbs 16:9; 20:24; 21:1; Luke 22:22; and Acts 2:23. James Packer observes, "God's control is absolute, in the sense that men do only that which He has ordained that they should do; yet they are truly free agents, in the sense that their decisions are their own, and they are morally responsible for them."[53]

How God can control the actions of people and yet not deprive them of their freedom and responsibility is, indeed, a mystery which defies our understanding. But since this is the teaching of Scripture, we must be contented to accept this truth by faith and to wait for more enlightenment, which will be given later (cp. I Cor. 13:11-12).

GOD'S DISPENSATIONS

Throughout human history God has given to people, both universally and particularly, certain responsibilities or duties, which we call "dispensations." While some minimize this truth, I believe that it is scriptural and is required for our pleasing God. Our understanding of the dispensations gives us insight into God's will for mankind and us.[54]

• Their Definition

The New Testament word "dispensation" basically means "a house rule" (Gk. *oikonomia*). In its usage the word may mean "management" of a household (Lk. 16:2-4), "administration" or "stewardship" (I Cor. 9:17; Eph. 3:2; Col. 1:25), "arrangement" or "plan" (Eph. 3:9, "fellowship"; 1:10), or "training" (I Tim. 1:4, "edifying").[55]

As Christ's apostle, Paul spoke of his duties as a stewardship ("dispensation"), for which he was endued with divine grace (Eph. 3:1-2; cp. Rom. 12:3). With this in view, I define a *dispensation* to be a stewardship, or the responsibilities, that God assigns to mankind or to certain people for a period of time.

While a dispensation involves time, the emphasis should be placed on the duties which the dispensation imposes on people. Although God works through these dispensations to accomplish His purpose (cp. Eph. 1:10; 3:9), our primary concern in this study is with the duties that these dispensations require of the people to whom they are given. Excepting the first one, these dispensations are not to be regarded as tests of obedience to the divine will. Rather, they are declarations of the divine will for the people to whom they are given.

---

[53] James I. Packer, *The New Bible Dictionary*, p. 1052.
[54] For an introduction to dispensationalism, see Charles C. Ryrie, *Dispensationalism Today* (Chicago: Moody Press, 1965), chs. 2, 3.
[55] William F. Arndt and F. Wilbur Gingrich, "oikonomia," *Greek-English Lexicon of the New Testament* (1957), p. 562.

A *dispensationalist* is one who recognizes the divine dispensations and interprets the Bible accordingly. Also, *dispensationalism* is the interpretation and application of the Scriptures that recognizes the dispensations, the particular *features* that distinguish between these dispensations, the people to whom they are given, and the portions of the Bible to which they relate.

- **Their Distinction from the Ages**

We should *distinguish* between a dispensation and an age and *not* use these terms synonymously. In the Bible the word "age" has several *meanings* relating to time. In addition to referring to the *age of a person* (I Chron. 23:3; Jn. 9:21), the word "age" has two meanings which have dispensational significance.[56] These meanings are characterized by the words "dynamically" and "ethically."

Dynamically, an age is a period of time that is characterized by some activity of God, man, or Satan. For instance, the period during which the Lord is building His Church is called the Church Age. According to the pre-tribulation rapture view, the period immediately after the rapture of the Church and before Christ's second coming to earth is called the Tribulation Age. This is because of the many judgments earth dwellers will experience during this time (Rev. chs. 6-19). The period during which God deals with Israel (the seventy-sevens of Daniel ch. 9) is sometimes called the Jewish Age (cp. Mt. 24:3, "world" = age). Also, our Lord's reign over the earth for a thousand years is called the Kingdom Age.

Ethically, an age is what the world is morally and philosophically at any moment of its history. For instance, when he writes, "Be not conformed to this world (age)" (Rom. 12:2), Paul is urging his Christian readers not to adopt the sinful lifestyle and thinking of the unsaved.

In its relation to a dispensation an age may be concurrent with only a part of a dispensation. For example, I believe that the Church Age and the Tribulation Age fall within the Dispensation of Grace. Also, an age may extend beyond the limits of a dispensation. For example, the Jewish Age covers parts of the Dispensations of Law and Grace.

- **Their Aid in Bible Interpretation**

The recognition and understanding of the dispensations are important to a right interpretation and application of the Bible, especially in the following ways:

One, this observes the distinctions between the divine stewardships and between the divine covenants, together with the people to whom they belong.

---

[56] Robert Cameron defines an age to be "a period of time, having a well defined beginning, and marked by certain moral and providential characteristics which distinguish it from all other periods of time..." (*The Doctrine of the Ages*, p. 18). The Bible speaks of God's creating the ages through Christ (Heb. 1:2; 11:3), His wisdom being ordained before the ages (I Cor. 2:7), the mystery of Gentile and Jewish equality not revealed in previous ages (Eph. 3:5; Col. 1:26), Satan's being the god of the present age (II Cor. 4:4) and his demon hosts as its rulers (Eph. 6:12), the present age being evil (Gal. 1:4; Rom. 12:2), the end of the age (Mt. 13:39-40; 24:3; 28:20), the age to come (Mt. 12:32; Lk. 20:34-35; Eph. 1:21), the ends of the ages (I Cor. 10:11; Heb. 9:26), the ages to come (Eph. 2:7). In KJV *aion* is often translated "world."

An example is the distinction between the nation of Israel and the church universal. Disregarding this distinction, non-dispensationalists regard Israel to be the church of the Old Testament and the church to be the Israel of the New Testament, with common spiritual blessings and functions. However, dispensationalists hold that each of these groups has its own particular stewardship, blessings, and function. Having the stewardship of grace, the church is not obligated to observe the Law of Moses, nor does it fulfill the same function as Israel.

Two, this also allows a literal interpretation of the Bible, especially in the area of unfulfilled biblical prophecy. This method of interpreting prophecy was established by the literal fulfillment of those O.T. prophecies that related to our Lord's first coming to earth. Non-dispensationalists, for instance, usually believe that Israel, by their rejection of Christ, forfeited their future place in God's program and that all prophecies about the future of the nation are to be interpreted allegorically as pertaining to the church. On the other hand, dispensationalists hold that Israel has a definite place in God's future program, as the prophecies indicate, and that they must experience the fulfillment of God's covenant promises to them.

Many dispensationalists hold that throughout human history there is only one method of salvation, that God's moral law is always the same, and that salvation brings basic, common blessings to all (the forgiveness of sins, the reception of eternal life, and a personal relationship with God (Jer. 31:33-34). On the other hand, the redeemed peoples of the various dispensations appear to have different functions in God's program. For instance, Israel had a special relation to the LORD as His wife (Hos. ch. 2). Although the nation has been unfaithful to Him, yet in the beginning of Christ's earthly kingdom they will be restored to Him and will again enjoy the blessings of this relation and function as the foremost nation on earth (Zech. 8:23; Mic. 4:1-7; Isa. 59:20-60:22). On the other hand, the church will function as the bride of Christ (Eph. 5:32; Rev. 19:7). This indicates that she will have a special relation to the Lord Jesus above all other redeemed peoples. Unlike Israel, the church will not have an earthly inheritance, but will be with Jesus forever (I Thess. 4:17; Jn. 14:3).

• Their Application to Life

One, we who are saved are to follow the Dispensation of Grace, which consists of most of the commands of the New Testament. This portion of the Bible was given by the Lord Jesus for the direction of His people (Jn. 16:12-15; Eph. 4:21; Col. 3:16; Gal. 6:2; Rev. 1:1-2).

Two, while our Lord's teachings recorded in the Gospels were given during the Dispensation of Mosaic Law, they also apply to us as well. By these teachings the Lord was preparing His disciples for life and service in the new dispensation which began on Pentecost. Examples of these teachings are found in the Sermon the Mount (Mt. chs. 5-7).

Three, we must recognize that while it is all profitable to us, the Bible is not all about us (II Tim. 3:16; Rom. 15:4; I Cor. 10:11). Most of the Old Testament concerns God's dealing with Israel under the Dispensation of the Mosaic Law. Since the New Testament gives God's dispensation for His people today, we may follow the instructions of the Old Testament in so far as these teachings reflect, or are in harmony with, those of the New Testament. For instance, we do not follow the levitical sacrificial ritual, for these have been fulfilled in and replaced by the sacrifice of the Lord Jesus. On the other hand, we read of the duty of fearing God (Ps. 34:9; Prov. 1:7; Eccles. 12:13), which is also commanded in the New Testament (Eph. 5:21; Heb. 12:28; I Pet. 2:17).

Four, there are prophetic passages in the New Testament which do not directly apply to us today such as Matthew chapters 24-25 and Revelation chapters 4-18. These passages will be of special value to God's people who will be living in the Tribulation Age.

Five, there are recorded in Acts certain events, experiences, and practices, that belong to the transition into the Dispensation of Grace and which are not normative for us today. These include waiting for the promise of the Father (1:14), the experience of the Pentecostal phenomena (2:1-4), the common holding of private property (2:45), and praying for the gift of the Holy Spirit (8:14-17). Today, we receive the Holy Spirit's indwelling, baptism, and anointing at salvation. Because of this, it is unnecessary to seek these as additional works, or blessings, of grace.

Some carry dispensationalism beyond the limits that are clearly indicated by the Scriptures. These people are called "ultradispensationalists." They hold that the Great Commission is Jewish (Mt. 28:19-20). They believe that while the "Jewish church" began on Pentecost (Acts ch. 2), "the Gentile church" began with Paul, either after his conversion (13:2) or after his arrival in Rome (28:28). They also teach that water baptism is not for the Church Age and that Acts 2:38 sets forth a works kind of salvation. These extreme views can be refuted by showing that the building of the church began on Pentecost, that water baptism was observed by the early church, that salvation is always by grace through faith in Jesus, and that the commission is self-perpetuating.[57]

• Their Relation to the Divine Covenants

We avoid confusion and misunderstanding when we clearly distinguish between God's dispensations and covenants. While a dispensation is a stewardship that God gives to certain people to fulfill, a covenant declares by promises what God will do for certain people. There are divine covenants within dispensational periods of time, but these promises are not

---

[57] In Acts 2:38 the phrase, "for the remission of sins," can also read "because of the remission of sins." The preposition "for" (eis) sometimes indicates a basis or ground, as in Matthew 12:41, "at the preaching of Jonah." Baptism follows salvation (Acts 18:8).

an essential feature of any dispensation, except the Mosaic Law, which functioned simultaneously as a dispensation and a covenant. The primary feature of the dispensation is the duties which God imposes upon certain people; that of the covenant is the promises which God makes to certain people.

- **Their Names**
  1. The Dispensation of Created Man (Gen. 1:28-29; 2:15-17)
  2. The Dispensation of Fallen Man (Gen. 3:16 – 4:7)
  3. The Dispensation of Governed Man (Gen. 9:1-7)
  4. The Dispensation of the Patriarachs (Gen. 12:1; 17:1; 26:5; 31:3, 13; 35:1; 46:1-4)
  5. The Dispensation of the Mosaic Law (Ex. 20:1-7; 21:1 – 23:19; Lev. chs. 1-27; Num. chs. 5, 6, 9, 10, 27-30)
  6. The Dispensation of Grace (Tit. 2:11-12; most commands of the New Testament)
  7. The Dispensation of Christ's Earthly Rule (Isa. 2:1-3)

- **Their Description**
  In our study of the dispensations, we shall observe the following features:

  1. *THE RECIPIENTS OF THE STEWARDSHIP*
  These are the people to whom the dispensation is given. Some dispensations are universal in that they are given to all people worldwide; others are restricted to certain people.

  2. *THE STEWARDSHIP ASSIGNED TO MAN*
  This concerns the duties, expressing God's will, which are given in the dispensation and which require obedience.

  3. *MAN'S RESPONSE TO THE STEWARDSHIP*
  The response is either disobedience or obedience. Each dispensation imposes upon its recipients the responsibility of fulfilling its stewardship.

  4. *GOD'S REACTION TO MAN'S RESPONSE*
  He blesses the obedient and punishes the disobedient. We shall see that the elect are sufficiently obedient (by divine grace) to allow God to accomplish His purpose through them.

  5. *THE DURATION OF THE STEWARDSHIP*
  This is the span of time during which the duties of a dispensation are in force.

  6. *GOD'S USE OF THE STEWARDSHIP*
  God works through people's lives according to their dispensation to carry out His purpose for mankind. Since redemption is a primary divine activity in the history of man, we shall look at this aspect of God's use of the dispensations.

- **Their Content**
  1. *THE DISPENSATION OF CREATED MAN (Gen. 1:28-29; 2:15-17)*
     a. *The recipients of the stewardship*
        These were Adam and Eve. That they were historical persons is indicated in the New Testament (Mt. 19:4; Lk. 3:38; Rom. 5:12; I Cor. 11:8-9; I Tim. 2:13-14). God created Eve to help Adam meet the requirements of the stewardship as well as to minister to his social needs (Gen. 2:18; I Cor. 11:9).
     b. *The stewardship assigned to man*
        This consists of the following duties:
  1. To be fruitful and fill the earth (Gen. 1:28).
     Man is to reproduce his kind and populate the earth. The word "replenish" (KJV) means "fill."
  2. To subdue the earth and have dominion over the lower forms of life (Gen. 1:28).
     This duty seems to apply particularly to the environment outside of Eden. Subduing the earth meant that man was to control his environment so as to make the best use of it for his needs and God's glory. This subjugation included his learning about his environment through exploration and study, his good use of earth's resources, and the domestication of animals to serve his needs. Animals did not fear man before the flood (9:2). The fact that God gave to man dominion "over all the earth" indicates that Satan had not yet fallen and seized world authority.
  3. To eat vegetables, grain, and fruit (Gen. 1:29).
     Man, as well as animals (vs. 30), was to eat vegetables, grain, and fruit. Man was not authorized to eat animal flesh until after the Flood (9:3).
  4. To dress the garden and keep it (Gen. 2:15).
     The garden was man's home. He was to work it and care for it. This work contributed to man's well-being, for it gave him opportunity to express his abilities and to provide for himself and his dependents. The woman's duty was to help the man and be his companion (Gen. 2:18).
  5. Not to eat the fruit of the forbidden tree (Gen. 2:16-17).
     There were two unique trees in Eden — the tree of life, which would have enabled man to live forever in his natural state, and the tree of the knowledge of good and evil, which was divinely selected as a test for man. Because Adam and Eve had moral awareness and self-determination, it was necessary that their ability of moral choice be tested. This test concerned their allegiance to their Creator. By obedience they would acquire an experiential knowledge of good and enter a permanent state of holiness (cp. the holy angels). By disobedience they would acquire an experiential knowledge of evil and enter a state of spiritual ruin and death. This test indicates that man was created to be ruled as well as to rule (I Cor. 11:3). To whatever controlling principle he would surrender, that principle (whether God or sin) would direct his life and use him for its expression (cp. Rom. 6:11-13, 16).

This test gave Adam and Eve the opportunity to choose voluntarily God's direction for their lives. Their obedience would have changed their mutable righteousness and holiness into permanent, immutable form. (In carrying out their stewardship until their sin, the couple acquired a personal righteousness and holiness which were subject to change.) Their obedience also would have given them a perception of evil like God's.

God's prohibition also declared what penalty disobedience would bring (Gen. 2:17). Although the couple knew God personally and had spiritual life, their disobedience would bring them immediate spiritual death and subsequent physical death.

c. *Man's response to the stewardship*

Both Adam and Eve chose to disobey God (Gen. 3:1-6). Eve's choice was preceded by satanic deception; Adam's was not (I Tim. 2:14). Satan led Eve to think that her disobedience would satisfy her natural, sinless desires (Gen. 3:6). But it did not.

d. *God's reaction to man's response*

God reacted to the couple's sinning with judgment (Gen. 3:7-19). The guilty pair immediately experienced the natural results of their sin, including spiritual death, the total corruption of their human nature, and their coming under sin's control. Furthermore, they were judicially examined by God (vss. 9-13) and received penal sentences (vss. 16-19). Eventually, they died physically (Gen. 5:5).

In spite of the necessity of this judgment, God graciously provided salvation for Adam and Eve (Gen. 3:20-24). His sentence upon Satan, who had used the serpent as a means to speak to Eve (Gen. 3:1; Rev. 12:9), contained the promise of the woman's Seed (the coming Saviour), who ultimately would deliver the devil a mortal blow (Rev. 5:5; Col. 2:15; Jn. 16:11). Adam's faith in this promise is manifest in his calling his wife "Eve," that is, "living" (Gen. 3:20). He believed that she would be the divine means not only of perpetuating the human race but also of providing through her Seed man's ultimate victory over Satan and death (Heb. 2:14-15). Eve's faith in the promise is indicated by her accepting her name and by her utterances at the births of Cain and Seth (Gen. 4:1, 25).

In response to the couple's faith in the promise of the Seed, God clothed them in garments of animal hides (Gen. 3:21). This was the first of many animal sacrifices that would be offered for the covering of human sins from God's sight and that would be typical of the sacrifice of God's Lamb (Lev. 17:11; Jn. 1:29). The making of these garments required the death of innocent animals and the shedding of their blood. By this action God established the arrangement for the precross atonement of human sins. Also, this portrayed the substitutionary character of Jesus' atoning death and the shedding of His blood, by means of which He paid the debt of our sins (Mt. 20:28; Rom. 6:23; 5:8). The garments portrayed the righteousness which believers receive at salvation and in which they stand before God (Rom. 3:22; I Cor. 1:30; II Cor. 5:21).

After providing these symbolic garments, God drove the saved couple from the garden in order that they might not eat from the tree of life and live forever in their unredeemed bodies (Gen. 3:22-24). This was an act of divine mercy.

e. *The duration of the stewardship*

It continued from the time of man's creation until his first sin, perhaps only a few days.

f. *God's use of the stewardship*

By this stewardship God allowed man to determine his spiritual allegiance and condition. The Creator used the opportunity afforded by man's disobedience to announce in veiled language the Saviour's coming and work, to demonstrate by symbols His method of atoning for human sins, and to begin saving the elect. His clothing Adam and Eve with animal hides and His evicting them from Eden set the stage for the outworking of His redemptive program.

2. *THE DISPENSATION OF FALLEN MAN (Gen. 3:16 - 4:7)*

Although Adam and Eve believed God's salvational promise and were saved, yet all future generations of their descendants would experience the effects of Adam's initial sin. They would be born sinners with wholly corrupted human natures (Rom. 5:12-19).

a. *The recipients of the stewardship*

These are Adam and Eve and all their posterity.

b. *The stewardship assigned to man*

Man's banishment from Eden ended his care of the garden. But he still had other duties that belonged to the first dispensation such as his filling the earth, subduing it, and eating vegetation and fruit. Moreover, man's dominion "over all the earth" (Gen. 1:26) was lost to Satan, who, I believe, was elevated by man's sinning to be the "prince of this world" (Jn. 12:31; Mt. 4:8-9). [It is noteworthy that man's dominion over the earth was not restated in the dispensation given to him after the Flood (Gen. 9:2 with 1:26)]. Also, the wife must continue to live in subjection to her husband (Gen. 3:16). This confirmed the principle of man's headship in human society, which was established by the woman's creation as his helper (Gen. 2:18; cp. I Cor. 11:3, 7-9).

The new dispensation brought mankind additional responsibilities:

1. Man must eke out a living from the divinely cursed ground (Gen. 3:17-19).

With the first sin of earth's noblest creature, God imposed a curse upon the ground and lower forms of life (Rom. 8:20-22; cp. Mk. 11:12-14, 21). With this divine curse, nature became subject to disease and death and it became hostile toward man. This made man's work toilsome and his life hazardous.

Both plants and animals developed defense mechanisms. Undomesticated animals became ferocious toward other animals and man. The blight of disease and death settled upon all forms of animal and plant life. Insects became destructive, and many forms of vegetation became inedible and hurtful. Both bugs and weeds were unwelcomed, tenacious "squatters" in man's fields and gardens. Disease and predators took their toll of his herds. Man now had to eat his non-meat diet by the sweat of his brow until he died.

2. Approach unto God must be by means of a substitutionary animal sacrifice (Gen. 4:1-5).

This was in keeping with the divine arrangement for dealing with human sins, established in Genesis 3:21. When God clothed Adam and Eve in the skins of animals, He must have revealed to them the gospel of the coming Redeemer and instructed them in the manner of approaching Deity by substitutionary animal sacrifice. Consequently, only by animal blood sacrifice could the offerer's sins be covered from divine view and he be accepted by God (cp. Heb. 9:22; Lev. 17:11). Cain failed to do this and was rejected by God. Abel was divinely received. His exercise of faith (Heb. 11:4) indicated the existence of God's revelation of His will in these matters. Abel believed God's word and followed His direction. Cain did not do this.

Although He did not accept Cain's vegetable offering, God graciously gave to him the opportunity to make the right sacrifice (Gen. 4:6-7). Had he done this, Cain's obedience would also have corrected his relationship with Abel (if the last clause of verse seven refers to his younger brother and if "sin" means "a sin-offering.")

3. Man must do well (Gen. 4:6-7).

Doing "well" (good) is doing the will of God, given by special revelation (cp. Heb. 13:21; Jas. 4:17). Since there is no record of His giving to the Gentile world a moral law like the law of Moses (Rom. 5:13), it seems that God has allowed man to follow his own moral instincts (2:14-15). Being made in the divine image with a sense of morality, unsaved Gentiles instinctively possess moral values, make moral evaluations, engage in moral conduct, and make moral judgments of one another. It appears that these people who have no formal moral code from God are responsible for obeying this "law written in their heart" and that they will be divinely judged according to this law (Rom. 2:1-3). Needless to say, sinners cannot keep laws of any kind in a way that pleases God (3:9-20).

c. Man's response to the stewardship

Most people, particularly Cain and his descendants, disobeyed God (Gen. 4:8, 16-24; 6:1-7, 11-12; II Pet. 2:5; Jude 11). By the grace of God a few (if not all) among the descendants of Seth obeyed the LORD (Gen. 5:6-32; 6:8). These were people of faith (Heb. 11:4-7).

d. God's reaction to man's response

God judged the disobedient by destroying all living flesh upon the earth, except Noah, his sons, and their wives (Gen. 6:13, 17; 7:21-23). The rapid growth of human wickedness (Gen. 6:5) appears to have been accelerated by evil angels (demons), who succeeded in corrupting the human race to such a degree that God's promise of the coming Saviour was threatened. From Jude 6, 7; I Peter 3:18-20; and II Peter 2:4 I infer that there was some kind of relation between these evil angels and human women that resulted in the birth of "giants" (literally "fallen ones," Gen. 6:4), the heroes and mighty ones of old. (The nature of these fallen ones is not clear. Were they human clones possessed by demons?) The judgment that followed was a devastating, worldwide flood, which prevailed for 150 days (Gen. 6:11-13, 17; 7:19-20, 24; II Pet. 3:6).

God blessed the obedient, who by His grace believed His Word and did His will (Gen. 4:4; 5:24; 6:8-9, 13-22; Heb. 11:4-7). He accepted Abel's sacrifice, translated Enoch, and delivered Noah and his family from the flood. Other godly people of this time died before the flood occurred (cp. Gen. 5:27, 31; Methuselah, Noah's grandfather, died the year of the flood; Lamech, Noah's father, died five years earlier).

e. The duration of the stewardship

It extended from man's fall to the end of the flood (Gen. 3:16-8:22), some 1,657 years if the fall occurred within the first year of man's creation.

f. God's use of the stewardship

Satan almost succeeded in corrupting the human race to the extent that the divine promise of the coming Saviour could not be fulfilled. But God in His sovereignty and grace prevailed to preserve a godly nucleus by whom to repopulate the earth and to assure the lineage of the Messiah-Redeemer.

3. THE DISPENSATION OF GOVERNED MAN (Gen. 9:1-7)

Upon their leaving the ark and offering burnt-offerings, Noah and his sons received a new stewardship for the new beginning of the human race.

a. The recipients of the stewardship

Noah and his family and their posterity (Gen. 9:1, cp. 12).

b. The stewardship assigned to man

The fact that God accepted Noah's offerings (Gen. 8:21) and later Abraham's (12:7) indicates that man was to continue approaching Him by animal sacrifices (cp. Gen. 3:21; 4:4). This need would continue until God's Lamb came and atoned for sin (Heb. 9:12-14; 12:24). Other requirements of the previous dispensations also continued such as subduing the earth, eking out a living from the cursed ground, the submission of the wife to her husband, and man's continuing to live by "the law written in his heart" (Rom. 2:14-15). The new dispensation imposed the following duties upon man:

1. To reproduce and fill the earth (Gen. 9:1).

The previous world population had been destroyed by the Flood (Gen. 7:21-22). Now man was to fill the earth not only by reproducing his kind but also by scattering over the face of the earth (11:4, 9).[58]

2. To have dominion over the lower forms of life (vs. 2).

Although he lost his world dominion to Satan, man still has the management and use of animals and other lower forms of life on earth.

3. Man may now eat animal flesh in addition to his vegetarian diet (vss. 3-4).

With this permission for man to eat flesh, God instilled in animals a fear of man (vs. 2). Wild animals must now be hunted and taken by force. The only prohibition relating to eating flesh was the consumption of blood. This may have been given because the physical animating principle, soul ("life" vs. 4), is associated with blood (Lev. 17:11). Thus the observation of this prohibition shows respect for human and animal physical life. Moreover, the shedding of blood together with the death of an animal substitute was the O.T. means of making atonement for sin. Finally, modern medical science shows that the blood is the carrier of most diseases which animals have in common with man.

4. To exercise capital punishment (vss. 5-6).

While mankind had family and civil government before the flood (cp. Gen. 3:16; 4:17), there was no mandatory capital punishment for capital crimes. Up to this time God reserved capital punishment to Himself (cp. Gen. 4:8-15). Now this new dispensation gave mankind the authority to take human life for homicide.[59] This would strengthen government's hand in the maintenance of law and order (cp. Rom. 13:1-6). It would make government more efficient in protecting life, repressing violence and deterring anarchy.

God's reason for capital punishment is this: "For in the image of God made He man" (vs. 6). To mutilate or destroy man who reflects the divine image is to outrage the majesty of God. God considers personhood, the divine image in man which distinguishes him from animals, to be sacred. Thus, malicious manslaughter requires the death of the murderer. It is noteworthy that fallen man still has this image which, I believe, is personhood (Jas. 3:9). In today's discussion about capital punishment, many people are overlooking the divine reason for it. While capital punishment may be a means of curbing crimes of violence (Rom. 13:4), the real reason is the nobility of man who still reflects God's image.

c. Man's response to the stewardship

Most people have disobeyed God. The earliest recorded action of human rebellion against God after the Flood was the building of a tower for

---

[58] See John Pilkey, *Origin of the Nations* (San Diego: Master Book Publishers, 1984, pp. 16 f., 115 ff.).

[59] The Bible gives several exemptions from capital punishment: accidental manslaughter (Num. 35:11), killing in self-defense (Ex. 22:2; cp. Lk. 14:31-32), and execution for the state (Rom. 13:4). In acting for the state, one must be convinced that the cause is just and in keeping with biblical principles. It is noteworthy that the Bible says nothing about the form government should take or the extent of its functions other than maintaining law and order by dispensing justice (Rom. 13:1-7).

the purpose of making for themselves a name (Gen. 11:1-9). God considered this to be a sinful act of self-will (vss. 6-8). Also, it appears that idolatry, with its perverse worship and conduct, began before man's dispersion and was carried throughout the earth (Gen. 11:9; Rom. 1:21-25; Rev. 17:5). Today, in addition to worshiping false gods, the unsaved who do not have God's Word ignore capital punishment, abuse civil authority, eat blood, and violate the "law written in their heart." This universal disobedience will reach its climax in the blasphemous reign of Satan's human agent during the last half of the coming tribulation period (Rev. ch. 13; II Thess. 2:3-10).

By the grace of God a few people have obeyed Him. The Bible speaks of several Gentiles, who living after the flood had a right relation with God, such as Job (Job 1:1), Melchizedek (Gen. 14:18), and Jethro (Ex. 3:1; 18:1-23). It seems that God directly revealed Himself to these people as He did to Abraham (Acts 7:2-3) or that they believed the promise of the coming Messiah-Saviour, preserved in their traditions (Ps. 145:4-7) and displayed by the stellar constellations (19:1-6).[60] This stewardship is observed today by them who are saved through faith in the Lord Jesus Christ (cp. Acts 15:19-20; Rom. 13:1-4).

d. God's reaction to man's response

God immediately judged those who were involved in the rebellion at Babel by confounding their language and dispersing them over the earth (Gen. 11:5-9). In time He also sent them various woes which arose out of their perverse worship and immorality (Rom. 1:21-32). Still, He sometimes exercised forbearance by not dealing with sinners severely before their cup of iniquity was full (Gen. 15:16; Rom. 2:4; 3:25). In the future God will release the awful judgments of the tribulation period upon wicked earth dwellers (Rev. chs. 6-19).

God blessed them who were obedient to His will (cp. Job 1:1-3). This is not to say that this obedience was meritorious or wholly a human work, for people cannot obey God apart from His grace (Eph. 2:8-9; I Cor. 15:10; Gen. 6:8-9). Both Noah and Job were imperfect (Gen. 9:20-23; Job 40:4; 42:6), yet they were men of faith and recipients of true righteousness (Heb. 11:7; Job 1:8; Ezek. 14:14; Gen. 6:9).

e. The duration of the stewardship

Being universal in its extent and having never been annulled, I believe that this stewardship continues in force for those people who do not have the New Testament, which presents the Dispensation of Grace. Not having access to this dispensation, these people are responsible for the duties of this third dispensation, preserved by their traditions, and for the law "written in their heart." To be saved, people who today live under this

---

[60] See E.W. Bullinger, *The Witness of the Stars* (Grand Rapids: Kregel, 1967); Joseph A. Seiss, *The Gospel in the Stars* (Philadelphia: Castle, 1884)

dispensation must hear and believe the gospel of the Lord Jesus. God will provide for them this opportunity as they respond favorably to His general revelation (cp. Acts ch. 10). This third dispensation, I believe, will continue until the Lord Jesus returns to earth, overthrows the present world order, and establishes His own worldwide kingdom, with its own stewardship (Isa. 2:1-3; see Acts 15:20; Rom. 13:1-7).

  f. *God's use of the stewardship*

  By giving human government the power of capital punishment and by directing men to fill the earth, this stewardship preserves humanity from anarchy and extinction. Thus, it assures the continuation of the Saviour's lineage (Lk. 3:23-36) and the fulfillment of God's program for mankind (II Tim. 1:10; Tit. 2:11).

  4. *THE DISPENSATION OF THE PATRIARCHS (Gen. 12:1; 17:1; 26:5; 31:3, 13; 35:1; 46:1-4)*

  With the preceding universal dispensation still in force, God gave an additional stewardship to a certain man and to selected members of his posterity — Isaac, Jacob, and his twelve sons. These people are called "the patriarchs" (Acts 7:8; Heb. 7:4).

  a. *The recipients of the stewardship*

  Throughout the period of His dealing with the patriarchs, God gave direction to Abraham (Gen. 12:1), Isaac (Gen. 26:1-3), and Jacob (Gen. 31:11-13). Also, the posterity of Jacob was to keep in touch with the LORD and obey Him, since He promised to be with them and make of them a great nation (Gen. 46:3-4). They were His people (Ex. 3:7, 10).

  b. *The stewardship assigned to man*

  This dispensation, which was given in several revelations, includes the following:

1. Abraham was to leave Ur and go to a land to which God would lead him (Gen. 12:1; 15:7; Neh. 9:7; Acts 7:2-3).
2. He was to walk before God and be perfect (Gen. 17:1).

  This means that he was to live in touch with God and be what he ought to be. The word "perfect" (Heb. *tom*) means "complete," "whole." It refers to a spiritual person like Jacob or Job (Gen. 25:27, trans. "plain"; Job 1:1) in contrast to a carnal or profane person like Esau (Heb. 12:16)

3. He was to obey the LORD's commands (Gen. 18:19; 26:5). These commands appear to be more directions than those that are preserved in the Genesis record. An example of Abraham's obedience is his offering his son Isaac (22:1-18). God also gave orders to Isaac (Gen. 26:1-3) and to Jacob (31:3, 11-13; 35:1; 46:1-4).

  c. *Man's response to the stewardship*

  In spite of temporary lapses (Gen. 16:2; 27:6-25) and unwise moves (Gen. 12:10; 20:1-18; 26:6-23), the patriarchs were men of faith (Gen. 15:6; Heb. 11:8-22) and obedience (Gen. 12:1-4; 18:19; 22:18; 26:5, 23-33). However, the descendants of Jacob almost lost their ancestral faith in Egypt (Josh. 24:14; Ex. 32:1-6; Ezek. 20:6-8). This faith was awakened through the ministry of Moses (Ex. 3:13-15; 4:29-31).

    d. *God's reaction to man's response*

He brought judgment upon the disobedient. He disciplined the patriarchs when they stepped out of line (cp. Gen. 20:1-18; 26:6-23). He also allowed their descendants to suffer slavery and hard labor in Egypt when they fell into idolatry (Ex. 1:8-14; Josh. 24:14).

He saved them who believed the promise of the coming Saviour (Gen. 15:6; Gal. 3:8, 16) and blessed them who obeyed Him (Gen. 24:35; 26:12-14; 32:28; 47:27). In fulfillment of His promise to Abraham (Gen. 15:13-14), God delivered Israel from Egyptian bondage (Ex. 3:7-10; 14:30; Deut. 7:7-8). However, this redemption was more physical than spiritual (Ex. 14:10-14). Israel's deliverance from Egypt did not give them eternal life.

    e. *The duration of the stewardship*

This dispensation extended from the call of Abram to leave Ur (Gen. 12:1) until Israel's reception of the Mosaic Law at Mt. Sinai (Ex. 19:8). This span of time in years is 430 years, plus the years between Abraham's call in Ur and his entrance into Canaan when he was 75 (Gen. 12:4-5). Israel's sojourn of 430 years (Ex. 12:40-41; Gal. 3:17) began with Abraham's entrance into Canaan. Stephen's reference to 400 years (Acts 7:6; Gen. 15:13) concerns the sojourn of Abraham's seed, starting with the weaning of Isaac and the casting out of Ishmael, 30 years after Abraham's entrance into Canaan (Gen. 21:5-12).

    f. *God's use of the stewardship*

Through this stewardship God maneuvered the patriarchs into a position where He could make of them an elect nation by which the Saviour was to come (Gen. 12:5; 15:5; Gal. 3:8, 16; Jn. 8:56; Mt. 1:1; Heb. 2:16). The Israelites entered Egypt as the family of Jacob and came out 210 years later as a nation.

    5. *THE DISPENSATION OF THE MOSAIC LAW (Ex. 20:1-7; 21:1 - 23:19; Lev. chs. 1-27; Num. chs. 5, 6, 9, 10, 27-30)*

While the third dispensation continued in force over the earth, God gave a special stewardship to the recently delivered Israelites for the purpose of forging them into a regulated, holy society.

    a. *The recipients of the stewardship*

Only the nation of Israel (Ex. 19:3; Neh. 9:13-14; Ps. 147:19-20).

    b. *The stewardship assigned to man*

1. The law given at Mt. Sinai: the moral laws (Ex. 20:1-17), the civil laws (Ex. 21:1-23:13), and the religious laws (Ex. 23:14-19; Lev. chs. 1-27).
2. Additional regulations: Numbers chapters 5, 6, 9, 10, 15, 19, 27-30.

The greatest of these 613 laws concerned the Israelites' loving God (Deut. 6:5) and their loving their neighbor (Lev. 19:18). See Mark 12:28-34.

c. Man's response to the stewardship

No one but the Lord Jesus Christ kept all of the law (Mt. 5:17; Heb. 7:26). Everyone else in Israel in some way violated it (Acts 7:53; 15:10; Jer. 31:32). There were several reasons for this failure. The people were sinners by nature (Rom. 3:9; 5:19). Moreover, the law did not provide enablement for its observance (Heb. 7:18-19). Finally, being unable to correct this condition, the law could only condemn and slay its violators (Rom. 3:19-20; Gal. 3:10, 21).[61] Being legal in character (Ex. 19:5-8; Lev. 26:3, 14), the law required God to deal with Israel as they deserved. Thus, the nation repeatedly came under divine judgment, as in the eighth and seventh centuries B.C. (II Chron. 36:15-16; Neh. 9:26-30) and in A.D. 70 (Jn. 1:11; Mt. 23:37-39; Acts 7:51-52).

Rather than allowing the law to humble them and to lead them to Christ as their Saviour (Gal. 3:19-24), Israel misused it. They made it a badge of pride, which distinguished them as being superior to other nations (Rom. 9:4; Eph. 2:14-15), and they attempted to use it to establish their own righteousness before God (Rom. 9:30-10:5). Under the instruction of the rabbis, they displaced the Mosaic Law by the Tradition of the Elders,[62] which became the major religious influence in their lives (Mk. 7:1-13). Consequently, the Judaism of the New Testament period was largely based on these traditions and consisted of their application to daily life.

It is noteworthy that the saved of Israel observed the commandments of the Mosaic Law (Lk. 1:6 cp. Ps. 119:51, 55, 56, 63). Although they were not sinless (Lk. 1:18-20), they were sufficiently obedient to allow God to work out His will in and through their lives. Now the law did not provide enablement for its observance, but the grace of God, which accompanies salvation, did. Consequently, these people were enabled to do what was pleasing in God's sight, just as we are today. (II Cor. 1:12; Phil. 4:13) But lacking this grace, unsaved Jews were not able to keep the law.

d. God's reaction to man's response

The Law of Moses carried its own penalties for the violation of its regulations. Some of these violations, such as Sabbath breaking, sins of defiance, and murder, required the death of the offender (Num. 15:30-36; Lev. 24:17). It seems that in the days of Israel's apostasy, the penalty of many violations was not carried out, though the nation superficially, inconsistently

---

[61] Under the Mosaic Law salvation was not by law observance (Rom. 3:20; Gal. 2:16; 3:21-22), but by God's grace through faith in the promise of a coming Saviour (cp. Gen. 15:5-6; Gal. 3:8, 16; Jn. 5:39; 8:39-40; Lk. 1:46-55; 2:25, 38). The Levitical offerings did not save people spiritually, but they were a gracious provision that allowed unintentional lawbreakers (guilty of non-capital crimes) the continuation of physical life within the covenant community. Failure to keep the required ritual resulted in one's being cut off from Israel (Lev. chs. 4, 5). Under the law David should have died for his sins (II Sam. ch. 11; 12:9; Lev. 20:10). But he repented, and God graciously spared his life (II Sam. 12:1-14; Ps. 32, 51; Rom. 4:6-8).

[62] Taught by the Pharisaic scribes, the Tradition of the Elders largely shaped N.T. Judaism. Beginning in the days of the Babylonian captivity, this tradition was developed by the Jewish scribes. It consisted of several ingredients: a restatement of the Mosaic Law, the application of the Mosaic Law to a new way of life such as that belonging to an urban or commercial people (the Mosaic Law was suited to a pastoral people), man-made regulations to prevent violations of the Mosaic Law, and an extensive commentary on the Mosaic Law.

observed the Levitical ritual (cp. Isa. 1:1-23). Consequently, God repeatedly chastened them by the hands of Gentile nations. Eventually, He allowed the Northern kingdom of Israel to be carried away captive into upper Mesopotamia and the Southern kingdom (Judah and Benjamin) to be taken to Babylon (Judg. 2:10-15; II Ki. 17:6-23; II Chron. 36:15-21). Finally, upon their rejection of Jesus as the Messiah, they were dispersed again in A.D. 70, when the Romans took Jerusalem (Lk. 19:41-44). Long before, Israel had been warned of the frightful results of their turning away from God (Lev. 26:14-39; Deut. 28:15-68).

In spite of these things, God graciously dealt with lawbreakers when they turned to Him, confessed their sins, obeyed His voice, and fulfilled the appropriate Levitical ritual (Deut. 4:30-31; II Sam. 12:13; Ps. 51:3, 16-17; Lev. chs. 4-5). He was motivated by the gracious promises of the Abrahamic Covenant (Deut. 4:31; II Ki. 13:23; cp. Mic. 7:19-20).

e. The duration of the stewardship

While the Mosaic Law as a covenant ceased with Christ's death, it appears that as a dispensation this stewardship extends from the giving of the law at Sinai until the present time for them who assume its obligations. Paul recognized that his Jewish contemporaries were still under the law (I Cor. 9:20; Gal. 4:4-5; 5:3). The law ceases for those Jews who become Christians and the recipients of the Dispensation of Grace.

To be a Christian and to assume the duties of the Mosaic Law is to fall from grace, with its liberty and requirements, and to place oneself under the principle of law-works (Gal. 5:3-4). While the Galatian believers were salvationally secure in grace, their following the false teachings of Judaizers was leading them to attempt to live their Christian lives by the principle of works. One cannot be saved by grace and live by works, that is, by self-effort. The grace of God that saved us is also available through faith to enable us to live godly lives (Jn. 15:5; I Cor. 15:10; II Cor. 1:12; 12:7-10; Gal. 2:20; Phil. 4:13).

f. God's use of the stewardship

God used the Mosaic Law to show Israel their need for the coming Saviour (Gal. 3:19-24). Giving sin the character of legal offence against God (Rom. 3:20; 4:15; 5:13), the law revealed to Israel their sinfulness before God.

God also used the law to make Israel a holy nation in the midst of Canaanite immorality, thus preserving the line by which the Saviour was to come (Ex. 19:5-6; Deut. 7:6). While most Israelites did not directly benefit spiritually from the law because of their unsaved state and disobedience, a few (the elect) did. The law caused them to cast themselves upon the sure mercies of God and to look for redemption in Jerusalem (cp. Dan. 9:1-19; Lk. 1:46-55; 2:25, 38). In this manner, the law had a sanctifying influence in their lives (Ex. 19:6; Rom. 7:12-13). While the law provided no enablement for its observance, the grace of God did. Such saved people as Zacharias and

Elisabeth were enabled to keep it (Lk. 1:6; Ps. 119:51, 55, 56, 63). Also, it was into this kind of a home that our Saviour was born (Mt. 1:19; Lk. 1:46-55; 2:21-24).

6. *THE DISPENSATION OF GRACE (Tit. 2:11-13; most commands of the New Testament)*

We must not allow the designation of this dispensation to lead us to think that God's grace did not operate during the Old Testament period. The testimony of God's people throughout history indicates that they had God's Word for their faith (Lk. 1:70) and His grace for their obedience (Gen. 6:8; Ex. 33:12). But with the coming of the Saviour, God's grace was fully manifested by Jesus' life, teachings, and work (Jn. 1:14; II Tim. 1:9-10). The duties of this dispensation rest upon this grace, express this grace, and are fulfilled by it (I Cor. 15:10; II Cor. 1:12). Meanwhile, it seems that the third dispensation continues in force over that portion of mankind that does not have the New Testament (there is no record of its being cancelled) and that the Mosaic Law (as a dispensation) continues to exert its domination over them who attempt to keep it.

a. *The recipients of the stewardship*

These are the unsaved and the saved (Tit. 2:11-12). All the unsaved who hear the gospel have the duty of obeying it. All the saved who have the New Testament have the duty of obeying its commands which relate to Christian life and service.

b. *The stewardship assigned to man*

This stewardship is more spiritual in content than that of Governed Man. Being universal in its extent, there are two aspects of it. One, there is the duty of the unsaved who hear the gospel to obey it (Tit. 2:11; Acts 17:30; 20:21; Rom. 1:5; 16:25-26; I Tim. 2:4; II Pet. 3:9; I Jn. 3:23). Second, there is the duty of the saved to follow all that Jesus reveals through the New Testament as being His will for them (Tit. 2:12-13). It is noteworthy that the Lord's commands to His disciples, who were still under the Mosaic Law, apply to us today, for He anticipated their living under the Dispensation of Grace. God's moral requirements are always the same, whether under grace or law.

The duties of the Dispensation of Grace consist of the Lord's teachings (commands) (Tit. 2:12; Eph. 4:20-21; Col. 3:16), or His law (Gal. 6:2; I Cor. 9:21; Jas. 1:25). Those commands that He gave during His earthly ministry are recorded in the Gospels; those that He gave through His servants after His return to Heaven are recorded in the remainder of the New Testament.

Some of these duties for His people are abiding in Christ (Jn. 15:4-5), being filled with the Holy Spirit (Eph. 5:18), loving others with Christ's love (Jn. 13:34), growing in the spiritual life (II Pet. 3:18), bearing witness to the lost (Acts 1:8), yielding body and mind to God (Rom. 12:1-2), understanding and doing God's will (Eph. 5:17, 10), giving God's Word its place in our hearts

(Col. 3:16), pleasing and glorifying God (II Tim. 2:15; I Cor. 10:31), living godly lives (Tit. 2:12), and looking for Christ's return (Mt. 24:42, 44; Tit. 2:13). Unlike the Mosaic Law, God's grace provides enablement for the observation of this stewardship (Jn. 14:16-17, "Comforter" means "Helper"; Gal. 5:25; II Cor. 1:12; II Pet. 1:3).

c. Man's response to this stewardship

By God's grace the elect among the lost are obeying the gospel (Jn. 6:37; Acts 13:48; I Cor. 1:26-29). Also, by God's grace many saved people are walking in obedience to the Lord. While it is possible for a believer to lapse into sin (I Cor. 3:1-3), it is likely that many who profess to be saved and who are living carnal lives have never been born again (cp. II Cor. 13:5; Mt. 7:21-23; I Jn. 2:3-4).

d. God's reaction to man's response

Regarding the unsaved, God saves all who exercise salvational faith in Christ (Jn. 6:28-29, 47; Acts 16:31; Rom. 10:9-13), and He will banish to Hell all who fail to do so (Jn. 3:18, 36; Mt. 7:21-23). On the other hand, God faithfully chastens His people who persist in disobedience (I Cor. 11:31-32) and blesses them who walk in His fellowship (I Jn. 1:7; Jn. 13:17).

e. The duration of the stewardship

Since there does not seem to be any special stewardship for the Tribulation Period [as today, the Law of Moses will be a dispensation during the Tribulation Period for them who assume its responsibilities (Mt. 24:20)], I believe that the Dispensation of Grace extends from the Day of Pentecost (Acts ch. 2) unto Christ's second coming to earth (Rev. ch. 19). Thus, in my opinion, it will be in force throughout the Church Age and the Tribulation Period which follows.

This view is based on the following considerations: Many people will be saved during the forepart of the tribulation, and these will have the New Testament for their guidance. Moreover, the lost will still have the duty of obeying the gospel, as today. Also, there is no duty of the Dispensation of Grace that would not apply to the Tribulation Period believer and that he would not be able to keep, for he will have the Holy Spirit, just as we do today. Finally, the Scriptures do not indicate any special dispensation being given for the Tribulation Period.

f. God's use of the stewardship

Having come to earth and returned to Heaven, the Lord Jesus is doing two things on the earth throughout this dispensation. One, during the present Church Age He is building His church. Second, during the Tribulation Period He will prepare the elect of Israel and the Gentiles, who will be on earth during those days, for His second coming and earthly rule. These activities are a part of His Messianic work, which He is doing in obedience to the Father.

7. THE DISPENSATION OF CHRIST'S EARTHLY RULE (Isa. 2:1-3)

Climaxing God's dealings with earth dwellers, this stewardship is the last that will be given to mankind. Our Lord's earthly rule, with its righteous government and curse-free environment, will complete God's current program for humanity and will fulfill man's longing for universal peace. It will replace all previous dispensations.

a. *The recipients of the stewardship*

These will be all who are on earth during Christ's rule (Ps. 72:8-11; Isa. 2:1-4; Zech. 14:9, 16-17).

b. *The stewardship assigned to man*

During the Kingdom Age mankind will receive this stewardship directly from King Jesus, perhaps by means of prophecy (Isa. 2:1-3; Joel 2:28). Because people born in kingdom days will need salvation, this stewardship will require their obedience to the gospel. Also, the Lord Jesus will teach earth dwellers His will for their lives (Isa. 2:1-3). Doubtless, this will include many of the precepts and principles that we find in the Scriptures, including those of the Dispensation of Grace.

The Sermon on the Mount (Mt. chs. 5-7) does not present laws that apply exclusively to the millennial kingdom, as some suppose. It presents the characteristics and duties of the citizens of Christ's kingdom (saved people) who are now living on earth (Col. 1:13). The sermon deals with conditions that will not exist during kingdom days, such as persecution, temptation, theft, and false prophecy (Mt. 5:10-12; 6:13, 19; 7:15). Indeed, God's will shall be done on earth during those days (Mt. 6:10).

c. *Man's response to the stewardship*

Disobedience to the King will be rare. The unsaved will give external lip service (Ps. 66:3, margin: "yield feigned obedience"; Mt. 15:8), and the saved will give loving heart obedience (cp. Mk. 12:30). Because there will be no temptation by Satan and his demons and there will be no open sin and moral pollution, apparently unsaved people will externally observe the laws of the kingdom. We know that many unsaved people will be on earth at the close of the Lord's rule (Rev. 20:7-9).

d. *God's reaction to man's response*

During His reign the Lord will slay those who openly violate His laws (Isa. 11:4; 65:20). The rest of the unsaved will be sifted out of the world population and will be destroyed at the close of the Kingdom Age when they revolt against the Lord (Rev. 20:7-9). The saved will live throughout the Kingdom Age and will enjoy the abundant blessings of the Lord (Mt. 25:34; Ps. 72:7).

e. *The duration of the stewardship*

The Lord's earthly kingdom will continue for a thousand years after His second coming to earth (Rev. 20:1-7). Then, there will follow the dissolution of the present universe (II Pet. 3:10-13) and the judgment of the unsaved (Rev. 20:11-15). After these events, Christ's earthly kingdom will merge with the universal kingdom of the Father, and together They will reign over the new heavens and earth forever (Rev. 21:1-3; I Cor. 15:23-28; Lk. 1:32-33).

f. God's use of the stewardship

Continuing His Messianic work as the Father's Servant, the Lord Jesus Christ will rule until He has achieved the divine objectives of His present work. These objectives include His subjugation of all rebels against God (I Cor. 15:25; Rev. 19:11-20:3, 7-15); His subjection of the earth and its creatures (Heb. 2:5-8; cp. Gen. 1:28); His restoration of the earth to its primeval state by lifting the divine curse upon creation and by reconciling to God all things involuntarily affected by man's sin (Rom. 8:19-22; Col. 1:20; Acts 3:20-21; Eph. 1:10; Isa. 11:6-9; cp. Gen. 3:17); His completing the salvation of the elect (Rom. 11:26-27; Joel 2:32; II Thess. 2:13); and His fulfillment of the divine covenant promises (Deut. 30:3-5; Jer. 31:31-34; Gen. 17:8; II Sam. 7:16).

In our seeking God's will for us and our interpretation of the Scriptures, it is important that we recognize these dispensational distinctions. While all the Scriptures are profitable to us (II Tim. 3:16), they do not all express God's will for us (II Tim. 2:15). Because of this, we should give special attention to the Dispensation of Grace, which God has given us to observe.

The Dispensations of...

Created Man • • • • •

Fallen Man   • • • • •

Governed Man   •

The Patriarchs   • • • • •

The Mosaic Law   • • • • • • • • • • •

Grace   • • • • •

Christ's Rule   • • • •

GOD'S COVENANTS

Throughout human history God has made great covenant promises that relate to His program for mankind. For a more accurate understanding of the Scriptures, it is important that we distinguish between a divine covenant and a divine dispensation. A covenant declares in the form of promise what God will do, but a dispensation states in the form of command what He wants people to do. Although God may make one or more covenants during the time a dispensation is in force, these are not necessarily a part of the dispensation's requirements. The single exception is the Mosaic Law which was both a dispensation and a covenant.

• Their Definition

Two kinds of covenants are found in the Bible—those between men and those between God and man. Let us look at these.

1. Covenants between men

The most common form in the Scriptures is the bilateral covenant. This is an agreement that is voluntarily made by two parties who commit themselves to the terms of the compact (cp. Gen. 31:44-55; I Sam. 18:3; 23:18; I Ki. 5:12). The rarer form is the unilateral covenant, which is undertaken by one of two parties. This may be a disposition in the form of a law imposed by a superior party like a king (Ezek. 17:13-14), or it may be a declaration in the form of a will made by a testator (Heb. 9:16-17).

2. Covenants between God and man

These are solemn statements, made to certain people, of what God promises to do. Notice that they differ from human covenants in two ways: first, they are never the result of both parties' bargaining; second, God Himself is never subject to any condition that is made by men.

• Their Names

1. The Noachian Covenent (Gen. 9:8-17)
2. The Abrahamic Covenant (Gen. 17:1-19; also 12:1-3; 13:14-17; 15:4-21; 22:15-18)
3. The Mosaic Covenant (Ex. 19:1-8; Lev. 18:5)
4. The Palestinian Covenant (Deut. 28:1-29:1; 30:1-10)
5. The Davidic Covenant (II Sam. 7:10-16)
6. The New Covenant (Jer. 31:31-40)

• Their Description

In our study of God's covenants, we shall observe the following features:

1. The recipients of the covenant
The people with whom the covenant was made.

2. The promises of the covenant
The statement of what God promises to do.

3. The obligations of the covenant
What man is to do, if anything, to experience the fulfillment of the covenant promises.

4. The character of the covenant
This indicates whether the covenant is gracious or legal, conditional or unconditional. "Gracious" and "legal" represent principles

by means of which God is motivated to fulfill His promises.[63] "Conditional" and "unconditional" indicate whether or not the recipient must meet certain conditions to experience the fulfillment of the covenant promises.

5. *The duration of the covenant*

The length of time during which the covenant is in force.

6. *The covenant sign or witness*

This assures the recipient that the covenant is in force and reminds him of the covenant promises.

7. *The importance of the covenant*

Like the dispensations, the covenants are a means through which God works in human affairs to accomplish His purpose. This description considers the importance or value of the covenant to God's program.

• Conditional Gracious Covenants

Though gracious in character, certain divine covenants impose certain obligations on their recipients for their experiencing the promised blessings. Nevertheless, the conditional character of these covenants does not conflict with the principle of grace or make these covenants legalistic. The reason for this is that God enables the recipients of gracious covenants to fulfill the covenant conditions. These recipients are enabled to exercise faith and obedience by God's gracious prompting and power (cp. Acts 11:18; 16:14; II Pet. 1:1; Phil. 2:13, with reference to the New Covenant). Because of this, the recipient's fulfillment of the gracious covenant condition is not a meritorious work that deserves the promised blessings as a reward or pay. His obedience by divine grace allows God to do what He has promised. Accordingly, all the credit and praise for this obedience belongs solely to God.

The one legal covenant is the Mosaic Law, which was given to Israel. God's fulfillment of the promises of this covenant was according to the principle of law or works (Ex. 19:5). This required the recipient to do his part (without divine assistance) if God was to do His. Because this was a two-party contract, the recipient by his disobedience to the covenant obligations

---

[63] These principles are contrasted as follows:

The principle of grace (involving a gift and responding to faith: Rom. 4:5; Eph. 2:8-9)	The principle of law or works (involving pay or debt and responding to meritorious works or worth: Rom. 4:4)
1. God deals favorably with people in a way they do not deserve.	1. God deals with people in a way they do deserve.
2. It does not recognize human merit, worth, or works. These do not contribute anything to the fulfillment of the promises.	2. It recognizes human merit, worth, and works. If possible, these would contribute to the fulfillment of the promises.
3. The fulfillment of the promises is wholly God's work and brings Him all the praise.	3. The fulfillment of the promises is partly man's work, bringing him part of the praise.
4. Human obedience (by God's grace) to the covenant conditions allows God to fulfill promise.	4. Human obedience to the covenant conditions compels God to fulfill promise.
5. The only principle that allows God to keep His promises to sinners or unworthy people.	5. This principle bars sinners or unworthy people from God's promised blessings.

could break the covenant and release God from His duty to fulfill His promises (Jer. 31:32; Lev. 26:14-16). However, God in His sovereign mercy continued to honor the broken covenant until it was replaced by the New Covenant (Ex. 33:19; Rom. 9:15, 25-27). He extended mercy and forgiveness to the repentant people of Israel on the basis of the Abrahamic Covenant (Mic. 7:18-20).

Being the work of God in man, the fulfillment of the gracious covenant's conditions cannot be regarded as a meritorious human work. In spite of their conditional character, these gracious covenants are not legalistic. Their conditions do not represent man's work but God's work in and through man.

• Covenantal Theology

Being the theology of the Reformed churches, the English Puritans, and the Scottish theologians, covenantal theology views God's dealing with man as being covered by two covenants—the Covenant of Works and the Covenant of Grace, and they interpret the Bible accordingly. This theology holds that God made a covenant of works with unfallen Adam. By this covenant Adam was constituted the representative head of the race so that he could act for his descendants, was temporarily put on probation so as to determine whether he would willingly subject himself to God's will, and was promised eternal life if he should obey God. Upon Adam's disobedience and his making the covenant void, God made a covenant of grace for the purpose of saving the elect of fallen mankind. Though this second covenant was offered right after man's fall, its details were not clearly stated until the giving of the Abrahamic Covenant and thereafter. This theology holds that all of the Old Testament covenants, including the Mosaic Law, are expressions and amplifications of the Covenant of Grace. Replacing ritual circumcision, baptism is regarded to be the sign and seal of the Covenant of Grace, certifying entrance into the covenantal community.

Covenantal theology holds that there is only one people of God. The people who were in covenantal relationship with Him during the Old Testament period made up His church then as well as those who are in covenantal relationship with Him today. Many covenantal theologians believe that the nation of Israel has no place in God's future, prophetic program and that the prophecies about this nation, which must be interpreted allegorically, are being fulfilled in the church today. Covenantal theology understands the Bible as teaching one covenant of grace, one chosen people of God, one general resurrection and final judgment upon Christ's one return to earth.

Opposing covenantal theology in favor of dispensationalism, I offer the following:

1. Distinguishing the various covenants from the dispensations, I see that God made special promises to Israel in the Abrahamic, Palestinian, Davidic, and New Covenants that will yet be fulfilled to this nation in the

future (cp. Isa. 54:7-8; Rom. 3:3-4; Heb. 6:13-20). For instance, consider the promise to Israel of a land (Acts 7:4-5; Heb. 11:9 with Gen. 13:15-17; 15:18).

2. While salvational blessings are essentially the same in every age (cp. Jer. 31:33-34), functional blessings differ among groups of redeemed peoples, as the church's being Christ's bride (Eph. 5:32) and Israel's being Jehovah's wife (Hos. ch. 2).

3. Paul distinguished between the Mosaic Covenant, which held people in bondage, and the New Covenant, which liberates (Gal. 4:19-31).

4. Being a bilateral, legal covenant, the Mosaic Law was broken by Israel's disobedience and apostasy (Jer. 22:9; 31:31-32; Ezek. 44:7). Dealing with them as they deserved, God had to administer judgment rather than His promised blessings.

5. Nowhere does the New Testament indicate that baptism is the sign of the New Covenant. Rather, following salvation, it is a witness to salvational faith (Acts 18:8). The Lord's Supper, with its cup, is the sign of the New Covenant (Lk. 22:20).

6. Christ's church could not have existed before His incarnation and exaltation. As part of His Messianic work, our Lord is building His church upon the foundation of His Person and work by the baptism of the Holy Spirit (Mt. 16:18; Eph. 2:20; I Cor. 12:13, 27; Eph. 1:22-23).

7. For saved Gentiles to be "Abraham's seed" (Gal. 3:29) does not mean that all or only Gentiles are his seed (Jn. 8:37; Rom. 9:6-8; Gal. 3:16). For Gentiles to be "the children of Abraham" (Gal. 3:7) means that they are saved and are people of faith as he was a person of faith.[64]

8. For Gentiles to be grafted into the stock of Abraham does not necessarily replace Israel in God's program or shut the door to their restoration to His favor and blessing (Rom. 11:11-15, 26-27). Since salvation is of the Jews (Jn. 4:22) and the covenant promises about the Saviour were given to Abraham and his descendants through Jacob (Rom. 9:4), it was necessary for the Gentiles, who had no hope (Eph. 2:12), to look to Christ, the Seed of Abraham, and by faith to partake of the promised blessing in Him (Gal. 3:14).

9. Paul's reference to saved Gentiles being "the Israel of God" (Gal. 6:16) does not indicate the cancellation of the great covenant promises relating to Israel's future. Meanwhile, all Jews who are saved during the present age are members of the church (Eph. 2:15; 3:6).

• Their Content

The usual dispensational view of the divine covenants holds that there were two covenants made with man before the first that is definitely recorded

---

[64] The phrase, "the seed of Abraham," has four meanings in the Scriptures, determined by its context: one, his natural descendants (Jn. 8:37); two, his natural descendants who are saved—the true Israel (Rom. 9:6-8); three, the Gentiles who are saved people of faith (Gal. 3:29; cp. "children" in vss. 6-9 means "children" or "sons" in character—people of faith as Abraham was (cp. Jn. 8:39); and four, the Lord Jesus Christ (Gal. 3:16).

in the Bible (Gen. 9:8-17).[65] These are the Edenic Covenant, allegedly made with Adam before his fall (Gen. 2:16-17), and the Adamic Covenant, after the fall (Gen. 3:15-19). In my opinion, this view is conjectural, based upon alleged evidence that fails to distinguish between a covenant and a dispensation. The directive concerning the trees of which man might or might not eat (Gen. 2:16-17) was a part of the dispensation that God gave to newly created man. Also, the veiled reference to the coming Seed, who would utterly defeat Satan (Gen. 3:15), was a part of God's judicial sentence upon the devil (it was addressed to Satan, not to man). These were not covenant promises.

I do not see any divine covenants recorded in Genesis before the Noachic Covenant (Gen. 9:8-17). The word "covenant" does not occur until Genesis 6:18. When God clothed Adam and Eve in response to their salvational faith (Gen. 3:21), He was not fulfilling a covenant promise as such, but He was honoring their faith in what this judicial sentence said about the coming Redeemer, brief as it was. How much they understood about the redemptive work of the Seed (the sentence speaks of His judicial work) is not clear.

Although it is unrecorded, when He clothed Adam and Eve with the skins of animals, God must have spoken about His provision of redemption from sin through the coming Redeemer. By this action He also established the O.T. means of atonement for human sins (Gen. 3:21). This is verified by Abel's offering his animal sacrifice by faith in divine revelation (Heb. 11:4). Again, these are not covenant promises. The reference to the coming Redeemer would be an amplification of the reference to the Seed of the woman, which was a part of a judicial declaration (Gen. 3:15). The establishment of the O.T. means of the atonement would relate to the second dispensation.

1. THE NOACHIAN COVENANT (Gen. 9:8-17; cp. 6:18)
   a. Its recipients
      Noah and his sons and their posterity (vss. 8-9), also all the animals that were with Noah in the ark (vss. 10-12).
   b. Its promises
      God promises never again to destroy all flesh with water (vss. 11, 15).
   c. Its obligations
      There are none since the covenant was made with animals as well as man.
   d. Its character
      The covenant is gracious and unconditional, for it was made with animals as well as with man.
   e. Its duration
      "For perpetual generations" (vs. 12), "everlasting" (vs. 16). These

---

[65] See The Scofield Reference Bible (New York: Oxford University Press, 1917), pp. 5, 6, 9.
The New Scofield Reference Bible (New York: Oxford University Press, 1967), pp. 5, 7.

words indicate that the promise will be effective as long as the present world continues (cp. Gen. 8:22). After our Lord's millennial rule, the earth will be destroyed by the dissolution of its elements (II Pet. 3:10-13), not by water.

f. *Its sign or witness*

God gave the rainbow as His assurance to man that He would not forget His promise (vss. 13-16).

g. *Its importance*

The covenant assures man and beast that God will not end the present natural world order until He has accomplished His purpose for it. God's objectives for the present world order will be achieved by Christ's millennial rule. Meanwhile, God promises never again to destroy life universally with water.

2. *THE ABRAHAMIC COVENANT (Gen. 17:1-19; also 12:1-3; 13:14-17; 15:4-21; 22:15-18)*

a. *Its recipients*

Abraham and his posterity (Gen. 17:7) through Isaac (17:19, 21; 26:1-4) and Jacob (28:10-15; 35:9-12; I Chron. 16:15-18).

b. *Its promises*

These were given to Abraham by a series of divine revelations (Gen. 12:1-3, 7; 13:14-17; 15:1-7, 13-16; 17:1-21; 18:9-19; 21:12-13 22:15-18; cp. 24:7).

(1) The promises relating to Abraham himself

(a) To bless Abraham and make him a blessing (Gen. 12:2; 22:17).

God made Abraham rich (Gen. 13:2; 24:35) and a mighty prince in the eyes of the inhabitants of Canaan (23:6).

(b) To give to Abraham a noble, invincible, numerous posterity through Sarah (Gen. 12:2; 13:16; 15:5; 17:5-6; 22:17).

This promise refers to Abraham's natural posterity (Jn. 8:37) by Sarah — the descendants of Isaac (Gen. 25:23).

(c) To be the God of Abraham and of his posterity (Gen. 17:7).

Referring to Abraham and his posterity — Isaac and Jacob, this promise concerns their having a special relationship with God, which was based on these covenant promises.

(d) To bless them that bless Abraham and to curse him who curses Abraham (Gen. 12:3).

History has shown the fulfillment of this promise in God's blessing and cursing both nations and individual persons according to their treatment of Abraham's descendants.

(2) The promises relating to Israel

(a) To give to Abraham and his posterity through Isaac and Jacob the land of Canaan (and more) for an everlasting possession (Gen. 13:15; 15:18-21).

The extent of the land that God promised to Abraham far exceeds that of the land of Canaan. It extends from the Nile River in Egypt to the Euphrates River in Mesopotamia (Gen. 15:18). Although Abraham never possessed the land in his lifetime, this promise was partially fulfilled in the days of Joshua (Jos. 21:43; cp. Gen. 17:8) and of Solomon (I Kings 4:21). It will be completely fulfilled in the future when the Lord sets up His earthly kingdom and restores the elect of Israel to their land (Deut. 30:1-5; Ezek. 34:11-13; 36:24, 28). Meanwhile, the LORD promised Abraham and other O.T. people of faith a heavenly city, which they now occupy until their possession of the promised land in the future millennial kingdom (Heb. 11:8-10, 13-16).

(b) To deliver Israel from Egyptian bondage (Gen. 15:13-16).

Centuries later, in keeping with this promise, God delivered Israel from Egypt (Ex. 6:5-8; Acts 7:17). Observe that the "400 years" (Gen. 15:13; Acts 7:6) refers to that span of time which started with the weaning of Isaac (30 years after Abraham entered Canaan (Gen. 21:5-12) and which included Israel's being in Egypt 210 years. The "430 years" (Ex. 12:40-41) was this span of time starting with Abraham's entrance into Canaan.

(3) The promises relating to Jesus the Messiah

    (a) To give to Abraham a seed (Gen. 15:5; 22:17-18).

In this promise the word "seed" has multiple meanings, referring not only to Isaac and his posterity through Jacob but also to Christ Jesus (Gal. 3:16). Those who believed the promise of the coming "Seed" were saved through this (cp. Gen. 15:6). This truth was the "John 3:16" of the precross period.

    (b) To bring universal blessing to mankind through Abraham's seed (Gen. 12:3; 18:18; 22:18).

By this promise God alluded to Jesus and to the blessing that man would receive through His work. This universal blessing is now being offered through the gospel, which speaks of our Lord's atoning work and the divine offer of salvation through faith in Him (Gal. 3:8). This promise will be universally experienced in the blessings of our Lord's rule over the earth during His millennial kingdom (Mic. 4:1-5).

Many of these promises were repeated to Isaac and Jacob (Gen. 26:3-4; 28:10-15; Lev. 26:42).

    c. *Its obligations*

Although the promises are fulfilled by God's grace, the actual realization of the personal promises required the people's faith and obedience (Gen. 17:9-10; 22:16-18; 26:3-5; Heb. 11:8-29). God's grace enabled these people to trust and obey.

    d. *Its character*

This covenant is gracious. While the fulfillment of the promises relating to the patriarchs' personal lives was conditioned upon their obedience to God, those promises relating to Christ and to national Israel appear to be unconditional. Having fulfilled His personal promises to Abraham, delivered Israel from Egypt, and sent the Redeemer, God will fulfill the remaining promises in His time.

e. *Its duration*

It is everlasting (Gen. 17:7; Ps. 105:8-10).

f. *Its sign or witness*

God's covenant with Abraham was solemnized by something He did and He required Abraham to do. It was solemnized by God's passing between sacrificial victims (Gen. 15:9-10, 17), which was a customary way to ratify contracts (Jer. 34:18-19). The burning firepot and the fiery torch indicated God's presence (Gen. 15:17). The covenant was also solemnized by the recipient's submitting to circumcision (Gen. 17:9-14). By this rite the recipient identified himself with the covenant and was thereafter constantly reminded of it. The reception of the covenant sign in his body did not spiritually save him, but it did prevent his being excluded from the temporal blessings (spiritual and material) that were enjoyed by the covenant community (vs. 14).

In Romans 4:9-12 Paul argues that the determining factor of Abraham's righteous status before God was not his circumcision, but his faith in God's justificatory promise (Gen. 15:6) before he was circumcised (Gen. 17:26). His circumcision was a seal, authenticating and confirming the genuineness of the righteous status that he had received by God's grace through faith. His circumcision did not create or enhance this status of righteousness, as the Jews of Jesus' day wrongly believed (Jn. 8:33-44; Rom. 4:9) and as some Christian Jews believed later (Acts 15:1). It was only a sign of this status to them who truly possessed the divine gift of righteousness through faith.

To my mind, there is no biblical basis for the covenantal concept that water baptism has replaced circumcision as the sign and seal of the Covenant of Grace. They who hold this view baptize infants in order, as they allege, to make them members of the covenantal community as circumcision did among the descendants of Abraham in the precross era. Contrariwise, we become members of the new covenantal community at salvation by the baptism of the Holy Spirit, who places us into Christ (Gal. 3:26-28) and into the Lord's body, the church (I Cor. 12:13, 27: Eph. 1:22-23).

g. *Its importance*

With the promise of the coming Seed (the Lord Jesus Christ), the covenant was the basis for the salvational faith of Abraham and his posterity, including those who lived under the Mosaic Law. Since it pointed to the coming Saviour and His work (Gal. 3:8, 13-16), the covenant promises of Genesis 12:3 and 15:5 gave something for these people to believe. These promises were a kind of Old Testament "John 3:16" (cp. Lk. 1:68-75; consider Paul's remarks in Gal. 3:8, 14, 16). People who lived beyond the reach of this revelation, given to Israel, still had whatever truth that persisted in their traditions and the witness of the stellar constellations. As time elapsed, however, these traditions became more distorted and the message of the constellations was less clear. Certainly, by the first century the world was ready for the universal proclamation of the gospel.

This covenant also provided a basis for God's gracious dealings with disobedient Israel during their history (Ex. 2:24-25; 6:1-8; Deut. 30:20; II Kings 13:23) and with the elect of Israel at Christ's second coming (Lev. 26:40-45; Jer. 30:3; Mic. 7:18-20; Ezek. 36:28). Israel's present occupation of Palestine is not a fulfillment of this covenant, nor can any aggression on their part ever be justified by it. The Lord Jesus will restore the elect of Israel to their land when He comes to earth again.

3. THE MOSAIC COVENANT (Ex. 19:1-8; 24:1-8; Lev. 18:5)

a. Its recipients

This covenant was given only to the nation of Israel (Ex. 19:3; II Chron. 6:11; Ps. 147:19-20). It has never been given to any other people.

a. Its promises

1. To make Israel a peculiar treasure for God's possession (Ex. 19:5).

This means that they were to be His special people above all other nations.

2. To make them a kingdom of priests to serve Him (vs. 6).

The elect of Israel served God by their being a witness to His existence and singularity, their being writers and guardians of the Old Testament Scriptures, their worshiping Him, and their giving birth to the Messiah.

3. To make them a holy nation (vs. 6).

The Mosaic Law gave to this group of recently delivered slaves national organization and political identity. Moreover, it made them different and separate from their grossly immoral neighbors.

4. To give them spiritual life (Lev. 18:5; cp. Deut. 8:1; Neh. 9:29; Prov. 4:4; Ezek. 20:11, 13, 21; Rom. 10:5; Gal. 3:12).

Although it promised spiritual life (not salvation) to anyone who could keep it (Mt. 19:16-17), the Mosaic Law could not save or give life to them who violated it (Gal. 3:21; Rom. 7:10). Since no one but Jesus fully kept the law (Acts 15:10), none received life from it. The law could not save or give spiritual life to sinners.[66] Only God in His grace can do this (Lk. 18:18-27).

5. To prosper Israel and to allow them to remain in the promised land (Lev. 26:3-12; cp. Deut. 5:33; 28:2-14).

The Mosaic Law required obedience of Israel for their remaining in the promised land (Lev. 26:3-13). Disobedience to God's law would bring them

---

[66] That the law was unable to help or save sinners (Rom. 7:10) was not due to any inherent defect in it (Rom. 7:12-13), but to the sinfulness of fallen people who could not keep a perfect moral law (Rom. 8:7-8). Demanding complete obedience (Gal. 3:10), the law could not compensate for this weakness (Rom. 8:3). It could only condemn and slay (Rom. 7:10-11; Gal. 3:10). It could not give its violators spiritual life.

divine judgment, including dispersion (vss. 14-33).

c. Its obligations

Israel's obligation was to keep the Mosaic Covenant by observing all that the LORD had commanded therein (Ex. 19:5-8; Lev. 26:3, 14-15). These commandments consist of the following: *the commandments,* stating the moral laws [Ex. 20:1-17 as well as Deuteronomy 6:5 and Leviticus 19:18 (see Mk. 12:28-31)]; *the judgments,* presenting the social laws (Ex. 21:1-23:19); *the Levitical ritual,* regulating Israel's approach unto God and prescribing the duties of the priests (Leviticus); and *additional regulations,* given in Numbers (chs. 5, 6, 9, 10, 15, 18, 19, 27-30).

d. Its character

The Mosaic Covenant was legal in character. The conditions of this covenant were expressed by its laws, or dispensational features. Based on the principle of law or works, it provided no divine enablement for its observance and required God to deal with its recipients as they deserved (cp. Ex. 19:5; Lev. 18:5; 26:3-4; Rom. 9:31-32; Gal. 3:11-12, 21-22).

If a person had been able to fulfill the covenant obligations, then his works would have required God to do what He had promised, for his obedience would have placed God in his debt (Rom. 4:4). On the other hand, were he to fail to fulfill his obligations, then he would break the covenant and incur divine punishment (Lev. 26:14-39; Gal. 3:10). Being weak and sinful, the unregenerated people of Israel broke the covenant continually during the time it was in force (Jer. 31:32; 11:7-10), even before they left Mt. Sinai (Ex. 32:1-10). Because the law was unable to minister to their spiritual need, it could not help these people. It could only condemn and slay them; it could not give them life (Rom. 7:9-10; Gal. 3:10). On the other hand, the saved of Israel like Elisabeth and Zacharias (Lk. 1:6) were able to keep the law sufficiently to be used of God. They did this, as we do, by the divine grace that accompanies salvation.

God graciously gave to Israel the Levitical ritual and offerings in order to provide a means to keep them alive physically when they sinned and to fulfill to them the covenant promises. But no provision was made for deliberate sins (Num. 15:30-31) or for such capital crimes as Sabbath breaking (Ex. 35:2) and murder (21:12). As always, the Jew was spiritually saved by faith in the promise of the coming Saviour (cp. Gen. 15:5-6; Gal. 3:6-14), not by law keeping or by observing the Levitical offerings. The offerings only covered certain sins and thereby kept the Israelite from suffering death by the law. Undoubtedly, the offerings had greater meaning to godly Jews who were looking for the promised Redeemer.

e. Its duration

In spite of Israel's repeated violations, by the sovereign mercy of God this covenant continued in force from its ratification at Mt. Sinai (Ex. 19:8; 24:7-8), throughout the remainder of the Old Testament period (Mal.

4:4), unto Christ's death (II Cor. 3:6-14; Gal. 3:19; Eph. 2:14-16; Col. 2:14; Heb. 10:9). It was replaced by the New Covenant, which was ratified by our Lord's death (Lk. 22:20; Heb. 10:5-10). Although the Mosaic Law as a covenant ended at the cross with the ratification of the New Covenant, it seems to continue as a dispensation to all who strive to fulfill its duties (cp. the Jews of Paul's day). In any case, God will no longer honor its covenant promises.

f. Its sign or witness

Being a two-party covenant, the Mosaic Law was ratified by the people and by God. The people agreed to the covenant when they promised to obey its obligations (Ex. 19:8; 24:3, 7). Later, individual submission to the covenant was expressed by accepting ritual circumcision (Ex. 12:43-49; Jn. 7:23; Acts 15:1, 5; 21:21; Gal. 5:2-3) and by Sabbath observance (Ex. 31:12-17; Ezek. 20:12). Ritual circumcision reminded its possessor of the promises of the Abrahamic and Mosaic Covenants; Sabbath observance was a token of continued obedience to the Mosaic Law. Meanwhile, acting as God's agent, Moses ratified the covenant when he sprinkled the people with sacrificial blood (Ex. 24:8).

g. Its importance

Paul sets forth the importance of the Mosaic Covenant in Galatians 3:19-25. He declares that it served as *a teacher* to establish and reveal the character of sin as transgression (Gal. 3:19; cp. Rom. 3:20; 5:20; 7:7-13; 4:15), *a jailer* to confine the people to the awareness of their sins and their need for the Redeemer (Gal. 3:23; cp. I Tim. 1:9-10; Heb. 10:2-3), and *a child-guardian* to restrain the people until they entered the freedom of sonship by faith in Jesus Christ (Gal. 3:24-25; cp. 4:1-5). The apostle also states that the law, together with the prophets, bore witness to Christ (Rom. 3:21). (Compare the Messianic prophecies and the symbolism of the offerings and tabernacle.)

While the law was ineffective in the lives of most Israelites, it was fruitful in the lives of the elect. Like David, the people who were chosen to salvation responded to its condemnatory and disciplinary work by casting themselves upon the grace of God, expressed in the Abrahamic Covenant (II Sam. 12:13; Lev. 20:10; Ps. 32, 51; cp. Lev. 26:40-42; Mic. 7:19-20). The Mosaic Law did not cancel or replace the Abrahamic Covenant, but it was given alongside to fulfill a disciplinary role in the lives of the Israelites and to point them to Jesus (Gal. 3:17-19).

God used the law in the hearts of the elect Israelites to create of them a holy nation (Ex. 19:6). Although the law itself could not save or give sinners spiritual life, it did show the elect their need for God's grace and for trusting the promise of the coming Saviour. Those who trusted the promise not only were saved but also were enabled by divine grace to observe the law's commandments. They did not keep the law perfectly, but they were obedient to the extent that they could be used of God to accomplish His purposes for Israel (cp. Lk. 1:6, 27-28; Mt. 1:19). Unsaved Israelites had no enablement through the law to observe its commandments, and so they violated it continually.

4. THE PALESTINIAN COVENANT (Deut. 28:1-29:1; 30:1-10)

a. Its recipients

God made this covenant in Moab with the second generation of the Israelites who came up out of Egypt (Deut. 29:1, 9), whose parents died in the wilderness, and with their posterity (vss. 14-15, 22-29).

b. Its promises

The covenant has two major parts: One is a restatement of what God had promised in Leviticus 26:3-39 (Deut. 28:1-29:1), promising blessing for obedience (28:1-14) and judgment for disobedience (28:15-29:1). The second part is a group of promises that the LORD will fulfill when Israel returns to Him and obeys His voice (Deut. 30:1-10; cp. Lev. 26:40-45; Ezek. 36:16-38). Let us consider this second group of promises, which present additional details of this gracious part of the covenant.

1. To restore Israel to their land (Deut. 30:3-5).

In the event that Israel is removed from their land because of their apostasy (this occurred twice in their subsequent history — during the 8th to the 6th centuries B.C. and A.D. 70), they will be restored again. A few Jews returned from Babylon to Palestine in the 6th century B.C., but the prophecy concerns both Judah and the Northern Kingdom when Christ returns to establish His kingdom (cp. Jer. 30:3-24; Ezek. 34:11-13; 36:24).

2. To bless and multiply them (vs. 5; cp. Jer. 23:3-4; Ezek. 37:26; Amos 9:11-15).

The Lord Jesus will bless the repentant of Israel in an unprecedented way when He restores them to their land.

3. To regenerate them (vs. 6; cp. Ezek. 36:25-27; 37:14).

For Israel to circumcise the heart means to humble herself, accept the punishment for her sins (Lev. 26:41), and renew her pledge of loyalty and obedience to God (Jer. 4:4; cp. Deut. 10:16). For God to circumcise the heart in response to Israel's fulfilling her part is a figurative expression for spiritual cleansing and renewal (Deut. 30:6). This results in their loving God and experiencing eternal life.

4. To curse their enemies (vs. 7; cp. Jer. 30:11, 16).

God promises to deal with Israel's enemies in judgment for their persecuting His people. This will take place particularly at the Battle of Armageddon (Rev. 19:11-21) and with Jesus' judgment of the nations, which determines who are qualified to enter His kingdom (Mt. 25:31-46).

5. To cause Israel to prosper (vs. 9) both spiritually and materially (Ezek. 37:26-27; Isa. chs. 35, 60).

God will cause restored Israel to flourish during our Lord's millennial reign. At that time, Israel will again be the wife of the LORD (Yahweh, Hos.

127

2:19-23). This means that above all nations she will enjoy a special relationship with God.

c. Its obligations

In the event of their disobedience and dispersion, it will be Israel's duty to return to the LORD and to obey His voice (Deut. 30:2, 8, 10). This will involve their repentance toward God and salvational faith in the Lord Jesus Christ (Acts 20:21; 2:38-39; Rom. 16:25-26; Jn. 6:28-29). This was the message that John the Baptist, Jesus, and Peter preached to Israel (Mt. 3:1-2; 4:17; Acts 2:38). By the grace of God the elect of Israel, living in that day, will do this (cp. Zech. 12:10; Joel 2:12-18; Jer. 32:27-44; Ezek 36:16-28; Acts 19:4). When they turn to Him, Christ will return to earth to establish His millennial kingdom (Deut. 30:2; Acts 3:19-21). These are the people Paul had in view in Romans 11:25-26.

d. Its character

The first major part of the Palestinian Covenant is legal in character, for it repeats a portion of the Mosaic Law (Deut. 28:1-29:1 with Lev. 26:3-39). Accordingly, God dealt with disobedient Israel as they deserved by dispersing them among the Gentiles.

The second major part is both gracious and conditional (Deut. 30:1-10). The elect of Israel will be graciously restored to their land and to God's blessing when they return to the LORD and receive Jesus as their Saviour. God will not have forgotten the gracious promise that He made to Abraham regarding the Land (Gen. 15:18; 17:8; Lev. 26:42; Deut. 30:20).

e. Its duration

The gracious promises of the Palestinian Covenant will endure forever (Ezek. 37:25; cp. Jer. 32:37-39). Indeed, in that day God will make an everlasting covenant (the New Covenant) with Israel which will assure them of a perpetual continuation of these blessings (Jer. 32:40).

f. Its sign or witness

This appears to be the survival of the people of Israel (cp. Jer. 31:35-37). Consider how God has preserved them through these many years while other nations, much greater than they, have perished. After many centuries, the political State of Israel was established in 1948 and continues to the present time.

g. Its importance

In the event of their dispersion, this covenant promises Israel their restoration to their land and God's blessing on them in the land. It also gives instruction regarding what they must do to experience this restoration.

5. THE DAVIDIC COVENANT (II Sam. 7:10-16)

a. Its recipients

This covenant was made with David and his posterity through Solomon (II Sam. 7:12-13, 16; cp. I Ki. 1:29-30; 2:45-46; 9:1-9; I Chron. 28:5-7).

b. Its promises

Called "the sure mercies of David" (Isa. 55:3; Acts 13:34; cp. II Sam. 7:15), these promises are listed as follows:

1. To *Israel* God promised a permanent place of habitation as well as deliverance from their enemies (II Sam. 7:10; cp. Deut. 30:2-5).

This concerns the future restoration of the elect remnant of Israel to their land, as promised by the Palestinian Covenant (Deut. 30:2-5), when the Lord Jesus comes to rule over the earth. God also promised that they would never be dispersed again.

2. To *David* He promised a perpetual house (dynasty), kingdom, and throne (II Sam. 7:16; cp. Ezek. 34:23-24; 37:24-25; Jer. 30:9).

This assured that David and his posterity through Solomon would be the ruling dynasty of Israel forever. During the nation's subsequent history, David's house under Solomon and Rehoboam ruled all of Israel; from Rehoboam through Jerhoiachin, it ruled the tribes of Judah and Benjamin (I Kings 12:17, 21; II Kings 24:12).

The promise also assured that David's house will be the ruling dynasty in our Lord's millennial kingdom. David himself will rule Israel (Ezek. 34:23-24; 37:24-25; Jer. 30:9) while the Lord Jesus will rule the whole earth, including Israel (Lk. 1:32-33; Acts 2:30; Ps. 2:8-9; 72:8.)

3. To *David's seed* (Solomon and his lineage) He promised mercy and the establishment of his kingdom forever (II Sam. 7:13-15). Of David's nineteen sons (I Chron. 3:1-9), God selected Solomon to be the successor to the throne. In contrast to the five dynasties that ruled the northern kingdom of Israel (I Ki. 12:20; 15:28; 16:16; II Ki. 9:13-14; 15:17-20), there was but one ruling dynasty of Judah (cp. Gen. 49:10; I Ki. 15:4). Later, a divine curse fell upon Solomon's line which thereafter prevented the members of this dynasty from occupying and prospering on the throne (Jer. 36:30; 22:30).

The title to David's throne was transmitted to the Lord Jesus through His legal father Joseph, a descendant of Solomon (Mt. 1:6-16). Our Lord's virgin conception and birth allowed Him to bypass the divine curse upon the royal line and to rule with divine favor. Because He had no sons and is alive forevermore, the Lord Jesus will possess this title forever (Lk. 1:31-33). See Acts 13:22-23, 32-39; Jeremiah 33:15; Romans 1:3; II Timothy 2:8.

c. Its obligations

While there were no obligations for the fulfillment of the covenant promises, obedience was required of any king to remain on David's throne and to enjoy God's blessing (I Kings 2:3-4; 9:4-9). God promised never to reject the dynasty of Solomon, but He did threaten to remove them who disobeyed His commands (II Sam. 7:14-15; Ps. 89:30-37; II Chron. 7:17-20).

d. Its character

The Davidic Covenant is gracious and unconditional. There are no conditions for man to meet for the promises to be fulfilled. God will bring all this about in His time.

e. Its duration

Upon their being restored to their land, Israel will never be threatened again with invasion or dispersion (II Sam. 7:10). Having sworn by His holiness, God will never break this covenant (Ps. 89:33-37). It will continue forever (II Sam. 7:16; 23:5).

f. Its sign or witness

This appears to be the continuation of David's house and the establishment of his throne in Solomon (I Chron. 28:1-7) and in Immanuel, the Virgin's son Jesus (Isa. 7:10-14; Lk. 1:30-33; Mt. 1:20-23).

g. Its importance

The Davidic Covenant establishes the legality of Jesus' future rule over the earth from David's throne (Lk. 1:32-33; Isa. 11:1-5). The Lord Jesus received the title to the throne from Joseph, His legal father, and was a descendant of David through Mary, His real mother. Being the last to receive the title, Jesus will possess it forever, for He has no natural posterity to whom it will pass. His title to the earth is by divine command (Ps. 2:6-9).

6. THE NEW COVENANT (Jer. 31:31-40)

a. Its recipients

These are all who are saved after the covenant became effective upon Christ's death and resurrection (Lk. 22:20; cp. II Cor. 3:6-18; Heb. 10:14-18; 12:24; 13:20). This will also include the elect remnant of Israel and Judah in the day of their restoration to God (Isa. 59:20-21; Jer. 31:31; Ezek. 37:26-27).

There are not two New Covenants, as some have taught, one for Israel and one for the church. The one New Covenant applies to all who receive the Saviour during the Church, Tribulation, and Kingdom Ages.

b. Its promises

The promises of the New Covenant are predicted in Jeremiah 31:31-40 and are repeated in Hebrews 8:6-13; 10:15-17. These promises concern salvation and its basic blessings as described in the New Testament (the portion of the Bible that deals with the New Covenant).

1. To put His law in their inward parts (Jer. 31:33).

Some have understood this to mean God's gracious prompting and enablement by which His people obey His Word (cp. Phil. 2:13). However, to my mind, it is better to interpret these words literally. When the salvation of the Lord's people is completed, with the redemption of their bodies, and the promises of this covenant are fulfilled, then the Lord will actually put His Word in their hearts. His people will not have to carry Bibles, for God's Word will forever exist in their memory as well as exert its influence on their lives.

2. To be their God (vss. 33b, 34a).

To know the LORD refers to one's having a right relationship with God, brought about by divine forgiveness and the new birth (cp. Jn. 17:3; 10:27; 1:12). This relationship with God also involves a right attitude toward Him — the fear of God (Jer. 32:39-40) To fear God is to revere Him (Ps. 33:8), be in agreement with Him (Prov. 3:7; 8:13), obey Him (14:2), trust His promises (14:26), and accept His instructions (1:7; 15:33).

3. To forgive their sins (vs. 34).

This means that the gospel believer's debt of sin is cancelled by the application of the value of Christ's atoning work (cp. Eph. 1:7; Acts 10:43). The declaration, "I will remember their sins no more," refers to God's judicial memory, that is, to His holding these sins against His people. This clause is parallel to the words, "I will forgive their iniquity." Not remembering sin means the same as forgiving sin, that is, releasing the sinner from the obligation to bear punishment for sin.

The prophecy of Jeremiah 31:31-40 looks forward to God's saving the elect remnant of Israel according to the promises of this covenant, which was ratified by Jesus' death and resurrection (Lk. 22:20; Rom. 11:26-27; Heb. 10:29; 12:24; 13:20). All who exercise salvational faith in the Saviour during the Church Age, Tribulation Period, and Kingdom Age will receive the promised blessings of the covenant. However, this is not to say that all the recipients of this covenant are one people with the same function in God's program. While the salvational blessings, offered by the covenant, are the same for all, these are to be distinguished from the functional roles (with their particular blessings) that various groups of redeemed people have. For example, while the church and the future elect of Israel will have the same salvational blessings, promised by the New Covenant, they will have different functional roles during the kingdom. The church will be Jesus' bride (Eph. 5:32) and Israel will be Yahweh's wife (Hos. ch. 2).

c. Its obligations

To enter the bond of the covenant and to experience its promised blessings, one must exercise salvational faith in Jesus, the Mediator of the New Covenant (Heb. 12:24; Acts 13:32-39). Observe that baptism is not required for participation in the covenant. As a minister of the New Covenant, Paul appealed to people to exercise salvational faith in Jesus (Acts 20:21; II Cor. 3:6; 5:18-20).

d. Its character

The New Covenant is gracious and conditional. It is gracious in that God offers salvation to undeserving people. It is conditional in that obedience to the gospel brings one into the bond of the covenant (Acts 13:32-39; Rom. 1:5). Obedience is also necessary for the daily experience of God's fellowship and blessings (I Jn. 1:5-7). This obedience is a work of divine grace (Eph. 2:2-9; II Cor. 1:12).

e. Its duration

The relationship between God and His people according to this covenant will continue forever (Jer. 31:35-37), for this covenant cannot be broken (vss. 31-32). Unlike the Law of Moses, this covenant cannot be annulled by people's disobedience. Actually, in their glorified state the Lord's people will never sin again. Meanwhile, all of their sins are judicially forgiven (Col. 2:13); therefore, none of these can threaten the continuance of the covenant.

Because of the perpetual quality of these promises, this covenant is described as being "everlasting" (Isa. 61:8; Jer. 32:40; Heb. 13:20) and "a covenant of peace" (Ezek. 37:26). All who become the recipients of this covenant through trusting Jesus as Saviour are justified forever (Rom. 8:30-34).

f. Its sign or witness

The initial sign was the shedding of our Lord's blood together with His death and resurrection, by which the covenant was ratified by God (Heb. 12:24; 13:20; Rom. 1:4). Today, this sign is symbolically portrayed by the "cup" of the Lord's Supper (Lk. 22:20; I Cor. 11:25-26), which reminds us of the Lord's atoning work — the central fact of our faith. In the coming millennial kingdom, this covenant sign will be displayed by the crucifixion marks in Jesus' body (Jn. 20:24-28) and by the various sacrifices that will be offered in the millennial temple (Ezek. chs. 43, 45, 46). Being commemorative rather than effective, these offerings will apparently remind His people of His atoning work, as the Lord's Supper does today.

g. Its importance

The importance of the covenant is manifest in its salvational promises. Being based on Christ's atoning work, the New Covenant fulfills and replaces the salvational aspect of the Abrahamic Covenant, which foresaw the coming Seed and the blessings that Jesus would bring to all who trust Him. But this covenant does not cancel or replace earlier covenants that promised other things, such as Israel's title to certain territory, and the like, which are yet to be fulfilled. The New Covenant only replaces the Covenant of the Mosaic Law (Heb. 8:6-13).

Observe the following distinctions in your study of these covenants:

1. All of these covenants relate to Israel (Rom. 9:4): the Noachian Covenant was given to all mankind; the Abrahamic Covenant gives Israel title to certain territory; the Mosaic Covenant states the condition of their remaining in the promised land; the Palestinian Covenant declares the conditions for their restoration to the land in the event of their dispersion; the Davidic Covenant assures Israel of the perpetuity of David's house and of their restoration to the promised land; and the New Covenant promises salvation to all who receive Jesus as Saviour.

2. The Abrahamic and New Covenants are salvational covenants: The

Abrahamic Covenant, which spoke about the coming Seed and the blessing He would bring, was the salvational covenant of the Old Testament period from Abraham's time onward. The New Covenant, based on Jesus' atoning work, is the current, final salvational covenant, fulfilling and replacing the salvational aspects of the Abrahamic Covenant.

3. Only the Noachian and New Covenants directly concern us who are saved during the present Church Age and Gentiles who will be saved in the future.

GOD'S SAVING WORK

Unquestionably, salvation is uniquely God's work (Isa. 45:22; Rom. 5:6; Eph. 2:8-9). While we shall examine this doctrine in greater detail later, it is fitting that we include it here with God's other works. This is His greatest work, for it displays certain qualities of His nature that no other work does. Because sinners were unable to deliver themselves from sin, God in His measureless grace was pleased to provide salvation. This saving work includes the following divine operations:

- **God's Choosing Whom He Would Save (II Thess. 2:13)**

This choice was not prompted by human works, worth, or merit (Rom. 9:11). It was solely by God's pleasure (Eph. 1:9, 11).

- **God's Atoning for Humanity's Sins (Jn. 1:29)**

Before He could save sinners, God's nature required Him to deal with their sins and satisfy His holy demands against them. This involved the joint activity of the Trinity. The Father gave His Son to appease His wrath by paying the debt of our sins (Jn. 3:16; I Jn. 4:10). In obedience to the Father, the Son atoned for our sins by His death and the shedding of His blood (Mt. 20:28; Jn. 10:18). This work was ratified by His resurrection. Finally, the Holy Spirit enabled the Lord Jesus to do all that the atonement required (Heb. 9:14; Rom. 8:11).

- **God's Saving the Elect (I Pet. 1:2)**

Drawn by divine action (Jn. 6:37, 44), the gospel believer receives the value of Christ's atoning work and experiences God's saving work in his life (Jn. 3:16).

Being wholly God's work (Eph. 2:8-9), salvation manifests God's wisdom, power, and grace. This work includes not only deliverance from the ruin, debt, and power of sin, but also the bestowal of the riches of God's grace. We who are saved shall never cease to praise Him for this gracious work in our lives.

GOD'S JUDGMENTS

As the Creator and Ruler of the universe, God is the Judge of all the earth (Gen. 18:25). In contrast to salvation, judgment is His "strange work" (Isa.

28:21). Still, it is required by His holy nature and the accountability of His personal creatures (Rom. 14:12; I Pet. 4:5). Paul describes the qualities of divine judgment as being factual (Rom. 2:2), fair (vs. 6), and impartial (vs. 11).

Although the word "judgment" has various meanings in the Scriptures, theologically it seems to represent three ideas, determined by its context: one, God's trial of accountable, personal creatures; two, His sentence upon them; and three, the execution of His sentence.

When Jesus says that the Father committed all judgment to Him (Jn. 5:22), He seems to have in view those judgments that are related to His Messianic work. (Compare the reason for this authority being given in verse 27, "because He is the Son of Man" — a Messianic title.) Because of this, I do not consider the divine judgments of the Old Testament period to be Messianic or the exclusive work of the Son since they occurred before His incarnation and the beginning of His Messianic work.

A partial list of divine judgments, with their particular aspect, follows:

- **In the Past**

Adam and Eve (Gen. 3:7-13 with 2:17: execution; vss. 14-19: trial and sentence); the Noachian flood (Gen. chs. 6, 7: execution); Sodom and Gomorrah (Gen. ch. 19: execution); plagues of Egypt (Ex. 12:12: execution); Jesus' bearing the divine judgment of our sins (Isa. 53:10; I Jn. 2:2: execution); the world and Satan at the cross [Jn. 12:31; 16:11: trial and sentence; their crime of crucifying the Creator was self-incriminating (Jn. 3:18)].

- **In the Future**

These will be Messianic judgments, including those of the Tribulaltion Period (Rev. chs. 6-19: execution); earth dwellers who survive this period (Israel, Ezek. 20:33-38, and the Gentiles, Mt. 25:31-46: trial, sentence, execution); and the judgment of the lost (Rev. 20:11-15: trial, sentence, execution).

The judgment of believers (Rev. 22:12; II Cor. 5:10) is not a judicial one. It is the Master's appraisal of the works of His servants for the calculation of their rewards. The believer will never come into judicial judgment for his sins, for the Lord Jesus bore this on the cross (Jn. 5:24; Rom. 8:1, 31-34).

One cannot reflect upon the excellency of our God's person and works, in contrast to the false, ineffective gods of this world, and not be filled with gratitude and praise for His self-revelation. The true and living God deserves more from His people than what the false gods of the world receive from their devotees (I Thess. 1:9-10).

Solomon declared that the whole duty of man is to fear God and keep His commandments (Eccles. 12:13). Although the unsaved do not fear God as they should (Rom. 3:18), this is the duty of us who are saved (Ps. 34:9; II Cor. 7:1; I Pet. 2:17; Heb. 12:28). This fear is not one of terror or dread, which is incompatible with love (I Jn. 4:18; II Tim. 1:7). Rather, it is expressed by a profound reverence for God's Being and majesty (Ps. 33:8), an agreement with His attitude toward good and evil (Prov. 3:7; 8:13), obedience to His will (14:2), confidence in His promises (14:26), and the acceptance of His instruction (1:7; 15:33). This fear not only prolongs our days (Prov. 10:27) but also equips us for life and service (Phil. 2:12; I Pet. 3:15).

A Review of Theology Proper

1. How may we define God?
2. How do we know that God exists?
3. Give the four witnesses to God's existence by means of general revelation.
4. Briefly explain the four rational arguments for God's existence. In what circumstances may these arguments be useful? Compare I Peter 3:15.
5. Why do we not have to prove to unsaved people God's existence?
6. To what extent is God's witness to mankind clear?
7. Give and describe the various non-Christian views of God.
8. What is the Christian view of God called?
9. Describe the active and passive forms of God's revelation.
10. Why is it necessary that God reveal himself to man?
11. What are the two kinds, or stages, of divine revelation?
12. Describe these stages and to whom they are given.
13. In what way is general revelation insufficient?
14. In what way is general revelation effective?
15. In what ways is special revelation sufficient?
16. In what ways is special revelation effective?
17. In what ways was special revelation given during the O.T. period?
18. In what ways was special revelation given during the N.T. period?
19. What was the unique manifestation of special revelation in the N.T. period?
20. Why do we say that new special revelation is not being given today?
21. When will new special revelation be given again?
22. How does religious liberalism view special revelation?
23. What is God's primary constitution, or make-up?
24. What features show that God has personhood?
25. Of what substance does the divine nature consist?
26. What are the qualities of the divine nature called?
27. Which of these qualities are communicated to saved people? By what means are they communicated?
28. Describe God's qualities, or attributes. Give a blessing that the truth of each attribute is to us who are saved.
29. Explain God's transcendence and His immanence.
30. How does God's love differ from human love?
31. What is the great expression of divine love toward the world?

32. How does God's hatred differ from human hatred?

33. What two kinds of wrath does God's hatred express?

34. Explain and give an example of each of the following terms: anthropomorphisms, anthropopathisms, and zoomorphisms.

35. Of what does the unity of God consist?

36. Why is the unity of God emphasized in the Old Testament?

37. Of what does the triunity (Trinity) of God consist?

38. Why is the triunity of God emphasized in the New Testament?

39. Give a four statement summary of the biblical doctrine of the Trinity.

40. Explain the three false views of the Trinity.

41. What makes each of the three Persons of the Godhead to be God?

42. What makes the three Persons of the Godhead to be together one God?

43. Why do the three Persons of the Godhead have equal attributes?

44. Explain the relationships among the Members of the Godhead with reference to the divine nature.

45. Explain the subordination that is manifest among the Members of the Godhead with reference to their internal relationships and to their relationships to the universe.

46. What three kinds of designations are there?

47. Give the three basic Hebrew names for God in the Old Testament, their meanings, and how they are expressed in the KJV of the Bible.

48. Give the three kinds of designations found in the New Testament for each Member of the Godhead.

49. What is the human personal name of God the Son? When did He receive this name?

50. What is God's decree? Give the biblical words that stand for His decree.

51. Give and explain the various qualities that characterize God's decree.

52. What actions of God are governed by His decree?

53. Explain the efficient and permissive aspects of God's decree.

54. What evidence shows that people are not mechanically determined like parts of a machine by God's decree?

55. For what aspect of His decree will God not assume responsibility?

56. State the difference between God's decree and His revealed will for mankind. With what should we be concerned?

57. What is the ultimate objective of God's decree?

58. How did sin have a place in God's decree?

59. What should be our attitude toward biblical doctrines we do not understand?

60. Define God's act of creating the universe.

61. Give the two steps that were involved in God's creative work.

62. Describe the roles of the Members of the Godhead in the creation of the universe.

63. Describe the events of the six days of God's creative activity.

64. What appears to be the purpose of accommodative interpretations of these six days of creative activity?

65. Describe these accommodative interpretations of Genesis one.

66. Why is it inadvisable to harmonize Scripture with scientific opinion?

67. What is scientism? Organic evolution? Chance?

68. List and explain the natural laws with which the theory of evolution conflicts.

69. What creative works is God doing today? In the future?

70. Describe God's acts of preservation and providence as these relate to the universe.

71. What problems come into view when we look at God's providence? How do we resolve these?

72. Define the terms "dispensation," "dispensationalist," and "dispensationalism."

73. Dispensationally, what two meanings does the word "age" have in the New Testament?

74. What is the difference between a divine dispensation and a divine covenant?

75. List the divine dispensations, their recipients, and their duties.

76. Some people to a large degree have obeyed God. By what means did they do this?

77. List the divine covenants, their recipients, and their promises.

78. What is covenantal theology? Why do dispensationalists reject this?

79. What covenants relate especially to Israel? What do they promise these people?

80. What dispensation and covenant particularly apply to us who are saved today?

81. Which dispensation was also a covenant?

82. List the sign of each covenant. What purposes do these signs serve?

83. In addition to creation, dispensations, covenants, and sovereign rule, give two other works of God.

84. Give the three theological meanings that the word "judgment" has in the Scripture and an example of each.

85. What does it mean to fear God?

Paterology

PATEROLOGY
The Doctrine of God the Father

This doctrine is usually included with Theology Proper, but its importance requires our special attention. The following study is largely from New Testament passages that unquestionably refer to the First Person of the Trinity. This is not to suggest that the Father is not mentioned or alluded to in the Old Testament (Isa. 63:16; Hos. 11:1; Prov. 30:4), but the designation "God" (Heb. *Elohim*) probably more often represents the Trinity collectively, as the plural form of the Hebrew word indicates. In the New Testament, the word "God" often represents the Father, especially in passages where references to the Son occur as well (cp. Rom. 1:1-3, 8-9; I Cor. 1:9; I Jn. 1:5-7).

THE FATHER'S NATURE

This concerns who and what the Father is.

HE IS A PERSON.

That the Father is a person is seen in His possessing features of personhood, such as selfhood, individuality, morality, and perpetuity. His selfhood is indicated by His self-consciousness (Jn. 4:23; Mt. 3:17) and self-determination (Jn. 6:38-39); His morality by His moral awareness (Lk. 10:21; Mt. 7:11); His individuality by His personal distinctiveness (Jn. 14:16); and His perpetuity by His living forever (Rev. 4:9). Other features, which many believe are qualities of personhood, are intelligence (Mt. 6:8; Mk. 13:32), emotion (I Jn. 4:9-10), and communication (Heb. 1:1-2; Mt. 3:17; Jn. 12:28).

The Father also functions as a person. He speaks (Mt. 3:17; Jn. 15:15), sees (Mt. 6:6), gives (Jn. 14:16), works (Jn. 5:17), blesses (Eph. 1:3), keeps (Jn. 17:11), sends (Jn. 20:21), promises (Lk. 24:49), comforts (II Cor. 1:3-4), directs (I Thess. 3:11), chooses (Eph. 1:4), calls (I Cor. 1:9), disciplines (Heb. 12:6-10), bears witness (Jn. 5:37), and forgives (Mt. 6:14).

HE IS GOD.

Possessing the divine nature in common with the other Persons of the Godhead, the Father is God. His deity is indicated by the following:

- **He is called God.**

See Romans 1:7; I Corinthians 1:3; Ephesians 4:6; and Philippians 2:11; I Thessalonians 3:13.

- **He manifests divine attributes.**

These include life (Jn. 6:57), self-existence (Jn. 5:26), omnipotence (Jn. 10:29), omniscience (Rom. 8:27; Mt. 6:8, 18), omnipresence (Jn. 14:23; 16:28, 32), sovereignty (Lk. 10:21), wisdom (Rom. 16:27), holiness

(Jn. 17:11), perfection (Mt. 5:48), righteousness (Jn. 17:25), love (Jn. 3:16), mercy (Lk. 6:36), grace (Eph. 1:6), faithfulness (I Cor. 1:9), and goodness (Mt. 6:25-30; Eph. 1:3).

- **He does the works of God.**

Being the Source of all created things, God the Father was active in the creation of the universe (I Cor. 8:6; Rev. 4:9-11). He is the Source of all divine revelation (Jn. 16:15; Rev. 1:1; I Cor. 2:9-10; Heb. 1:1-2). He initiated our salvation (Eph. 1:4-5). He gave His Son for the atonement of sin (Jn. 3:16; I Jn. 4:10) and raised Him from the dead (Gal. 1:1). He begets them who believe the gospel (I Pet. 1:3). He forgives sins (Mt. 6:14). Finally, He reigns supremely over all (Lk. 10:21; Eph. 4:6) and judges (I Pet. 1:17).

- **He receives supreme honors.**

He receives worship (Jn. 4:23; Eph. 3:14-21; Rev. 4:10) and adoration (Gal. 1:5; Phil. 2:11; 4:20; Rev. 1:6; 5:13). Moreover, the Lord Jesus honored the Father (Jn. 8:49) by obeying Him (8:29; 6:38) and glorifying Him in all that He did (12:28; 17:4).

These truths clearly show that the Father is God and is worthy of our worship, adoration, and service.

THE FATHER'S RELATIONSHIPS
TO THE OTHER MEMBERS OF THE TRINITY

Being God, the Father is equal to the other Members of the Godhead in the nature and extent of His attributes since the three Persons commonly possess the same divine nature (essence). However, we observe the following regarding the Father's relationship to the other Persons:

- **His Ontological Relationship**

The Father is the Generator of the Son. He is generator by an eternal act, whereby He makes the one divine essence common to Himself and to the Son (cp. Jn. 5:26; 3:16). There is no creation of the personhood of the Son or of new essence, nor is there a division of the existing essence. By this act of generation the eternally existing essence is modified so that it is communicated to the Son in such a way that it remains undivided, yet wholly possessed by the Father and the Son individually. Jesus' human nature was generated by the Holy Spirit, not by the Father (Lk. 1:35; Mt. 1:18, 20).

With the Son the Father is the Spirator of the Holy Spirit. Through the Son He communicates (by spiration, not generation) the divine essence to the Holy Spirit in such a way that it remains undivided, yet wholly possessed by the three Persons individually. The Scriptures never say that the First Person is the father of the Holy Spirit.

- **His Ontological Ascendancy**

As to order or rank the Father is first (Mt. 28:19). This does not imply that there are qualitative differences in attributes or substantive differences in nature among the Persons of the Godhead, for each possesses the same substance wholly and simultaneously with the Others. This order concerns only their constitutional relationship, with the unbegotten Father being first.

TO THE UNIVERSE
The Father's relationship to the created universe is as follows:

- **He is the Source of all created things (I Cor. 8:6; Rev. 4:9-11).**

While the Son is the creative Agent (Jn. 1:1-3), the Father is the creative Source from whom all things, excepting sin, proceed. This does not mean that the universe is an emanation of the divine nature and thus is a part of God. Yet, He has a metaphysical relationship with them by which He gives and sustains their existence. In this sense, all human beings are described as "the offspring of God" (Acts 17:29), and He is called "the Father of spirits" (Heb. 12:9, probably a reference to believers in contrast to our earthly fathers).

- **He is the Ruler over all things (Lk. 10:21).**

All creatures (including Satan and fallen angels) and things are under His authority (cp. Job 1:12; Mt. 11:25). By His determinate and benevolent rule (Acts 17:24-28), He is carrying out His decree (Eph. 1:11). He will be the supreme Ruler forever (I Cor. 15:24-28).

TO HIS ELECT PEOPLE

- **To Israel**

Israel was identified collectively as God's son and individually as His children (Ex. 4:22; Deut. 14:1; 32:6; Isa. 1:2; 63:16; 64:8; Jer. 3:4, 19; 31:9; Hos. 11:1; Mal. 1:6). While the whole nation enjoyed certain material and spiritual blessings because of their special relationship to God under the Mosaic Law (Ex. 19:5; Deut. 7:6-11), their disobedience broke the covenant and prevented their experiencing all that God desired for them. On the other hand, the few saved Israelites enjoyed a personal relationship with God (Ps. 103:1-5, 13; 89:20-26), as promised by the Abrahamic Covenant (Gen. 17:8; 12:3).

- **To Christians**

1. *The nature of the relationship*

Each saved person has a personal relationship with God the Father as His child (Jn. 1:12-13; Rom. 8:16; Gal. 3:26). However, this relationship is not the same as that between God the Father and God the Son (cp. Jn. 20:17). Because of this, Jesus never said "our Father" when He spoke about His relationship to the Father and that of His disciples. There are two reasons for this: One, the relationship between the Father and the Son is an eternal one. And two, the Son, inherently having the divine nature, is essentially identical to the Father in His qualities and powers.

We who are saved are *children* of God in the sense that by the new birth the Father has given us a new kind of life, called "eternal life" (Jn. 1:12-13). But this life is not God's own self-existent life, for He does not make our human nature divine. God the Father is like a father to us because He has imparted to us this new life and cares for us. By divine adoption we were given the position of full-grown *sons* in God's family (Eph. 1:5; Gal. 4:1-7).

2. The beginning of this relationship

A saved person's relation with God comes about at his salvation by the new birth, not by adoption (Jn. 3:3-6). Upon believing the gospel, we experienced the cleansing and renewal of our inner human nature (soul and spirit), received God's gift of spiritual life, and became God's children (Jn. 1:12-13; Rom. 6:23; Gal. 3:26).

At this time, God took up His residence within us (I Cor. 6:19; Jn. 14:23); and by this we became partakers of the divine nature (II Pet. 1:4). However, this does not mean that we became God. Although we became new creatures in Christ (Eph. 2:10; II Cor. 5:17), we shall forever be human beings, fashioned after the likeness of Jesus' glorified humanity (Rom. 8:29; Phil. 3:20-21; I Jn. 3:2).

3. The blessings of this relationship

The concept and reality of God's being our heavenly Father is a great blessing to us who are His children (Mt. 5:16, 45, 48, 6:1, 6, 8, 9, 18, 32; 7:11). This is shown by the fact He cares for us (Mt. 6:25-33; 10:29-31), keeps us (Jn. 17:11), gives us good things (Mt. 7:11; Jas. 1:17), fellowships with us (I Jn. 1:3, 7), desires our spiritual maturity (Mt. 5:48), disciplines and trains us (Heb. 12:5-11), makes us His heirs (Rom. 8:16-17), loves us (Jn. 16:27), invites our prayers (Jn. 16:23), speaks to us (Heb. 1:1-2), sees us (Mt. 6:6), knows us (Mt. 6:32; II Cor. 11:31), forgives us (Mt. 6:14), indwells us (Jn. 14:23), sanctifies us (Jn. 17:17; Jude 1), comforts us (II Cor. 1:3-4), blesses us (Eph. 1:3; Mt. 6:31-34), judges us (I Pet. 1:17), commands us (II Jn. 4), and gives us a place in His house (Jn. 14:2). How blessed it is to be His children!

4. The demands of this relationship

Our being children of this heavenly Father imposes upon us certain duties such as the following: We are to obey Him (I Pet. 1:14-15), to submit to His discipline (Heb. 12:7, 9), to share our cares with Him (I Pet. 5:6-7), to glorify Him in all that we do (I Cor. 10:31), to worship Him (Eph. 1:3), to imitate Him with Jesus as our human example (Eph. 5:1-2), to walk in His fellowship (I Jn. 1:5-7), to serve Him (I Thess. 1:9), to pray to Him (Mt. 6:6, 9), to trust Him (Mt. 6:25-34), and to love Him with our total being (Mk. 12:30).

Nowhere does the Bible teach the erroneous idea of God's universal fatherhood, in the sense that He is the spiritual Father of all people, saved and unsaved alike. The fallen human race is alienated from God by their sins (Eph. 2:1; 4:18). In their spiritual state, unsaved people are the product of Satan (Jn. 8:44) and sin (Rom. 1:21-32). They are characterized as being the children of disobedience and wrath (Eph. 2:2-3).

THE FATHER'S WORKS

In other sections we have considered the Father's involvement in the creation (I Cor. 8:6) and government (Lk. 10:21) of the universe and in the giving of special revelation (Rev. 1:1). Let us briefly consider two other activities of the Father.

IN SALVATION

While the Trinity is involved in this great work, it seems to be the Father's role to choose who should be saved (II Thess. 2:13-14), to predestinate us to adoption (Eph. 1:5) and to Christ-conformity (Rom. 8:29), to give His Son to atone for our sins (I Jn. 4:10), to draw us to Himself (Jn. 6:44), to call us to His kingdom and glory (I Thess. 2:12), to beget us again unto a living hope (I Pet. 1:3), to keep us safe (Jn. 17:11-12), and finally to bring us to glory (Heb. 2:10).

IN JESUS' MESSIANIC WORK

Upon His baptism Jesus was anointed with the Holy Spirit for the work that He came to do as the Father's servant (Jn. 1:32; 3:34; Phil. 2:7-8). In the roles of Prophet, High Priest, and King, the Lord Jesus must accomplish certain goals, set by the Father, during His first and second advents and the intervening time. He is achieving this in the power of the Holy Spirit by doing the Father's will (Jn. 6:38; 8:28-29) and by speaking the Father's words (Jn. 12:49-50).

Jesus' Messianic works (the works He is doing as man) are really the Father's works, for He is doing what the Father commanded Him to do and what He saw the Father do (Jn. 5:36, 19). Jesus is doing these works in a relationship that allows the Father to do them through Him (Jn. 14:9-11) by the power of the Holy Spirit (Acts 10:38). Being done in the sphere of Jesus' humanity (Jn. 5:17-36), these works serve to glorify the Father (Jn. 12:28; 17:4). When His present Messianic work is completed, Jesus as man will continue to be in subjection to the Father so that God may be all in all (I Cor. 15:20-28).

THE FATHER'S LOCATION

Being God, the Father is everywhere present in and throughout the universe. However, Jesus spoke about the Father's being in Heaven (Mt. 5:16; 6:9, 14, 26, 32; 7:11, 21). Perhaps the Lord referred to the Father's being in Heaven so as to distinguish Him from our earthly fathers. Or, perhaps He was referring to a visible manifestation of the Father, which is seen by heavenly creatures. Being Spirit in nature, the Father, as well as the Holy Spirit, is invisible to created eyes (Col. 1:15; I Tim. 1:17). However, in Heaven His presence is indicated by a theophany, seated upon a throne (Rev. 4:2-3; Heb. 1:3; 12:2). When the present universe is replaced by a new heaven and earth, then God will live forever with His people on earth (Rev. 21:1, 3). Since the Father does not have a body, as Jesus does, He will then, as now, assume some visible form to indicate His presence with His people.

THE FATHER'S DESIGNATIONS

Designations are names and titles that are ascribed to God the Father in the Scriptures.

HIS GENERIC NAME

Generic names describe one's kind of being.

He is called "God" in O.T. Messianic passages which also refer to God the Son (Ps. 22:1; 45:2, 7; Isa. 42:5; 49:4-5). He is also called "God" in the New Testament (Rom. 1:9; I Cor. 8:6; Eph. 4:6), especially in passages that also refer to Jesus (Jn. 3:16; II Cor. 13:14; Phil. 2:9-11). He is "the Lord God Almighty" (Rev. 21:22).

HIS TITLES

Titles relate to one's functions or offices.

1. Some Old Testament Titles

Again, in Messianic passages we find references to the Father as "the Ancient of days" (Dan. 7:9, 13, 22), "the Lord" or *Adonai* (Isa. 48:16); "the Redeemer of Israel" and "their Holy One" (Isa. 49:7).

2. Some New Testament Titles

"Father" with the definite article or an adjective (Mt. 5:48; Eph. 3:14; Rev. 1:6.), "Lord" (*Depostes* meaning absolute owner; Lk. 2:29; Acts 4:24; Rev. 6:10), "Lord" (*Kurios* meaning one supreme in authority and power; Acts 4:29; Rev. 11:17), "Husbandman" (Jn. 15:1), "Saviour" (I Tim. 1:1), and "the Almighty" (Rev. 21:22).

HIS PERSONAL NAMES

A personal name is that which distinguishes one from others within a given order or class of beings.

1. In the Old Testament

The personal name for God in the Old Testament is "LORD" (*Yahweh,* or *Jehovah; Jer. 33:2). That this was the personal name of God the Father is seen in Psalm 2:7; 110:1; and Isaiah 48:16, "GOD"; 49:1, 5.

2. In the New Testament

As with the other Persons of the Godhead (the Son and the Holy Spirit), the title "Father" without the article or an adjective may also be, in N.T. usage, a divine personal name of the First Person of the holy Trinity (Jn. 12:28; 17:1). Other than this, no personal name has been revealed for our heavenly Father. We find the O.T. personal name in quotations such as

Matthew 22:44 (Ps. 110:1, "LORD").

How grateful we are for the truths that our heavenly Father has revealed about Himself and for the indescribable blessings we enjoy as His children through faith in Jesus. May we seek to honor Him in all things by our lives and ever walk in His fellowship daily (Mt. 5:16; I Jn. 1:5-7). If the reader should not know the Father personally, he may come to know Him through trusting Jesus as his Saviour from sin (Jn. 1:12-13; 3:5, 16; 17:3).

A Review of Paterology

1. Describe the Father's nature.
2. What features show His having personhood?
3. What features indicate that He is God?
4. What is the Father's ontological relationships with the other Members of the Godhead?
5. What is the Father's ontological ascendancy over the other Members of the Godhead?
6. What is the Father's relationship to the universe?
7. What is the Father's relationship to Israel?
8. What is the Father's relationship to saved Christians: its nature, beginning, blessings, and demands?
9. How does the relation of God the Son to the Father differ from our relation to the Father?
10. Why is the idea of the universal fatherhood of God in error?
11. In what works relating to the universe is the Father involved?
12. How is the Father involved in our Lord's Messianic works?
13. What is the Father's location?
14. If the Father is invisible, how does He appear to people in Heaven?
15. What generic name is given for the Father in the Old and New Testaments?
16. What titles do we find for Him?
17. What are His personal names in the Old and New Testaments?

Christology

CHRISTOLOGY
The Doctrine of the Lord Jesus Christ

We now focus our attention upon the Person and work of God the Son, the Lord Jesus Christ. Because of the importance of Jesus' atoning work and the objective of the Holy Spirit to exalt Him (Mt. 1:21; Lk. 2:11; Jn. 16:14), we are not surprised to find an abundance of detail in the New Testament about our Lord's earthly life and work. Indeed, from the fall of man onward, the biblical revelation anticipated the coming of the promised Messiah-Saviour (Gen. 3:15, 21; 15:5; Isa. 49:1-7; Jn. 5:39; 8:56; Gal. 3:8, 16). Consisting of the Old Testament anticipation and New Testament fulfillment, this revelation has been preserved that we might believe in Jesus' deity and atoning work and that we might receive eternal life through faith in His name (Jn. 20:30-31). As we study this truth, may our faith in Him be deepened and our esteem for Him be increased.

THE DEITY OF THE LORD JESUS CHRIST

The fact that the Lord Jesus Christ is God the Son is fundamental to Christianity and to salvational faith in Him. As we shall see, no one but God could be the Saviour. The Scriptures teach that Jesus is God, the Second Person of the holy Trinity, and that all that can be said of God can be said of Him. The following bears witness to this truth.

HIS DIVINE NAMES

- **God**

  He is called "God" (Isa. 9:6; Jn. 1:1, 18 Gk.; 20:28; Rom. 9:5; 14:7-12; I Thess. 4:14; I Tim. 3:16; Tit. 1:3; Heb. 1:8; I Jn. 5:20). The Greek text identifies Him to be God (Eph. 5:5; II Thess. 1:12; I Tim. 5:21; Tit. 2:10, 13; II Pet. 1:1).[1] He exists in "the form of God (Phil. 2:6); He is "the image of the invisible God" (Col. 1:15); and He is "the express image of His (God's) Being" (Heb. 1:3).

- **Lord**

  A comparison of certain New Testament passages with their Old Testament equivalents shows that Jesus is sometimes identified as LORD (Yahweh or Jehovah), the personal name of God (see Lk. 1:68 with Ps. 106:48; Lk. 3:4-6 with Isa. 40:3-4; I Cor. 1:30 with Jer. 23:5-6; Rev. 1:7 with Zech. 12:1, 10; Eph. 4:8-10 with Ps. 68:4, 18; Heb. 1:10-12 with Ps. 102:12, 25-27. He is

---

[1] The Granville Sharp rule: "When the copulative *kai* connects two nouns of the same case, if the article *ho* or any of its cases precede the first of the said nouns or participles, and is not repeated before the second noun or participle, the latter always relates to the same person that is expressed or described by the first noun or participle; i.e., it denotes a further description of the first-named person." — quoted by H. E. Dana and J. R. Mantey, *A Manual Grammar of the Greek New Testament* (New York: The Macmillan Company, 1941), p. 147.

also identified as the Lord *(Adonai)*, the primary O.T. title of God (see Mt. 22:41-46 with Ps. 110:1; Jn. 12:37-42 with Isa. 6:1).

- **The Word**

A spoken or written word expresses one's feelings or thoughts. As the Word (Jn. 1:1, 14; Rev. 19:13), the Son has always expressed what the invisible God is and what truth God communicates to man (Col. 1:15; Mt. 11:27). Before His incarnation (His coming to earth and taking on Himself a human nature), He expressed certain qualities of God's nature by His creative work (Ps. 19:1; Jn. 1:1-3) as well as God's thoughts by His words (it seems that He gave the Old Testament revelation as well as the New; cp. Rev. 1:1). With His incarnation He manifested the Father by His words and actions (Jn. 1:14, 18; 5:19; 12:49-50; 14:8-11). Only one who is God can fully reveal God (Mt. 11:27; Heb. 1:3; Col. 1:15; 2:9).

- **Son of God**

This title is used of angels (Job 1:6) and men (Lk. 3:38; Rom. 8:14; cp. Ps. 82:6), for they are made in God's image. But when it is used of Jesus, it expresses His eternal relationship to and equality with God the Father (Jn. 5:18-26). Observe that He was the Son of God before His incarnation (Ps. 2:7; Gal. 4:4). The Jews regarded this designation to be a title of deity (Jn. 5:17-18; 10:31-36). In biblical language to be son of someone or something is to have the character of that one or thing (cp. Jn. 17:12; Eph. 2:2-3). In the case of Jesus, He manifested the character of the Father, for He and the Father were one (Jn. 10:30). The neuter predicate adjective indicates one thing rather than one person. This emphasizes their essential unity, their possessing in common the single divine nature. Thus Jesus is the Son of God because He inherently possesses the divine nature.

Closely related to the concept of Jesus' sonship are the following designations:

1. *He is the First Begotten.*

This designation marks His priority in time or rank, as in the following examples: He is prior to and ranking above all creation (Col. 1:15). (The self-consistency of the Scriptures requires us to regard "of creation" as a genitive of reference rather than a genitive of identification; thus, He is above all with reference to creation, not as a part of creation; cp. Col. 1:16-17). He is Mary's firstborn son, being born before her other children (Mt. 1:25; Lk. 2:7). He is the first to rise from the dead, never to die again (Col. 1:18; Rev. 1:5). And He is the first member of the new humanity, as its pattern and head, whose human likeness all the redeemed will share (Rom. 8:29; I. Cor. 15:47-49; I Jn. 3:2). It is the first of these examples that speaks of His deity as the divine Creator (Col. 1:15).

2. *He is the Only Begotten Son.*

This designation (Jn. 1:14, 18; 3:16, 18; I Jn. 4:9) emphasizes the uniqueness of the Son in His relation to God the Father. As the only Offspring of the Father, Jesus is the Only Begotten in a sense that no one else is: He is eternally the Son and possesses the divine essence in common with the Father. (Compare Lk. 7:12; 8:42; 9:38; Heb. 11:17).

HIS ETERNAL PREEXISTENCE

There are many passages that speak of the Son's existence before His incarnation (Jn. 1:1, 14, 30; 6:33, 38; Gal. 4:4; Heb. 10:5). However, it is the fact of His eternal preexistence which underscores His deity. This is stated emphatically in Micah 5:2 and is implied in Isaiah 9:6 ("Father of eternity"); John 1:1; Colossians 1:16-17; Revelation 1:11; and John 17:5.

HIS DIVINE ATTRIBUTES

We should expect that He, in whom "dwelleth all the fulness of the Godhead bodily" (Col. 2:9), "who being in the form of God thought it not robbery to be equal with God" (Phil. 2:6), "who is the image of the invisible God" (Col. 1:15), and "who is the express image of His Being" (Heb. 1:3), possesses all the attributes of God. Some of these are eternality (Mic. 5:2; Jn. 1:1; Rev. 1:11); omnipresence (Mt. 28:20; Jn. 3:13; Col. 1:27); omnipotence (Jn. 1:1-3; I Cor. 1:24; Heb. 1:3); omniscience (Jn. 2:24-25; 6:64; Col. 2:3); truthfulness, being real and reliable (Jn. 7:18; Rev. 19:11; 3:14) as well as the Truth (the revelation of God, Jn. 1:14, 17; 14:6; Eph. 4:21); righteousness (II Tim. 4:8; Acts 3:14; 22:14; I Jn. 2:1); goodness (Acts 10:38); holiness, transcending all things (Isa. 6:1-3; Jn. 12:41) as well as being sinless and pure (I Jn. 3:3, 5; Heb. 7:26; Acts 3:14); love (Jn. 13:1, 34; 15:9; Rev. 1:5); grace (II Cor. 8:9; Jn. 1:14); mercy (I Tim. 1:12-16; Heb. 2:17); longsuffering (I Pet. 2:18-24; Rev. 1:9); and sovereignty (Acts 10:36).

In addition to these, there is immutability (Heb. 1:10-12; 13:8). Although by His incarnation God the Son assumed a complete human nature, His divine nature remained unchanged. Something was added to His personhood, but not to His deity.

The Lord Jesus Christ is alive (Jn. 6:51). He is self-existent (Jn. 5:26; Col. 1:16-17). He is the giver of all life, both physical (Jn. 1:3-4; 5:28-29) and spiritual (Jn. 14:6; 11:25; 17:3; Col. 3:3; I Jn. 5:11-12, 20). He experiences both physical and spiritual life in His humanity.

HIS DIVINE WORKS

The Trinitarian view of God sees the Members of the Godhead being active before time in formulating the divine decree (by which all events of the universe are rendered certain) and in time administering its details. Being the Instrumental Cause of all things, the Son is involved in every aspect of God's total work relating to the universe.

- **His Creating All Things**

Acting with the other Members of the Godhead, the Son was the Father's Agent, or Instrumental Cause (I Cor. 8:6; Jn. 1:3; Col. 1:16).

- **His Sustaining All Things**

  He not only "holds together" all things (Col. 1:17) but also "upholds" all things (Heb. 1:3).

- **His Receiving Worship**

  The Lord Jesus receives worship (Mt. 8:2; 28:9, 17; Jn. 5:23; Phil. 2:9-11; Rev. 5:11-13). Neither the apostles nor holy angels allowed men to worship them (Acts 10:25-26; Rev. 22:8-9).

- **His Revealing the Father**

  As the eternal Word the Son revealed the Father (Mt. 11:27). He did this by His creative work (Jn. 1:1-3; Rom. 1:19-20) and His words (assuming that the Old Testament is the Word of the Son as is the New; Rev. 1:1).

- **His Forgiving Sins**

  Only God can forgive people of their sins since all sin is against Him and He is sovereign over the universe. Jesus exercised the authority of forgiveness, which the Jews understood as belonging only to God (Lk. 5:20-25). He demonstrated the reality of His having this authority by healing the man He had forgiven. Also, see Luke 7:47-49.

- **His Giving Life**

  In addition to bestowing life in His creative work (Jn. 1:3-4), the Son of God also has the power to give spiritual life to them who trust Him as their Saviour (Jn. 6:32-40) as well as to raise the dead (5:21, 25). During His public ministry Jesus had the power to restore the dead to their former physical life (Lk. 7:14-15; 8:54-55; Jn. 11:43-44).

- **His Exercising Judgment**

  Only God can justly exercise judgment and give to people what they deserve, for He knows their motivations and intentions as well as their overt acts (Rom. 2:2, 6, 11, 16). Knowing the hearts of men (Jn. 2:24-25), the Son of God will judge all people (5:22-23). The Lord will appraise His people upon His coming for them (II Cor. 5:10; Rev. 22:12). He also will judge earth dwellers after His return to earth (Rev. 19:11-15; Mt. 25:31-46). Furthermore, He will judge the unsaved after His millennial rule (Rev. 20:11-15; Acts 17:31).[2]

- **His Authoring Salvation**

  Only One who was God could be the instrumental "Cause" of salvation ("Author," Heb. 5:9) because of the magnitude of sin's power and ruin in human lives and of its debt to God. The Lord Jesus is the only Saviour from sin (Mt. 1:21; Lk. 2:11; Acts 4:12; I Jn. 4:14).

---

[2] Observe that His doing miracles is not listed as a divine work. He did these by the power of the Holy Spirit (Acts 10:38) as did also the apostles (Heb. 2:3-4). Satan, too, can do miracles (II Thess. 2:9; Rev. 13:13-14). Nevertheless, we should expect Jesus who was God as well as man to do wonders.

HIS DIVINE ASSERTIONS

Jesus made assertions that would have been most blasphemous if they were untrue. On the other hand, only One who was God could have said these things without lying.

- **He affirmed His being equal to the Father.**

He asserted equality in receiving honor (Jn. 5:23), in being the object of faith (Jn. 14:1; 12:44), in His words and works (Jn. 5:19; 14:10, 24; 12:49-50), and in revelation (Jn. 12:45; 14:9). When He says that the Father is greater than He (Jn. 14:28), Jesus is referring to His humanity and to His Messianic role of being the Father's slave (Phil. 2:7). In His deity He is equal to the Father in every way.

- **He affirmed His having a unique relation to the Father.**

This is seen in His being the Father's revelator (Mt. 11:27; Jn. 12:45); His imitator (Jn. 5:17, 19-20); His intimate (Jn. 14:7-10, 20); His Son (Jn. 10:36). He also said that He and the Father were one (Jn. 10:30). The neuter gender of the predicate adjective "one" indicates oneness of purpose and nature rather than person. They are distinct, divine Persons but one God.

- **He affirmed His ability to satisfy man's deepest needs.**

Unlike Paul (II Cor. 4:5), Jesus proclaimed Himself as the One who could provide for people's needs. See John 6:35; 4:14; 7:37-38; 10:9-10; Matthew 11:28-30.

- **He affirmed His ability to give eternal life and safety to His people.**

See John 10:27-29; 6:37-40.

HIS WITNESSES

The testimony of competent witnesses is allowed in our courts as evidence. Various ones gave testimony to Christ's deity, including God the Father (Jn. 5:17-18, 31-39), John the Baptizer (Jn. 1:34; 3:31), Nathanael (Jn. 1:49), Peter (Mt. 16:16-17; Jn. 6:69), the apostle John (Jn. 20:30-31; I Jn. 5:20), the centurion (Mk. 15:39), Satan (Mt. 4:3, 6; "if" here views the condition as a fact); and demons (Mk. 1:24).

All of these truths demonstrate clearly and conclusively that the Lord Jesus Christ is God the Son and that everything which can be asserted about God can be asserted about Him.

THE HUMANITY OF THE LORD JESUS CHRIST

This portion of our study is concerned with God the Son taking upon Himself a complete, sinless human nature and becoming the God-man. We shall direct our attention to His first coming to earth, long ago, particularly looking at His condescension, humiliation, and exaltation.

HIS CONDESCENSION

The condescension of God the Son refers to His stooping to come to earth, to assume a human nature [this was lower than that of His servants, the angels (Heb. 2:9)], and to live among sinful people In this section we shall examine His incarnation, His human character, and His human activity.

• His Incarnation

The word *incarnation* speaks of the initial action and following condition of assuming a human nature and being embodied in flesh. (Jn. 1:14). The incarnation of God the Son was His taking upon Himself a complete, sinless human nature (body, soul, and spirit), so that everything that can be asserted of sinless man can be asserted of Him. Several aspects of His incarnation follow:

1. HIS SELF-EMPTYING

The Greek text of Philippians 2:7 reads "He emptied Himself" for the KJV reading, "made himself of no reputation." What does His emptying Himself mean? Some hold the erroneous view that in His incarnation God the Son, in some sense, laid aside certain attributes that belonged to His divine nature. My objections to this view are these: First, it is impossible to discard any manifest quality (attribute) of an essence without changing the fundamental nature of the essence. Second, it is illogical to say that some attributes are more essential to deity than are others since all the attributes of deity are possessed and determined by the divine essence. Third, this view conflicts with the Scriptural teaching that the Son continues to be God during His incarnation (I Thess. 4:14; I Jn. 5:20).

My understanding of our Lord's self-emptying is this: When He took upon Himself a human nature, there were certain features of His deity that, with rare exception (Jn. 1:48; 18:6; Mk. 6:48; Lk. 5:20-21), He did not bring into His human experience. Still, these features remained with His divine nature and continued to express themselves in His divine experience such as His upholding the universe (Heb. 1:3).

Some of these features of His "self-emptying" are these:

One, as a man the Lord Jesus rarely manifested His preincarnate glory (cp. Jn. 17:5). I am not speaking about the glory of His character, which was manifest throughout His earthly life (Jn. 1:14). Rather, in His humanity He did not radiate the visible glory of God, which shines as a blinding light (exception, Mt. 17:2), nor did He occupy the glory of position, which is above angels (Heb. 2:9; Lk. 22:43). These glories were given to His humanity upon His ascension into Heaven (Acts 26:13; Eph. 1:20-22).

Two, as a man He did not exercise His inherent divine power. Being the

Messiah (the Anointed One), He did, and is doing, all of His human works in the power and by the direction of the Holy Spirit (Lk. 4:1, 14, 18; Acts 10:38; cp. Isa. 61:1; 11:1-5).

Three, as a man He did not exercise certain divine attributes, such as omnipresence (Jn. 11:6-7), and omniscience (Mk. 13:32; Jn. 8:26, 28, 40), which are not compatible with human nature. In His human experience He was physically localized. He was not able physically to be in more than one place at a time. Although He seemed to be aware of what was going on beyond the range of His physical senses (Jn. 1:48; 2:24-25), this perception may have been given Him by the Holy Spirit (cp. Acts 5:3; 13:9). As a child He developed in human knowledge (Lk. 2:40, 52). His knowledge of spiritual truth was given Him by the Father (Jn. 8:26, 28).

Four, as a man He did not exercise independent, divine authority. He was the Father's servant (slave; cp. Phil. 2:7; Isa. 42:1-7; 49:1-6; 52:13-53:12; Jn. 6:38; 8:28-29). Only in this sense was He less than the Father (Jn. 14:28). Being subordinate to the Father's authority, Jesus never acted in His human experience independently of Him (Jn. 8:28; 12:49; 14:9-10) or disobeyed Him (Jn. 17:4; 8:29). Yet, being God, He possessed equal authority with the Father (Jn. 1:3; 17:24; Heb. 11:3).

Five, on the other hand, in His human experience the Lord Jesus displays the moral attributes of deity, which are compatible with humanity. These include holiness (Jn. 8:46; I Pet. 2:22), righteousness (Jn. 8:29), love (Jn. 15:9), mercy (Lk. 18:31-43), holy hatred (Mk. 3:5; cp. Mt. ch. 23), grace and truth (Jn. 1:14). By the Holy Spirit these qualities can be displayed in us as well (Gal. 5:22-23.)

2. HIS CONCEPTION AND BIRTH

a. Its Nature

Ordinarily, conception takes place when a male sperm unites with a female ovum. This union results in the beginning and development of human life. The unique feature of Christ's birth is that it was a virgin birth; that is, His conception was not the result of human generation. Mary did not conceive by the agency of a man (Mt. 1:18, 25; Lk. 1:34-35), with or without divine help (cp. Elisabeth, Lk. 1:5-7, 24-25). In the case of Jesus, Mary conceived by the agency of God the Holy Spirit (Mt. 1:20; Lk. 1:35). It is this fact that makes Jesus' birth a virgin one. While the prenatal development of the holy Child within Mary and the subsequent birth event were natural processes, Jesus' conception was uniquely and radically different from all others. It was wholly of the Holy Spirit, who generated of Mary's substance a complete human nature, consisting of body, soul, and spirit (Mt. 26:12, 38; 27:50).

This work of the Holy Spirit did not include the creation of Jesus' personhood, for this, together with His divine nature, existed from eternity (Mic. 5:2; Gal. 4:4; Jn. 8:42; 1:1). With His incarnation God the Son did not acquire another personhood, so that He was a combination of two persons, one divine and the other human. Rather, He acquired another nature (a human nature), so that there were united in Him (the one Person) the nature of God and the nature of man.

With this truth in view, we can understand why the angel described that which was conceived in Mary as being a holy "thing" (Lk. 1:35; also Mt. 1:20, "that" is a neuter demonstrative pronoun). The neuter gender indicates that Mary was only the mother of Jesus' human nature. She was not the mother of His eternal personhood and deity; she was not the mother of God.

b. Its Importance

Our Lord's virgin birth was necessary for His saving work (Mt. 1:21). It preserved His sinlessness and gave Him the ability to die. It was necessary for Him to become a man in order that He might be identified with mankind and experience death, the penalty for humanity's sins (Heb. 2:9, 14-18). Yet, as a man He had to be sinless, for a sinner can neither discharge himself from the debt of his sins nor deliver others from their obligation. The Lord's unique conception prevented His receiving from a human father the hereditary corruption and imputed guilt of Adam's initial sin (Rom. 5:12-19; Gen. 5:3; I Cor. 15:22). It also preserved His human nature from any contamination of Mary (Lk. 1:35). Being absolutely sinless (I Pet. 2:22; I Jn. 3:5), Jesus was qualified to bear our sins and to pay their awful debt (Rom. 5:8; I Pet. 2:24; Heb. 9:26).

The Lord's virgin birth also made it possible for Him to rule one day from David's throne over Israel and the world (Mt. 2:2; II Sam. 7:12-17; Lk. 1:32-33). It allowed Him to receive the title to David's throne without the divine curse. The title to the throne was transmitted through Solomon and his posterity (I Chron. 28:4-7; Mt. 1:1-16, 20). However, in the days of king Jehoiakim of Judah, a divine judgment decreed that none of his posterity would sit or prosper on the throne (Jer. 36:30). This was repeated to his son, Jehoiachin or Coniah (Jer. 22:30). By His virgin birth Jesus avoided the curse, became a true relative of David, and received the title to the throne. He did not come under the divine judgment, for He was not Joseph's actual son. Yet, being Joseph's eldest legal son, He inherited the title to the throne.

Jesus' birth also established Him as a true descendant of David through Mary and her ancestor Nathan, a son of David (I Chron. 3:5; Lk. 3:21-23; Rom. 1:3; II Tim. 2:8). Luke gives Mary's lineage through her father Heli (3:23), which should read, "And Jesus began to be about thirty years of age, being (as it was popularly supposed the son of Joseph) the (grand)son of Heli". Matthew shows Jesus' legal connection to Joseph through Mary (1:16). Consequently, because of His legal connection with Joseph, the lineal heir to David's throne, and His blood relation to David through Mary, Jesus is the last heir to David's throne and the only one who can rule with God's blessing. In fulfillment of divine prediction, Jesus will rule over the earth when He comes again (Rev. 19:11-16; Lk. 1:32-33; Gen. 49:10; Isa. 9:6-7).

3. THE FACT OF HIS HUMANITY

We have seen that God the Son assumed a complete, sinless human nature within the virgin Mary. He will continue forever to be the God-man (I Tim. 2:5). Early heretics denied Christ's humanity (I Jn. 4:3), but the Scriptures show that it was real and unique.

a. Its Reality

This is shown by His prenatal development and birth, which were normal, natural processes (Lk. 2:5-7; cp. 1:57). The Lord also had a complete human nature: body (Mt. 26:12), soul (Mt. 26:38), and spirit (Mt. 27:50; Jn. 11:33). (Observe that the human spirit is not the same as the essence of God which is Spirit [Jn. 4:24]). Jesus had human appearance (Jn. 4:9; 8:57; 10:33). He experienced normal human development in body, in human knowledge (Lk. 2:40, 52), and in spiritual awareness (vss. 46-50). He manifested His spiritual awareness at the age of twelve when He spoke of His personal relation to God the Father and of the necessity of being about the things of His Father. Being sinless, He did not develop morally. However, He did develop socially (Lk. 2:51-52), submitting Himself to the authority of His parents and advancing in favor with God and man. This means that He pleased the Father (Mt. 3:17) and maintained people's admiration and respect.

The reality of Jesus' humanity was also manifest in His living an ordinary human life in Nazareth, fulfilling His domestic, vocational, and religious duties (Mt. 13:55-56; Mk. 6:3; Lk. 4:16). Moreover, He experienced the sinless limitations of human nature, such as hunger (Mt. 21:18), sleep (Mt. 8:24), weariness (Jn. 4:6), and confinement to place (Jn. 11:6-7). There is no indication that He was ever sick (this results from the inherent corruption of fallen physical nature). He experienced human emotions, such as grief (Mk. 3:5; Jn. 11:35), love (Jn. 11:36), agitation (Jn. 12:27), exultation (Lk. 10:21), anger (Mk. 3:5), trust (Lk. 23:46), suffering (I Pet. 3:18), and compassion (Mk. 9:36). He was tempted as we are yet without sin (Heb. 4:15). Finally, He died (Heb. 2:9, 14-17). While physical death is a natural result of sin, Jesus did not die naturally. Uniquely, He laid down His life in obedience to the Father (Jn. 10:17-18).

b. Its Uniqueness

While Jesus possesses a complete human nature as we do, it differs qualitatively from ours in its being perfect and sinless. Concerning the perfection of Jesus' human character, He fully displayed the moral qualities of God in His humanity (Jn. 1:14). W. H. Griffith Thomas writes, "He embraces all the good elements which mark other men...He possesses all these in a higher degree than any one else, and with perfect balance and proportion. There is no weakness, no exaggeration or strain, no strong or weak points, as is the case with the rest of mankind. There are certain elements and traits of character which are not found elsewhere, such as absolute humility, entire unselfishness, whole-hearted willingness to forgive, and the most beautiful and perfect holiness."[3]

Regarding the sinlessness of Jesus' humanity, the Scriptures testify that He never sinned, nor was He a sinner. He never confessed sin, nor did He ever seek forgiveness (cp. Mt. 27:4; Lk. 23:47; Jn. 8:46; 19:4, 6; Acts 3:14; Rom. 8:3; II Cor. 5:21; Heb. 4:15; 7:26; I Pet. 1:19; 2:22; I Jn. 3:5). Although Jesus submitted to John's baptism (Mt. 3:13-17), this rite was not indicative of His repentance (cp. Mk. 1:4). It was the occasion of His divine anointing (Jn. 1:32).

We who are saved look forward to the time when our bodies will be delivered from inherent corruption and the sin-principle (Rom. 8:10, 23). Then we shall be like Him in His humanity (I Jn. 3:2; Phil. 3:20-21; Rom. 8:29).

4. THE UNION OF JESUS' TWO NATURES

What is the relation of Jesus' divine and human natures to each other and to His personhood? A *nature* refers to the essence (substance), with its qualities and powers, that gives to the person possessing it particular identity and character. *Personhood*, or *self*, is that unique, self-conscious, self-asserting, responsible subject who possesses a certain kind of nature and whose qualities are determined by this nature.

From eternity God the Son was a Person who possessed the divine nature (the nature of God). Upon His incarnation He took upon Himself a human nature, divinely generated of Mary's substance. But He continued to have His divine nature. The union of these two natures (the divine and the human) in the one personhood is called "the hypostatic union." "Hypostatic" is from the Greek word *hupostasis*, meaning "that which stands under." Theologically, the word *hypostasis* can refer to God's nature or to His personhood as follows:

Regarding God's nature: In Hebrews 1:3 (KJV) this word, translated "person," would be more clear if it were translated "essence" or "nature" since "person," referring to one's total being, may include personhood. The Son bears the exact impress of the divine nature, for this nature is equally possessed by each Member (personhood) of the divine Trinity. Thus in Hebrews 1:3 the *hypostasis* is the divine nature, which underlies the three Members (personhoods) of the Trinity — the Father, the Son, and the Holy Spirit.

Regarding the Son's personhood: The doctrine of the hypostatic union of Jesus' two natures states that these two natures (the divine and the human) are united in His personhood. Here, the *hypostasis* is His eternal personhood, which underlies His divine and human natures and which unites them within Himself.

a. Features of the Hypostatic Union

One, the divine and human natures are united in the one personhood. The Lord Jesus is not two persons, one human and the other

---

[3] W. H. Griffith Thomas, *Christianity Is Christ* (London: Longmans, Green and Co., 1909), p. 12.

divine, but He is one Self. In His incarnation God the Son did not assume a human person, but a human nature, divinely made of Mary's substance (Lk. 1:35). His incarnation made Him human; but still possessing the divine nature, He is also divine. Thus He is a personal being with two natures, making Him to be the God-man.

Two, the two natures are inseparably united in His personhood, yet not mingled or confounded. Our Lord's incarnation does not affect His divine nature in any way, for there is no interaction or exchange between the two natures. The properties of one nature never become the properties of the other. They are never mixed or combined so as to lose their distinctiveness or to form a third nature. On the other hand, these natures do not function independently of His personhood like separate persons. They continuously and simultaneously communicate their powers and qualities to His person-hood without conflict.

When He was on earth, Jesus' personhood had complete control over the manifestations of His deity in the realm of His human experience (Mt. 17:1-2). But when He did not display the visible qualities of His divine nature, He still possessed it. When He expressed His deity with speaking the divine name in Gethsemane (Jn. 18:5-6), He was still a man, whom they bound and led away (vss. 12-13). When He manifested His humanity by sleeping in a boat (Mt. 8:24), He was no less God, upholding the universe by the word of His power (Heb. 1:3). With this in view we can understand Paul's reference to the blood of God (Acts 20:28). Although blood is not a part of the divine nature, it was an essential element of Jesus' unglorified human nature. Being God and man, God the Son purchased His church with His own sacrificial, human blood (Eph. 5:25).

b. Problems of the Hypostatic Union

These problems are not inherent in the union itself, but belong to our understanding of this union.

One, there is the problem of Jesus' limited knowledge (Mk. 13:32). As God the Lord Jesus knows all things (Col. 2:3), but as man His knowledge is limited to what the Father has revealed to Him (Jn. 5:19-20; 8:26, 28, 40). Having the two natures, He has both divine knowledge and human knowledge, each determined by its respective nature. Of course, the mystery is how one Person can experience both unlimited and limited knowledge at the same time. It has been suggested that His divine knowledge was below the level of His human consciousness. Because there were certain things which He was not given to know or teach as a man, He did not allow them to flow into His human consciousness.[4]

Two, there is the problem of His being tempted. Could Jesus have sinned? If not, why was He tempted? By itself unfallen human nature is capable of sinning, as the fall of Adam and Eve show (Gen. 3:1-6). However, because

---

[4] J. Stafford Wright, *What Is Man?* (London: The Paternoster Press, 1955), pp. 185 f.

Jesus' human nature was united to His divine nature within His personhood, I firmly believe that He could not have sinned. Keep in mind that it is one's personhood that sins, not one's nature alone (we are responsible for our actions). Since He possessed the divine nature which made Him to be infinitely holy, Jesus could not sin. It was impossible for Jesus to have sinned, for He was God as well as man.

On the other hand, His temptations were externally real (Heb. 4:15; Mt. 4:1). But there was no evil within Him to which these temptations could appeal. He never experienced a struggle of conflicting inner moral forces as we do (Rom. 7:14-23). Jesus was completely sinless in His human nature and His commitment to the Father's will was absolute (Heb. 10:7; Jn. 6:38). Also, His human will was supported by His divine will in this commitment (cp. Mt. 26:39). Finally, there was no need or lack within Him to which temptation could successfully appeal. As His temptations in the wilderness demonstrated (Mt. 4:1-10), any amoral need, such as the need for food, to which the tempter appealed was superceded by the greater need of pleasing the Father (cp. Jn. 4:34).

It is obvious that Satan thought that Jesus could sin (sin causes irrational, absurd thinking) and that he could conquer Him as he had Eve and Adam. But he grossly underestimated his Opponent and was utterly defeated on every count.

Three, there is the problem of Jesus' death. How could One who was God die, especially when God cannot die and death is a result of sin (Jas. 1:14)? Jesus' death was entirely a human experience; He died as a man. However, because He was God, it can be said that God the Son died. For like reason, Paul can speak of the blood of God (Acts 20:28).

While He was upon the cross, Jesus experienced separation from the Father in spiritual death (Mt. 27:46). His words, "My God," indicate that this was a human experience. In His separation from the Father (the experience of Hell), there was no division of the divine essence, which each Person of the Godhead wholly possesses in common with the other Persons, else Jesus would have ceased to be God. The separation was between the Persons (personhoods) themselves — between the Father and the Son in their fellowship, not in their ontological relationship.

In His physical death Jesus did not die naturally from sin as we do. When our sins were laid on Him (I Pet. 2:24) and He was made sin (II Cor. 5:21), He was identified with them only in a forensic (legal) manner for the purpose of atoning for them. But He Himself did not become a sinner or subject to sin's debilitation so as to die from its natural effects. As a man He died uniquely by deliberately laying down His life in obedience to the Father and with His authority (Jn. 10:18).

These explanations do not remove all the mystery which surrounds the union of the two natures in Jesus, but they may shed some light for our understanding.

c. False Views of the Hypostatic Union

Since our Lord's incarnation, certain people have held wrong views about the hypostatic union. These false views have spawned erroneous teachings about Jesus, which in turn hinder salvational faith in Him. One cannot be saved and refuse to accept all that the Scriptures teach about Him (I Jn. 4:1-3; Rom. 10:9).

One, there are those who assert Christ's deity but deny His humanity. The Docetae (2nd c.) denied the reality of His body (cp. I Jn. 4:3). They held that Christ was too divine to suffer agony and death and that He only seemed to do so. Some taught that the divine Christ came upon Jesus at His baptism and left Him at His death.

The Apollinarians (4th c.) denied the completeness of Christ's human nature. They held that He had a human body and soul but no human mind or spirit. This was replaced by the divine Logos (Word).

Two, there are those who assert Christ's humanity, but deny His deity. The Ebionites (2nd c.) denied Jesus' virgin birth, holding that He was the offspring of Mary and Joseph. The Arians (4th c.) held that the Son was a creature (the first created being), infinitely transcending all other creatures, with definite beginning and liability to change and sin.

Three, there are those who deny the one personhood of Christ. The Nestorians (5th c.) denied that the two natures are united in the one Self. They held that there are two selves.

Four, there are those who deny the two natures of Jesus. The Eutychians (5th c.) confused the two natures, making them one, which was more divine than human. Sometimes this is called "Monophysitism." The Monothelists (7th c.) held that Jesus acted as one unitary energy with one will.

We need to be on the alert today for such false views concerning the natures of Christ, especially as held by them who profess to be Christians.

• His Human Character

1. Its Description

While *personality* is the manifestation of one's personhood in or through his human nature, *character* is a description of the qualities of a person's human nature in daily life. Some inner qualities of Jesus' humanity are His meekness and humility (Mt. 11:29), compassion (Mt. 9:36), obedience (Jn. 8:29), love (Jn. 13:1), industry (Jn. 9:4; 17:4), patience (Jn. 14:1-9), grace (II Cor. 8:9), forgiveness (Lk. 23:34), tenderness (Jn. 8:3-11), firmness and courage (Lk. 9:51), and holiness (Mk. 1:24). These qualities are available to us who are saved through the Holy Spirit (Gal. 5:22-23).

2. Its Importance

Our Lord's character was very important to His work. It showed that He was qualified to be our Saviour (Heb. 7:26-27; cp. I Jn. 3:5; I Pet. 2:22). It manifested the moral character of God the Father (Jn. 1:14, 18; 14:9). It set forth the ideal standard for His people to follow (Eph. 5:1-2; I Pet. 2:21). Finally, it exposed and rebuked wickedness (Jn. 3:19-20; 15:22-24).

• His Human Activity

A purpose for our Lord's being man is that being the Father's Servant and the Last Adam, He might carry out the divine will for mankind. A summary of this activity follows:

During His first advent to earth the Lord Jesus presented Himself to Israel for their acceptance or rejection (Isa. 49:4-7; Lk. 4:42-44; Jn. 1:11). By allowing Himself to be crucified, He confirmed the divine sentence of condemnation against God's enemies (Rom. 8:2; Jn. 16:11; 12:31). He also gave His life for the provisional atonement of humanity's sins (Mt. 20:28) and arose in triumph over death and Satan (Acts 2:24; Heb. 2:14). Finally, He prepared the apostles for their ministry of establishing Christianity in the world (Mt. 15:21-18:35; Acts 1:3).

During His physical absence from the earth, He is building His church (Mt. 16:18) during this age, preparing a place for His people (Jn. 14:2-3), and interceding for them at the Father's right hand (Rom. 8:34; Heb. 7:25). During the tribulation period He will prepare earth dwellers for His return by having the gospel preached universally (Mt. 24:14), dealing with the elect of Israel (Deut. 30:1-3), and pouring out awful judgments upon the wicked (Rev. chs. 6, 8, 9, 12, 13, 16).

During His second advent to earth He will destroy Israel's enemies (Rev. 19:11-21), judge the surviving nations to determine who are qualified to enter His kingdom (Ezek. 20:33-38; Mt. 25:31-46), and rule over the earth for a thousand years, completing all that the Father has given Him to do (Rev. 20:4; I Cor. 15:24-25). Details of these activities will be examined later.

HIS HUMILIATION

The humiliation of the Lord Jesus refers to the inexpressible shame and degradation that He experienced in His obedience to the Father unto death (Phil. 2:8). He suffered gross indignities at the hands of sinful men. Moreover, He was the Father's offering for humanity's sins.

The indignities that He suffered at the hands of wicked men included their mocking Him, striking Him, spitting upon Him, scourging Him, and finally crucifying Him (Mt. 26:63; 27:26-35). Although they did not contribute to Jesus' atoning work, these abusive indignities revealed the true spiritual state and the just condemnation of all who were involved in these heinous crimes (Acts 4:27; Lk. 2:34-35). When He made atonement for our sins, our Lord experienced further humiliation in bearing our sins and their judgment.

Our Lord's atoning death and triumphant resurrection are the foundation of the Christian faith and message (I. Cor. 15:1-3). Since God's gracious provision of salvation rests upon these truths, it is imperative that we thoroughly understand their meaning, not only for our own edification and that of others but also for the clear presentation of the gospel to the lost.

The *Oxford Dictionary* defines atonement as "the condition of being at one with others...The action of setting at one, or being set at one." Theologically, *atonement* represents our Lord's dealing provisionally with humanity's sins by His sacrifice to satisfy divine justice and to establish harmony between God and the gospel believer. This had to be done before God could save sinners. In fulfillment of prophecy (Lk. 24:25-26; Ps. 22:1-21; Isa. 53:1-12), God the Son came to earth for this purpose (I Jn. 3:5; 4:9-10; Jn. 1:29; Mt. 20:28). The apostolic witness, given of the Holy Spirit and preserved in the New Testament (Jn. 16:12-14; Acts 2:32), reveals the historicity and meaning of the atonement. Let us look more closely at this.

- **False or Incomplete Theories of the Atonement**
  Throughout the present age theologians have tried to state the meaning of Jesus' death. Although the following theories do not correctly or sufficiently state what the Scriptures teach about the atonement, our acquaintance with these views will help us to recognize them when we meet them and will also help us to understand better the Scriptural view.

   1. *The Recapitulation Theory of Irenaeus*
      He believed that Christ reversed the course of human life by repeating in Himself all its stages and experiences, including those of sinners. By His obedience He compensated for Adam's disobedience and became the transforming agent of mankind.

      This theory is incomplete, for it fails to state the basis of the atonement other than Christ's obedience.

   2. *The Ransom Payment-to-Satan Theory of Origen*
      He taught that Christ's death was a ransom paid to Satan for the purpose of delivering humanity from his claim.

      This theory is wrong, for it ignores that the debt of sin was owed to God since it was His law which was violated (I Jn. 3:4).

   3. *The Commercial Theory of Anselm*
      This holds that Christ's death by way of satisfaction restored God's honor, which was violated by sin. He also secured a merit that He Himself did not need and that is passed on to all who obey the gospel.

      This view overlooks the truth that sin incurs a divine penalty that must be paid. God's holiness, rather than offended honor, demands this.

   4. *The Moral Influence Theory of Peter Abelard*
      He believed that Christ's death was not a ransom but was a revelation of God's love, which awakens a response in the sinner and delivers him from the power of sin.

      This view fails to explain the substitutionary and propitiatory character of Christ's death (Rom. 5:8; I Jn. 2:2; 4:10).

5. *The Theory of Thomas Aquinas*

He held that the atonement was not necessary and that God could have redeemed man without it. He also believed that Christ's total life contributed toward His atoning work.

This view makes the atonement arbitrary. Actually, God cannot act contrary to His holiness and justice. Although Christ's obedience and sinlessness were necessary qualifications of His saviorhood, salvation rests upon His obedience unto death (Phil. 2:8).

6. *The Acceptilation Theory of Duns Scotus*

Similarly to Aquinas, Scotus believed that the method of atonement was entirely arbitrary (God could have chosen another person or way to atone for sin) and that there was no inherent necessity for rendering satisfaction.

This view ignores the truth that the necessity for the atonement lay in God's nature rather than in His will.

7. *The Example Theory of Faustus Socinus*

He held that Christ did not bear the exact, full penalty of the law since this would require Him to die as many deaths as there are sinners. He believed that forgiveness of sins is an act of pure mercy, based on man's repentance and obedience.

This theory ignores the connection between Jesus' death and the salvation of sinners (Mt. 20:28; 26:28). God could not save sinners without their debt of sin being paid.

8. *The Governmental Theory of Hugo Grotius*

He held that Christ's death was symbolic, showing God's hatred of sin.

This denies that the Lord's death fully paid the debt of our sins.

9. *The Mystical Theory of Edward Irving*

Rejecting penal satisfaction, he associated the atonement with Jesus' purifying human nature. He believed that Jesus assumed a corrupt, evil human nature, purified this by His sufferings and obedience, and reunited it to God. People are saved by becoming partakers of Jesus' purified humanity by faith.

This ignores the need for a divine propitiation for sin (I Jn. 4:10).

10. *The Vicarious Confession Theory of John McLeod Campbell*

He believed that Christ offered to God on behalf of humanity the repentance that was necessary to fulfill the condition of divine forgiveness. Christ made this confession by His death, which showed His agreement with the Father's condemnation of sin.

There is no scriptural support for this theory.

- **The Nature of Jesus' Atoning Work**

    1. An Analysis

    Atonement had to be made before God could deliver sinners from sin's debt, ruin, and power and could bring them into a right relation with Himself. This is expressed by the words of John 3:16: "For God so loved the world that He gave His only begotten Son that whosoever believes on Him should not perish but have everlasting life." What does it mean for God to give His only begotten Son? Why must the sinner believe in the Saviour to receive everlasting life? The answers to these questions are found in the atonement. Let us look at this subject more closely. Atonement involves the principles of substitution and satisfaction.

    a. Our Lord's sacrifice was substitutionary (Rom. 5:8).

    The idea of substitution is that Jesus died for sinners (Mk. 10:45; II Cor. 5:14-15). With "for" meaning "on behalf of," this emphasizes the truth that Jesus took our place on the cross. As our substitute He bore the punishment of our sins (I Pet. 3:18).

    The question that confronted God in saving man was this: How can God who is holy and just deal with sinners as they deserve and still deliver them from the punishment of their sins? Since the debt of sin had to be paid, then a substitute had to be found if sinners were to be delivered from this obligation. Only God himself was qualified to be this substitute. According to divine plan, God the Son came to earth, assumed a sinless human nature, submitted to crucifixion, and received the divine stroke for our sins as our substitute. There is no other substitute or way that God will accept (Acts 4:12).

    b. Our Lord's death was satisfactory (I Cor. 15:3).

    With "for" meaning "concerning," this emphasizes the truth that Jesus' death related to our sins. The Scriptures teach that by His death Jesus satisfied God's demands against us. God's law required the death of sinners (Ezek. 18:20; Rom. 6:23). By His substitutionary death Jesus satisfied this requirement on our behalf.

    There are two features of this satisfaction that we should consider. One, Jesus' death for our sins was propitious (I Jn. 2:2; 4:10). A propitiation is a sacrifice that appeases, or placates, the wrath of Deity. God the Father was angry with us because we had broken His laws and offended His person. However, with unparalleled grace and love God the Father gave His Son to appease His own wrath against us so that we should not be punished. As the divine propitiation for our sins, the Lord Jesus received the punishment that was due us. By this sacrifice God's wrath against us was placated and His demands were satisfied.

    Two, Jesus' death for our sins was provisional (Jn. 3:16, 18, 36). By His atoning work the Lord Jesus secured a value which He did not need for Himself and that could be divinely applied to the account of others (II Cor.

169

5:18-20). That His death was provisional means that the value of His atoning work is not divinely accredited to the sinner's account until he exercises salvational faith in the Saviour (Acts 10:43). This means that the sinner's debt for his sins was not paid to God at the time Jesus died. If it were, then all for whom Jesus died would have been saved at that time. When He died, Jesus secured the value that God demanded of sinners and that is now offered through the gospel. This value is applied when the sinner trusts Jesus as his Saviour. Until he trusts the Saviour, the sinner is still obligated to pay the debt of his sins in spite of our Lord's atoning work. Only when the sinner trusts the Saviour is the Lord's atoning work credited to his account and it is rendered "paid in full." This is the meaning of divine forgiveness (Eph. 1:7).

We now can understand why the sinner must place His trust in Jesus for His salvation. The Lord Jesus was his substitute. If the sinner is satisfied with the Lord's atoning work on his behalf and accepts this by salvational faith, God makes the atonement effective in his life (Jn. 3:36; Acts 4:12).

2. Some Observations

a. The means of the atonement was determined by God's nature rather than His will, that is, it was not subject to divine whim or option. While God's love motivated Him to find a way to deliver sinners from sin's ruin, power, and debt, His holiness and justice determined what this way should be — by penal satisfaction (Ezek. 18:20; Jn. 3:16; Rom. 3:25-26). God always acts in agreement with His nature; He cannot deny Himself (II Tim. 2:13). He had to deal with our sins before He could set us free.

b. Christ not only bore our sins (I Pet. 2:24; Isa. 53:6) but He also was made sin (II Cor. 5:21). He was more than just an instrument for exposing our sins to divine wrath. Being made sin, He personally received and experienced the full measure of God's wrath against our sins (cp. Mt. 27:46; 20:28).

c. Christ's atoning sufferings were penal. This means that they were judicial afflictions from the hand of God the Father, which served to satisfy the claims of His nature and law (cp. Isa. 53:10; Ezek. 18:4; Rom. 5:8). While Jesus suffered from the pain and indignities of crucifixion, these did not have atoning value. Also, He did not suffer from the natural results of sin, such as disease, while on the cross.

d. Our Lord's physical death was deliberate and voluntary. He did not die from the natural results of sin or from loss of blood. He was not a suicide, dying from self-infliction. He was not killed. He uniquely, voluntarily laid down His life (Jn. 10:18).

e. Christ's atoning work was wholly confined to the time He was on the cross (cp. Mt. 20:28; Col. 1:20; Jn. 19:30). His sinless, obedient human life, which He lived since His incarnation, demonstrated His worthiness to be the Saviour, but it did not itself atone for our sins. His atoning work took place on the cross where He bore our sins and gave His life in death (Mt. 20:28). Moreover, this work was confined to the activity of the divine Trinity. The

Father made Jesus' soul an offering for sin (Isa. 53:10; Mt. 27:46); and the Son gave His life (Jn. 10:17-18) in the power of the Holy Spirit (Heb. 9:14).

f. Jesus' enemies did not contribute to His atoning work, for only God could make atonement for human sins. Their crucifying Jesus was humanity's greatest crime. This wicked act supported the justice of their divine condemnation. The atonement does not rest on this crime.

Furthermore, it should be carefully noted that man's shedding Jesus' blood did not in itself make atonement any more than it did in the case of Levitical animal sacrifices. Sacrificial blood, representing the life of the substitute, had to be offered upon the altar (cp. Lev. 17:11). The shedding of sacrificial blood was done by the offerer (Lev. 1:2-5). Jesus' blood was shed in volume by His enemies after He had died (Jn. 19:34). Unlike the animal sacrificial victims which died by bloodshedding, Jesus himself uniquely gave His life in death (Jn. 10:18). He did not die from loss of blood or by self-infliction. Keep in mind that the offerer of Jesus' life and shed-blood was God, not sinful men (Isa. 53:10; Jn. 3:16; see p. 189, fn. 22). The wages of sin which Jesus paid was His life given in death (Rom. 6:23).

Jesus' work was done when He cried with a loud voice, "It is finished," and gave up His life (Jn. 19:30). To fulfill the O.T. typology and to assure His death, it was necessary that His blood be shed, but this was not the cause of His death. It expressed the wicked intention of man to slay Him. Both God and man were active at Calvary: the One, exercising the greatest measure of grace and love; the other, manifesting the greatest expression of hatred and rebelliousness.

g. By His atoning work Jesus secured a value for sinners. Being personally free from sin Himself, His atoning work secured a value or result that He did not need for Himself and that could be divinely applied to others (II Cor. 5:18-20). This value, which is sufficient for all people, is offered through the gospel and is divinely applied to the elect when they exercise salvational faith in the Saviour (Acts 10:43).

h. It was necessary that the substitute be God and man. Only one who was God could qualify morally for the atonement and do its work; only one who was a man could identify with the human race and could die (Heb. 2:14; Rom. 5:6; II Cor. 5:18; Ps. 3:8; cp. Job 9:32-33).

i. The atonement was the combined work of the Members of the Trinity: the Father (II Cor. 5:19; Jn. 3:16; I Jn. 4:10) the Son (Mt. 20:28; Jn. 1:29; I Pet. 3:18), and the Holy Spirit (Heb. 9:14). The Son offered Himself in obedience to the Father and through the power of the Holy Spirit; the Father gave His Son as a propitiation for our sins and for those of the world.

j. We must distinguish between the atonement and salvation as expressed by the first and second halves of John 3:16. God could not save sinners until He dealt with their sins by atoning for them. Jesus' atoning work cleared the way for God to save. Salvation is the product of divine grace, based upon our Lord's atoning work. It is His gracious work in response to them who exercise salvational faith in the Saviour. The atonement precedes faith and must be believed; salvation follows faith with divine deliverance from sin and the bestowal of God's gracious blessings.

• The Validity of Substitutionary Atonement

Liberal theology and other forms of unbelief reject the biblical view of substitutionary atonement. Since this rejection concerns such an important doctrine, let us consider some of its objections and the replies that H. E. Guillebaud so ably gives.[5]

> 1. *Objection: It is wrong for a judge to sentence an innocent man to die for a guilty person.*

In reply Mr. Guillebaud points out that the objector sees four distinct parties involved in this case besides the guilty criminal (we'll say the murderer). These are the judge, the innocent substitute, the wronged party (the family of the murdered man and through them the whole community), and the king, representing the law of the land, to whom the judge is under oath to administer justice. It is observed that, if the innocent substitute could by his voluntary consent surrender his own rights, the judge's action would be a double outrage against the wronged party and the law that he had sworn to administer. He would be committing a crime against both of these by releasing the murderer and ordering the execution of an innocent person.

However, in the teaching of substitutionary atonement, the case is different. Mr. Guillebaud writes,

> There is the condemned criminal, the guilty sinner. But beside him there is only One, who is Judge, Wronged Party, King (or Law), and Substitute. God was not administering someone else's law, but His own, and the sin was not committed against someone else, but against Him; and above all He did not take someone else and accept him as a substitute for the condemned sinner, but He came Himself, took upon Himself the nature of the guilty ones, and bore the penalty of His own law. The Substitute who died on Calvary expressly declared Himself to be the Judge of the world. Instead, therefore, of a judge punishing an innocent third party in place of the criminal, we have a Triune Judge, One of whose Persons identified Himself with the nature of the criminal in all except his sin, then takes the sin itself upon Him, and suffers the penalty of His own Law, which indeed has no existence independent of Him. Moreover, not only is there this identity between the Substitute and the Judge, but also in a mysterious sense between the Substitute and the criminal, when the latter becomes willing to accept the identification. Can this be termed immoral?[6]

---

[5] H. E. Guillebaud, *Why the Cross?* (London: Inter-Varsity Fellowship, 1954), pp. 146-63.
[6] *Op. cit.*, pp. 147 f.

One problem of unbelief is its refusing to accept the truth that Jesus is more than a man. He is the God-man. Were He only a man, His substitutionary atoning work would be immoral.

2. Objection: How could a few hours of suffering by the Substitute be equivalent to Hell for sinners?

This objection disregards the fact that quantity, bulk, length of time, and distance are conceptions that have little significance in the spiritual world in contrast to quality.

Mr. Guillebaud writes,

> The reply to this objection is that the importance of the sacrifice of the Son of God is not measured by the duration in time of His sufferings, but by their quality, and above all by the quality of Him who suffered...Quantity is a conception wholly out of place in considering the sufferings of the Saviour: the very idea of balancing those sufferings in quantity against the doom of lost mankind is entirely alien to the Bible...But if we think in terms of spiritual quality, surely it is not incredible that such sufferings endured by the Judge Himself should be adequate to "propitiate" His eternal justice and make it possible for Him righteously (and gladly) to forgive the sinner who truly turns to Him.[7]

L. S. Chafer observes that the value of the sacrifice is not discovered in the intensity of the Saviour's anguish but in His dignity and infinite worth.[8]

3. Objection: Guilt cannot be transferred from one person to another.

This objection rests upon the misunderstanding that guilt is the same as the evil effects of sin upon one's life. Guilt really concerns one's obligation to God to pay the penalty which his sins have incurred. At the cross our sins were judicially transferred to the Saviour; and He bore their guilt, that is, the obligation to pay their judicial debt which was death. He did not experience the natural results of sins, such as disease. Mr. Guillebaud asks, "Is it incredible that He [God], under conditions that seem right in His eyes can lift that responsibility from us and take it upon Himself in Christ?"[9]

• The Kinds of Death Jesus Experienced

Since the wages of sin is death (Rom. 6:23; Gen. 2:17) and the divine arrangement for atoning for sin was death and the offering of blood (Lev. 17:11), it was necessary for the Saviour to die that He might atone for our sins (Mt. 20:28; Rom. 5:6, 8). When Adam and Eve sinned, they immediately died spiritually (Gen. 2:17) and later died physically (Gen. 5:5). Our Lord also experienced these kinds of death when He was upon the cross. (Note that the word "shedding" in Hebrews 9:22 includes the offering of the shed-blood.)

---

[7] *Op. cit.,* pp. 160 f.
[8] L. S. Chafer, *Systematic Theology,* III, p. 68.
[9] *Op. cit.,* p. 163.

1. His Spiritual Death (Mt. 27:46)

During the awful hours of darkness (Mt. 27:45), our Lord bore humanity's sins (I Pet. 2:24; Isa. 53:6; I Jn. 2:2) and was made sin (II Cor. 5:21). The full fury of God's wrath fell upon Him and crushed Him (Isa. 53:10). As a man Jesus was separated from the Father, as His cry, "My God, My God, why hast Thou forsaken Me?" indicates (Mt. 27:46). (Observe that there was no division of the divine essence during these hours; it was a separation of Persons.) Jesus experienced Hell and its indescribable desolation (cp. Ps. 22:1-5). The Father forsook Him, for His holy nature reacted against the sin-bearer (Hab. 1:13).

2. His Physical Death (Lk. 23:46)

When He had exhausted God's wrath against our sins, Jesus was restored to fellowship with the Father. This is indicated by His addressing God "Father" (Lk. 23:46). Being made alive in His human spirit (I Pet. 3:18 Gk.), He cried out triumphantly, "It is finished!" (Jn. 19:30), commended His human spirit to the Father, and died physically (Lk. 23:46).

The manner of our Lord's physical death was unique in that He deliberately laid down His life in obedience to the Father (Jn. 10:18). Having borne the wrath of God against our sins, He voluntarily, decisively laid down His life. No one took it from Him, though His enemies were charged with His murder (Acts 2:23; 3:15; 5:30). Our Lord did not die from exhaustion (Lk. 23:46), disease (the penalty was legal, not natural), loss of blood (Jn. 19:33-34), or a broken heart. Neither was He a suicide, for He did not take His life by self-affliction. But with authority from and in obedience to the Father (Jn. 10:17-18), He deliberately laid down His life by giving up His human spirit (Jas. 2:26; Mt. 27:50). It appears that He simply stopped breathing.

While it was necessary for the atonement, our Lord's physical death was not associated with divine wrath as was His spiritual death. Being in complete fellowship with the Father, Jesus voluntarily laid down His physical life to gain power over death, Satan, and Hades by His resurrection (Acts 2:23-32; Heb. 2:14). He aggressively invaded the realm over which Satan and sin held power (Heb. 2:14; I Cor. 15:56) and challenged them, as it were, to bind Him as they had bound the human race. But since they had no claim on Him (Acts 2:24), He broke their power forever. They could not hold Him, for He was personally sinless (I Jn. 3:5; Jn. 14:30). As the Messiah He now has authority over these powers (Rev. 1:18).

Our Lord's atoning work involved His spiritual and physical deaths, and required His resurrection. While His deaths satisfied the demands of divine holiness and justice, His resurrection ratified His atoning work and broke the power of the enemy that held mankind in its grip.

• The Crucifixion of Jesus

The sacred record simply says, "they crucified Him" (Mt. 27:35), sparing us the painful details, which to my mind have been overplayed to the extent of eclipsing from our view God's atoning work. That which Jesus suffered at the hands of evil men did not contribute to His atoning work, but it did reveal the spiritual state and just condemnation of all who were involved in this heinous crime (Acts 4:27; Lk. 2:35). As God was about to do His greatest work in making His Son an offering for humanity's sins, fallen angels and rebellious humanity were committing their greatest crime against Him (Mt. 27:26-44; Ps. 2:1-3). They subjected their Creator to a shameful, humiliating, painful execution with the intention of murdering Him (Jn. 11:53; Acts 3:15; 5:30). Their heinous act revealed the gross depravity of their character and the malignant nature of sin.

Death by crucifixion was the most shameful punishment that was inflicted in those times. To be crucified was to be identified with the lowest criminals. Roman law forbade the crucifixion of Roman citizens. The lowest term of reproach that a Roman could apply to another was "crucifer" or "cross-bearer."[10]

Death by crucifixion was an agonizing experience with the victim living from two to seven days. Torn flesh and infected wounds, taut muscles and swollen tissues, the unnatural position of the body, the heat of the sun and the cold of night, the bites of insects and the attacks of animals combined to make this a most excruciating experience.

The Jews regarded anyone who was crucified to be cursed of God (Deut. 21:23; Gal. 3:13) and thus a stumbling block to them (I Cor. 1:23). So great was the scandal of the cross to Gentiles that they considered the Christian teaching which gave to a crucified person a place in the Godhead and the role of Saviour sheer madness (vss. 18, 23).

While the New Testament has preserved for us the indignities which were done to Jesus before His execution, Psalm 22:6-21 prophetically speaks of those which He experienced while upon the cross. His spiritual sufferings are expressed by His awful cry (vs. 1). His mental suffering is indicated by His being despised (vs. 6), mocked (vss. 7-8), and the object of immodest gaze (vss. 17-18; crucified victims were naked). Our Lord also suffered physically (vss. 12-18). But in faith He looked to God for help (vss. 19-21a, c). And when it seemed that He could no longer endure, God intervened. The Saviour's work was done. His spirit revived; He sighed, "Thou hast heard Me!" (vs. 21b); He cried, "It is finished!" (Jn. 19:30). His work ended when He gave up His spirit. The judgement of humanity's sins was borne.

- **Jesus' Work While on the Cross**

1. JESUS MADE AN ATONEMENT FOR SINS.

Just before He died physically, Jesus triumphantly cried out, "It is finished!" (Jn. 19:30). He died with the awareness that His atoning work was

---

[10] See William Wood Seymour, *The Cross in Tradition, History, and Art* (New York: The Knickerbocker Press, 1898), Part I, ch. III.

done. This work did not begin until He was upon the cross, and it was completed with His physical death. His resurrection ratified this work and made it effective (I Cor. 15:14-19). In our study of His atoning work, we must distinguish between the atonement (that which He did on the cross) and salvation (the benefits of the atonement which are divinely applied to the gospel believer).[11] At this time let us look at the atonement. What did Jesus do by His atoning work?

    a. He dealt with humanity's sins.

        He did this decisively by putting sin away (Heb. 9:26; Jn. 1:29) — by paying their debt (I Cor. 15:3). As we noted earlier, Jesus dealt with humanity's sins propitiously and provisionally. Let us look at these concepts again.

        To understand His dealing with humanity's sins propitiously (I Jn. 2:2; 4:10), we must ask this: How could God who is holy and just deal with sinners in a way that they deserve and yet satisfy His love by delivering them from sin's penalty and ruin? Motivated by gracious love, He sent His Son to be the propitiation for our sins and for those of the world (I Jn. 4:10). Although He could not change His holy demands against sinners, He could perfectly and justly satisfy these demands on their behalf and by this appease His wrath. Pagans seek to propitiate the anger of their deities by offering them gifts, but God Himself was propitious. He gave the necessary sacrifice that would satisfy His demands and placate His wrath against us. The Lord Jesus dealt with humanity's sins propitiously when He received their punishment and satisfied God's holy demands.

        Jesus also dealt with humanity's sins provisionally. This means that the value of His atoning work was secured by His death but it is not credited to the sinner's account until he exercises faith in the Saviour and His work (Acts 10:43). Until he does this, the sinner is obligated to pay the debt of his sins in spite of the Lord's atoning work. Only when he believes the gospel is the value of the atonement divinely applied and his account is rendered "paid in full." Then, he receives the salvational blessings that are based upon the atonement, such as regeneration (I Jn. 4:9; 5:11), justification (Rom. 5:1, 9), redemption (Eph. 1:7), and reconciliation (Col. 1:20-21). We who are saved can look back to our Lord's atoning work and see that by this He obtained for us these benefits (cp. Heb. 9:12). But no one can claim these before he trusts the Saviour and receives on his account the value of the atonement. If the sinner does not accept the Saviour, he remains indebted to God for his sins as though Christ had not died.

    b. He took away the sins of precross saints.

        By His atoning work the Lord Jesus dealt with the sins of those people who were saved during the Old Testament or precross period (Rom.

---

[11] See W. G. T. Shedd, *Dogmatic Theology,* II, 469.

3:25; Heb. 9:15). While their sins had been covered by the blood of animal sacrifices (Gen. 3:21; Lev. 17:11), they had not been dealt with in a final, permanent way (Heb. 10:4, 11). Because of this these believers did not receive the promised inheritance and go to Heaven when they died (Heb. 9:15-17; 11:8-16). Instead, they went to "Abraham's bosom" in Hades to await the atonement (cp. Lk. 16:22; Gen. 25:8; I Ki. 2:10). Upon His death, resurrection, and ascension into Heaven, the Lord took these disembodied people with Him, to await the time of the resurrection of their bodies (cp. Eph. 4:8).

    c. *He secured the basis of parental forgiveness.*

Jesus' atoning work is the basis not only of "judicial" forgiveness (Col. 2:13), but also of "parental" forgiveness (I Jn. 1:9). Judicial forgiveness concerns the cancellation of divine retribution, which is everlasting separation from God in Hell (Rev. 20:14). Parental forgiveness concerns the cancellation of the chastisement that God imposes upon believers for failure to deal with known sins (I Cor. 11:27-32). Since Jesus dealt with the family aspect of our sins (I Jn. 1:7) as well as with the judicial aspect (Eph. 1:7), our heavenly Father is able to grant us parental forgiveness of known sin, which removes the threat or the experience of chastisement (I Jn. 1:9). It appears that we are automatically forgiven of sins that are unknown to us (I Jn. 1:7). But when we learn of these sins or commit them knowingly, then we must deal with them by repentance and confession for divine forgiveness (Rev. 2:5; I Jn. 1:9).

2. *JESUS CONFIRMED THE CONDEMNATION OF GOD'S ENEMIES.*

In keeping with the demands of justice and orderly judicial procedure, an accused offender must be found guilty of an alleged crime before he is sentenced to punishment by a court. God had already handed down a sentence of condemnation against His enemies (cp. Jn. 3:18; Rom. 3:19; 5:18). But their guilt was fully established and clearly manifested by their wicked actions against the Lord Jesus during His trial and execution. The gross injustice of the Jewish and Roman courts, the physical abuse associated with these trials, and their nailing Him to a cross with the intention of murdering Him proved to be the greatest crime of fallen angels and humans against their Creator. These heinous actions were self-incriminating, exposing their hatred, rebellion, and guilt (Jn. 3:20; Lk. 2:35). Their actions confirmed the justice of the divine verdict of condemnation.

The value of this condemnation is two-fold: One, it gives Christ the legal right and basis to deal with God's enemies (the sin-principle, fallen angels, and lost mankind) as they deserve. He will do this when He returns and rules over the earth (I Cor. 15:25-26; Rev. 19:15, 20-21; 20:7-15). And two, it allows Him to deliver His people from bondage to these enemies when He saves them and to grant them occasions of victory in daily life. (cp. Rom. 14:9; Rev. 12:11).

Although this condemnation does not appear to be part of the atonement, it did take place at the cross. Let us look more closely at this.

a. *The condemnation of the sin-principle (Rom. 6:10; 8:3)*[12]

Energizing those who were involved in Jesus' trials and crucifixion, the sin-principle manifested its abhorrent character in their abusive, shameful actions (cp. Mk. 14:61-65; Lk. 23:32-37; Acts 2:23). These actions were self-condemnatory. They proved that the sin-principle was the impelling, impersonal force that caused men and angels to do these wicked things.

Upon His confirming the divine sentence of condemnation against the sin-principle and breaking its power of death by His resurrection (Jas. 1:15; Acts 2:24; I Cor. 15:56-57), the Lord Jesus sets His people free from its claims (Rom. 6:6-7, 16-22) and is able to grant them occasions of victory over it in their lives (Gal. 5:16; Rom. 6:1-13). Although the inherent power of this sin-force in us remains undiminished, it will one day cease to exist in the lives of God's people with their death or with the change in their bodies at Christ's return (Rom. 8:10-11, 23), and in the universe, with the death of the last unsaved person (Rev. 20:9).[13]

b. *The condemnation of fallen angels (Jn. 12:31; 16:11; Mt. 25:41)*

The Scriptures imply that Satan tried to keep Jesus from going to the cross (Mt. 4:8-10; 16:21-23; cp. 26:36-39). (Was this because of the ancient prophecy of Genesis 3:15?) When he failed, the devil and his demons did all within their power to make Jesus' cross experience as odious and painful as possible (cp. Ps. 22:12-21). Their involvement in our Lord's trial, crucifixion, and harassment while on the cross reveals their guilt before God (cp. Jn. 13:27; Lk. 22:53).

Because He confirmed the divine sentence of condemnation against the enemy and broke his power by His death and resurrection (Heb. 2:14), Jesus now sets His people free from Satan's authority (Col. 1:13; Acts 26:18) and can give them occasions of victory over temptations (Jas. 4:7). At the close of His earthly rule, Jesus will banish Satan and his angels to Hell forever (Rev. 20:1-3, 10; Mt. 25:41).

c. *The condemnation of the world (Jn. 12:31).*

In the Scriptures the word "world" has various meanings, determined by the context. Here it refers to the world-system of lost

---

[12] The Bible teaches that sin is a principle, force, or law (not an essence) that motivates people and energizes them to do evil (Rom. 7:23, 25; 8:2).

[13] The sin-principle is confined to and operates only in humans and fallen angels. Because of the fall of certain personal creatures, the impersonal creation is under a divine curse (Gen. 3:17-19; Rom. 8:20-21). Since the sin-principle is resident in the body's flesh, it perishes with the body's death and dissolution (Rom. 7:17-21). In my opinion, the resurrected lost will not have the sin-principle. Also, Satan and his angels will be divested of it as well. I do not think of Hell as a place where fallen personal creatures continue to exist in sin's grip and express their hostility toward God. Though they continue forever in conscious suffering and desolation, they will still bow the knee to Jesus and acclaim Him to be Lord (Phil. 2:11). Sin had a beginning; it will have an end when death is abolished (I Cor. 15:25-26).

mankind, including their philosophy and works. This system is headed by Satan (Jn. 12:31), and its works are evil (Jn. 7:7). The world's representative peoples (Acts 4:27)—their religion (traditional Judaism), government (Roman imperialism), and culture (Greek Hellenism) — united to crucify the Lord Jesus. By this crime they expressed their guilt before God.

Upon His confirming the divine sentence against the world, the Lord now delivers His people from its constituency and power (Jn. 15:19; Gal. 6:14) can give them occasions of victory over its influence upon their lives (I Jn. 2:15-17; Mt. 6:19-24; Col. 3:1-3) and one day will deliver them physically from it (I Thess. 4:17; cp. Gal. 1:4). Moreover, the Lord will replace the present world order with a new one, when He sets up His kingdom on earth (Dan. 2:44-45; Rev. 11:15-18; 19:11-16; Isa. 2:1-5; 11:1-9).

3. JESUS RATIFIED THE NEW COVENANT.

By His death the Lord Jesus brought an end to the Mosaic Covenant, which God made with Israel (II Cor. 3:6-14; Gal. 3:25; Eph. 2:14-16; Col. 2:14; Heb. 7:18-19; 10:9). While the Mosaic Law continues as a dispensation for them who submit themselves to it (Acts 15:21; 21:21), its covenant promises (Ex. 19:5-6; Lev. 18:5) are no longer honored by God.

When He brought the old covenant of law to an end, the Lord Jesus also brought into force the new one that was predicted in Jeremiah 31:31-34 and that is given in the New Testament portion of the Bible (Lk. 22:20; Heb. 10:9-18; 12:24). The promises of the New Covenant are fulfilled to all who receive Jesus as their Saviour (cp. II Cor. 3:6; Acts 20:21).

4. JESUS LAID THE BASIS FOR RECONCILIATION.

By His atoning work Jesus laid the ground for the reconciliation to God of all impersonal creatures and things that were involuntarily affected by the divine curse (Col. 1:20; cp. Eph. 1:10). Paul is not speaking about universal salvation (he is careful not to refer to things under the earth, cp. Phil. 2:10),[14] for this would contradict the doctrine of the everlasting punishment of the lost (Mt. 25:46; Jn. 3:36). He anticipates the time when the Lord Jesus will return to establish His earthly kingdom. Then the Lord will lift the divine curse, which rests upon creation (Gen. 3:17-18; Rom. 8:20) and will restore the earth to its primeval, pristine state (Rom. 8:19-23; Eph. 1:10; Acts 3:21; cp. Isa. 11:6-9; ch. 35; Amos 9:13; Ps. 8). Whatever has been involuntarily affected by the divine curse and creaturely sin, whether on earth or in the heavens, will be restored to its original harmony with God and with itself. Just how the Lord's atoning work relates to this reconciliation is not clear to me, but the whole creation waits for this glorious deliverance (Rom. 8:19-21).

---

[14] "Under the earth" refers to Hades, the prison of the unsaved dead and many fallen angels (cp. Lk. 16:22-23; I Pet. 3:18-20; II Pet. 2:4; Rev. 20:13). There is no salvation for these. When He went to Hades after His death (Mt. 12:40; Rom. 10:7), Jesus made a proclamation, but He did not evangelize (I Pet. 3:19).

5. HE PURCHASED THE WHOLE HUMAN RACE

By His sacrifice the Lord Jesus purchased all of mankind, both the unsaved (II Pet. 2:1) and the saved (I Cor. 6:20; 7:23). By this purchase mankind became His property to do with as He pleases, in keeping with the divine plan. As the Messiah, the Lord Jesus is truly Lord of all (Acts 10:36) by divine gift (Jn. 3:35; Ps. 2:8) and by purchase. He is also sovereign over the universe as Creator God (Jn. 1:3; Ps. 24:1).

When He returns to earth again, the Lord Jesus will take possession of earth as its owner, not as the usurper Satan did. He will take possession of His property and will rule over His subjects (Rev. 19:11-16). Moreover, He to whom all people are accountable will judge mankind, both at the beginning of His millennial kingdom (Mt. 25:31-46) and in the final judgment (Jn. 5:22; Rev. 20:11-15). He will judge His people when He comes again (Rev. 22:12).

• The extent of Jesus' atoning work

In His dealing with human sins on the cross, did Jesus atone for the sins of all mankind or for those of the elect alone? W. G. T. Shedd observes that the word "extent" has two meanings in usage: passively, it means value, such as the extent of one's property; actively, it speaks of the act of extending.[15] With reference to the atonement, the word "extent" passively refers to its value which is sufficient to satisfy God's demands against the sins of all mankind. Actively, "extent" refers to the application of the atonement's value to them who believe. Thus, in the passive sense, the atonement is unlimited; in its active sense it is limited to the elect. Although Christ died for all mankind, the salvational benefits of His atoning work will be experienced only by the elect.

The following propositions set forth my understanding of this doctrine:

One, Christ died for all mankind (Heb. 2:9; I Jn. 2:2; II Cor. 5:14-15; Jn. 3:16-17; I Tim. 2:1-6).

Two, He is the Saviour of the world (I Jn. 4:14; Jn. 1:29; I Tim. 4:10).

Three, His death seems to include a wider purpose than only the salvation of the elect. It also provided a value for the non-elect to reject, to their added condemnation (Jn. 3:18; II Pet. 2:1). While it is God's intention to save the elect when they believe, it seems also to be His intention by Jesus' atoning work to make the gospel's universal appeal real and true (Jn. 3:16; Acts 17:30; 20:21; Col. 1:23). We can carry the word of reconciliation to anyone in the world with the assurance that Jesus provisionally died for him (II Cor. 5:18-20; I Jn. 2:2). God does have something to say to the non-elect through the gospel. They are not relieved of their duty to receive the Saviour by a limited atonement. Because the Lord Jesus died for the non-elect, they can never say that they could not have been saved if they had chosen to receive Him. On the

---

[15] *Op. cit.,* II, 464.

other hand, if He did not die for them, how can they be guilty of rejecting a value that does not exist for them?

Four, although universal in its extent, the Lord's atoning work was provisional in the sense that the benefits derived from it are not received and possessed until one exercises salvational faith in the Saviour (Acts 16:31; 10:43). While the Lord Jesus atoned for the sins of the whole world by bearing their punishment, yet in the reckoning of God the sinner's debt is considered to be paid only when he receives the Saviour. There is no transference of value before he believes. Until he trusts the Saviour, this value remains with God and the sinner is obligated to pay the debt of his sins. There is no double payment of the debt of the non-elect, for the value of Jesus' atoning work is not put to the sinner's account as payment until he believes. If he fails to receive the Saviour, the sinner himself must pay the debt as though Jesus had not died. The awful debt of sin remains.

Five, we must distinguish between Jesus' atoning work (His dealing with humanity's sins) and salvation (the benefits derived from the atonement). Timewise, people receive salvation when they trust Jesus and His atoning work rather than when He died on the cross. Salvational faith precedes the personal reception of the components of salvation such as regeneration, redemption, justification, and reconciliation (Acts 10:43; 16:31). The value of the atonement, with its salvational blessings, is not divinely applied until the sinner believes.

Six, a distinction must be recognized between God's unrevealed decree or purpose and His revealed will or desire for sinners. His revealed will for all people is that they believe the gospel and be saved (II Pet. 3:9; I Tim. 2:4). This is indicated by the universality of the gospel's appeal (Acts 17:30; Jn. 3:15-16). But God's secret decree is to save only them whom He has chosen (II Thess. 2:13; Acts 13:48).

Seven, since Christ died for the whole world and secured thereby a value, now offered by the gospel, for everyone to receive or reject, we can present the gospel to everyone with the assurance that God will save all who exercise salvational faith in Jesus. The "whosoever" of the gospel appeal is to be taken literally, for God who cannot lie means what He says. When speaking about the word and ministry of reconciliation, Paul observed that God did not reckon the sins of the world to them and send them to Hell (II Cor. 5:18-20). Rather, He laid them on Jesus for the purpose of provisionally reconciling the world unto Himself. Consequently, anyone in the world can be reconciled to God by receiving the message of reconciliation. Because of this, we can beseech men everywhere to be reconciled to God. They who fail to receive this message will go to Hell. As we present the gospel to people everywhere, God will work according to His sovereign purpose (Lk. 24:47; Mk. 16:15; Acts 18:9-11).

Eight, in summary it can be said that the Lord's atoning work was unlimited in its value for He died for all people. However, in the divine application of this value, His atoning work is limited to those who believe the gospel. Jesus did not actually pay the debt of humanity's sins while He was on the cross. By His death He secured a value that is now offered through the gospel and which is divinely applied when people place their trust in the Saviour. They who do not receive the Saviour must themselves pay this debt.

- ## The blood of Christ

In its New Testament usage "the blood of Christ" has both literal and theological meaning. Literally, it is that which flowed from His body in Gethsemane (Lk. 22:44), in His trial (Jn. 19:1; Mt. 27:29-30), in His crucifixion (Jn. 19:18; 20:24-27), and after His death (Jn. 19:34). But let us seek to understand the theological meaning of Jesus' blood, especially His shed blood.

1. Its Necessity

The shedding of blood and its being offered on an altar together with life given in death was God's O.T. arrangement for dealing with humanity's sins (the atonement) and for providing salvation. He ordained this when He clothed Adam and Eve (Gen. 3:21); He honored this when He accepted Abel's offering (Gen. 4:4; Heb. 11:4); and He stated this in the Mosaic law (Lev. 17:11; Heb. 9:22). Although the animal blood sacrifices could only cover sins from God's sight, they pointed to the coming Lamb of God who by His sacrifice would put them away (Jn. 1:29; Heb. 10:4-10; 9:26).

2. Its Purpose

Since the wages of sin is death (Gen. 2:17; Rom. 6:23), not the shedding of blood, one wonders why God required bloodshedding for the atonement during the precross period. Perhaps it served as proof that the sacrificial victim had died. It is impossible for one to live with the blood removed from his body (except, of course, with artificial support). The shedding of our Lord's blood after His death assured that He was dead (Jn. 19:34). Were it not for this precaution, there might be the possibility that He did not really die and the atonement was not completed. Also, the blood, which is the vehicle of the soul (the animating principle of the body), was the material representative of life (given in death) upon the altar (Lev. 17:11)[16]. The life which is resident in the blood can be offered in sacrifice only as the blood is shed and poured out at the base of the altar or sprinkled upon the altar, as the offering requires (Lev. 4:7). Otherwise, the life remains intangible.

3. Its Significance[17]

Throughout the Bible the shedding of blood is a sign or symbol of violent death. Jacob understood this when he saw Joseph's gory coat (Gen.

---

[16] See Franz Delitzsch, A System of Biblical Psychology (Grand Rapids: Baker Book House, 1966), 281 ff.
[17] See A. M. Stibbs, The Meaning of the Word 'Blood' in Scripture (London: The Tyndale Press, 1954), pp. 9 f., 16-19.
Leon Morris, The Apostolic Preaching of the Cross (London: The Tyndale Press, 1955), ch. III.

37:33). A murderer was said to have upon him the blood of the person he killed (II Sam. 1:16; cp. Mt. 27:24-25). Stephen's death was described as his blood being shed (Acts 22:20). When murder provoked revenge, the one who retaliated was a "revenger of blood" (Num. 35:19). If death was the result of a person's own folly, his blood was said to be upon his own head (Josh. 2:19).

With the exception of two references to bloodshedding (Lk. 22:44; Jn. 19:34), five references to blood used as a sign of violent death (Mt. 27:4, 6, 24-25; Acts 5:28), and one reference to blood as a part of His unglorified human nature (Heb. 2:14), all of the remaining thirty-three references[18] to Jesus' blood are to be understood as having theological meaning.

In those references where it has theological meaning, the word "blood," as well as "death," is a figurative expression (synecdoche, see Addenda) for His atoning work (cp. Rom. 5:9-10). Keep in mind that Jesus provisionally paid the debt of humanity's sin by His death (Rom. 6:23). While the shedding and offering of blood was not a wage of sins, it was required in the atonement process (Lev. 17:11; Heb. 9:22). In the case of Jesus, the shedding of His blood did not bring about His death as in the case of the O.T. animal sacrifices, but it did assure His death and the fulfillment the O.T. typology. Bloodshedding was by man; atonement was by God.

An example of a passage where Jesus' blood is to be interpreted theologically is the words, "the blood of Jesus Christ, His Son cleanses us from all sin" (I Jn. 1:7). John is not speaking about the application of Jesus' blood in a physical way. Rather, he is speaking about the divine application of the value of Christ's atoning work which was accomplished by His substitutionary death and the offering of His blood. (cp. Jn. 6:53-56).

4. Its Importance

In the following passages our Lord's blood should be understood in its theological sense, namely, as referring to His sacrifice by which He atoned for our sins. Its importance to us who are saved is evident when we look at its relation to our salvation and to our Christian life.

Through Jesus' blood, at salvation, we received spiritual life (Jn. 6:53), we were redeemed (Eph. 1:7; I Pet. 1:19), we were judicially forgiven of all our sins (Eph. 1:7; Rev. 1:5), we were justified (Rom. 5:9), we were reconciled to God (Col. 1:20), we had a propitiation for our sins (Rom. 3:25), we were made near to God (Eph. 2:13), we were cleansed from sin's defilement (Heb. 9:14), we were purchased (Acts 20:28), we were sanctified (Heb. 13:12), and we were made recipients of the promises of the New Covenant, which was ratified by His blood (Lk. 22:20; I Cor. 11:25; Heb. 12:24; 13:20; I Pet. 1:2).

Through the blood of Jesus we experience during our Christian lives

---

[18] Mt. 26:28; Mk. 14:24; Lk. 22:20; Jn. 6:53-56; Acts 20:28; Rom. 3:25; 5:9; I Cor. 10:16; 11:25, 27; Eph. 1:7; 2:13; Col. 1:14, 20; Heb. 9:12, 14; 10:19, 29; 13:12, 20; I Pet. 1:2, 19; I Jn. 1:7; 5:6, 8; Rev. 1:5; 5:9; 7:14; 12:11.

divine parental forgiveness of sins (I Jn. 1:7), spiritual renewal (Jn. 6:54-56), fellowship with Christ and His people (I Cor. 10:16), approach unto God (Heb. 10:19), and victory over our spiritual enemies (Rev. 12:11).

Needless to say, the blood of Jesus is an important theme of the Scriptures. It is no wonder that Satan hates it so and ever seeks to discredit it.

• The Atonement and Healing

Is physical healing in the atonement? Some believe that one can trust Christ for physical healing just as he can for salvation, with the confidence that the Lord will always heal the body. This belief is based on the erroneous view that our Lord made atonement for our diseases as well as for our sins and that our body is now redeemed. If true, then a believer should never be sick. Should he suffer from some disease or illness, then (so the theory goes) it is because he has failed to appropriate fully the benefits of the atonement through faith or he is guilty of some personal sin for which sickness is a divine judgment. This theory holds that it is always God's will to heal, at least until we reach three score and ten years (Ps. 90:10), if we deal with our sins and believe in Jesus' atoning work. Advocates of this view look to Isaiah 53:4-5 and James 5:14-15 for their support.

I believe that this theory is unbiblical, for Isaiah 53:4-5 represents a double prophetic outlook: One, to an atonement of sin (cp. vs. 5 with I Pet. 2:24). "With His stripes we are healed" refers to spiritual healing (Ps. 41:4; 147:3). And two, to the healing of disease (cp. vs. 4 with Mt. 8:17). Our Lord's healing ministry fulfilled this prophecy before and apart from His atoning work.[19]

Another reason for rejecting this theory is that while on the cross Jesus bore the judicial penalty of our sins, which is death. He did not bear their natural consequences, such as disease (Rom. 6:23; 5:8). In this regard A. J. McClain writes, "Sickness is not sin; it is rather the result of sin. We punish men for sinning, but not for getting sick...Christ died for our sins, not for our diseases. He was made sin for us; He was not made disease for us. Christ never forgave disease; He forgave sin and healed diseases. Death is the divine penalty for sin, not for disease. Therefore, the death of Christ as our Substitute was penal, not pathological."[20]

If healing is in the atonement and our body is now redeemed, then why do the Scriptures portray the body as still being unredeemed (Rom. 8:10, 23)? Since redemption concerns the total person, we who are saved will experience the redemption of the body (its deliverance from inherent corruption, sin, and death) when Jesus comes for His church (Rom. 8:11; Phil. 3:20-21; Rom. 13:11; I Cor. 15:50-57).

---

[19] H. W. Frost, *Miraculous Healing* (London: Marshall, Morgan & Scott, 1951), p. 59.
[20] A. J. McClain, *Was Christ Punished for our Diseases?* (Winona Lake: The Brethren Missionary Herald Co., n.d.), pp. 7 f.

If we can be healed by exercising faith, it is strange that the apostle Paul did not receive healing in answer to his prayers (II Cor. 12:7-10). He also advised Timothy to take medication for his infirmities (I Tim. 5:23).

Finally, this theory ignores the fact that sickness serves divine purposes for the Lord's people. It may be for divine chastisement (I Cor. 11:30-32), for spiritual productivity (II Cor. 12:9-10), or solely for the glory of God (Jn. 9:3).

HIS EXALTATION

Our Lord's humiliation ended with His death. The Father did not allow any more indignities to be done to Him or His body. Ordinarily, the bodies of crucified persons were left on the cross until devoured by carrion birds and animals as a shocking, impressive warning against crime, or they were cast into a refuse dump. But God overruled by moving Joseph of Arimathaea to take the body of Jesus and to place it in his new, unused tomb (Lk. 23:50-53).

Theologically, Jesus' burial was proof of His death and a prerequisite to His resurrection. Upon His death Jesus' personhood and immaterial human nature (soul and spirit) immediately went to the Paradise region of Hades to await the time of His resurrection (Mt. 12:40; Lk. 23:43; Acts 2:31; Rom. 10:7). While He was in Hades, Jesus made an undisclosed announcement to the fallen angels who were active in the days of Noah (I Pet. 3:19-20). Meanwhile, His entombed body did not deteriorate (Acts 2:27; 13:37) as did that of Lazarus (Jn. 11:39).

Having completed the divine purpose for His condescension and humiliation, our Lord as man was exalted to the supreme majesty by the Father (Phil. 2:9-11; cp. Heb. 2:9). This exaltation was a partial reversal of His condescension, with the restoration of His visible, preincarnate, radiant glory (Jn. 17:1, 5; Mt. 17:1-2; Acts 26:13). Moreover, as man He was exalted above all creatures and things (Eph. 1:20-22). Being delivered from the humiliation of His death by the burial and resurrection of His body, He is now released from the limitations of unglorified human nature and will forever possess His glorified human nature, with its new constitution and powers (Rom. 8:11; Jn. 20:26; cp. I Cor. 15:42-49). Being the Father's anointed Servant, He will as man remain in subjection to the Father forever (I Cor. 15:28).

Our Lord's exaltation includes His resurrection, ascension, enthronement, and second coming to earth. Let us look at these.

● **His Resurrection from the Dead**

1. *ITS DEFINITION*

Jesus' resurrection consisted of the reunion of the immaterial parts of His human nature and personhood with His body, which was made alive by the Holy Spirit (Rom. 8:11), and His physically rising from the grave, never to die again (Lk. 24:5-6; Acts 2:32; 26:23; Rev. 1:18).

2. *ITS FEATURES*

a. It was brought about by the combined activity of the Members of the Trinity (Gal. 1:1; Jn. 2:19; 10:18; Rom. 8:11).

b. It was a physical resurrection (Lk. 24:36-40; I Cor. 15:3-4). The burial of our Lord's body shows the reality of His death and resurrection, for only the bodies of the dead are buried, not their immaterial parts. Resurrection concerns the reunion of the person with his body and its being made alive. Jesus demonstrated that His resurrection was physical by showing His disciples His hands and feet (Lk. 24:39; I Jn. 1:1), and His eating before them (Lk. 24:41-43) and with them (Acts 10:41).

c. It was a unique resurrection (I Cor. 15:23; Rev. 1:18). He was the first to be restored to physical life, with a reconstituted physical body, never to die again (Acts 26:23; Rom. 6:9; Rev. 1:18). Others had been restored to natural life (II Ki. 4:32-37; Mk. 5:35-43), but these restorations were only reanimations. These people died again, for Satan who has the power of death had not yet been conquered (Heb. 2:14). As a kind of "first fruits" (I Cor. 15:23), Jesus' resurrection was the first of everlasting duration and the pledge of the resurrection of His people.

3. ITS IMPORTANCE

Together with His atoning death and the shedding of His blood, our Lord's resurrection is the keystone of the Christian faith. This is evident in the following:

a. *Its importance to Himself*

One, Jesus' resurrection was the seal of the Father's satisfaction with His life and atoning work (Acts 2:22-24). If this were not true, He would not have risen.

Two, it was the mark of His divine Sonship and human Messiahship (Rom. 1:4; Acts 2:36). It was His greatest Messianic sign (Jn. 2:18-21; cp. Mt. 12:38-40).

Three, it reconstituted His body for everlasting existence (Acts 2:31). With His resurrection, Jesus will forever possess His complete human nature and be the God-man (I Tim. 2:5). Moreover, His body was adapted to the laws and conditions of life in Heaven and in the eternal state. For instance, His resurrected body is vitalized by a new life principle, the Holy Spirit (Rom. 8:11). Moreover, it manifests new powers that it did not have before His death, such as the ability to appear and disappear at will (Lk. 24:15-16) and to enter closed rooms without difficulty (Lk. 24:36; Jn. 20:19).

Four, it made possible His future Messianic work, such as His building the church and His millennial rule (Mt. 16:18, 28).

b. *Its importance to His people*

One, Jesus' resurrection gave value and force to His atoning work on the cross (I Cor. 15:14, 17). It was the essential complement to His atoning death. If He had not risen, then His death would be of no value in the salvation of sinners and the gospel would be ineffective. A saviour still dead cannot save. But He did rise, and by this He activated all that He died to achieve. For example, His death made justification possible, and His resurrection made it actual for all who receive Him (Rom. 4:25; cp. I Pet. 3:21).

Two, it made possible the release of new life and power by which His people can live and serve (Jn. 14:19-20; Rom. 6:4; Eph. 1:18-20).

Three, it gives His people a living hope (I Pet. 1:3; Tit. 2:13), which includes the expectation of Christ's imminent return for His church and the blessed events that are associated with His coming (cp. I Thess. 4:13-17; I Pet. 1:3-5; Tit. 1:2).

Four, it guarantees the resurrection of His people (I Cor. 15:20-23; Rom. 8:11). Jesus' resurrection assures the resurrection of His people, for it was the first-fruits of all resurrections and the resurrecting Spirit now indwells them.[21]

Five, it made possible His present work on behalf of His people. This includes His building the church (Mt. 16:18), His preparing a home for His people (Jn. 14:2-3), His interceding for them (Heb. 7:25), His teaching them (Eph. 4:20-21), and His ruling over them (Col. 1:13).

Six, it established the prototype for the changed bodies of His people (Phil. 3:21). The bodies of the Lord's people will be delivered from their inherent corruption and mortality and will be changed to His kind of body (I Cor. 15:42-53). This change will prepare them physically for the eternal state.

c. Its importance to His enemies

One, Jesus' resurrection gave Him final victory over them. The world crucified Him with the intention of removing Him forever from their midst (Ps. 2:1-3; Acts 2:23). But God raised Him up (Acts 2:24) and gave to Him the kingdoms of the world and the power to destroy them who destroy the earth (Rev. 11:15-18; 19:11-21; Ps. 2:4-12).

Moreover, before his defeat Satan had the power of death (Heb. 2:14), in that he ruled the sphere in which the unsaved abide (Acts 26:18; I Jn. 5:19). Also, he had the power to inflict physical death according to God's permissive decree (I Cor. 5:5; Job 1:12-19). By His unique physical death Jesus aggressively invaded death's domain; by His resurrection He broke the power of sin and death and of Satan's grip on mankind. He also became the Warden of death and Hades (Acts 2:24; Heb. 2:14; Rev. 1:18).

Although Satan continues to hold the unsaved in death's power, this is only temporary, for the Lord will raise them from their graves (Jn. 5:28-29). Also, the Lord will deliver His people from death (Heb. 2:15; I Cor. 15:51-57).

---

[21] The resurrection of the redeemed, which is called "the first resurrection" (Rev. 20:5-6; Jn. 5:28-29), includes three resurrection events: one, that of the dead church saints (I Thess. 4:16); two, the precross saints (Lk. 13:28; Gen. 17:8; 28:13; Heb. 11:13; Dan. 12:2-3; Ezek. 34:23-24); and three, the Tribulation Period martyrs (Rev. 20:4; cp. 6:9-11; 7:9-17; 12:17; 13:7, 15; 15:2). The word "first" (Rev. 20:5) concerns the kind of resurrection events rather than their number (cp. Jn. 5:28-29). "The second resurrection" will be that of the unsaved after our Lord's millennial rule (Rev. 20:6, 12; cp. Jn. 5:28-29).

Since He has conquered His enemies and will live forever, Jesus will bring all His enemies to their final doom (I Cor. 15:25-26; Rev. 20:10, 13-15).

Two, the Lord's resurrection guarantees the resurrection and judgment of the unsaved (Jn. 5:28-29; Acts 17:31). Their judgment is certain, for the Judge is alive and Satan, their leader, has been judged (Jn. 16:11). Paul preached this truth to pagans (Acts 24:25).

d. Its importance to His new world order

Our Lord's resurrection will allow Him to fulfill all of the Scriptural predictions about the new world order that He will establish when He rules over the earth (Acts 3:20-21; cp. Isa. 11:1-9).

e. Its importance to salvational faith

Belief in our Lord's resurrection is an essential part of salvational faith (Rom. 10:9), for His resurrection gave value to His atoning work. Paul argued that if Christ did not rise, then the gospel would be false, being without content (I Cor. 15:14-15) and ineffective (vss. 16-19); also, faith in such a gospel would be futile and they who have trusted Christ would be still in their sins. There is nothing to trust for salvation if Jesus did not rise from the dead. But since He did rise from the dead, the gospel is true and the atonement of which it speaks is effective toward all who receive the Saviour (vs. 20). The apostles in their preaching emphasized the Lord's resurrection as well as His atoning death (Acts 2:24-33; 3:15; 4:33; 5:30; 10:40-41; 13:30; 17:3, 18, 31; 28:31). No one is saved who rejects the truth of Jesus' physical resurrection, for a saviour still dead is not a saviour at all.

• His Ascension into Heaven

1. ITS DEFINITION

Forty days after His resurrection the Lord Jesus, as man, departed physically and visibly from the earth and was immediately received into Heaven (Mk. 16:19-20; Lk. 24:50-53; Acts 1:6-12; I Tim. 3:16).

2. ITS FEATURES

a. Like His resurrection the Lord's ascension was a human experience, which transferred His human residence to Heaven (Heb. 4:14-15; 1:3). However, as God He is everywhere present on earth (Jn. 3:13; Mt. 28:20).

b. His ascension was not merely a disappearance or a change of state but an actual passing from earth to Heaven, where He was received by the Father (Acts 1:9; see vs. 11; 2:33; 3:21; 7:55-56; Rom. 8:34; Eph. 1:20; Phil. 3:20; I Thess. 1:10; 4:16; I Tim. 3:16; Heb. 8:1; 9:24; 10:12; 12:2; Rev. 5:5-12; 19:11).

c. He ascended forty days after His resurrection (Acts 1:3-9). Some teach that He also ascended to Heaven and returned to earth on His resurrection day, as implied in John 20:17 and Hebrews 9:6-12. Support for this view is the typology of the high priest's entering the Holy of Holies on Atonement Day and his sprinkling the sacrificial blood upon the mercy seat (Lev. 16:14). It is argued that, in a similar way, Christ went to Heaven and presented the blood of His sacrifice before the Father.[22]

If this is true, how could He say that His work was finished while He was still on the cross (Jn. 19:30)? We read in Hebrews 9:12 (Gk.) that He entered into the Holy Place "through" His blood, not "with" it. I believe that His shed blood went into the ground when it had accomplished the divine purpose. The Lord's words to Mary Magdalene (Jn. 20:17) can be translated, "Stop clinging to me." Her spontaneous action was improper and stands in contrast to that of the other women who worshiped at His feet (Mt. 28:9). In His exalted state the Lord no longer has the same relation with His people as He did when He was with them during His earthly ministry (cp. Jn. 14:20).[23]

3. ITS IMPORTANCE

a. It marked the end of His first advent and earthly mission (Jn. 17:4). He did all that He came to do.

b. It made possible His present human work in Heaven. This includes His building the church on earth through His people on earth (Mt. 16:18; I Cor. 6:15; 12:27; Eph. 4:11-12), His governing the church (Eph. 1:22), His preparing a place for His people (Jn. 14:2), His acting as our intercessor and advocate (Heb. 7:25; I Jn. 2:1), and His communicating His life to His people (Jn. 14:6; Col. 3:4).

c. It allowed the localized Christ as man to become universal in the lives and ministries of His people (Jn. 14:20). He does this through a union with His people that is effected by the baptism with and indwelling of the Holy Spirit (Gal. 3:27; Jn. 14:16-18). Because the bodies of His people on earth are His members, (I Cor. 6:15), the Lord Jesus as a man can build His church on earth while He himself is seated at the Father's right hand in Heaven.

d. It allowed the Holy Spirit to perform His work during this dispensation, which includes regeneration, baptism, anointing, indwelling, and the giving of N.T. revelation (Jn. 16:7; see Jn. 3:3-6; Acts 1:5, 8; Jn. 14:16; 16:13).

- **His Enthronement**

1. ITS DEFINITION

As man the Lord Jesus was given the position of highest rank at the Father's right hand, far above all created beings and things and their authority (Acts 2:33; Heb. 1:3; Rom. 14:9).

2. ITS FEATURES

a. This exalted position concerns Jesus as man, not as God. When He took upon Himself the nature of man, God the Son assumed in His humanity a position lower than His servants, the holy angels (Heb. 2:9). With His

---

[22] It appears that the cross was the altar upon which the divine atonement was made. The Father was there, making Jesus' soul an offering for sin (Isa. 53:10), delivering Him up for us all (Rom. 8:32), and reconciling the world unto Himself (II Cor. 5:19).

[23] See John F. Walvoord, *Jesus Christ Our Lord*, pp. 220 f.

enthronement at the Father's right hand, the Lord Jesus was exalted to the highest position, far above all angelic and human beings and their authority (Eph. 1:20-22; I Pet. 3:22). With this exaltation, Jesus was exalted in His humanity to be Lord of all (Acts 2:36; 10:36; Phil. 2:9-11).

b. Although He is so exalted, the Lord Jesus as man remains the Father's Servant (slave) forever, in keeping with His continuing role as the Messiah (I Cor. 15:28).

3. ITS IMPORTANCE

a. Jesus' enthronement marked the completion of His glorification as a man. This glorification consists of His moral glory (Jn. 1:14), His physical glory (Phil. 3:21; Acts 26:13), and His achievement glory. The last includes His being the Mediator of the New Covenant (Heb. 12:24), the Redeemer of God's people (Rev. 5:5-10), and the Builder of the church (Mt. 16:18). In addition to these glories He also has positional glory since He occupies the place of supreme authority, far above all created persons, creatures, and things (Phil. 2:9-11). In His humanity He is now "Lord of all" (Acts 10:36) and is worthy of the highest honor (Jn. 5:23; Phil. 2:10-11; Rev. 5:8-14).

b. His people will share in all of these glories (Jn. 17:22, 24), including that of His achievement glory. However, this glory will be that which is restricted to our working with Him in the building of the church (Jn. 17:22, 24; cp. Phil. 3:20-21; Eph. 5:27; 2:7; I Thess. 2:19-20; I Cor. 15:49).

• His Second Coming to Earth

Unlike His first coming to earth, Jesus' second advent and millennial rule will be with power and great glory, marking the final phase of His exaltation (Mt. 24:30; II Thess. 1:7-10). As the earth was the scene of His great humiliation, so will it be that of His triumphant exaltation. He will come as "the Lion of the tribe of Judah" (Rev. 5:5) and as "the King of kings and the Lord of lords" (Rev. 19:16) to destroy His enemies and to rule over His people in fulfillment of the great covenant promises (Rev. 19:11-15; Rom. 11:26-27). His house will be exalted above all others (Isa. 2:2), and His rule will be without parallel in human history (Isa. 11:1-9). This, as well as the other aspects of His exaltation, will glorify God the Father (Phil. 2:11; Jn. 12:28; 13:31; 17:1).

THE MESSIANIC WORK OF JESUS

Our understanding of Jesus' life and work as man rests upon our grasping the meaning of His being "the Christ" or "the Messiah." As we examine this truth, let us look to the Holy Spirit to illuminate and bless our hearts.

HIS BEING THE MESSIAH

• The Meaning of This Title

As an official title of Jesus (Mt. 1:1; Lk. 2:11), the word "Messiah" (from the Hebrew) or "Christ" (from the Greek) means "Anointed One." This title points us to the Old Testament practice of anointing prophets (I Ki. 19:16), high priests (Ex. 29:7; Lev. 8:12), and kings (I Sam. 9:21-10:1) with oil.

• The Significance of His Anointing

1. THE MEANING OF ANOINTING

The meaning of the anointing rite is revealed in Saumel's anointing young David to be king of Israel (I Sam. 16:1, 13). Here the anointing rite represented God's appointment of a person to an office (vs. 1). It also represented God's giving to the anointed person the Holy Spirit for divine enablement for the duties of his office (vs. 13). Essentially, this anointing action represented God's consecration of a person to service (Ex. 28:41; 40:9-15; Lev. 8:10-12) such as those vocations (prophet, priest, and king) that required this anointing.

The anointing oil was a symbol of the Holy Spirit, who set apart the anointed person unto God's service and who empowered him to do God's will in his divinely appointed office (I Sam. 16:13). After his grievous sin with Bathsheba, David was concerned with the possibility of losing his anointing and thus his kingdom as Saul had lost his (I Sa. 16:14; Ps. 51:11).

2. THE MEANING OF JESUS' ANOINTING

One, by His anointing Jesus as man was appointed by God the Father to the office of servant, or slave (Acts 4:27). This is the teaching of N.T. revelation (Phil. 2:7-8; cp. Jn. 6:38; 8:28-29; 17:4) and of O.T. prophecy (Isa. 42:1-2; 49:1-6; 52:13 – 53:12).

Two, as man Jesus now does all of His Messianic work in the power of the Holy Spirit rather than in His own inherent divine power (Acts 10:38; cp. 1:2; Lk. 4:1, 14; 5:17; Mt. 12:28; Isa. 42:1-7; 61:1-2 with Lk. 4:16-21; Rom. 15:19).

Three, all of Jesus' Messianic work is done in union with the Father to the extent that this work is actually that of the Father in and through Him (Jn. 5:17, 19-20, 30; 14:8-11).

Four, Jesus as man was set apart by His anointing from a secular vocation of private life to the work that He came into the world to do (Mk. 6:3; Mt. 20:28). After His anointing, Jesus never returned to His carpentry work and private life in Nazareth.

• The Time of His Anointing

Jesus received His anointing as the Messiah at His water baptism when the Holy Spirit descended upon Him (Lk. 3:21-22). Witnessing this event, John the Baptizer declared that the Holy Spirit descended upon Jesus and remained on Him (Jn. 1:32-33).

In this case, the symbolic medium of anointing was water, not oil as in the O.T. examples (cp. Jn. 7:37-39). Jesus' submission to baptism and His praying (Lk. 3:21) represented His complete surrender to the anointing work of the Holy Spirit and to all that this anointing meant. Jesus gladly and willingly assumed this permanent, subordinate human role of being the Father's slave

(Heb. 10:5-7). The Father responded favorably to Jesus' obedience to this rite (Mt. 3:17), for He had chosen Jesus for this office (Isa. 42:1; I Pet. 2:4).

With this event marking the division between His private life as a citizen of Nazareth and His public ministry as the Messiah, Jesus went forth to do His divinely appointed work. It was His resolution to do all of the Father's will and to glorify Him in everything (Jn. 4:34; 6:38; 8:29; 12:28; 17:4).

HIS WORK AS THE MESSIAH

As the Servant of the Father, Jesus is carrying out His Messianic work in the roles of Prophet, High Priest, and King, as suggested by those who were anointed in the Old Testament period. His Messianic work covers the time of His first advent to earth, the present time of His absence, and the period of His second advent. It also relates to more than His dealings with Israel. It embraces all that the Father has given Him to do as man in order that He might accomplish certain divine objectives (see pp. 461 f.).

- **Jesus' Work as Prophet (Deut. 18:18; Heb. 1:1-2)**

A prophet was not essentially a preacher or a teacher; he was God's spokesman. He was one through whom God spoke His Word. As the Prophet greater than Moses, Jesus spoke the words of the Father (Jn. 8:28; 14:10, 24).

He did this during His first advent in all His teaching and preaching (Jn. 3:34; 7:15-17; 12:49-50). He said only what the Father directed Him to say and gave forth the Father's words.

During His present absence from earth He has given His servants the New Testament revelation (Jn. 16:12-15; Eph. 4:20-21; I Tim. 6:3; Rev. 1:1-2), by which the Father speaks to us (Heb. 1:1-2) and makes known His will for us today (II Tim. 3:16-17).

When He comes to earth again to rule, He will give whatever divine revelation is needed, in addition to the Bible, to make known God's stewardship (dispensation) for earth dwellers during the kingdom (Isa. 2:1-3).

- **Jesus' Work as High Priest (Ps. 110:4; Heb. 5:5-6; 4:14)**

The basic function of the high priest in Israel was to be a mediator between God and the people. As a mediator his work included teaching (Deut. 33:8-10; II Chron. 15:3), offering sacrifices for the sins of the nation (Lev. 16:3-16), and making intercessory prayer (I Sam. 12:23). The Lord Jesus also does these things.

Jesus exercised these priestly functions during His first advent. He taught the people about God (Mt. 9:35; Lk. 19:47); He gave Himself for our sins (Mt. 20:28; Heb. 9:14); and He prayed for His people (Jn. 17:9-24; Lk. 22:31-32).

During His present absence from earth, the Lord Jesus is teaching His people by means of the Scriptures (Eph. 4:20-21; Col. 3:16). Moreover, having given Himself for our sins, He is now distributing the benefits of His atoning work to those who trust Him as their Saviour, according to the promises of the New Covenant (Jn. 6:35, 47: Heb. 9:11-15). Finally, He unceasingly makes intercession for His people (Heb. 7:25). This means that He prays for them and attends to all of their needs during their pilgrimage in this world (Jn. 17:9-24; Lk. 22:31-32). His present work of building the church involves the priestly functions of evangelism, saving those who believe the gospel, baptizing them into the church by the Holy Spirit, and teaching them God's truth.

When He returns and rules over the earth, He will continue the priestly functions that He is doing today (Ps. 110:4; Heb. 5:6; 7:24-25; Zech. 6:12-13).

- **Jesus' Work as King (II Sam. 7:10-16; Isa. 9:6-7; Lk. 1:31-32; Jer. 23:5)**

Revelation 19:15 indicates that Jesus' regal functions are to rule and to judge. The executive, legislative, and judicial branches of government unite in Him.

His regal work during His first advent did not concern itself with politics (Jn. 18:36-37) or with the execution of divine judgment (Jn. 3:17). He did, however, rule over nature (Mk. 4:39-41), demons (Mk. 1:32-34), disease (vs. 34), and the lives of people who were committed to Him (Mk. 1:17-18).

During His present absence from earth, the Lord Jesus is the Head of the church, which He is now building (Eph. 1:22-23; 4:15-16). He is also the believer's King since all who are saved are members of His kingdom, in its present spiritual, non-political form (Col. 1:13). Being Lord of all, He is the Sovereign of His people as well as the Potentate of the universe (Acts 10:36; I Tim. 6:14-15)

When He returns to the earth, He will judge His enemies and will rule the world for a thousand years (Rev. 19:11-16; 20:4; Ps. 2:6-9; 72:8-11; Isa. 11:1-9; Zech. 14:9).

These activities represent our Lord's Messianic work in keeping with the Father's present program for humanity. In the ages to come (Eph. 2:7), our Lord will continue these Messianic roles in other programs which the Father has for Him. He will forever convey divine revelation, function as high priest, and govern His people. All who are saved will work with Him in these unrevealed programs.

SOME DESIGNATIONS OF CHRIST JESUS

Designations are names and titles that are ascribed to the Lord Jesus Christ in the Scriptures.

HIS GENERIC NAMES

Generic names describe one's kind of being.

1. He is called "God" in the Old Testament (Isa. 9:6; 7:14; Ps. 45:6-7) and in the New Testament (Rom. 9:5; I Tim. 3:16; Heb. 1:8; I Jn. 5:20).

2. With His incarnation, He is also called "man" (I Tim. 2:5).

HIS FUNCTIONAL NAMES

These are titles which relate to His offices and works.

1. Some Old Testament Titles
    a. Those relating to His deity
"Lord," meaning "My Master" (*Adonai,* Ps. 110:1); "Son" (Ps. 2:7); and "Father of eternity" (Isa. 9:6).
    b. Those prophetically relating to His humanity
"The Branch" (Isa. 11:1; Jer. 33:15), "Counselor" (Isa. 9:6), "Immanuel" (7:14), "King" (Ps. 2:6), "Messiah" (Dan. 9:26), "Priest" (Ps. 110:4), "the Prince of peace" (Isa. 9:6), "the Prophet" (Deut. 18:15-18), "the Seed" (Gen. 3:15; 15:5), "the Servant of the LORD" (Isa. 42:1), "the Son of man" (Dan. 7:13), "the Stone" (Ps. 118:22), and "Wonderful" (Isa. 9:6).

2. Some New Testament Titles
    a. Those relating to His deity
"Lord" in O.T. quotations referring to *Adonai* (Mt. 22:43-45 with Ps. 110:1), "the Word" (Jn. 1:1-3, 14); "Son" (Mt. 3:17); and "the Son of God" (Mt. 26:63-65; cp. Jn. 10:33, 36; 20:31).
    b. Those relating to His humanity
"Apostle and High Priest" (Heb. 3:1), "the Bread from Heaven" (Jn. 6:32), "Christ" meaning "Anointed One" (Acts 2:36), "the Door" (Jn. 10:9), "the Faithful Witness," "the First Begotten of the dead," and "the Prince of the kings of the earth" (Rev. 1:5), "the Good Shepherd" (Jn. 10:11), "Judge" (Acts 10:42), "the King of kings and the Lord of lords (Rev. 19:16), "the Lamb of God" (Jn. 1:29), "the Last Adam" (I Cor. 15:45), "the Light of the world" (Jn. 8:12), "the Lion of the Tribe of Judah" (Rev. 5:5), "Lord" (*Kurios,* Acts 2:36; 10:36) referring to His human exaltation to supremacy in authority and power, "Lord" (*Despotes* II Pet. 2:1; Jude 4) referring to His absolute ownership, "Master" meaning "Teacher" (Mt. 8:19), "the Resurrection and the Life" (Jn. 11:25), "the Rock" (Mt. 16:18), "Saviour" meaning "Deliverer" (Phil. 3:20), "the Second Man" (I Cor. 15:47), "the Son of Man" speaking of His identification with mankind (Mk. 10:45), "the True Vine" (Jn. 15:1), "the Way, the Truth, and the Life" (Jn. 14:6).

HIS PERSONAL NAMES

A personal name is that which distinguishes one from others within a given order or class of beings.

1. Before His Incarnation
The personal name for God in the Old Testament is "LORD" (*Yahweh,* or *Jehovah;* Jer. 33:2). That this was the personal name of God the Son is seen in Isaiah 2:2-5; 40:3, 10, "GOD"; and Jeremiah 23:6.

2. Since His Incarnation
    a. With reference to His deity

He is called "Lord" in Luke 2:11, which seems to be a reference to the O.T. divine personal name "LORD," or *Yahweh* (see Mt. 3:3 and Jn. 1:23 with Isa. 40:3). As with the other Persons of the Godhead (the Father and the Holy Spirit), the title "Son" in N.T. usage possibly may be a divine personal name, especially when it occurs alone without other designations (I Cor. 15:28; Gal. 4:4, 6; I Thess. 1:10).

    b. With reference to His humanity

    His human personal name is "Jesus" (Mt. 1:21; Lk. 1:31; 2:21).

His full human name is "the Lord Jesus Christ" (I Thess. 1:1), "Jesus Christ our Lord" (Rom. 5:21), or "Christ Jesus our Lord" (I Cor. 15:31). While "Jesus" is His human personal name and "Christ" is a human title which speaks of His being the "Anointed One," "Lord" (Gk. Kupios) in this case is a human title that means "one who has power, or authority" (Abbott-Smith). This is the title of Jesus' human exaltation (Phil. 2:9-11; Acts 2:36; 10:36). Needless to say, being God, He is also "Lord" (*Adonai*) in the Old Testament sense (Mt. 22:41-45; Ps. 110:1; cp. I Cor. 15:47).

What a wonderful Saviour and Lord we have! May we increasingly live unto Him and allow Him to work and to manifest His character through our lives so that others may be attracted to His light and life.

A Reveiw of Christology

1. What does the deity of Christ mean?
2. What basic truths bear witness to His deity?
3. What does His being "the Word" mean?
4. What do "First Begotten" and "Only Begotten Son" mean?
5. What is the meaning of eternal preexistence?
6. Why does the Son have the same attributes as the Father?
7. What works of the Son bear witness to His deity?
8. What assertions did He make that speak of His deity?
9. Give the names of five people who bore witness to Christ's deity.
10. What does the humanity of Christ mean?
11. What does the condescension of God the Son emphasize?
12. What is the meaning of His incarnation?
13. What is the basic idea of His self-emptying?
14. Why would it be erroneous to say that in His self-emptying Jesus laid aside some of His divine attributes?
15. Who was the father of Christ's human nature? Who was the father of His divine nature?
16. Of what parts did our Lord's new human nature consist?
17. How was His human nature different from ours?
18. Why was Mary not the mother of God? Of what was she the mother?
19. What was the importance of Christ's virgin conception and birth as it related to His saviourhood? Kingship?
20. Explain the doctrine of the hypostatic union of the two natures in Jesus. What is the hypostasis of this union?
21. How could the Lord Jesus have limited knowledge and yet have at the same time unlimited knowledge?
22. Why could Jesus not sin?
23. Give several ways which show the importance of Jesus' unique human character.
24. How long did, or will, Christ possess His human nature?
25. What is the meaning of Jesus' humiliation?
26. What is the theological idea of atonement?
27. Why must atonement be made for human sins before God could save people from their sins?
28. Jesus' atoning work was substitutionary and satisfactory. What do these terms mean?

29. What is the meaning of propitious and provisional?

30. What is the value that Jesus secured for all people by His atoning work and that is now offered through the gospel?

31. Since Jesus died for everyone, why will not everyone be saved?

32. Why could not God take a perfect human being from among men to be our substitute?

33. What two kinds of death did Jesus experience on the cross? Which of these was associated with divine wrath?

34. What was unique about His physical death?

35. Why was the crucifixion of Jesus man's greatest crime against God?

36. What five things did Jesus accomplish while He was on the cross?

37. By His death Jesus confirmed the divine condemnation of God's enemies. What were these enemies?

38. How is this confirmation of condemnation helpful to us who are saved?

39. What is the New Covenant that Jesus mediated by His death?

40. Explain how our Lord's atoning work is unlimited and how it is limited.

41. What is the theological meaning of the blood of Christ?

42. Give some of the blessings that saved people have because of His blood in its theological sense.

43. In establishing the atonement, why did God include the shedding of blood when the wages of sin is death?

44. Some say that we can be healed physically through faith just as we are saved through faith. Why is this view in error?

45. What is the theological importance of Jesus' burial?

46. Give the four steps in Jesus' exaltation.

47. Define each of these steps and describe their importance. How do each of these benefit to us?

48. How did Jesus' resurrection differ from those who were earlier restored to life?

49. How many days after His resurrection did Jesus ascend to Heaven? Was this a divine or a human experience?

50. What outstanding event did He experience in His humanity upon His return to Heaven?

51. What did anointing in O.T. times mean?

52. What does the anointing medium (oil or water) represent?

53. When was Jesus anointed? To what office was His appointed? How long will He continue in this office?

54. In what roles is He now fulfilling this office?

55. Explain His activities in carrying out these roles: when He was here, during His present absence, and when He comes to earth again.

56. What are Christ's generic names?

57. What are some of His titles in the Old Testament?

58. What are some of His divine titles in the New Testament? His human titles?

59. What was His personal name before His incarnation?

60. What is His divine personal names since His incarnation? His human personal name?

61. What is the meaning of "the Lord Jesus Christ"?

62. Is your trust in Jesus' atoning work for your salvation?

Pneumatology

PNEUMATOLOGY
The Doctrine of God the Holy Spirit

With the growing emphasis on the work of the Holy Spirit and the spreading influence of the charismatic movement, it is urgent for the Lord's people to understand what the Bible teaches about this wonderful Person and His activity. It is Satan's strategy to deceive the unwary by part-truth doctrine and counterfeit experience, which are widely accepted as being of God. A careful study of the Bible's teaching about the Holy Spirit will help us to avoid error and to cooperate with Him, so that He will be able to do His work in and through our lives.

THE NATURE OF THE HOLY SPIRIT

This concerns who and what He is. He is a Person and He is God.

HE IS A PERSON.
Unitarians, false cultists, and company deny the personhood (personality) of the Holy Spirit. But the Bible teaches otherwise, though the word "spirit" has neuter gender in the Greek New Testament. The personhood of the Holy Spirit is manifested by the following propositions:

• He possesses certain features of personhood, including a unique selfhood that is seen in His self-awareness (Acts 13:2, "me," "I") and self-determination (I Cor. 12:11); individuality (Jn. 14:26); moral awareness (Acts 5:3; Rom. 1:4; Gal. 5:16-17); and perpetuity (Heb. 9:14). Other qualities that are often attributed to personal beings are found in Him, such as intelligence (I Cor. 2:10-12), emotion (Rom. 15:30; Eph. 4:30), and will (Acts 13:2, 4).

• He does work that only persons can do, such as teaching (Jn. 14:26), reproving or convicting (Jn. 16:8), interceding (Rom. 8:26), and calling (Rev. 22:17), and bearing witness (Rom. 8:16).

• His responses to human actions and needs indicate His personhood, such as His grieving over sin (Eph. 4:30), His giving satisfaction (Jn. 7:37-39), His helping (Jn. 14:16), and His imparting power (Gal. 5:16; Acts 1:8; Eph. 1:19).

• Certain things may be done to the Holy Spirit which point to His personhood, such as His being obeyed (Acts 10:19-21), lied to (Acts 5:3), resisted (Acts 7:51), blasphemed (Mt. 12:31), and insulted (Heb. 10:29).

• Both John and Paul sometimes use masculine pronouns for Him, contrary to normal Greek usage ("spirit" is neuter). A masculine demonstrative pronoun occurs in John 15:26; 16:13-14. A masculine relative pronoun is used in Ephesians 1:14. The masculine personal pronoun is used in John 16:7.

- His relation to other persons indicates His personhood, such as to Christ (Jn. 16:14) and believers (Acts 15:28; 16:6-7).

These evidences of personhood show that the Holy Spirit is more than an impersonal influence. In all of our thinking about Him and our relationship with Him we should regard Him to be a Person as we are persons.

HE IS GOD.

The Holy Spirit is a Person who possesses the divine nature, which makes Him to be God. Like His personhood (personality), the deity of the Holy Spirit is also widely denied today. That He is God is shown by the following:

- **He is called God.**

Peter refers to the Holy Spirit as being God (Acts 5:3-4). Paul writes of Him as "the Spirit of our God" (I Cor. 6:11), "the Lord is the Spirit," and "the Spirit of the Lord" (II Cor. 3:17-18). His indwelling His people, "the temple of God," also indicates that He is God (I Cor. 3:16). See Jeremiah 31:31-34 with Hebrews 10:15-18; Judges 15:14 with 16:20; Matthew 12:28 with Luke 11:20.

- **He has the attributes of God.**

These are life (Rom. 8:2; Jn. 3:5-6), eternality (Heb. 9:14), omnipresence (Ps. 139:7; I Cor. 6:19), omnipotence (Job 33:4; Ps. 104:30; Gen. 1:2), omniscience (I Cor. 2:10-11; Jn. 16:13), truthfulness (Jn. 14:17; 15:26; 16:13; I Jn. 2:27; 5:6), holiness (Rom. 1:4), righteousness (Rom. 8:4), grace (Heb. 10:29), love (Rom. 15:30; 5:5), and sovereignty (I Cor. 12:11; Acts 10:19-20).

- **He does the work of God.**

The Holy Spirit was active in creation (Gen. 1:2; Ps. 33:6; Job 26:13); He inspired the prophets (II Pet. 1:21); He brought about the conception of Jesus' human nature (Lk. 1:35); and He produces the new birth (Jn. 3:3-8).

These Scriptural evidences point to the fact that the Holy Spirit is God in every respect as are the other Members of the Trinity.

THE HOLY SPIRIT'S RELATION TO THE OTHER MEMBERS OF THE TRINITY

Being God, the Holy Spirit is equal to the other Persons of the Godhead in His nature and in the extent of His attributes since the three Persons commonly possess the single, divine nature. However, regarding subordination the Holy Spirit has the following rank: One, that based on the internal relationship of the Persons (ontological subordination) — the Holy Spirit proceeds from the Father through the Son and thus is third in order (Mt. 28:19). And two, that based on the external work of the Persons (economical subordination) — the Holy Spirit is the Dynamic Cause, or the means by whom the Son carries out the will of the Father as determined by the divine decree (cp. creation, Job 26:13; Ps. 33:6; Gen. 1:2; and revelation, Jn. 16:12-15; II Pet. 1:21).

The relation of the Holy Spirit to the other Persons of the Godhead is expressed theologically by the terms *spiration* and *procession*. *Spiration* represents the process by which the Father through the Son[1] communicates to the Holy Spirit the divine nature in such a way that each Person wholly possesses it and that there is but one God. *Procession* represents the result of this process.

DESIGNATIONS OF THE HOLY SPIRIT

These designations are titles that are ascribed to the Holy Spirit in the Scriptures. I do not know of any generic name such as "God" for the Holy Spirit in the Old or New Testaments although He is identified as being God in both Testaments (Gen. 1:2; I Cor. 3:16). Also, I do not know of any personal name that is attributed directly to Him in either Testament. Possibly, the titles "Holy Spirit," "the Spirit of God," or "the Spirit of the LORD" are used as personal names in certain contexts (cp. Jn. 14:26). Consider the following titles that are descriptive of His relationships, attributes, and works.

THOSE DESCRIBING HIS RELATIONSHIPS

- **To the Father**
  Spirit of God (Mt. 3:16), Spirit of our God (I Cor. 6:11), Spirit of the LORD (Isa. 59:19), Spirit of your Father (Mt. 10:20), Spirit of the living God (II Cor. 3:3); and Spirit of the Lord GOD (Isa. 61:1).

- **To the Son**
  Spirit of Christ (Rom. 8:9), Spirit of Jesus Christ (Phil. 1:19), Spirit of His Son (Gal. 4:6). These are not references to Jesus' human spirit (cp. Jn. 14:16, 26), nor do they imply that there is more than one divine Spirit (cp. I Cor. 12:11, 13; Eph. 4:4). They refer to the Third Person of the Trinity. These designations may derive from the fact that Jesus' spiritual life is conveyed to His people at salvation by the Holy Spirit who regenerates them (Jn. 3:6; Tit. 3:5).

THOSE DESCRIBING HIS ATTRIBUTES

One Spirit (Eph. 4:4), the Lord the Spirit (II Cor. 3:18, Gk.), eternal Spirit (Heb. 9:14), Spirit of glory and of God (I Pet. 4:14), Spirit of life (Rom. 8:2), Spirit of holiness (Rom. 1:4), Spirit of wisdom and revelation (Eph. 1:17), Spirit of truth (Jn. 14:17), Spirit of grace (Heb. 10:29).

THOSE DESCRIBING HIS WORKS

Spirit of adoption (Rom. 8:15), Spirit of faith (II Cor. 4:13), Comforter or Helper (Jn. 14:16), the Anointing (I Jn. 2:27). Isaiah 11:2 indicates some of the

---

[1] At the Council of Frankfort (794) the Western Church adopted the view that this procession was from the Father and the Son. The Eastern Church retained the original concept that it is from the Father through the Son.

Holy Spirit's ministries to the Lord Jesus during His millennial rule. He will give to Jesus wisdom, understanding, counsel, might, knowledge, and the fear of the LORD.

SYMBOLS AND THEOPHANIES OF THE HOLY SPIRIT

SOME SYMBOLS

Symbols are things that represent something else. Some symbols of the Holy Spirit are oil (I Sam. 16:13; Heb. 1:9), an earnest[2] (II Cor. 1:22; Eph. 1:14), a seal[3] (Eph. 1:13; 4:30), and water (Jn. 3:5; 4:14; 7:38-39).

SOME THEOPHANIES

A theophany is a temporary appearance of God in some visible form. Several theophanies of the Holy Spirit are a dove (Mt. 3:16; Jn. 1:32), wind and fire (Acts 2:2-4).

"The seven Spirits" (Rev. 4:5) perhaps is a figurative expression indicating the Spirit's simultaneous presence and work in each of the seven churches in the province of Asia (2:7, 11, 17, 29; 3:6, 13, 22) or in the Messiah (Isa. 11:2).

THE WORK OF THE HOLY SPIRIT

It is supremely important to understand the work of the Holy Spirit, especially that which relates to the present time. The following surveys His work in eternity past as well as throughout human history.

HIS WORK IN ETERNITY PAST

Together with the other Members of the Godhead, the Holy Spirit was active in formulating the divine decree (cp. Gen. 1:26; Acts 2:23; 4:28; Eph. 1:11). This means that He is involved in the total work of God, not only in devising the decree but also in administering it. This includes the aspects of the decree which concern creation, preservation, providence, revelation, and salvation.

HIS WORK DURING THE OLD TESTAMENT PERIOD

Keep in mind the roles that the Persons of the Godhead have with reference to their dealings with the universe: God the Father is the Originating Cause of all things (I Cor. 8:6), God the Son is the Instrumental Cause of all things (6), and God the Holy Spirit is the Dynamic Cause of all things. In all of the transitive actions of the Trinity, God the Father works through God the Son by the power of the Holy Spirit.

---

[2] In purchases an earnest is a token or pledge such as a down-payment, which assures that the balance will be paid.

[3] This is a device that bears a design which can impart an impression on a soft substance, such as clay or wax. It also designates the substance which has received the impression. As we shall see, a seal may indicate authority, ownership, security, or a finished transaction.

- **Regarding Creation**

  That the Holy Spirit was active with the other Members of the Godhead in the work of creation is stated in the Scriptures (Gen. 1:2; Job 26:13; 33:4; Ps. 33:6; 104:29-30; Isa. 40:12-14). This is also implied in the plural designation "God" (Elohim) and the personal pronoun "us," which point to the plurality of the Members of the Godhead (Gen. 1:1, 26).

- **Regarding Divine Revelation**

  The Holy Spirit enabled certain men to receive God's special revelation and to convey it orally or to record it verbally, without error or omission, as the very Word of God. This work of the Holy Spirit upon men is divine inspiration (see II Pet. 1:21; II Sam. 23:1-2; Mic. 3:8; Acts 1:16; 28:25; I Cor. 2:13; Heb. 10:15).

- **Regarding Men**

  1. *His striving with men*

  The LORD said, "My Spirit shall not always strive with men" (Gen. 6:3). While the meaning of the Hebrew word which is translated "strive" is uncertain, some believe that it refers to the Holy Spirit's striving with men to restrain them from their evil ways.[4] The moral character of mankind had so deteriorated that God determined to cease this striving and to destroy the human race in 120 years (cp. Rom. 1:24, 28; in the future, II Thess. 2:6-7).

  2. *His helping men*

  The Holy Spirit came upon people, or anointed them, for the purpose of enabling them for some ministry (Judg. 13:25; 14:6, 19; 15:14; 16:20; I Sam. 16:13). He also filled certain people for special work (Ex. 31:3; 35:31). He even entered some but not permanently (Ezek. 2:2; 3:24).

  Although He did not indwell people permanently as He does today, the Holy Spirit was with His people (Jn. 14:17; cp. Ps. 139:7-10; Dan. 4:8-9, 18; 5:11-12). He was with them to do many of the things that He does for us today such as giving understanding (Neh. 9:20), wisdom (Ex. 31:1-6), administrative ability (Num. 11:16-17; Deut. 34:9; I Sam. 16:13), physical strength (Judg. 14:19), and the ability to do miracles (II Ki. 2:9-15). After his sin with Bathsheba, David feared losing his anointing to rule over Israel, as Saul had lost his (Ps. 51:11; cp. I Sam. 16:13-14). The Holy Spirit enabled these precross saints to walk with God and to serve Him.

HIS WORK DURING THE SON'S INCARNATION

With the coming of God the Son into the world, the person and work of both the Son and the Holy Spirit were brought into focus to a greater degree than ever before (cp. II Tim. 1:10). The Holy Spirit had, and will forever have, a very important part in the life and ministry of Jesus as a man.

---

[4] H. C. Leupold, *Exposition of Genesis* (Grand Rapids: Baker Book House, 1953), p. 256.

- **Jesus' Conception (Mt. 1:20; Lk. 1:35)**

  The conception of Jesus' human nature came about by the generative act of the Holy Spirit rather than by the agency of a man. In a manner beyond our understanding, He made of Mary's substance a complete, sinless human nature, which was assumed by God the Son at the time of this unique conception. By this God the Son became man. He is forever the God-man.

- **Jesus' Private Life (Lk. 2:40)**

  Although it is nowhere stated what Jesus' relationship to the Holy Spirit was throughout His private life in Nazareth, the fact that God's grace was upon Him implies that His life was affected by this divine Person (Heb. 10:29). We know that He pleased the Father during these years (Mt. 3:17).

- **Jesus' Messianic Work (Lk. 4:16-21)**

  At His baptism Jesus received the anointing of the Holy Spirit for His Messianic work (Lk. 3:21-22; Jn. 1:32; 3:34). This means that as man Jesus began to do all that the Father had commissioned Him in the power of the Holy Spirit (Acts 10:38; Isa. 42:1; 61:1; cp. Mt. 12:28; Lk. 4:1, 14). The Holy Spirit will forever enable Jesus to work in obedience to the Father (Isa. 11:1-5).

- **Jesus' Death (Heb. 9:14)**

  The Holy Spirit enabled Jesus to endure the sufferings that were inflicted on Him by the Father (Mt. 27:46; Isa. 53:5-10) and man (Mt. 26:67; 27:26-35) and to lay down His life for our sins (Jn. 10:18; Mt. 20:28).

- **Jesus' Resurrection (Rom. 8:11)**

  In cooperation with the Father (Gal. 1:1) and the Son (Jn. 10:18), the Holy Spirit participated in bringing about Jesus' resurrection from the dead (cp. Eph. 1:17-20). He is the new life principle that now animates Jesus' resurrected body and will animate the changed bodies of His people (cp. I Cor. 15:44).

- **Jesus' Ascension and Enthronement (Eph. 1:17-22)**

  As man Jesus ascended into Heaven and sat down at the Father's right hand by the power of the Holy Spirit.

- **Jesus' Building of the Church (Mt. 3:11; 16:18; Acts 1:5)**

  Although as man He is in Heaven, Jesus is building His church on earth through the Holy Spirit, who transmits the Lord's life and power to His people (cp. Jn. 15:1-5). This power connection is formed by the Holy Spirit, who baptizes us into Christ and who indwells us (Gal. 3:27; I Cor. 6:19; Col. 1:27). This results in our being in Jesus and His being in us (Jn. 14:20). The Holy Spirit also baptizes us into Christ's mystical body to form the church (I Cor. 12:13, 27; Eph. 1:22-23), which now serves as the Lord's body on earth.

- **Jesus' Earthly Rule (Isa. 11:2-5)**

  The Lord Jesus will continue His Messianic work on earth during His millennial, earthly kingdom by the Holy Spirit's power (Isa. 42:1-4), as during His first advent. In fact, the Holy Spirit will continue to energize the Lord Jesus for His Messianic works throughout all eternity (I Cor. 15:28; Lk. 1:33).

HIS WORK DURING THE CHURCH AGE

The Holy Spirit is currently active on earth in restraining evil, ministering to the lost, and working in the lives of His people.

• His Restraint on Lawlessness

This is implied in II Thessalonians 2:7, "For the mystery of iniquity does already work, only He who now restrains will restrain until He be taken out of the way." A "mystery" is a sacred secret or a divine truth that was hidden from men during previous generations and that is now revealed to the Lord's servants as part of the New Testament revelation (see Appendix 0). "Iniquity" is lawlessness—that evil principle which aserts itself against God and violates His law (cp. I Jn. 3:4). The manifestation of lawlessness in this world is not a secret, for it is seen in every part of fallen, human society (cp. Mt. 7:21-23; 23:28). The "mystery of lawlessness," unknown to the world but revealed to God's people, is the fact that the source and guiding genius of this lawlessness is Satan and that it will peak in the career of his human agent, the Beast (II Thess. 2:3-12; Rev. ch. 13).

Although the Holy Spirit is not named in II Thessalonians 2:7, the interpretation that identifies "he" as referring to Him, in my opinion, best fits the context. He alone is capable of holding Satan and sin in check until God's time for their full, unbridled expression.

When the Lord's present work of building His church is completed, then the Holy Spirit will relax His restraint upon lawlessness and will allow the Beast ("the lawless one") to pursue his prophetic career under Satan's direction (vss. 8-10). The Holy Spirit's relaxation of restraint, described as His being "taken out of the way," does not mean that He will be removed from the earth. (Being God, He is omnipresent; God's program and people will need His continued ministry.) It means that He will allow lawlessness to run its full, natural course, without interruption.

In restraining evil today, the Holy Spirit uses the lives of godly people (Mt. 5:13), human government (Rom. 13:1-4), and the influence of the Scriptures (Jn. 17:17) as well as His own sovereign power.

• His Presalvational Ministry to the Lost

The Holy Spirit ministers to the lost by showing them their spiritual need and, in the case of the elect, by bringing them to salvational faith in Jesus. This presalvational ministry of the Holy Spirit to the elect is described as a kind of presalvational "sanctification" (I Pet. 1:2; II Thess. 2:13).

1. HIS MINISTRY OF CONVICTION
Jesus speaks of this in John 16:8-11.

a. *Its meaning*

The verb "reprove" (vs. 8) may also be translated "convince," "convict," or "rebuke." It bears the connotation of bringing something to light, exposing, setting forth, of pointing out something (Jn. 3:20). The reproving work of the Holy Spirit seems to include His showing the sinner his spiritual need, the atoning work of Jesus, and the duty of receiving the Saviour.

b. *Its necessity*

This arises from the fact that the unsaved are spiritually blind to the essential facts of the gospel (II Cor. 4:3-4). Moreover, they are insensitive to God and to spiritual values and truth (Eph. 4:18-19; cp. Rom. 3:18, 11; 1:21-23). Finally, they are totally depraved (Rom. 3:10-12). Sin has affected their total person. In their natural state the unsaved neither want God nor can move toward Him (cp. Jn. 5:40; 6:44; Rom. 1:18; 3:10-12).

c. *Its content*

The Holy Spirit convicts sinners of sin, righteousness, and judgment (Jn. 16:8-11). What does this mean?

(1) Man's problem—"sin" (vs. 9)

The Holy Spirit shows the unsaved their sinfulness before God. Because of their unbelief toward the Saviour, they are still in their sins, both original and actual, which bring on them divine condemnation (Rom. 5:18; 3:9-20; Jn. 8:24, 34; 3:18).

(2) Man's lack—"righteousness" (vs. 10)

The Holy Spirit shows their lack of righteousness — that quality of condition and life which God requires of His personal creatures (Rom. 3:10). The sinner has nothing wherewith he can commend himself to God. Even his religion is insufficient to provide the required righteousness. The Saviour's returning to the Father points to His atoning work and the divine sentence of justification, with its imputation of His righteousness, which is now available through faith in Him (Rom. 3:21-24; 5:1; I Cor. 1:30).

(3) Man's accountability — "judgment" (vs. 11)

Having moral awareness and self-determination, people are accountable to their Creator for their actions. With the divine sentence of condemnation already given and with the Judge's being forever alive, the sinner's accounting of himself to God is certain (Rom. 5:18; Jn. 3:18; Acts 17:31). The devil's condemnation has already been confirmed at the cross and his execution is sure (Rev. 20:10; I Jn. 2:17). The unsaved who remain on the devil's side are serving a lost cause and will share their leader's doom (Mt. 25:41, 46).

When we speak to the unsaved about the gospel, we can cooperate with the Holy Spirit by emphasizing these truths, which He uses to show them their spiritual condition.

2. *HIS TESTIMONY TO JESUS (Jn. 15:26)*

The Holy Spirit not only shows sinners their spiritual condition before God but also points to the Lord Jesus as the only one who can provide for this need. Because of His atoning work, the Lord Jesus can save people from sin (its guilt, ruin, and power), provide them with true righteousness, and deliver them from divine retribution.

We can cooperate with the Holy Spirit by speaking to the unsaved about the substitutionary death of the Lord Jesus and His triumph over death by resurrection (I Cor. 1:23-24; 2:1-5; 15:1-3). He is the only one who can save sinners (Acts 4:12; Jn. 3:16). However, the non-elect will reject this witness (Acts 5:32-33; 7:54; Heb. 10:26).

3. HIS IMPARTATION OF REPENTANCE AND FAITH

Left to himself, the sinner would never receive the Saviour, though he may be aware of his spiritual need. Because of his complete depravity and inability, he neither desires nor is able to take the initiative to move toward God (Jn. 5:40; 6:44; Rom. 3:11). However, according to His sovereign purpose the Holy Spirit gives the elect the disposition of heart to repent (Acts 5:31; 11:18) and to believe the gospel (II Pet. 1:1; Acts 3:16).

Calvinists identify this influence of the Holy Spirit that results in the salvation of the elect as efficacious, or irresistible, grace. Wesleyans hold the doctrine of prevenient grace. This states that God has bestowed His grace upon all people, that this grace sets aside the guilt of original sin and creates in men the beginning of spiritual life (this leads on to further life if people respond to it), and that this grace can be successfully resisted unto one's damnation. Thus, according to the Arminian view which sees man's will as free, the sinner has the final say about his salvation. This view sees salvation as a two-party contract, which is entered voluntarily and which can be annulled by sinning. In keeping with the concept that salvation is wholly God's work, I prefer the Calvinistic view here.

• His Ministry to the Believer

Since the Holy Spirit is our Helper (Jn. 14:16), it is of utmost importance that we understand His ministry to His people in order that we might cooperate with Him and allow Him to do all that He desires in and through our lives.

1. AT THE TIME OF SALVATION

When we received the Lord Jesus as our Saviour, we experienced several works of the Holy Spirit.

a. He regenerated us (Tit. 3:5; cp. Jn. 3:3-8).

(1) Definition

Regeneration is the act of God the Holy Spirit whereby in response to salvational faith He cleanses and renews the gospel believer's soul and spirit and imparts to him spiritual life.

(2) Features

One, like every other part of salvation, regeneration is an act of God (Jn. 1:13)—the Father (I Pet. 1:3), the Son (Jn. 10:28), and the Holy

Spirit (Gal. 5:25).

Two, contrary to the teaching of Calvinistic theology, I believe that regeneration follows salvational faith. This divine gift of faith itself imparts the dynamic for the elect person to believe the gospel (Jn. 6:53-57). While it is true that unsaved people are totally depraved and are naturally unwilling and unable to receive the Saviour, the elect are given salvational repentance and faith so that they can and will believe (II Pet. 1:1; Acts 3:16; 11:18). However, this gift of salvational faith is not to be regarded as the gift of eternal life. The unsaved are not made spiritually alive before they believe the gospel (cp. Jn. 1:12; Acts 16:31). They are made alive upon believing the gospel (Jn. 6:53).

Three, although it requires human response to the gospel (Jn. 3:36; Acts 17:30), regeneration takes place apart from human means (Jn. 1:13). The Holy Spirit regenerates the gospel believer after He has used the Word (I Pet. 1:23; II Tim. 3:15) and has imparted salvational faith (Acts 3:16; 5:31) to secure this human response — the reception of God's gift of salvation (Eph. 2:8-9).

Four, regeneration occurs instantly in response to salvational faith, whereas the presalvational work of the Holy Spirit may cover a period of time, sometimes many years (cp. Jn. 1:13; 3:3, 5, 7, aorist tense).

Five, regeneration is nonexperiential in that it is not derived from, based on, or a part of human sensuous experience. Being the instantaneous act of God, regeneration does not impart any sensation. Yet Christian experience proceeds from the new life and the inward renewal that are produced by this act of God (Acts 16:34).

Six, by this act the Holy Spirit not only imparts spiritual life (Rom. 8:2, 10) but also cleanses (I Cor. 6:11) and renews (Tit. 3:5, not replaces) the immaterial part (soul and spirit) of our human nature by delivering it from inherent corruption (Acts 15:9; I Pet. 1:22) and recreating it in righteousness and holiness (Col. 3:10; Eph. 4:24). This renewal of soul and spirit gives us the capacity to understand spiritual truth, to express godly emotions and have right attitudes, and to make right moral decisions (cp. Lk. 5:37-38). Thus we are inwardly saved (Heb. 10:39; I Pet. 1:9; I Cor. 5:5) and are made new creatures (Eph. 2:10; II Cor. 5:17). Although the body is still subject to death (Rom. 8:10), we anticipate its future deliverance (vss. 11, 23). In spite of the fact that our saved soul and spirit are still susceptible to the sin-principle, resident in the body's flesh, we can yield our total being to the Holy Spirit and allow Him to use us as an instrument of righteousness (Rom. 6:11-13).

Seven, the everlasting life that the Holy Spirit imparts is more than the perpetuation of life's experience in this world. It is a new kind of life, which the Lord Jesus is and gives (Jn. 14:6; Col. 3:4; I Jn. 5:11-12) and which springs from an intimate relation with God (Jn. 17:3). This new life brings us a new dynamic (Phil. 4:13; Jn. 14:6), a new rule of conduct (Gal. 6:2; II Tim. 3:16-17), a new life objective (I Cor. 10:31), a new knowledge (I Cor. 2:12), a new association (I Cor. 1:9; I Jn. 1:3), a new character (Gal. 5:22-23), a new resource (Heb. 13:5-6; Jn. 7:37-39), a new desire and activity (Phil. 2:13), a new life-direction (Eph. 2:10; 5:17), a new interest (Col. 3:1), a new citizenship (Phil. 3:20), and a new expectancy (Tit. 2:13) with its destination (Jn. 14:2-3).

Eight, by regeneration we are born into God's family as children (Jn. 1:12; Eph. 2:19; 5:1) and are made members of His kingdom as citizens (Jn. 3:3; Col. 1:13). Following our entrance into God's family by the new birth, adoption gives us the place of adult-sons in this family (Eph. 1:5).

Nine, by regeneration God imparts to the believer a new kind of life which is Jesus' human spiritual life, not His divine life (Jn. 14:6). Second Peter 1:4 seems to mean that we are partakers of the divine nature in the sense that we have received God the Holy Spirit (Acts 5:32; I Jn. 3:24). He communicates to us this new life to the extent that Christ and His life are now in us (Col. 1:27; I Jn. 5:12). We shall never become God in any way, but we are members of the new human race, of which Jesus is the head and pattern (I Cor. 15:22; II Cor. 5:17; Rom. 8:29).

    b. *He baptized us (I Cor. 12:13; Gal. 3:27-28).*

    (1) Definition

        The baptism of the Holy Spirit is that work whereby He brings the gospel believer into spiritual union with Jesus and with all other believers who are in Him and who are saved during this age.

    (2) Features

        One, the Lord Jesus does this baptizing (Lk. 3:16; Jn. 1:33), using the Holy Spirit as His Agent of baptism (cp. the instrumental *en* in Mt. 3:11; Lk. 3:16; Jn. 1:33; Acts 1:5; 11:16; I Cor. 12:13).

Two, we must distinguish between the baptism with the Holy Spirit into Christ (Gal. 3:27; Rom. 6:3) and ritual baptism into water in the name of the Lord (Acts 2:38; 8:16; 10:48).

Three, this baptism is instantaneous and nonexperiential, occurring beyond the range of our sensation and feeling.

Four, this baptism occurs once for all to all believers at the time of their salvation (I Cor. 12:13; Gal. 3:27). There is no command for people to seek this or receive it.

Five, the initial baptism with the Holy Spirit took place on the Day of Pentecost, ten days after Jesus' ascension to Heaven. This is indicated by the Lord's prediction (Acts 1:5) and by Peter's interpretation of the phenomenal events of Pentecost which indicated that this Spirit baptism had occurred (Acts 11:15-16 with 2:1-4). While some hold that all believers who were living at this time were baptized into Christ on Pentecost, it is more likely that only the 120 believers, gathered in an upper room in Jerusalem, received this initial baptism (Acts 1:12-15). Believers in other places did not receive this baptism until they were contacted by the apostles (cp. Acts 19:2-6). Today, this baptism takes place involuntarily at salvation (Gal. 3:26-28; II

Cor. 5:17; Eph. 2:10). We are never commanded to seek it as a second work of grace. Furthermore, we are never commanded to seek the Pentecostal signs of this event since we now have the N.T. Scriptures which indicate that believers are baptized with the Spirit at salvation.

Six, it appears that the Old Testament believers were also baptized into Christ after the completion of His atoning work (perhaps before His ascension), for He is the redemption and righteousness of His people (I Cor. 1:30; cp. I Cor. 15:22; II Cor. 5:17; Eph. 2:10; see Appendix D).

Seven, the spiritual union of the Lord's people with Himself, resulting from this baptism, is the basis for their positional blessings (see "in Christ," Eph. 1:3, 7, 11; 2:6, 10; Col. 2:10-13; I Cor. 1:2, 30).

Eight, during this Church Age the baptism of the Holy Spirit not only places the believer into Christ (Gal. 3:27) but also places him into the mystical body of Christ (not His human body), which is His church (I Cor. 12:13, 27; Eph. 1:22-23; Col. 1:18). This baptism unites all believers who belong to the Church Age to form an organism, of which Jesus is the life and head (Eph. 1:22; 4:14-15; 5:23; Col. 1:18; 3:4). Although as man Jesus has a physical body in Heaven, yet He lives in and works through His people on earth to build His church (I Cor. 12:13, 27; 6:15; Rom. 12:4-5; Jn. 14:20; 15:1-5). This means that He is working through his "body" on earth to build the church (cp. Eph. 4:11-12).

Nine, the baptism with the Holy Spirit must be distinguished from His filling believers (Eph. 5:18). Being distinct, separate works, this baptism occurs once for all at salvation, whereas His filling takes place repeatedly throughout the believer's lifetime (cp. Acts 1:5 with 2:4; 4:8, 31).

Ten, the only relation that water baptism (immersion) has to the Holy Spirit's baptism is that water baptism is a symbolic reenactment of the believer's participation in Christ's death, burial, and resurrection, which becomes a reality to us by the Holy Spirit's placing us into Christ (cp. Rom. 6:1-4; Eph. 2:5-6).

    c. He indwelt us (Jn. 14:16-17; Rom. 8:9, 11).

        (1) Definition

            The indwelling of the Holy Spirit is His taking up His residence within the gospel believer and His abiding in him forever.

        (2) Features

            One, being instantaneous and nonexperiential, this action occurs once for all at salvation (Rom. 8:9; Acts 5:32; 19:2). However, the Lord's disciples received the Holy Spirit on resurrection evening (Jn. 20:22).

    Two, this action results in our having the Holy Spirit as God's promised gift (Jn. 14:16-17; Rom. 5:5; I Cor. 2:12; 12:13; II Cor. 5:5; Gal. 3:2; 4:6; I Jn. 3:24; 4:13). This giving of the Holy Spirit must be distinguished from His baptizing and anointing the disciples on Pentecost (this anointing with power for service was the result of their being brought into union with Christ, Acts 1:5,

8; 2:4). Today, the indwelling, baptism, and anointing of the Holy Spirit are simultaneous events, occurring at salvation (cp. Acts 10:44-47; 11:15-16; 19:1-6). The irregular events of Acts 8:14-17 may refer to the Samaritan believers' receiving the Holy Spirit's baptism and/or His anointing rather than His person. (See p. 229, fn. 12.)

Three, it is impossible to be saved and not have the Holy Spirit (Rom. 8:9; Jude 19).

Four, the Holy Spirit indwells His people forever (Jn. 14:16).

Five, while He did not permanently indwell precross believers (Ezek. 2:2; 3:24), the Holy Spirit was continually with them to perform all the ministries that He does for us today (cp. Jn. 14:17; Lk. 2:25-27). Our Lord's emphasis on the Holy Spirit's abiding with His people forever was to assure His disciples that the Spirit would not leave them as He was about to do (Jn. 14:16; 13:33).

Six, the bodies of the Lord's people are the sanctuaries of the Holy Spirit (I Cor. 6:19). Observe that He lives within our body, whereas the sin-principle is resident within the flesh of the body (Rom. 7:18-20). The Holy Spirit is not a part of the body as sin is.

Seven, besides the Holy Spirit, God the Father and the Son indwell believers (I Jn. 4:12-13; Col. 1:27).

Eight, the Holy Spirit's indwelling seems to be complementary to His baptizing work. In keeping with Jesus' prediction, "I in you and you in Me" (Jn. 14:20), the Holy Spirit's baptism placed us into Jesus and His indwelling brought Christ into us (Col. 1:27; I Jn. 5:12). By this two-fold work the Holy Spirit becomes a lifeline, transmitting the vitality and power of the exalted Lord Jesus to each of His people. This seems to be the only purpose for His indwelling, for He does not have to be in us to minister to us, as the lives of the precross saints show.

Nine, the Holy Spirit's presence is the pledge and foretaste of our future blessings in Christ (II Cor. 5:5; Eph. 1:14 "earnest" means a down payment given as a pledge that the balance will be paid).

    d. *He sealed us (Eph. 1:13; 4:30; II Cor. 1:22).*

        (1) Definition

            The sealing of the Holy Spirit is the work of God the Father who sets the Holy Spirit as a seal upon each gospel believer to preserve him until the redemption of his body, which completes his salvation.

        (2) Features

            One, a seal is a device that bears a design and imparts an impression on a soft substance like clay or wax. It may also be the substance that has received this impression.

        Two, in the Bible a seal signifies several things: a completed transaction (Jer. 32:9-10), security (Mt. 27:66), ownership (II Tim. 2:19), approval (Jn. 6:27), authenticity (I Cor. 9:2), and intimate dearness (S. Sol. 8:6). The primary significance of the Holy Spirit's sealing seems to be security (Eph.

1:13-14; 4:30), which anticipates the completion of our salvation experience—the redemption of our bodies from inherent corruption, sin, and death (Rom. 8:23, 10-11). This will take place when the Lord Jesus returns for His church (Phil. 3:20-21). Meanwhile, not one of His people will be lost during their lifetime on earth (Jn. 17:11-12), for they are preserved by this divine Seal. Although the primary significance of this sealing is security, it also conveys the other truths that are listed above.

Three, this sealing occurs at salvation (Eph. 1:13 should read, "When you believed, you were sealed...").

e. He anointed us (II Cor. 1:21-22; I Jn. 2:20, 27).

(1) Definition

The anointing of the Holy Spirit signifies our being divinely appointed to be Jesus' servants (slaves) and our receiving divine enablement to do God's will.

(2) Features

One, this anointing is by God the Father (II Cor. 1:21), who uses the Holy Spirit as the anointing agent (cp. I Sam. 16:13; Isa. 61:1; Lk. 3:21-22; 4:16-21).

Two, as in the cases of David and Jesus, this anointing relates to service. It signifies the divine appointment of a person to an office and his divine enablement for this office (I Sam. 16:1, 13; Isa. 42:1; Phil. 2:7; Jn. 6:38; Acts 10:38). We who are saved are Jesus' servants (Mt. 6:24; I Cor. 6:19-20; Rom. 1:1; 6:22; 14:8-9), and we have His power by the Holy Spirit to do His will (Jn. 14:16-17; 15:1-5; Phil. 4:13).

Three, the early church was anointed with the Holy Spirit for service on Pentecost (Acts 1:8). Today, this takes place at salvation (II Cor. 1:21-22). We are not commanded to seek or ask for it.

These works of the Holy Spirit at salvation are permanent and involuntary. They never need to be sought for or repeated. We are also filled with the Spirit at salvation, but this is not an abiding spiritual reality.

2. THROUGHOUT THE CHRISTIAN LIFE

The basic function of the Holy Spirit in the lives of them who receive the Saviour is Helper (Jn. 14:16-17). He communicates to them the life and power of the Lord Jesus. We Christians soon learn that the Christian life demands of us far more than what our human resources can provide. This life consists of superhuman character (Eph. 5:1-2), warfare (6:12), service (II Cor. 5:20), and worship (Jn. 4:24). In short, it is the expression of Christ's living in and working through His people (Gal. 2:20; Phil. 1:21; Col. 3:4).

How, then, can we live such a life? By means of this divine Helper, the Holy Spirit. He stands ready to help us to be and to do all that God requires of us. He produces in us Christian character (Gal. 5:22-23); He enables us to wage victorious warfare against our spiritual enemies (Gal. 5:16); He energizes us to perform Christian service (Acts 1:8); and He quickens us to render acceptable worship (Phil. 3:3). The Holy Spirit ministers to us who are saved for the purpose of making real in our daily experience all that comprises our relationship with God and of enabling us to please and glorify God (I Cor. 6:19-20). It is consistent with our new life in Christ that we live by means of the Holy Spirit who imparted this new life to us (Gal. 5:25).

As we examine the various ministries of the Holy Spirit that relate to our Christian life, we should keep in mind that some of these, as His praying for us and His convicting us of sin, are unconditional and involuntary on our part. Others such as His filling us, teaching us, and exercising certain gifts through us, are conditional and voluntary on our part, being dependent upon our surrender and faith.

a. *He prays for us (Rom. 8:26-27).*

The Holy Spirit prays within us with inaudible, inexpressible sighs. While this takes place below the level of our awareness, from time to time it rises to our consciousness as the yearnings of our human spirit. This intercession is effective, for the Father knows the mind of the Holy Spirit, who always prays according to the divine will (vs. 27). He also enables us to pray effectively (Jude 20).

b. *He convicts us of sin (I Jn. 3:20).*

Since He convicts the unsaved of their sins (Jn. 16:8-11), it is reasonable to assume that He also shows us our sins. He points to known sins by our conscience, the vehicle of moral awareness. He also shows us through the Scriptures sins in our life that are unknown to us or that we have forgotten (cp. Ps. 139:23-24).

c. *He bears witness to us (Rom. 8:16).*

The Holy Spirit bears witness to our human spirit — the seat of our human understanding (I Cor. 2:11-12; Eph. 4:23; Rom. 12:2) In this witness He uses the promises and declarations of God's Word which certify our relationship to God (cp. I Jn. 5:6-12). He makes these statements of Scripture meaningful to us who are saved. He also gives us the inclination to call God "Father" (Rom. 8:15; Gal. 4:6).

d. *He teaches us (I Jn. 2:27).*

Sometimes called "divine illumination," this is the activity whereby the Holy Spirit gives His people an understanding of divine truth (Jn. 14:26; I Cor. 2:11-12). He also gives His people discernment to distinguish between truth and error (cp. I Jn. 4:1-6). The apostle John points to the fact that God's people are not abandoned to the necessity and fallibility of human teachers, for they themselves are taught by the Holy Spirit (I Jn. 2:27). Apart from this ministry, it is impossible for anyone to understand the spiritual teachings of God's Word (I Cor. 2:11-12, 14; II Cor. 4:3-4). Whenever we approach the Scriptures, our prayer should be, "Open Thou my eyes that I may behold wondrous things out of Thy law" (Ps. 119:18).

e. *He guides us (Rom. 8:14).*

The verb "led" probably means management as well as showing the way (cp. vs. 5). As we look to Him for direction, the Holy Spirit shows us and leads us in the will of God (cp. Acts 16:6-10). He renews our mind in order that we may recognize and approve God's will for us (Rom. 12:2; Eph. 5:10, 17; I Thess. 5:21-22).

The Holy Spirit leads us by different means: He uses the Scriptures, which by their commands, guiding principles, and examples indicate what is God's will for us (Ps. 119:11, 105; II Tim. 3:16-17; Rom. 15:4; I Cor. 10:11). He also leads by inward impressions or urges (Isa. 30:21; Lk. 2:27). However, we must discover the source of any urge before yielding to it. Also, we must test it by the teachings of the Scriptures and seek its confirmation by prayer. Finally, the Holy Spirit guides us through our circumstances, including people (Acts 11:24-26; 17:13-14) as well as events (Gal. 4:13 with Acts 13:14). As we give ourself to the leadership of the Holy Spirit and look to Him for direction, we shall receive His guidance (Prov. 3:5-6).

f. *He sanctifies us (II Cor. 3:18).*

To be sanctified is to be set apart unto God for His manifestation and use. This not only occurs positionally when we are saved (I Cor. 1:2; 6:11) but also practically throughout our Christian life as we yield ourself to God's control and do His will (Rom. 6:11-23). Our God who is holy must have a people who are holy in their daily behavior (I Pet. 1:15-16; I Thess. 4:3, 7).

To be holy in behavior is to become increasingly like the Lord Jesus. It is to move away from the old moral life-style we had when we were unsaved and to conform to the will of God, displaying the moral qualities of Jesus (Eph. 4:17-5:20). To experience this sanctification, we must separate ourself from attitudes and behavior that are unlike Jesus and give ourself to those that express Him (Col. 3:8-14). The Holy Spirit brings this about as we respond to His prompting, instruction, and discipline (Jn. 17:17; 15:3; Heb. 12:10; Rev. 2:7; cp. Rom. 8:2-4; Gal. 5:16, 22-23; Eph. 5:9).

g. *He fills us (Eph. 5:18).*

This does not concern our receiving more of the Holy Spirit, for being a person He wholly resides in us. To be filled with the Holy Spirit is to be under His control, not in an absolute sense so that we are passive and our personal faculties cease to function (cp. demon possession), but in a relative sense (see Appendix Q) in which we cooperate with Him by doing our part and by depending upon Him to do His work (cp. Acts 2:4; 4:8, 31; 6:3, 5, 8-11; 11:24; 13:52; contra 5:3). This cooperation allows Him to energize us and to do through us all that He desires. While His filling is an intermittent experience, we should seek to be under His control continuously (Eph. 5:18, "be filled" is in the present tense). What must we do, then, to be filled with the Holy Spirit and remain filled?

(1) Our becoming filled with the Holy Spirit

To come under the Holy Spirit's control requires our

adjusting ourself to His presence, or our cooperating with Him. This allows Him to do His part as our Helper. We do this by the following steps:

First, we come under His control by judging known, personal sins (Eph. 4:30; cp. I Cor. 11:31). Sins known to us hinder His ministry in our life. When we become aware of these sins, we must deal with them by repentance and confession to God (Rev. 2:5; I Jn. 1:9). When we neglect to deal with known sins, we grieve the Holy Spirit. This grieving is a conscious experience which causes us to be very unhappy (Ps. 32:3-4). Our adjustment to the Holy Spirit's presence requires us to deal with any sin of which we are aware.

Second, this adjustment requires our giving ourself to His control (I Thess. 5:19; cp. Rom. 6:11-13). To "quench" the Holy Spirit is not to extinguish Him as one puts out a fire, for He indwells us perpetually. It is to stifle Him, to limit or hinder His activity in our life by our refusing to cooperate with Him. We do this when we oppose or resist His control and give ourself to sin. We can correct this by dealing with our rebellious attitude and by giving ourself to the Spirit's direction and enablement. We yield to His control by heart decision and prayer. Isaiah said "Here am I" (Isa. 6:8).

Third, this adjustment requires our exercising faith that He will do His part as we do ours (Acts 6:5). Since we do not see Him or feel Him, we must rest on the Lord's promise that He will help us (Jn. 7:37-39). This promise gives us something to believe. This invitation is extended to all who thirst, that is, who have inner desire rising from some spiritual need (e.g. for salvation or qualities of spiritual life). Our new life in Christ has spiritual desires for righteousness, understanding, courage, and the like, that can only be satisfied by the Lord through the activity of the Holy Spirit. We experience the satisfaction of these needs when we appropriate the divine provision by faith in Jesus (Jn. 6:35).

All who have spiritual thirst are invited to go to Jesus and drink (Jn. 7:37). We go to Him by prayer. We drink when we receive from Him what we desire by the exercise of faith in His promise (Jn. 7:38). In response to this, the Lord provides for our thirst through the activity of the Holy Spirit, who resides within our inner being ("belly"). The powerful energy by which the Holy Spirit ministers to our need is vividly described as "rivers of living water." This powerful torrent flows from within us and abundantly satisfies our spiritual thirst. This exercise of faith, by which we look to the Holy Spirit and depend upon Him to provide for our need, allows Him to control us.

When we cooperate with Him in this manner, we allow the Holy Spirit to fill us. His filling does not eliminate our reasoning, decision-making ability, or physical activity, for He requires us to use our total being (Rom. 12:2; I Cor. 14:15). And as we do, He wants us to rely upon Him and the Scriptures in every circumstance for the direction and enablement we need to do God's will. Also, His filling is not registered by our physical senses, but it is indicated outwardly by Christlikeness and inwardly by such fruits as peace, joy, patience, and self-control (Gal. 4:19; 5:22-23). L. L. Legters writes, "The chief need is not that you know it [His filling], but that others know it...We are generally unconscious of the fruit in our lives, but others are conscious of it...There is an evidence to you when you are filled with the Holy Spirit...[It] is that Jesus becomes everything to you. You see Him. You are occupied with Him. You are fully satisfied with Jesus. He becomes real..."[5]

We experience variation in the frequency and scope of the Holy Spirit's control, or influence. In addition to a growing understanding of spiritual truth, this is due to the frequency of our surrender to God and of the exercise of our faith. Also, when we are under the Spirit's control, other areas of our life of which we are unaware may remain under the control of sin until we learn about them and give them over to the Lord. We shall not knowingly sin as long as we remain yielded to the Holy Spirit (Gal. 5:16).

Since the believer's power of choice is free, his control by the Holy Spirit or by sin is not absolute. When he is under the Spirit's control, he can still choose at any time to give himself over to the sin-principle and to its demands. At that moment, the believer ceases to be under the control of the Holy Spirit and comes under the control of sin. In like manner, when he is under sin's control, the believer can give himself over to the control of the Holy Spirit and do what is right in God's sight. In any case, the believer has liberty to yield to either controlling principle, God or sin, that would dominate his life. During his conscious periods he is never without the influence of one or the other upon his life. Because of this, he is responsible to God at these times for his actions (II Cor. 5:10).

(2) Our remaining filled with the Holy Spirit

God not only wants us to be filled with the Holy Spirit but also to remain filled with Him (Eph. 5:18, "be filled" is in the present tense). We remain filled with Him as long as we do not yield to sin but do the following:

First, we continue to be filled with the Holy Spirit by remaining adjusted to Him. We experience His control as long as we faithfully deal with those sins of which He makes us aware (I Jn. 1:7, 9), as we give ourself to Him whenever we consciously have need of His ministry (Jn. 7:37-38; Jas. 4:7), and as we exercise practical faith in Him (Gal. 5:25), sharing with Him all that concerns us and depending upon His direction and enablement. (Observe this distinction between "practical" and "salvational" faith.)

Second, we remain filled by obeying Him (Rom. 6:16-22). Desiring to manage our life (Jas. 4:5), the Holy Spirit will fill us as long as we walk in obedience to His direction. When we refuse to cooperate with Him, we come under the control of sin and walk in spiritual darkness (I Jn. 1:5-7).

Third, we stay under the Holy Spirit's control as long as we give ourself

---

[5] L. L. Legters, *The Simplicity of the Spirit-Filled Life* (Philadelphia: Pioneer Mission Agency, 1939), pp. 48-50.

to those things that He uses to sanctify and mature our life. He uses Bible study and meditation, fellowship with God and His people, church attendance, involvement in the Lord's service, submission to His discipline, and spiritual cleansing (Jn. 17:17; Ps. 1:1-3; I Jn. 1:7; Heb. 10:25; II Tim. 2:21; Heb. 12:9-11; II Cor. 7:1). We remain filled as we regularly and diligently give ourself to these spiritual exercises. On the other hand, we must avoid those things that are morally unlike Jesus, that hinder our spiritual life, and that compromise our testimony (Col. 3:8; Gal. 6:7-8; Heb. 12:1; II Cor. 6:14-18; II Tim. 2:19-22).

To be filled with the Holy Spirit is like closing an electric circuit that supplies power to a lamp. The lamp will shine as long as the circuit is closed. In like manner, the Holy Spirit will control us as long as we remain adjusted to Him, follow His direction, and give ourself to those things that He uses to make us more like Jesus. Such a relationship with the Holy Spirit is, indeed, a very intimate one. We can address our needs to Him and confirm our trust in Him at all times, for He is always with us as our Helper (Jn. 14:16-17; Phil. 2:1; II Cor. 13:14). We cannot have fellowship with one if we do not interact with him.

Someone has given us a timely reminder: "We are warned to remember that there is no separate Gospel of the Spirit. Not for a moment are we to advance, as it were, from the Lord Jesus Christ to a higher or deeper region, ruled by the Holy Spirit." I would add that we should be suspicious of any movement or ministry that exalts the Holy Spirit above the Lord Jesus. It is the Holy Spirit's purpose to bear witness to Jesus and to exalt Him (Jn. 16:14-15; 15:26).

    h. *He imparts to us spiritual gifts (I Cor. 12:4-31).*

        (1) Definition

        Spiritual gifts are measures of divine grace, by which the Holy Spirit enables believers to do special ministries, which today are involved in the building of the church.

        (2) Features

        One, these gifts must be distinguished from native abilities, which are natural powers belonging to our human nature. These abilities are capable of training and development. They may be used in Christian service as we yield them to God and use them according to His will and way. Some native abilities, like teaching and leadership, are similar to certain spiritual gifts, but they are not identical.

Two, the word "gifts" (I Cor. 12:4; Rom. 12:6) means "grace-gifts." This indicates that these gifts are measures of divine grace, or specific manifestations of divine power, by means of which the Holy Spirit enables the believer to minister in certain capacities in response to corresponding measures of faith (Eph. 4:7-8; Rom. 12:3-6; I Pet. 4:10). The given measure of faith seems to be suited to the gift of grace that determines a particular spiritual gift.

Three, when he discusses the nature and use of spiritual gifts (I Cor. 12:4-11), Paul points out that they are manifestations of the Holy Spirit (vs. 7), distributed to each believer according to His sovereign will (vs. 11) for the profit of the congregation (vs. 7; 14:12, 26). This means that they are not arbitrarily selected by His people, nor are they given for self-exaltation or self-edification. All spiritual gifts are for our ministry to others in the building of the church, quantitatively and qualitatively, during this age (I Cor. 14:26; Eph. 3:2; 4:7-16). They are not given for self-edification although personal edification often results from their ministry to others.

Four, it is unlikely that any one spiritual gift is possessed by all believers. Paul likens the Lord's people to the organs of the body, with their particular functions (Rom. 12:6-8; I Cor. 12:12-31). As members of the body of Christ, each of us who are saved has his own particular function in special service, which is determined by his spiritual gifts and native abilities. It is wrong to make the possession of any gift a mark of spirituality. Incidentally, only the Lord Jesus as man has all of the spiritual gifts to an unlimited degree (Jn. 3:34).

Five, the spiritual gifts which belong to the present age will function until there is no longer need for them (cp. I Cor. 13:8)[6]. As we shall see, some of the gifts ceased with the completion of the New Testament Canon.

Six, as certain gifts were exercised in the Old Testament Period (I Sam. 10:10; 16:13-14), so certain ones will function beyond the Church Age (Rev. 11:3; Joel 2:28-29). However, we shall focus our attention upon those which relate to the present age.

(3) Categories

This study assumes that the only spiritual gifts that are functioning during the Church Age are those given in the New Testament lists (Rom. 12:6-8; I Cor. 12:8-11, 28-30; Eph. 4:8, 11). We must be alert not to confuse spiritual gifts with native abilities, which include verbal comprehension, reasoning, physical skills, manual dexterity, mechanical comprehension, space visualization, mathematical ability, clerical ability, linguistic ability, creative ability, artistic ability, dramatic ability, speaking ability, musical ability, writing ability, persuasive ability, leadership ability, teaching ability, and the like.

Although there is uncertainty about the function of certain gifts, here is a description of the N.T. gifts as I understand them.

(a) *Gifts that relate to God's Word and its ministry.*
- *Prophecy (Rom. 12:6; I Cor. 12:28)*

---

[6] I Corinthians 13:8 should not be used as proof that certain gifts like tongues have ceased. Paul seems to say that certain gifts, in contrast to love, are transitory. They exist only as long as there is need for them. He indicates what this need is by referring to what is partial, which to my mind, is the present earthly spiritual experience of the Lord's people. These gifts minister to the edification of saved people in their present incomplete state. In the future, these gifts will no longer be needed, for God's people will have entered the fullness of spiritual life [Tit. 1:2; cp. Paul's illustrations (I Cor. 13:11-12)].

This gift enabled a person to speak or to write God's Word under divine inspiration.

In biblical times, the prophet spoke or wrote God's words as he was inspired by the Holy Spirit (Deut. 18:15, 18; Heb. 1:1-2; II Pet. 1:21). N.T. prophets spoke God's words to the local church congregations (Acts 13:1-2; cp. Eph. 2:20). However, with the completion of the N.T. Scriptures and their distribution to the churches, prophecy ceased, for it was no longer needed to convey the N.T. truth that the Lord wanted His people to know.

The gift of prophecy should not be equated with preaching. Observe that I Corinthians 14:3 does not necessarily define prophecy but describes how God used His Word through the N.T. prophets to minister to the needs of His people. Together with interpretation and application, preaching consists of the proclamation of God's Word, already produced by divine inspiration through prophecy. Unlike prophecy, preaching has nothing to do with the production of God's Word.

To my mind, preaching itself is not a spiritual gift. It is the native ability of speech combined with the gifts of exhortation and teaching and/or evangelism.

- Pastoral care (Eph. 4:11)

This office indicates the gift of pastoral care, which enables a person to care for and to lead the Lord's people, such as those who constitute a local church.

The basic idea of pastoral care is one's shepherding, or tending, the Lord's people (Acts 20:28; I Pet. 5:2; "feed" means to shepherd, tend). With the authority, direction, and use of God's Word (II Tim. 4:2a; 3:15-17), this ministry includes supervising the Lord's people (Heb. 13:7, 17), teaching, exhorting, and reproving them (II Tim. 4:1-2), protecting them from spiritual enemies (Acts 20:28-31), being an example to them (I Pet. 5:3), and serving them by ministering to their needs (Mk. 10:42-45). This ministry also involves evangelizing the lost (II Tim. 4:5).

This gift seems to have other applications beside pastoring a local church. One with this gift may care for the spiritual needs of a group of the Lord's people within or outside of a local church.

- The utterance of knowledge (I Cor. 12:8)

It appears that this gift enables a person to understand, formulate, and state Bible doctrine.

In I Corinthians 14:6, Paul indicates that prophecy and doctrine are the outward expressions of their internal counterparts — revelation and knowledge. Thus the apostle seems to associate knowledge with doctrine. The utterance of knowledge seems to be the statement of Bible doctrine. If this is so, we should distinguish between teaching doctrine and formulating it from references to it in the Scriptures. The gift of knowledge, I believe, refers to the latter. The person with this gift can recognize, sort out, and put together in systematic order the teachings of the Scriptures. Not all teachers have this ability.

- *Teaching* (Rom. 12:7; I Cor. 12:28)
This gift enables a person to explain God's truth clearly and effectively.

While the gift of the utterance of knowledge enables one to systematize and state Bible doctrine, the gift of teaching enables one to explain this doctrine to others. The spiritual gift of teaching should be distinguished from the native ability of teaching. The spiritual gift of teaching enables one to grasp and to convey to others the meaning of God's Word, which is wholly different from human disciplines. The teaching of God's Word gives the Holy Spirit the opportunity to illuminate people's hearts (I Cor. 2:12; Acts 16:14; Eph. 1:18) and to work in their lives according to the divine purpose (Acts 16:15; Rom. 10:17; I Thess. 2:13; II Tim. 3:15-17).

- *The utterance of wisdom* (I Cor. 12:8)
Since wisdom often refers to the practical use of knowledge (cp. Eccles. 2:13-14), it appears that this gift enables a person to discern the needs of others and to apply God's truth to their lives in a practical way.

Those who have this gift can relate the teachings of God's Word to the everyday needs of God's people (cp. Acts 6:3; Eph. 5:15-17).

- *Evangelism* (Eph. 4:11)
The office of evangelist suggests the gift of evangelism which enables a person to present the gospel clearly and effectively to the unsaved.

We should distinguish between this gift and the duty of witnessing to Jesus and His work. All believers are to be witnesses in the sense that they tell what the Lord Jesus has done for them (Acts 1:8; Mk. 5:19). However, as Jesus' distinction between sowing and reaping indicates (Jn. 4:35-38), not all have the gift of evangelism. Witnessing is largely sowing the gospel seed. Evangelists are reapers as well as sowers. This gift has a wide range of application.

- *Exhortation* (Rom. 12:8)
This gift enables a person to use the Scriptures to motivate people to respond to God's will, to encourage the fainthearted, and to comfort the afflicted and the bereaved.

This gift has a wide range of application, including preaching (I Thess. 5:14; I Tim. 6:2; II Tim. 4:2).

Keep in mind that God always uses His Word to minister to the spiritual needs of people (II Tim. 3:15-17; 4:2; I Pet. 1:22-24; Rom. 10:17). The gift of apostleship may also belong to this category (Eph. 3:1-12).

(b) *Gifts that relate to the administration of the Lord's work.*

- *Apostleship* (I Cor. 12:28)

This gift enabled certain men to fulfill their commission as Jesus' authorized representatives in this world (Rom. 12:3; 15:15; cp. Mk. 3:13-19; Mt. 10:1-4).

The apostles' commission was to introduce Christianity to the world after Jesus' returned to Heaven. They did this by preaching the gospel and teaching Jesus' doctrines (Lk. 24:46-48; Jn. 16:12-15; Acts 8:25; Rom. 1:1-6; Eph. 4:20-21), by bearing witness to Jesus' death and resurrection (Acts 2:32; 3:15; 5:32), by planting and supervising the first local Christian churches (Acts 14:27; 15:41; II Cor. 11:28; Tit. 1:5), and by giving the official account of Jesus' life and ministry (Jn. 15:27; Lk. 1:2).

With the completion of the N.T. Scriptures, which gives the apostles' account of Jesus and His doctrines and their supervision of the churches, this gift is no longer needed nor does it now exist.

- *Administration* (Rom. 12:8; I Cor. 12:28)

This gift enables a person to serve in some leadership capacity in the Lord's work.

The management know-how of the secular world does not itself qualify one to administer the Lord's affairs, for His work involves spiritual principles and goals (cp. I Cor. 10:31; 3:5-10; Acts 14:26-27). On the other hand, there may be helpful applications of this knowledge to the Lord's work, especially in organizing people and procedures for dealing with problems and needs.

The gift of pastoral care may also belong to this category since pastors have the supervision of their churches (Heb. 13:7, 17).

(c) *Gifts that relate to practical forms of service.*

- *Helps* (I Cor. 12:28)

This gift seems to enable a person to render some form of assistance to others in their ministry.

In addition to its application in rendering assistance, especially in ministry (in contrast to giving or showing mercy to those who are in physical or temporal need), this gift may be associated with many native abilities, like clerical skill, which God uses in His work.

- *Service* (Rom. 12:7, "ministry")

This gift enables a person to function in the office of deacon in a local church.

This word (Gk. *diakonia*) refers to a work that covers a wide range of activity in serving others, especially in temporal affairs as suggested by Acts 6:2; 19:22. However, a cognate word (Gk. *diakonos*) is used for an officer in the local church (Phil. 1:1; I Tim. 3:8, 12; cp. Rom. 16:1). From this, it appears that one must have the gift of service if he is to function effectively in this office. Like the gift of helps, the gift of service may enable one to exercise certain native abilities as those used in the ministry of music.

That this gift enables certain people to minister to the temporal needs of others is indicated by the fact that its possessor is not required to have the gift of teaching (I Tim. 3:2, 10-13). Those, like pastors, who minister to the spiritual needs of others must be able to teach God's Word.

- *Showing mercy* (Rom. 12:8)

This gift enables a person to minister compassionately to the temporal needs of others who are experiencing some kind of economic, physical, or psychological lack or distress.

This gift has a broad range of application, especially in the form of medical and social services. The exercise of this gift differs from similar services of the world in that it is accompanied by the fruit of the Spirit (Gal. 5:22-23) and often provides opportunity for the ministry of God's Word to the afflicted person's spiritual needs (II Tim. 3:15-17). While all of the Lord's people are to express concern for others who have need and seek to alleviate this need (I Jn. 3:16-18), they who have this gift are more efficiently and widely used.

- *Giving* (Rom. 12:8)

This gift enables a person to give above ordinary measure.

This giving may involve goods as well as money. In II Corinthians 8:1-15, Paul distinguishes between two kinds of ordinary giving: *non-sacrificial giving* out of that which one does not need for himself and *sacrificial giving* from that which he needs for himself. The spiritual gift of giving appears to be something other than these. It has to do with giving as a special ministry which God uses in a special way to carry on His work in the building of the church, quantitatively and qualitatively. This is in addition to ordinary giving, which all believers are to do (Gal. 6:6; I Jn. 3:16-18).

(d) Gifts that served as signs and proofs.

Being more spectacular in their expression, these gifts had a special function during the time when the New Testament had not yet been completed and was not yet available to the churches. As *signs* these gifts conveyed certain meaning to skeptical people; as *proofs* they authenticated certain spiritual facts.

- *Healings* (I Cor. 12:9)

This gift enabled one to impart healing to others, apart from therapeutic means.

This gift did not prohibit or replace the use of medical means in treating illness (cp. I Tim. 5:23). And it was not exercised in every case of illness (cp. II Tim. 4:20). It served to authenticate the commission of the apostles (Acts ch. 3; 5:12-16; 28:8-9).

We should distinguish between miraculous healing, which illustrates this gift, and divine healing in answer to prayer.[7] In *divine healing,* God is active

---

[7] For a fine discussion on divine healing, see Henry W. Frost, *Miraculous Healing* (London and Edinburgh: Marshall, Morgan & Scott, 1951) pp. 114-17.

in the healing process, whether by medical means, by rest or change of activity, or by divine power alone. In cases of *miraculous healing,* God directly brings about an immediate, complete, and final cure, apart from any medical or other human means. Again, God may be pleased to heal miraculously, apart from any means, in unusual circumstances. But this would not mean necessarily that the gift of healing was required, present, or exercised.

- *Miracles* (I Cor. 12:10)

This gift enabled one to perform superhuman works in the external world, apart from and contrary to natural law.

Expressions of this gift included healing the sick, raising the dead, casting out demons, and showing immunity to poisonous venom (Acts 3:1-8; 9:37-41; 16:18; 28:1-6; Mk. 16:17-18) as well as other wonders (Acts 5:12). It served to authenticate the divine commission of the apostles (II Cor. 12:12; Heb. 2:4; Jn. 14:12).

We do not need this kind of confirmation today, for our commission of Christian ministry is given in the New Testament (Mt. 28:18-20). On the other hand, God may be pleased, at times, to perform miracles today, but this would not require the exercise of the gift of miracles.

- *Speaking in tongues* (I Cor. 12:10)

This gift enabled one's human spirit to express praise and thanks to God by a special, nonrational utterance, which was unique to each speaker.[8]

The N.T. references to the gift of tongues show that this gift served several purposes: one, as *proof* of the fact of the early believers' baptism by and their anointing with the Holy Spirit (Acts 1:5, 8; 2:1-4; 10:45-46; 19:6); two, as a *sign* to skeptical Jewish people of certain spiritual truths regarding Jesus (Acts 2:4-6, 29-36), believing Gentiles (10:23, 34-36, 45), and the contemporary value of the message and ministry of John the Baptizer (19:1-7); and three, as a *means of edification* of others (I Cor. 14:4-5).

I believe that the spiritual gift of tongues has ceased, for the New Testament now assures us of the truths that this gift confirmed. Moreover, we can give adequate praise unto God in our native language. Today, some profess to speak in tongues in their worship, but this religious phenomenon should not be construed as the gift of speaking in tongues.

(e) *Gifts that relate to other needs.*

- *Interpretation of tongues* (I Cor. 12:10)

This enabled one to understand and explain to the congregation the meaning of what was uttered by speaking in tongues.

It appears that the one who spoke in tongues was not always able to interpret his expressions of praise and thanksgiving to others. If the

---

[8] See Appendix A.

congregation was to be edified, someone with the gift of interpretation had to do this (I Cor. 14:5, 13-19, 27-28). If there was no interpreter, then the speaker was to remain quiet (28).

• *Discerning of spirits* (I Cor. 12:10)

This gift enabled one to perceive whether or not an alleged prophet spoke under divine inspiration.

With many false prophets uttering their demonic messages, there was need for a quick, accurate discrimination between true and false revelations. Because of this, every congregation had at least one, if not two, with this gift for the recognition of the source of the prophecy, whether of the Holy Spirit or of a demon.

We do not need this gift today, for we have the Scriptures by which we can test all alleged prophecies, or messages, from God (I Jn. 4:1-3). However, we should distinguish this gift from the ability of spiritual discernment, or insight, which all believers who are taught of God in the Scriptures have.

• *Faith* (I Cor. 12:9)

This gift enabled one to be a confessor and martyr like Stephen (Acts ch. 7) or to do unusual deeds like the people of Hebrews 11:32-35.

This kind of faith should be distinguised from salvational faith and practical faith which all believers have. There may be times today when God gives to certain people unusual faith, especially in uncommon circumstances where His name would be magnified by this expression.

The foregoing spiritual gifts are all that are listed in the Scriptures. I do not believe that there are others than these that are being exercised today, for the Scriptures provide us with the means to examine and evaluate all spiritual activity in order to discern whether or not it is of God. That which people identify as extrabiblical gifts are really native abilities.

According to these descriptions of the spiritual gifts, a Sunday school teacher should have the gift of teaching and possibly wisdom. A youth camp director should have the gift of administration, exhortation, and possibly teaching and/or evangelism. Every pastor should have the gift of pastoral care and teaching. Needless to say, there are many applications of those gifts which are operating today in the building of the church.

(4) Recognition

Since each believer has one or more spiritual gifts (with the gifts of helps and service covering his native abilities) and their exercise is required for special service in the building of the church,[9] it is important for us believers to learn what our gifts are and to cooperate with the Holy Spirit

---

[9] The Lord seems to be building His church through His people by two kinds of ministries (cp. Eph. 4:11-12). There is the general ministry that belongs to all believers alike, such as prayer, Christian living, giving, etc. There is also the special ministry, based on native abilities and spiritual gifts, that is unique to each believer (cp. Rom. 12:3-8).

in their use.[10] You will learn what your spiritual gift (or gifts) is by the following steps: Become acquainted with the gifts by studying those which are listed in the New Testament (Rom. 12:6-8; I Cor. 12:8-11, 28-30; Eph. 4:8, 11). Then give yourself to the Holy Spirit and ask Him to show you your gift. You must be willing to do whatever God has for you. Next, ask Him to give you a desire for the ministry for which your gift enables you (cp. I Tim. 3:1; Jas. 1:5). When you have the opportunity and as the Lord leads, try various kinds of service in which you are interested and for which you may be gifted. Evaluate the results of these trials and the witness of godly people to your ministry. If you are gifted for a particular work, you will feel comfortable with it and be blessed in it. Finally, seek those gifts that most edify the church quantitatively or qualitatively (I Cor. 12:31; 14:26).[11]

When you learn what your gift or gifts are, seek opportunities to exercise them where you are until the Holy Spirit leads you forth unto some other place of service (Acts 11:25-26; 13:1-4). If your gifts are not needed where you are, you may ask God for other gifts (I Cor. 12:31), or you may seek out a place where they are needed. Whatever gifts and abilities you may have, ever seek to use them under the Holy Spirit's control and for the glory of God (Eph. 5:18; I Cor. 10:31). Do not attempt to use your gift apart from the Holy Spirit and His love (I Cor. 13:1-3), for this will not be fruitful or profitable in the Lord's work. In fact, to attempt to minister apart from God is to sin (Rom. 14:23; cp. Jn. 15:5). Also, avoid allowing these gifts and abilities to become dormant (II Cor. 6:1; I Tim. 4:14; II Tim. 1:6; I Pet. 4:10-11).

• His Ministry in Acts

Any study of the Holy Spirit must recognize that the book of Acts covers an important transition period in sacred history. It bridges the gap between the Gospels, which deal primarily with the Messianic ministry of Jesus, and the Epistles, which deal with Christian doctrine, life, and service.

While the book of Acts is a vital link in the transition from life under the Mosaic Law to life under the new Dispensation of Grace, certain events of this transitional period are not normative for Christians today. These include waiting for the baptism and the anointing of the Holy Spirit (1:4-5, 8), experiencing the Pentecostal phenomena (2:1-4), the common holding of private property (44-45), and praying for the gift of the Holy Spirit (8:14-17). Today, we receive the Holy Spirit's baptism, anointing, and indwelling at salvation. Since we have the teachings of the New Testament that assure us of these truths, it is not necessary for us to pray for these blessings of grace or to experience their evidential phenomena such as speaking in tongues.

Although the church began on Pentecost, a number of years passed before

---

[10] One can go through the outward motions of exercising certain spiritual gifts; but unless they are done by the power of the Holy Spirit, they accomplish nothing.

[11] The Lord is building His church quantitatively by saving people and adding them to it, and qualitatively by promoting the spiritual growth of His people.

the permanent pattern and character of the new age were established. For this reason, we should be cautious in seeking for or adopting a work of the Holy Spirit that was characteristic in those days.

Roy L. Aldrich offers helpful observations regarding the transition problem of Acts:

1. A transition period was necessary to overcome the natural psychological resistance to change. It took a special revelation to Peter to convince him of the universality of Christianity.

2. A special period of preaching the gospel first to the Jew was necessary to confirm the promises made unto the fathers. The "no difference" pattern of ministry developed gradually after the conversion of Cornelius. It should be remembered that in Acts the gospel was preached *exclusively* to the Jew first about seven years (Acts 11:19). No one would argue for such a program today.

3. The signs and wonders can be partially explained as God's method of dealing with Israel. That these public miracles were intended to be temporary is proved simply by the historical fact that they were temporary — Pentecostalism to the contrary.

4. The signs and miracles were also apostolic in the broader sense to attest the authority of the messengers and their message for the new age. There was no personal apostolic succession. The appearance of the New Testament gave permanent inspired form to apostolic doctrine.

5. A transition period was necessary to reach all living believers with the new message and its accompanying Pentecostal experience. The inspired historical record indicates that only 120 believers were baptized by the Spirit at His initial coming. The church began with this small nucleus out of thousands of living saints. The others were subsequently united to the church by the baptism of the Spirit when they were contacted by the apostles or their associates. Thus Acts 19:1-7 (the incident about the disciples of John) is a sample of the common experience of believers who passed from one dispensation to the other without immediately hearing the Pentecostal message. Those who were saved after Pentecost received the Spirit at the time of faith. The one exception in the case of the Samaritans has been noted and explained. Paul's experience was not an exception, for it is distinctly stated that what he received in the house of Ananias was a filling of the Spirit (Acts 9:17).

   In the transition period there was an interval between regeneration and the baptism of the Spirit only for the Samaritans and for the living saints who passed into the new age without immediately hearing of Pentecost. For all others since Pentecost, regeneration and Spirit baptism are simultaneous (I Cor. 12:13).[12]

- **His Part in the Production of the New Testament**
  The New Testament revelation had its source in God the Father (Rev. 1:1-2; Jn. 16:15; 14:10; 12:49-50), was given through the Lord Jesus Christ (Jn. 16:12-15; Eph. 4:20-21; Heb. 1:1-2; Rev. 1:1-2), and was inspired in its production and content by the Holy Spirit, like the Old Testament canonical books (II Pet. 1:21; II Tim. 3:16). This means that the Holy Spirit so controlled the writers of the New Testament books that, without setting aside the human factor, He enabled them to receive the divine revelation and to record it verbally, without error or omission, as the very Word of God. This work of the Holy Spirit was predicted by Jesus (Jn. 16:12-15), asserted by the apostles (I Cor. 2:9-13; II Pet. 1:16-21; 3:2, 15; Rev. 1:1-2, 10-11), and testified to by the Holy Spirit himself (Rev. 2:7; 14:13).

HIS WORK DURING THE PROPHETIC FUTURE

After the church has been completed and removed to Heaven, the Holy Spirit will continue His work on earth as He does today, with the exception of baptizing people into the body of Christ (I Cor. 12:13, 27). During the Tribulation Period He will withdraw His restraint upon the forces of evil in this world (cp. II Thess. 2:7-8). Yet at the same time, He will continue His work of saving the elect (Mt. 24:13-14) and will help them in their Christian lives (Mt. 10:16-23; cp. Rev. 12:13-14).

During the Lord's millennial kingdom, the Holy Spirit will continue His salvational work (Ezek. 11:19; 36:26; 37:9-10; Zech. 12:10) and will minister to the needs of His people (Isa. 30:21; 59:21). He also will enable Jesus for His Messianic work (Isa. 11:2-3; 42:1-7) and will make known the new dispensation given by Jesus (Isa. 2:3) to the people of earth by prophecy (Joel 2:28-29). Meanwhile, He will continue to indwell His people (Jn. 14:16), doing for them all that is required.

We are grateful for the person and ministry of the Holy Spirit. It is urgent and fitting that we cultivate an intimate relationship with this incomparable Helper that we might realize in our life all that He came to do, to the glory of the Father and the Lord Jesus.

---

[12] Roy L. Aldrich, "Transition Problems in Acts," *Bibliotheca Sacra,* Vol. 114, No. 455 (1957), pp. 241 f. Dr. Aldrich's explanation of the experience of the Samaritans is this: "Peter and John ministered the Spirit to them sometime subsequent to their initial faith in Christ (Acts 8:14-17). The reason for this exception is not stated, probably because it is so obvious. The traditional conflict between the Jews and the Samaritans about which people possessed the truth had to be settled in accord with the Lord's dictum, 'Salvation is of the Jews' (John 4:22). The ministration of the Spirit by the official leaders from Jerusalem was necessary to avoid a destructive schism in the apostolic church." (p. 240).

A Review of Pneumatology

1. Give five reasons for believing that the Holy Spirit is a person.

2. Give three reasons for believing that He is God.

3. Why does the Holy Spirit have attributes that are equal to those belonging to the other Members of the Godhead?

4. In what ways is the Holy Spirit subordinate to the other Members of the Godhead?

5. Give three symbols found in the Scriptures that represent the Holy Spirit.

6. What theophanies of the Holy Spirit were manifest on the Day of Pentecost? At Jesus' baptism?

7. What role did the Holy Spirit have in the transitive actions of the Trinity in creating the universe and in the giving of divine revelation?

8. In what ways did the Holy Spirit help people during the Old Testament period?

9. Briefly explain the Holy Spirit's activity in the following aspects of God the Son's incarnation: His conception, Messianic work, death, and resurrection; also, in His building the church and His earthly rule.

10. How long will the Holy Spirit continue to empower Jesus for His Messianic works?

11. Why do many believe that the Holy Spirit is the Restrainer of II Thessalonians 2:7?

12. When this restraint upon evil is removed, why is it incorrect theologically to say that the Holy Spirit is removed from the earth?

13. Give three things that the Holy Spirit does to bring people to salvational faith in Jesus.

14. What does it mean for the Holy Spirit to convict people?

15. Give and explain the three things that the Holy Spirit does to convict the unsaved of their need for salvation.

16. Of what does the Holy Spirit bear witness to Jesus in His dealing with unsaved people?

17. Why are not unsaved people able and willing to place their trust in Jesus apart from the Holy Spirit's ministry?

18. Give the meanings of "irresistible grace" and "prevenient grace."

19. Give and explain the five things that the Holy Spirit does for the gospel believer at salvation.

20. What part of the gospel believer's human nature does the Holy Spirit renew by regeneration?

21. What kind of life does the Holy Spirit impart?

22. What is eternal life? List several new features that this new life brings into the believer's experience.

23. Does regeneration precede or follow salvational faith?

24. How can people who are spiritually dead respond to the gospel without their being made spiritually alive first?

25. Into what family and kingdom have regenerated people entered?

26. Give the two aspects of the baptism of the Holy Spirit. Which of these is essential for membership in Christ's universal church?

27. When did the first baptism of the Holy Spirit occur? When does it occur in our lives today?

28. How do we know whether or not we have been baptized with the Holy Spirit if we are not to seek signs of this event?

29. Which of these two aspects of the Holy Spirit's baptism will continue to occur in those who believe the gospel after the rapture of the church?

30. How long will the Holy Spirit indwell believers today?

31. Explain the meaning of John 14:20b. By what actions of the Holy Spirit are we in Christ and He is in us?

32. What does the sealing work of the Holy Spirit mean? Why is this work important to our salvation?

33. What does the anointing work of the Holy Spirit mean?

34. What is the basic function of the Holy Spirit in the saved person's life?

35. What other ministries does He perform in our lives?

36. By what means does the Holy Spirit guide us?

37. What does the sanctifying work of the Holy Spirit mean? How can we cooperate with Him in this?

38. What does it mean to be filled with Holy Spirit?

39. What must we do to become filled? To remain filled?

40. What immediately ends the filling of the Holy Spirit? How can we recover the Spirit's filling?

41. Describe the nature of spiritual gifts. Native abilities. What is the purpose for spiritual gifts?

42. List the spiritual gifts that are given in the New Testament and describe each one.

43. Which ones are useful in ministering God's Word? In administrating the Lord's work? In doing practical forms of service?

44. Which gifts should a pastor of a church have? A Sunday-school teacher?

45. What purposes did the gift of speaking in tongues serve in the N.T. church?

46. Why do we not need the gift of tongues today?

47. Why should we not make the possession of any one gift a test of spirituality?

48. How can we learn what our spiritual gifts are?

49. What spiritual gift may cover the use of native abilities in the Lord's work?

50. Do you know what your spiritual gift (or gifts) is? What should we do with our spiritual gifts?

51. Why should we be cautious in seeking to experience all that is recorded of the Holy Spirit's activity in the book of Acts?

52. What will be the work of the Holy Spirit during the Tribulation Age? The Kingdom Age?

53. Is it proper to talk to the Holy Spirit? Give a reason for your answer.

54. What kind of a relation are you now having with the Holy Spirit? Is He filling you daily?

Angelology

ANGELOLOGY
The Doctrine of Angels

That there are other rational, personal beings in our world besides us humans provokes our curiosity and alarm. Who are these creatures and what is their intention? Are they friendly or hostile? Will they do us good or harm? The Scriptures reveal that these creatures are angels, both holy and evil, who live beyond the range of our means of detection and yet are active in our lives. Let us consider what is revealed about them.

THEIR ORIGIN

Angels are created beings (Col. 1:16-17; Neh. 9:6; Ps. 148:2, 5). As part of the initial creation of the universe (Gen. 1:1), they were created before the earth, perhaps before any material thing (Job 38:4-7).

THEIR NATURE

These creatures are personal beings with angelic nature.

THEY ARE PERSONS.
Angels are personal beings, for they have personhood (the divine image). Their personhood is manifested by such features as self-awareness (Dan. 10:11-14), self-determination (Acts 12:7-8; Rev. 22:8-9), moral awareness (Mt. 13:41; Lk. 15:10), perpetuity (Mt. 25:41), as well as intelligence (II Sam. 14:20; Rev. 22:16), desire (I Pet. 1:12), emotion (Job 38:7; Rev. 12:12), and accountability (I Cor. 6:3). Their personhood is also indicated by their being called "sons of God" (Job 38:7).[1]

THEY HAVE ANGELIC NATURE.
Unlike us humans with body, soul, and spirit, angels have a spirit kind of nature (Lk. 24:37-39) that makes them "spirits" (Heb. 1:7, 14). However, we must not equate their spirit nature with God's uncreated essence that is spirit (Jn. 4:24) or with our human spirit (I Cor. 2:11). Their spirit nature is unique, yet it has some kind of bodily organization or form (cp. Lk. 24:4; Mt. 28:2-3; Dan. 10:5-6). Although they express reason, emotion, and will, there is no indication that they have soul and spirit as essential parts of their nature as we humans have.

THEIR CHARACTER

Some characteristics of angels follow:

---

[1] See Franz Delitzsch, *A System of Biblical Psychology* (Grand Rapids: Baker Book House, 1966), 78.

THEY ARE INVISIBLE.

Normally, angels are invisible to our present sight (cp. Num. 22:22-31; II Kings 6:17; Ps. 34:7). They have the ability to appear and disappear at will (cp. Acts 12:7, 10).

THEY ARE MANY.

See Daniel 7:10; Matthew 26:53; Hebrews 12:22; Revelation 5:11.

THEY ARE POWERFUL.

Endowed with superhuman strength (Ps. 103:20; II Pet. 2:11), they can do things that we humans cannot do (cp. II Ki. 19:35; Acts 5:19, 23). However, they do not have infinite power as God does.

THEY ARE SUPERIOR IN ORDER.

They belong to a higher order of life than humans (II Pet. 2:11). In His incarnation the Lord Jesus assumed for a little while a lower order of life than that of angels (Heb. 2:9). But in His exaltation as man, He was elevated above them in position and order (Eph. 1:20-23; Phil. 2:9-11; I Pet. 3:22). As new creatures in Christ (II Cor. 5:17) and members of the new humanity of which He is pattern and head (Rom. 8:29; I Jn. 3:2), we who are saved now share this exalted position and order (Eph. 2:6).

THEY ARE CAPABLE OF LEARNING.

They are learning about God's infinite wisdom and grace, as manifested in His redemptive work and program for the elect of mankind (Eph. 3:10; 2:7; I Pet. 1:12).

THEY ARE MASCULINE IN GENDER.

Throughout the Scriptures masculine gender is ascribed to them (cp. Rev. 10:1-3). This may indicate the reason they do not marry (Mt. 22:30).

THEY ARE INDESTRUCTIBLE.

Being created personal creatures with definite beginning, they will exist forever (Lk. 20:36) — the holy angels with God (Heb. 12:22-23) and the evil angels in Hell (Mt. 25:41, 46).

THEY ARE UNREDEEMABLE.

There is no scriptural evidence that Christ's atoning work extends to fallen angels. In fact, Hell was prepared for them (Mt. 25:41). The elect, holy angels have no need for redemption.

THEIR CLASSIFICATION

The basic classification of angels relates to their moral character — holy or evil. Within each group of angels there is a hierarchy of rank (Eph. 1:21; 6:12; Col. 1:16), with Michael as the foremost holy regular angel (Rev. 12:7-

8) and Satan as the leader of evil angels (Mt. 25:41). In Ephesians 1:21, the words "principality" (rule), "power" (authority), "dominion" (lordship), and "might" (power) indicate various angelic positions of authority in the administrations of God and Satan. While their generic designation is "spirit" (Heb. 1:7, 14), most of their other designations, including "angel" meaning "messenger," are titles which express their functions.

THE HOLY ANGELS

• The Regular Angels

With the title "angel" meaning "messenger," holy angels are active in the service of God: rendering worship (Rev. 5:11-12), delivering divine messages (Lk. 1:11, 26-27), conveying divine revelation (Acts 7:53; Rev. 1:1), inflicting divine judgments (II Sam. 24:16-17; II Kings 19:35; Rev. chs. 8-9), influencing the leaders of governments (Dan. 10:12-11:1), bearing dead humans to their destinies (Lk. 16:22), caring for God's people (Gen. 19:1-22; Ps. 34:7; 91:11-12; Acts 5:19-20; Heb. 1:14), observing believers (I Cor. 4:9; 11:10), and warring against the forces of Satan (Rev. 12:7-9).

Michael, the archangel, seems to have a special commission relating to the care of the nation of Israel (Dan. 12:1; 10:13, 21; cp. Jude 9; Rev. 12:7).

• The Cherubim

Perhaps the highest order of angelic beings, these are closely associated with the throne of God (Ezek. 28:14; II Ki. 19:15). If these are the "living creatures" of Ezekiel chapter one and Revelation chapters four and five, they bear God's throne (Ezek. 1:26; 10:1; Ps. 18:10; 99:1) and engage in His worship (Rev. 4:6-9; 5:8, 14).

• The Seraphim

Stationed near God's throne (Isa. 6:2, 6), these appear to be responsible for proclaiming the glory and holiness of God. One was an agent in Isaiah's purification (vss. 5-7).

• The Twenty-Four Elders

These are seen sitting around God's judgment throne (Rev. 4:4, 10; 5:8-10). While many believe that these angelic beings are redeemed humans who represent the Old and New Testament saints, I prefer the view that they are an order of angelic beings.[2] These appear to hold some kind of administrative position in God's government, for they sit on thrones and wear crowns (Rev. 4:4).[3] Moreover, they serve in a priestly capacity, engaging in worship (Rev. 4:10; 11:16-17) and presenting prayers (5:8; cp. 6:9-10; 8:3-5). Also, they engage in prophetic activity, perceiving God's purpose for creation (Rev. 4:11), recognizing Christ's atoning work (5:5, 9), and anticipating the future

---

[2] See Revelation 5:9-10 in *The Greek New Testament*, edited by Kurt Aland, Matthew Black, Bruce M. Metzger, and Allen Wikgren. This text translates "them" and "they" rather than "us" and "we."
[3] "Crown" (stephanos) may represent rule and authority as well as a victor's garland (Rev. 6:2).

blessings of the tribulation martyrs (7:13-17) and of Jesus' Messianic rule (11:16-18). (For the Angel of the LORD, see p. 77.)

THE EVIL ANGELS

These are the angels who followed Satan in his rebellion against God (Mt. 25:41; Rev. 12:4, 7-9). Some of these are now confined, others are free.

• The Confined Evil Angels

These angels left their proper place and went after a different kind of flesh for immoral purposes (II Pet. 2:4; Jude 6-7; cp. I Pet. 3:18-19). These may have been the "sons of God" who had sexual relations with human women before the Noachic flood (Gen. 6:1-4). These fallen angels are confined to Tartaros, a region of Hades (II Pet. 2:4 Gk.), and they serve as an example of divine vengeance (Jude 7).

If the "locusts" of Revelation 9:1-10 are evil spirits, then these too are confined to the Abyss, another region of Hades (cp. Rom. 10:7), until the time of their release for tormenting earth dwellers in the tribulation period. Their king, named Destroyer, is probably a holy angel who has charge of the Abyss. In verse fourteen we read of four angels who are bound at the Euphrates River. When loosed, these will lead an army of 200 million superhuman horsemen to destroy a third of the earth's population (Rev. 9:15).

• The Free Evil Angels

Loyal to their leader, Satan, these angels actively oppose God and His people and influence world affairs (Rev. 12:7-9; Jn. 14:30; Eph. 6:12). The common biblical designations of these evil angels are "demons"[4] and "spirits" (Mt. 8:16).

Displaying personality features (Mk. 5:8-13) and superhuman strength (Mk. 9:18; Acts 19:16), these evil spirits cause certain physical, emotional, and mental disorders (Mt. 12:22; Lk. 13:11; Mk. 5:1-5), cause self-destruction (Mk. 9:17-22), teach false doctrine (I Tim. 4:1), inspire false prophets (I Jn. 4:1, 3), incite wickedness (Mt. 12:42-45), influence human political leaders (Dan. 10:12-11:1), hinder God's people (I Thess. 2:18), tempt (3:5) and project evil thoughts (cp. Mt. 16:22-23).

They are called "unclean spirits" (Mt. 10:1), "deaf and dumb spirit" (Mk. 9:17, 25), "foul spirit" (Mk. 9:25), "evil spirits" (Lk. 7:21), "spirit of divination" (Acts 16:16), "spirit of error" (I Jn. 4:6), "seducing spirits" (I Tim. 4:1), and "lying spirits" (I Ki. 22:22).

THE FALL OF SOME ANGELS

God created all angels good (Gen. 1:31; cp. Ezek. 28:14-15). Since they

---

[4] This is "devils" in the KJV, an unfortunate translation as there is only one devil, who is Satan (Rev. 12:9; 20:2).

possessed personhood with its moral self-determination, they were given the choice of remaining loyal to God and serving Him forever or of rebelling against God and serving sin.

- **The Fall of Lucifer**
  Satan was created "the anointed cherub," one appointed to carry out God's will (Ezek. 28:13-14). His name was "Lucifer" (Isa. 14:12; Heb. "the shining one"). Moreover, he was perfect in all of his ways until he sinned (Ezek. 28:15). As the "covering cherub," he was the highest and most beautiful of all creatures (vss. 13, 17). He was stationed in "Eden the garden of God," or "the mountain of God" (vss. 13, 14, 16, a reference to Heaven), next to the throne of God (1:26).

  Having personhood, Lucifer had the abilities of moral choice and worship. However, struck by his dazzling beauty, he chose to exalt himself rather than his Creator (Ezek. 28:17). This wrong choice and subsequent action engendered within him the sin-force, brought him moral ruin, led to pride, and resulted in his eviction from God's presence (vs. 16; I Tim. 3:6). Motivated by sin, Satan set out on an irrational course to seize for himself God's position and authority (cp. Isa. 14:12-14).

  I believe that Satan's first sin occurred after the creation week (Gen. 1:31) and before man's sin (3:1-6). It appears that Satan became the ruler of this world when he led man, the ruler of earth, to sin (Gen. 1:26) and by this brought Adam and his posterity under his dominion (Jn. 12:31; Acts 26:18; I Jn. 5:19).

- **The Fall of Other Angels**
  Apparently responding to Satan's example and persuasion, as many as a third of the angelic host chose to revolt against God and to follow the devil (Rev. 12:4). Their wrong choice and action engendered within them the sin-force and brought to them spiritual death and moral ruin, as their designations indicate (see above). Their rebellion also brought them under Satan's authority (Mt. 25:41).

THE ETERNAL FUTURE OF ANGELS

Being personal, responsible beings, angels are accountable to God for their conduct and will exist forever.

THE FUTURE OF HOLY ANGELS
Being elected of God to remain unfallen (I Tim. 5:21), they will worship and serve Him forever (cp. Heb. 12:22-23; Rev. 5:11-12; 21:12).

THE FUTURE OF EVIL ANGELS
These will be judged (I Cor. 6:3; II Pet. 2:4) and will experience conscious torment in Hell forever (Mt. 25:41; Rev. 20:10). They are aware of the doom

that awaits them (Mt. 8:29; Mk. 5:7; Lk. 8:28).

Nowhere do the Scriptures teach that redemption has been provided for evil angels. Colossians 1:20 seems to refer only to that which was involuntarily affected by sin. Paul does not refer to the things under the earth that belong to Hades.

SATAN

While it is urgent for us to learn what God has revealed about His archenemy Satan, we must be careful not to give the adversary honors which belong only to God. Moreover, we must take care not to allow an unhealthy curiosity about the devil and his works to involve us beyond what is lawful. God has revealed all that we need to know about the devil. It is safe and wise to be contented with this information.

HIS DESIGNATIONS

Before his fall Satan was called "Lucifer" which is Latin for "light-bearer" (Isa. 14:12) and which in Hebrew means "the shining one" (cp. Ezek. 28:13). Since his fall the leader of evil angels is called "Satan," meaning "adversary" (Job 1:6; Mt. 4:10; Acts 5:3; Rev. 12:9); "the devil," meaning "slanderer" (Mt. 4:1; Jn. 8:44; I Pet. 5:8); and "Beelzebub," meaning "lord of flies" and suggesting all that is vile and loathsome (Mt. 12:24-26). Other designations are "dragon" (Rev. 12:9; 20:2), "the old serpent" (Rev. 12:9; 20:2), "the tempter" (Mt. 4:3), "the prince of this world" (Jn. 12:31), "the father of lies" (Jn. 8:44), and "the prince of demons" (Mt. 12:24), and "the god of this age" (II Cor. 4:4).

HIS NATURE

Although many deny his personhood and regard him as being only an evil force, the Scriptures reveal what Satan is.

- **He is a person.**

His personhood is indicated by his self-awareness (Mt. 4:9), self-expression (Isa. 14:13-14), moral awareness (Mt. 4:1), perpetuity (Rev. 20:10), as well as his craftiness (Eph. 6:11; II Cor. 2:11) and emotion (Rev. 12:12).

- **He is an angel.**

He was created the supreme angel, called "the anointed cherub" (Ezek. 28:13-14; cp. Job 1:6; II Cor. 11:14). Like all created beings, he is finite and is subject to God's supreme authority (Job 1:12; Rev. 12:9-12).

HIS CHARACTER

The Scriptures show that Satan is wicked (Jn. 17:15), murderous (Jn. 8:44), deceptive (Rev. 12:9; Jn. 8:44), proud (I Tim. 3:6), powerful (Job 1:12-19; 2:7; II Thess. 2:9); insolent (Mt. 4:9), cunning (II Cor. 2:11; Eph. 6:11), persevering (Lk. 4:13), and crazy, being obsessed with the absurd idea that he can unseat God (Isa. 14:12-14).[5]

HIS ACTIVITY

- ### After his Fall
Upon man's fall God judicially declared that the Seed of the woman would crush Satan's head (Gen. 3:15). Early in human history, the tempter tried to thwart this sentence by attempting to destroy the human line of descent into which the Redeemer would be born [cp. the evil antediluvian days (Gen. 6:5)]. Later, he led Israel to rebel against God (Isa. 1:1-9) and plotted against the life of the Lord Jesus (Mt. 2:1-16).

Today, he is doing all he can, within the limits of God's permissive decree, to hinder the ministry of the Lord's people. It irks him to see his former subjects serving the Lord Jesus and bearing witness to the message and effectiveness of the gospel. Untiringly, he seeks to stop this and to render their lives ineffective (Eph. 6:11-14; I Pet. 5:8).

- ### In the Future
In the middle of the coming Tribulation Period, Satan and his angels will be evicted from the celestial heaven and will be cast unto the earth (Rev. 12:7-10; cp. Isa. 14:12-17). Realizing that his time is short, the devil will attempt to achieve his infamous ambition through a human agent, the Beast, through whom he will rule the earth and will require world worship (Rev. 12:12; 13:3-8). But Satan will not succeed. His human confederates will be destroyed in the battle of Armageddon, and he and his evil angels will be cast into the Abyss for a thousand years (Rev. 20:1-3).

After Christ's millennial rule over the earth, the devil will be released from the Abyss and will lead a final revolt of unsaved earth dwellers against the King in Jerusalem. But the rebels will be destroyed by fire, and Satan will be cast into the Lake of Fire (Rev. 20:7-10). God will gloriously triumph, not only in putting away the enemy forever but also in accomplishing His purpose for the devil's existence (Rom. 9:22; Rev. 11:15-18).

HIS DEFEAT BY JESUS

God's judicial sentence upon Satan in Eden was that the Seed of the woman (Jesus) would crush his head (Gen. 3:15). When God the Son came to earth and by His incarnation became the last Adam (I Cor. 15:45), He had the title to everything, including this world (Mt. 11:27; Jn. 3:35; 13:3; Heb. 1:2; Ps. 2:7-9). Therefore, the usurper prince of this world tried to secure the Heir's

---

[5] Like Ezekiel 28:11-19, Isaiah 14:12-17 looks beyond its subject, the human political ruler, to Satan, the ruler of this world. This prophecy anticipates the time when Satan and his angelic confederates will be cast into Hades (Rev. 20:1-3). This will take place after his 3½ years rule over the earth through his human agent the Beast (13:1-10) and before our Lord's millennial kingdom. Isaiah 14:13-14 may refer to the devil's words after his confinement to earth in the middle of the Tribulation Age (Rev. 12:7-9).

allegiance and inheritance as he had gained man's (Mt. 4:1-11), but he did not succeed. Our Lord defeated him in every encounter.

- **Jesus defeated Satan during the years He lived in Nazareth.**
The Father's words testify to His pleasure in Jesus' life during this time (Mt. 3:17). Jesus was tempted as we are, yet without the inner desires of the sin-principle (Heb. 4:15) for no sin was in Him (I Jn. 3:5).

- **Jesus defeated Satan at the beginning of His Messianic work.**
The devil tested Jesus' commitment to the Father's will about His physical condition, physical situation, and Messianic vocation (Mt. 4:1-11).

- **Jesus defeated Satan throughout His public ministry.**
The devil approached Jesus through friends (Mt. 16:22-23) and enemies (Mk. 10:2; Jn. 8:6).

- **Jesus defeated the adversary at the cross.**
There the divine sentence of condemnation against the adversary was confirmed (Jn. 16:11), for the crucifixion of Jesus was a self-condemnatory act. It was the greatest crime of creatures against their Creator.

- **Jesus defeated the devil by His death and resurrection.**
Uniquely, Jesus voluntarily laid down His life, invaded Satan's domain, and broke the enemy's power by His resurrection (Jn. 10:18; Heb. 2:14; Acts 2:24).

- **Jesus now defeats Satan in the lives of His people.**
The Lord not only delivers all who receive Him from Satan's authority (Col. 1:13) but He also gives them occasions of victory in their daily life and final victory over death (Jas. 4:7; I Cor. 15:51-57).

Because of these victories, the Lord will one day cast the devil and his demonic associates into the Lake of Fire (Rev. 20:10). We who are saved are looking forward to this triumphant event (Rom. 16:20).

HIS DEFEAT IN OUR LIVES

Although he is a defeated enemy who ultimately will be cast into the Lake of Fire, the devil is still very active in his warfare against the Lord's people, who were his former subjects (Col. 1:13). However, we who are saved can have occasions of victory over him as we prepare for the conflict and take those steps which lead us to victory. I say occasions of victory, for if we fail to do our part, we shall be defeated by the adversary. While our Lord will ultimately prevail over the enemy, He can only give us victory in the skirmishes we experience with Satan as we look to Him. Happily, our defeats here do not determine the outcome of the campaign, though they do hinder our testimony and spiritual progress.

- **Our Preparation before Satan Attacks**
To be victorious, we must do certain things before the enemy launches his

attack against us.

1. LEARN ABOUT HIM FROM GOD'S WORD

We must not be ignorant of his devices, or designs (II Cor. 2:11). The enemy takes advantage of our spiritual immaturity and ignorance (Eph. 4:11-15).

2. CONSTANTLY STRENGTHEN OURSELVES IN THE LORD (Eph. 6:10)

When we daily feed on the Scriptures and walk in fellowship with the Lord, we then can meet the enemy in the Lord's strength. Because of this, the enemy seeks to disrupt our daily communication with the Lord.

3. PUT ON THE WHOLE ARMOR OF GOD (Eph. 6:11-18)

This armor consists of spiritual realities which we are to appropriate to our daily life. These realities are spiritual qualities that are found in Christ and that manifest Him in our lives (Rom. 13:11-14). They are qualities that express the very opposite of what Satan would have us to be. Since these qualities belong to Christ and are reproduced in our life by the Holy Spirit, they are put on by prayer, self-surrender, and the exercise of faith (cp. Jn. 7:37-38). Whenever we appropriate these qualities by faith, we put on Christ and allow Him to express Himself in our life (Rom. 13:14; Gal. 2:20). Jesus is this complete armor. He lacks nothing that is essential for our pleasing God and our defeating the enemy.

Paul compares these spiritual qualities to the battle gear of the Roman soldier. Let us consider what we are to put on each day.

a. The Belt of Truth (Eph. 6:14; cp. Jn. 14:6)

While this truth may refer to God's Word (Jn. 17:17), which we are to read, understand, and apply, it more likely refers to truthfulness and honesty in daily life. The enemy, who is a liar (Jn. 8:44), would have us to be dishonest and deceitful. When we have the belt on, we are truthful.

The soldier's belt was a broad leather one, covering the lower part of the body and reaching down to the middle of the thighs.

b. The Coat of Righteousness (Eph. 6:14; cp. Phil. 1:11)

Righteousness is a state of being or doing right. We become righteous when we are saved (Rom. 5:1; I Cor. 1:30). Now it is our duty to do what is right in God's sight (I Tim. 6:11; II Tim. 2:15; I Jn. 3:7). Satan would have us disobey God. When we have the coat on, we do God's will.

The soldier's coat of mail consisted of two parts: one covering his chest and stomach, the other his back. This was usually made of leather plated with metal. It protected the body from wounding blows.

c. The Sandals of Preparation (Eph. 6:15; cp. II Cor. 5:20)

This may represent a willingness of heart (Rom. 1:14-16) and a promptness of action (Acts 16:30-31) to bear witness to the lost when the opportunity arises. Satan would have us remain silent. When we put on these sandals, we are prepared to witness to the content and the effectiveness of the gospel.

Paul alludes to the heavy, hobnailed military sandals which protected the feet from road bruises.

   d. *The Shield of Faith (Eph. 6:16; cp. Gal. 2:20)*

   This seems to refer to practical faith which rests upon God's promises. Satan shoots at us flaming arrows like fear, bitterness, and doubt. But by faith in such promises as Isaiah 41:10, Romans 8:28, and Hebrews 10:23, we can quench these arrows and experience the victories of peace, praise, and confidence. Satan would have us lean upon our own resources rather than God's Word. When we use this shield, we quench the arrows of the adversary.

Paul speaks of the large Roman shield, which was semi-cylindrical and which measured four by two-and-a-half feet. It was made of boards, covered with coarse cloth under an outer layer of rawhide. The arrows were tipped with pitch and were set on fire before they were discharged.

   e. *The Helmet of Salvation (Eph. 6:17; cp. Heb. 13:6)*

   This may represent the essential knowledge of salvation and the experience of its deliverance in our daily life. Our Lord would have us to know what the Scriptures teach about the plan, components, and assurance of salvation. He also would have us to experience its power in daily deliverance from our spiritual enemies and in continual realization of its new life. Satan would have us remain ignorant of these things so as to keep us in doubt and bondage.

The Roman helmet was made of leather or metal. It covered the head, brows, cheeks, and neck, protecting these vulnerable parts of the body.

   f. *The Sword of the Spirit (Eph. 6:17; cp. Jn. 1:14)*

   This is the Word of God, wielded in the power of the Holy Spirit. To use the word effectively against the enemy, we must learn its content, obey its commands, and depend upon the Holy Spirit to help us to apply it to the various needs of life. Since the Scriptures reveal God's will for us, Satan would have us to ignore them and to follow his evil suggestions (cp. Mt. 4:1-10). We must confront the adversary with the Word in the power of the Spirit as Jesus did.

The Roman sword was a short, two-edged one that the soldier carried as a side arm and used in close combat.

   4. *MAINTAIN COMMUNICATION WITH GOD (Eph. 6:18a)*

   This involves our regularly reading the Scriptures and praying. Since this is the means by which the Lord provides direction and strength, Satan seeks to disrupt this or cause us to neglect it.

   5. *BE ALERT FOR THE ENEMY (Eph. 6:18b)*

   The enemy is ever searching for unwary prey (I Pet. 5:8). His "roaring" is a deception, indicating that he, like a filled beast, is harmless, but this is not true. How then can we detect his presence? He is near when he suggests doubts about God and behavior that does not agree with God's will for us; when he would have us hurry in making some decision without our seeking God's will; when he gets us worked up over some issue; when he seeks to inflate us with pride; when he casts over us fear, depression, or mental torment; and when in our thinking he seeks to push things to an extreme so that they are out of balance with everything else.

- **Our Course when Satan Attacks**

If we have prepared ourselves to meet the enemy, then we shall experience victory by taking the following steps:

1. REMEMBER THAT THE LORD WILL GIVE US VICTORY as we look to Him (I Cor. 10:13; Heb. 2:18; Phil. 4:13). Since the Lord defeated Satan during the course of His earthly life, He can now defeat the enemy through us as we allow Him.

2. REMEMBER GOD'S WILL FOR US about our circumstances (Eph. 5:17). Jesus did this when He faced the enemy (Mt. 4:4, 7, 10). God's will for us is revealed in the Scriptures by precepts and principles, which we may apply to any circumstance of life.

3. IMMEDIATELY GIVE OURSELF TO GOD FOR VICTORY (Jas. 4:7). As we give ourself to the Lord and believe that He will help us as He promises, we allow Him to confront the enemy through us (Phil. 4:13).

4. RESIST SATAN'S ATTACK BY DEPENDING UPON THE LORD and by saying no to the devil (Jas. 4:7; I Pet. 5:8-9). We cannot, however, successfully say no to the devil until first we have said yes to Jesus.

By faith in God's promises we can experience what Jesus won for us. In His name we can resist the enemy and refuse to submit to his evil suggestions and relentless assaults. If the attack comes through some person, we can rebuke the person (Mt. 16:23) or leave his presence (Gen. 39:12). If it comes in the form of a thought, we can turn it over to Jesus and think on right things (II Cor. 10:5; Phil. 4:8).

5. REMEMBER AND REST UPON THE PROMISE OF VICTORY (Jas. 4:7). Victory is certain if we follow the course that leads to it. Defeat is certain if the enemy finds us unprepared and unwilling to follow these steps.

- **Our Remaining Alert for the Next Attack**

The enemy will not leave us for long (Lk. 4:13). The fact that we are attacked by him does not make us blameworthy, nor is it to be feared. Although we are aware of Satan's craftiness and power, we should consider his attacks as opportunities to defeat him in Jesus' name. Each victory strengthens our spiritual life (Jas. 1:1-3).

HIS STRATEGY

Satan's strategy is indicated by the words "wiles" (Eph. 6:11) and "devices" (II Cor. 2:11). His "wiles" are his methods of procedure that he follows to achieve his goals; his "devices" are his designs, plans, or plots. His strategy against the Lord's people is shown by the kinds, manner, and timing of his approach. Let us look at these.

- ### The Kinds of Approach

  1. ### HE TEMPTS US.

  He seeks to gain our consent to his proposals that would lead us to act contrary to God's will for us (I Thess. 3:5). We do not sin by being tempted; we sin by yielding to temptation. Henry Drummond wrote, "It is only when a man sees temptation coming and goes out to meet it, welcomes it, plays with it, and invites it to be his guest that it passes from temptation into sin."[6]

  2. ### HE ASSAULTS US.

  With this approach Satan attempts to injure or harass us without our consent. His assaults against the Lord's people include their experiencing various losses (Job 1:14-19), unfounded criticism (Job 4:7-8), physical illness (Job 2:7; Lk. 13:11, 16; II Cor. 12:7), hindrance to spiritual endeavor (I Thess. 2:18), violence (Acts 7:57-58), mental obsession and torment (I Sam. 16:14), and satanic control (Acts 5:3).

  We must distinguish between demonic influence and demonic possession. Demonic influence means for one to be subjected to or affected by the power of a demon, yet not indwelt by him. The subject has self-determination and expresses his own personality under this influence. On the other hand, demonic possession means for one to be indwelt by a demon and to be wholly under his control to the extent that the subject is completely passive, having no self-determination and expressing the personality of the demon.[7] Being unconscious, the possessed subject is not aware of what he says or does.

  Bible students are not agreed upon the possibility of a believer's being possessed by a demon.[8] Many do not believe that this is possible, for the body is the temple of the Holy Spirit (I Cor. 6:19). But this ignores the fact that, being omnipresent, the Holy Spirit is with evil spirits continually. Missionaries bear witness to known believers being possessed. There remains the possibility that these possessed people were not really saved or that the possession was mistakenly identified. If believers can be possessed, then it seems that this takes place in the unredeemed part of their human nature — their body. Inducing unconsciousness, the demon uses their body for his expression. In any event, it behooves us who are saved to avoid any contact with devices, situations, or activities where we come under demonic influence

---

[6] Quoted by James Strahan, *Hebrew Ideals* (Grand Rapids: Kregel Publications), 289. This book is the finest I know on the lives of the Patriarchs in Genesis chs. 12-50.

[7] For the stages of obsession and possession, see John L. Nevius, *Demon Possession and Allied Themes* (New York: Fleming H. Revell Company, 1893), pp. 285-90.

[8] See Merrill F. Unger, *Demons in the World Today* (Wheaton: Tyndale House Publishers, 1971), pp. 116 f. Merrill F. Unger, *What Demons Can Do to Saints* (Chicago: Moody Press, 1977), ch. 4.

and to shun the attitude of passivity which makes us vulnerable to this influence.[9]

- ### The Manner of Approach

Genesis 3:1-6 reveals much about the procedure that Satan follows when he seeks to secure our consent to his proposals.

1. *HE APPROACHES IN DISGUISE (vs. 1).*

Being the archdeceiver, he aims at making things to look different from what they really are. He approaches behind members of the animal kingdom (Gen. 3:1) and people (Mt. 16:21-23; Job 2:9; II Cor. 11:13-15). Moreover, he appeals to natural physical and mental appetites (Mt. 4:3) and to religious duty (Ex. 32:4-6; I Cor. 10:20).

2. *HE SEEKS TO UNDERMINE OUR TRUST IN GOD (vss. 1-5).*

Our exercise of faith in God and His Word allows Him to minister to our needs and enables us to do His will. If Satan can divert our faith to some other object, then he renders us powerless and defenseless. His words to Eve indicate several ways by which he undermines this practical faith in God. He does this...

a. *By asking a question which raises doubt about God's goodness (vs. 1).* The question implies that God is unduly strict.

b. *By speaking a lie which raises doubt about God's integrity (vs. 4).* The lie suggests that God does not mean what He says and that He is trying to intimidate man.

c. *By making an insinuation which raises doubt about God's motives (vs. 5).* The devil hints that God is keeping something good from man, namely, that one can be like God by exercising independent self-determination.

3. *HE SHOWS WHY WE SHOULD DISOBEY GOD (vs. 6).*

Looking at the fruit and seeing what the devil wanted her to see, Eve yielded to the tempter's proposal and sinned against God. When Satan succeeded in turning Eve's attention away from God, he then appealed to her native physical, aesthetic, and intellectual desires (which were in themselves sinless) and offered her satisfaction of these desires in a way that was contrary to God's will (cp. Jesus' temptation, Mt. 4:1-10). Eve's initial mistake was to talk to the devil, for he convincingly gave her reasons for following his suggestions.

- ### The Time of Approach

While the devil may attack at any time, he will do so when he thinks it is to his advantage. He may approach us when we are in the wake of a great spiritual experience (Mt. 3:16; 4:1-2), when we are at the beginning of some spiritual endeavor (vs. 17), when we are in a state of physical weakness or

---

[9] See Appendix Q: Passivity and demonic possession.

mental exhaustion (vs. 2), or when we are alone (vs. 1). We can expect Satan to challenge our commitments to the Lord as he challenged Jesus throughout His ministry (Mt. 4:1-11; 16:21-23). We must always be alert for him (I Pet. 5:8), for he generally attacks unexpectedly (Mt. 16:21-23).

We thank God for the victory we can experience through Jesus over our adversary. We can have the expectation of Paul when he declared that the Lord would deliver him from every evil work and would preserve him unto His heavenly kingdom (II Tim. 4:18).

We thank God, too, for the ministry of His holy angels in our lives. Although it is not given to us to know our guardian angels or to ask them for help (they are God's servants to carry out the divine will), we are grateful for this provision for our lives. We must always look to God for help. He will respond in the way that is best for us.

A Review of Angelology

1. Where did angels come from?
2. Describe the nature (make-up) of angels.
3. How do we know that angels have personhood?
4. What is the basic description of angelic nature?
5. In what way are angels like God?
6. Why does their having a spirit kind of nature not make them like God?
7. Describe the characteristics of angels.
8. What is the generic designation of angels?
9. What is the meaning of "angel"?
10. What is the basic moral classification of angels?
11. What is the primary function of holy angels?
12. What are some of the duties of holy angels in this role?
13. In addition to "regular" angels, what other kinds of holy angels are there?
14. What two kinds of evil angels are there?
15. What is a common biblical designation for free evil angels?
16. How could Lucifer sin when this evil force did not exist?
17. What did Lucifer choose to do? What did the angels who sinned choose to do?
18. What is the future of holy angels? Sinful angels?
19. Give several biblical designations for Satan.
20. What does the word "Satan" mean? "The devil"?
21. What evidence is there that Satan has personhood and thus is a personal creature?
22. Describe the character of the devil.
23. What has been the activity of Satan since his fall? What are his future activities?
24. While Jesus defeated Satan many times, what was His greatest defeat of the devil?
25. When will the devil be cast into the Lake of Fire?
26. What preparations must we make in order to be ready for Satan's attacks? How often should we make these preparations?
27. What is the armor of God? How do we put this on?
28. What do the parts of the armor represent in the Christian life?
29. How can we detect the devil's presence?
30. What are the steps to victory when the devil attacks us?

31. Why does the devil flee when we face him in dependence on the Lord?

32. Give the two kinds of Satan's approach to a Christian.

33. When does temptation become sin?

34. What is the difference between demonic influence and demonic possession?

35. What can we learn about the manner of Satan's approach from his tempting Eve?

36. At what times in our life does Satan seem to prefer to attack us?

37. How can these attacks be beneficial to us?

38. When shall we be permanently delivered from Satan's attacks?

39. Will the devil always retain his power? When will he be deprived of it?

40. Did you thank God today for the ministry of holy angels in your life?

41. Should we try to communicate with our guardian angel? Give a reason for your answer.

Anthropology

ANTHROPOLOGY
The Doctrine of Man

The Bible gives us exclusive information not only about God but also about ourselves. Ignoring this revelation, modern scientific opinion regards man as being a higher kind of animal, which has slowly evolved to its present form over millions of years. However, the facts of man's origin and nature cannot be known apart from what God has revealed in His Word. Any opinion that is not grounded upon and governed by this revelation will be conjectural and faulty. Being human beings, we should seek to learn what the Creator has revealed about us; being Christians, we should accept this revelation as absolute truth and base our understanding of this doctrine on it. Throughout this study, the word *man* is used generically for both male and female humans, except in those passages where it obviously represents the male gender.

THE ORIGIN OF MAN

ITS MANNER

Man was created by the direct, personal act of God, apart from any organic evolutionary process (Gen. 1:27; 2:7, 21-22; 5:1-2; 9:6; Ps. 100:3; Eccles. 7:29; Mt. 19:4).[1] This creative work was the joint action of the Persons of the Godhead in fulfillment of Their earlier determination, expressed by Their decree (Gen. 1:26-27).

Regarding the two accounts of man's creation, the second (Gen. 2:7) completes the first (Gen. 1:26-27). The account in chapter one presents the creation of man in his relationship to his environment, while the account in chapter two presents the creation of man in his relation with his Creator.

- ### The Creation of Adam (Gen. 2:7)

Following a two-step process that He seems to have used in the creation of animals (Gen. 2:19; cp. 1:20, 24; 7:21-22), God directly created man in this way: First, He made Adam's body from existing material — "the dry, fine crumbs of earth"[2] (cp. Gen. 3:19; Job 4:19; 33:6; Ps. 103:14; Eccles. 3:20; 12:7). "Adam" means "red arable soil."[3] Second, God breathed into Adam's nostrils "the breath of lives," with the result that man "became a living soul" (i.e., a living being or creature; cp. Gen. 1:20-21, 24; 2:19). It appears that God did several things in this second step of man's creation. He animated man's body by imparting a human spirit (Gen. 6:17; 7:21-22; cp. Ps. 104:29) and soul (I

---

[1] The verb "created" (Gen. 1:27; Heb. *bara*) does not mean to create something out of nothing, as Genesis 1:20-21 shows, but to create something new. It is joined with "made" (Heb. *asah*) in Genesis 2:3. See Franz Delitzsch, *A New Commentary on Genesis* (Edinburgh: T. & T. Clark, 1899). I, 74.
[2] Ludwig Koehler, "aphar," *Lexicon in Veteris Testamenti Libros* (1953), p. 723.
[3] _____ , "adam," op. cit., p. 13.

Kings 17:21-22). He also imparted the divine image (Gen. 1:26), which I believe is personhood,[4] and spiritual life (2:17), rising out of a personal relationship with God (Lk. 3:38).

Upon the completion of this creative process, "man became a living soul." While other passages, as we shall see, show that man has a soul as a separate component of his makeup, this clause seems to emphasize his becoming a living creature.[5]

- ## The Creation of Eve (Gen. 2:18-25; I Cor. 11:8-12)

God created Eve on the same day that He created Adam (Gen. 1:27; 5:1-2). This also was a two-step process. First, God made Eve's body from Adam's rib (Gen. 2:21-22). Creating her body from living tissue, God did not have to impart to her the physical life-animating principles of soul and spirit as in the case of Adam. Second, God imparted to Eve the divine image (i.e., her unique personhood, Gen. 5:1-2; 9:6) and spiritual life (2:17). By this creative process Eve became a living human being, with the same essential parts as Adam — personhood and human nature, consisting of body, soul, and spirit (5:1-2; cp. 7:21-22).

God created Eve for Adam in order that she might fulfill certain needs in his life (I Cor. 11:9; Gen. 2:18-25). Being lonely, the first man needed a companion like himself, yet differing, with whom he could have an intimate relationship and by whom he could be completed. He also needed a helper with whom he could share the service of God and the labors of life and with whom he could reproduce his kind (Gen. 1:28; 2:15). The words "a help meet for him" (2:18) literally read "a helper corresponding to him."

Adam became aware of his need for a companion and helper when he named the animals and birds (2:19-20). He observed that each creature had its mate, yet he did not find any among them that corresponded to him or suited him physically, intellectually, and emotionally. But God met his need. Placing him in a deep sleep, He took one of Adam's ribs, of it made Eve, and presented her to him. Indeed, it was love at first sight (2:22-25)!

Why did God make Eve from a rib? Perhaps it was to remind Adam of the affection that he should have for his wife. That God made Eve of Adam's substance was for woman's humility and glory. "It is humbling to the woman to know that she was created for the man, but it is for her glory to know that she alone can complete him. Likewise, it is humbling to the man to know that he is incomplete without a woman, but it is to his glory to know that the woman was created for him."[6]

---

[4] See Appendix C.

[5] That man became a living creature by God's creative breath refutes any theory that holds that man was another kind of creature before this act which, it is said, made him human.

[6] Dwight Hervey Small, *Design for Christian Marriage* (Westwood: Fleming H. Revell Company, 1959), p. 32.

ITS TIME

The Bible states that God created man on the sixth day of creation week (Gen. 1:24-31), but there are differences of opinion among scholars about how long ago this was. Bible chronologists James Usher, Martin Anstey, Philip Mauro, Richard Niessen, and Eugene W. Faulstitch offer the dates 4004, 4124, 4025, 4174, and 4001 B.C., respectively.[7] Today many feel that more time is needed for man's dispersion over the earth and for the scholar's accommodation to scientific opinion about man than what a face-value computation of Bible chronology allows. (Incidentally, if people migrated three miles a day, in ten years they would travel ten thousand miles, the length of North and South America.) Therefore, they assume the possibility of gaps in the Genesis genealogical records (chs. 5, 10, 11) or hold that the names listed in these represent the first ancestor of a clan or family.

These arbitrary interpretations of the genealogical records create problems. It opens the door to all kinds of conjecture regarding the antiquity of man, and it assumes that the Bible does not present an unbroken line of descent from Adam to Christ (Lk. 3:23-38).[8] Actually, as the forenamed chronologers show, the Bible does give a complete chronology from Adam to Christ with sufficient detail to compute accurately the span in years. We should remember that there are no absolute means of verification of any date earlier than 3500 B.C., the beginning of recorded history. In spite of current opinion to the contrary, I prefer the witness of Bible chronology.

Regarding the discovery of Pleistocene hominid fossils, the question remains whether any of these are human. Some believe that these hominids were pre-Adamic races of creatures that resembled man but which were not made in God's image. However, the Bible nowhere hints at pre-Adamic races, nor does the creation week, as I understand it, allow for their existence. All remains of true humans must be the descendants of Adam. Without doubt, some human races became extinct, particularly with the Noachic flood.

Although early man may have made extensive use of stone implements, this does not necessarily mean that he was an ignorant savage, as people with stone age culture show today. Also, we must distinguish between civilization (an advanced state of material and social well-being) and spirituality (a state of fellowship with God). Though early man may have had a simple culture, yet by God's grace some were able to please Him and walk in His fellowship

---

[7] Thomas Hartwell Horne, An Introduction to the Critical Study and Knowledge of the Holy Scriptures (Boston: Littell and Gay, 1868), II, 556. Martin Anstey, Chronology of the Old Testament (Grand Rapids: Kregel Publications, 1973), p. 149. Philip Mauro, The Chronology of the Bible (Boston: Hamilton Bros., 1922), p. 22; Richard Niessen, Creation Research Society Quarterly, Vol. 19, June, 1982, pp. 60 ff; Eugene W. Faulstitch, It's About Time, (Spencer, Iowa: Chronology-History Research Institute), January, 1987, p. 11; March, 1987, p. 13.

[8] With reference to our Lord's actual genealogy through Mary (Lk. 3:23-38), there is the problem of Cainan (vs. 36) who is not found in the Masoretic text of Genesis 11:10-12 and who may never have existed. He is listed in the Septuagint version (vs. 12). Still if authentic, this would not account for a gap of thousands of years which some require for their theories.

(Gen. 2:15; 4:4; 5:24; 6:9). History has repeatedly demonstrated that a complex civilization often serves as a substitute for God and may be a hindrance to true spirituality (cp. Gen. 4:16-24; Lk. 16:15; I Jn. 2:15-17; Rev. chs. 17, 18).

THE NATURE OF MAN

Having examined what the Scriptures reveal about man's origin, let us look at man himself to learn what he is and what his makeup is.

MAN IS A CREATURE.

In his unfallen state, man was a product of God, produced by direct creation (Gen. 1:26-27). While fallen man remains God's property and creature (Ps. 24:1), he is Satan's product (Jn. 8:44), for his present fallen condition (physically, psychologically, and spiritually) is the result of Satan's activity (Gen. 3:1-6; Eph. 2:2; Jn. 8:44). Having been recreated by God, we who are saved are His workmanship (Eph. 2:10; II Cor. 5:17). However, this divine work begun in us will not be completed until Jesus returns for His church (Phil. 3:20-21). In our glorified state, we who are saved shall forever be like Jesus in His humanity (I Jn. 3:2). We shall never become God; we shall always be creatures.

MAN BEARS THE IMAGE OF GOD.

Man was deliberately made in God's image (Gen. 1:26-27; 5:1). While both "image" and "likeness" express correspondence to God, "likeness" indicates that this correspondence is one of similarity, not identicalness. That the image of God in man is not identical is the fact that the divine image in man is created while God himself is uncreated. Being made in the image of God does not mean that man is God. Indeed, we humans shall never be God. It means that man (and woman) has a created feature which is like that belonging to God and which distinguishes him from lower creatures. This correspondence gives human life a sacredness, dignity, and value that do not belong to lower forms of life (Gen. 9:6; Jas. 3:9; cp. II Pet. 2:12).

Incidentally, God the Son is "the express image" of the Father's substance (Heb. 1:3, not "personhood"). Possessing the one divine nature, yet being distinct Persons, the Father and the Son are fully and equally God.

• The Nature of This Image

Of what does this image consist? Many believe that it includes such features as reason, emotion, and will (cp. Isa. 1:18; Jn. 3:16; Eph. 1:11). However, these features in man, as we shall see, are expressions of the human soul and spirit, and God does not have these components of nature. Moreover, these features to a lesser degree are manifest in higher forms of animal life as well as in man. As I see it, the image of God is not to be found in human nature, although similarities to the Creator's moral qualities are manifest in man's nature.

I believe that the divine image in man consists of personhood — that unique personal entity which at conception is created by God (Mal. 2:10) and which is immediately and forever joined to one's propagated human nature. It is the self, or I, as being distinct from the soul and spirit (Job 7:11; Isa. 26:9), which are components of human nature.[9] It appears that angels also have this image since they express the characteristics of personal creatures and, like humans, are called sons of God (Job 1:6; 38:7; Lk. 3:38; cp. 20:36).[10] Thus man and angels are like God in that, having personhood, they are persons. Having the one divine nature, the true God consists of Three Persons, — the Father, the Son, and the Holy Spirit. Humans and angels, with their particular natures and personhoods, are human and angelic persons.

We should not confuse the divine image in man (personhood) with the image of the Lord Jesus Christ, after which we who are saved are made in salvation (Eph. 4:24; Col. 3:10; Rom. 8:29). In His humanity the Lord Jesus is the head and pattern of a new human race, of which we who are saved are members (I Cor. 15:22; II Cor. 5:17; Heb. 2:11). By His sanctifying work in our lives, the Holy Spirit is reproducing in us the moral qualities of the Lord Jesus as we submit to His Word and His dealings with us (II Cor. 3:18; Heb. 12:10; Jn. 17:17; II Tim. 3:16-17). When He comes again, the Lord will deliver our bodies from inherent corruption and will make them like His body of glory (Rom. 8:23; Phil. 3:20-21; I Cor. 15:45-53). Then we shall be fully like Him in His human nature.

• **The Duration of This Image**

While man was created in God's image (with personhood), does he still have this image in his fallen state? The Scriptures show that he does (Gen. 9:6; Jas. 3:9). Man's sinning did not cause him to cease being a person, although it radically affected his entire being (personhood and nature). All humans, both saved and unsaved, will possess their personhood forever, for they will exist and will experience either God's blessing or judgment forever (Mt. 25:46).

MAN EXISTS AS MALE AND FEMALE (Gen. 1:27; 5:2; cp. Mt. 19:4).

God created man and woman, with their peculiar sexual distinctions and drives, in order that they might complete one another and fulfill His purpose for their existence in this world (Gen. 1:26; 2:23-25). The Bible never suggests that these distinctions and drives are in themselves evil or base. (Fallen man's and woman's nature is wholly corrupted by sin.) Being given of God, these

---

[9] See Franz Delitzsch, *A System of Biblical Psychology* (Grand Rapids: Baker Book House, reprinted 1966), pp. 179-181.
[10] Op. cit., pp. 78 f.

distinctions fulfill their role most completely in the marriage state. The relationship between man and woman is fully manifest in the marriage state and in the social order that God has established for humans.

- **The Institution of Marriage**

Marriage is a formal, legal commitment before God to an exclusive love between a man and a woman. Its sanctity rests upon its being instituted by God and its bond being effected by Him (Gen. 2:22-25; Mt. 19:4-6). Although marriage is given to the human race, it is God's will that believers marry only believers (II Cor. 6:14; I Cor. 7:39). On the other hand, when a spouse becomes saved, his union with his unsaved spouse is still sacred in God's sight (I Cor. 7:12-14). The marriage bond can only be broken by adultery or death (Mt. 19:9; Rom. 7:2).

God forbids premarital and extramarital sexual relations (Eph. 5:3-5; I Thess. 4:3-7; I Cor. 6:15-18). The reason may be that these illicit relations portray a spiritual union (the marriage bond) that really does not exist, and thus they perpetrate a lie. Furthermore, adultery violates one's pledge of exclusive love to his spouse.

In spite of the teaching of pagan philosophy about the body and sexuality, the marriage state is as holy and good as the single state (cp. I Cor. 7:14; Heb. 13:4). However, in certain circumstances, such as persecution or the demands of certain services, marriage may not be as desirable (cp. I Cor. 7:26-35).

In addition to perpetuating the race and providing a home for offspring, the purpose of marriage is to provide a couple with the opportunity to experience that completeness which is achieved by sexual union, reciprocal love, and mutual trust and sharing. In marriage a man and a woman are brought together into a unique oneness of life, by means of which both find completion in each other (Gen. 2:24). This oneness is expressed by the words "one flesh." Within the marriage state the husband and his wife are united to the extent that former natural ties are severed and a new tie is made by God (Mt. 19:5-6). The sexual relation is a symbol of this union and is its unifying factor. The sex function is not merely the means of continuing the race; it is the deepest symbol of personal understanding and love. It expresses the meaning and quality of the relationship between a husband and his wife. It expresses the depth of communion where one surrenders himself to and for the other. Thus, the sexual relation in marriage is not something that is evil and shameful, but holy, pleasurable, and purposeful. It promotes the growth of mutual understanding and love.

The union between a husband and his wife portrays that between the Lord Jesus and His church (Eph. 5:22-32). Being espoused to Christ at salvation (II Cor. 11:2), we have the duty of remaining faithful to Him (Jas. 4:4). In the future we who comprise His church shall become His wife (Rev. 19:7-8).

- **The Order of Headship**

Contrary to the world's view, God has established what the human social order should be. He has given the leadership of human society to men (I Cor. 11:3). This is not to say that women are inferior to men spiritually, mentally, or skillfully (Gal. 3:28), but from the beginning God has given to woman the position of social subordination as man's helper (Gen. 2:18; I Cor. 11:9). When Eve abandoned this position and assumed that of leadership, she brought sin to the human race (Gen. 3:1-6). With sin she brought upon her female descendants sinful man's cruel despotism and lustful exploitation. A punishment for her sin was the continuation of her subordination to man (vs. 16).

The subordination that women are to express to men is not in the nature of bondage or to the extent of disobeying God's commands, which supercede those of man (Acts 5:29). It is a voluntary subordination that puts the interests and goals of the man, for whom she was created as helper, above those of herself and that exalts the man (I Cor. 11:7-9; cp. 10:31).

Paul gives God's social order for mankind in I Corinthians 11:2-16, where he points out that the woman was made of and for the man (vss. 8-9). Elsewhere he affirms man's leadership in the home (Eph. 5:22-23), the local church (I Cor. 14:34; I Tim. 2:11-12), and civil government (Rom. 13:4). When God's social order is honored, it brings His blessing. When it is ignored, it incurs trouble and unhappiness.

MAN IS A COMPLEX BEING.

Man's essential makeup consists of personhood and human nature. Having personhood, humans are like God. Having a body, soul, and spirit, they are like animals.[11] Let us look at these essential parts more closely.

- **Man Has Personhood.**

Unlike animals, man is a personal being, for he has personhood, which, I believe, is the image of God in man (Gen. 1:26-27). What is personhood and what are its qualities?

1. Its description

Personhood is that basic, personal entity that we call "self" and which is identified by the personal pronouns "I" and "me." This entity, the image of God in man, provides the capacity within the framework of human existence for personal self-awareness, self-determination, and self-expression.

By self-awareness I mean that one is aware of himself and is aware that

---

[11] That animals have soul and spirit is not commonly recognized. In Genesis 1:20-21, 24, the word "creature" is a translation of the Hebrew "soul" *(nephesh)*. That they have spirit is indicated in Genesis 7:21-22 and Ecclesiastes 3:19, 21. Among other functions, both soul and spirit animate the body in its present living state.

he is distinct from other persons and things. By self-determination I mean that one can make moral choices and is responsible for his actions. And by self-expression I mean that one can function and thus can manifest himself by means of his human nature.

2. Its distinction from human nature

Job's distinction between his personhood ("I") and his body ("mouth"), his spirit, and his soul (Job 7:11), indicates that personhood, or self, is something other than human nature (cp. Isa. 26:9).[12] While body, soul, and spirit are the essential parts of human nature, personhood is an entity in man that is other than human nature.

As I see it, personhood is that unique, personal entity, or self, which at one's conception is created by God (cp. Mal. 2:10) and which is permanently joined to one's human nature. Personhood could hardly be propagated, for by this, derived from and consisting of the personhoods of the parents, it would not be unique or distinct from their personhoods. On the other hand, human nature, consisting of body, soul, and spirit, is at conception transmitted from the parents to their child by propagation. Possessing the genetic code of one's ancestors and the effects of Adam's initial sin, human nature qualifies personhood and makes the person to be the kind of person that he is, generically and morally — a human and a sinner.

I believe theologians make a mistake when they equate personhood with the soul. While it sometimes represents human beings (Gen. 46:26; Acts 27:37), the soul should never be equated with personhood.[13] To do so is to create theological confusion. For example, this would make Jesus, having a human soul (Mt. 26:38), to be two persons.

3. Its qualities

While the propagated human nature imparts human qualities to personhood and makes the person to be human, it appears that personhood itself has inherent qualities. Not found in nonpersonal forms of life such as animals, these qualities of personhood correspond to features in God's personhood. These qualities include individuality, morality, and perpetuity.

a. Individuality

Individuality here refers to that peculiarity of being, not of character, which distinguishes one from other beings of his kind.[14] For example, in the case of identical twins who have similar human natures, they still are distinct persons. Thus each human being is uniquely distinct from all other humans, not only in personality (the expression of human nature through one's personhood) but also in personhood itself.

Individuality is seen in the Godhead. While possessing the one divine

---

[12] See Appendix C; also see Franz Delitzsch, *A System of Biblical Psychology*, pp. 179-181.
[13] See Franz Delitzsch, p. 181.
[14] Franz Delitzsch, p. 180.

nature, the Members of the Godhead, having separate personhoods, are distinct Persons who are equal in their qualities and powers (Jn. 14:16; Mt. 28:19).

b. Morality

It appears that personhood gives to human nature the quality of morality, which is the ability to recognize and to distinguish between good and evil, right and wrong. This quality also enables us humans to make moral evaluations and moral decisions or choices and to engage in moral activities, for which we are responsible to God and to man (Rom. 2:6, 16; 13:1-5).

God also has a similar quality of morality. This is seen in His recognition of good and evil (Gen. 3:22; Prov. 15:3) and in His judging mankind (Acts 17:31).

c. Perpetuity

Perpetuity concerns one's existing forever. Having personhood, we humans shall survive death and exist forever, either with God or apart from Him in Hell (Mt. 25:46). It is our personhood that gives perpetuity to our human nature, for our personhood requires the continuance of our human nature for its expressions and impressions in our afterlife experiences. On the other hand, not having personhood, animals have no need for the perpetuation of their natures. There is no biblical evidence that they survive death.

God also has the quality of perpetuity (Ps. 102:12). The Persons of the holy Trinity continue forever.

• Man Has a Human Nature.

In addition to personhood, man has a human nature that makes him to be a human person. One's human nature provides the means by which his personhood can express itself and receive impressions.

1. Its description

Human nature is that propagated essence, with its qualities and powers, that is united to our personhood and interacts with it and that makes us to be human persons, physically, rationally, emotionally, and volitionally. Wholly transmitted to us by our parents, with the genetic code of our ancestors, our human nature consists of human body, soul, and spirit. However, in its unsaved, natural state human nature from its conception bears Adam's image (Gen. 5:3; I Cor. 15:49) and the effects of his initial sin, or original sin (Rom. 5:12).[15]

When we think of human nature, we must distinguish it from the divine nature and from angelic nature. Each kind of personal being has his own kind of nature that makes him to be what he is.

---

[15] Fallen humans have a complete, functioning human nature. However, this is wholly, inherently corrupted and is unresponsive (dead) toward God and the things that concern Him: heart (a metaphor for man's inner nature, Mk. 7:21-22; Jer. 17:9; Eccles. 9:3), soul (I Pet. 1:22; Prov. 21:10), spirit (Prov. 16:2, 18; 25:28; Ps. 78:8), and body (Rom. 8:10; I Cor. 15:50). See Ephesians 2:2-3; 4:17-19; Romans 1:18-32; 3:9-18.

2. Its essential parts

Human nature consists of material and immaterial parts. Obviously, the material part is the physical body, but the immaterial parts (soul and spirit) are not clearly defined in the Scriptures. These parts are so similar in their functions that one would regard them to be synonymous if they were not spoken of as separate entities (Heb. 4:12). To the Hebrews the various parts of man's nature were not considered to be contrasting elements, as in pagan thought, but differing aspects of one, vital personality. They regarded the immaterial parts as being almost physical and the physical parts as having psychological functions, so that whatever activity man engaged in, the predominant aspect represented the whole person (cp. Gen. 2:7; Ps. 51:8).[16]

a. THE MATERIAL PART OF HUMAN NATURE

(1) Its Substance

The body was originally made from dust of the ground (Gen. 2:7; 3:19), Because of this, it needs elements that are found in soil for its sustenance. We ingest these elements through food. When it dies, the body returns to dust to await its resurrection (Gen. 3:19; Jn. 5:28-29). Although the body in its natural state has such lowly origin and ending, medical science is still learning about its wonders, for which David long ago gave praise to God (Ps. 139:14).

While Paul distinguished between human flesh and animal flesh (I Cor. 15:39), both are animated by the same means. Living bodies are presently animated by the soul (Gen. 35:18; Mt. 26:38; Lk. 12:20) and by the spirit (Gen. 7:22; Ps. 104:29; Lk. 8:55; 23:46; Jas. 2:26). When it is abandoned by these animating principles, the body dies and returns to dust. Physical life, now transmitted by the propagated human spirit and soul, returns to God who imparted it in the beginning (Gen. 2:7; Eccles. 12:7; Job 34:14-15).

(2) Its Condition

Since Adam's first sin, human bodies have been inherently corrupt and mortal (Rom. 8:10; I Cor. 15:53). This means that, being affected by sin, human bodies are subject to aging, weakness, degeneration, disease, and death (cp. I Cor. 15:42-44). Moreover, the sin-principle resides in the flesh of the body and energizes it as well as the other parts of human nature for its evil expressions (Rom. 7:17-18, 23; 3:9; Gal. 5:19-21).

While they have yet to be delivered from corruption and mortality, the bodies of living saved people no longer have to be the tools of sin's evil expressions. This is because saved people no longer have the same relation to sin as they did when they were unsaved. To God's mind, we who are saved have died to sin and to its claim to us (Rom. 6:2). Thus we are to regard our bodies to be like broken tools which have been rendered useless to sin (vs. 6)

---

[16] W. David Stacey, *The Pauline View of Man* (London: Macmillan & Co. Ltd., 1956), p. 85.

and like remade tools that have become the instruments of God and of righteousness (vs. 13). Having been acquitted of sin's claim to us (vs. 7), we can now ignore sin's urges and yield ourselves to God to do His will (vss. 11-13).

Our bodies will be delivered from their inherent corruption and the resident sin-principle when the Lord Jesus returns for His church (Phil. 3:20-21). At that time, He will instantly recreate these bodies to prepare them for the eternal state. He will raise the bodies of dead believers to incorruptibility, never to die again; and He will change the bodies of living believers to immortality, never to face death again (I Cor. 15:50-53). Presently, our bodies are subject to the laws and conditions that govern physical life in this world. But when they are changed, these bodies will be prepared for life off this planet and for the eternal state (I Cor. 15:50-55; I Thess. 4:16-17; Rev. chs. 21-22).

These changes will be substantive, not ethereal as certain cults teach (cp. Lk. 24:39). Being energized by the Holy Spirit, these changed bodies will differ from our present ones in their qualities, powers, and animating principle (I Cor. 15:35-44; Rom. 8:11). Because of this, Paul speaks of the changed body as being "spiritual" rather than "natural" (soulish, I Cor. 15:44-50). "Spiritual" and "soulish" seem to refer to the principles by which the body is animated: presently by the soul ("soulish") and in the future by the Holy Spirit ("spiritual").

Being made like the glorified body of the Lord Jesus in its essential construction (Phil. 3:20-21), our changed bodies will allow us to experience all that God has for us in the eternal state and to express Jesus' human intellectual, emotional, and volitional qualities (see Appendix V). Having His kind of body, we shall truly be like Him. Presently, in their unsaved state, our bodies are like fallen Adam's body and those of our intermediate ancestors. They presently express the qualities of Adam's sinful state and the genetic features of our ancestors. But all of this will be changed when Jesus comes for His church (Phil. 3:20-21).

(3) Its functions

The body is our mechanical means of perception, expression, and reproduction in this world. It also is the instrument of the principle, or force, that presently dominates our life, whether God or sin (Rom. 6:12-13). The sin-principle wholly dominates the life of unsaved people and uses their total human nature for its evil expressions (Jn. 8:34; Rom. 3:9; 6:16; Gal. 5:19-21; Eph. 2:2-3; I Jn. 3:8). In principle, sin's domination over the lives of God's people was broken when they were saved. At that time, they died to sin and were made alive to God and to His authority (Rom. 6:1-10). Hence it is now their duty to yield themselves daily to their new Master and to do His will (vss. 11-13; 12:1-2).

In spite of his body's present corruption, the believer should possess his body in sanctification and honor (I Thess. 4:4), for it can now by the power of God serve holy purposes, including the following (I Cor. 6:12-20):

One, the believer's body is an earthly member of Christ (vs. 15). As His body on earth, the Lord's people collectively are the means by which Jesus works to build His church. He uses us and our bodies in this ministry (Rom. 12:1).

Two, the believer's body is a temple of the Holy Spirit (vs. 19). Because the Third Person of the holy Trinity lives within the bodies of His people forever (Jn. 14:16-17), we must respect them and care for them as His property.

Third, the believer's body is the only means he has by which to glorify God in this world (I Cor. 6:20; 10:31). He cannot express himself or function apart from his body.

(4) Its care

Because of these truths, we should never abuse our body or regard it as our enemy as pagan philosophy and practice do. Rather, we should daily care for our body, nourish it, discipline it, and yield it to God for His holy purposes (Rom. 13:14; Eph. 5:28-29; I Thess. 4:3-7; I Cor. 9:26-27; Rom. 6:16, 19; 12:1-2).

Since our physical condition directly affects the quality of our life and ministry, it is important that we maintain our physical well-being (Mk. 6:31; Lk. 8:55; Acts 27:33-35). It is sinful to disregard the laws and means of physical health, such as proper food and sufficient rest, unless circumstances force us to do so. Traditional self-mortification (affliction or denial) of the body rises from pagan thought which considers the body to be inherently evil and a threat to the soul.[17] While there are times when spiritual duty or some crisis transcends our physical needs (Mt. 4:1-4; Acts 13:2-3), ordinarily we should maintain our physical well-being. A body that is racked by pain or bound by weakness is a handicap to one's efficiency in thought and action. On the other hand, when God in His wisdom sends affliction, we can look to Him for the grace to rise above this and to do His will (II Cor. 12:7-10).

(5) Its designation "flesh"

While we do not have difficulty in understanding the word "body," the meaning of "flesh" in the Bible is more complicated. The word "flesh" (Heb. basar, Gk. sarx) has different meanings, as determined by its biblical-usage and context.

One, the physical structure of human and animals (Ex. 29:14; Dan. 1:15; Lk. 24:39; Rom. 7:18; I Cor. 5:5).

Two, living humans and animals (Gen. 6:17; 7:15-16; Acts 2:17).

Three, representing what is human in nature. This is in contrast to what is divine (Mt. 16:17) and what is angelic (Eph. 6:12).

Four, one's relatives, ancestors, or posterity (Gen. 29:14; Acts 2:30; Rom.

---

[17] See W. David Stacey, pp. 73 f.

1:3; 9:3).

Five, man's frailty and temporariness (Ps. 78:39; Isa. 40:6; Rom. 6:19).

Six, man's responsiveness to God (Ezek. 36:26). This is in contrast to stone which represents man's obstinacy to God.

Seven, Christ's atoning work (Jn. 6:53-56; Eph. 2:15). "Flesh" represents our Lord's physical death which was involved in the atonement (Heb. 10:5, 10; 2:9) and by which He defeated Satan who had the power of death (2:14).

Eight, one's total being (II Cor. 7:5; Heb. 9:13).

Nine, human nature dominated by the sin-principle (Rom. 8:3, 8, 9; Eph. 2:3, second occurrence of "flesh"). In this usage, the emphasis is on the human nature of unsaved people which is absolutely dominated by sin.

Ten, the sin-principle dominating one's human nature (Rom. 8:1, 12-13; Eph. 2:3, first occurrence of "flesh"). In this usage, the emphasis is on the sin-principle, sometimes in contrast to the Holy Spirit (Gal. 5:16) or to Jesus (Rom. 13:14).

When we come upon the word "flesh" in the Bible, we should consider which one of these meanings best fits the passage and its context.

b. THE IMMATERIAL PART OF HUMAN NATURE

These immaterial parts of human nature are soul and spirit. What these parts are is not clear. Although the Bible uses designations that indicate that they are distinct, simultaneous entities (I Thess. 5:23; Heb. 4:12), they may be references to the same thing, for they have similar functions. Their separate designations, "soul" and "spirit," may rise from the ways in which the single immaterial entity of human nature is related to the body: its relation to the body in association with blood being soul and its relation to the body in association with breath being spirit. However this may be, the soul and spirit give to personhood the capacities of intelligence, emotions, and will. Also, they impart to our present body physical life. To facilitate our study, I have sorted these immaterial parts of human nature into two groups — those that have their own names and those that are represented by bodily parts.

(1) Parts Having Their Own Names

(a) The human soul

The Bible reveals that humans have a soul as a part of their human nature (Ps. 3:2; Lk. 1:46). When He created man, God imparted to him soul (and spirit) with the result that Adam became a living soul (Gen. 2:7), or a living creature (cp. 1:20-24).

The soul's relation to the body appears to be in its association with the body's blood.[18] Blood itself is not the soul, but it is the vehicle of the soul. Soul resides in the blood and conveys life to the cells of the body (Lev. 17:11, 14, "life" in KJV should read "soul").[19] Also, the soul survives death (Rev. 6:9), for

---

[18] See Franz Delitzsch, pp. 281-285.

[19] It is in this sense that we must understand Genesis 9:4 and Deuteronomy 12:23. The eating of blood was prohibited, for to eat blood was to eat the vehicle of the soul.

it is needed by personhood in the afterlife to provide the human capacities of intelligence, emotion, and will.

The functions of soul in the Old Testament (Heb. *nephesh*, occurring about 750 times) and in the New Testament (Gk. *phyche*, occurring about 100 times) are similar.

One, representing human beings (Gen. 46:22-27; Acts 27:37) and one's total self (Ps. 120:6; Lk. 12:19).

Two, being the physical life force of the body (Job 2:4, 6; I Kings 17:21-22; Jonah 4:3 "life"; Jn. 10:11, 15, 17; Acts 20:10).

Three, the seat of the intellect like thinking (Gen. 23:8 "mind"; Prov. 23:7 "heart") and knowing (Ps. 139:14; Prov. 24:14). Compare Acts 14:22; 15:24.

Special Greek words are used for the intellect and its functions in the New Testament. These include *nous*, with the ideas of making moral judgments (Rom. 7:23, 25; 12:2), understanding truth (I Cor. 14:14, 19; Phil. 4:7; Rev. 13:18), a frame of mind (I Cor. 1:10; II Thess. 2:2), and thinking (Rom. 14:5); and *dianoia* with the ideas of the organ of thought or understanding (Mk. 12:30; Eph. 2:3; 4:18) and a kind of thinking or disposition (Col. 1:21; I Pet. 1:13).

Four, the seat of the emotions like distress (Gen. 42:21; Job 30:16; Jn. 12:27; Mk. 14:34), desire (Ps. 42:2; Rev. 18:14), joy (Ps. 35:9; Mt. 12:18), and love (S.S. 1:7; Mk. 12:30).

Five, the seat of the will (Ps. 27:12 "will"; Acts 4:32).

(b) The human spirit

Human beings also have spirit as a part of their human nature (Gen. 41:8; Eccles. 3:21; II Tim. 4:22). This human spirit must be distinguished from angelic spirits [holy (Heb. 1:14) and evil (Mt. 8:16)], from God the Holy Spirit (Gal. 5:16), and from the substance of which God's nature consists (Jn. 4:24).

The spirit's relation to the body appears to be in its association with the body's breath (Gen. 7:21-22). This is not to say that spirit itself is breath and consists of the air we breathe. Rather, it is the means by which physical life is somehow imparted to the body by breath. Like the soul, the spirit survives death (Heb. 12:23), for it too is needed by personhood in the afterlife to provide the human capacities of intelligence, emotion, and will.

The functions of spirit in the Old Testament (Heb. *ruach*, occurring about 80 times) and in the New Testament (Gk. *pneuma*, occurring about 55 times) are similar.

One, representing human beings (I Cor. 5:5; II Tim. 4:22; Heb. 12:23) and the total self (II Cor. 7:13).

Two, being the physical life force of our present body ("breath" in Gen. 6:17; 7:15, 22; Job 27:3, Ps. 104:29; Isa. 42:5; Lk. 8:55; Jas. 2:26).

Three, being the seat of the intellect (Eph. 4:23) like thinking (Eph. 4:23; Col. 2:5), understanding (Job 20:3; I Cor. 2:11), and perceiving (Mk. 2:8).

Four, being the seat of the emotions like distress (Job 7:11; Jn. 13:21), grief

(Gen. 26:35 "mind"; Ex. 6:9), joy (Lk. 10:21), anger (Jud. 8:3 "anger") and of such dispositions (II Cor. 12:18) as meekness (I Cor. 4:21), humility (Ps. 34:18; Mt. 5:3), fervor (Rom. 12:11), faith (II Cor. 4:13), patience and pride (Eccles. 7:8; Prov. 14:29).

Five, being the seat of the will (Ex. 35:21).

Here are some observations about soul and spirit: One, the soul and spirit depart from the body at death (Gen. 35:18; Jas. 2:26). However, the personhood of the deceased still retains these parts of his immaterial human nature and continues to be made human by them (Lk. 16:19-25; Rev. 6:9-11).

Two, the seat of spiritual life within the believer is not the human spirit or soul but the Holy Spirit, who transmits to us who are saved the spiritual life of Jesus (Jn. 14:6; Rom. 8:2, 9-10; I Jn. 5:12). "Spirit" in Romans 8:10 probably refers to the human spirit, which is made alive by regeneration.

Three, at first glance it may appear that the conscience (see Appendix B) is another part of our immaterial human nature. However, this does not appear to be the case. The conscience is a part of our memory bank, located in the brain, with its input of moral values by instruction.[20]

Four, Paul speaks of the soul and spirit of the believer as the "inner man" (Rom. 7:22; II Cor. 4:16; Eph. 3:16). This is in contrast to the "new man" which we are in Christ (Eph. 4:24).[21]

Five, the believer's soul and spirit, together with his personhood, is the part of his makeup that is now saved (I Pet. 1:9; Rom. 8:10, with "spirit" referring to the human spirit[22]). This, together with his saved personhood, makes him to be a new creature in Christ (II Cor. 5:17; Eph. 2:10). The body, which is still unsaved, has yet to be delivered from inherent corruption, mortality, and the resident sin-principle (Rom. 8:10; 7:18).[23]

Six, as long as the believer's soul and spirit are exposed to the influence of the sin-force within and of evil without, they are just as susceptible to the influence of evil as they are to that of the Holy Spirit. When we yield our total self to the Holy Spirit, we can think holy thoughts, have right attitudes, feel

---

[20] There is no special Hebrew word for the conscience in the Old Testament. It is represented by the words "heart" (I Sam. 24:5), "spirit" (Prov. 20:27), and "reins" (Ps. 73:21). In the New Testament, the conscience is usually represented by its own word ("conscience," Gk. *suneidesis;* see Acts 23:1; Rom. 2:15; 9:1; I Cor. 8:7; Heb. 10:22) and by "heart" (Acts 2:37; 7:54; I Jn. 3:20-21).

[21] Observe that the "old man" is what we were in Adam when we were unsaved; the "new man" is what we are now in Christ (II Cor. 5:17). This "putting off" and "putting on" took place at salvation, as indicated by the aorist tense of these verbs in the Greek text (Col. 3:9-10; Eph. 4:22, 23). Because of this truth, we are not to put off sins and put on Christlike qualities to *become* new men. Rather, we are to put off sins (Col. 3:8-9) and to put on these qualities (12-17) because we *are* new men in Him.

[22] In I Corinthians 5:5, Paul seems to have in view the final salvation of the sinning saved person, whom he represents by the word "spirit," as the purpose for the disciplinary destruction of his body (cp. 11:30, 32).

[23] What does it mean for the soul and spirit to be saved? First, they are delivered from inherent corruption, with its bent toward sinning (I Pet. 1:22) and from spiritual death (Rom. 8:10). Second, being divinely renewed [not replaced (Tit. 3:5)], they are created in righteousness and holiness (Col. 3:10; Eph. 4:24) and given new life. Being made righteous and holy, the believer's soul and spirit have the bent toward pleasing God. Also, being divinely renewed, they give the believer the capacity to understand spiritual truth and think right thoughts, to express right emotions such as God's love, and to make right decisions in harmony with God's will (I Pet. 1:22).

proper emotions, make God-honoring resolutions, and do those things that please Him (Rom. 8:4). On the other hand, when we yield to the sin-force within or to evil without, this results in our having evil thoughts, emotions, attitudes, purposes and our doing evil deeds. The soul and spirit are defiled by our sinning and have need for daily cleansing (II Cor. 7:1; I Jn. 1:9). But our sinning does not radically and permanently affect the soul and spirit as did Adam's first sin, for we are now delivered from the awful judicial effects of sinning through our Lord's sacrifice (Rom. 8:31-34).

Seven, that both soul and spirit are saved when we receive the Saviour is indicated by the following truths: By the renewed *human spirit* we worship God (Lk. 1:47; Jn. 4:23; I Cor. 14:14-16; Phil. 3:3), serve Him (Rom. 1:9), and know Him (Eph. 4:23; Rom. 8:16). Also, by the renewed *human soul* we worship God (Lk. 1:46), love Him (Mk. 12:30), thirst after Him (Ps. 42:2), follow after Him (Ps. 63:8), bless Him (103:2; 146:1), wait for Him (130:5), obey Him (119:129), and enjoy spiritual prosperity (III Jn. 2). Salvational faith results in the saving of the soul (Heb. 10:39). The believer's spirit "is life" in contrast to his body which is still mortal (Rom. 8:10).

Eight, the human soul and spirit survive death (Rev. 6:9; Heb. 12:23), and continue to make their indigenous personhoods human. However, they will not provide the changed body with the physical life-principle, as they do now, for the Holy Spirit will do this (Rom. 8:11). But they will continue to provide their possessors with the human capacities of intelligence, emotion, and will. All physical life returns to God upon death (Eccles. 12:7).

Nine, the Lord Jesus gave His human soul (Mt. 20:28; Jn. 10:11, 15, 17; I Jn. 3:16, "life") and His human spirit (Lk. 23:46) in atonement for our sins. In His separation from the Father during the hours of darkness on the cross, the Lord Jesus humanly experienced spiritual death in His soul and spirit, which were alienated from the Father by humanity's sins (Mt. 27:46). (There was no separation between the Father and the Son, with the division of the divine nature. His words, "My God" are words of His humanity.) Then, when His human spirit was revived, He gave up His soul and spirit in physical death (I Pet. 3:18; Jn. 19:30).

(2) Parts Represented by Bodily Organs

In biblical times people often attributed the meanings or functions of soul and spirit to various organs of the body. The following are found in the Bible:

(a) HEART

The word "heart" is the most comprehensive term in the Bible for the non-physical parts and functions of man. It is used to represent the human soul, spirit, mind, conscience as well as one's total inner being. Of the many occurrences of this word in the Bible, very few literally mean the physical organ (II Sam. 18:14; II Kings 9:24; Ps. 45:5).

In the Old Testament the word "heart" (Heb. *leb*, 598X; *lebab*, 252X) has various functions or meanings: the seat of physical energy and life (Ps. 22:14; Isa. 1:5); the seat of the emotions (Ex. 4:14; Jud. 18:20; II Ki. 6:11; Ps. 61:2) and desire (Prov. 6:25); the seat of one's disposition or mood (Ex. 4:21; II Sam. 17:10; I Ki. 8:23; 11:3; 12:27; Ezek. 21:7); the seat of the will (II Sam. 7:27; II Ki. 12:4); the seat of reasoning (Gen. 6:5), perception (Deut. 29:4), and understanding (I Ki. 3:9; Prov. 28:26); the self (Gen. 17:17; I Ki. 8:47, "themselves"; Eccles. 2:1); and the conscience (I Sam. 24:5; II Sam. 24:10).

In the New Testament the word "heart" (Gk. *kardia*) occurs about 155 times and has functions or meanings similar to its Old Testament usage: the seat of physical life and energy (Jas. 5:5); the seat of the emotions (Jn. 14:1; 16:6; Acts 2:26; II Cor. 2:4); the seat of the will (Acts 11:23; II Cor. 9:7) and desires (Rom. 10:1); the disposition (Mt. 11:29; 13:15; I Pet. 1:22); the seat of reasoning (Lk. 12:45) and the mind (Acts 7:23; I Cor. 2:9); the self (Mt. 15:8; Rom. 6:17; 10:10); and the conscience (I Jn. 3:20-21).

In many passages the heart is seen as the control center of a person's life (Prov. 4:23; Mt. 6:21; 12:35; Mk. 7:21-23). Whatever principle (whether God, Satan, or sin) governs the heart also expresses itself in one's life. The heart itself has no active moral qualities. Being inherently corrupted, the heart of unsaved people is inclined toward sin (Jer. 17:9; 18:12). On the other hand, being purified by Christ's blood, the heart of the saved person is inclined toward righteousness (Acts 15:9; II Tim. 2:22; Heb. 10:22; cp. I Pet. 1:22). From the heart springs both good and evil conduct, as determined by the principle — God, Satan, or sin — that acts upon it (Ps. 119:11; Acts 5:3; Rom. 5:5; Col. 3:15-16; Eph. 3:17; Rev. 17:17). In Mark 7:21-23 the Lord has in view the heart that is dominated by sin (cp. Mt. 12:34-35; Lk. 8:15).

The Holy Spirit's being given to our heart (II Cor. 1:22; Gal. 4:6) simply means that He was given to us at salvation and now indwells us (I Jn. 3:24; Jn. 14:16-17). God's being the searcher of hearts indicates that He knows all about us, especially our inner thoughts, purposes, motivations, desires and feelings (Rom. 8:27). His trying our hearts means that He examines our inner life, looking for that in our daily life which He can approve (I Thess. 2:4). To believe with the heart is to exercise salvation faith with our total inner being — our reasoning, emotions, and will (Rom. 6:17; 10:10; cp. Mt. 15:8). Again, to act with the heart means to act with one's whole being (Col. 3:23; Mk. 12:30; Mt. 15:8).

(b) BELLY

In addition to its physical meaning, the word "belly" (Heb. *beten*) in the Old Testament represents the seat of the emotions (Job 20:20; Ps. 31:9) and thought (Job 15:35), and one's self (15:2). In the New Testament the word (Gk. *koilia*) means one's inner being (Jn. 7:38) or self (Rom. 16:18). Generally, it refers to the physical organ (Lk. 15:16).

(c) BOWELS

Sometimes, this refers to the physical organ, but more often it has psychical or spiritual functions. In the Old Testament the bowels (Heb. *meim*) are the seat of the emotions (Isa. 16:11; Jer. 31:20; S. Sol. 5:4; Lam. 1:20). In the New Testament the word (Gk. *splagchna*) represents the seat of the emotions (II Cor. 6:12; Phil. 1:8; 2:1; Col. 3:12; Philem. 7) and the self (Philem. 12, 20).

(d) REINS OR KIDNEYS

In the Old Testament "reins" (Heb. *kelayoth*) refers to the seat of the emotions (Prov. 23:16); the mind (Ps. 16:7); the inner self with its thoughts, purposes, and motivations (Ps. 7:9; 26:2; Jer. 11:20; 12:2; 20:12); and the conscience (Ps. 73:21). In the New Testament the word (Gk. *nephros*) occurs only as the inner self with its thoughts, purposes, and motivations (Rev. 2:23).

(e) BONES

Only in the Old Testament do the bones (Heb. *estem*) sometimes function as the seat of the emotions (Ps. 51:8; Prov. 12:4; 15:30; 16:24; Isa. 66:14; Jer. 20:9; Lam. 1:13; Hab. 3:16). Usually, it keeps its physical meaning (Gen. 50:25; Lk. 24:39).

Observe that the biblical view of man is synthetic (sees man as a whole) as expressed in Hebrew thought, rather than analytic (sees man in parts) as expressed in Greek thought. This means that the Scriptures portray man as a unity that is seen in the several aspects of one, vital human personality, not as a combination of contrasting elements. Behind each aspect of human nature (body, soul, and spirit) is the whole person. For example, the mind is not seen as an isolated faculty, but as man knowing, understanding, and judging. Man is described as a living soul, not simply one who has a soul. Moreover, man's personhood is inseparably and forever related to his human nature. He will never be divested of it, except of his body during the interim of death. Because of this union, whatever our human nature experiences or expresses, our personhood experiences or expresses. As human persons, we ourselves think, act, speak, become weary, rejoice, feel pain, have sexual desires, plan, sin, die, and are resurrected.

The Greeks thought of the body and soul as being antagonistic toward each other. They held that the body, being material, was inherently evil; therefore, it corrupted and imprisoned the soul. But the Bible does not present this antagonism. Our enemy is not the body or self, but the sin-principle resident within the body's flesh (Rom. 7:17, 18, 23). While fallen man is wholly corrupted by original sin, his salvation brings to his total being, excepting his body, deliverance from sin's ruin and power and renewal by God's power (Rom. 8:10-11; I Cor. 6:11; Eph. 4:22-24; Phil. 3:20-21; I Thess. 5:23; Jas. 1:21). As we yield ourself to Jesus, our total being becomes in His hand an instrument of righteousness (Rom. 6:13, 19).

- **Traditional Views About Man**

Throughout the Christian era scholars have presented views regarding man's essential parts and the origin of his soul. However, much of this, to my mind, is unscriptural, for they have equated personhood with the soul. The Bible teaches that personhood, as a separate entity, is to be distinguished from the soul and spirit (Job 7:11; Isa. 26:9, "I" is distinct from soul and spirit).

1. *ABOUT HIS PARTS*

While all agree that man consists of material and immaterial parts, not all concur on the divisions of his immaterial part and their functions.

   a. *Trichotomy*

Proposing that man consists of body, soul, and spirit, this theory was held by the earlier Greek church fathers, and for some time it was the prevailing view of the Eastern church. Today, many trichotomists explain man's threefold construction as follows: The body is the means by which man attains world or sense consciousness and by which he makes contact with his physical environment. The soul is the means by which he attains self-consciousness and self-expression in his relation with other humans. And the spirit is the means by which he attains God-consciousness. This view also regards the spirit of unsaved people as not functioning since these people are dead toward God and divine things.

As our study has shown, this explanation of the functions of man's essential parts is not entirely in accord with the biblical teaching of man's nature. Also, it ignores that the total being of fallen man functions, but not toward God. Furthermore, it fails to see personhood as a separate part of man's makeup.

   b. *Dichotomy*

From the first this view prevailed in the west, being held by Tertullian and Augustine. This says that man's nature consists of body and soul, with the soul representing the higher or spiritual element in man. Personhood and spirit are regarded as aspects of the soul.

I prefer the view that man's makeup consists of personhood and human nature; that human nature consists of body, soul, and spirit; and that the immaterial part of human nature consists of soul and spirit, which have similar functions but which are separate entities (Heb. 4:12). In I Thessalonians 5:23, Paul seems to emphasize that our whole being is preserved unto the coming of Jesus (cp. Deut. 6:5; II Ki. 23:25).

2. *ABOUT HIS SOUL*

Philosophers and theologians have given considerable attention to the origin of the soul, which they equate with personhood. They have proposed the following theories:

   a. *The Theory of Preexistence*

This holds that all human souls were created simultaneously as angels at the beginning of time, before the creation of matter and man. However, because of their apostasy, they are being given human bodies as punishment and are confined to earth until their restoration to their former angelic state.[24] The leading proponent of this theory was Origen (185-251?). This theory has been universally rejected by the church.

   b. *The Theory of Creationism*
      This holds that the body alone is propagated, whereas the soul is directly created by God and is placed in the body at birth. This theory was dominant in the Eastern church and became so in the Western church during the Middle Ages. It continues in the Roman Catholic and Eastern Orthodox Churches today. In support of this theory the Scriptures seem to teach that the soul (?) is created (Eccles. 12:7; Zech. 12:1; Isa. 42:5; 57:16; Heb. 12:9). This theory is more consistent with the popular (unbiblical) view that relates the soul to man's higher nature and the body to his lower nature. (Nowhere does the Bible make this distinction.)

   My objections to this theory follow: It makes God the creator of sinful souls (Prov. 21:10). It ignores the fact that God is indirectly the creator of the body as well as of the soul (Ps. 139:13-14; Jer. 1:5). It does not account for posterity being in the loins of their ancestors (Heb. 7:4-10). Also, the Bible does not say there are higher and lower parts of human nature as the ancient Greek philosopher Plato taught.[25]

   c. *The Theory of Traducianism*
      With its designation coming from the Latin verb *traduco* (lead, bring across or over), this theory holds that the soul was created on the sixth day of creation week with the creation of man (Gen. 2:7) and is transmitted and individualized by propagation. This was the view of the early Western church, being first stated by Tertullian (born c. 160) and established by Augustine (354-430). During the Middle Ages creationism prevailed over traducianism. The revival of Augustinian anthropology during the Reformation led to the appearance of traducianism in Lutheran and Calvinistic teachings. Today, advocates of creationism and traducianism are found among Protestant teachers and preachers.

   Advocates of traducianism point out that Adam begat a son in his own likeness (Gen. 5:3) and that descendants are said to be in the loins of their ancestors (Gen. 46:26; Heb. 7:4-10). This theory best explains the inherent corruption of fallen human nature and mankind's participation in Adam's initial sin (Rom. 5:12-19; I Cor. 15:22).

   The principle objection to this theory is that it implies a division of substance. How can the immaterial soul be propagated in this way?
W. G. T. Shedd replies:

   When it is said that that which is divisible is material, divisibility

---

[24] W. G. T. Shedd, *A History of Christian Doctrine* (New York: Charles Scribner Co., 1868), II, 4.
[25] See W. David Stacey, p. 73.

by man is meant. It is the separation of something that is visible, extended, and ponderable, by means of material instruments. But there is another kind of divisibility that is effected by the Creator, by means of a law of propagation established for this purpose. God can divide and distribute a primary substance that is not visible, extended, and ponderable, and yet real, by a method wholly different from that by which man divides a piece of clay into two portions.[26]

Observe that these theories of the origin of the soul do not deal with personhood as a separate element of man's makeup. They assume that the soul is man's personal entity or self. It is more in accord with the Scriptures to regard personhood as being distinct from human nature (body, soul, and spirit, cp. Job 7:11; Isa. 26:9). I prefer the view that personhood is at conception directly created by God and is immediately and permanently joined to one's propagated human nature. Upon this union one's personhood assumes all the qualities of his human nature and is made human. In turn, personhood communicates to human nature the qualities of individuality, morality, and perpetuity. This view allows God to be the Creator of unique, personal individuals who were created morally neutral and who were corrupted by their fallen, propagated human nature. This also explains how descendants were in the loins of their ancestors. Since one's human nature qualifies his personhood and makes him to be everything that his nature represents, in effect people were in the loins of their ancestors because their nature was involved in the lives of their forefathers. The solidarity of the race rests upon their having a commonly derived human nature, not in their having common personhood (Acts 17:26; I Cor. 15:45, 47, 49; see Appendix C).

MAN IS BOTH UNITED AND DIVERSE

• The Unity of Mankind

In spite of man's multiple racial distinctions, speech communities, and political states, all human beings have sprung from a common ancestry and thus form a unity. God uses the words "man" and "Adam" to speak collectively of Adam and Eve (Gen. 1:26-27; 5:2). Moreover, the whole human race descended from this couple (Acts 17:26; Gen. 3:20; chs. 4-5) and later from Noah's three sons after the flood (Gen. 9:1, 19; ch. 10). Paul describes Adam as "the first man" (I Cor. 15:45, 47). He also speaks of the solidarity of the human race with and in Adam when mankind participated in his first sin and inherited its woeful results (I Cor. 15:22; Rom. 5:12-19).

• The Diversity of Mankind

Biblical history reveals that God destroyed the earth's population with a flood of universal extent (Gen. 7:17-24). It has been conservatively estimated

---

[26] W. G. T. Shedd, *Dogmatic Theology*, II, 83.

that after eighteen generations, with only one previous generation still living, the world population at the time of the flood was over 1,030 million people.[27] If the remains of prehistoric man-like creatures are truly human, they may indicate a diversity of preflood races, similar to what exists today.

The diversity of races and languages, since the flood, began with the confounding of man's original language and his dispersion over the earth (Gen. 11:7-9). This was completed with their being confined to their divinely allocated areas of habitation (Gen. 10:32; Deut. 32:8; Acts 17:26).

Evolutionists account for racial distinctions as being the result of certain mechanics of change, such as mutation, adaptation, selection, and isolation.[28] It is believed that racial distinctions did not express themselves in man until the isolation of groups, which resulted in intermarriage, the strengthening of the gene pools, and the triggering of the forces of adaptation and selection.

Some creationists hold a similar view, believing that racial differences rapidly came about within small, isolated populations which were acted upon by the forces of natural selection, mutation (to a lesser extent), and genetic drift.[29] William J. Tinkle, a creationist, believes that God created man with mixed genes.[30] This gave man latent possibilities which were later expressed in various types of human beings. Similarly, creationist John Pilkey points out that Noah and his three sons could not be the key to race origin because the three sons shared the racial character of their father. He believes that racial distinctions were embodied in the four wives who were divinely selected for this purpose from four antediluvian stocks, including a red matriarch, a yellow matriarch, a black matriarch, and a white matriarch. He believes that these primary racial types, which already existed before the Flood, came about by the genetic potential of Adam and Eve. He also holds that the radical diversities within each color group after the Flood (for example, there are four kinds of blacks) derived from a process of eugenic polygamy within Noah's immediate family.[31]

While mutations can cause changes, this does not appear to be the principal method of adding variety to living things, for mutant individuals lack vigor and most die out in natural selection. Most varieties probably came about by the regrouping of the genes. These changes are not "evolutionary," for they create not higher types but variety within the species.

There is no factual basis for the theory that the racial characteristics of negroid or black people are the result of the curse that Noah placed on his grandson Canaan (Gen. 9:25). The descendants of Canaan were never black. The prophetic curse was that the Canaanites were to become a servile race

[27] Whitcomb and Morris, The Genesis Flood, p. 25 f.
[28] What Is Race? (Paris: United Nations Educational, Scientific, and Cultural Organization, 1952), pp. 11-36.
[29] R. Daniel Shaw, "Fossil Man," in A Symposium on Creation III, ed. by Donald W. Patten (Grand Rapids: Baker Book House, 1971), pp. 132-4.
[30] Heredity, pp. 85-99.
[31] John Pilkey, The Origin of the Nations, (San Diego: Master Book Publishers, 1984), pp 11-16.

(Gen. 9:25-26). This was realized in the conquest of Palestine by the Hebrews, Philistines, and Arameans. Later, the Greeks and the Romans subjugated the great Phoenician colonies. People who are some color other than ruddy (Adam means "red soil") are so because of God-given mechanics of change, not because of some curse.

THE WORK OF MAN

When He created Adam and placed him in the garden, God gave man work to do (Gen. 2:15). This work extended beyond his caring for the garden. Man also was to subdue the earth, making it subservient to his will (Gen. 1:28). God also created and appointed Eve to be Adam's helper (Gen. 2:18). However, with man's sin his work became wearisome, sorrowful toil (Gen. 3:17-19). From the divinely cursed ground man was to eke out his living and eat its produce in the sweat of his face.

Yet, in spite of these things, work still contributes to man's good (Eccles. 2:24). It gives him opportunity to express his ability and creativity, to provide for his livelihood and that of his dependents, and to achieve certain goals that minister to the general well-being of mankind.

From its beginning Christianity has condemned idleness (I Thess. 4:11; II Thess. 3:10-12). The Lord taught the principle that the laborer is worthy of his hire (Lk. 10:7). Hard, legitimate work, suited to one's abilities and temperament, not only is personally satisfying but also is a means by which one can bring blessing to others (I Tim. 5:8; 6:17-19; Eph. 4:28).

In his instructions to Christian slaves regarding their work, Paul presents principles which apply to us who are Christian employees (Eph. 6:5-8). He speaks of our duty to carry out the will of them for whom we work (Eph. 6:5-6; Col. 3:22; I Pet. 2:18), of our work as a service to Christ (Eph. 6:5-7), of holding right attitudes toward God (Col. 3:22; Eph. 6:5-6) and our employer (Eph. 6:7), and of anticipating a reward (Eph. 6:8; Col. 3:24-25). Work, done rightly, will bring double pay (I Cor. 15:58)! Paul also has something to say to Christian masters or employers (Eph. 6:9; Col. 4:1).

Since secular work makes up the larger part of life for most saved people, we should look at this more closely. Ordinarily, believers think of their secular occupation in one of several ways, so as to give it spiritual significance. Some think of it as an opportunity to witness to the unsaved whom they contact on the job. Others think of it as a means of providing for their material needs while they serve the Lord in their local church or elsewhere. Still others consider it as a way of securing money to finance the Lord's work. While these are valid views, I believe that the saved person should also regard his secular work, when done in God's will and way, as a service with and unto the Lord. Paul exhorts Christian slaves, "Be obedient...as unto Christ" (Eph. 6:5); "as the servants of Christ, doing the will of God from the heart" (vs. 6); "with good will doing service as to the Lord" (vs. 7).

Actually, the believer's total life should be regarded as a service to God (Rom. 12:2; II Cor. 5:15). As we abide in the Lord, we allow Him to express Himself in all we do (Jn. 15:4-5). While we pursue our secular employment, we can allow Him to minister through us to others, according to His sovereign purpose. On the other hand, there is still need for people to enter "full time" gospel ministries as God directs.

THE REPRODUCTION OF MAN

Unlike angels, humans have power to reproduce their kind. Needless to say, this places upon us a great responsibility. Both God and man take part in this awesome event, which begins with human conception (Ps. 51:5; Gen. 5:3; Jer. 1:5; Ps. 139:13-15).

GOD'S PART IN HUMAN REPRODUCTION

God gives or withholds the fruit of the womb according to His sovereign purpose (Gen. 16:2; 30:2; I Sam. 1:5-6, 19-20; Job 1:21; Lk. 1:24-25). The view that one's personhood is directly created by God and his human nature is propagated by human parents points to human reproduction as being something more than the operation of a natural law.[32]

MAN'S PART IN HUMAN REPRODUCTION

Although it is God's right to give and to take life, this does not relieve man of his responsibility in the exercise of his procreative powers. Because of this, many people believe that any interference with natural processes is an interference with the providence of God and is therefore sinful, regardless of what the motivation may be. Actually, man's subjugation of the earth and dominion over it require him to interfere with the processes of nature so that his environment may serve higher human purposes (Gen. 1:28).

The Bible does not provide specific guidance for family planning in the present dispensation. The case of Onan is entirely irrelevant (Gen. 38:6-10). Onan incurred the Lord's displeasure by his disobeying his father's command and his brother's desire, thus refusing to perpetuate the family (Messianic) line. Later, this levirate custom became a law in Israel (Deut. 25:5-10). The Scriptures leave the matter of birth limitation and family planning to the individual conscience and to the motivation of New Testament principles that govern Christian conduct. Married believers need to develop the concept of responsible parenthood, which takes into consideration the physical, emotional, spiritual, and economical conditions of the home.[33]

---

[32] See Appendix C.
[33] See Dwight H. Small, *Design for Christian Marriage*, p. 101. M. O. Vincent, "Moral Considerations in Contraception," in *Birth Control and the Christian*, ed. by Walter O. Spitzer and Carlyle L. Saylor (Wheaton: Tyndale House Publishers, 1969), pp. 248-53.

While both God and man have part in human reproduction, this concurs in such a way as not to rob God of His sovereignty and man of his responsibility. God allows man to do what he wills, but man must bear the consequences of his actions. The Lord is pleased when His people seek His guidance for their lives and seek to glorify Him in all they do.

THE PHYSICAL DEATH OF MAN

The practice of organ transplantation has required doctors and theologians to define more precisely death. With modern life-support machines, it is sometimes difficult to determine when a person dies, for there is no precise moment of biological death. Consequently, physicians look for evidence of meaningful life. The criteria of the American Medical Society for death are these: lack of response to external stimuli, no movement or breathing during a one-hour observation period, no reflex action, and a flat electroencephalogram to confirm the other tests.[34] Since any understanding of physical death must include what the Scriptures reveal about it, let us examine the following:

ITS DEFINITION

Medical science recognizes several kinds of death, including clinical death in which the respiration and heart beat stops; brain death in which the functions controlling consciousness and the nervous system, heart, and lungs cease; biological death which consists of the permanent end of bodily life; and cellular death which is the final termination of all life processes in the body. Theologically, physical death occurs when the spirit (Ps. 146:4; Eccles. 12:7; Jas. 2:26; Mt. 27:50) and the soul (Gen. 35:18; I Ki. 17:21) depart from the body. This triggers the beginning of total decay which reduces the body to dust (Gen. 3:19; Ps. 16:10; I Cor. 15:50-54). Thus, physical death is an event which introduces the state of body corruptibility. (See fn. 15, p. 262.)

ITS ORIGIN

Being the product of sin (Jas. 1:15), death entered the human race by Adam's initial transgression (Gen. 2:17; 3:19; Rom. 5:12). Consequently, it has affected all of mankind as an inevitable experience of life (Gen. ch. 5: Ps. 90:9-10; 103:15-16; Eccles. 3:19; 9:2-3; Heb. 9:27). Still, two have escaped it (Gen. 5:24; II Ki. 2:11). Also, believers living at the time of the rapture (I Thess. 4:17) and at the time when the Lord's kingdom will be established on earth (Mt. 25:34, 46), will not experience it. Death is an enemy (I Cor. 15:25-26) feared by the unsaved (Heb. 2:14-15).

Apparently, there was no death among animals before man sinned and God placed a curse upon nature (Gen. 3:17; Rom. 8:20-21). Newly created man and animals were not to eat flesh (Gen. 1:29-30). The divine curse upon

---

[34]Janet Rohler Greisch, "Organ Transplants," in Our Society in Turmoil, ed. Gary R. Collins (Carol Stream, Ill.: Creation House, 1970), p. 184.

nature brought death to nature, including animals.

ITS MASTERS

To various degrees God, Satan, and Jesus exercise authority over physical death. Being the creator of life, God has absolute authority over death (Deut. 32:39; I Sam. 2:6; II Ki. 5:7; Job 1:21; Ps. 68:20). As the Creator He can take life and not be guilty of murder.

On the other hand, Satan is a murderer (Jn. 8:44), for he brought death to mankind that was not his creation. Satan now has the power of physical death (Heb. 2:14), not in an absolute sense so as to inflict it on whom he pleases, but according to God's permissive decree (I Cor. 5:5; Job 1:12-19). He also rules the sphere of spiritual death in which the unsaved now abide (Acts 26:18; I Jn. 5:19; Jn. 5:24). Satan will continue to have this power until his confinement in the Abyss and later in the Lake of Fire (Rev. 20:1-3, 10).

By His death Jesus invaded Satan's domain, yielded to death's power, and by His resurrection broke death's grip. It was not possible for death to hold Him, for He was sinless and death had no claim on Him (Acts 2:22-24). By His resurrection triumph our Lord broke Satan's power and became the Warden of death and Hades (Rev. 1:18; Heb. 2:14). While Satan still has the power of death over the lost, he does not have this authority over the saved (Col. 1:13). The Lord delivers His people from Satan's authority at salvation, saves them from the fear of death, receives them safely at death, and one day will deliver their bodies from death (Heb. 2:15; Jn. 14:3; Phil. 1:23; I Cor. 15:51-57). In His time He will bring both Satan and physical death to their final doom (I Cor. 15:25-26; Rev. 20:10, 13).

ITS EXPERIENCE

Upon death the unsaved go to Hades until the resurrection of their bodies and their judgement (Lk. 16:23; Jn. 5:28-29; Rev. 20:13). At death we who are saved go to be with the Lord until the resurrection of our bodies at His coming (II Cor. 5:8; Phil. 1:21, 23; 3:20-21; I Thess. 4:16).

Some hold that the dead are asleep during the interval between their death and resurrection (cp. I Thess. 4:14), but the Bible does not really support this view (cp. Lk. 16:22-23; Phil. 1:23; Rev. 6:9-10). The concept of death as sleep seems to rise from the appearance of the body in death and the temporariness of this state (cp. Jn. 11:11-14). It seems that all the dead are in a state of consciousness and are aware of their surroundings, whether in Hades or Heaven (Lk. 16:19-32; Rev. 7:9-17). There is no scriptural indication that the dead are able to view earthly events or to contact earthly people, save the single case of Samuel, whom God used to pronounce a sentence on Saul, king of Israel (I Sam. 28:1-20).

A person may hasten his death by attempting suicide (I Sam. 31:4-5) or by defiant sinning (I Cor. 11:30; I Jn. 5:16). But this would only be effective according to God's permissive decree.

From this study we have seen that man is a complex, noble being, made in the image of God. Because of this, we should treat ourselves and others with respect (Mk. 12:31). The ungodly idea which sees man as a higher form of animal undermines his dignity and encourages the inhumanity of selfish exploitation and cruel domination, often with violence. People behave according to what they believe they are.

A Review of Anthropology

1. Why is the biblical record of man's creation more accurate and more to be accepted than man's scientific opinions?

2. Describe the two-step process of Adam's creation.

3. What did God do in the second step beside imparting to man's body physical life (soul and spirit)?

4. What does it mean when it says that man became "a living soul" (Genesis 2:7)?

5. How do we know from Genesis 2:7 that pre-Adamic races of humans did not exist?

6. What was the process in God's creating Eve?

7. What did God not do in creating Eve that He did in His creating Adam? Why did He use Adam's rib?

8. What were the two purposes for God's creating Eve?

9. When did God create Eve?

10. Distinguish between civilization and spirituality.

11. What is the image of God in man? What human beings have this image?

12. What leads us to think that angels have this image too?

13. Distinguish between the image of God in humans and the image of Christ in the believers.

14. What is marriage?

15. Give three purposes for marriage.

16. Why does God forbid premarital and extramarital sexual relations?

17. What spiritual relationship does marriage portray?

18. What is God's social order for mankind?

19. To what areas of human life does the Bible show that this social order applies?

20. What is a purpose of woman's subordination to man?

21. What is man's essential make-up or constitution?

22. What is personhood?

23. How do Job's words in Job 7:11 indicate that personhood exists?

24. What qualities does personhood have and contribute to our humanity? Explain these qualities.

25. What is human nature? What are its three parts?

26. What is the present condition of the bodies of all living humans?

27. When will the believer's body be saved, or changed?

28. What appears to be the primary functions of the body in living humans?

29. In addition to these, what are the holy functions of the believer's body?

30. Although the believer's body is still corrupt and mortal, why is it no longer the proper instrument of sin?

31. Why is it important to care for the body?

32. Give the meanings of "flesh" in the Scriptures.

33. What two parts make up the immaterial part of our human nature?

34. What reason is there to believe that these parts may be one entity?

35. How is the soul related to the body? How is the spirit related to the body?

36. Give the five basic functions of the soul and spirit.

37. What is the seat of spiritual life in the believer?

38. What part of the believer is saved?

39. What does it mean to say that soul and spirit are saved?

40. What part of human nature survives death? Why?

41. What is the most comprehensive term in the Bible for the inner part of man?

42. What is the conscience?

43. To what part of our being does conscience belong?

44. What other faculty of moral judgment do we have beside the conscience? (See Appendix B)

45. Which of these two faculties is stronger than the other?

46. Why is it sinful to act contrary to your conscience?

47. How can we reprogram the conscience?

48. What does it mean to have a seared conscience?

49. What does it mean to do something with the heart?

50. In what circumstances is man's heart evil? When is the believer's heart evil? Pure?

51. What are the theories of dichotomy and trichotomy?

52. Give the theological theories for the origin of the soul (personhood).

53. What is the writer's theory?

54. What part of our make-up is created by God? What part is propagated?

55. What accounts for the unity of the human race? Its diversity?

56. How does work contribute to man's good?

57. In what ways may secular work have spiritual significance?

58. In human reproduction there is a concurrence of divine and human activities. What are these activities?

59. Why is it not wrong to interfere with natural processes? When is it wrong to do so?
60. What is physical death theologically?
61. How are God, Satan, and Jesus related to physical death?
62. Why can God take life and not be a murderer?
63. How did Jesus break Satan's power over death?
64. Where do unsaved people go when they die? Saved people?
65. What biblical evidence is there against soul-sleep?
66. Why should not a person commit suicide?

Hamartiology

HAMARTIOLOGY
The Doctrine of Sin

Contrary to popular opinion, the Bible teaches that man is not now normal (what God created him to be), but he is a sinner. Adam's disobedience to God brought about a ruinous change in his total being and generated within him the sin-principle. These cataclysmic results also extend to all his posterity. Therefore, it is urgent that we understand the dynamics of sin and how we can experience deliverance from its disastrous effects and victory over its tenacious power.

THE NATURE OF SIN

The Scriptures teach that sin is an impersonal, temporal, evil force, which is confined to fallen angels and all earthly humans and which expresses itself through their natures. Thus, there are two aspects of sin: *sin* as an evil principle, force, or energy, and *sins* as the evil expressions of this energy in the evil activities of fallen angels and earthly humans.

SIN AS A PRINCIPLE[1]

1. Its Description

According to this aspect, sin is an evil law, force, or principle that impels angels and humans to sin (Rom. 7:23; 8:2). It is the root, of which sins (the expressions of this force through human and angelic natures) are the fruit (cp. Gal. 5:19-21, "flesh" represents this sin-force dominating one's self and nature). In the New Testament this principle is represented by the singular word "sin" in passages that are not speaking of some particular expression of sin (cp. Jn. 8:34; Rom. 3:9; 5:20-21; 6:1-2, 6-7, 10-14, 16-18, 20, 22; 7:14, 17, 20, 23, 25; 8:2-3; Gal. 3:22; I Jn. 1:8). In James 1:14, this evil force is represented by the word "lusts," or the inner desires, by means of which this evil energy induces people to sin. "Lusts" here is a figurative expression (synecdoche) for the sin-force (cp. Rom. 6:12; 13:14; Gal. 5:16, 24).

---

[1] While this aspect of sin is commonly called "the sin-nature," it is more accurate to speak of it as "the sin-principle" or "the sin-force," as does the Bible (Rom. 7:23, 25; 8:2). A principle is "a primary element, force, or law which produces or determines particular results" (*Oxford Universal English Dictionary*, p. 1585). Contrariwise, I understand "nature" to be the created essence or substance that determines generic kind of being, such as human nature or angelic nature. Mankind, whether saved or unsaved, has only human nature. In its unredeemed state, the human nature is sinful and corrupted. All humans on earth have within their bodily flesh the sin-principle that would use their human nature as its instrument of expression. Observe that "flesh" often means in the New Testament the sin-principle, dominating the human nature (Gal. 5:19-21; Rom. 8:4). Also, see A.T. Robertson, *Word Pictures in the Greek New Testament* VI, p. 208, I John 1:8; and W.F.Arndt & F.W. Gingrich, *A Greek-English Lexicon of the New Testament*, "nomos," p. 542.

2. Its Distinctions

It is important that we distinguish between the sin-principle and human nature (body, soul, spirit). While this evil force is resident within the flesh (the cells) of our mortal bodies (Rom. 7:17-18, 23, 25; 8:2), it must not be equated with our human nature. Being self-generated by rebellious angels and humans, this evil energy was never an essential part of the newly created angelic and human natures. The sin-principle is the active force that induces and energizes personhood to express through its nature, whether angelic or human, sinful actions, words, thoughts, motives, emotions, intentions, and attitudes. Human nature is its passive instrument (cp. Rom 6:13).

Moreover, we must distinguish between the sin-principle and self (our personhood), as Paul does when he says, "It is no more I that do it but sin that dwells in me" (Rom. 7:17, 20). Our enemy that leads us to sin is neither our human nature nor our self (personhood), but sin which would dominate us and energize both us and our nature for its evil expressions.

3. Its Distribution

The sin-principle completely dominates the lives of the unsaved to the extent that they are ever its slaves (Rom. 3:9-12; Jn. 8:34). In spite of the relatively good things that they do, their whole bent of life is toward sinning and the total output of their lives consists only of sins in God's sight (Rom. 3:10, 12; cp. 14:23). They have neither the will nor the ability to do what is right before God.

Every saved person on earth still has the sin-principle within his bodily flesh (Rom. 7:18; 6:11-13; I Jn. 1:8). This accounts for the evil, inner urges we feel (Jas. 1:14; Rom. 13:14; Gal. 5:24), our ability to sin (I Jn. 2:1), and God's exhortations against our sinning (Rom. 6:12; Col. 3:8). However, because of the radical change that salvation has made in our lives, we no longer sin continuously as the unsaved do (I Jn. 2:29; 3:4-10, observe the present tense). We now commit acts of sin and acts of righteousness, according to the dominating principle (God or sin) to which we surrender.

As we shall see more clearly later, it is natural for unsaved people to sin, for their human nature, wholly corrupted by original sin, is bent toward sinning and is wholly dominated by the sin-principle. On the other hand, saved people sin contrary to their human nature, for their nature (excepting the body) has been renewed by regeneration and is now bent toward doing righteousness (Col. 3:9-10; Eph. 4:24; Rom. 6:18-19, 22). Having a new dynamic principle (the Holy Spirit) within us, it is now fitting and required that we who are saved yield our self and human nature (including our body), with its actions, words, thoughts, emotions, attitudes, and intentions, to God as an instrument of righteousness in His hand. However, as long as we have the sin- principle, we shall be susceptible to its urges and shall be in need of victory over it.

SIN AS AN EXPRESSION

As we have observed, specific sins of word, action, thought, will, emotion, attitude, and motive are the fruit of the sin-principle as it energizes our personhood and human nature for its evil expressions. Without an instrument of expression, this evil force could not manifest itself by these evil works. It is like a musician who must have an instrument to play if he is to produce music. We shall look at this more closely when we consider actual sins.

THE CHARACTER OF SIN

The character of sin is revealed by divine revelation and is determined by its contrast with the character of God. Sin is not only unlike God in its character but it is also opposed to Him in its direction (I Jn. 1:5; Ps. 51:4; Gen. 39:9; Isa. 59:2; Rom. 8:7). It is dynamic rather than static.

We see the character of sin in the following biblical terms that are used for its designations.

IN THE OLD TESTAMENT

- "Sin" (Deut. 19:15; Heb. *hatta:* to fail, miss; *hattah:* failure). Sin is recognized as a failure or a clear violation of a given command or prohibition.

- "Iniquity" (II Sam. 22:24; Heb. *awon:* acting crookedly). Sin is an action which is not straight or right. It originates with wrong intention.

- "Transgression" (Mic. 1:5; Heb. *pesha:* rebellion, revolt). Sin is a revolt of the human will against the divine will.

- "Trespass" (Lev. 5:15; Heb. *maal:* faithlessness). Sin is acting contrary to one's duty.

- "Unrighteousness" (Lev. 19:15; Heb. *awel:* unrighteousness). Sin is wrong doing, acting against God's will.

- "Evil" (Gen. 2:9; Heb. *raw:* bad, evil). This word has a wide range of applications including the concepts of disaster (Gen. 44:34), illness (Deut. 7:15; cp. 28:27), and that which is unpleasant (Gen. 28:8). It is used with ethical meaning in Genesis 2:9; Deuteronomy 1:39; II Samuel 14:17; I Kings 3:9; and Psalm 34:14.[2]

IN THE NEW TESTAMENT

- "Sin" (Jn. 1:29; Gk. *hamartia:* missing a mark or goal, failure to attain an end). Sin is to miss the standard which is fixed by God (Rom. 3:23).

---

[2] See Ludwig Koehler, *Old Testament Theology,* pp. 169-71.

- "Disobedience" (Rom. 5:19; Gk. *parakoe:* failing to hear, hearing amiss). Sin is a failure to hear which results in disobedience.

- "Iniquity" (Mt. 7:23; Gk. *anomia:* lawlessness). Sin is to act contrary to the law.

- "Transgression" (I Tim. 2:14; Gk. *parabasis:* overstepping). Sin is a violation of law.

- "Trespass," "offence" (Mt. 6:14-15; Rom. 5:15-18, 20; Gk. *paraptoma:* a falling behind, lapse, or deviation). Sin is a deviation from truth or righteousness.

- "Unrighteousness" (Rom. 1:18; Gk. *adikia:* unrighteousness). Sin is doing wrong, acting against God's will.[3]

SOME OBSERVATIONS ABOUT SIN

- Being a unique force, sin is positive, absolute evil, not a lesser degree of goodness (Gen. 2:9; cp. I Jn. 1:5-6).

- Sin is not only unlike God in its character but it also is actively opposed to Him and His will (Gen. 39:9; Isa. 42:24; Jn. 3:20; Rom. 8:7; I Jn. 1:5; 3:4).

- Actual sins may be greater or lesser in the punishment it incurs (Mt. 11:20-24; 23:14; Mk. 3:28-29; Jn. 19:11). This seems to be determined by the amount of spiritual knowledge against which one sins as well as the intrinsic character of the sin itself (cp. murder v. lying).

- Being an energy rather than a generic nature, sin was not a part of original creation (Gen. 1:31). It was the product of rebellious angels and humans.

- Sin always produces death, both spiritual and physical (Jas. 1:14-15; Gen. 2:17; Gal. 6:7-8). It can never impart life.

- Having definite beginning, sin will cease to exist when all mortal bodies die or are changed. When death is abolished (I Cor. 15:26, 54), its parent, sin, will also be abolished, as the account of the rich man in Hades indicates (Lk. 16:22-28; cp. Phil. 2:10-11). Apparently, fallen angels are deprived of the sin-force at the time of their judgment. I do not believe that the lost will perpetually sin in Hell, though they will forever pay the penalty of their sinning during their former life (Mt. 25:46; cp. Phil. 2:10-11; I Cor. 15:25-26). It appears that the resurrection body of the lost, which will be reconstituted for the eternal state, will not have the sin-principle. I understand Revelation 22:11, 15 to describe the continuing character of the lost, as determined by their lifetime, not their continuing actions.

---

[3] See Kenneth S. Wuest, *Studies in the Vocabulary of the Greek New Testament* (Grand Rapids: Wm. B. Eerdmans Publishing Co., 1945), pp. 95-100.

- An actual sin consists of the decision to do wrong and the actions which follow. When one decides to do wrong but is not able physically to do it, he still is guilty of this sin, for with his decision he carried it out in his mind (cp. Mt. 5:27-28).

THE ORIGIN OF SIN

Contrary to philosophical dualism which sees good and evil as eternal principles, the Scriptures reveal that sin had a definite beginning. Let us see what the Bible says about this and sin's relation to God and His creatures.

SIN'S ORIGIN AND GOD

• God Included Sin in His Decree.

With only limited understanding of this profound doctrine, we have observed that God's decree includes everything that comes to pass, whether good or evil (Rom. 11:36; cp. Acts 2:23; 3:18, 4:27-28). Evil belongs to the permissive aspect of God's decree. This means that, while He actively chose sin to be a part of His decree and thus made it certain, God was not compelled to accept sin as a foreseen evil, nor does He Himself bring it to pass or assume the responsibility for it.

• God Did Not Create Sin.

The Scriptures do not suggest that sin was a part of the original creation, which God saw to be "very good" (Gen. 1:31). However, when He created angels and humans with the ability to make moral choices, He gave to them the ability to sin. They had the free choice of obeying their Creator or rebelling against Him.

Nevertheless, we cannot credit God with being the author (efficient cause) of sin, for this would attribute to Him a quality that contradicts His self-revelation (II Tim. 2:13). With reference to character He is unlike sin (I Jn. 1:5; Ps. 92:15; Hab. 1:13), and with reference to ability He cannot sin (Jas. 1:13; Tit. 1:2). God cannot be or act contrary to what He is.

• Possibilities for God's Choosing to Allow Sin

1. *The capability of doing evil was a necessary alternative to the creature's choosing to do good.* There could be no true moral choice if good were the only option. Being free moral agents with self-determination, angels and humans were allowed to choose the ruling principle that would govern their lives.

2. *Sin was a means for manifesting certain divine qualities.* These qualities of God's nature were His holiness which makes Him to be wholly unlike sin and without sin (I Jn. 1:5), His hatred toward evil as expressed by His wrath (Rom. 9:22), His power as manifested in His

judgments (Rom. 9:17, 22), His righteousness and justice as exercised in His judgments (Rom. 2:5), and His mercy and grace as displayed in salvation (Eph. 2:4, 7). These divine qualities could only be displayed in His dealing with sinful creatures who deserved His wrath. The glories of God's character radiate more brightly against the dark backdrop of sin. This is not to say that sin contributes to His glory, but it does stand in striking contrast to His glory and enhances it.

SIN'S ORIGIN AND PERSONAL CREATURES

We must not think of sin as being like a radioactive cloud, which floats about the universe and pollutes everything with its fallout. Actually, sin exists and functions in a closed system. This means that it is confined to fallen angels and to earthly humans, with whom it originated. In spite of all appearances, I believe that sin does not reside in impersonal creation such as vegetation and animals. This aspect of the universe is temporarily afflicted with degeneration, disease, and death, resulting from a divine curse which God placed upon it when men sinned (Gen. 3:17; Rom. 8:20-22; cp. Mt. 21:18-19). When He sets up His earthly kingdom, the Lord Jesus will lift this curse and will restore the earth to its pristine state (Isa. 11:1-9). Just how God is implementing this curse is not clear.

• Sin and Angels

Lucifer (Satan) was the first creature to sin (Ezek. 28:11-19). Being the anointed cherub who was perfect in all of his ways, Lucifer's first sin was his exalting himself rather than God. Resulting from a wrong choice, this sinful act generated within him the sin-principle, which has dominated him ever since. In response to his beauty, Lucifer misused his God-given powers of choice and worship by choosing to admire and exalt himself rather than the Creator (Ezek. 28:15, 17). This sinful act of self-exaltation led to pride and to the irrational ambition to take God's place over the universe (I Tim. 3:6; Isa. 14:13-14).

Following Lucifer's example, other angels chose to revolt against God and to give their allegiance to the devil (Mt. 25:41; Rev. 12:4, 7-9). Their sinful act of rebellion generated within them the sin-principle, which now dominates their lives. As in the case of humans, it appears that angels were given a probationary period to choose the leadership they would follow. The angels who are now fallen chose to follow Satan rather than God (cp. Rev. 12:4).

Observe that in the case of angels as well as humans, their initial sin was more than their decision to revolt. It also included the action resulting from the decision (cp. Jas. 1:14-15; Rom. 5:19). Their sinning was the natural outcome of their wrong decision.

• Sin and Humans

Eve was the first human to sin. But the disastrous effects of sin and its principle were transmitted to the human race through Adam, its lineal head

(Rom. 5:12; I Cor. 15:21-22). Let us examine man's fall more closely.

1. MAN'S PROBATION (Gen. 2:17)

God's prohibition against man's eating the fruit of the tree of the knowledge of good and evil was a test, which man's moral self-determination required and which stimulated his free choice as a moral being. It required Adam and Eve to choose the ruling principle (the authority of God or the power of sin) that would govern their lives. This test gave the couple opportunity to choose God's direction for their lives and to experience permanent moral development. By obeying their Creator during this period, they would have expressed their love for Him, chosen Him as their life manager, and passed from a state of mutable righteousness and holiness to one of moral immutability. Also, they would have received an innate knowledge of good and evil. Meanwhile, God warned Adam of what would take place if he should disobey this prohibition.

2. MAN'S DISOBEDIENCE (Gen. 3:1-6)

This is the only literature of antiquity that explains how the human race became sinful. Liberal theologians regard this record as a fable or myth, which is to be interpreted allegorically. But Edward J. Young observes that there is a great difference between this record of man's fall and well-known fables. The record of man's moral fall has no moral attached to it; the passage is not poetry but prose; the historicity of the event is underscored by Paul's reference to it (Rom. 5:12-19; I Tim. 2:13-14); and God's curse upon the snake indicates that it was more than a symbol of evil.[4] Being a historical event, man's fall probably occurred very soon after his creation, perhaps within several days.

a. Eve's Sin (Gen. 3:1-6a)

Eve's sin was self-generated, not contracted like some disease. Rather than obeying God, she chose to satisfy her natural desires for food, beauty, and wisdom in a way which was contrary to God's will (cp. I Jn. 2:16). Her sin brought into being within her the sin-force.

Eve was encouraged to make this choice by Satan's deceptive strategy (II Cor. 11:3; I Tim. 2:14). First, the devil attracted her attention by speaking through the snake (Gen. 3:1). Then, he undermined her confidence in God. He did this by discrediting God's goodness with a question (vs. 1): "Yea, hath God said, 'Ye shall not eat of every tree of the garden?' ("Fruit was made to be eaten, but God will not let you eat it.") Also, by discrediting God's integrity with a lie (vs. 4): "Ye shall not surely die." ("This is only a threat; God does not mean what He says.") And by discrediting God's intention with a suggestion (vs. 5): "For God doth know that in the day ye eat thereof, then your eyes shall be opened, and ye shall be as God, knowing good and evil." ("God is selfish; He does not want you to be like Him.") Finally, Satan used

---

[4] Edward J. Young, *Genesis 3* (London: The Banner of Truth Trust, 1966) pp. 10-14.

this part-truth to motivate her.

Stripped of her spiritual defence and motivated by the hint that she could be like God, Eve sought to satisfy her natural desires by taking the forbidden fruit and eating it in disobedience to God's command. But she was deceived, for she did not experience the benefits that Satan and the fruit seemingly offered (I Tim. 2:14).

Several possibilities may be offered for Satan's approaching Eve first. Being subordinate to her husband and dependent upon him, she may have been more susceptible to Satan's strategy. Since she had not received the prohibition directly from God (when it was given, she had not yet been created), she may have been more vulnerable to satanic argument and doubt. Also, being Adam's wife and helper, she was the most effective agent in leading him to sin, for he dearly loved her.

b. Adam's Sin (Gen. 3:6b)

Adam was not deceived (I Tim. 2:14). With full knowledge of the consequences, he deliberately sinned. He chose to accept Eve's offer (Gen. 3:6) rather than to follow God's command (2:16-17). His sin was outright disobedience (Rom. 5:19). It generated within him the sin-principle.

Eve's sinning made a difficult choice for her husband. Would he express his love for his wife by following her direction? Or would he express his love for God by following His command? Rather than leaving the problem of his fallen wife to God (cp. Lk. 1:38) and expressing greater love for Him, Adam accepted the fruit and ate it.

As in the case of fallen angels, the initial sins of Eve and Adam resulted from a wrong choice, and this in turn brought into being within them the sin-principle. Unlike angels, man propagates his kind. Adam transmitted the corrupting, ruinous results of his initial sinning to his posterity (Gen. 5:3; Rom. 5:12-19; I Cor. 15:21-22). This means that unlike Adam and Eve who were created without sin, all their descendants (excepting Jesus) are born sinners and receive from their parents a wholly corrupted human nature with the sin-principle.

THE RESULTS OF SIN

Satan's rebellion seems to have led to the fall of a third of the angelic host (Rev. 12:4). He also deceived Eve and encouraged her to sin. In turn, Eve persuaded Adam to eat the forbidden fruit. This introduced sin, with its devastating results, into the human race.

THE FALL'S EFFECT UPON ADAM AND EVE

There were both immediate and subsequent effects.

- **Their Sins' Immediate Effects[5]**

The immediate effects were the spontaneous, natural results of their sinning.

1. *Spiritual Death*

In their unfallen state the couple possessed spiritual life. With their newly created lives involuntarily organized about their Creator, they enjoyed His fellowship and began to carry out their stewardship. But the moment they sinned, they died spiritually (Gen. 2:17). Their conscious, spiritual relationship to God was severed. Sin disorganized them spiritually and cut them off from vital, personal relation to God. Choosing to sin, they became sinners and began to experience a different kind of existence, characterized by spiritual death, guilt, and fear (Gen. 3:7-10).

2. *Total Corruption of Human Nature*

Their sinning brought about the total corruption of their human nature, which ultimately led to physical death (Gen. 3:19; 5:5). This ruinous change gave their human nature the inclination toward and capacity for expressing sinful human actions, thoughts, feelings, and the like. Their sinning also generated within them the sin-force that would incite and energize them to sin.

3. *An Acute Sense of Guilt*

Upon sinning, they became keenly aware of their nakedness before God (cp. Gen. 2:25), for their eyes were now opened to an experiential knowledge of sin and its guilt (Gen. 3:7-8). Their sense of nakedness and feeling of fear were symptoms of their awareness of having violated God's command. Therefore, they attempted to alleviate their guilt feelings by dealing with the symptoms. They tried to cover their nakedness and hide from God (Gen. 3:7-8), but human means of dealing with guilt are not sufficient.

- **Their Sins' Subsequent Effects**

These effects were the judicial results of their sinning. It was inevitable that the sinful pair would be confronted by their Creator and would be required to give an account of their disobedience (Gen. 3:9-13). In spite of their efforts to shift the blame to others, they were found guilty and sentenced to punishment.

1. *God's Sentence Upon Eve (Gen. 3:16)*

God's sentence upon Eve was especially severe because, leaving her

---

[5] I believe that at this time Adam lost his world authority to Satan. Jesus declared that the devil is the prince of this world (Jn. 12:31; 14:30; 16:11); and He did not contest the validity of the devil's offer to give to Him the kingdoms of earth (Mt. 4:8-9). Since he set man up to sin (Gen. 3:1-6) and is the invisible ruler of the lost (Acts 26:17-18), it appears that Satan seized world dominion from Adam at this time and in this way. It is noteworthy that after the Flood God did not say that man had dominion over the earth as He did when He created man (Gen. 9:2 with 1:26). The Lord Jesus will evict the usurper Satan from earth when He establishes His earthly, millennial kingdom (Rev. 20:1-3).

role as his helper, she was instrumental in Adam's sinning (Gen. 2:18; 3:6). The sentence included not only an increase of the pain and distresses which are peculiar to women and of the frequency of conception but also a continuation of the woman's subjection to the will and domination of man. Eve was already subordinate to her husband as his helper (Gen. 2:18; I Cor. 11:9), but now she was placed in permanent subjection to him. She would not be free to attain her desire (will) without his permission, for he would rule over her. Whereas this subordination brings to women shameful, cruel exploitation and oppression by evil men, it brings blessing to believers who are motivated by obedience and love (Eph. 5:21-33; I Cor. 11:7).

   2. *God's Sentence Upon Adam (Gen. 3:17-19)*

   Although God addressed Adam, it appears that His words apply to both men and women. For man's sake God cursed the ground so that the soil would be less productive and that it would bear such nuisances as thorns and thistles.[6] Thus, man's work became sorrowful toil. He was required to eke out a living from the field, with pain and sweat, all the days of his life. History bears continual witness to man's struggle to overcome this sentence, but the curse remains and work is toil. It appears that God did not want man to become too attached to this world. God wanted man to anticipate something better beyond this world that he would ultimately receive through salvation.

   Another part of this sentence is that man's body must return to the soil (vs. 19). This speaks of physical death and of the disorganization (corruptibility) that death brings to the body (cp. I Cor. 15:42, 50-53).

   By ejecting the couple from the garden and barring them from it (Gen. 3:22-24), God dramatically asserted that He would not allow humans to live on earth forever in their sinful state. They must prepare for death and for what lies beyond it. To insure this, He mercifully prohibited the couple's access to the tree of life, which would have given them perpetual physical life in their unredeemed bodies.

THE FALL'S EFFECT UPON THE SERPENT (Gen. 3:14)

   God cursed the serpent above all wild and domesticated animals. If it should appear strange that God should curse an impersonal creature for being Satan's tool (cp. Rev. 12:9; 20:2), the Scriptures reveal that it is a part of God's order for animals to be punished for any harm they may do to man (Gen. 9:5; Ex. 21:28-32), for human beings are made in God's image.

   God also decreed that the serpent should crawl on his belly and eat dust. These actions are signs of defeat or degradation (Lev. 11:42; Ps. 72:9; Isa.

---

[6] When God cursed the ground, it seems that He also cursed all of creation, at least relating to earth (Rom. 8:20-21). This accounts for the disease, ferocity, depredation, decay, and death that we see in animal life and vegetation. As God has imposed this curse, He will also remove it for the earthly kingdom (Rom. 8:19-22; Isa. 11:6-9; ch. 35; Hos. 2:18; Amos 9:13). Besides making man's work laborious and his life hazardous, this curse was necessary if man (God's highest earthly creature) was to retain his superiority over his environment after his fall (cp. Gen. 9:2).

49:23; Mic. 7:17). This sentence will continue through Christ's earthly kingdom as seen in the serpent's continuing to eat dust (Isa. 65:25).

THE FALL'S EFFECT UPON SATAN (Gen. 3:15)

Since Satan approached Eve through the serpent (Rev. 12:9; 20:2), God pronounced a sentence on the devil. Speaking words that went beyond the serpent to Satan (cp. Ezek. 28:11-12), God placed a state of hostility between Satan and Eve, which is perpetuated between their seed. If we think of "seed" as meaning "spiritual product" rather than "natural offspring," then the seed of Satan would be fallen angels (demons) and unsaved humans (Jn. 8:44; Mt. 25:41). Also, the seed of Eve would be saved humans, redeemed through the atoning work of her descendant, the Lord Jesus Christ (Isa. 53:10). In a prophetic sense, the seed of the woman is a veiled reference to Jesus, the son of the virgin Mary (Isa. 7:14; Mt. 1:20-23; Lk. 1:31). In this case, the woman also represents the nation of Israel, through which God the Son entered the human family (Rom. 1:3; Rev. 12:4).

The hostility of which the prophecy speaks is seen throughout human history. It is expressed in the world's and Satan's unceasing antagonism toward the Messianic line (cp. Gen. 4:8), the nation of Israel (cp. Ex. 1:7-14), and the Lord's people today (Jn. 15:18-21). Furthermore, this state of hostility is indicated in God's declaration that the woman's seed would "bruise" (lit. crush) Satan's head. This is a mortal blow, which speaks of the devil's final defeat at the hand of the Lord Jesus. Our Lord defeated Satan by His death and resurrection (Jn. 16:11; Heb. 2:14) and will execute him at the close of His earthly rule (Rev. 20:7-10). We also shall share in this triumph (Rom. 16:20).

The LORD also declared that Satan would crush the heel of the woman's seed. This seems to be a reference to Jesus' crucifixion — a most shameful and painful experience and fallen creatures' greatest expression of hatred toward God. But the crushing of a heel is not a mortal blow. Crucifixion did not slay our Lord, for He laid down His life voluntarily and uniquely (Jn. 10:18). The shame and pain of crucifixion were soon eclipsed by the glory of His resurrection, ascension, and enthronement at the Father's right hand (Ps. 22:22-31; Phil. 2:9-11; I Pet. 3:22).

THE FALL'S EFFECT UPON THE HUMAN RACE

Adam's sin completely affected all of his posterity. We shall look at this when we consider original sin.

THE KINDS OF SIN

Theologians distinguish between original sin and actual sins. Original sin refers to Adam's first sin and its effects upon himself and his posterity. Actual sins refer to the sins that people commit during their life experience on earth. Let us look at these.

ORIGINAL SIN

• Its Source

We gain a better understanding of original sin and its relation to mankind when we look at the actions of Adam and Jesus and the far-reaching results of their actions upon their kinds of people. The Scriptures show that there are two Adams — the first man and the last Adam, the Lord Jesus Christ (I Cor. 15:45, 47). Paul implies that these Adams hold unique, identical positions in relation to two groups of human beings. He indicates that the human race consists of two groups — they who are in Adam and they who are in Christ (vs. 22). Because of their union to the respective head of their group, these people share the action and character of the Adam who heads their group (cp. I Cor. 15:45-49; Rom. 5:12-19).

They who are in the first Adam are his natural posterity (unsaved mankind). They share his kind of human nature, which is soulish ("natural")[7] and earthy (cp. Jn. 3:6) and which became corrupted and dominated by sin. They also share his disobedience and the results of his first sin.

They who are in Christ are all who are redeemed, recreated and placed in Him by God (Eph. 2:10; II Cor. 5:17; Gal. 3:27-28).[8] When a person is saved, he is severed from Adam and removed from his group. Also, he is joined to Christ and brought into His group — the new human race of which He is the head and pattern (II Cor. 5:17; Eph. 4:15; Rom. 8:29). Being in Christ, the believer shares His kind of human nature (with the prospect of having His kind of body), His obedience unto death, and the blessed results of this obedience.

In a complex passage (Rom. 5:12-19), Paul contrasts the actions of Adam and Christ and their results. He describes Adam's first action against God's will to be a "sin" (vs. 12), a "transgression" (vs. 14), an "offence" (vss. 15, 17-18), and "disobedience" (vs. 19). By contrast, he speaks of Jesus' action as being an exercise of divine grace (vs. 15), a righteous deed (vs. 18, "righteousness"), and "obedience" (vs. 19). This act of obedience, supported by a lifetime of compliance to the Father's will, was expressed in His atoning death (Phil. 2:8).

Paul also writes about the results of these actions. Because of the relations of these Adams to their respective groups, their actions directly involved their people. Adam's sin brought to his posterity sin and its penalty death, which became a ruler over mankind (Rom. 5:12, 14, 17). While the apostle seems to be speaking primarily of physical death, his words also allow for spiritual death (vs. 15). Adam's sin also incurred for himself and all in him the divine sentence of condemnation (vss. 16, 18). Both he and his posterity in him were

---

[7] "Soulish" does not itself imply sinfulness, but the manner in which our body is presently animated (see "Soul"). "Spiritual" implies that our changed body will be animated by the Holy Spirit (Rom. 8:11).

[8] See Appendix D regarding who are in Christ.

found guilty of his first sin and were sentenced to punishment. Finally, his action resulted in his becoming a sinner and the race in him being constituted sinners (vs. 19). Because of their relation to Adam, all unsaved people are born sinners, are under divine condemnation, and are ruled by death.

The result of our Lord's obedience unto death upon all who are in Him is dramatic. We who are saved have God's gracious gift of righteousness (vss. 15, 17) and are thereby made righteous (vs. 19). Because of this, the divine sentence regarding us is justification — we were divinely acquitted of the verdict of condemnation and were declared to be righteous in God's sight (vss. 16, 18). This sentence results not only in our having life (spiritual and physical) but also in our reigning in life through Christ Jesus (vss. 18, 17).

Observe that the same principle of solidarity or union that brings the devastating results of Adam's sin upon the lost also brings the blessed results of Christ's obedience upon the saved (I Cor. 15:22). This solidarity differs in that the union between Adam and his posterity is physical while that between Christ and His people is spiritual (6:17). Nevertheless, in both cases the union is real and conductive.

- **Its Meaning**

Original sin refers to Adam's initial sin and its effects upon himself and his posterity.[9] Notice that his subsequent sins did not affect his descendants as did his first one. The effects of original sin that now belong to lost mankind are spiritual death, the corruption of human nature, the sin-principle, and guilt.

1. Spiritual Death

Upon his sinning, Adam spiritually died (Gen. 2:17). This means that he ceased being alive toward God and became alive toward the sin-force that was generated within him by his disobedience. Consequently, all of his posterity are conceived spiritually dead, being spiritually alienated from God and naturally unresponsive to the things of God (Eph. 2:1-3; 4:17-19).

2. The Corruption of Human Nature

What does the corruption of human nature mean? To corrupt is to ruin constitutionally and to defile morally. Constitutional corruption means that sin changed human nature (body, soul, and spirit) by giving it the capacity for and inclination toward sinning. Because of his sin, Adam's human nature was ruined as an instrument of righteousness. Now, the human nature of his posterity can only function as the tool of sin in expressing unrighteousness (cp. Rom. 6:12-13, 19)). Because of the ruinous effect of sin, the body experiences degeneration, disease, and death. Human nature is also morally defiled because of this ruinous condition. The soul and spirit of unsaved

---

[9] The only member of Adam's posterity who did not partake of the effects of original sin was the Lord Jesus (I Jn. 3:5). His divine-virgin conception avoided the transmission of this sin and its effects to His human nature (Lk. 1:35).

people, represented by the word "heart," are deceitful and desperately wicked (Jer. 17:9). Out of this corrupted inner nature, dominated by sin, flows all kinds of morally defiling sewage in the form of evil thoughts, actions, words, attitudes, and the like (Mk. 7:20-23).

Because Adam's sin totally corrupted his human nature, each of his children received from him a corrupted human nature (Gen. 5:3). Moreover, each succeeding generation received from their parents (the father) a wholly corrupted human nature (cp. Gen. 6:5; Job 14:4; Ps. 51:5; Eccles. 9:3; Jer. 17:9; Rom. 1:21-32; 3:9-18).

This corruption of nature is often called "total depravity" and "total inability." Total depravity means that this inherent corruption extends to every part of the unsaved person's human nature (body, soul, and spirit). It affects his thinking (Gen. 6:5; 8:21; Rom. 1:21-23; 3:11; 8:5-8; I Cor. 2:14; Eph. 4:17-18), his emotions and attitudes (Jn. 3:19-20; Rom. 1:24-32; 3:18; Eph. 4:18), his will (Jn. 5:40; 8:44; Eph. 2:2-3), and his body (Rom. 8:10; I Cor. 15:50). Jesus alluded to this when He spoke about the spiritual character of unsaved people's hearts (Mt. 12:33-35; Mk. 7:15-23). Total depravity does not mean that an unsaved person is as evil in his conduct as he can be, for common grace (God's restraining, benevolent influence on mankind) and his innate morality (Rom. 2:14-15) now prevent this (cp. II Thess. 2:7-8; Acts 14:17). On the other hand, there is no part of the unsaved person's being that has escaped the corruption and ruin of original sin (Rom. 3:12). He possesses this corruption from his conception (Ps. 51:5).

Total inability means that of himself the unsaved person neither desires nor is able to do the will of God (Jn. 3:19-20; 5:40; 6:44; 8:44; Rom. 8:7-8). Prompted by common grace and innate morality, he can do relatively good things which are in accord with the ethical standards of fallen man, but he cannot of himself do absolute good (the will of God), nor does he desire this (Rom. 3:12, 18). The unsaved person's relatively good deeds have no merit in God's sight, for they are sinful to Him (Eph. 2:8-9; Rom. 14:23; Heb. 11:6).

While the human nature of unsaved people is wholly corrupted by sin and is sinful, it is not the force that produces sins. This force is the sin-principle which is resident in their nature.

3. The Sin-Principle

When Adam and Eve sinned, there was generated in them the sin-principle ("the law of sin," Rom. 7:23, 25; 8:2), which would dominate them and their posterity throughout their unregenerate, earthly lives. This evil force completely energizes and dominates the lives of the unsaved to the extent that all they do is sinful in God's sight (Rom. 3:9-19; I Jn. 3:8, 10). We who are saved still have this force within us (I Jn. 1:8), but we no longer have to regard it as our master or yield to its demands since we are dead to it and are alive unto our new master, the Lord Jesus Christ (Rom. ch. 6).

The Scriptures reveal that the sin-principle is resident within the body's flesh (Rom. 7:17-23; cp. Eph. 2:3; Col. 3:5) and can exert its evil energy upon one's total being (Rom. 3:9). It is not like a disease that is contracted at an early age, but it is propagated together with our human nature and remains with us until our body's dissolution in death. Because it will not be revived in the changed or resurrection body (cp. I Cor. 15:50), I believe that this principle will be wholly eradicated with the dissolution of the universe (II Pet. 3:10, 13; I Jn. 2:17). Moreover, it appears that people in Hell will neither have this principle nor will sin (cp. Phil. 2:10-11).[10]

4. Guilt

Adam's sin brought him the divine sentence of condemnation (Rom. 5:16). This means that God found him guilty of sinning and sentenced him to punishment. Since this sin involved Adam's posterity, it also brought them this guilt (Rom. 5:12; 3:23). When Paul writes that all sinned (aorist tense in Gk.), he seems to be speaking about the involvement of the human race with Adam's first sin. This implication was not one of voluntary transgression within the life experience of each member of humanity. It was an involuntary participation which came from humanity's corporate union with Adam, resulting from the propagated human nature. Because of this union, God judicially imputed to (reckoned to the account of) each member of the race the guilt of Adam's first offence as his own sin. This imputation is manifest in God's condemning the whole race (Rom. 5:18). Unlike the first three features of original sin which are propagated, the guilt of Adam's sin is divinely imposed upon each member of the race directly as a legal sentence.

Sometimes the objection is raised against this imputation that people are not accountable for the sins of others (cp. Ezek. 18:19-20), but this overlooks the fact that people are not as independent as they think they are. Everyone has participated in Adam's sin (Rom. 5:12) because of their corporate union with him and the responsibility which this relationship incurs. Still, as we shall see, no one will go to Hell solely because of Adam's sin. In my opinion, infants who die before they are personally accountable for their actions are covered by the Lord's atoning work. People who go to Hell are guilty not only of original sin but also of sins which they have committed during their lifetime (see pp. 367 f.).

It is not agreed among those who hold the imputation of Adam's sin how the justice of God is vindicated in this act. The chief theories are federalism and realism. *Federalism* is the theory that Adam was divinely appointed to be the representative of the human race; therefore, when he sinned, he involved the race representatively, but not actually. But I see no biblical evidence for Adam's acting as an agent for the race. *Realism* is the theory that all humans, having germinal existence in Adam, actually co-sinned with him.

---

[10] Two effects of original sin — the corruption of human nature and the sin-principle — together are called "hereditary corruption."

Although we were not present as persons, our human nature existed in him and participated in the act. Since this nature qualifies our personhood, we virtually sinned with him. (The unifying element of the race is not personhood but human nature.) Consequently, his sin and its guilt are reckoned by God to all of Adam's posterity. The realism theory seems to be more in accord with the statements of Scripture (cp. Heb. 7:9-10).

Some teach that our Lord's atoning work removed from the whole human race the guilt of original sin and that people are now guilty only of actual sins. If this were true, why are all, including infants and imbeciles who have not committed actual sins, still condemned in God's sight (Jn. 3:18; Rom. 5:12, 18)?

- **Historical Views on Original Sin**

The doctrines of sin and grace did not seriously engage the attention of the church until the beginning of the fifth century.[11] While the church universally rejected the view of Pelagius, the Eastern branch accepted the doctrine of inherited corruption and the Western branch also accepted the doctrine of imputed guilt. Gradually, however, the Western church embraced the semi-pelagian view stated by the Council of Trent. Following Augustine, the Reformers Luther and Calvin supported the doctrine of inherited corruption and imputed guilt, while Zwingli leaned toward the semi-pelagian position. After Protestantism became established, the old antagonism between these doctrines revived in the Calvinist-Arminian controversy and continues to this day. During the latter part of the eighteenth century, liberal elements among American Calvinists (John Taylor, Jonathan Mayhew, Samuel Webster, and Charles Chauncey) voiced their objection to imputed guilt. Today only a few Protestants accept this biblical doctrine.

1. *THE VIEW OF PELAGIUS (360-420, a British monk)*

He held that man, being unaffected by Adam's sin, is morally well. Like newly created Adam, each person determines his moral state by his own actions.

2. *THE VIEW OF AUGUSTINE (354-430, Bishop of Hippo, North Africa)*

In keeping with the teachings of the Scriptures, he regarded man as being morally and spiritually dead. Believing in man's total depravity, he asserted that the human race was wholly affected by Adam's sin and that the guilt of his sin was divinely imputed to each person.

3. *THE VIEW OF THE SEMI-PELAGIANS*

This arose in certain French churches in the fifth century. They held that man, being greatly weakened physically and morally by Adam's sin, is

---

[11] See William G. T. Shedd, *History of Christian Doctrine* (New York: Charles Scribner & Co., 1868), II, 50-186.

spiritually sick, but not dead or totally depraved. Although man needs the assistance of divine grace to attain salvation and to produce holiness, yet his freedom of will and native power to do good were not lost by the fall. There is sufficient power in the will to set in motion the beginning of salvation, but not enough to complete it. Water baptism removes imputed sin and its guilt.

4. THE VIEW OF ROMAN CATHOLICISM

This was formulated at the Council of Trent (1545-1563). This regards man as being imperfect at his creation because of the inherent antagonism that existed between his body and soul. To correct this, God added to man a gift of righteousness so that his body might be kept in subjection to his soul. When man fell, he lost this righteousness and reverted to his former state of conflict. The effect of Adam's sin upon the race is their experiencing this conflict between the body and the soul. This state of unrestrained physical desires provides fuel for sin and weakens the will, but it is not one of sin and guilt. Baptism removes the guilt of Adam's sin.

5. THE VIEW OF THE REFORMERS

Both Luther and Calvin followed Augustine in their views of hereditary corruption and imputed sin and its guilt. On the other hand, Zwingli held that Adam's sin was not truly sin for his posterity, for they had not committed a crime against law. According to his view, the race's sin in Adam should be regarded as the disease of self-love and the condition of bondage. There was no imputation of sin and its guilt.

6. THE VIEWS OF THE ARMINIANS

a. The Earlier View[12]

This represents the view of James Arminius and later of John Wesley. They held that original sin involved man in guilt and exposed him to divine wrath. However, this guilt was removed by the atonement, which made it possible for all people to cooperate with God through the Holy Spirit. While Arminius believed that the ability that enables man to cooperate flows from God's justice, Wesley believed that it was conferred by prevenient (going before) grace. By this gift of grace everyone is released from the guilt of Adam's sin and has created in him the beginning of life, which will lead him on to further life if he responds favorably to it. This grace gives to everyone the power to choose the good and incentive to follow the good.[13] In spite of this, man can resist this grace and be lost, for he makes the final decision about salvation.

b. The Later View

This view was held by the Remonstrants who protested extreme Calvinism. They held that original sin did not include imputed guilt with its

---

[12] H. Orton Wiley, Christian Theology (Kansas City: Beacon Hill Press), II, 108, 136 ff.
[13] See Leo G. Cox, "Prevenient Grace — A Wesleyan View," Journal of the Evangelical Theological Society (1969), pp. 143-49.

punishment and that inherited depravity affected the body and the intelligence, but not the will. Man's will is competent of itself to cooperate with the assistance of the Holy Spirit in the keeping of God's law.

Observe that the earlier Arminianism accepts the view that inherited depravity is of the nature of sin, while the later Arminianism denies this. The earlier view held that man is totally depraved and cannot cooperate with God apart from grace; the later view held that the fall did not affect man's will. While the errors of the later view are obvious, the belief of the earlier view, which holds that the imputed guilt of all men is removed by Christ's atoning work and that all men are given grace to release the will from depravity and to give it power to choose the good, is unscriptural.

7. THE VIEW OF RELIGIOUS LIBERALS

Prior to 1750 the New England Puritans held the doctrine of original sin as given in the Westminster Confession of Faith, which speaks of hereditary corruption and imputed guilt (Articles VI, IX). However, with the infiltration of the rationalism of the European Enlightenment into New England, this doctrine was modified under the label of the New School Theory among Congregationalists and Presbyterians. This theory denied the doctrine of imputed guilt.

With the publication of the Darwinian theory of evolution, there developed within the New England school of Calvinism a theology that discounted the idea of original sin altogether. This school of thought viewed man as emerging from lower forms of life and becoming aware at some moment in his development of a conflict between his lower and higher natures. The concept of sin became that of inherited disabilities, which are not sinful in themselves and which are capable of moral improvement. World War I shattered the optimism of this theology of moral and social progress. In its place there was revived in liberalism a false view of original sin, which interpreted the fall as a myth rather than a literal fact. It understood the fall to illuminate the psychological situation in which man encounters temptation and becomes a victim of sin.[14]

In spite of the unpopularity of original sin, the Scriptural view, as I understand it, is that all members of the human race (with the exception of Jesus) receive by propagation spiritual death, a totally corrupted human nature and the sin-principle and have divinely imputed to them Adam's sin and its guilt. Because of this, all unsaved people are sinners by human constitution and are guilty by divine imputation.

ACTUAL SINS

These are the sins that people commit during their lifetime on earth.

---

[14] See H. Shelton Smith, Changing Conceptions of Original Sin (New York: Charles Scribner's Sons, 1955), ch. 9.

- **Their Sources**

Actual sin as well as the sin-principle came into existence within certain newly created angels and humans when they misused their powers of choice and worship. Since Adam's first sin, actual sins result from our yielding to the demands of the sin-principle, the temptations of Satan and his demonic agents, and the influence of the world. Let us look at these sources more closely.

1. *The Sin-Principle*

This is the evil, nonpersonal energy, resident in the flesh of our bodies, that impels us to sin (Rom. 7:17, 23; 3:9). While the initial sin of angels and humans generated in them this evil force, all members of the human race (after Adam and Eve) receive this principle by propagation (cp. Ps. 51:5). They also receive a corrupted human nature, but it is the sin-principle which is the active cause in man's sinning.

The Bible reveals the mechanics of actual sin, or how a person sins (Jas. 1:14-15). It starts with the desire ("lust") of the sin-principle to express itself through our human nature (our words, thoughts, actions, emotions, attitudes, and intentions). When we yield ourself (including our human nature) to sin's enticement, we sin. Our surrender to the desires of the sin- principle allows it to conceive and bring forth actual sins through our being (cp. Gal. 5:19-21).

Living continuously under sin's domination, unsaved people commit sins all the time (Eph. 2:3; Rom. 3:9). We who are saved no longer have to give in to sin's demands; in fact, we are not to sin at all (Rom. 6:1-13; I Jn. 2:1). Nevertheless, we do sin intermittently.

2. *Satan and His Demon Host*

Satan and his demon confederates (fallen angels) tempt humans to sin (Lk. 4:2; I Cor. 7:5). Through temptation they seek to gain our consent to their proposals, which would lead us to act contrary to God's will. Being cunning, personal beings, Satan and his demons plot and execute strategies and devices against us (Eph. 6:11; II Cor. 2:11). It is not sinful to be tempted; we sin when we yield to temptation and act contrary to God's will for us.

3. *The World*

The world is that system which embraces the total society, culture, and philosophy of lost mankind. This is headed by Satan (Jn. 16:11); its works are evil (Jn. 7:7); it is condemned by God (Jn. 12:31; I Jn. 2:17); and it fails to satisfy man's spiritual need (I Cor. 1:21).

Since we who are saved are no longer a part of this world system (Jn. 15:19; Col. 1:13), we are continually threatened by its hostility (Jn. 15:18) and evil influence (Rom. 12:2; I Jn. 2:15-16). It solicits us to satisfy our physical, emotional, mental, and spiritual needs in ways that are contrary to God's will for us. John describes these solicitations as "the lust of the flesh, and the lust of the eyes, and the pride of life" (I Jn. 2:16; see Appendix U). When we yield ourself to this influence and seek to satisfy our needs in these ways, we express the world's sinful lusts and pride. But being dead to the world (Gal. 6:14), we should have a different life-style than this (Rom. 12:2; Ps. 1:1-3). It is in keeping with our new creaturehood that we express the life-qualities of the Lord Jesus (Eph. 5:1-20).

It is difficult to trace the source of some actual sins. The sin-principle, Satan, and the world are so closely allied that they often work together (so it seems) to bring about actual sins in our life. It is probable that the sin-principle, supplying us the energy to sin, is active in all of our sinning while the world and the devil externally solicit our will to yield to their sinful suggestions. Even so, we are still responsible for our sinning, for it is we that sin, not just our human nature. Also, we would not sin if we did not yield to these evil forces, and allow them to use us for their wicked expressions (Rom. 6:11-13; 12:2; Acts 5:3). On the other hand, we do what is right when we yield ourself to Jesus and allow Him to use us as an instrument of righteousness (Rom. 6:16-19; Gal. 5:16). We believers can choose the principle that would use us for its expression. This choice, which incidentally unsaved people do not have, is an aspect of Christian freedom (Gal. 5:13).

- **Their Diversity**

  Since our entire human nature is susceptible to the sin-principle, our nature's parts and functions may be used by this evil force to express various actual sins, such as evil actions (Eph. 4:28), thoughts (Mt. 5:28), feelings or attitudes (Jn. 3:20; Eph. 4:26), words (Eph. 4:31; Mt. 12:36-37), motivations (Acts 5:3-4), and desires (Col. 3:5).

  In addition to these evil expressions of human nature, there are other classifications of actual sins such as the following: Regarding awareness, there are known sins and unknown sins (Rom. 7:7-8). Regarding activity, there are sins of action and sins of inaction (Jas. 4:17). Regarding intent, there are deliberate sins (Isa. 1:20) and compulsory sins (Rom. 7:15-20). Regarding ethical standards, there are violations of divine law (Rom. 5:14; 7:7-8), man's law (13:4), and moral training, or the conscience (14:14, 20). Regarding offence, there are sins against one's self (Mt. 5:30), one's human nature — body (I Cor. 6:18), soul (II Pet. 2:7-8), and spirit (II Cor. 7:1) — and other people (I Cor. 8:12).

  Observe that all sins are against God (I Cor. 8:12; Gen. 39:9). Also, the most common sin of believers probably is acting independently of God, which is what unsaved people do (Rom. 14:23). (For such problem sins as the unpardonable sin and the sin unto death, see Appendix E.)

THE DIVINE REACTION TO SIN

God's stern, inflexible reaction to sin rises from His holiness of character (Hab. 1:12-13) and His hatred of evil (Prov. 6:16-19). Thus His justice compels Him to deal with sin and sinners as they deserve. This includes His condemning sinners and His punishing them.

GOD CONDEMNS SINNERS.

Condemnation is the judicial sentence which after examination declares one to be guilty of an alleged crime. God has condemned the whole human race for original sin (Rom. 5:12, 18) and those of moral accountability for actual sins (Jn. 3:18; Rom. 3:9-19). On the other hand, saved people are acquitted of condemnation and are declared to be righteous in God's sight (Rom. 8:30-34).

• The Meaning of Guilt

Guilt is the fact or condition of one's having committed a crime. A convicted person's being guilty concerns not only the fact of his having committed a crime but also of his obligation to satisfy justice by bearing the punishment of the offense.

We must distinguish between being guilty and having guilty feelings. Guilty feelings do not always indicate guilt. The believer's experience of guilty feelings, after he has dealt with his sins, may arise from Satan or from a wrongly programmed conscience. The divine forgiveness of sins, whether judicial or parental, includes the removal of guilt (Heb. 9:14). Real guilt is determined and dealt with by judicial process, not by one's feelings.

• The Incurrence of Guilt

All members of the human race (except the Lord Jesus) are guilty of Adam's first sin because of their corporate union with him by human nature (Rom. 5:18). On the other hand, people do not inherit the guilt of their ancestors or others, although they often suffer the natural results of these people's sins (Ezek. 18:20; II Chron. 25:3-4; Deut. 24:16).

All who have sufficiently developed in their nature to have moral awareness and self-determination at some time in their life are guilty of the sins they knowingly commit (Lev. 5:1-4; Rom. 3:19; cp. Jon. 4:11). On the other hand, I believe that people who die in infancy or who are imbeciles do not have this guilt. Also, their guilt of original sin is covered by Jesus' atoning work (I Jn. 2:2).

GOD PUNISHES SINNERS.

• The Meaning of Punishment

Divine punishment is the active expression of God's anger toward the sinner and his sins in the form of judgment (Rom. 2:5-6). Sometimes this punishment is viewed as a penalty, or debt, that one must pay for breaking God's law.

God's anger is the expression of His holiness against sinners and their sins. Passively, this divine wrath expresses itself as a hostile attitude toward sinners (Rom. 1:18; Jn. 3:36). Actively, it expresses itself as destructive judgment (Ps. 5:5-6; Rev. 14:19; 15:1; 19:15).

- **The Kinds of Punishments**
  Human beings experience several kinds of punishment.

  1. Natural punishments
  These include economic, physical, and emotional problems including death, resulting from the violation of economic, physical, and psychological laws (Eccles. 4:5; 10:18; Prov. 5:22; 23:1-3).

  2. Societal punishments
  These include fines, imprisonment, restitution, and death, incurred by violating man's laws (Rom. 13:2-4).

  3. Divine punishments[15]
  The violation of God's law incurs retribution upon the lost and the chastisement of the saved.

    a. Divine retribution
    This is God's punitive dealings with the unsaved. They proceed from His holiness and give to sinners what they deserve. Divine retribution is not remedial, that is, it does not have for its purpose the sinner's restoration and well-being. This is not to say that others cannot profit from visitations of divine retribution on sinners (cp. Josh. 2:9-13), but these are not given to improve the condition of the ones on whom they fall. The wicked are cut off without remedy (Prov. 29:1). On the other hand, God sometimes uses the natural consequences of sin to draw unsaved people to Himself (Lk. 18:35-43). Divine retribution assumes the form of severe woes in this life (Rom. 1:22-32) and of Hell in the eternal state (Mt. 25:46). It exhibits God's judicial power and His holy character (Rom. 2:5; 9:17, 22; Heb. 12:18-29).

    b. Divine corrective chastisement
    This is God's punitive dealings with His people. Proceeding from His holiness, they are tempered by His love (Rev. 3:19) and are remedial in purpose. They intend to restore the wayward believer to the place of God's fellowship and blessing and to preserve him from divine condemnation (I Cor. 11:31-32). When His people are unresponsive to His corrective

---

[15] The violation of God's laws ultimately brings death (Rom. 5:12; 6:23; Gen. 2:17; Jas. 1:15). Presently, human beings suffer spiritual and physical death for their sins. *Spiritual death* is the event that severed Adam's and Eve's relationship with God (Gen. 2:17; 3:7-8). It is also the state of alienation from God in which all unsaved people exist (Eph. 4:18; 2:1). *Physical death* is the event of man's immaterial part leaving his body (Jas. 2:26; Gen. 35:18). It is also the state of corruptibility that follows this event, in which the body is reduced to dust (Gen. 3:19; I Cor. 15:50, 53). In the future, the penalty of sin will be *everlasting death*, or "the second death" (Rev. 20:14). This event takes place when the unsaved are cast into Hell, or the Lake of Fire. They will enter the everlasting state of unrelieved suffering and absolute isolation from God (Rev. 20:15; Mt. 25:46).
    The present state of the unsaved differs from their final state in Hell in that they are not yet abandoned by God. They who are alive still enjoy the blessings of common grace (see the Addenda) and have opportunity to be saved. They who have died are in Hades and are aware of the awful judgment that lies ahead (Lk. 16:23-24).

chastisement and set themselves against it, God prematurely removes them from the earth (Jn. 15:2a; Heb. 12:9).

THE DIVINE FORGIVENESS OF SINS

In His marvelous, loving grace, God has acquitted all who are saved of their condemnation and has forgiven them of their sins. As we shall see, this acquittal is related to justification and this forgiveness to redemption. Both are benefits of our Lord's atoning work.

THE ACQUITTAL OF CONDEMNATION

We believers were divinely justified when we received the Saviour (Rom. 5:1, 9). This means that God dropped His verdict of condemnation against us and declared us to be righteous. In other words, we are no longer guilty before Him (Heb. 9:14; 10:22; Rom. 5:16-20). Because of this, we should not allow Satan to torment us with guilty feelings about our forgiven sins. Rather, we should rest on the truth of our justification through Christ (Rom. 5:1, 9). Yet, as a part of His convicting work, the Holy Spirit causes us to feel guilty about present sins which we need to judge (cp. I Jn. 3:20).

THE FORGIVENESS OF SINS

Forgiveness concerns the release from an obligation, or the cancellation of a debt (Mt. 18:23-27). In divine forgiveness, God releases a person from the obligation of bearing the punishment, or paying the debt, of his sins. He is able to do this on the basis of Jesus' atoning work (Eph. 1:7). As their substitute the Lord bore the punishment of humanity's sins and provisionally paid their debt (I Pet. 3:18; Rom. 5:8). Because of this, God is able to extend judicial forgiveness and parental forgiveness to all who fulfill the conditions of forgiveness. These kinds of forgiveness are implied in John 13:10.

• **Divine Judicial Forgiveness of the Gospel Believer**

This kind of forgiveness relates to the court and sees God as a judge and the sinner as a criminal. God forgives the gospel believer of all his sins — past, present, and future (Acts 10:43; Eph. 1:7; Col. 2:13). By this action the sinner is released from the punishment of divine retribution for original sin and his actual sins (Jn. 5:24).

Since we have taken refuge in the Lord Jesus and His atoning work, any charge that may be brought against us now involves Him (Rom. 8:31-34). Being in Christ, we are beyond the reach of any charge that may be made against us before God. The requirement for one's receiving judicial forgiveness is the exercise of salvational faith in Christ and His atoning work (Acts 10:43).

• **Divine Parental Forgiveness of the Child of God**

This kind of forgiveness relates to the family and sees God as a father and the offender as a child. God forgives His children of the known sins which they judge by repentance and confession (I Cor. 11:31; Rev. 2:5; I Jn. 1:9). By this divine action the believer is released from the punishment of chastisement. If he deals with his sins immediately when they occur, he will be spared corrective chastisement; if he deals with his sins while he is in the throes of corrective chastisement, his punishment will cease.

In His dealings with us, God first speaks to us about the things in our life which displease Him and gives us opportunity to judge them. But if we are unresponsive to His voice, He disciplines us (Rev. 3:19). When we deal with our sins the moment we become aware of them, we continue in His fellowship (I Jn. 1:7). The sins of which we are not aware are automatically cleansed away by the blood of Jesus, else imperfect people could not walk in fellowship with an infinitely holy God. As we adjust to Him by dealing with known sins and by obeying His will, we walk in the light as He is in the light. If we fail to do this, we walk in darkness alone (vss. 5-6).

What must we do to receive divine parental forgiveness? Remembering that the Lord's atoning work is sufficient for this as well as for judicial forgiveness, we must repent (have a change of mind; Rev. 2:5), confess our sin to God (I Jn. 1:9), admit our sin to others if we have wronged them (cp. Mt. 5:23-24), and be forgiving toward others who have wronged us (Mt. 6:12, 14-15) when they have fulfilled the condition of forgiveness (Lk. 17:3; see the Addenda, "Christian Forgiveness"). Then, God immediately applies to us the value of our Lord's atoning work and forgives us as He promises (I Jn. 1:9). Observe that all sins are forgivable.

With this distinction between judicial and parental forgiveness in view, we can understand how a believer who dies with known sin in his life is still justified and is taken to Heaven. When he was saved, he was judicially forgiven of all the sins that he had committed and that he would commit throughout the remainder of his life. Therefore, he could never again be condemned by God or owe the judicial debt of his sins. Parental forgiveness is needed during the course of a believer's life on earth for his fellowship with God, but this is not required for his going to Heaven.

We should ever be grateful to God for the fact of divine forgiveness. Of all the people in the world who seek forgiveness, only the child of God knows beyond any doubt that he has been forgiven of his sins. Blessed be the Lord Jesus who was willing to pay this awful debt on our behalf!

THE BELIEVER AND SIN

Although it seems contrary to our experience, we who are saved are no longer related to sin as we once were. It is very important for us to learn what God has revealed about this, so that we might avoid unnecessary misery and irreparable loss and that we might live holy and victorious lives.

THE BELIEVER'S RELATION TO ORIGINAL SIN

When Paul wrote that the old things had passed away and all things had become new (II Cor. 5:17), he was declaring that we who are saved have been separated from Adam and the consequences of this relationship and that we have everything new in Christ (cp. Rom. 5:15-19). In part, this means that we are no longer related to original sin as we once were.

- **He has been forgiven imputed sin and its guilt.**

We can say that Adam's initial sin and its guilt are no longer imputed to us for two reasons: One, we have been divinely, judicially forgiven of all sins, both original and actual (Eph. 1:7; Col. 2:13); and two, we have been justified by God (Rom. 5:1, 9; 8:30, 33). We could not now be righteous in God's sight (justified) if we were still guilty of original sin. In fact, we cannot now be successfully charged with or condemned for sin because of the atoning work and intercession of our substitute, the Lord Jesus (8:34).

Observe that imputed sin, with its guilt, is not removed by water baptism, as most of Christendom believes. It is taken away by the divine application of the value of our Lord's atoning death and the shedding of His blood (Rom. 3:21-25; Eph. 1:7; Heb. 9:26; Rev. 1:5).

- **He has been made spiritually alive.**

With his regeneration, the gospel believer is made spiritually alive (Jn. 3:16; Eph. 2:1). This means that upon his receiving the Lord Jesus as his Saviour, the believer is given eternal life, which rises out of his new personal relationship with God (Jn. 17:3). Being the spiritual life of the Lord Jesus (Jn. 14:6; I Jn. 5:12), this new life is communicated to God's people by the Holy Spirit (Rom. 8:2; Gal. 5:25). This new life in Christ provides for the believer the dynamic for interaction with God and for the display of Christlikeness in daily life.

- **His immaterial nature has been delivered from hereditary corruption.**

Since the material part of our human nature still remains corrupted, we still suffer physical weakness, sickness, aging, and death (I Cor. 11:30; 15:53; Rom. 8:10-11; I Tim. 5:23). But in spite of its inherent corruption, our body in its function does not have the same relation to sin as it did have, for we who are saved do not have the same relation to sin as we did in our unsaved state (Rom. 6:6-7, 11). Thus the body of a saved person no longer properly functions as the instrument of sin. It is now a member of Christ and a temple of the Holy Spirit (I Cor. 6:15, 19-20). God now uses it as an instrument of righteousness as we yield it to His control (Rom. 6:13, 19). The body will remain in its corrupt condition until it is changed at Christ's coming (Rom. 8:11; Phil. 3:20-21; I Cor. 15:50-53).

On the other hand, the Scriptures show that the immaterial part of our human nature (soul and spirit) has been redeemed from hereditary corruption (Acts 15:9; II Pet. 1:4). Paul alludes to this when he states that we did put off the "old man" (what we were in Adam when we were unsaved) and that we did put on the "new man" (what we are in Christ as new creatures), "which after God was created in righteousness and true holiness" (Col. 3:9-10; Eph. 4:22-24). The apostle also speaks of our being renewed in the spirit of our mind (Eph. 4:23) and of people's calling on the Lord out of a pure heart (II Tim. 2:22). Moreover, he declares that the spirit "is life" (Rom. 8:10). Peter speaks about our soul's being purified in obedience to the gospel (I Pet. 1:22) and its being saved (I Pet. 1:9; cp. Heb. 10:39). He also describes Lot's soul as being righteous (II Pet. 2:8). With the salvation of soul and spirit, we who are saved now have the capacity to understand spiritual truth, to express holy emotions, and to make right decisions. Because of this, we can now worship and serve God with our spirit (Phil. 3:3; Rom. 1:9; cp. I Cor. 14:15).[16] The virgin Mary worshiped God with her soul and spirit (Lk. 1:46-47; cp. Ps. 103:1-2).

Although our soul and spirit are delivered from hereditary corruption, they are still susceptible to the influence of our spiritual enemies. Peter writes about "fleshly lusts which war against the soul" (I Pet. 2:11), and about Lot's soul being tortured ("vexed") by what he saw and heard in Sodom (II Pet. 2:8). Paul writes of the spirit's being defiled by our sins and of the need for its being cleansed (II Cor. 7:1). Both the Scriptures and our experience show that our redeemed immaterial nature can come under the temporary domination of the sin-principle, Satan, and the world and be used as their instrument of expression (Gal. 5:19-21; Eph. 4:25-31; I Pet. 2:11; I Jn. 2:15; Acts 5:3). But this does not mean that our immaterial nature is in itself inherently evil or corrupted, though it is still susceptible to these evil influences. Being unredeemed, our body has resident in its flesh the sin-principle, hereditary corruption, and mortality — the forces of sin, deterioration, and death. But our immaterial nature does not have these forces resident in it, though it remains open to the attack of these spiritual enemies.

It is our duty to yield our total human nature to the control of the indwelling Holy Spirit and to allow Him to produce His holy fruit in our life (Gal. 5:16, 22-23). He can keep our spiritual enemies in check as well as enable us to do what is pleasing in God's sight (Gal. 5:16; Rom. 8:2-4).

- **He is no longer a slave of the sin-principle.**

Since our unredeemed body still harbors the sin-principle, we shall have this evil force resident within our flesh throughout our earthly life. This is indicated by the teaching of Scripture (Rom. chs. 6, 7; I Jn. 1:8), God's appeals against our sinning (I Jn. 2:1; Col. 3:8), and various case histories (I Cor. 3:1-3; Eph. 4:28-31).

---

[16] In I Corinthians 5:5 Paul is not necessarily suggesting that the believer's spirit is not now saved. The discipline that he directs the church to administer is remedial to the extent that the sinning person may remain saved and experience final salvation when Jesus comes (cp. Rom. 13:11; I Cor. 11:32).

Although we are able to sin, we no longer have to give in to sin's lusts or demands because of the radical change in our relation to it, which took place when we were saved. Paul speaks of this in Romans 6:1-13. He argues that if grace superabounds where sin abounds (5:20), then the logical inference would be to keep on living in sin's grip (6:1). But the apostle recoils from this conclusion (vs. 2). How can people who have died to the sin-principle continue to live under its domination? He then explains the inconsistency and impropriety of our yielding ourself to sin's demands. First, he says that, as God sees it, we died to the sin-principle (vss. 2-3; I Pet. 2:24). This death is one that we came to share with Christ when we were united to Him by the baptism of the Holy Spirit (Gal. 3:27). Being dead to sin, we should no longer respond to its demands.

In the next place, he says that we arose with Christ to walk in newness of life (Rom. 6:4-5). As we shared our Lord's death and died to sin, we also share His resurrection and are alive to God. Paul draws an analogy between our Lord's physical experience of death and resurrection and our spiritual participation in these events (vs. 5). As our death with Him was effective in severing our relation to the sin-principle, so our resurrection with Him is effective in our experiencing now the principle of spiritual life (vs. 4). Being now dead to sin and alive unto God, it is our duty to live unto God's glory (I Cor. 10:31) and to be responsive to His will (II Cor. 5:15).

In view of this truth, what then is our relation to the old life under sin's grip and to our new life in Christ (Rom. 6:6-10)? Our death with Christ severed all our spiritual ties with the old life (vss. 6-7). "Our old man" refers to what we were in Adam before we were saved (Col. 3:9; Eph. 4:22). But when we were saved and put into Christ, we participated in His death, and the "old man" died. Being new creatures in Christ, we now possess the new life-principle (Christ's life), which is manifest in our life whenever we cooperate with the Holy Spirit.

Paul points out that our sharing Christ's death has done two things for us: One, it has rendered our body with reference to sin powerless (Rom. 6:6). Keep in mind that the sin-principle would use our human nature for its expression. Before we were saved, our human nature was continually under sin's domination. But upon our participating in Christ's death, with the subsequent death of our "old man," our human nature, like a broken tool, was made ineffective as the instrument of sin (cp. vss. 12-13). Paul is not saying that our human nature is no longer susceptible to sin's use, but that this is not God's purpose for it. It is neither fitting nor proper for us who are alive unto God to give ourself over to sin for its evil expressions.

Two, our participating in Christ's death has also ended our having to serve sin (Rom. 6:6-7, 15-18). Since our "old man" (what we were in Adam) died and our body has been legally rendered useless to sin, we no longer have to serve sin (vs. 6). We now stand freed (Gk. justified) from this evil force (vs.

7). This means that we have been divinely acquitted of sin's claim to us and of the divine penalty that sin incurs. Just as a corpse is relieved of all earthly obligations and does not respond to external stimuli, so we who have died to sin must ignore its demands. Observe that we have died to sin; sin is not dead.[17] Its force is very active in our members, but we do not have to give ourself over to its demands ("lusts"). Our duty is to be responsive to the direction and pleasure of our new master, the Lord Jesus Christ (vss. 11-13). Unlike unsaved people, we are freed from sin's bondage so that we can now choose the principle which will dominate our lives. However, we only experience the divine purposes for our freedom as we give ourself to the Holy Spirit (cp. I Pet. 2:16; Gal. 5:13; II Cor. 3:17-18).

Salvation has radically altered our relation to original sin. We have been forgiven of imputed sin with its guilt. Also, the immaterial part of our human nature has been delivered from hereditary corruption and has been made righteous for holy purposes, although it is still susceptible to the evil influences of our spiritual enemies. Since we have died to these and are alive unto God, it is now our duty to quit submitting ourself to their demands and to yield ourself to our new Master, for His use and glory.

THE BELIEVER'S RELATION TO ACTUAL SIN

Although we who are saved are able to sin and do sin, we no longer have to sin, nor are we able to sin continuously as we once did when lost (I Jn. 3:8-9, the present tense indicates continuous action). We now commit righteous acts as well as sinful ones (I Jn. 2:3; 3:7). In fact, we cannot sin continuously over an extended period of time as we once did because of our new creaturehood (II Cor. 5:17; Eph. 4:22-24, the new birth has renewed our inner nature), our having God's Seed (I Jn. 3:9, Jesus our new life), our relation to Christ who is sinless and who has dealt with our sins (I Jn. 3:5; 5:12), our having innate desire to obey God (Phil. 2:13), our ability not to sin (I Jn. 3:6; Gal. 5:16), and our having been set free from sin's claim to us (Rom. 6:6-7). John argues that if a person sins continuously, that is all the time, he is not saved (I Jn. 3:4-10). Actual sins are inconsistent with and contrary to the new life we have in Christ. Having put off what we once were ("the old man") and put on what we are now in Christ ("the new man"), it is fitting that we allow Him to express Himself in our life (Col. 3:1-17). It is God's desire that we put off actual sins by ceasing to commit them (Col. 3:8) and that we cleanse

---

[17] Some refer to Galatians 5:24 as supporting the idea that the flesh, or the sin-force, with its passions and desires, has been put to death in the believer and that he must consider it to be inactive. Since other passages clearly state that we believers died to this evil force (Rom. 6:1-2, 11) and that this force is still active in us (7:19-20), it appears that the passage in question must be understood with these truths in view. As God sees it, our participation in Christ's death, which condemned sin (Rom. 8:3), broke the power of sin in our life so that in a sense we can regard it as being crucified. What we were in Adam, dominated by sin's power, died (Rom. 6:6). Thus through death we were set free from this force (vss. 7, 17-18, 22). While the sin-force is as active as ever, in God's sight its power is broken in our life since we died to it. Now we must consider this to be true and live unto God and His demands.

ourself from their defilement by repentance and confession (II Cor. 7:1; Rev. 2:5; I Jn. 1:9). We pay a high cost when we neglect these.

• Our Paying the Toll of Sin

While our conscious sinning does not require us who are saved to pay the divine penalty of sin, it does take a spiritual toll and incurs natural penalties.

1. *It interrupts our fellowship with God (I Jn. 1:6-7).*

To fellowship with God is to live in conscious touch with Him by sharing with Him all that concerns us, drawing from Him all that we need, communicating with Him by prayer and the reading of His Word, participating with Him in His work, living according to His will, and resting on His promises. Our sinning can interrupt this fellowship by turning our heart away from God and bringing us His displeasure.

We can have fellowship with God only as we walk in the light as He is in the light (I Jn. 1:7). This does not demand our perfection, but it does require us to conform to His will and adjust to His character. It requires us to be responsive to His Word and to seek to be and do what He desires for us. It is possible for imperfect people to have fellowship with God because of the means of cleansing and enablement He has provided for us. When the Word or our conscience points to some sin in our life, then we must repent and confess it to God (Rev. 2:5; I Jn. 1:9). Moreover, we must depend upon the Holy Spirit to enable us to do those things that are pleasing to God (Gal. 5:16). When we fail to do these, our fellowship ceases until we have dealt with our sins and have given ourself anew to His will. If we sin unknowingly and God does not make this sin known to us, then it seems that the value of the atoning work of Christ is automatically applied to us for our cleansing (cp. I Jn. 1:7). However, it is of utmost importance that we deal with known sins when we become aware of them, lest neglecting to do so causes our fellowship with God to cease.

2. *It hinders certain ministries of the Holy Spirit (I Thess. 5:19).*

Sin stifles the Holy Spirit's work, which enables us to experience the fruit of Christian character (Gal. 5:22-23) and to participate in Christian service (Acts 1:8; Eph. 4:12). Furthermore, our conscious sinning causes us to be very unhappy, for it grieves the Holy Spirit (Eph. 4:30; cp. Ps. 32:3-4; Mt. 26:75) and it is contrary to our saved, inner human nature, which is righteous and holy (II Cor. 5:21; Eph. 4:24; I Pet. 1:22). This is a high price to pay when we consider that it is through His work we experience all the blessings of the new life we have in Christ (cp. Eph. 1:14).

3. *It arrests spiritual growth (I Pet. 2:1-2).*

It is God's command that we grow in our spiritual lives, for our new life in Christ has this capacity and need, just as the physical life does (II Pet. 3:18). This growth occurs in the areas of Christian character (I Thess. 3:12), spiritual knowledge (Col. 1:10), and spiritual activity (II Cor. 9:8). The purpose of this growth is that we increasingly become like Jesus (Rom. 8:29; II Cor. 3:18). However, sin which is unlike Christ arrests this growth. Paul rebuked the Corinthian believers for acting like unsaved people (I Cor. 3:1-3) and described them as being "carnal" (ones living under the domination of the sin-principle) and "babes" (infants in spiritual maturity). Peter admonishes his readers to lay aside sin and to desire the Word in order that they may grow (I Pet. 2:1-2). God wants us to be mature and strong (Eph. 4:14-15; 6:10). Sin retards and weakens.

4. *It brings us God's corrective chastisement (I Cor. 11:28-32; Rev. 3:19).*

When we fail to deal with known sins in our life, we invite God's corrective discipline. In chastening His people, God deals with them so as to correct what He disapproves and to direct them to walk in the way He approves. Not all adversity is the result of unjudged sins, but this must be our first consideration when it strikes (cp. Ruth 1:20-21). If we promptly deal with the sin that is made known to us, then we avoid God's corrective action. We would evade much trial if we kept short accounts with God by dealing promptly with that in our life that displeases Him.

5. *It incurs the loss of reward (II Cor. 5:10; I Cor. 3:13-15).*

Since each of us who are saved is Christ's slave and has the responsibility of doing His will, we must give an account of our stewardship to Him (Rom. 14:12). All that we have done in keeping with His will and in His strength will bring us His approval and reward. But all else will bring us His reprimand and loss, for not being shared with Him, He had no part in it (Jn. 15:4-5; Rom. 14:23; II Cor. 5:10; Col. 3:24-25). This is not a judicial judgment but our Master's appraisal of His servants for the purpose of giving them suitable rewards for their lives on earth.

6. *It energizes us to manifest spiritual death (Gal. 6:8).*

During every conscious moment, we who are saved are manifesting either spiritual life or spiritual death. This is determined by the principle (God or sin) that is energizing our life. If we yield to the Holy Spirit, we allow Him to manifest through us spiritual life by our doing righteous works (Rom. 6:22). In this way we reflect Christ. On the other hand, when we give ourself to sin and allow it to energize us as an instrument of unrighteousness, we not only commit sins but we also manifest spiritual death, which is the product of sinning (Jas. 1:15; Rom. 6:21). This does not mean that we lose eternal life; it means that we do not always manifest our new life in Christ in our daily life. At any conscious moment we are manifesting either spiritual life or spiritual death. There is no neutrality in the Christian experience (Gal. 6:7-8).

• Our Cleansing from Sin's Defilement

Sin in the Christian's life does not change him constitutionally, as it did Adam and Eve, but it does temporarily corrupt or defile him. This means that it energizes us for its evil expressions and leaves the residue of a defiled conscience and a polluted record of sinful activity. It appears that the blood of Jesus (the value of His atoning work applied to us) automatically cleanses us from the defilement of sins of which we are not aware (I Jn. 1:7). On the other hand, when we knowingly sin or when the Holy Spirit shows us that some action is sinful, we must then deal with this sin and cleanse ourself from its defilement (II Cor. 7:1; I Cor. 11:31). However, we cannot by ourself remove this defilement. The cleansing agent is Jesus' blood, which in biblical usage often means the value of His atoning work that is divinely applied to us. Applying the value of our Lord's atoning work to us, God forgives and cleanses us when we take those steps which allow Him to do so. Let us consider these steps.

1. *We must repent of the sin (Rev. 2:5).*

This is a change of mind or attitude toward the sin. This rises from a sorrow that is prompted by God (II Cor. 7:10; cp. Eph. 4:30). Rather than justifying, rationalizing, excusing, or ignoring his sin, the repentant person looks at it as God does and repudiates it (Prov. 28:13).

2. *We must confess the sin to God (I Jn. 1:9).*

This is to acknowledge the sin to God in prayer, calling it what He says it is. Observe that we do not have to ask Him to forgive us our sin. He promises to do this when we fulfill the condition of confession. Also notice that there cannot be true outward confession if this is not preceded by inward repentance, for God searches the heart (Ps. 139: 23-24; Rom. 8:27). He is faithful to forgive truly confessed sin, as He promises. Also, He is righteous in doing this because of the Lord's atoning work. All sins that a believer may commit are forgivable (I Jn. 1:9).

3. *If we have wronged others, we must admit this to them and seek*
   their forgiveness (Mt. 5:23-24; Jas. 5:16).

Perhaps James has this in view when he exhorts his readers to confess their faults to one another (cp. Lk. 15:21). The faults that we confess publicly should be those that are known to or involve the public. Private sins, which are unknown to others, should be the concern only of God and the sinning believer.

4. *If we have been wronged by others, we must have a forgiving*
   spirit toward them (Mt. 6:12, 14-15).

God will not forgive us the sins that we confess to Him when we have an unforgiving spirit toward others, for this attitude which manifests an unrepentant heart is sinful in His sight. Because of God's manifold forgiveness toward us when we repented and trusted Jesus as Saviour, we should express immeasurable forgiveness toward others when they repent and fulfill their obligation to us (see "Christian Forgiveness" in the Addenda; cp. Mt. 18:21-35; Eph. 4:32; Lk. 17:3).

Upon our taking these steps, we immediately receive the divine application of the value of Jesus' atoning work and are forgiven. Moreover, we are cleansed from sin's defilement and relieved of its guilt (II Cor. 7:1; Heb. 10:22).

In response to God's promise to forgive us, we should believe it, act upon it, express our thanks to Him, and give ourself anew to His control. (We sinned because we yielded to sin's control.)

Do not allow this gracious provision for cleansing to encourage you to sin or to make your sinning easier. Although we are cleansed of sin's defilement and relieved of divine chastisement, its record still stands and it (also our handling of it) will be considered in the calculation of our reward (Col. 3:24-25). We cannot sin with impunity, though our judicial judgment is past. God's Word bears witness to the sins of His people unto this day (Jn. 18:25; II Tim. 4:10).

• Our Victory Over Sin

We sin when we yield ourself to the demands or urges of the sin-principle, which resides in the fleshly part of our body (Rom. 7:17, 23; 6:11-12; Jas. 1:14-15). But since we do not have to yield to these demands, we can experience occasions of victory over this evil force. I speak of "occasions" of victory, for there is no permanent victory over our spiritual enemies in this life, in the sense that they cease troubling us. While we are in this world, we are susceptible to their attacks and influences. How then can we experience victory over the sin-principle when we sense its urge to use our nature contrary to God's will? By following Paul's instruction in Romans 6:1-13. Although we have considered the forepart of this passage earlier, let us look at it again with God's provision of victory in mind. This victory is realized by our knowing certain truth and our acting upon it.

1. *God wants us to know certain truth (Rom. 6:1-10).*

He wants us to know that we died to the sin-principle and its demands (vss. 2-3, 6-7). We died at salvation when we participated in the Lord's death. This took place by our being joined to Him by the baptism of the Holy Spirit (Gal. 3:27). By this union we came to share in His death (and resurrection), dying to the sin-principle and its claim to us. This death rendered our human nature ineffective as the legal instrument of sin and set us free from sin's claim (Rom. 6:6-7).

God also wants us to know that we are alive unto our new master, the Lord Jesus Christ (vss. 4, 10). As our sharing the Lord's death was effective in severing our bondage and duty to sin, so our sharing His resurrection now enables us to experience our new life in Him and to fulfill our duty of living unto God (II Cor. 5:14-15).

2. *God wants us to reckon this truth to be so (Rom. 6:11).*

To "reckon" means to consider the facts that God wants us to know to be true and to act accordingly. In Christ we not only died to the sin-principle but we also remain dead to it. Therefore, reckoning this to be so, we are to be unresponsive to its demands. On the other hand, being alive unto God, we now have the duty of believing this to be true and of giving ourself to His control. This reckoning gives stimulus and direction to our moral choices and actions. It reminds us that we should no longer yield to the urges of the sin-principle, to which we have died, but that we should now give ourself to the will of God, to whom we are alive. It is our privilege to give Him the place in our life which sin once held. Our reckoning this truth reminds us who our owner is and prompts us to take appropriate action.

3. God wants us to take appropriate action (Rom. 6:12-13).

What does God want us to do? He wants us to quit yielding ourself to the sin-principle (vss. 12-13). To yield to sin is to allow this evil force to use us as a tool of unrighteousness. This is not fitting to us who have Christ as our life.

God also wants us to yield ourself to Him (vs. 13). This places our self under His control for His holy expressions through our human nature. When we fail to do this, we cannot avoid yielding to sin and sinning, for sin is stronger than we are alone.[18]

4. God wants us to practice the holy alternative (Rom. 6:16-22).

Upon our yielding ourself to God, it is our duty then to obey Him and do His will (righteousness) in the energy of the Holy Spirit (Gal. 5:16, 25). Our doing righteousness results in practical holiness and the expression of eternal life (Rom. 6:22). Whatever sin would have us to do, there is a holy alternative that God wants us to do in its place. It is important that we know what this is (II Cor. 5:9; Eph. 5:17; cp. 4:25 – 5:5, 15-18).

When we become aware of the urges of the sin-principle within us, we can experience victory by yielding ourself to God, rather than to sin, and by doing His will in His strength (Phil. 4:13). When we do this, we allow the Holy Spirit to hold the sin-principle in abeyance and to enable us to do what is right in God's sight (Gal. 5:16; I Jn. 3:6). Sinful habits are unwound and holy ones are formed as we yield ourself to the Holy Spirit and do God's will in His strength. When we sin, we must apply to ourself the means of cleansing and give ourself anew to God's control.

Observe again that the believer has the liberty to choose what principle will energize his life, God or sin. If he is walking in the power of sin, he can choose to yield himself to God. If he is walking in the power of the Holy Spirit, he can choose to yield himself to sin. No matter how strong a hold sin seems to have on a believer's life, it can be broken immediately by the decision and action to yield one's self to God. But with this submission to God there must also be the faith that the Holy Spirit will provide the energy for the believer to do God's will (cp. Jn. 7:37-39).

---

[18] Observe that, unlike demon possession (see Appendix Q), our yielding to the control of God or sin does not make us inactive. Our total human nature continues to function in association with the principle to which we yield ourself, but it receives energy and direction from this principle. At any time, our self (personhood) can stop yielding to the one principle and give our human nature to the other. In demon possession there is complete passivity of one's self and nature, so that the demon expresses his personality apart from the human personality, using only the physical part of one's human nature.

We thank God for this marvelous truth — our being dead to sin and alive unto Him. We no longer have to sin; we can now do righteousness. Just as we once were slaves of sin, ever ready to do its bidding, so now are we the Lord's slaves to do His bidding. Let us daily yield ourself to Him as His instrument of righteousness and seek to glorify God in all we do (I Cor. 10:31; 6:20; Phil. 1:11).

THE LAW AND SIN

A characterization of sin is that it is a transgression of divine law (I Jn. 3:4). If men are to be aware of sin as transgression and be convicted of violating law, they must have God's Law (Rom. 3:20). Where there is no law, this guilt cannot be imputed (Rom. 4:15; 5:13). On the other hand, people without divine law are guilty of actual sins on grounds other than transgressing divinely revealed law.

PAGANS WITHOUT DIVINE LAW

Paul points out that pagans who do not have divinely revealed Law (e.g., the Law of Moses or the New Testament, with its record of the Dispensation of Grace) sometimes instinctively do the things that are in the law (Rom. 2:14-15). The reason for this seems to be that, being made in the image of God, they possess innate morality which expresses itself in their moral evaluations and decisions. Although pagans do not have a written divine law, they are guilty of actual sins on the basis of violating the laws of their communities, which reflect the "law written in their hearts."

Being responsible moral creatures, pagans also have the obligation to respond favorably to God's self-revelation in nature and to fulfill certain basic duties that personal creatures owe the Creator, such as worship, gratitude, and service, and that they owe to one another (cp. Rom. 1:18-23; II Tim. 3:2-3). When Paul preached to pagans, he did not use divine law, such as the Mosaic Law, to bring them under the conviction of sin (Acts 14:6-18; 17:15-34; 24:25). Rather, he reminded them of their creaturehood (Acts 17:24-26, 28-29) and their guilt of dishonoring God by neglecting to seek after Him (vs. 27) and by regarding Him to be less than what He is (vss. 24-25, 29). He also declared their duty to seek the Lord (vs. 27), repent (i.e., exercise salvational faith, vs. 30, cp. vs. 18), and prepare for coming judgment (vs. 31).

MEN AND THE TEN COMMANDMENTS

While the Mosaic Law was given to Israel as a dispensation, its moral precepts, such as the Ten Commandments, may be used universally to bring people under the conviction of sin. Being absolute and timeless, God's moral Laws transcend dispensational boundaries. They apply to people of every age. Observe that nine of the Ten Commandments are covered by the Dispensation of Grace (I Jn. 5:21; Eph. 6:2-3; I Thess. 4:3-5; Eph. 4:28; Col. 3:9, 5).

The exception is Sabbath-keeping. Being a rabbi, Paul was keenly aware of the Mosaic Law in his early Christian life (Rom. 7:7-14). It made him conscious of the activity of the sin-principle, but it could not deliver him from the domination of this evil force (vss. 15-24). He was to learn that only God can do this by His grace in response to the believer's submission and faith (Rom. 7:25-8:4; Gal. 2:20; 5:16).

BELIEVERS AND CHRIST'S LAW

We who are saved are under Christ's Law (I Cor. 9:21; Gal. 6:2), which consists of the precepts and principles given in the New Testament (the Dispensation of Grace, cp. Jas. 1:25). We experience the fullest expression of this law when we allow the Lord Jesus' love to work in our hearts and to govern our relations with others (Jn. 13:34-35; Rom. 5:5; 13:8-10; Gal. 6:2; I Jn. 3:16-23).

The Old Testament is profitable to the saved person (see p. 24). But we should remember that, although all of the Bible is profitable to us who are saved (II Tim. 3:16), not all of it relates to us. Most of the Old Testament concerns God's dealings with Israel under the Mosaic Law. Since the Lord Jesus' commands for His people today are presented in the New Testament, we should follow only those O.T. directions which reflect, or are in harmony with, these N. T. commands. For instance, we are not obligated to observe the ritual of the Mosaic law, but we are required to fear God (Eccles. 12:13; I Pet. 2:17).

For Christ's people all other laws are subordinate to His law (Acts 5:29). This does not mean that we should disregard man-made laws, but we recognize that in dying with Christ we have died to man-made laws and customs to the extent that we must give His law priority above all others (Rom. 7:1-6). Paul sought to accommodate himself to man's ideas so as to win them to Christ (I Cor. 9:19-23) and to live conscientiously as a citizen (Acts 23:1). Yet, he was ever mindful of his being "inlawed to Christ" (I Cor. 9:21). When we know the good that is prescribed by our Lord's law and fail to do it, we sin (Jas. 4:17). But as we look to Him for strength, we can obey Him (Phil. 1:11; 4:13). To obey God is to do righteousness, which is an evidence of our salvation (I Jn. 2:29).

Our study of sin has shown us its enslaving and destructive force in the lives of personal creatures who have chosen to disobey God. But we who are saved from sin rejoice in God's provision in Jesus for His forgiving us of sin's debt, cleansing us from its defilement, and giving us victory over its power. It is to God's glory that we daily respond to this truth and anticipate the time when we shall be forever delivered from the presence of our spiritual enemies.

Notes

A Review of Hamartiology

1. What are the two aspects of the nature of sin?
2. Explain what the sin-principle, or sin-force, is.
3. To what part of human nature is the sin-principle most closely related?
4. How do we know that the believer still has the sin-principle?
5. What determines the evil character of sin? Give several basic characteristics of sin.
6. How do we know that God did not create sin?
7. Why did God include sin in His decree?
8. How did sin begin in angels and humans?
9. Why did God create these personal creatures with the ability to commit their first sin?
10. How was Adam's first sin like Eve's? How was his sinning different from hers?
11. What was the immediate effects of their first sin?
12. What punishments did God mete out to Eve, Adam, the serpent, and Satan?
13. In His judgment on Satan, what did God declare that would take place?
14. Why did God banish Adam and Eve from the garden of Eden?
15. What is "original sin?" What are its effects upon the human race?
16. What are the two human races and their heads?
17. What does the corruption of human nature mean?
18. What is total depravity? Total inability?
19. By what principle do the members of each human race participate in the actions of their head?
20. What are the two theories as to how the guilt of Adam's initial sin was imputed to the human race?
21. According to the author of this book, which theory is more biblical?
22. What does imputation mean? Give the three events of imputation given in the Scriptures (see Index).
23. Distinguish between the Pelagian, Semi-Pelagian, and Augustinian views of man's depravity.
24. What are "actual sins"?
25. Describe the mechanics of sinning.
26. What other evil influences lead us to sin?
27. From what does God's reaction to sin proceed?

28. What is the meaning of condemnation? Guilt? Punishment?

29. What is the ultimate punishment of sin? Give its three expressions.

30. What two kinds of punishment does God mete out to people who sin? To what kind of people is each of these given?

31. Which kind of punishment is remedial and what does this mean?

32. What is the basic idea of forgiveness?

33. What two kinds of forgiveness does God extend to repentant people?

34. What must one do to receive judicial forgiveness? Parental forgiveness?

35. What is the believer's present relation to the effects of original sin?

36. Why is the radication of the sin-principle unnecessary in this present life?

37. Our soul and spirit have been delivered from the corruption of original sin. What does this mean? Why do we still sin?

38. Why cannot a believer sin continuously as he did before he was saved?

39. What toll does a believer's sinning take in his life?

40. What must we do to experience cleansing from sin as Christians? What must unsaved people do?

41. Describe Christian forgiveness (see the Addenda).

42. What steps must we take to experience victory over sin in our life?

43. Although pagans do not have a written moral code from God, by what code do they live (see the Dispensation of Fallen Man)? Of what sins may they be convicted?

44. Why may the preaching of the Ten Commandments bring people under the conviction of sin even though they do not live under the Mosaic law?

45. What law has absolute jurisdiction over Christians today above all other laws? Where do we find this law in the Scriptures? How can we keep this law?

Soteriolology

SOTERIOLOGY
The Doctrine of Salvation

Paul exhorted the Ephesian believers to put on the helmet of salvation, as a part of their armor against Satan (Eph. 6:17). This helmet seems to represent an essential knowledge of salvation and its delivering power in daily life. Because of our familiarity with the gospel, it is easy for us to treat this doctrine lightly. However, it is urgent that we learn all that God has revealed about it for our personal blessing and the benefit of others. Having been given the ministry of reconciliation, it behooves us as Christ's ambassadors to learn all we can about the work of reconciliation (II Cor. 5:18-20). A fuller understanding of salvation's method, components, function, and assurance will help us to be more efficient witnesses to a lost world (Acts 1:8).

THE NATURE OF SALVATION
ITS BIBLICAL DESCRIPTION
Essentially, salvation is a deliverance. To save is to rescue, or to deliver, someone from calamity, loss, or destruction. In the Bible the word has both secular and spiritual meanings.

- **Its Secular Meaning**

Secular salvation is a deliverance from some natural or physical danger or affliction (Ex. 14:30; Ps. 34:6; Mt. 14:30; Acts 27:42-44).

- **Its Spiritual Meaning**

Spiritual salvation is one's deliverance from his spiritual enemies and their works in his life. These spiritual enemies are sin (Mt. 1:21), Satan (Col. 1:13), and the world (II Pet. 2:20).

ITS THEOLOGICAL DESCRIPTION
Theologically, salvation is a blanket term for all that takes place spiritually in a person at the time of and resulting from his receiving Jesus as his Saviour. A full theological statement of salvation is this: Salvation is the gracious work of God whereby He delivers undeserving, gospel believing sinners from their spiritual enemies and their works; brings them into a right, vital relationship with Himself; and bestows upon them the rich benefits of His grace.

THE ASPECTS OF SALVATION
With reference to time, salvation has different phases or tenses.

IN THE PAST (II Tim. 1:9)

When we trusted Jesus as our Saviour, we were immediately and forever delivered from the guilt, judicial punishment, corruption, and bondage of our sins (Rom. 5:9; 6:6-7; I Pet. 1:22), from bondage to Satan (Acts 26:18), and from being a part of this world system (Jn. 15:19).

DURING THE PRESENT (Jas. 1:21)

We can now experience occasions of deliverance from the power of the sin-principle, the temptations of Satan, and the evil allurement of the world (Gal. 5:16; Jas. 4:7; 1:27). Moreover, we can now express the reality and qualities of our new life in Christ as we cooperate with the Holy Spirit (Phil. 2:12-13; Gal. 5:25) and obey His Word (Ps. 119:11).

IN THE FUTURE (Rom. 13:11)

We anticipate the deliverance of our body from the effects of sin (its inherent corruption and resident sin-principle, Phil. 3:20-21) as well as our removal from this world (Gal. 1:4) when Jesus comes (I Thess. 4:13-17).

THE NECESSITY FOR SALVATION

People's need for salvation is marked by the lack of necessary spiritual realities in their lives as well as the presence of undesirable realities. Before one can be saved, he must be made aware of his spiritual need before God (cp. Jn. 4:15-19; 6:34-36). While he may feel more pressing needs, such as physical or material ones, the sinner's primary need concerns his sins and his deliverance from their ruin, guilt, power, and penalty. Keep in mind that Jesus came to be the Saviour from sin (Mt. 1:21; I Jn. 3:5). Only when the matter of sin is divinely settled in a person's life can he look to Jesus to minister to his other needs. In their natural, unsaved state all people are as follows:

1. **Sinners by constitution (Rom. 5:19) and by practice (Eph. 2:3; Rom. 1:21-32).** They are born sinners and in time commit sins. They sin by breaking God's laws (I Jn. 3:4) and by failing to attain His moral standard for His personal creatures (Rom. 3:10, 23).

2. **Slaves of sin (Jn. 8:34; Rom. 3:9; 6:16-17),** Their lives are wholly dominated by sin as well as by Satan (Acts 26:18; I Jn. 5:19, "in the wicked one") and by the world, of which they are a part (Jn. 15:19). See Ephesians 2:1-3.

3. **Condemned by God (Jn. 3:18).** The unsaved have already been found guilty by God and sentenced to Hell for original sin (Rom. 5:18) and their actual sins (Rom. 3:9-19). Their future judgment concerns their accountability for their lives and the degree of punishment they must receive (Rev. 20:11-

15; Mt. 11:22).

4. Spiritually dead toward God and the things of God (Eph. 2:1; 4:18; Rom. 1:21-23; 3:11; I Cor. 2:9, 14). This means that they are naturally unresponsive to the things of God. On the other hand, they are very much alive, or responsive, to sin, Satan, and the world (Eph. 2:2-3).

5. Lost (Lk. 19:10; Rom. 3:9-18; II Cor. 4:3). This means that they are spiritually ruined, not lost to God's view. Being wholly affected by sin, they are not now as God created man.

6. In debt to God for their sins (Gen. 2:17; Ezek. 18:4; Rom. 6:23). They are obligated to bear the punishment of their sins. They can never pay off this debt in Hell and gain release (Mt. 25:46).

7. Helpless to correct their condition or to provide for their spiritual needs (Rom. 5:6). They need a rescuer — the Saviour!

Observe that this is the spiritual condition of all humans who are not saved. This description and our Lord's commission to us to evangelize the lost (Lk. 24:47) indicate that all humans are lost, including those who have never heard the gospel. Having the continual witness of general revelation, they who have not heard the gospel are without excuse for their not seeking the Creator and their not fulfilling basic duties to Him (Rom. 1:19-20; Acts 17:23-29). Yet, they who respond favorably to the witness of creation will in time hear the gospel, which informs sinners how they can know God and be rightly related to Him (cp. Acts 10:1-43).

THE BENEFITS OF SALVATION

While we shall consider these blessings more thoroughly later, let us see the extent to which salvation ministers to a person's spiritual need who receives Jesus as His Saviour.

1. The saved person is no longer a sinner but is a saint (I Cor. 1:2; 6:11). He no longer belongs to the category of sinner though he still sins. Set apart in Christ, he is a holy (or sanctified) one.

2. He is no longer a slave of sin, Satan, and the world but is a slave of Jesus and righteousness (Rom. 6:16-18). His duty is to live unto Jesus and to do His will.

3. He is no longer condemned by God but is justified (Rom. 5:1, 9, 18). He has been acquitted of condemnation and has been declared righteous by God (Rom. 8:30-34; II Cor. 5:21).

4. He is no longer spiritually dead but is alive toward God (Eph. 2:1). He is now a member of God's family and a citizen of His kingdom (Jn. 1:12; Col. 1:13).

5. He is no longer a spiritual ruin but is a new creature in Christ (II Cor. 5:17; Eph. 2:10; 4:24).

6. He is no longer in debt for his sins but is forgiven (Eph. 1:7; Col. 2:13). He is forever released from the judicial punishment of all His sins.

7. He is no longer helpless but is empowered by the Holy Spirit (Jn. 14:16-17). This Helper ("Comforter") enables him to be and do all that God requires of him (II Pet. 1:3).

How we thank God for the radical change that He brings about in all who receive the Saviour. This change is manifest in all who walk in obedience to God and in His power.

THE PROVISION OF SALVATION

This explains why God gave His only begotten Son and why sinners must believe on Jesus to be saved (Jn. 3:16). Since sinners cannot deliver themselves from their spiritual plight, God has graciously provided His Son to be their Saviour (Mt. 1:21; Jn. 14:6; Acts 4:12; I Jn. 4:9-10). To help us understand this provision, let us ask a question and answer it.

THE QUESTION

How can God who is holy and just rightly deliver sinners from what they deserve (divine retribution) and bring them into a right relation with Himself? His holiness moved Him to oppose and condemn sinners and their sins; His justice required Him to deal with them as they deserve. Contrary to the view of sentimentalists, God could not in love override His holiness and ignore His justice (cp. Lk. 19:41-44). How, then, could God rightly justify sinners?

THE ANSWER

While He could not change His holy demands against sinners, as their substitute God Himself could satisfy these demands on their behalf. In a deliberate exercise of love and grace (Rom. 9:15; Eph. 2:4-5), God the Father gave His Son to atone for humanity's sins (Isa. 53:10; Jn. 1:29; 3:16), and God the Son gave His life to pay provisionally the debt of these sins (Mt. 20:28; I Cor. 15:3-4; I Pet. 2:24; Rom. 5:8; Heb. 9:26). His atoning work required His bearing these sins and being made sin, as well as His experiencing spiritual and physical death, the offering of His blood, and His rising physically from the dead. On the basis of this finished, substitutionary work, God can freely and justly save everyone who exercises salvational faith in the Saviour and His atoning work (Jn. 3:16, 18, 36; Rom. 3:21-26).

Paul describes this answer as "the cross" and the gospel declaration as "the preaching of the cross" (I Cor. 1:18, 22-23; 2:1-2). Any ministry that omits this truth is not the gospel. This is what people must believe about Jesus if they are to be saved. He is the only Saviour from sin and the only Way unto God (Acts 4:12; Jn. 14:6).

THE APPLICATION OF SALVATION

This concerns the divine and human activities that are involved in a sinner's being saved. These activities are described in II Thessalonians 2:13 as "sanctification by the Spirit and (man's) belief in the truth" and in I Peter 1:2 as "obedience (man's belief in the gospel) and the sprinkling of the blood of Jesus (the divine application of the atonement to the gospel believer)".

GOD'S PART IN THIS APPLICATION

Although the sinner has something to do within the area of conscious decision and duty (Jn. 6:28-29; Rom. 10:9-10), his salvation is wholly God's work (Eph. 2:8-9). Salvation is God's gift, freely offered to all through the gospel; and it is His work wrought in the elect according to His eternal purpose. God's part in this application follows:

- **Before the Beginning of Time**

    1. *GOD ELECTED (Eph. 1:4; II Thess. 2:13; cp. Rom. 8:28, "purpose").*
    a. *Definitions*
    Election is the sovereign act of God whereby He freely chose certain human beings to be saved. Preterition is His passing by those whom He did not choose to save (see Appendix J).
    b. *Features*
        (1) His election was sovereign.
        This means that He freely chose according to His good pleasure (Eph. 1:9, 11). He was not prompted or influenced by people's works, merit, or worth, of which there was none (cp. Rom. 9:11, 15-16).[1]
        (2) His election was gracious.
        It was an act of undeserved favor toward a people who because of their total depravity wholly deserved the penalty of their sins (Rom. 11:5).
        (3) His election was eternal.
        Being a part of His eternal plan (Eph. 1:4), election logically

---

[1] That God's election was determined by His foresight of what people would do is a wrong understanding of I Peter 1:2. "Foreknowledge" is equated with and preceded by His "determinate counsel" in Acts 2:23. Thus God's foreknowledge is based upon His counsel, or decree.

follows God's decree to create man and permit his fall (see Appendix J).

(4) His election was in Christ.

All of God's purpose for the elect (as well as for everything not voluntarily affected by sin, cp. Eph. 1:10; Col. 1:20), is in Christ (Eph. 3:11), including their being made alive (I Cor. 15:22), their blessings (Eph. 1:3), and their election (1:4). As God's Agent in carrying out the efficient aspect of the divine plan (I Cor. 8:6), the Lord Jesus encompasses the whole program of God, as it relates to the salvation and the destiny of the elect. They are and have nothing apart from Him (I Cor. 1:30; II Cor. 5:17; Eph. 2:10).

b. Objections

(1) "His choosing only some to be saved is not fair." God's choice is not unjust, for all people deserve Hell. Had they deserved Heaven and were not chosen, then such discrimination would have been unjust. Moreover, the Creator, who is absolutely just, has the right to do whatever He pleases with His creatures (Rom. 9:14-24). Also, His pleasure is always in harmony with His nature. His choice was sovereign and gracious.

(2) "If He chose some to be saved, then He also elected the remainder to be lost."

This view is called the "decree of reprobation." God's selecting some to be saved inevitably left the rest to suffer for their sins. However, His passing by the nonelect did not necessitate, or bring about, their perdition, although His decree made it certain. While divine election is an efficient cause in the salvation of the elect, preterition is not an efficient cause in the perdition of the nonelect. God simply decided to leave the nonelect alone to their self-chosen sins and their consequences.[2] Paul sees this distinction in Romans 9:22-23. He says that God prepared the vessels of mercy unto glory (a reference to saved people), but he does not say that God fitted the vessels of wrath unto destruction (the fate of the nonelect). Man fitted himself for divine judgment.

(3) "Divine election concerns only service."

This statement ignores II Thessalonians 2:13, Ephesians 1:4, and Romans 11:5-6. The principle and character of divine election remain the same, regardless of its application (cp. Rom. ch. 9).

2. GOD PREDESTINATED (Rom. 8:29; Eph. 1:5, 11-12).

a. Definition

Predestination is the sovereign act of God whereby He determined beforehand what He would do with them whom He elected to salvation.[3]

b. Features

Keep in mind that in its narrow sense salvation refers to

---

[2] See W. G. T. Shedd, I, 444 ff. and A. H. Strong, p. 789.

[3] Observe that Reformed theology holds that predestination covers election and reprobation. It is more scriptural to regard it as a distinct, separate act of God in addition to election and preterition.

deliverance from sin. Upon choosing whom He would save from sin, God then made several decisions regarding what He would do with these elect people when He saved them.[4]

(1) He predestinated them to adoption (Eph. 1:5).

This determined what the elect would be. While the new birth makes us God's children by bringing us into His family, adoption gives us the status of adult-sons. This means that we have all the privileges and duties that belong to this position.

(2) He predestinated them unto conformity to Christ (Rom. 8:29).

This determined what kind of adult-sons we would be. God decided that we should be like Jesus (Heb. 2:10-12). While we shall never share in our Lord's deity, we are being made in the image of His glorified humanity (II Cor. 3:18). This is because He is the head and pattern of the new humanity, of which we are a part (I Cor. 15:45-49). This conformity will be completed when our bodies are changed at His return (I Cor. 15:50-53; Phil. 3:20, 21; I Jn. 3:2; see Appendix V). This image also includes His moral likeness (Eph. 1:4; 5:27; I Cor. 1:8).

(3) He predestinated them unto the praise of His glory (Eph. 1:11-12).

This determined what the ultimate purpose for our existence would be. The glory of God consists of some manifestation of His attributes (Ps. 19:1; Jn. 2:11; 17:4). We glorify God when we allow Him to manifest in us His character and to do through us His works (Phil. 1:20; 4:13) and when we give to Him praise (Rom. 11:33-36; Mt. 5:16). Also, by our salvation we glorify God in a way that angels can never do. We who are saved will forever be the supreme manifestation of His grace (cp. Eph. 1:12; 2:7). God decided that our very existence should glorify Him and how this should be done (Eph. 1:18, 23; 2:7, 10; 3:10).

- **During the Lifetime of the Elect**

1. *GOD CALLS*[5] *(Rom. 8:30; Acts 2:39; I Tim. 6:12)*

   a. *Definition*

   This is the act of God whereby He commands sinners through the gospel to receive His salvation through Jesus.[6]

   b. *Features*

   Calvinists recognize two kinds of divine calls to salvation: a

---

[4] With reference to the nonelect, predestination concerns only their action toward Jesus (Acts 4:27-28; cp. 13:27-29). Still, these people were responsible for their infamous deed (Lk. 22:22). This action was predestinated, for the Lord's death was determined by God (Acts 2:23).

[5] There are other divine calls beside the initial one to salvation such as those to discipleship (Mk. 1:17), fellowship (I Cor. 1:9), holiness (I Thess. 4:7), and service (II Tim. 1:9). The calls to glory (II Thess. 2:14; I Pet. 5:10) and God's kingdom (I Thess. 2:12) relate to salvation. In I Corinthians 7:20-24, "calling" probably refers to the social position which one has when he is "called," or saved.

[6] That people are commanded by the gospel to receive the Saviour is indicated in John 3:36; Acts 5:32; 17:30; Romans 1:5; 16:26; II Thessalonians 1:8; and I Peter 1:22; 4:17.

general call and a special call. The general call through the gospel is that which extends to the nonelect (Mt. 22:14; cp. 11:28; Mk 16:15; Isa. 45:22). This call does not result in their salvation. The special call through the gospel is that which extends to the elect and which results in their salvation (I Cor. 1:2, 9, 24; Rom. 8:28, 30; I Thess. 2:12). This is sometimes identified as God's effectual call.

This special call to the elect appears to be more than a command to receive the Saviour. It seems also to embrace the whole presalvational work of God in bringing them to exercise salvational faith in Jesus, including the following divine activities: One, God sweeps away satanic blindness (II Cor. 4:3-6) and gives understanding of the gospel (Acts 16:14; 8:30; II Cor. 4:6). Two, He convicts the elect of their sins (Jn. 16:8-11). And three, imparting repentance (Acts 5:31; 11:18; II Tim. 2:25) and faith (II Pet. 1:1; Acts 3:16), He draws the elect person to Himself (Jn. 6:37, 44). Since this occurs below the level of human awareness, the person's desire and decision to receive the Saviour are, in effect, his own.

Steps one and two seem to apply also to the nonelect as a part of God's general call. Hebrews 6:4-6 may illustrate the case of one who is brought to the threshhold of salvational faith. He is warned not to fall away from going on to faith in Christ. To fall away would result in his hardening to such a degree that he would never be restored to this place again. On the other hand, the works of us who are saved bear witness to our salvational faith and salvation (vss. 9-10; Jas. 2:14-26).

Holding that the sinner must be made spiritually alive before he can believe, Calvinists speak of this presalvational work as "regeneration" and the experience of salvation as "conversion." However, the Scriptures teach that the impartation of spiritual life follows faith in Christ (Jn. 1:12; 3:16, 36; 6:53). God can give salvational faith to one who is spiritually dead just as readily as He can make inanimate stones cry out (Lk. 19:40). The divine gift of salvational faith itself has the dynamic to enable its recipients to trust the Saviour just as the gift of life enables one to live.

    c. Questions

       (1) "Is God's general call genuine and sincere?"

       Regardless what His secret decree may be, God's revealed desire for all men is that they be saved (I Tim. 2:4; II Pet. 3:9). Therefore, He sincerely extends to the nonelect the general call through the gospel, which He knows will be refused. On the other hand, anyone who wants to be saved may respond to the call and be saved (Jn. 3:16; Acts 10:43; 17:30). Because of the provisional character of the Lord's atoning work, there is something substantive for the nonelect to believe or to reject (I Jn. 2:2; II Cor. 5:19).

       (2) "Is God's special call irresistible?"

       God's presalvational work does not sensibly coerce man's will. It is not an outward constraint upon the will, but a nonexperiential compulsion that works from within man's nature. God's special call to salvation is irresistible, not in the sense that it is never consciously resisted but in the sense that it is never resisted successfully. On the other hand, this truth never annuls a person's duty to believe the gospel (Lk. 13:3; Acts 20:21).

2. *GOD JUSTIFIES* (Rom. 8:30).

Upon exercising salvational faith in Jesus, the believer experiences God's saving work, of which justification is a part. Doing all that He promises through the gospel, God delivers the gospel believer from the penalty and ruin of his sins and imparts to him spiritual life. (Later, we shall look at justification as a component of salvation.)

• In the Future

Paul writes that they whom God justified He also glorified (Rom. 8:30). Glorification speaks of the completion of our salvation experience when God delivers our body from mortality (corruptibility, if dead), inherent corruption, and the resident sin-principle and changes it for the future state (I Cor. 15:50-53). This takes place when Jesus returns for His church (Phil. 3:20-21; I Thess. 4:13-17). Paul uses the past tense (constative aorist) because of the certainty of its coming to pass. He sees it as having taken place although experientially it is still future (cp. Rom. 8:23; 13:11).

Observe that these divine activities show that salvation is wholly God's work from start to finish (Eph. 2:8-10; Lk. 18:24-27). Sinners cannot make it, earn it, or buy it. Because of his total depravity (Rom. 3:10-12), inability (Jn. 6:44), and unwillingness (5:40), the sinner, left to himself, would never seek God (Rom. 3:11). Thus God gets all the credit for salvation (I Cor. 1:26-31). We readily give Him praise and thanksgiving for what He has done.

MAN'S PART IN THIS APPLICATION

Although salvation is wholly the work of God, yet within the conscious sphere of moral decision there is something for man to do to be saved (Mt. 7:21; Jn. 6:28-29). He must obey the gospel's command to receive the Saviour (Acts 16:31; 17:30; 20:21). This exercise of salvational faith should not be regarded as a meritorious work, for which God gives salvation as a reward or pay. Rather, it is the personal acceptance of God's gracious gift of life in Christ Jesus. Furthermore, the believer cannot receive any credit for believing the gospel, for salvational faith is God's gift, even when this faith seems to be his own (II Pet. 1:1; Acts 3:16; 11:18). Let us look more closely at this salvational faith, especially its parts and its expression.

• The Parts of Salvational Faith

What does it mean to believe the gospel, to receive Christ, or to exercise salvational faith in Jesus? It is more than one's asking Jesus to come into his heart. This belief consists of several ingredients — assent, repentance, and trust.

1. Assent to the Facts of the Gospel (Acts 16:14, 32; I Cor. 15:1-4)

These facts are what the gospel says about man's spiritual need, God's gracious provision of salvation in Christ, and what the sinner must do to be saved. To give assent to these facts is to acknowledge their truthfulness. Rather than being a nonrational leap into some undefined experience, salvational faith embraces what God says in His Word about Jesus and His atoning work (Rom. 10:8, 17; II Tim. 3:15; 4:2, 5; I Pet. 1:23, 25). The presentation of these facts should be accompanied with explanation so that they may be more meaningful to the unsaved heart (Acts 17:2-3; 8:30-35).

2. Repentance (Lk. 13:3; Acts 20:21)[7]

This is a change of mind and attitude toward God and the things of which the gospel speaks (cp. Mt. 21:29). The sinner normally is rebellious toward God, is hostile or indifferent toward the things of God, and exalts himself above God (Jn. 3:20; Rom. 3:11-12, 18; I Cor. 2:14). Also, he seeks to justify his wrongdoing or makes excuse for it. But when he repents, he humbles himself before God and repudiates his sins (cp. Prov. 28:13). A keen awareness of the holiness of God and the enormity of his sins causes him sorrow of heart, from which true repentance rises (II Cor. 7:10). This change of mind and attitude is brought about by God (Acts 5:31; 11:18; II Tim. 2:25). Without it there is no salvation (Lk. 13:3).

3. Trust in Christ and His Atoning Work (Jn. 1:12; Gal. 2:16)

Being more than a general faith in God or Jesus, this is to place one's complete trust in Jesus and His atoning work for the specific purpose of being delivered from sin and receiving God's gift of spiritual life. It is here that many miss salvation. Thinking that they are saved by some physical action, like raising a hand or walking an aisle, they fail to trust Jesus' substitutionary work for their salvation. They place their trust in something or someone other than Him. But one's trust must be wholly in Jesus and His atoning work, for He alone is the sinner's Substitute and Saviour (Acts 4:12).

Salvational faith consists of these ingredients. If any of these is missing, then one does not experience salvation.

• The Expression of Salvational Faith

How does one believe the gospel? Observe what Paul says about this in Romans 10:10. Inwardly, one believes the gospel by giving assent to its facts, repenting, and making a heart response to trust Jesus and His atoning work. This heart response involves the total self, including the will and the mind. Outwardly, by prayer to God the gospel-believer confesses his spiritual need and his trust in Jesus as His Saviour. Upon this expression of salvational faith, God immediately applies to the believer the value of Jesus' atoning

---

[7] Being a part of salvational faith, "repentance" and its verb form "repent" often occur as figurative expressions (synecdoche) for salvational faith (Lk. 24:47; Acts 2:38; 3:19; 5:31; 11:18; 17:30; 26:20; II Pet. 3:9).

work, forgives him of his sins, imparts to him spiritual life, makes him a member of His family and kingdom, and bestows on him the wealth of His grace (vs. 13). Since God knows the heart, the outward confession appears to be for the benefit of the believer, who by this concretely expresses his abstract, inner faith. When it marks the exercise of true salvational faith, this confession definitely indicates the time of one's salvation, ever to be remembered.

On the other hand, continual refusal to receive the Saviour results in one's hardening his heart toward the gospel (Acts 19:8-9). There seems to be a point in the life of the gospel hearer when he makes a final decision to accept or to reject the gospel. If he decisively rejects it, then he will never again be renewed unto repentance (Heb. 6:4-6).

So much evangelistic preaching today is not gospel preaching. It does not proclaim "the cross," which represents our Lord's atoning work; it does not speak of sin as being people's greatest problem before God; and it does not demand repentance toward God and toward sin. Moreover, it fails to portray God's holiness and anger toward sinners. Such insufficient preaching produces misdirected faith, false hope, and unreal "conversions," with the result that people think that they are saved when they are not. Their profession is not supported by their works (Jas. 2:26; Mt. 3:8; Eph. 2:10; I Jn. 2:3). Is the reader really trusting Jesus and His finished work for his salvation?

• Additions to Salvational Faith

In spite of the Bible's teaching that we are saved by God's grace through faith (Eph. 2:8) — "plus nothing, minus nothing," many insist that there is more to do than to believe the gospel.

1. *Some say that one must submit to water baptism.*

There are two aspects of the view that water baptism is necessary for salvation:

a. *Baptism is the instrument of salvation.*

This holds that baptism, imparting grace, is the instrument by means of which the Holy Spirit effects regeneration. In the case of infants, baptism washes away original sin and imparts faith (Lutheran), is the beginning of new life in Christ (Anglican High Church), or is the grace of adoption (Roman Catholic). In the case of adults, baptism also washes away actual sins.

Contrariwise, I believe that the death of Jesus, along with the offering of His blood, was sufficient to deal with all our sins and formed an adequate basis for divine forgiveness and cleansing (Col. 2:13; Heb. 9:14, 26; I Jn. 1:7; Rev. 1:5). The grace of God in salvation responds to faith, not baptism (Eph. 2:8; cp. Acts 16:31). The new birth, adoption, and placement into Christ's church follow personal, salvational faith in Christ (Jn. 1:12; Gal. 4:6; I Cor. 12:13, 27).

b. Baptism completes salvation.

This holds that water baptism, following faith and repentance, completes the salvational process (Disciples of Christ). The moment the gospel believer is immersed, he is saved.

Contrariwise, I believe that the gospel believer is saved the moment he exercises salvational faith in Jesus (Acts 16:31; Jn. 3:16). Baptism should follow salvation as one's formal, public witness to his faith in Christ (Acts 18:8; Mt. 28:19-20).

The few New Testament passages that appear to support the view that baptism is needed for salvation have alternate translation or explanation.

Acts 2:38 — "Repent, and be baptized every one of you in the name of Jesus Christ for the remission of sins..." "Repent" refers to exercising salvational faith (cp. Acts 17:30). "For the remission of sins" can read "because of the remission of sins." The remission of sins is not a result of baptism but the basis for baptism. Baptism is a formal witness to the truth that our sins were forgiven when we believed on Jesus (Acts 10:43).

Acts 22:16 — "Arise and be baptized, and wash away thy sins, calling on the name of the Lord." "Calling" (an aorist middle participle, "having called") indicates that Paul called upon the Lord, as an expression of his faith (Rom. 10:9-10, 13), before he was baptized.

A. T. Robertson writes, "The use of 'wash away thy sins,' in Acts 22:16, in connection with 'baptize,' cannot be properly insisted on as teaching baptismal salvation, since the Oriental symbolism often put the symbol to the forefront in descriptions when, as a matter of fact, the experience preceded the symbol in order of time. We know, in fact, that this was the case here, for Saul not only was already converted, but had received the Holy Spirit before his baptism (Acts 9:17, f.)."[8]

John 3:5 — "Except a man be born of water and of the Spirit, he cannot enter into the kingdom of God." From the context we know that entrance into God's kingdom is by the new birth, which is effected by the Holy Spirit (vss. 6-8). While some believe that "water" is a metaphor for physical birth (Jn. 1:13) or for the Scriptures (Eph. 5:26), I prefer the view that it represents the Holy Spirit (Jn. 7:37-39; Tit. 3:5) as the context teaches. The word "and," joining "water" and "the Spirit," may be interpreted as an explanatory copulative. If this is true, then the passage should read, "Except a man is born of water, namely the Spirit, he cannot enter the kingdom of God."

I Peter 3:21 — "The like figure whereunto even baptism doth also now save us (not the putting away of the filth of the flesh, but the answer of a good conscience toward God) by the resurrection of Jesus Christ." "Baptism" is in apposition with "figure" (the counterpart of reality). Peter is careful to explain that he is not teaching baptismal regeneration, for he says, "not the putting

---

8 A. T. Robertson, *Epochs in the Life of Paul* (New York: Charles Scribner's Sons, 1930), p. 55.

away of the filth of the flesh." Baptism is "the answer of a good conscience toward God," that is, the external witness to one's conscience that he has done what God requires for salvation.[9]

Mark 16:16 — "He that believeth and is baptized shall be saved; but he that believeth not shall be damned." Although baptism, according to this verse, seems to be necessary for salvation, failure to be baptized is not stated as a cause for being damned. If baptism were really necessary, it seems that it would be repeated here.

2. Others say that one must submit to the Lordship of Christ.

This view holds that salvational faith must also include the confession that Jesus is one's Lord (cp. Rom. 10:9; Mt. 11:28-30). I do not discount the fact that the sinner who asserted his independence of God must surrender his autonomy when he receives the Saviour. This appears to be involved in repentance, which is a change of attitude, and in trust, which is a redirection of faith. Still, the recognition of the lordship of Christ must not be allowed to eclipse or replace the emphasis on His saviourhood. People can only be saved as they see and trust Jesus to be the Saviour from their sins (Mt. 1:21). Salvational faith requires one to confess that Jesus is everything the Scriptures say about Him, though one may not understand what all of this means (I Jn. 4:15). The total commitment of discipleship follows salvation (Rom. 12:1-2; 6:11-13; Col. 3:1-3; II Cor. 5:14-15; cp. Lk. 14:25-27, 33). Also, "Lord Jesus" (Rom. 10:9) is a common designation of Christ (Acts 1:21; 7:59; 8:16; 9:29; 19:5, 10, 13, 17; 20:35; I Cor. 6:11; 11:23).

3. Still others say that one must do good works as well as believe in order to gain final salvation.

These hold that salvation is a two-party contract, which is entered by faith and maintained by good works. If one willfully sins and fails to repent, he breaks the contract and forfeits salvation. Only by faithfully doing good works can one hope to achieve the final salvation of his soul in glory.[10]

This view is a faith-plus-works kind of salvation, which is contrary to the teaching of Scripture (Eph. 2:8-9). Good works are an important evidence that one is saved, for they bear outward witness to one's inner salvational faith (Jas. 2:14-20). But they never are a condition of or make a contribution to salvation, initially or finally. The two-party contract (synergistic) concept of salvation is not, in my opinion, a biblical one as we shall see. People are saved initially and forever through faith in the Lord Jesus and His atoning work. No human works of any kind are involved.

• Household Salvation

Some have understood Acts 16:31 to teach that, if parents believe the

---

[9] See Kenneth S. Wuest, First Peter in the Greek New Testament (Grand Rapids: Wm. B. Eerdmans Publishing Company, 1942), p. 109.

[10] See R. Larry Shelton, " Initial Salvation" in A Contemporary Wesleyan Theology (Grand Rapids: Francis Asbury Press) I, pp. 497 f.

gospel, this guarantees that their children will be saved. The common biblical teaching is that each unsaved person must himself place his trust in Jesus for his salvation (Jn. 3:16). Paul also gave God's word to the household who obviously themselves believed (Acts 16:32). Humanly speaking, children who are raised in a Christian household are more likely to be saved because of the Christian teaching and example that they receive than those who do not have this privilege.

SCHOLASTIC OPINION ABOUT THIS APPLICATION

Throughout this age scholars have been divided about the extent man's will plays in the exercise of salvational faith. Some like Augustine and Calvin held a monergistic view — that the unsaved person, being totally depraved, does not effectively cooperate in his salvation by believing. They regarded salvation to be wholly God's work, including His gift of salvational faith. On the contrary, the Arminians hold a synergistic view — that salvation is a joint work of God and man. This means that assisted by divine grace, the sinner can effectively cooperate with God in his salvation. The Arminians (Wesleyan) believe that grace releases the human will from bondage to sin so that one with his freed will can accept or reject the Saviour. Thus, according to this view, man has the final say about his salvation; moreover, he is able to fail in his perseverance of faith and to lose salvation.

I prefer the concept of monergistic salvation. Although the sinner must believe the gospel to be saved, yet he cannot receive credit for this, for all of salvation (including salvational faith) is wholly God's work. In the application of salvation the sinner does cooperate with God in the sense that he must receive the Saviour (Acts 16:31). But this response does not contribute anything to salvation by completing it, adding to it, effecting it, or meriting it. The sinner does not even make the final decision to be saved. Left to himself, he would neither desire salvation nor respond to the gospel (Rom. 3:11; Jn. 6:44). When the elect person is effectually called of God, he freely responds by receiving the Saviour. But his decision to accept the Saviour is not one of absolute freedom or independent cooperation. It is a conscious, personal response that is prompted and carried out by the inward activity of God, below the level of human consciousness. The elect's obedience to the gospel is initiated and completed by the concurrent action of God in the impartation of salvational faith.

THE PRINCIPLE INVOLVED IN SALVATION

There are only two principles by which God deals with people — grace and law. Throughout human history God has saved people by His grace (Eph. 2:8-9; Ps. 103:10-12; Gen. 6:8; 15:5-6; Rom. 4:1-5, 16; 11:5-6). According to this principle God deals favorably with people in a way they do not deserve. The only other principle by which God can deal with people is law (sometimes called "works"). This principle requires Him to deal with people in a way they deserve. Since sinners deserve death and Hell, they cannot be delivered from this penalty by this principle (Rom. 3:20; 8:3; Gal. 2:16; 3:10-12; Heb. 7:18-19). The spiritual blindness of the unsaved is evident in that all their religions teach that people are saved by their works, the very principle which bars them from acceptance with God. No one can ever be saved from his sins apart from God's grace.

The principles of grace and law are opposite in their manner of operation (Rom. 11:6; 4:4-5). Observe the following contrasts between them:

The Principle of Grace or Gift	The Principle of Law or Debt
(This responds to faith: Eph. 2:8-9; Gal. 2:16; Rom. 1:17; 4:16.)	*(This responds to works, merit, or worth: Ex. 19:5; Gal. 3:12.)*
1. God deals favorably with people in a way they do not deserve.	1. God deals with people in a way they do deserve.
2. This is the only way sinners can be saved from sin.	2. This bars sinners from salvation.
3. This does not recognize human merit, works, or worth as causing, earning, or contributing to salvation.	3. This recognizes human merit, works, or worth as causing, earning, or contributing to salvation.
4. The human response of faith *allows* God to work graciously, as He promises.	4. The human response of meritorious works, which make a claim on God, *compels* Him to fulfill His obligation.
5. Salvation is wholly God's work; He receives all the credit and praise.	5. Salvation is a cooperative endeavor of God and man, thus both receive praise.
6. Being solely God's work, salvation by this method cannot fail.	6. Relying on man's doing his part, salvation by this method would never be absolutely certain.
7. This is the only principle which is effective in saving sinners.	7. This principle can never save sinners.

Observe that apart from salvation God deals with sinners according to their works, or as they deserve. The gracious principle of divine dealing only relates to salvation. God follows the meritorious principle of works when dealing with people in judgment. They justly receive what they deserve — the awful punishment of their sins.

Observe that the principle of grace also applies to our living the Christian life and to service. This means that we must look to the Lord by faith in His promises for the enablement and direction we need to please Him (I Cor. 15:10; II Cor. 1:12; Gal. 2:20). We cannot please Him in our own strength (Jn. 15:5; Phil. 4:13).

THE ASSURANCE OF SALVATION

It is God's desire that His people know that they are saved (I Jn. 5:13a). Satan uses unfounded doubt to cause us inner unrest and to hinder our spiritual development and service. On the other hand, we should not take our salvation for granted without valid evidence of its reality in our lives (II Cor. 13:5). The assurance of salvation rests upon two lines of evidence. These are the witness of the Holy Spirit and the signs of new life.

THE WITNESS OF THE HOLY SPIRIT (I Jn. 5:6b, 10a)

The Holy Spirit indwells every saved person (I Jn. 3:24; 4:13; Rom. 8:9). One of His ministries is to bear witness to the saved person's relationship to God (Rom. 8:16; Gal. 4:6). The agency that He uses is His Word (I Jn. 5:9-13a). Taking the promises and declarations of Scripture that relate to salvation, He impresses these upon our human spirit, the seat of our understanding, and makes them meaningful to us. These declarations certify that we have been born again and now have eternal life if we have exercised salvational faith in the Saviour (II Tim. 3:15; I Jn. 5:13a).

THE SIGNS OF NEW LIFE (I Jn. 5:11-12)

Upon our receiving the Saviour, we are made new creatures in Him, possessing a new kind of life and experiencing the renewal of our inner human nature (Jn. 1:12; II Cor. 5:17; Col. 3:9-10). It is impossible to have this new life and to experience this change in nature without manifesting this in daily life (cp. Acts 16:33-34). Although this manifestation may vary and at times be eclipsed by sin, nevertheless the signs of this new life will be expressed in them who have it. Let us consider some of these signs.

- **The Sign of Fellowship with God and His People (I Jn. 1:3)**

Being members of God's family, saved people have an affinity for Him and His people. They desire and enjoy their fellowship, for they share a common spiritual life and interests. On the contrary, unsaved people, being rebels, oppose God and hate His people (Jn. 3:20; 15:19; Rom. 3:11, 18).

- **The Sign of Obedience to God (I Jn. 2:3)**

Saved people have an innate desire to obey God, although at times they feel the rebellious disposition of the sin-principle within and yield to it (Phil. 2:13; Rom. 6:12-13). Our response to the command of the gospel is the beginning of a life of obedience to our new master, the Lord Jesus Christ (II Cor. 5:15). On the contrary, unsaved people never willingly obey God (Rom. 3:12; 8:7-8; Eph. 2:2).

- **The Sign of Doing Righteousness (I Jn. 2:29)**

To do righteousness is to do the will of God in His power (Heb. 13:21; Phil. 1:11). Having a renewed inner nature and the Holy Spirit, saved people have the inner desire and strength to do God's will as they yield themselves to Him

(Rom. 8:4; Phil. 2:13; 4:13). On the contrary, unsaved people never do what is right in God's sight because of their depravity and hostility (Rom. 3:10, 12; I Jn. 3:10).

- **The Sign of Love for God's People (I Jn. 3:14)**

This is Christ's love reproduced in our hearts by the Holy Spirit (Rom. 5:5; Gal. 5:22). It manifests itself by our desire and effort to minister to the well-being of others, even at personal cost (I Jn. 3:16-18). This manifestation of love is a mark of true discipleship (Jn. 13:34-35). On the contrary, unsaved people do not love God's people in this way (Jn. 15:17-19), nor do they love God, which requires their obedience (Jn. 3:20; 14:15).

- **The Sign of Confessing Christ (I Jn. 4:15)**

This confession is the agreement of our inner conviction and public declaration with what the New Testament says about Jesus. Saved people readily receive God's witness about His Son and willingly confess their belief in this truth (I Jn. 5:6, 9-10). On the other hand, nonelect people reject the witness that God has given of His Son (I Jn. 4:1-3).

In addition to these signs, there is the concern for our Lord's work in this world — the salvation of the lost and the growth of His people — which is an expression of His love (Rom. 10:1; I Thess. 1:8). Also, a true believer can no longer knowingly sin comfortably and derive real pleasure from it, for sinning is no longer compatible with his renewed, inner human nature (Col. 3:8-14).

While sin may temporarily conceal some of these signs, the sinning believer will incur God's chastisement if he should fail to judge himself. This, too, is a sign of his relationship to God (Heb. 12:6; I Cor. 11:28-32). A saved person can be assured of his relationship with God (see how John deals with this in his First Epistle). If one is not certain of his salvation, following Romans 10:10 he should make a definite decision to trust the Lord Jesus and His atoning work for his salvation and express this trust to God by prayer. Having definitely trusted the Saviour, he then can be assured of his salvation by the promises of Scripture such as Romans 10:13 and John 1:12.

THE PERMANENCE OF SALVATION

Can one who is truly saved involuntarily or voluntarily lose his salvation? I believe that it is the teaching of the Scriptures that the saved person is forever safely kept, regardless of what he may do or experience. Let us look at this permanence as it relates to God and to ourselves.

AS IT RELATES TO GOD

Consider the following propositions:

- **God wills to keep His people.**

This is the will of the Father (Jn. 6:39-40) and of the Son (Jn. 17:11-12, 24), whose petitions have never been denied by the Father. Jesus declared that He had so kept His apostles that none was lost, except Judas, the son of perdition. The Scriptures show that the betrayer was never saved (Jn. 6:70-71; 13:10-11).

- **God is able to keep His people.**

Sometimes people are not able to carry out their purpose, but this is not a problem to the omnipotent God. He is able to fulfill His purpose for us and to finish His work (II Tim. 1:12; Jude 24; Jn. 10:28-29; Phil. 1:6). There is no power or creature that is able to hinder Him or cause Him to fail (Isa. 46:10). Since salvation is wholly His gracious work from start to finish, human failure does not render void the New Covenant or jeopardize the salvational enterprise (cp. Rom. 3:3-4; Jer. 31:31-37).

- **God is free to keep His people.**

Since the judicial debt of all our sins — past, present, future — has been paid by our Lord's atoning work, we who are saved can never again incur divine condemnation by sinning (Rom. 8:1a, 32-34). Any condemnation which may be brought against us now falls on our substitute, Jesus, who perfectly and fully paid our debt. Being justified by God and reconciled to Him, we are forever saved by Jesus' ongoing life (Rom. 5:9-10) and His intercession for us (8:31-34; Heb. 7:25).

- **God has provided for the safekeeping of His people.**

Their safekeeping is secured by the following provisions:

1. *Christ's Advocacy for Us (I Jn. 2:1)*

Jesus, our righteous advocate, pleads our case before the Father when we are accused by Satan of some sin (Rev. 12:10). Our Lord neither begs the Father to be lenient with us nor makes excuse for us. Instead, He presents the value of His atoning death as grounds for Satan's accusation being thrown out of court (Rom. 8:31-34). Our Lord's advocacy does not make it easier for us to sin; indeed, it is revealed so that we do not sin (I Jn. 2:1). It is not easy to sin when we know that this is an open matter in Heaven and requires this special ministry of Jesus our Lord.

2. *Christ's Intercession for Us (Heb. 7:25)*

While the Lord's intercession includes His advocacy and praying for us, it is more than this. As our great high priest, He is our official representative before the Father, who looks after all that concerns our well-being while we are here on earth (Heb. 4:14-16; Jn. 17:9-24; Lk. 22:31-32). Because of this, He is able to keep us to the very end.

3. *The Father's Corrective Dealings with Us (I Cor. 11:31-32)*

God faithfully deals with His sinning people who fail to heed the warnings and appeals of His Word (Rev. 3:19). This corrective chastisement (there are also other purposes for divine chastisement, such as instruction, maturation, productivity, and sanctification) indicates that we are God's children and that we shall not be condemned with the world (Heb. 12:6; I Cor. 11:32). To be condemned with the world would be to share the guilt and penalty of their sins. But this is impossible for us who are saved, for we are covered by the atoning work of the Lord Jesus (Rom. 8:31-34). God does not chasten them who are not His people. To them He deals out retribution (judgment).

4. *The Holy Spirit's Presence as a Seal (Eph. 4:30)*

God the Holy Spirit is the divine seal that preserves us until the completion of our salvation—the redemption of our body from inherent corruption, the sin-principle, and mortality, or in the case of dead believers corruptibility (Rom. 8:23, 10-11). Ordinarily, any process is vulnerable until it is completed. But in this case, the Holy Spirit keeps us secure until God's redemptive work is finished in us.

- **God promises to keep His people.**

God's offer of eternal life through the gospel is based on the promises of the New Covenant, which Jesus mediated by His death and ratified by His resurrection (cp. Heb. 8:6-12; Jer. 31:31-34; Lk. 22:20). Being gracious in character, this covenant is everlasting (Jer. 31:35-37; Heb. 13:20; Rom. 4:25). Unlike the Covenant of the Mosaic Law which Israel broke by their disobedience, the New Covenant cannot be annulled by human failure. By this covenant God promises its recipients everlasting life (cp. Jn. 3:15-16; 10:28-29).

AS IT RELATES TO OURSELVES

The permanence of salvation not only rests upon God but also upon the believer's continuance or perseverance in salvational faith (I Pet. 1:5). However, this continuance of salvational faith is not solely a human achievement. Unlike practical faith, salvational faith is sustained by the prayers of Christ (Lk. 22:31-32; Heb. 7:25). While he may not always exercise practical faith, the believer is never without salvational faith. It is noteworthy that the Lord never accused His disciples of having no faith (Mt. 6:30; 8:26; 14:31; 16:8), except on one occasion when he was speaking about practical faith (Mk. 4:40).

This truth distinguishes between those who profess to be saved and those who are really saved. The professor will not continue in salvational faith; the possessor will persevere until the final aspect of his salvation (Mt. 24:13). This principle is confirmed by several passages, which at first glance seem to teach the possibility of losing salvation. From Colossians 1:21-23 the inference is occasionally drawn, "If we do not continue in the faith, we shall be lost." Actually, we have not been saved if we do not continue in the faith. The past fact of our being reconciled to God (vs. 21, aorist tense) will be manifest by our continuing in the faith. Again, from Hebrews 3:6 the inference is sometimes drawn, "If we do not hold fast, then we shall cease to be Christ's house and be lost." But the verse does not say this. It says that if there is no perseverance of faith in the future, we are not now Christ's house. Our failure to meet the future condition is due to our not experiencing the past conclusion (cp. Heb. 3:14).

OBJECTIONS

- **"This doctrine grants believers a license to do what they please while guaranteeing their perpetual salvation."**

While believers can do as they please, this doctrine does not give them permission to sin. It is God's will that we not sin (I Jn. 2:1). God has counterbalanced this doctrine with those of divine chastisement (I Cor. 11:30-32) and unprofitable reward (II Cor. 5:10; I Cor. 3:15; Col. 3:25). We are accountable to God the Father and Jesus our master for our conduct. Anyone who sins with insensitivity and abandon may never have been saved (II Cor. 13:5; cp. Phil. 2:13; I Jn. 3:8-9).

- **"Some passages indicate that we can lose salvation."**

John 15:2, 6 — In this allegory the Lord is speaking, not about salvation but of the relation that His people must have with Him to be spiritually fruitful. Verse two may refer to premature physical death due to divine chastisement (I Cor. 11:30; Prov. 15:10; Heb. 12:9). Verse six may concern the believer's works being appraised by the Lord and the unacceptable ones being burned (I Cor. 3:15; cp. Jn. 15:16).

Hebrews 6:4-12 — The writer seems to distinguish between the readers who are saved (vss. 9-12) and others who are at the threshold of salvation and who are experiencing the convicting work of the Holy Spirit (vss. 4-8). He warns the latter against rejecting Christ and returning to Judaism.

I John 3:6-10 — The present tense of the verbs points to the general character of life that unsaved people have rather than to particular acts of sin. Having been set free from bondage to the sin-principle (Rom. 6:1, 6-7), the believer no longer continually sins as he once did when lost. He now commits only acts of sin (I Jn. 2:1). It is impossible for the saved person to be in character what he was in his unsaved state, for he is a new creature in Christ (II Cor. 5:17), possesses God's Seed (I Jn. 3:9, probably Jesus, his life), and has a renewed inner nature (Col. 3:9-10; Eph. 4:22-24, we "did put off" the old man and we "did put on" the new man at salvation). While the believer is capable of sinning and does, this is not in accord with his regenerated state (Col. 3:1-17). He no longer sins all the time as unsaved people do.

SOME OBSERVATIONS

- Like salvation there is a concurrence of God's sovereign action and the believer's duty to persevere in salvational faith for his safekeeping (I Pet. 1:5).

- This perseverance of faith serves as proof that one is saved. Perseverance indicates the reality of a person's salvation; nonperseverance indicates that he was never saved. We should never take salvation for granted. Paul exhorts his readers to examine themselves to see if they be in the faith (II Cor. 13:5). The faith of too many rests upon the words of men or some physical response to a gospel invitation, rather than on God's Word (cp. I Cor. 2:1-5).

- Again, salvational faith should be distinguished from that trust which we are to exercise in the Lord for matters of daily life (Prov. 3:5-6; Mt. 17:19-20; Mk. 11:22; I Tim. 6:17). Because it is God's gift and is supported by Christ's intercession, salvational faith is always consistent, but practical faith varies in its strength and expression.

THE DIVINE GOALS OF SALVATION

Whatever God's objectives for saving the elect may be, they seem to include His creating a new human race and His bringing glory to Himself.

TO CREATE A NEW HUMAN RACE

The Holy Spirit is doing this by His ministries of regeneration (Jn. 3:6; Tit. 3:5) and baptism into Christ (II Cor. 5:17; Eph. 2:10; Gal. 3:27). This creative work is not the creation of new personhood but rather the renewal of persons who formerly were members of Adam's race. It involves the recreation of human nature, not the replacement of its parts (Eph. 4:22-24; I Pet. 1:22).

God was pleased to create Adam and Eve in His image with mutable holiness and righteousness. But their sin brought them and their posterity total ruin and divine condemnation (Rom. 5:12-19; I Cor. 15:22). Today, God is creating a new human race in Christ with elect members of the old race. The members of this new race are identified as new creatures (II Cor. 5:17). In addition to possessing the image of God (personhood), this new race bears in their human nature Jesus' image (Col. 3:10; Rom. 8:29; I Jn. 3:2; II Cor. 3:18), for He is the head and pattern of the new humanity (I Cor. 15:22, 45-49; Eph. 4:15). With personhood and our inner human nature (soul and spirit) saved, this renewal will be completed when our body is changed at the Lord's return (I Cor. 15:50-53; Phil. 3:20-21).

TO BRING GLORY TO GOD

God is glorified by some manifestation of Himself in creation (Ps. 19:1). He will be glorified forever by the new humanity, for saved humans will manifest the exceeding riches of His grace and mercy, which He exercised in their salvation (Eph. 1:12; 2:4-7). These glorious divine qualities could only be expressed toward undeserving people who were sinners (I Tim. 1:12-17). God's saving the elect of humanity displays His grace and wisdom to the holy angels (I Pet. 1:10-12; Eph. 3:10), who will give Him endless praise for redeeming people from every nation (Rev. 5:8-12, ASV). We who are saved should seek now to glorify God by our lives in all that we do (I Cor. 10:31). We exist for this purpose.

THE COMPONENTS OF SALVATION

The word "salvation" is a blanket term for all that occurs to a person at the moment that he receives Jesus as his Saviour. The components of salvation are the various parts or aspects of salvation that the elect receive when they believe the gospel. The ones that we shall study are only part of the blessings that comprise salvation (Eph. 1:3; 2:7). The more we understand these blessings, the more meaningful salvation will be to us and the more cause we shall have to rejoice in them and to be grateful for what God has done.

REGENERATION

This word is used in Titus 3:5, and the truth is taught in John 3:3-7 and I Peter 1:3, 23.

- **Its Definition**

Regeneration is the act of God whereby He cleanses the gospel believer, renews the immaterial part of his human nature, and imparts to him spiritual life.

Observe that the sinner must be prepared for the reception of eternal life (cp. Lk. 5:38). This preparation involves his cleansing from the defilement of sin and the renewal of his morally ruined soul and spirit (Tit. 3:5). This renewal of soul and spirit gives him the capacity to experience and to express this new life intellectually, emotionally, and volitionally.

- **Its Timing**

Calvinistic and Lutheran theologians regard regeneration as including the presalvational work of God in the sinner's heart as well as its completion in conversion. I prefer the view that regeneration consists of the impartation of spiritual life following salvational faith in Christ (Jn. 1:12-13; 3:16; 6:53). Though totally depraved, the sinner does not have to be regenerated to believe the gospel since salvational faith is God's gift and has within itself the dynamic to cause people to believe (II Pet. 1:1) (Acts 3:16). Any inclination of the heart toward God is a part of the Holy Spirit's presalvational work in drawing people to God (Jn. 6:44).

- **Its Means**

Regeneration is wrought by the Holy Spirit (Jn. 3:5-8; Tit. 3:5) through the agency of God's Word (I Pet. 1:23; Rom. 10:17), following salvational faith in Jesus (Jn. 1:12). In evangelism it is important for us to present the gospel as it is given in the Scriptures and to depend upon the Holy Spirit to work according to the divine purpose. We must refrain from attempting to do the

Holy Spirit's work when making gospel appeals. The Arminian view which sees the sinner as having a free will and as making the final choice in salvation leads one to use coercion in his evangelistic appeals. With whatever means it takes, it compels people to receive Christ. Needless to say, such means is counterproductive. We must leave it to the Holy Spirit to do that work which only He can do.

- **Its Necessity**

The need of the unsaved for regeneration is indicated by their being spiritually dead and members of Satan's kingdom.

1. *They are spiritually dead.*

Being spiritually dead, the unsaved exist in a state of alienation from God (Eph. 2:1; 4:18) and are a spiritual ruin (Lk. 19:10, "lost"; I Cor. 1:18, "perish"; Rom. 3:12). This means that they are so disorganized by sin that they are naturally unresponsive to God and divine things and are responsive only to sin and the world (Eph. 2:1-3).

2. *They are members of Satan's kingdom.*

Unsaved people have Satan's moral character (Jn. 8:44; Eph. 2:2) and are under his authority (I Jn. 5:19; Acts 26:18). However religious they may be, they are not members of the Lord's kingdom (Mt. 7:21-23).

- **Its Basis (I Jn. 4:9; Jn. 3:14-15)**

In his unsaved state the sinner cannot impart to himself spiritual life or admit himself to God's kingdom. But by His atoning provisionally for the sins of the world (I Jn. 2:2), Jesus made it possible for God to forgive gospel believers of their sins, which barred them from His kingdom, and to give them eternal life, which is required for His kingdom (Jn. 3:5-6).

- **Its Blessings**

By divine regeneration the believer receives a new kind of life and is brought into a new relation with God.

1. *HE RECEIVES A NEW LIFE.*

Regeneration renews our immaterial human nature (Tit. 3:5) by delivering it from inherent corruption (I Pet. 1:22), recreating it in righteousness and holiness (Col. 3:10; Eph. 4:24), and imparting to it spiritual life, which makes us responsive to God (Rom. 8:10; Ps. 63:1).

In contrast to physical life, this new life is called "spiritual life" or "eternal life." This eternal life is fully expressed in the Lord Jesus (Jn. 14:6; I Jn. 5:12; Col. 3:4) and is communicated to the believer by means of the Holy Spirit (Rom. 8:2). Some features that this new life conveys to us who are saved are a new power (Gal. 5:25; Jn. 14:16), a new rule of conduct (Gal. 6:2, the New Testament), a new knowledge (I Cor. 2:9-12), a new association (I Jn. 1:3; I Cor. 1:9), a new life purpose (Mt. 6:33; I Cor. 10:31), a new resource (Heb. 13:5-6; Phil. 4:13), a new desire and activity (Phil. 2:13), a new character (Gal.

5:22-23), a new interest (Col. 3:1), a new direction (Eph. 5:17), a new citizenship (Phil. 3:20; Col. 1:13), a new expectation (Tit. 2:13), and a new destination (Jn. 14:2-3). Thus, having eternal life is more than living forever. It is to have a new kind of life, with its many features, which is made real to us by the Holy Spirit as we walk in the Lord's fellowship (I Jn. 1:7; Jn. 8:12).

2. HE IS BROUGHT INTO A NEW RELATION WITH GOD.

Jesus speaks about eternal life as springing from a new, right relation with God whereby we know Him in a personal way (Jn. 17:3). Two aspects of this relation follow:

a. *He is a member of God's family.*

By the new birth a person becomes a child of God (Jn. 1:11-13), and God the Father becomes his heavenly Father (Jn. 20:17; II Thess. 2:16; Mt. 6:8-9), but this does not mean that we become God. To partake of the divine nature (II Pet. 1:4) is not to partake of the divine essence in a way that it becomes a part of our essential nature. It may mean that our renewed human nature is the product of God's creative work (Eph. 2:10) or that we received God's Seed (I Jn. 3:9), which may be the Lord Jesus Christ, our eternal life (Jn. 14:6; I Jn. 5:12), or that we received God into our being so that our body is His temple (I Cor. 6:19; Col. 1:27; Jn. 14:23). God is our Father in the sense that He has given to us this new life in Christ; He did not impart to us His own inherent, self-existent life.

Some blessings which spring from this relationship follow:

(1) We Know God (Jn. 17:3).

Our inward renewal and our new life in Christ gave to us who are saved the capacity and the opportunity to know God in a personal way. This new life, which is capable of growth (II Pet. 3:18), is cultivated by our study of the Word and by His dealings with us (II Tim. 3:16-17; Heb. 12:5-11; cp. Job 42:5).

(2) We Have Fellowship with God (I Jn. 1:3, 7).

This is the normal parent-child relationship. When we consider all that this relationship with God includes, we find it to be the highest experience in the Christian life. It includes our sharing with Him our life and all that it contains, our drawing from Him all that we need, our talking to Him in prayer and our listening to Him as we read His Word, our trusting Him and His promises in every situation, our participating with Him in His work on earth, and our living in complete agreement with His revealed will. To fellowship with God, we must walk where He is — in the light given by His Word (I Jn. 1:5-7; Ps. 119:105).

(3) We are Subject to His Discipline (Heb. 12:5-7).

Our heavenly Father deals with us, not only to correct us (I Cor. 11:32), but also to lead us to submit to His authority (Heb. 12:9), to produce in us His holiness (vs. 10), and to make us more spiritually productive (vs. 11; cp. Jn. 15:2). He does this with infinite wisdom and love. Therefore, we should not faint because of His dealings or ignore them (Heb. 12:5), but we should endure them patiently (vs. 7) in order to receive the benefit He has for us.

(4) We are the Objects of His Loving Care (Mt. 6:31-33; 10:29-31).

Our heavenly Father lovingly cares for us every moment we are on earth. Although powerful forces are arrayed against us, a multitude of details engage our attention and tax our human resources, and much else escapes our notice, yet our God is ever aware of our needs and ministers to us continually. He has provided for all that we need for our pilgrimage through this world and for our achieving all that He desires for us (II Pet. 1:1-4). We must be careful, however, not to think of Him as our servant, who responds to our every whim (Jas. 4:3). He is our God, whom we worship and serve forever. As we delight ourself in Him, He satisfies our heart's desires (Ps. 37:4).

(5) We are His Heirs (Rom. 8:17).

In the Scriptures an inheritance is something that is given for a possession (cp. Ezek. 44:28, Lk. 12:13, 15:12). Today the Lord Jesus Christ is our inheritance (Eph. 1:11). In Him we have wisdom, righteousness, sanctification, redemption (I Cor. 1:30), peace (Eph. 2:14), grace (II Cor. 12:9), life (Col. 3:4), help (Heb. 13:5-6), satisfaction (Jn. 6:35), and every spiritual blessing (Eph. 1:3). In the future we shall share His earthly inheritance when He returns to take possession of it (Rom. 8:17; Heb. 1:2; Mt. 11:27; Ps. 2:8-9). Meanwhile, another portion of this future inheritance is reserved for us in Heaven. This seems to consist of the untold blessings that God has prepared for His people (I Pet. 1:4-5; Heb. 10:34; Jn. 14:1-3). The profusion of this future inheritance is indicated by the present, blessed ministries of the Holy Spirit, which represent only the first installment of that which awaits us (Eph. 1:14).

b. He is a citizen of God's kingdom.

As a newborn person automatically becomes a citizen of the country to which his parents belong, so likewise the child of God is a subject or citizen of God's kingdom by being born into God's family. The new birth is the only means by which sinners can enter this kingdom (Jn. 3:2-7).

While "the kingdom of God" has various meanings in the Scriptures,[11] here I believe it is the realm where God's authority is acknowledged and His grace prevails. Its citizenship extends to everyone in Heaven and on earth who is rightly related to God and who obeys Him. Presently, this kingdom, which is also Christ's kingdom (Col. 1:13), is located in Heaven (Phil. 3:20; II Tim. 4:18) as a spiritual, invisible, non-political entity. When Jesus returns to earth, His kingdom will become visible, geographical, political, and earthly.

As subjects of God's kingdom, we enjoy many blessings. Among these, we have unrestricted access to our Sovereign (Eph. 2:18; I Thess. 5:17); we enjoy His loving direction and care (Prov. 3:5-6; I Pet. 5:7); and we anticipate the

---

[11] See Appendix R.

benefits of His coming earthly rule, both during the millennium (Isa. 11:1-9) and throughout eternity (II Pet. 1:11; I Cor. 15:24-28). Also, we have the duty of submitting to His authority in everything (II Cor. 5:14-15; Mt. 7:24-25). Furthermore, as His ambassadors, we have the privilege of representing the Lord to the world and proclaiming His message of reconciliation (II Cor. 5:18-20).

ADOPTION (Rom. 8:15, 23; Gal. 4:5; Eph. 1:5)

• Its Definition

Adoption (Gk. *huiothesia*) means "placing as a son." In Bible usage it is the two-fold action of God whereby He now gives the gospel believer the position of adult-son in His family and will in the future, with the redemption of his body, make his human nature suitable for this position. Observe that we do not enter God's family by means of adoption; we enter by the new birth (Jn. 1:12-13, "sons" should read "children").

• Its Necessity

Our need for adoption is seen in our position in God's family upon the new birth as newborn children and in the present condition of our body. Without adoption we would still have the status of children who require strict, detailed discipline and who are vulnerable to the hurtful forces ("elements of the world") that would take advantage of our minority (Gal. 4:1-7). Also, without adoption our body would remain under the power of inherent corruption (Rom. 8:10). Rather than remaining as children in God's family, adoption gives us the position of adult-sons. Also, its future aspect assures us of that deliverance and change which will make us physically suitable to this position of adult-sons.

• Its Basis

The basis of adoption is redemption, by which the Lord Jesus has delivered us who are saved from these world forces (like legal ordinances, Rom. 7:1-6) and will deliver our body from its corruption (Gal. 4:5; Rom. 8:23).

• Its Blessings

1. In the Present

The present blessing of adoption concerns our position. By adoption we who are saved have been given the privileges and duties of adult-sons, regardless of our spiritual age or rate of spiritual growth. This means that all believers have the same law of Christ (given in the New Testament), which expresses His will for their lives. Moreover, since adoption eliminates our spiritual childhood and adolescence, we are not restricted in the use of our privileges or in fulfilling our duties. Within the sphere of their understanding of spiritual truth, all believers have the same obligations to fulfill as well as the same rights and privileges to enjoy. Some of the privileges of this position are immediate access to God (Eph. 2:18; Heb. 4:16), partnership with the Father and Christ in the building of the church (I Cor. 3:9; Jn. 15:1-5), and the liberty of free decision and action relating to matters that are not specifically dealt with in the Scriptures (Rom. 14:1-8).

The indwelling Holy Spirit is called "the Spirit of adoption" (Gal. 4:6; Rom. 8:15). By His activity in our life and through the Scriptures, we are made aware of our position in God's family, instinctively address God as our Father, make use of our spiritual privileges and rights, and fulfill our duties. Without His enablement, the privileges and duties of adult-sonship would be beyond our reach.

2. In the Future

In addition to having the position of adoption, we who are saved will also have a body that is suited to adult-sonship. This anticipates the time when we shall experience the completion of salvation with the redemption of our body from corruption, sin, and death (Rom. 8:23). Our adoption assures us that, being made like Jesus' glorified humanity, we shall be forever physically prepared for the full experience of all that adult-sonship involves (I Jn. 3:2; I Cor. 15:50-57).

In spite of our position as adult-sons, our present experience on earth is like that of children because of our unsaved bodies. Due to the great restrictions that our unredeemed bodies place on us, we now need God's care and supervision while we are here in this world. However, with the redemptive change of our bodies, this restriction will be lifted and we shall fully experience all that God has for us as sons (see Appendix V).

JUSTIFICATION (Rom. 3:24; 5:1, 9, 18; 8:30; I Cor. 6:11)

• Its Definition

Justification is the act of God whereby He acquits the gospel believer of the divine verdict of condemnation and declares him to be righteous.

• Its Necessity

The unsaved person's need for justification is seen in his condemnation by God and his lack of acceptable righteousness.

1. The unsaved person stands condemned before God (Jn. 3:18)

To be condemned is to be found guilty of a crime and sentenced to punishment. God has already found unsaved people guilty of original sin (Rom. 5:16, 18) and actual sins (Rom. 3:9-19) and has passed sentence on them (Jn. 3:16, 18, 36; Mt. 7:13-14). In the case of them who hear the gospel, this condemnation is increased if they should refuse to receive the Saviour (Jn. 3:18).

2. The unsaved person is without acceptable righteousness (Rom. 3:10).

Righteousness means the condition of being right in God's sight or the act of doing right. Unsaved people fall short of the righteousness that God requires of His personal creatures (Rom. 3:23). In their rebellion against Him, they substitute their own ethical standard and conduct for what He requires of them. But this self-righteousness is not acceptable to Him (Isa. 64:6). His Word declares that no one is righteous without His gift of righteousness (Rom. 3:10; I Cor. 1:30).

- **Its Basis**

We were graciously justified by Jesus' blood, that is, by His atoning work (Rom. 5:9). In our unsaved state we could neither deliver ourselves from divine condemnation nor attain the righteousness that God required of us. But in His gracious love, God provided a way whereby He could be just (or righteous) and still justify sinners (Rom. 3:24-26). By His atoning work, the Lord Jesus dealt with our sins and paid their awful debt (Rom. 5:8; I Pet. 2:24; Heb. 9:26). Upon our faith in His atoning work, we were acquitted of condemnation and declared to be righteous (Rom. 5:16-17). While His death atoned for our sins, the Lord's resurrection made this work for our justification effective (Rom. 4:25). Like all other aspects of salvation, justification is a gracious work (Tit. 3:7).

- **Its Blessings**

Justification brings the following blessings to us who are saved:

1. *We are forever acquitted of the sentence of condemnation.*

(Rom. 8:1, 33-34). We shall never again come under God's judicial wrath (Rom. 5:9; cp. I Thess. 1:10; 5:9), for we have peace with God (Rom. 8:1). Having judicially forgiven us, He no longer sees us guilty of any sin (Col. 2:13).

2. *We are declared righteous in God's sight.*

This is more than a pardon, which implies that one is still guilty of a crime, though exempted from its punishment. God has declared us who are saved to be righteous, for He actually regards us to be righteous. He sees us in His Son who is our righteousness (I Cor. 1:30). This position grants us two divine applications of Jesus' human righteousness, which consists of His perfect obedience to the Father, even unto death (Rom. 5:19; Phil. 2:8; Jn. 8:29).

One, God has made us righteous in Christ (II Cor. 5:21; cp. Rom. 5:19). This constitutional righteousness is a quality of our renewed inner nature (Eph. 4:24; cp. I Pet. 1:22; Acts 15:9). Justification consists not only of the divine declaration that one is righteous but also the divine work that makes the gospel believer righteous.[12]

Two, God has given us His righteousness (Rom. 3:22; Phil. 3:9). This righteousness was imputed to us (Rom. 4:1-4, 20-24), that is, it was credited to

---

[12] See John Murray, *The Epistle to the Romans* (Grand Rapids: Wm. B. Eerdmans Publishing Co., 1959), I, 349 f. (Appendix A).

our account in the place of our sins.[13]

Thus, in justifying us, God not only made us righteous but also gave to us true righteousness, with the result that in His sight we are forever righteous in Christ. How blessed is this truth!

3. *We are assured of future glorification and inheritance.*

(Rom. 8:30; Tit. 3:7). Justification guarantees the permanence of our salvation (Rom. 8:31-34). In turn, it assures us of the completion of our salvation experience with the redemption of our body (vss. 23, 30) and our participation in Christ's glory (Jn. 17:22; Col. 3:4; Rom. 8:18) as well as the reception of our inheritance (I Pet. 1:3-4).

4. *We are able to do righteousness (I Jn. 2:29; 3:7).*

Being righteous (not sinless), we are now able to do what is right in God's sight by the power of Christ through the Holy Spirit (Phil. 1:11; 4:13; Rom. 14:17). This requires our abiding in the Lord and obeying His Word, which allows Him to express His righteousness through our lives (Jn. 15:4-5; II Tim. 3:16).

REDEMPTION (Rom. 3:24; I Cor. 1:30; Eph. 1:7; Heb. 9:12)

• Its Definition

Redemption is the act of God whereby on the basis of ransom payment He releases the gospel believer from bondage to his spiritual masters and from the penalty of his sins and brings him into bondage to Christ, his benefactor.

• Its Necessity

The need of the unsaved for redemption is manifest by their being in bondage to their spiritual masters and by their being in debt to God for their sins.

1. *Their bondage to their spiritual masters*

Unsaved people are in bondage to sin, Satan, the world-system, and law. They are slaves of the sin-principle, which dominates their total being (Eph. 2:3), and of actual, habitual sins (Jn. 8:34). Also, they are slaves of Satan, for they live under his authority (Acts 26:18; Col. 1:13) and are continually subject to his influence upon their lives (Eph. 2:2). Again, they are in bondage to the world-system of which they are a part (Jn. 15:19). Paul states that the lost walk "according to the course of this world (age)" (Eph. 2:2) — that particular time during which they live under the domination of the world's philosophy, fads, moods, and works, all of which are evil in God's sight (Jn. 7:7). Finally, they are slaves of the religious laws and ethical principles that are part of their culture (Acts 15:10; Rom. 2:14-15; Gal. 4:1-10).

---

[13] Imputation is God's reckoning or putting something to a person's account (cp. Phile. 18). The Scriptures teach the imputation of Adam's first sin to the whole race (Rom. 5:12-19), the imputation of humanity's sins to Christ (II Cor. 5:19, 21), and the imputation of Jesus' righteousness to believers (Rom. 4:1-8, 20-24).

2. Their indebtedness to God for their sins

Unsaved people are guilty before God of original sin (Rom. 5:16, 18) and of their actual sins (Rom. 3:9-19). The divine penalty for sin is everlasting punishment in Hell (Rev. 20:12-15; Mt. 25:46). This debt is such that no sinner can ever discharge himself from this obligation by his merit or works and secure for himself everlasting life (Mt. 25:41; Jn. 3:36).

• Its Basis

Redemption is essentially concerned with a release that is secured by the payment of a ransom. In ancient times people were often released from slavery or prison by ransom payment (Ex. 6:6; Ps. 107:2). A person who, because of poverty, sold himself to another, could redeem himself or could be redeemed by a relative (Lev. 25:47-49).

God's requirements for the kinsman (relative) redeemer were these: He must be a relative of the person needing redemption (Lev. 25:47-49; cp. Ruth 3:12-13); he must be able and willing to redeem (cp. Ruth 4:4-6); and, obviously, he must be personally free of the calamity that befell his unfortunate relative. (How can an indebted person, who cannot meet his own obligation, redeem another?) In meeting these requirements, God the Son became identified with mankind by His incarnation (Heb. 2:9, 14, 16). He was able and willing to give His life as a ransom to pay (provisionally) the debt of humanity's sins (Jn. 10:11, 18; Mt. 20:28). Also, He was personally free of sin and its debt (I Pet. 2:22; II Cor. 5:21; I Jn. 3:3, 5; cp. Acts 2:24).

In his unsaved state man could not deliver himself from this bondage and debt. But by His death and atoning work, the Lord Jesus confirmed the divine sentence against humanity's spiritual masters (Rom. 8:3; Jn. 12:31; 16:11) and provisionally paid the awful debt of man's sins (Rom. 5:8; 6:23; Mt. 20:28). On the basis of this atoning work, God is now able to deliver all who believe the gospel from this bondage and indebtedness forever (Eph. 1:7; Heb. 9:12).

• Its Blessings

Upon trusting the Lord Jesus as our Saviour, we received the following redemptive blessings:

1. We were released from the judicial debt of our sins.

Upon the basis of our Lord's atoning work and resurrection, God canceled the judicial debt of all our sins (both original and actual), past, present, and future (Eph. 1:7; Col. 2:13; Rev. 1:5). Never again will we incur divine condemnation, spiritual death, and the awful penalty of everlasting separation from God in Hell (Jn. 5:24; Rom. 8:1a). We have been justified by the highest Court — by God Himself (Rom. 8:33).

2. We were released from bondage to evil spiritual masters.

Contrary to what we may experience, the Scriptures teach that we have been set free from the domination of the sin-principle (Rom. 6:7, 18), Satan's authority (Acts 26:18; Col. 1:13), and the world-system of lost mankind (Jn. 15:19), with its ethical and religious regulations (Rom. 7:1-16; Gal. 3:13; 4:3-5; Col. 2:8-23). Participating in Jesus' death, we were delivered from bondage to these former masters by our dying to them (Rom. 6:2-3; Gal. 6:14). Because of this, we do not have to sin, to yield to Satan's temptations, to conform to the world's evil ideas, or to obey its laws which clearly conflict with God's will for us. Redemption has delivered us from these dominating forces.

3. Our immaterial nature was delivered from hereditary corruption.

As we have observed elsewhere, we not only were delivered from the guilt of original sin but also its impact upon the immaterial part of our human nature. Though still susceptible to the lusts of the sin-principle, the soul and spirit are no longer inherently corrupted and inclined toward sin. They have been released from inherent corruption and sin's domination (Acts 15:9; Tit. 2:14); also being renewed, they are the instruments of righteousness (I Pet. 1:9, 22; Rom. 6:13; 8:10; Eph. 4:24, this should read "did put on"). While our body is still inherently corrupt, it too can be an instrument of righteousness as we yield it to God.

4. We were released for holy purposes.

Our redemption is the basis of our Christian liberty (Jn. 8:36). We have been set free from bondage to our former spiritual masters in order that we might serve God (I Pet. 2:16), express His love to others (Gal. 5:13), and grow in Christlikeness (II Cor. 3:17-18). This freedom is not exemption from external authority, but it is the liberty to give our human nature to those holy purposes for which God has set us free. We also can misuse this liberty by giving ourself to sin for its evil expressions (Rom. 13:14). At no time do we lose this liberty of self-surrender to the principle, God or sin, to which we yield. We continue to have the ability of self-surrender regardless of the principle that dominates our life. Thus when we are walking in sin, we can at any time yield ourself to God and in His strength do His will.

We experience this freedom when we yield ourself to the limitations that are imposed upon us by the Scriptures (I Cor. 9:21; Jas. 1:23-25) and by the Holy Spirit (II Cor. 3:17; Rom. 8:14; Gal. 5:16). As we yield to their direction, we allow the Lord to express Himself in and through our life by holy character and good works (Phil. 1:11, 21; Gal. 2:20; Jn. 15:4-5). We temporarily come under the domination of our former evil masters when we give in to their demands or fail to conform to these divine limitations. Being completely dominated by these evil forces, unsaved people do not have this freedom to choose what principle will govern their lives.

Although we often yield to the demands of our former evil masters, this is not right, for they no longer have lawful claim to us. Purchased by His blood, we are now Christ's property (I Cor. 6:19-20; Mt. 20:28). It is our duty and privilege to yield ourself constantly to His authority, as we formerly did to sin's demands (II Cor. 5:14-15). When we do, we exercise our freedom in the right way and with holy results.

RECONCILIATION (Col. 1:20-21; Rom. 5:10-11, "atonement")

- ### Its Definition

Reconciliation is the act of God whereby He does away with the hostility between the gospel believer and Himself and establishes peace.

- ### Its Necessity

The unsaved person's need for reconciliation is manifest by the state of hostility that exists between God and him (Rom. 5:10; Col. 1:21).

1. *The sinner is rebellious toward God.*

Rejecting God's claim to him, the sinner violates the Creator's laws and is indifferent toward the injury that these offenses bring (Rom. 3:10-11, 18; 1:18). Moreover, he hates the searching, penetrating light of divine revelation that is brought to bear on him. This exposes his sinfulness (Jn. 3:19-20) and reminds him of his accountability (Mt. 12:36-37).

2. *God is angry toward the sinner.*

God's holy nature strongly reacts to the unsaved person to the extent that He hates him (Ps. 5:5; 11:5; Hos. 9:15; Mal. 1:3) and his sins (Prov. 6:16-19) and that He is angry with him (Rom. 1:18; Jn. 3:36). This hatred and anger do not lead God to act irrationally, as they do man, but they move Him to punish man for his sinfulness (Rom. 2:1-11). That God should choose to love sinners and to provide salvation through His Son is an expression of pure grace (I Jn. 4:10; 2:2).

- ### Its Basis

In his unsaved state the sinner has neither the desire nor the means to remove the hostility that exists between God and him. Only God could do this by dealing with the cause of this hostility (humanity's sins) and by putting it away (Col. 1:20; Jn. 1:29; Heb. 9:26). Motivated by infinite love and grace, God did this by sending His Son to be a propitiation[14] for humanity's sins (I Jn. 2:2; 4:10; cp. Jn. 1:29). While pagans seek to propitiate (appease) the anger of their deities by offering them gifts, God Himself was propitious. He provided the necessary sacrifice for the appeasing of His own wrath against sinners when He gave His Son to atone for their sins. Bearing their sins and being made sin (Isa. 53:5-6; II Cor. 5:21), Jesus bore the full stroke of God's anger in their place (Isa. 53:10; Mt. 27:45-46).[15] By His death and the shedding

---

[14] A propitiation is the turning away of divine wrath by an appeasing sacrifice. The divine propitiation for humanity's sins was Jesus' atoning sacrifice, which provisionally appeased the demands of God's holiness and justice against sinners and turned away His wrath from them. However, this propitiation is effective only in the case of those who receive the Saviour. They who fail to receive the Saviour will suffer divine wrath and retribution for their sins.

[15] Many unsaved people are unwilling to accept the fact of God's wrath, for it does not square with their sentimental, humanistic concept of His love. But this wrath is not the fitful, sporadic, irrational anger that we find in humans. It is the stern reaction of His holiness against sinners and their sins. Today this divine wrath generally assumes the form of a strong settled opposition against the sinner (Jn. 3:36; Rom. 1:18), but in the future it will take the form of angry heat poured out in terrible judgments (Rev. 14:10-11; 15:1; 19:15). In His love God provided the sacrifice that provisionally satisfied His holy demands against sinners and opened the way for Him to save them who believe the gospel (I Jn. 4:9-10).

of His blood, Jesus dealt with these sins by paying their debt and appeased God by satisfying His demands (Jn. 1:29; Heb. 9:26; Rom. 3:25). Thus, by His sacrifice He made peace by removing the aggravating thorn of sin between God and sinners (Col. 1:20-21). That God was completely satisfied by this sacrifice was demonstrated by His raising Jesus from the dead (Acts 2:22-24; Rom. 4:25). On the basis of this propitious, atoning work, God is now able to reconcile to Himself all who receive the Saviour. Keep in mind that the Lord's atoning work was provisional in the sense that the value He secured for everyone is now offered by the gospel and is divinely applied only when people believe on Him (II Cor. 5:18-20).

• Its Blessings

Salvation brings the following blessings of reconciliation to them who receive the Saviour:

1. *We have peace with God (Col. 1:20-21; Rom. 5:1, 10).*

Praise God, the war is over! We now enjoy a harmonious relation with God as well as personal well-being. With Christ Jesus as our propitiation (I Jn. 2:2), we shall never again be exposed to God's judicial wrath (Jn. 5:24; Rom. 5:9; 8:1, 31-34; I Thess. 1:10; 5:9). (This does not, however, grant us immunity to man's wrath [II Tim. 3:10-12; Jn. 15:18-21; I Jn. 3:11-13].) With the confidence of children we can approach God with reverent boldness (Heb. 4:16; Eph. 2:18), even with our sins (I Jn. 1:9), without fearing divine hostility. While unjudged sins may temporarily eclipse heart-peace (a fruit of the Spirit; Gal. 5:22) and bring on us God's corrective chastisement (I Cor. 11:32), our reconciliation to Him remains steadfast forever (Rom. 5:10-11).

2. *We have peace with others who are reconciled to God (Eph. 2:14-19).*

Throughout their history a state of hostility has existed between Jews and Gentiles because of the Law of Moses. Having the law, the Jews felt superior to the Gentiles. Also, the Gentiles regarded the Jews as religious bigots. By His death the Lord Jesus removed the cause of this hostility (the partition wall that separated them) and atoned for their sins, including those that were expressed by their bitter attitude toward each other. The "partition" was the Law of Moses; the "wall" was the things of the law that kept Jews and Gentiles apart like ritual circumcision, restricted diet, Sabbath keeping, and religious ceremonies. The Lord brought the Law of Moses to an end, as a viable covenant, and ratified the New Covenant. By this both saved Jews and Gentiles are brought peacefully together in Him and have a common relation to God (Gal. 3:26-28). By their reconciliation to God, people who are traditional enemies become reconciled to each other. This is God's solution to the unrest that permeates this world. We who are saved are responsible for giving to others this message of peace which is in and through the Lord Jesus (II Cor. 5:18-20). Also, when their hearts are filled with the Holy Spirit, God's people experience this peace in their church and social relationships.

3. *The peace of God is available to us (Isa. 26:3-4; Jn. 16:33; II Thess. 3:16).*

This peace is a garrison to our hearts in the midst of life's trials and adversities (Phil. 4:6-7). Since it is a fruit of the Holy Spirit (Rom. 14:17; Gal. 5:22), we experience this peace only as we are rightly adjusted to Him and are trusting God's promises. Unjudged known sins bar this peace from our hearts and cause us unrest and unhappiness. Heart peace is restored when we deal with these sins.

4. *We can anticipate God's reconciling all things to Himself (Col. 1:20; Acts 3:21; Eph. 1:10).*

This seems to concern those things that were involuntarily affected by God's curse upon creation when man fell (Gen. 3:17; Rom. 8:19-23). These verses do not teach universalism (the idea that everyone eventually will be saved). In his listing that which is reconciled to God (Col. 1:20), Paul omits those who are under the earth in Hades (the lost). When He comes to establish His earthly kingdom, the Lord will lift this curse and will restore creation to its primeval state (Isa. 11:6-9; Ps. chs. 8, 98).

5. *We have the ministry of reconciliation (II Cor. 5:18-20; Mt. 5:9).*

Since the Lord regards us as His ambassadors and has given us His message of reconciliation, we have the duty of sharing the good news with others so they can be reconciled to God through faith in Jesus. This ministry, determined by our gifts and calling, ranges from formal gospel proclamation to informal personal witness to Jesus' saving work in our life. It is a privilege to be co-laborers with the Lord and to possess such an effective message (I Cor. 3:9; Rom. 1:16). Are you faithfully representing Him and sharing His message of peace?

NEARNESS TO GOD (Eph. 2:10-13)

- **Its Definition**

This is the divine act whereby the gospel believer is brought near to God in Christ.

- **Its Necessity**

The need of unsaved Gentiles for this aspect of salvation is dramatically stated by Paul in Ephesians 2:12:[16]

1. *We were without Christ.* We had no relation with Him who is the only Way to God, the personification of absolute Truth, and the essence of spiritual

---

[16] While Israel nationally had a special relation with God, based on the covenant of law (Ex. 19:3-6; Rom. 9:4-5), they severed this relationship by breaking the covenant (Jer. 31:32; Hos. 1:9). In the future God will make a new covenant with the elect Jewish remnant (Jer. 31:31-34), which promises them a perpetual relation with Him. Meanwhile, individual saved Jews are near to God in Christ (Eph. 2:14-18) and enjoy the relation with God as promised by the New Covenant.

Life (Jn. 14:6).

2. We were shut out from the commonwealth of Israel. Being Gentiles, we had no share in the blessings that belonged to God's ancient, chosen people (Rom. 9:4-5).

3. We were foreigners to God's covenant promises to Israel, such as those relating to their land (Gen. 13:15; 15:18-21; Deut. 30:1-5) and king (II Sam. 7:10-16).

4. We had no hope or expectation of divine blessing in or beyond this life (I Thess. 4:13).

5. We were destitute of God (I Cor. 1:21; Eph. 4:18). This is life's most tragic experience. G. G. Findlay writes, "To be without God in this world is to be in the wilderness without a guide; on a stormy ocean without harbor or pilot; in sickness without medicine or physician; to be hungry without bread, and weary without rest, and dying with no light of life. It is to be an orphaned child, wandering in an empty, ruined house."[17]

- **Its Basis**

In our unsaved state, we had neither the desire nor the ability to draw near to God. Our being made near is wholly God's work.

1. *It was made possible by Christ's sacrifice (Eph. 2:13, "by the blood of Christ").*

His atoning work removed our sins, which separated us from God (Heb. 9:26). Putting away the alienating cause, Jesus cleared the way to bring us near to God.

2. *It was made real by our baptism into Christ (Eph. 2:13, "in Christ Jesus").*

The Holy Spirit's baptism placed us into Christ (Gal. 3:27; Eph. 2:10; II Cor. 5:17). In Him we are as near to the Father as He is (Col. 3:3). No other created beings have such an exalted position as this (Eph. 1:3; 2:5-6).

- **Its Blessings**

Our being made near to God in Christ forms the basis of two important doctrines, which in turn point to the blessings of this position: our standing and state and our sanctification.

1. *THE BELIEVER'S STANDING AND STATE*
   a. *His Standing*

This refers to the believer's position in the sight of God. Our standing is in Christ Jesus (Eph. 1:1). We received this position at salvation by the creative work of God (II Cor. 5:17-18; Eph. 2:10) and the baptism of the Holy Spirit (Gal. 3:27).

---

[17] G. G. Findlay, *The Expositor's Bible: The Epistle to the Ephesians* (New York: Hodder & Stoughton, n.d.), p. 126.

This position grants us the blessings of sharing what Jesus has done and what He has as man. In sharing what He has done, we participate in His death, resurrection, and obedience unto death (Rom. 5:16-19; Rom. 6:1-4). This results in our being dead unto sin and alive unto God. Moreover, we possess His righteousness (I Cor. 1:30). In sharing in what He has, we are made wealthy (Eph. 1:3; cp. vs. 11; Heb. 1:2; Rom. 8:17), are accepted (Eph. 1:6; cp. Rom. 8:31; I Pet. 3:18), are made secure (Col. 3:3; cp. Jn. 10:28-29), and are complete (Col. 2:10). This position is radically different from that which we formerly had in Adam when we were unsaved (II Cor. 5:17; Rom. 5:15-19; I Cor. 15:22). Then, we shared Adam's kind of human nature, his sin, his condemnation, and his death.

b. His State

This refers to the condition of the believer's daily life. This is imperfect and changing because of our spiritual immaturity and ignorance, the opposition of our spiritual enemies, and our failure to apply consistently the provisions that God has granted for a fruitful, victorious life. It is God's desire that we increasingly conform to our standing in Christ (Eph. 4:1; Col. 3:1-17). To this end, God deals with us (Heb. 12:5-13) and teaches us (II Tim. 3:16-17; Eph. 4:11-15), and the wise person submits to these. The truth of our standing and state resolves the contradictory reality of carnal saints (cp. I Cor. 1:2-9; 6:11 with 3:1-4). On the other hand, carnality in a believer's life should not be tolerated, for professing believers who are living in sin may not be saved at all (II Cor. 13:5). And if they are saved, they will incur divine chastisement if they persist in their sins (Rev. 3:19).

2. THE BELIEVER'S SANCTIFICATION

In Scripture usage divine sanctification may be either an action or a state (condition) as determined by the context. As an action it is the activity of God whereby He sets His people apart unto Himself for His manifestation and use (cp. Eph. 5:26). As a state it is the condition of being set apart that results from this divine action (cp. Eph. 5:27; I Cor. 1:2). Therefore, the basic ideas of sanctification are the action of setting apart and the state of having been set apart (Lev. 20:26).

Some Bible words, translated from the same root words in the Hebrew and Greek texts, that relate to sanctification are these: verbs — "sanctify" and "hallow"; nouns — "saint," "sanctification," "holiness" and "Holy One"; and adjective — "holy."

The concept of sanctification was held by pagans in their setting apart people and things for their deities (cp. I Kings 14:24, "sodomites"). In the Scriptures we find God sanctifying people, days, places, and things (Gen. 2:3; Ex. 29:44; 19:23); man sanctifying God, himself, and things (I Pet. 3:15; Ex. 19:22; Jn. 17:19; I Tim. 4:5); and a thing sanctifying other things (Mt. 23:19).

In addition to that sanctification that relates to the presalvational work of the Holy Spirit in us (II Thess. 2:13; I Pet. 1:2; cp. Heb. 6:4-6; 10:29), there are three aspects of divine sanctification that relate to us who are now saved: positional, practical, and final.

a. Positional Sanctification

This concerns our having been set apart unto God in Christ (I Cor. 1:2). It is related to our position or standing in Him (1:30; 6:11). Observe several features of positional sanctification:

1. It takes place at salvation, with the result that we are in the permanent state of sanctification (I Cor. 6:11), with Jesus as our sanctification (I Cor. 1:30).

2. It is the instantaneous work of God the Father (Eph. 2:10), based on Christ's death (Heb. 13:12), wrought by the Holy Spirit (I Pet. 1:2; I Cor. 6:11; cp. Gal. 3:27), and done in response to salvational faith (Acts 26:18).

3. It belongs to every saved person alike, regardless of the condition of his daily life (I Cor. 6:11; cp. 3:1-4).

4. Being perfect and complete for every believer, it will continue forever (Heb. 10:10).

5. This makes every saved person a "saint" or a "holy one" (I Cor. 1:2; Phil. 1:1; Col. 1:2).

b. Practical Sanctification

This concerns the believer's condition of daily life (I Pet. 1:15). Since God is holy, He would have His people increasingly to express holiness (moral perfection, or sinlessness) in their daily lives (Mt. 5:48; I Jn. 2:1). We express this holiness when we separate ourselves from that which is morally unlike God, yield ourselves to Him, and do His will (Rom. 6:19, 22; 12:1-2). The relation of positional sanctification to this is that our sainthood should motivate us to live holy lives (Eph. 4:1; 5:8; Col. 3:1-14).

Notice several features of practical sanctification:

1. Being closely related to spiritual growth, this aspect of sanctification takes place throughout the believer's life. In this life we never reach the place where we have no further need for more sanctification.

2. It involves our separation from sin as well as our dedication to God and our doing His will (I Thess. 4:3, 7; Rom. 6:19, 22; 12:2; I Pet. 1:14-15).

3. It is a process that involves an increase in the frequency and duration of our expressing holiness. This takes place not only as we walk in obedience to God but also as we favorably respond to those divine activities which allow God to effect holiness in our daily life. These activities are His giving us victory over sin (Rom. 6:11-13, 22), His making us more like Jesus in character and works (II Cor. 3:18; Rom. 8:2-4), His using His Word to influence our lives (Jn. 17:17; 15:3), and His dealing with us (Heb. 12:10). As we respond favorably to these ministries, we advance in practical sanctification.

4. Its progress varies among believers and within the life of each believer. In this way some people are more holy than others; we are more

holy at one time than another. This variation in holiness is not one of degree but of frequency and duration. Like other fruits of the Holy Spirit, holiness is an absolute and does not express itself in varying amounts. Practical holiness is something that we are to express more often and for longer periods of time in daily life.

5. By this process we become more saintly in character and conduct (I Thess. 4:1-10; Rom. 6:19, 22). Actually, we become more like Jesus, who is our spiritual life (II Cor. 3:18; Gal. 4:19; Col. 3:4).

Note the following comparisons:

POSITIONAL SANCTIFICATION	PRACTICAL SANCTIFICATION
1. It relates to our standing in Christ.	1. It relates to our condition of life.
2. It occurs at salvation.	2. It occurs throughout life.
3. It is God's instantaneous work.	3. It is God's progressive work.
4. It is complete, absolute.	4. It is incomplete, relative.
5. It is the same for every believer.	5. It varies with each believer.
6. It makes the believer a saint.	6. It makes the believer saintly.

c. *Final Sanctification*

We who are saved shall experience this aspect when the Lord returns for His church. Then, our body will experience redemption, and we shall be brought into complete conformity to the character and human nature of our Lord Jesus Christ (Phil. 3:20-21; I Jn. 3:2). From then on, we shall be as holy in our condition as we are in our position (I Cor. 1:8; Eph. 1:4; 5:26-27; I Thess. 5:23; Jude 24).

Again, we should keep in mind the distinction between the atonement that Jesus accomplished on the cross and the benefits of this work that are granted to the gospel believer when he receives the Saviour. The components of salvation, which we have just reviewed, are the benefits or fruit of our Lord's atoning work. We who are saved can look back to the cross and say that for us He obtained eternal redemption (Heb. 9:12), sanctification (Heb. 10:10), completion (Heb. 10:14, "perfected"), and reconciliation (Rom. 5:10; Col. 1:20). However, these benefits are not divinely given until one believes. The Lord's atoning work, with its benefits, is provisional in the sense that it is not effective in the life of a person until he receives the Saviour. Should he not do so, then he himself must pay the debt of his sins as though Christ had not died.

THE DUTIES OF SALVATION

In our study of salvation, we have examined its parts—regeneration, adoption, justification, redemption, reconciliation, and our being made near to God. These salvational blessings are absolute, in the sense that they belong to every believer alike. But how do they relate to daily life? For many believers salvation is simply a means of preparing them for Heaven. But in reality it is much more than this. God intends that it have an impact upon the lives of His people, not only in the changes it brings about in our life but also in the duties it imposes on us. Let us look again at the components of salvation and learn the duties they place on us.

REGENERATION
This concerns our being made spiritually alive and our having a new relationship with God.

• The Duties of Our New Life
Our new life in Christ should be manifest in our daily experience by new attitudes and character (Gal. 5:22-23), new activity in keeping with God's will (Phil. 2:13; Eph. 5:17), new understanding of spiritual truth (I Cor. 2:10-12), new fellowship with God and His people (I Cor. 1:9; I Jn. 1:3), new purpose to please God (II Cor. 5:9), and new interest in the things of our Lord (Col. 3:1-3). It is our duty to cultivate these areas of our new life (II Pet. 3:18), as the commands of Scripture and the example of godly men indicate. We experience these things as we submit to the Lord Jesus, search out His Word, appropriate by faith what we need, and do what He commands (Phil. 4:13; Jn. 7:38-39; Gal. 2:20; Jn. 13:17).

• The Duties of Our New Relationship
Being members of God's family and subjects of His kingdom (Jn. 1:12; Col. 1:13), we have the duty of learning His will and truth (Eph. 5:17; Ps. 1:1-3), walking in His will and fellowship (I Jn. 1:7), depending upon His provision and care (yet, He will not do for us what we can do for ourselves, I Pet. 5:7; Mt. 6:8, 25-34), and yielding to His discipline (Heb. 12:1-15).

ADOPTION
This relates to our adult position in God's family. Having the position of adult-sons, we must determine what God's will is for us in every life-situation (compare the precepts of the Dispensation of Grace [the New Testament] and the guiding principles of I Cor. 10:31; Rom. 14:23; Col. 3:17; I Cor. 8:9, 13, 1; I Thess. 4:4). Also, we must assume the responsibility of our doing God's will and of our actions (Rom. 14:12; II Cor. 5:10). Adoption means, among other things, that God does not do all our thinking for us or give specific orders for every detail of our lives. With our renewed minds and the resources of the Scriptures and the Holy Spirit, we can learn what His will for us is (Rom. 12:2; Ps. 119:105; Rom. 8:14; see Appendix F).

JUSTIFICATION
This concerns our being acquitted by God of His sentence of condemnation and our being declared righteous in His sight.

• The Duty of Acquittal
Since God has forgiven us of all our sins, we should no longer feel guilty about them (Heb. 9:14). Satan often brings to our mind the past and tries to

make us feel guilt-ridden. This, in turn, makes us feel unfit for life and service. However, God wants us to claim the fact of our forgiveness and of our being guiltless in His sight. On the other hand, we should feel guilty of known sin in our life until we deal with it in the way that God prescribes in His Word (Rev. 2:5; I Jn. 1:9).

• **The Duty of Being Righteous**
God expects us who are righteous in Christ (I Cor. 1:30) to do right things, that is, to do His will in His way (Phil. 1:11; II Tim. 2:22; 3:16-17; Heb. 13:21; Rom. 6:13, 19; I Jn. 2:29).

REDEMPTION
This concerns our being delivered by the ransom payment of Christ's death and shed blood from sin's debt and from bondage to evil spiritual masters.

• **The Duty of Being Delivered from Sin's Debt**
Having been divinely forgiven of all our sins, we should now be forgiving toward others who have hurt us or are indebted to us morally (Eph. 4:32; Mt. 6:14-15; 18:21-35) when they have met the conditions of repentance (Lk. 17:3; see "Christian Forgiveness" in the Addenda). Harboring grudges, holding resentment, and seeking revenge have no proper place in the Christian life (I Cor. 13:5; Rom. 12:17-21).

• **The Duty of Being Delivered from Former Spiritual Masters**
Having been freed from enslavement to sin, Satan, and the world, it is our duty to yield ourself to our new master, the Lord Jesus (Rom. 6:11-13; Jas. 4:7; I Jn. 2:15; Rom. 12:2). He alone has absolute claim to our life (II Cor. 5:14-15; I Cor. 6:19-20).

RECONCILIATION
This refers to our being at peace with God. Being His friends, we should show ourselves friendly by loving obedience to His will (Jn. 15:14; 14:15). Furthermore, we should live peaceably with other believers (Eph. 4:31-32; 4:3; I Thess. 5:13) as well as with the world (I Tim. 2:2). Being at peace with God, we are peacemakers (Mt. 5:9), for we have the ministry and message of reconciliation (II Cor. 5:18-20).

NEARNESS TO GOD
This concerns our being made near to God in 'Christ. Because of our positional sanctification in Christ, it is our duty to live a holy life (I Pet. 1:15). This means that increasingly we must set ourself apart from that which is unlike Jesus (Col. 3:8; II Thess. 3:14-15; Rom. 6:17-18; II Cor. 6:14; I Jn. 2:15) and give ourself to Him in obedience and trust for His manifestation and use in this world (II Cor. 5:15; Rom. 12:1; Col. 3:1; Jn. 15:1-5). This involves our

resolute decision and hearty dedication by prayer (Isa. 6:8).

THE METHOD OF SALVATION IN OTHER AGES

How were people saved during the precross period? How will they be saved during the coming Tribulation Period and the Millennial Kingdom? While much information is lacking, the Scriptures give sufficient detail to answer these questions. The principle may be stated here that in every age of human history God saves people in the same way — by His grace through salvational faith in the divine revelation about the Redeemer (Eph. 2:8).

DURING THE PRECROSS PERIOD

Both Adam and Eve believed God's promise of the coming Redeemer (Gen. 3:15). Adam's faith is indicated by his naming his wife "Eve," which means "Life" or "Living," as she would be the means of perpetuating the race and of its ultimate victory over Satan and death (3:20). Eve's faith is manifest in her accepting this name and in her words upon the births of Cain and Seth (4:1, 25). In response to their faith, God clothed Adam and Eve with the skins of animals (3:21). It appears that by this action He established the principle of atonement as being by the death and the offering of the blood of an innocent substitute.

By faith Abel offered a more excellent sacrifice than Cain (Gen. 4:4; Heb. 11:4). By His acceptance of this gift, God bore witness to Abel's righteousness. The reference to Abel's faith presupposes a divine revelation to which his faith responded. This revelation (probably given at the time God clothed Adam and Eve) concerned the right approach to God through animal substitutionary sacrifices (cp. Gen. 8:20) and pointed to the coming Saviour. As always, Abel's righteousness was the divine gift of righteousness which accompanies salvation (cp. Gen. 15:6).

Abraham's faith in the coming Seed (Saviour) was divinely reckoned to him for righteousness (Gen. 15:5-6). It appears that he had believed the salvational revelation earlier than this (Gen. 12:3; Gal. 3:8-9) and rejoiced in the truth of the coming Saviour (Jn. 8:56).

Other people of faith who believed God's salvational revelation were Enoch (Gen. 5:22; Heb. 11:5-6), Noah (Gen. 6:8; Heb. 11:7), Zacharias and Elisabeth (Lk. 1:6, 41-45, 68-79), and the virgin Mary (vss. 46-55). Observe that both Zacharias and Mary refer to the Abrahamic Covenant (vss. 55, 72-73), which might be regarded as the "John 3:16" of the Old Testament.

During this time salvation was by grace (Ps. 103:10; Gen. 6:8; Rom. 11:5 through faith in God's revelation about the coming Redeemer (Gen. 3:15; 15:5 6; 12:3; cp. Gal. 3:8, 14, 16). Obedience to God was an outward manifestation of salvational faith (Heb. 11:4-30; Jas. 2:21-26). How much detail God gave about the Redeemer is not certain. It probably was more than the Old

Testament indicates (Jn. 8:56; Heb. 11:10, 13, 14).[18] However this may be, He revealed all that was necessary for salvational faith.

These precross saints possessed the same basic salvational blessings that we enjoy today, such as the presence of the Holy Spirit (Ps. 51:11; Jn. 14:17), righteousness (Gen. 15:6), forgiveness of sins (II Sam. 12:13; Ps. 32:1), redemption (Isa. 29:22), faith (Heb. ch. 11), joy (Ps. 51:12), the fear of God (Ps. 89:7; Job 1:1), grace to please Him (Gen. 6:8; 17:1; 26:5; cp. Lk. 1:6), fellowship with Him (Gen. 5:22; 6:9; Deut. 34:10; Ps. 16:8-11), and the prospect of blessing beyond this life (Heb. 11:13-16).

While these precross believers enjoyed the blessings of salvation, they did not go to Heaven at death (Gen. 25:8; Ps. 16:10). They went to paradise in Hades (cp. Lk. 16:22) to await their resurrection, for the atonement upon which their salvation rested had not yet been made (Heb. 9:15-17). Meanwhile, they anticipated the fulfillment of God's promises to them. These concerned Christ's first coming and His atoning work (Acts 13:23, 32-34; 26:6, 22-23; Gal. 3:16-19; Eph. 3:6) and an everlasting inheritance (Heb. 9:15; 10:34-36; 11:13-16), which is a city (cp. Rev. 21:10 ff.).

DURING THE TRIBULATION PERIOD

During the first half of the Tribulation Period, there will be an intensive evangelistic ministry by 144,000 born again Israelites, who will be saved immediately after the rapture of the church (Rev. 7:1-8; 14:3-4; 12:17). Apparently immunized against the divine judgments of this period, they will preach the gospel of the kingdom with unprecedented results (Mt. 24:14; Rev. 7:9, 14). This gospel will be the same as we proclaim today, with additional emphasis on the Lord's soon return to establish His earthly kingdom and the need to prepare for this event (Acts 20:24-25; cp. Mt. 24:42-44).

What does the Lord Jesus mean when He says, "But he that shall endure unto the end, the same will be saved" (Mt. 24:13)? He certainly is not suggesting the possibility of these people's losing their salvation or of their being saved by good works. The Scriptures reveal that most gospel believers will be required to deny their faith in Christ or to accept death (Rev. 13:7-8,

---

[18] That people were saved during the O.T. period outside of the Messianic line and of Israel is evident in Job (Job 1:1; Ezek. 14:14), Melchizedek (Gen. 14:18), and Jethro (Ex. 3:1). During some 2,500 years before the first written Scriptures, the good news of the coming Redeemer was preserved in human traditions (cp. Ps. 145:4-7) and was portrayed in the constellations, which God set in the heavens as "signs" (Gen. 1:14; cp. Ps. 19:1-3).

The longevity of life helped to preserve the accuracy of these traditions: From the creation of Adam to Abraham was 2,008 years. Adam was a contemporary of Methuselah for 243 years; Methuselah's life overlapped that of Shem for 98 years; Shem was a contemporary of Abraham for 150 years (Philip Mauro, The Chronology of the Bible, p. 32). There were five generations between Abraham and Moses, covering about 250 years.

See Don Richardson, Eternity in Their Hearts (Ventura, CA: Regal Books, 1981); E.W. Bullinger, The Witness of the Stars (Grand Rapids: Kregel Publications, 1893, 1967); J.A. Seiss, The Gospel in the Stars (Philadelphia: Castle Press, 1884); C.H. Kang & Ethel R. Nelson, The Discovery of Genesis (St. Louis: Concordia Publishing House, 1979): How the Truths of Genesis Were Found Hidden in the Chinese Language.

15; Mk. 13:9-13). They who remain faithful to Jesus "unto the end" (unto their death or His return) will experience the final phase of their salvation (Rom. 13:11), either by their resurrection if they are martyred (Rev. 20:4) or by their deliverance from their enemies if they survive until Jesus comes (Rev. 19:15). All who deny their professed faith in Christ and who embrace the Beast (Satan's human agent) will indicate by this that they never were saved and will commit an unforgivable sin (Rev. 14:9-11; 13:8). All who reject this gospel ministry during the forepart of the Tribulation Period will be caused to believe Satan's lie, that is, follow the Beast (II Thess. 2:8-12).

DURING THE KINGDOM PERIOD

From such passages as Matthew 7:21-23; 25:31-46, we infer that only saved people will be allowed to enter the Lord's earthly kingdom when He establishes it. However, during His millennial rule, the earth will be repopulated by saved earth dwellers who survived the Tribulation Period and who entered the kingdom in their unredeemed bodies (as ours are today). Born with original sin, the children of these people will need to be saved, as children do today. These will have unprecedented opportunity and encouragement to trust Jesus for salvation, for "the earth shall be full of the knowledge of the LORD as the waters cover the sea" (Isa. 11:9). As always, salvation will be by grace through faith in Jesus and His atoning work, according to the terms of the New Covenant (Jer. 31:31-34; Deut. 30:6; Ezek. 36:24-38). But in spite of this, there will be many unsaved people on earth at the close of the thousand years (Rev. 20:7-9).

Since God can only save sinners by the principle of grace, we can assert that people in every age are saved in the same way — by the grace of God through salvational faith in the divine revelation about the Saviour. The precross believers looked forward to Jesus' coming and atoning work; the postcross believers look back to His coming and work. All the saved of every age have the same, basic salvational blessings — a personal relationship with God with its product of eternal life and the divine forgiveness of sins (Jer. 31:33-34), but not all will have the same function in service, as we shall see.

THE SALVATION OF INFANTS

Contrary to a large segment of Christendom that believes that unbaptized infants who die are lost, I believe that they are saved upon death. While the Bible is not unquestionably clear about the fate of infants who die, the following inferences may be drawn:

1. All people, including infants, are lost because of their participation in Adam's initial sin (Rom. 5:12, 18-19; I Cor. 15:22).

2. The Lord Jesus died for everyone, including infants who die (Heb. 2:9; I Jn. 2:2; Jn. 1:29; 3:16-17; I Tim. 4:10). He provisionally paid the debt of the

sins of the whole world.

3. God is not willing that anyone, including infants, should perish (II Pet. 3:9; I Tim. 2:4; Mt. 18:14). Whereas all humans who fail to respond favorably to God's general revelation are without excuse (Rom. 1:18-20), it seems that infants, being incapable of making moral decisions (Deut. 1:39; Jonah 4:11; Rom. 9:11), are exempted from this responsibility until they develop moral awareness and self-determination.

4. Since salvation is wholly God's work, it is reasonable to assume that He saves all infants who die before reaching the state of moral awareness and self-determination, which results in accountability. Applying to them the value of Christ's atoning work, God graciously saves them at death (cp. Mk. 10:13-16).

5. While people are guilty of Adam's initial sin, they do not go to Hell solely because of this. They are condemned for their actual sins as well (Rom. 1:18-21; 3:9-19; Jn. 3:18).

In summary, it appears that infants who die, though born lost because of original sin, are saved upon death by God's application of the value of Christ's atoning work. Being infinitely righteous and just, God always acts in conformity to His nature (Gen. 18:25). Infants who die before the awakening of accountability are part of the elect whom God has chosen to save.

We can never reflect upon salvation without thanking God for such a wonderful Saviour and His provision. All is of His grace. There was nothing in us that meritoriously prompted this divine work. All is of God and to His glory. After serious reflection on these things, Paul reached the settled conclusion that he owed the Lord Jesus his life (II Cor. 5:14-15) and others the gospel message (Rom. 1:14-16). We have this debt as well. Like the lepers of old who in a time of famine stumbled across the spoils of the Syrians, we do not well to hold our peace in a day of salvation's good news (II Kings 7:9). Incumbent upon all of us who are saved is our continual witness of Christ to others (Acts 1:8). We must be prepared not only to interpret our spiritual experience to others (I Pet. 3:15) but also to share with them the gospel message, which they must believe to have this experience in their lives (Acts 11:19-20). We must support our witness by a consistent, growing Christian life that reflects the reality of what we are saying to our unsaved friends. A witness that is rooted in God's Word, watered with prayer and love, and energized by the Holy Spirit will be effective to God's glory.

A Review of Soteriology

1. What is the basic idea of salvation?
2. Give its secular meaning and its biblical meaning.
3. Give a theological description of salvation.
4. Give the three aspects of salvation with reference to time.
5. List the needs that unsaved people have for salvation.
6. List the corresponding benefits that salvation brings to them who receive the Saviour.
7. Explain the terms "condemned," "spiritually dead," and "lost."
8. What question about divine justice confronted God when He contemplated saving sinners?
9. What was the answer to this question?
10. What is the preaching of the "cross"?
11. Give the steps of God's part in the application of salvation. Explain each of these steps.
12. How does preterition differ from reprobation?
13. To what did God predestinate those whom He elected?
14. Distinguish between God's general and special calls to salvation.
15. What divine activities make up His special call?
16. In what way is God's special call to salvation irresistible?
17. In what way is the gospel more than an invitation?
18. What must the sinner do to be saved?
19. If there is something for the sinner to do to be saved, why is his salvation not of works?
20. Give and explain the parts of salvational faith.
21. How can the gospel believer express his salvational faith to God?
22. What does God immediately do in response to salvational faith?
23. What are the two erroneous views regarding the place of water baptism in salvation?
24. What is the biblical purpose of water baptism?
25. What place does one's confession of the lordship of Christ have in salvation?
26. What does monergistic salvation mean? Synergistic salvation?
27. Which of these two kinds of salvation is biblical?
28. By what principle of dealing does God save people?
29. Why can He not save sinners by the principle of works?

30. What two primary lines of evidence provide assurance of salvation?

31. List the signs of new life which indicate that a person is saved.

32. What might temporarily eclipse these signs of new life in one's daily life?

33. Explain the difference between the assurance of salvation and the permanence of salvation.

34. What does God do to give permanence to our salvation?

35. What provisions has He made for this permanence?

36. What is our part in maintaining salvation?

37. Explain how we are able to persevere in salvational faith.

38. How has God counterbalanced the doctrine of "eternal security" so that people do not think of this as a license to sin?

39. Explain the difference between salvational faith and practical faith.

40. Which of these two faiths is constant, or remains the same, and which fluctuates, or comes and goes?

41. What are the two ultimate goals for God's saving people?

42. List and define the six components of salvation.

43. What is the need for these components? What blessings do they bring the saved person?

44. What is Christian freedom, or liberty? What purposes does it serve in the saved person's life?

45. Distinguish between the believer's standing and state.

46. How do the Corinthians believers illustrate this?

47. What is the basic idea of sanctification, or holiness?

48. Describe the three aspects of the believer's sanctification.

49. What does it mean to live a holy life? How can we do this?

50. What activities of God contribute to our practical holiness?

51. What duties rest upon us who are saved?

52. How were people saved during the O.T. period?

53. By what means were people reminded of the promise of the coming Redeemer during the centuries before the incarnation of God's Son?

54. How will people be saved during the Tribulation Age and the Kingdom Age?

55. Why is a person unsaved at the time of his conception?

56. Give reasons for believing that people who die in infancy or before the time of accountibility are saved at death.

57. Are you wholly and solely trusting Jesus and His atoning work for your salvation?

Ecclesiology

ECCLESIOLOGY / Contents

ECCLESIOLOGY
The Doctrine of the Church

A blessing of salvation is our being called unto the fellowship of our Lord Jesus Christ and other believers (I Cor. 1:9; I Jn. 1:3). The doctrine of the church reminds us that we who are saved are not isolated bits of humanity, scattered about the world. But united to all saved contemporaries, we belong to a great spiritual fellowship, which, exceeding denominational boundaries, has a special relation to the Lord Jesus and which engages in worship, edification, and evangelism. In this section we shall examine the universal and local aspects of the Christian church as well as the nature and practice of the Christian life, which are necessary for the church's growth and function.

THE MEANING OF "CHURCH"

The New Testament word "church" (Gk. *ekklesia*, a "called out" assembly) has both secular and sacred meanings, depending upon its context. Its secular meaning concerns a public assembly gathered for secular purposes (Acts 19:32, 39, 41). With sacred meaning it twice refers to Israel (Acts 7:38; Heb. 2:12), and in the remainder of its occurrences it refers to groups of Christians: a local congregation of believers (Acts 8:1; 14:27; I Cor. 1:2), the totality of believers in a region (Acts 9:31 Gk., "church"; Phil. 3:6), or Christ's universal church, which is His body (Eph. 1:22-23). Notice that the N.T. word "church" never refers to a building. Our study concerns the universal and local aspects of the church, which consists of people.

THE UNIVERSAL CHURCH

A valid distinction between Christ's universal church and a local Christian church is seen in their compositions and in the people's relation to the Lord. The universal church consists only of saved people who are joined to Jesus by a spiritual union, while a local church might have among its members people who have not been born again (cp. Rev. 2:14-15).

ITS DEFINITION
The true universal Christian church is that company of people who have been saved and joined by the Holy Spirit's baptism to Christ and to one another in Him to form a body of which He is the head and life.

ITS ORIGIN
The universal church of Christ was not a subject of Old Testament

prophecy (cp. Eph. 3:1-6). This truth was kept secret until Jesus declared His purpose to build His church (Mt. 16:18; cp. Jn. 10:16; Eph. 3:3-6). His use of the future tense ("I will build") indicates that this program had not begun. He declared that He himself would be the builder and the foundation of the church (cp. I Pet. 2:3-6; I Cor. 3:11). Referring to the church as His possession, He asserted that the gates of Hades would not prevail against it.[1] Still, He did not say what the church would be or when its construction would begin. This was left to later revelation (Acts 1:5; Eph. 3:6; cp. I Cor. 12:13, 27, Eph. 1:22-23).

Since the Lord's announcement pointed to the future, the construction of the church began at a point between this disclosure and the first occurrence of the word "church" in Acts (KJV, 2:47). It appears that this construction began on the Day of Pentecost, ten days after our Lord's ascension into Heaven. This view is supported by Peter's reference to the events of Pentecost as "the beginning" (Acts 11:15-16) and by the first occasion of the baptism of the Holy Spirit, which is essential to the church's construction, as being on that day (Acts 1:5; 11:16; cp. I Cor. 12:13, 27). The nature and the construction of the church are such that it could not have existed before the Lord's exaltation and the subsequent baptizing work of the Holy Spirit (Jn. 14:20; 16:7; Acts 1:5). If a contractor begins the erection of a building, we need not be told that the work has started since this will be evident. The empirical evidence for the Holy Spirit's starting this special work was the Pentecostal phenomena (Acts 2:1-4), consisting of sound (wind), sight (fire), and expressions of praise (tongues). We do not need this kind of evidence today, for we have the teachings of the New Testament which are more certain than empirical evidence (II Pet. 1:16-19).

ITS FORMATION

The Lord's building of His church is a part of His Messianic work during the present age. This means that as a man He is carrying out this aspect of the Father's will.

• The Manner of its Construction

The Lord is building His church quantitatively by ministry to the unsaved and qualitatively by ministry to the saved. His building the church quantitatively means that He is doing this by saving all who exercise salvational faith in Him and by bringing them into union with Himself and with all others in Him. He does this through the Holy Spirit's work of

---

[1] While the phrase, "the gates of Hades" (often interpreted, "the forces of death") may imply that the church will not be permanently bound by death (cp. I Cor. 15:20-23, 51-57), it seems better to understand the words to mean that the members of Christ's church upon dying will not go to Hades at all. Later revelation shows that they go immediately to be with Him (Phil. 1:21, 23; II Cor. 5:6, 8). Contrary to the experience of precross saints, the church saints will never come under Hades' power.

regeneration and baptism to form a body of which He is the head (Acts 2:47; I Cor. 12:13, 27; Col. 1:18). His building the church qualitatively refers to His promoting the spiritual growth of His people (Acts 9:31; 15:41; I Cor. 14:26; II Cor. 12:19; Eph. 4:11-15).

• The Means of its Construction

Since He is doing this work as a man, seated at the right hand of the Father in Heaven, the Lord Jesus is using several means to save the lost and to cultivate the spiritual growth of His people.

1. He uses the Scriptures.

The Lord Jesus uses God's Word in His ministry to the unsaved (II Tim. 3:15; Rom. 10:17; I Pet. 1:23; I Thess. 1:8) and to the saved (I Pet. 2:2; II Tim. 3:16-17). For this reason, it is important in our ministries that we share with others God's Word. This allows Him to minister to their spiritual needs (II Tim. 4:2; Acts 8:4; 11:1; 16:32).

2. He uses the Holy Spirit.

In addition to the Holy Spirit's ministry of regeneration and sanctification, the Lord Jesus is using the Holy Spirit's baptism, which occurs at salvation, to form His church. By this baptism the believer is not only brought into spiritual union with Christ, with the result that he is in Jesus (Gal. 3:27; II Cor. 5:17), but he also is placed into the body of Christ, the church (I Cor. 12:13, 27). By this the believer is brought into union with all other believers who are in the body to form the church (cp. vss. 12-27; 10:17). To be distinguished from His physical body, this mystical body of believers is Christ's church (Eph. 1:22-23; Col. 1:18, 24), of which He is the head and life (Eph. 5:23; 4:15-16; Col. 1:18; 3:4). "Head" is a figurative expression (metaphor) for authority and supervision; "life" refers to the spiritual life of His people.

3. He uses His people who are on earth.

United to Jesus (Jn. 14:20), believers who are on earth are His ambassadors (II Cor. 5:20), and their bodies are His members, individually (I Cor. 6:15) and collectively (12:27), through which He works in this world. It is urgent that we who are saved recognize our part in His great enterprise and cooperate with Him by our yielding to His management and following His direction (Mt. 11:29; Rom. 12:1-2).

• The Extent of its Construction

From the nature of salvation and the renewal which it brings (Eph. 2:8-10; II Cor. 5:17), it appears that all the saved of mankind are baptized with the Holy Spirit into Christ so as to participate in what He has done (I Cor. 1:30; 15:22; see Appendix D). If this is true, then the dead precross saints were brought into Him upon the completion of His atoning work and resurrection (cp. Heb. 9:14-15). The saints of the present Church Age and future Tribulational and Kingdom Ages experience this at their salvation. The

Scriptures teach that the salvational blessings of the redeemed — a personal relationship with God and the forgiveness of sins — are the same for all, according to the promises of the New Covenant (Heb. 8:6-13).

Although all the redeemed of all ages are or will be in Christ, I believe that only the believers of the present age are baptized into His body to form the church (I Cor. 12:13, 27). The peculiar feature of Christ's church is not its union with Him, but the union of its members to one another to form His body, which Paul describes the church to be (Rom. 12:4-5; I Cor. 10:16-17; Eph. 1:22-23; Col. 1:18, 24). While union with Jesus is essential for one's justification and sanctification (I Cor. 1:30), union with one another in Jesus to form this body is not essential to one's salvation.

According to this view, I understand the universal church to be that company of saved people who by the baptism of the Holy Spirit are joined together with Jesus and with one another in Him to form His mystical body, of which He is the head and life. The church's formation continues from the Day of Pentecost until its rapture at Christ's return (I Thess. 4:13-17). It consists only of them who are saved during this time, together with those saints who were alive on earth when the church began on Pentecost.

ITS FUNCTIONS[2]

Whereas all the redeemed of humanity have common salvational blessing, promised by the New Covenant (Heb. 8:6-13), and positional blessings in Christ (Eph. 1:3; I Cor. 1:30), not all have the same function in God's program. For example, in the past the nation of Israel bore witness to the unity of God and gave birth to the Redeemer. In the coming millennial kingdom, she will be the wife of Yahweh as the foremost of earthly nations (Hos. 2:16-23; Mal. 3:12; Zech. 8:23). But the church has other functions that make her distinctive.

• Its Function as a Body

The present function of the church is to serve as Christ's body on earth (I Cor. 12:27; Eph. 1:22-23; Col. 1:18, 24). By this means the Lord Jesus at the Father's right hand is working in this world to build His church. Individually, the believer's body is the Lord's member (I Cor. 6:15); collectively, the church saints on earth form His body through which He works (12:27). As our body is a means by which we express ourselves, so the church on earth is the means by which the Lord Jesus expresses Himself and acts in this world (Rom. 12:3-8; Acts 14:27; 15:4; I Cor. 15:10; Phil. 4:13).

---

[2] Observe that in spite of the woeful state of Christendom, the universal church of Christ is the most powerful institution on earth. Protected by the Father's name (Jn. 17:11) and energized by the Holy Spirit (14:16-17), the church is the salt of the earth (Mt. 5:13), the light of the world (14-16), the body of Christ on earth (I Cor. 12:13, 27), His ambassador to the world (II Cor. 5:20), which will finally triumph over her enemies (Rom. 16:20). Her message is the power of God unto salvation (Rom. 1:16). She is one entity in Christ despite denominational differences (Gal. 3:28). In spite of the forces of evil, the Lord's construction of the church is on schedule and can never be thwarted.

• Its Function as a Bride

The future function of the church is to be Jesus' bride, or wife (II Cor. 11:2; Eph. 5:22-33). This means that all who comprise His church will have a special, spiritual relationship with Him that will be analogous to that between a husband and his wife. As Israel, the wife of Yahweh, will be foremost among the nations on earth, so the church, the wife of Jesus, will be the foremost among the redeemed.

1. THE STAGES OF THIS RELATIONSHIP

These stages are reflected by those observed in Bible times.

a. The Betrothal

This was the act of the father or guardian in giving the maiden to her future husband. Being done before witnesses, this was binding (cp. Deut. 20:7). It could not be broken except by divorce (Mt. 1:18-19). The betrothal was usually accompanied with a payment to the bride's father.

The church is the Father's gift to His Son (Jn. 17:24). This involved the cost of our Lord's giving His life as a ransom (Mt. 20:28; Eph. 5:25). While this gift was made before the foundation of the world (cp. Eph. 1:4), the contract was sealed in our life's experience when we received Jesus as our Saviour (II Cor. 11:2; cp. Gen. 24:58).

b. The Preparation

This was a period during which the prospective bride and groom prepared themselves for the wedding day (Rev. 19:7; Heb. 10:12-13). The groom set the date and sent his bride-to-be gifts to remind her of his love.

Needless to say, we should be preparing ourselves for the time of Jesus' return by studying His Word and doing His will. What gifts of love is He giving to you during your lifetime on earth?

c. The Wedding

When the time of marriage arrived, the bridegroom escorted his bride from her home, where her parents pronounced a blessing, to his own home (Gen. 24:60; Mt. 25:6, 10). There did not seem to be any formal religious wedding ceremony.

The Lord Jesus Himself will escort the church to Heaven (I Thess. 4:16-17). After His appraisal of the lives of His people, He will take the church as His wife before He returns to earth to establish His kingdom (Rev. 22:12; 19:7).

d. The Marriage Feast

Continuing a week or more, the marriage festivities included feasting and competitive games (Gen. 29:22; Jn. 2:2). The guests were seated at the table according to rank (Lk. 14:8-9), and they wore appropriate clothing (Mt. 22:11).

Our Lord's wedding feast will take place on earth after His return and the establishment of His authority over the earth (Rev. 19:9). By then, all the redeemed dead will have been resurrected and will be able with earth dwellers to join in the wedding festivities (cp. Jn. 3:29; Rev. 20:4; Mt. 8:11; Dan. 12:2-3).

2. THE GLORIES OF THIS RELATIONSHIP

The relationship between the Lord Jesus and His wife will involve His humanity as the head of the church. Although these glories surpass our comprehension, the Scriptures suggest what they will be.

a. The church will be blessed beyond measure.

She will partake of the Lord's fabulous inheritance (Heb. 1:2). Being joint-heirs with Him, we shall possess all things (Rom. 8:17; I Cor. 3:21-22). The church will also share the glory of His exalted humanity (Jn. 17:22, 24). This glory consists of His changed body (cp. I Cor. 15:49; Phil. 3:20-21) and His exalted position at the Father's right hand, far above all (Eph. 1:20-22; 2:4-6). Finally, the church will forever participate in His love and fellowship (Jn. 14:3; 17:24; I Thess. 4:18; cp. S. Sol. 2:4-6). This will not include sexual love (cp. Mt. 22:30).

b. The church will be Jesus' fulness.

As Eve completed Adam, so the church will complete the Lord Jesus, the glorified last Adam (Gen. 2:18; Eph. 1:23; I Cor. 15:45). How will the church be essential to His completeness? She will perfect His joy (Jude 24) and will satisfy His love (Eph. 5:25-27). We can imagine the eagerness with which He looks forward to receiving the church to Himself as His bride. Read again the Song of Solomon, which symbolically portrays this loving relationship. (1:9-2:17; 4:1-5:1, 9-16; 7:6-8:4).

ITS DISTINCTIVENESS

Since the church is a particular group of saints who serve presently on earth as Jesus' body and in the future as His wife, I believe that we should distinguish her from other groups of redeemed peoples, living outside of the Church Age. This distinction does not lie in the salvational and positional blessings that all the redeemed possess alike, such as regeneration, justification, and redemption. Rather it is manifest in the special distinctive function that each group has and in the particular blessings that attend this function.

• The church is distinct from Israel.

Some hold that Israel and the church are the same people of God, with Israel's being the church of the old covenant period and the church's being the Israel of the new covenant era. Some also hold that there is no prophetic future for the nation of Israel because of their rejection of Jesus and that all that was prophesied about the future of this nation is now being fulfilled in the church.

I prefer the view that sees the true Israel and the church as separate entities, consisting of redeemed people who have their own special function and place in the prophetic future. This view is supported by the following:

Paul distinguished between the church and the Jews in I Corinthians 10:32. Moreover, referring to himself as an example, he argues in Romans chapter 11 that God has not thrust away Israel, but in the future He will restore a remnant of the nation to Himself (vss. 1-6, 11-12, 25-27). This foresees the time when Jesus will return to earth, gather Israel from among the nations, and judge them, sifting out the apostates and saving them who trust Him as Saviour (Jer. 31:31-34; Ezek. 11:17-21; 20:33-44; 36:24-30; 37:21-27; Deut. 30:3-8). Although today Israel is both the enemy and the beloved of God (Rom. 11:28), they will not remain His enemy forever. As God is now showing mercy to Gentiles, so He will show mercy to the elect of Israel in the future by saving them (vss. 26-27, 30-31).

Paul calls believers "the children of Abraham" and his "seed" (Gal. 3:6-7, 29), but this does not necessarily mean that we who are Gentiles are the patriarch's actual posterity. Whether Jews or Gentiles, saved people are characterized as being people of faith (cp. Eph. 1:1; Acts 5:14). Being an outstanding example of faith (Rom. 4:13-21), Abraham may be regarded as the head of a class of persons who are characterized by this kind of faith (Gal. 3:9).

When the apostle uses the phrase, "Israel of God" (Gal. 6:16), he probably is referring to saved Jews, in contrast to the saved Gentiles to whom he is writing (cp. Gal. 3:14; Acts 13:46-48). Even his reference to his Gentile readers as "the circumcision" (Phil. 3:3) does not necessarily mean that God considers them to be Jews since elsewhere he uses circumcision to speak symbolically of the inner operation of the Holy Spirit upon the heart at salvation (Rom. 2:28-29; Col. 2:11-13).

When James quotes from the prophecy of Amos to relate God's intention of saving Gentiles (Acts 15:13-18; Amos 9:11-12), he seems unwittingly to be used of the Holy Spirit to speak also of Christ's future return and His restoration of the house of David, of which Gentiles are not a part (cp. Ezek. 37:19-28).

In contrast to the church's future function as the wife of Jesus,[3] saved Israel as the wife of Yahweh will be foremost among the nations on earth during the millennial kingdom (Hos. 2:7, 13-23; 3:1-5). Furthermore, Israel's inheritance will be earthly, for they will possess the land that was promised by the Abrahamic Covenant (Gen. 15:18; Deut. 30:5; Jer. 16:14-15; 24:6-7). Like the Levites of old (Num. 18:20), the church's inheritance is the Lord Jesus himself and all that has been given to Him (Eph. 1:11; Rom. 8:17; Heb. 1:2). Unlike Israel the church will not have a national entity or territorial possession.

The universal church could not have existed during O.T. times for the

---

[3] To be the wife of one is to have an exclusive relationship with this person. As in O.T. times, Israel above all other nations will have a special relationship with God (Ex. 19:5; Deut. 7:6; 14:2; Jer. 3:14; 31:32). Also, the church above all other redeemed peoples will have a special relationship with Jesus.

following reasons: One, its reality was future of Jesus' declaration in Matthew 16:18. Two, its construction is a Messianic work which began after Jesus' glorification (I Cor. 12:13, 27; Eph. 1:22-23). Three, it is built upon the teachings of the apostles and N.T. prophets, with Jesus as the chief cornerstone (Eph. 2:20). Four, it is related to Jesus as man, not as God (Jn. 17:22, 24; 14:20; Rev. 19:7). And five, there is no biblical evidence for its primary feature of construction, the baptism with the Holy Spirit (I Cor. 12:13, 27), as having occurred in human history before Pentecost (Lk. 3:15-16; Acts 1:5).

- **The church is distinct from the redeemed Gentiles of other ages.**

Nowhere do the Scriptures teach that the saved Gentiles of other ages are members of Christ's body, the church. While, in my opinion, the redeemed of all the ages will be brought into Christ (I Cor. 15:22; Eph. 1:10; see Appendix D), this is not the same as their being brought into His body, which is essential to membership in His universal church (I Cor. 12:13, 27). While the church will have a special relation to Christ Jesus as His wife, the saved Gentiles who survive the Tribulation Period, for instance, will comprise the nations that will exist on earth (together with Israel) during the millennial kingdom (Zech. 14:16; Mt. 25:31-34).

- **The church is distinct from Christ's kingdom.**

Believers who belong to Christ's universal church are a part of His kingdom (Col. 1:13; cp. Jn. 3:3-7; Acts 20:25; 28:31), but the kingdom also includes all of the saved of other ages as well. Our Lord's earthly kingdom will embrace all of the redeemed, including the Old Testament saints (Lk. 13:28-29), the saved Tribulation Period martyrs (Rev. 20:4), and the saved Tribulation Period survivors (Mt. 25:31-46) (including the elect remnant of Israel, Ezek. ch. 36), as well as the church saints.

Presently the church is a part of Christ's kingdom, which now is invisible, nonpolitical, and nongeographical. In the future it will be a part of His earthly kingdom, not in the sense that it will have a political entity like Israel or the Gentile nations but in the sense that it will be Christ's wife and therefore subject to His authority.

THE LOCAL CHURCH

With the beginning of Christ's universal church on Pentecost, there sprang up a local manifestation of the church in the form of an assembly of believers (Acts 2:41-47). Loosely organized, these believers met regularly in Jerusalem to hear the apostles' teachings, to fellowship, to observe the Lord's Supper, and to pray. When the need arose, they adopted more organization (Acts 6:1-6). Upon the faithful witness of their members, other local churches were established throughout Palestine and at Antioch (Acts 9:31; 11:19-21), continuing a chain reaction to the present.

ITS DEFINITION

From the New Testament we learn that a local Christian church is

- **In Content**

A company of baptized people, belonging to a certain place, who profess to be saved by trusting in Jesus and His atoning work (Acts 2:41, 47; 11:20-26; 18:8-11);

- **In Organization**

Who are in agreement in doctrine, policy, and practice (Acts 2:46; Eph. 4:1-6) and who are organized according to N.T. church offices (Phil. 1:1);

- **In Practice**

Who, recognizing the Lord's presence (Mt. 18:20), assemble regularly to worship God (Acts 2:47; 13:2), to observe the Lord's Supper (Acts 2:42; 20:7; I Cor. 11:23-26), to fellowship together in the study of the Word and in prayer (Acts 2:42; 4:23-31), to exercise their spiritual gifts for the edification of one another (Acts 9:31; 13:1; I Cor. 12:1-31; 14:23-26), to do good works (Acts 11:27-30; Gal. 6:10; Rev. 2:5), and to exercise corrective discipline when it is needed (Mt. 18:15-20; I Cor. 5:4-5);

- **In Mission**

Who bear witness to the gospel at home (I Thess. 1:8) and abroad (Acts 8:4; Phil. 4:10-18);

- **In Hope**

And who are looking for the return of Jesus (I Thess. 1:10; Phil. 3:20; Tit. 2:13).

ITS MEMBERSHIP

A local Christian church consists of persons who profess salvational faith in Jesus and His atoning work, who are organized according to N.T. principles, and who are obedient to the Lord's ordinances (Eph. 1:1; I Cor. 6:11; Acts 2:41-42; 11:20-26; 18:8-11; Mt. 28:19-20). To my mind, Christian parachurch organizations like schools, camps, study groups, and mission agencies do not constitute local churches, for this is not their declared purpose of existence and their organization. Therefore, it would not be fitting for the constituency of these organizations like a home Bible study group or a summer Bible camp to observe the church ordinances of believer's water baptism and the Lord's Supper apart from the supervision of a local church.

Without doubt, there are unsaved people who are members of local churches upon a false profession of faith in Jesus. But these are known to the Lord (Rev. 2:13-15), and He does not regard them to be His people (Mt. 7:21-23; cp. Jn. 10:27). In these days of deepening religious apostasy, there are in Christendom many local churches that are not truly Christian, for they neither manifest the qualities of a biblical local church nor confess the Christian faith as given in the New Testament.

Did the early local churches have formal memberships? There is no record in the Scriptures of believers' uniting with a local church. But there is evidence that they were formally a part of their churches, for they elected their own officers and delegates (Acts 6:3, 5; 11:29-30; 15:2, 3, 22; II Cor. 8:19) and were subject to excommunication (I Cor. 5:13).

There are people who profess to be saved and who attend local churches but who are not members of these churches. Except for unusual circumstances, this practice is not recommended. Why, then, should one who is saved belong to a Bible believing and teaching local church? Consider these advantages:

One, his being a real part of the local church and, if it has congregational government, his participating in its direction. Membership allows one to speak and to vote on the policies and matters pertaining to the church.

Two, his having opportunity to exercise his spiritual gifts. Many churches do not allow people to teach or to hold key positions without their being members.

Three, his having accountability for his belief and conduct. All believers need to be accountable to someone for these things.

Four, his sharing the support of the local church and its ministries. It is hardly equitable for a person to benefit from the ministry of a local church for an extended time and not become involved in its full support.

Five, his being a member identifies to others his doctrinal position and practice. By his membership outsiders know what one is and what to expect of him.

Six, his being a member makes him eligible to receive the loving care and support of fellow members. While we are to do good unto all, we have a special duty to those with whom we are associated in the local church.

Seven, His being a member is required by many Christian organizations, with which he might seek association.

Eight, his being a member is expected by the unsaved. Lack of membership can be a hindrance to one's testimony.

A Christian in this hostile world without church membership is like a ship without a home port. He is, indeed, alone and vulnerable to the assaults of his spiritual adversaries.

ITS GOVERNMENT

The Lord Jesus Christ is the supreme leader (Eph. 1:22-23) of both the local church and the universal church (I Pet. 5:4; cp. Rev. chs. 2, 3). Whenever His people gather in His name, He is present (Mt. 18:20). His Word (the New Testament) is the supreme authority of His people's faith and practice (Mt. 28:20; Jn. 16:12-15; Eph. 2:20 ["prophets" are N.T. prophets]; 4:20-21; Col. 3:16; Rev. 1:1-2; 2:7). Let us look more closely at the local church's officers and polity (government).

- ## Its Offices

The Lord's supervision of the local churches through His apostles and their representatives (Acts 6:1-6; 8:14; 15:36; 16:4; Gal. 2:7-10; I Tim. 1:3; Tit. 1:5) appears to have continued until the New Testament, which preserves His message and directives, was completed and distributed. Because of this, there was no need for apostolic succession. Indeed, there is no biblical evidence of its existence today.

The New Testament describes two church offices: the pastorate and the diaconate (Phil. 1:1).

1. The Pastorate

Under Christ, the general care and oversight of the local church belongs to spiritually gifted men who are divinely called to this office (Eph. 4:11; II Tim. 1:9, 11; Rom. 1:1; I Cor. 1:1) and who are spiritually qualified for their work (I Tim. 3:1-7; Tit. 1:6-9). These men are described by three titles: "elder" (Acts 20:17, Gk. *presbuteros*), "bishop" meaning "overseer" (I Tim. 3:1, Gk. *episkopos*), and "pastor" meaning "shepherd" (Eph. 4:11, Gk. *poimen*). These titles emphasize certain qualities and duties of this officer. "Elder" emphasizes that he is to be spiritually mature and wise; "bishop," that he is to preside over the affairs of the church, and "pastor," that he is to care for the church as a shepherd cares for his flock. That these designations relate to the same office and order of persons is indicated in Acts 20:28, 17; Titus 1:5, 7; and I Peter 5:1-2. It is noteworthy that the early churches often had more than one pastor or elder (Acts 14:23; 15:2; 20:17; Phil. 1:1; Tit. 1:5; Jas. 5:14).

The duties of the pastor include his ministering the Word by teaching and evangelism (II Tim. 4:2, 5; I Tim. 3:2), reproving the wayward (II Tim. 4:2; Tit. 1:9), equipping the saints for service (Eph. 4:11-12), leading the people (Heb. 13:17, "rule" means "lead"), protecting the flock from false teachers without and ambitious people within (Acts 20:28-30), being an example (I Pet. 5:3; Heb. 13:7; cp. I Tim. 4:12), and serving the spiritual needs of the flock (Mt. 20:24-28; II Cor. 11:28).

The pastor's authority is prescribed by the duties of his office as given in the New Testament and by the grant of the local church in its constitution. He expresses this authority when he follows the N.T. Scriptures in carrying out the duties of his office and when he uses their teachings in ministering to the spiritual needs of his people (Heb. 13:7; II Tim. 4:2; Tit. 1:9). Although he does not inherently have apostolic authority, the pastor has N.T. authority to lead God's people (Heb. 13:7, 17, 24, "rule"), to preside over them (I Tim. 5:17, "ruling"; cp. 3:4-5), and to care for them (3:5; cp. Lk. 10:34-35). Still, he is not to exercise dominion over them as an autocrat (I Pet. 5:3; cp. Mt. 20:25-28). Whatever authority he has, the pastor must use it only for the edification of the Lord's people, not for their destruction or for self-serving purposes (II Cor. 1:23-24; 10:8; 12:19; 13:10; I Pet. 5:3).

2. The Diaconate

This refers to the office of deacon. The word "deacon" (Gr. *diakonos*) means "servant," "attendant," or "minister." While the noun does not occur in Acts, the verb form occurs in the record of the formation of this office (Acts 6:1-6; "serve" in vs. 2). Paul speaks of the spiritual gift of ministry (Rom. 12:7) and gives the qualifications of this office (I Tim. 3:8-13).

Although many churches have deacons to assist the pastor in the spiritual oversight of the church, it would be more accurate to call them elders, or pastors. The need leading to the formation of the office (Acts 6:1-6) and the absence of the ability to teach in the requirements for deacons (I Tim. 3:8-13; contra 2) indicate that the duties of N.T. deacons were more temporal (dealing with people's physical and material needs) than spiritual. The spiritual needs were met by their pastors. This being so, it was appropriate for women to serve, at least unofficially, in this office as well, in keeping with the need for women to deal with females and their peculiar needs (Rom. 16:1-2; I Tim. 3:11).

Today, in addition to pastors and deacons we have the office of trustees. This office is required by the state to represent the local church in financial and legal matters.

• Its Polity

Polity concerns church government. Although the early churches were under the supervision of the apostles and the leadership of pastors (elders), there was considerable congregational democracy. This is seen in their election of officers and delegates (Acts 6:3, 5; 11:29-30; 15:2, 3, 22; II Cor. 8:19) and their exercise of corrective discipline (Mt. 18:17; I Cor. 5:4, 5, 7, 13).

Today, church polity differs widely throughout Christendom. The basic forms are these: congregational (e.g. Baptist), republican (e.g. Presbyterian), episcopal (e.g. Methodist), oligarchical (e.g. Eastern Orthodox), and monarchical (e.g. Roman Catholic). In congregational polity officers are chosen by the congregation and act in their name, but the authority still remains with the congregation. In republican polity the church's authority is constitutionally delegated to its elected officials, who function as a committee. In episcopal polity the authority of the church resides in the bishops. In oligarchical polity the government of the church resides in several contemporary patriarchs such as those of Constantinople and Jerusalem, And in monarchical polity all authority resides in the Pope at Rome, whom Roman Catholics consider to be God's vice-regent.

ITS ORDINANCES

While the Roman Catholic and the Eastern Orthodox churches practice seven sacred rites, called "sacraments," the New Testament gives only two rites which believers are commanded to observe. These are Water Baptism and the Lord's Supper (Mt. 28:19-20; Lk. 22:19-20; I Cor. 11:23-26). The "sacraments" are regarded by their observers to be visible signs of invisible grace and channels through which divine grace flows from the church to them as salvation and blessing. Many Protestants prefer to call the New Testament rites of Water Baptism and the Lord's Supper "ordinances," for they are commanded by the Lord and they do not minister saving grace to the observer. Actually, these rites bear witness to God's grace as manifest in the atonement and in the lives of them who receive the Saviour. Let us examine them.

- **The Ordinance of Water Baptism**

In Matthew 28:19-20, the Lord commissioned His people to do three things: to make disciples of all people through gospel presentation, to baptize them who believe the gospel, and to teach these to observe the instruction that He gave to His apostles (these are preserved in the New Testament). This commission and the practice of the early church in Acts (2:41; 8:38; 10:46-47; 18:8) show that water baptism is an ordinance that is binding upon all believers who are physically able to comply. It involves one's obedience to the Lord Jesus.

1. THE KINDS OF BAPTISM

Of the various baptisms that are mentioned in the New Testament, only the baptism with the Holy Spirit and water baptism are of immediate concern to the Lord's people. The involuntary baptism with the Holy Spirit, which places the believer into Christ and into His body (the universal church), takes place at salvation. Believers' water baptism is to be observed in obedience to the Lord after salvation as a witness to the observer's salvational faith in Christ and his union to Him. Other baptisms of which the New Testament speaks are these:

a. *The Baptism unto Moses (I Cor. 10:2)*

This refers to Israel's recognition of Moses' divine commission and to their submission to his leadership in the cloud and sea.

b. *The Baptism of Jesus (Mt. 3:13-17)*

This was symbolic of His obedience to the Father and of His giving Himself to the anointing of the Holy Spirit, whereby He was given all the gifts and powers that His Messianic work required (Lk. 3:22; Jn. 1:32-33; 3:34; Acts 10:38; Isa. 61:1; Lk. 4:16-19).

c. *The Baptism of the Cross (Mk. 10:32-38)*

This refers to the intense suffering that Jesus was to experience when His soul was made an offering for our sins (cp. Lk. 12:50; Mt. 26:42; Isa. 53:10). In Mark 10:39, the Lord seems to be referring to His people's participating with Him in His death and resurrection, which is the basis for their being dead to sin and alive unto God (cp. Rom. 6:1-11).

d. *The Baptism of Ceremonial Washings (Heb. 6:2; 9:10)*

These were rites, required by the Mosaic Law, for external purification and sanctification (cp. Ex. 29:4; 30:19-21; 40:12; Lev. 14:8-9; 16:4, 24; 17:15-16; 22:6; Num. 19:7-21; Deut. 21:6; 23:11).

e. *The Baptism of Fire (Mt. 3:10-12)*

This seems to concern Jesus' future Messianic judgment upon His enemies, especially the apostates of Israel, when He sets up His kingdom (Ezek. 20:33-38; Mal. 3:1-3; 4:1-3).

f. *The Baptism Because of Repentance*[4]

This was practiced by John the Baptizer (Mt. 3:1-2, 11) and Jesus' disciples (Mt. 4:17; Jn. 4:1-2). The immediate establishment of the Messianic kingdom depended upon Israel's repentance and return to the LORD (Deut. 30:2-3; Hos. 5:10-6:3; 14:1-2). Both John and Jesus called for repentance and faith in the Messiah and for their public confession in baptism (cp. Acts 19:4). This message anticipated the Messiah's appearance and the work that He would do.

g. *The Baptism for the Dead (I Cor. 15:29)*

This isolated instance has been subjected to many interpretations. Since "for" (Gk. *huper*) may also mean "account of" or "because of," this verse seems to refer to people who are saved and baptized because of the witness of believers who are now dead.

2. THE CANDIDATES FOR WATER BAPTISM

Contrary to the teachings of Roman Catholicism, Anglicanism, and Lutheranism, which advocate infant baptism, I believe that the only proper candidates for Christian water baptism are people who have trusted Jesus as their Saviour and who, thereby, have been born again (Acts 2:38, 41; 18:8). The erroneous notion that water baptism effects or completes salvation does not agree with New Testament teaching. The blood of Jesus, not baptismal water, cleanses us from all sins (I Jn. 1:7; Eph. 1:7; Heb. 9:14; Rev. 1:5).

Furthermore, there is no biblical evidence that water baptism has replaced ritual circumcision as a sign of the Covenant of Grace, as Reformed theologians insist. They hold that infant baptism is equivalent to O.T. ritual circumcision and is the means by which an infant becomes a member of the covenant community. Actually, the sign of the New Covenant is the Lord's Supper (Lk. 22:20). People become members of the New Covenant, Christian community by trusting Jesus as their Saviour (Jn. 1:12).

3. THE MEANING OF WATER BAPTISM

Contrary to the view of most of Christendom which holds that baptism washes away sins and works salvational grace in one's life, I believe that it bears witness to certain spiritual realities which God has wrought in the believer's life or to which the believer aspires. It is "the answer of a good conscience toward God" (I Pet. 3:21). By his water baptism the believer bears witness —

---

4 "Unto" (Gk. *eis*) in Matthew 3:11 and "for" in Acts 2:38 should be translated "because of" or "at" as in Matthew 12:41, for repentance and divine forgiveness are the ground of baptism, not its result. In keeping with Ephesians 2:8-9; Acts 16:31; John 1:12; 3:16; and I Corinthians 15:1-2, we should regard baptism as a witness to these realities rather than as the means of bringing them about.

a. *To his salvational faith in Christ (Acts 18:8)*

Water baptism provides the opportunity for a saved person to confess formally and publicly his salvational faith in the Lord Jesus Christ and His atoning work.

b. *To his union with Christ (Rom. 6:1-4)*

Water baptism is the outward, visible, symbolic portrayal of the results of one's baptism with the Holy Spirit into Jesus (Gal. 3:27; Rom. 6:1-4; Col. 2:10-13, 20; 3:1). Because of his union with Christ and his position in Him, the believer participates in the Lord's death, burial, and resurrection. By his immersion in baptismal water and his emersion from it, the believer demonstrates his union and participation with Christ in these events.

c. *To his desire to obey Christ (Mt. 28:19-20)*

The believer's observance of the ordinance of Water Baptism expresses his obedience to his new master, the Lord Jesus Christ. To be aware of this ordinance and to refuse to submit to it (except in cases of physical disability) is to sin against the Lord. This refusal disqualifies one from partaking of the Lord's Supper and incurs His chastisement. When he submits to baptism, the believer by this testifies to his desire to obey the Lord in everything.

d. *To his intention to follow Christ (Rom. 6:4)*

The believer's baptism should mark his final break with his old life and his start in his new life as Jesus' disciple. Although he will experience lapses from time to time, yet by his baptism he has started in the right direction. Incidentally, a believer needs to be baptized only once after he has been saved, not every time he sins or wishes to make a new commitment to the Lord Jesus.

e. *To his cleansing from sin (Acts 22:16)*

While baptism does not wash away sin, it does portray the believer's cleansing from sin's defilement and guilt by the divine application of Jesus' atoning work (Eph. 1:7). This judicial cleansing from sin at salvation is final, once-for-all, and complete, never to be repeated again (Col. 2:13; Heb. 9:14; 10:10, 12; Rom. 8:31-34).

If the believer has this understanding of water baptism, he will more appreciate this rite when he submits himself to it or recalls its experience.

4. THE MODES OF WATER BAPTISM

There are various opinions about how water baptism should be administered. The most common forms are pouring water on the candidate's head (affusion, first mentioned in *The Didache*, written about 150), sprinkling water on the head or face (aspersion, reported in 251 but not commonly practiced until the 13th century, only in the West),[5] and dipping the candidate completely in water (immersion, practiced since the conception

---

[5] "Baptism," Schaff-Herzog, *Encyclopaedia of Religious Knowledge* (1891), I, 201.

of the Christian church).

There are several reasons for my holding that immersion is the proper, biblical mode. First, there is the meaning of the word *baptize*. Coming from the Greek word *baptizo*, it means to dip or immerse. In non-Christian Greek literature the word was used for dipping, plunging, or sinking.[6]

A. T. Robertson writes, "It may be remarked that no Baptist has written a lexicon of the Greek language, and yet the standard lexicons...uniformly give the meaning of *baptizo* as dip, immerse. They do not give pour or *sprinkle*. The presumption is therefore in favor of *dip* in the N.T."[7] Johannes Warns adds, "The Greek language has distinct words for 'sprinkle' and 'immerse.'"[8]   In English versions of the New Testament the Greek word *baptizo* is not translated but is transliterated. To have translated the word would have shown that the practices of pouring and sprinkling are neither apostolic nor biblical.

Immersion was the prevalent mode until the Council of Trent (1545), when the Roman Catholic church abandoned the practice. The Reformer John Calvin wrote, "It is evident that the term *baptise* means to immerse, and that this was the form used by the primitive church."[9] However, he felt that sprinkling was as effective as immersion.

A second reason for holding immersion is that it was the practice of the New Testament church. The only description of water baptism in Acts is Philip's baptizing the Ethiopian official (Acts 8:38-39). They both entered the water, where Philip baptized the Ethiopian, and they came up out of the water. Although predating the church, John's baptism was also by immersion (Jn. 3:23; Mk. 1:5-10).

A third reason for holding immersion is that it portrays the results of the Holy Spirit's baptism. Immersion is the symbolic enactment of the believer's participation in Christ's death, burial, and resurrection, resulting from his union with Jesus (Rom. 6:3-4). While cleansing from sin and the outpouring of the Holy Spirit, symbolically portrayed by aspersion and affusion, are important to the Christian life, these do not present the ground of every spiritual blessing which we have in Christ (Eph. 1:3). Immersion alone portrays our union with the Lord, which is the basis of these blessings.

Incidentally, notice that to be baptized "in the name of the Lord Jesus" (Acts 8:16; 19:5) or "in the name of the Lord" (10:48) represents water baptism, while the baptism of the Holy Spirit is described as being baptized "into Jesus Christ" (Rom. 6:3), "into Christ" (Gal. 3:27), or "into one body" (I

---

[6] H. G. Liddell and R. Scott, *A Greek-English Lexicon* (London: Oxford University Press, 1940), p. 305.

[7] "Baptism," *The International Standard Bible Encyclopaedia* (1949), p. 386.

[8] Johannes Warns, *Baptism* (London: The Paternoster Press, 1957), p. 52.

[9] John Calvin, *Institutes of the Christian Religion* (Grand Rapids: Wm. B. Eerdmans Publishing Company, 1962), II, 524.

Cor. 12:13). "Name" represents a person and his work. To be baptized in Jesus' name is a public witness to one's faith in Him as Saviour and in His atoning work as being the sufficient basis for divine forgiveness.

The early church departed from the practice of immersion when the false teaching arose in the second century which alleged that baptism washes away sins. This error led to the false conclusion that all people, including infants, had to be baptized if they were to be saved. Thus, modes other than immersion were used if the candidates were infants or infirm people.

• The Ordinance of the Lord's Supper

The Lord instituted this rite on the eve of His death when He ate the Passover meal with His apostles (Mt. 26:26-29; Mk. 14:22-25; Lk. 22:14-20; I Cor. 11:23-25). That the Lord's people are to observe this rite today is indicated by the imperatives which the Lord used, regarding eating and drinking, when He instituted this memorial.

1. ITS SYMBOLISM

The Lord Jesus clearly stated that "the (unleavened) bread" was His body and (the content of) "the cup" was the blood of the New Covenant that was shed for His people (Lk. 22:19-20). However, there is not universal agreement about the meaning of the bread and cup. According to the Roman Catholic view, the bread and cup are changed by priestly consecration into the very body and blood of Jesus, and this consecration is a new offering of Christ's sacrifice. This view is called "transubstantiation." The Lutheran view holds that the bread and cup remain what they were, but the communicant consumes the actual body and blood of Christ "in, with, and under" these elements. This view is called "consubstantiation."

I prefer the view that the bread and cup are and remain symbols of the Lord's broken body and shed blood (I Cor. 11:24-25). This view is supported by the fact that when He instituted this rite, the Lord was physically present with His apostles and His blood had not yet been shed. Also, the linking verb is can be used with symbols as well as with actual things, as demonstrated by Galatians 4:22-26 and John 6:55. In fact, the Lord said that the cup was the New Covenant in His blood (Lk. 22:20). Representing the means by which the New Covenant was ratified, the cup is a symbol of our Lord's blood, or atoning work (Jn. 10:18; Eph. 1:7; Rom. 5:8-9). The bread is a symbol of our Lord's body, or His incarnation, which made possible His dying for our sins (Heb. 2:14; 10:10). Thus, the Lord's Supper, with its symbols, is a witness to His atonement, which is the basis of our relationship to God.

2. ITS PREREQUISITES

a. Salvation and Baptism

Since the Lord gave this to His disciples (Mt. 26:26), it is obvious that one must be saved and baptized to qualify for its observance. Some churches practice "closed communion" where only the members are allowed to participate. They who practice "open communion" hold that the Lord's table is open to all of His people even if they should not be members of the church in which the rite is held. All hold that one who refuses water baptism is disqualified for this rite.

b. *Heart Preparation*

A prerequisite, which is often ignored, is heart preparation. Paul rebuked the Corinthian believers for their unworthy observance of this rite (I Cor. 11:22-34). Because of sins that they committed during a common meal before the Lord's Supper, these people were guilty of insulting the Lord (vss. 20-22, 27). They were partaking of the elements of the rite without counting their meaning and value. This brought upon them the Lord's corrective chastisement (vss. 28-32). With this in view, our heart preparation requires our self-examination and adjustment and our having attitudes of commitment and expectation.

(1) *Self-examination and adjustment (I Cor. 11:28)*

This refers to our assessing our spiritual state by asking ourself questions like the following: Am I saved? Is there any known sin in my life with which I have not dealt? What does God approve in my life? What should I be doing that I am not doing? What place does God have in my life? Have I wronged others or hold an ill-feeling toward them?

Upon completing this assessment, we must make whatever correction is necessary such as repenting of and confessing any sins that are known to us (Rev. 2:5; I Jn. 1:9) as well as righting any wrongs that we have done to others (Mt. 5:23-24).

(2) *Committal and expectation (Mt. 11:28-30)*

These are attitudes of submission and faith. It is fitting that we submit ourself anew to the Lord's authority (II Cor. 5:14-15) and look to Him to impress upon us the truths that are appropriate for the occasion and to bless us.

3. *ITS WORTHY OBSERVANCE*

The worthy observance of the Lord's Supper requires our meditation and worship.

a. *Blessed Meditation (I Cor. 11:24-25)*

As we participate in the Lord's Supper, we should think about the meaning of its symbolism as a memorial, proclamation, and a fellowship. As a *memorial* (I Cor. 11:24-25, "in remembrance of Me"), the elements remind us of the atoning work of our Lord, upon which rests our salvation and our relationship to God (Rom. 5:9; Eph. 1:7; Jn. 6:53). As a *proclamation* (I Cor. 11:26), this rite declares the fact and central truth of our faith. By this we say that we have received the Saviour and have found Him truly to be the Redeemer. Having experienced its salvational benefits, we assert that His atoning work is effective. As a *fellowship* (I Cor. 10:16-17), this rite provides the Lord's people the opportunity to fellowship with Him and with one another. As the "one loaf" He is the spiritual life and nourishment of His people (Jn. 6:35, 55-57, 63), and as the "one body" we who are saved bear witness to our having partaken of Him.

b. *Joyful Worship (Acts 2:46-47)*

One cannot approach the Lord's table and reflect upon its meaning without gratitude and joy. Here we are brought face to face with the God of grace and the highest expression of His grace, manifest in our Lord's atoning work. When we consider what He has done for us, we are motivated to renew our commitment of love to Him and to praise Him for all that He is (II Cor. 8:9; 5:14-15).

ITS DISCIPLINE

Corrective church discipline of sinning members is always difficult, and failure to exercise it never resolves its need. Those churches that neglect this will become carnal, powerless, and short of God's blessing.

- **Its Value**

Corrective discipline, administered with proper spirit and purpose (Gal. 6:1), is good for the offender. Hopefully, it will lead to his shame, repentance, and restoration (II Thess. 3:14; Gal. 6:1). To ignore his sin is to confirm him in it by encouraging him to continue with it.

Corrective discipline is also good for the church. Disciplinary action toward sinning members will halt the corrupting influence of sin in the church (I Cor. 5:6-7). A morally clean church is a powerful one (Acts 5:1-16); a corrupt one is paralyzed (I Cor. 3:1-4; 15:34). Prompt corrective discipline is also a warning to others (I Tim. 5:20; Eccles. 8:11).

- **Its Duty**

The church is obligated to discipline its wayward members, for this is commanded by the Lord (Mt. 18:15-22; I Cor. 5:1-13; II Thess. 3:6, 14-15).

- **Its Procedure**

Needless to say, it is important that it be fully established that a person is really sinning or that he is violating the church's articles of faith and practice, which he agreed to uphold, before any disciplinary action is taken against him. If he is guilty, then the Scriptures give the following directions:

1. *We must pray for the offender (I Jn. 5:16).*

We should pray that he will deal with his sin and gain victory over it. Also, we should pray that he will respond favorably to counsel, if this should be needed. If we discern that he is committing a sin that will irrevocably lead to the divine judgment of premature physical death, then we should not pray for him. He will not be helped by prayer (cp. Prov. 15:10; Heb. 12:9).

2. *We must counsel with him (Mt. 18:15).*

At first alone. We are directed to point out his sin for the purpose of restoring him (Gal. 6:1). Observe the spiritual qualifications of this ministry: spirituality (our being filled with the Holy Spirit), meekness (our human spirit softened with love and clothed with humility), alertness (our watching lest we fall into temptation), and a knowledge of the Word (II Tim. 4:2). If he responds favorably, we have won him. If he should reject this counsel, then we must go again with one or two others (Mt. 18:16), and repeat our efforts. If he fails to respond favorably to this attempt, then his rebellious attitude will be attested by those who are with us.

3. *We must report the matter to the church if he fails to heed counsel (Mt. 18:17).*

At this point the pastor should be informed of the situation so that he, with members of the official board, may counsel with the sinning member in an effort to restore him. If this fails, then the matter must be presented to the congregation or its official representatives and the following action should be taken:

a. *Remove the offender's name from the church membership (I Cor. 5:13).* He is no longer qualified for this relation.

b. *Have no more association with him (II Thess. 3:6, 14; I Cor. 5:2, 7, 9-12, 13b).* Still, we must continue to have contact with him so that we can minister to him and can seek his restoration.

c. *Yet, do not count him as an enemy (II Thess. 3:15).* The church must continue to seek his restoration by admonition and prayer.

d. *Forgive and restore him upon his repentance (II Cor. 2:7-11).* Needless to say, it is very important that the church not hold against these offenders the judged sins of the past. We are to be forgiving like our Lord (Eph. 4:32). The blood of Jesus (His atoning work) does cleanse His people from all sins, when they are dealt with according to scriptural principles (I Jn. 1:7, 9; Rev. 2:5). To their shame, churches often either ignore their fallen members or refuse to forgive, reinstate, and love them.

THE ECUMENICAL MOVEMENT

The word *ecumenical* (from Gk. *oikoumene*, "inhabited earth") means "worldwide." This movement strives to reverse the fragmentation of Christendom that came about with the Protestant Reformation. It seeks a visible, organizational unity of all of Christendom under one head for the fulfillment of Jesus' prayer, "that they all may be one" (Jn. 17:21), and for the legislation of righteousness throughout the earth.

The movement began in England with the formation of The Evangelical Alliance (1846) for the purpose of promoting Christian union and religious liberty. This was followed by The World Student Christian Federation (1895) and The First International Missionary Conference (Edinburgh, 1910).

Theological differences soon divided the spirit of these international conferences. Religious liberalism made inroads; Quakers, Unitarians, and mainstream Protestants met to consider economic, social, and industrial problems as well as spiritual matters. These earlier conferences consisted of prominent church leaders and theologians.

In 1948 a merger of the World Conference on Faith and Order (1927, 1937) and the Universal Christian Council for Life and Work (1925, 1937) resulted in the formation of the World Council of Churches, the first international council of churches. Meeting in Amsterdam, this council consisted of some 150 denominations of Protestant, Anglican, Eastern Orthodox, and Old Catholic confessions from more than forty countries and represented about 150 million professed Christians. This council has characterized the ecumenical movement as one that is willing to sacrifice doctrine and conviction for the sake of unity.

Originally, the leadership of the World Council of Churches was dominated by Protestant liberalism. But since 1961, with the admission of the Russian Orthodox church and its satellite churches, it has broken away from its Protestant mooring and its western heritage and is swinging toward the Catholic orbit. A keen observer reports that in policy and practice the council has (1) disowned an authoritative Bible, (2) rejected the idea that man is lost in sin and can only be saved by accepting and obeying the Christian gospel, (3) repudiated the fundamentals of the Christian faith in favor of an inalienable religious intuition comparable to that faith, and (4) accepted the establishment of God's kingdom (a redeemed society) as the mission of the church. It proposes that the church should be freed from the obligation of preaching a distinctive gospel for the converting of individual souls so that it can cooperate with all agencies, both sacred and secular, for social improvement and the building of a better world.[10] It should also be pointed out that the council has never recognized the threat of Marxist communism to Christianity.

There is no indication in the Scriptures that the present ecumenical movement is of the Lord. The Lord Jesus was not praying for the organizational, ritualistic unity of His people, as ecumenism holds. He was praying for the inner, spiritual unity of His people, which transcends personal individuality and its expression in denominational distinctives and preferences. The unity for which He prayed (Jn. 17:21) does not find its reality in any device of man, but in God and in the union of His people with Himself (Jn. 14:9-10, 20; Gal. 3:27-28; I Cor. 10:17; 12:13, 27). This union is being effected by the baptism of the Holy Spirit which occurs at salvation. Its reality is

---

[10] James DeForest Murch, "Where Is the Ecumenical Movement Headed?" *Moody Monthly*, November 1969, pp. 26-29.

expressed in the universal church which the Lord is building during this age (Mt. 16:18). True believers cannot have spiritual fellowship with apostates and teachers of religious error (Rom. 16:17-18; Tit. 3:9-11; II Jn. 10-11).

The Lord's church, both its universal and local aspects, is indeed a unique institution. The universal church is a living organism, with Jesus as its head and life. The local church is a regional organization, consisting of professed Christians, who in spite of different personalities, origins and vocations agree in doctrine and purpose to worship and serve the triune God. It is our duty to belong to and be active in a local church, especially one that honors our Lord's teachings and authority and that promotes His work in this world.

THE CHRISTIAN LIFE

In this section we shall focus on those elements that are essential to Christian growth and fruitfulness and that are necessary for the health of the local church and the edification of the universal church. May the Holy Spirit not only give us understanding of these truths but may He also enable us to experience them in daily life to the end that our spiritual vitality might abound to God's glory.

THE EXPERIENCE OF THE CHRISTIAN LIFE

When we who are saved trusted Jesus for salvation, we received a new kind of life and entered a new life experience. This new life is spiritual ("eternal" or "everlasting") life (Jn. 3:15-16). Since the Lord Jesus Christ is the expression of this life (Jn. 14:6)[11], to have Him is to possess this life (I Jn. 5:11-12) and to allow Him to express Himself in and through us is to experience this new life (Gal. 2:20; 4:19; Phil. 1:21).

Having this new life, the Holy Spirit, and a renewed soul and spirit, the saved person has the capacity and apparatus that are necessary for Christian experience. Being an interaction with God and the things of God, Christian experience rests upon one's personal relationship with God, is brought about by the Holy Spirit's work in our lives, and is understood by the teachings of Scripture. Unlike mysticism which seeks contact with God by immediate intuition apart from Scripture, Christian experience conforms to and is understood by the Bible's teaching about spiritual reality.

Some aspects of Christian experience follow:

- **An awareness of one's filial relationship with God (Gal. 4:6).**

We experience this awareness when we are filled with the Holy Spirit and walk in obedience to the Lord (Jn. 14:21-23).

---

[11] Eternal life springs from a personal relationship with God (Jn. 17:3). This life has its source in the Father (Rom. 6:23), is through or in Jesus (Rom. 6:23), and is communicated to us believers by the Holy Spirit (Rom. 8:2). In our glorified state, we shall also have His present kind of physical life (vs. 11).

- **A growing knowledge of God and of spiritual truth (Jn. 17:3; Col. 1:10; Eph. 1:17-19).**

This knowledge is gained from the Scriptures and from God's dealings with us, interpreted in the light of His Word (cp. Job 42:5-6).

- **The knowledge of divine forgiveness (Col. 2:13; I Jn. 1:9).**

Only the saved person knows that his sins are forgiven, his debt to God is cancelled.

- **Various ministries of the Holy Spirit (Jn. 14:16-17).**

Such as His teaching, guiding, enabling us, and His producing His fruit in our lives (I Cor. 2:12; Rom. 8:14; Jn. 14:15-16; Gal. 5:22-23).

- **Love for God and for others (I Jn. 4:7).**

Our love for God is expressed by our obedience to His Word (Jn. 14:15, 21, 23). Our love for others is manifest when we seek to minister to their needs (I Jn. 3:16-18).

- **A sensitivity toward and dissatisfaction with sin (Eph. 4:30).**

Sin no longer brings us the pleasure it once did, for our renewed nature reacts against it (cp. I Jn. 3:9; 1:5-7).

- **Answers to prayer (Jer. 33:3).**

In keeping with His many promises, God answers our prayers when we meet His conditions (Jn. 14:13; 15:7; I Jn. 5:14-15).

- **The fulfillment of God's promises (II Pet. 1:4).**

Our faith in God's promises allows Him to do for us what He says He will do (cp. Heb. 13:5-6).

- **Occasions of victory over our spiritual enemies (Gal. 5:16; Jas. 4:7).**

To ignore sin's urges, Satan's temptations, or the world's evil influences and to yield to God and do His will are blessed experiences.

- **Involvement in Christ's service (I Cor. 3:9).**

The Lord is ministering through His people to build His church quantitatively and qualitatively (Jn. 15:4-5; cp. Acts 14:27).

- **Christian fellowship (I Jn. 1:3-4).**

Our fellowship with God and with others of like faith in the love and unity of the Holy Spirit is blessed, indeed.

THE GROWTH OF THE CHRISTIAN LIFE

This new life in Christ has a capacity for growth in its expression in our daily life; therefore, we have the duty of cultivating it (II Pet. 3:18). When Paul rebuked the Corinthian believers for their carnality, he described them as "babes" (I Cor. 3:1-3). They were infants in their spiritual development, not in age. Their living under the domination of the sin-principle had blighted their spiritual life and had retarded their spiritual growth (cp. Gal. 6:8; I Pet. 2:1-

2). This points to the fact that at any particular time in our life we are either progressing or retrogressing in our spiritual development, for there is no standing still. Let us consider what the Scriptures say about spiritual growth.

• Its Definition

Like all growth, spiritual growth is a progressive increase in certain areas of our spiritual life. These areas include spiritual character as expressed by the fruit of the Holy Spirit (I Thess. 3:12), practical faith in God and in His promises (II Thess. 1:3), spiritual knowledge of God and the things of God (Col. 1:10), spiritual activity within God's will (II Cor. 9:8; cp. Heb. 13:21; Jas. 4:17), and veneration for the Lord Jesus (Jn. 3:30; cp. Phil. 1:21).

Since this is brought about by the activity of the Holy Spirit, spiritual growth is quantitative rather than qualitative; it is absolute rather than relative; it is one of frequency rather than one of refinement. All that the Holy Spirit does is absolute, not being subject to refinement or improvement. For instance, growing in faith and in love means expressing these virtues more often rather than experiencing a refinement of them. This is true, also, of our gaining spiritual knowledge, engaging in spiritual activity, and venerating the Lord Jesus. These experiences, too, seem to be absolute and increase quantitatively in frequency. As we grow, we have these spiritual experiences more often. In the case of growing in spiritual knowledge, we more often add to the fund we already possess and by this gain greater spiritual insight. The Holy Spirit produces this growth as we cooperate with Him and allow Him to do this work in our life.

• Its Goal

The goal of spiritual growth is that we increasingly become like the Lord Jesus, who is this life (Eph. 4:11-16). We were predestinated to this (Rom. 8:29), and it is brought about by the activity of the Holy Spirit (II Cor. 3:18). It will be completed when our bodies are made like Jesus' risen body and we share His glory at His coming (I Jn. 3:2; Phil. 3:20-21; Col. 3:4).

• Its Means

How are we to cooperate with the Holy Spirit to cultivate this new life and promote its growth? There is a similarity between the means of natural growth and spiritual growth. These means include our eating, exercising, resting, and submitting to authority and instruction. As the natural life requires regular nourishment so the spiritual life requires the nourishment of God's Word (I Pet. 2:1-2; Jn. 6:63; II Tim. 3:16-17; Ps. 1:1-3). As the natural life needs exercise so does the spiritual life in the form of obedience to God (I Jn. 2:5). As the natural life calls for rest so does the spiritual life require faith in God and His Word (Gal. 2:20; 5:25; Rom. 1:17). (This practical faith is not one of inactivity but of joint activity with God, relying on Him to do His part as we do ours.) Finally, this growth is fostered by our submitting to God's authority, heeding His instruction, and patiently bearing His dealings with us

(Heb. 12:6-11).

When we faithfully appropriate these means of growth, we experience spiritual development. When we neglect these means, we come under the control of the sin-principle and allow it to express its evil works in our lives (Gal. 5:19-21). This carnality not only will hinder growth but also will cause retrogression in one's spiritual life if it is allowed to continue (I Pet. 2:1-2; I Cor. 3:1-3). The more we grow spiritually, the more we become like Jesus and manifest Him (Gal. 5:22-23; Rom. 6:16-22).

Since the spiritual life has an infinite capacity for growth, we should never be satisfied with our present spiritual condition. It is God's desire that we keep on growing throughout our lifetime (II Pet. 3:18). Although we shall never attain absolute maturity in this world, we can be relatively mature for our spiritual age as we continually give ourselves to those means that God uses to bring this about.

THE MAINTENANCE OF THE CHRISTIAN LIFE

God has given us everything that we need for our pleasing and glorifying Him (II Pet. 1:3). These provisions include the Bible, the Holy Spirit, prayer, cleansing from sin, and the ministries of other believers. However, to receive benefit from these provisions, we must apply them to our life. Let us see how we may make profitable use of these.

• The Bible

The profitableness of the Bible to our life cannot be overstated. Consisting of the Old and New Testaments, it is God's complete written revelation to man. Needless to say, it is of supreme importance to us who are saved. It is food for our spiritual nourishment (I Pet. 2:2), a lamp for our guidance (Ps. 119:105), a weapon against our spiritual enemies (Eph. 6:17), and equipment for every good work (II Tim. 3:17). Furthermore, by the Scriptures the unsaved learn about salvation and how to be saved (II Tim. 3:15; Rom. 10:17; I Pet. 1:23).

More and more I am impressed with the fact that God uses the Scriptures to minister to the spiritual needs of people. Paul not only exhorted Timothy to preach the Word (II Tim. 4:2), but he also declared that the Scriptures are profitable (3:16-17) for doctrine (teaching us what we should know), reproof (pointing to what is wrong in our life), correction (showing us how we should deal with this wrong), and instruction in righteousness (teaching us what is God's will and how we are to do it). Being God's Word, the Bible effectively works in all who believe its truth (Heb. 1:1-2; I Thess. 2:13). It is essential to our well-being and fruitfulness that we learn what God says and apply this truth to our lives daily.

1. HOW TO READ THE BIBLE FOR PERSONAL PROFIT

One can read the Scriptures and receive nothing from them. However, this is not the fault of the Scriptures, but of us and the manner in which we read them. The following formula may be helpful in making your devotional reading more profitable:

a. *Pray*, asking God to help you understand His message for you (Ps. 119:18).

b. *Read* the passage straight through so as to get an overview of it.

c. *Study*, trying to understand each part of the passage and to discover its spiritual instructions. As time allows, look up the marginal references, for unfamiliar words consult a dictionary, and find the meaning of difficult verses in commentaries.

d. *Reread* the passage with your personal needs in mind.

e. *Select* some truth or part which stands out or impresses you. God speaks through the Scriptures in this manner.

f. *Think* how this impressive part relates to your life.

g. *Pray again*, asking God to help you apply this truth to your life, giving Him thanks for speaking to you, and yielding yourself anew to Him. Do not leave the Word until He has given you something. Look to the Lord to minister to you through His Word, not only as you read it but also as you recall what you have read. There is no adequate substitute for daily reading of the Scriptures (Jn. 6:63; Mt. 4:4). Beware of allowing devotional aids to take the place of this.

2. *HOW TO UNDERSTAND THE SCRIPTURES*[12]

The following rules of interpretation will help you to understand God's Word:

a. *Follow the customary usage of language.*

Interpret the Bible literally, except where figures of speech, such as simile and metaphor, are given.[13] Learn the biblical usage of words and recognize the main ideas of the passage, as indicated by the independent clauses, and their relationships to one another, as indicated by the introductory clause conjunctions.

b. *Interpret in the light of the context.*

The context of a passage is the surrounding portion. Disregarding chapter and verse divisions, discover who is speaking, to whom the words are addressed, the antecedent of any pronoun, the historical and geographical setting, and the writer's theme, purpose and plan.

c. *Interpret Scripture by Scripture.*

The Bible often gives its own explanation of words and phrases. With the aid of marginal references or a concordance, see how the words or

---

[12] See F.H. Barackman, *How To Interpret The Bible*. (Grand Rapids: Kregel Publications, 1991)

[13] David L. Cooper's "Golden Rule of Interpretation" follows: "When the plain sense of Scripture makes common sense, seek no other sense; therefore, take every word at its primary, ordinary, usual, literal meaning unless the facts of the immediate context, studied in the light of related passages and axiomatic and fundamental truths, indicate clearly otherwise." *What Men Must Believe* (Los Angeles: Biblical Research Society, 1943) p. 63.

phrases are used elsewhere in the Bible and what light is cast upon their meaning.

d. *Recognize dispensational distinctions.*

While all Scripture is profitable (II Tim. 3:16), recognize that God has given particular stewardships, which express His will, to certain peoples throughout history. His stewardship for us is given in the New Testament. While all the redeemed of human history have the same salvational blessings, groups of redeemed peoples, such as Israel and the church, have separate functions and duties. It is important to keep in mind what people are being addressed in the portion of the Bible you are reading.

e. *Recognize the progress and unity of God's revelation.*

Every part of the Bible makes a contribution toward our understanding of a biblical subject, but by itself a single passage will be doctrinally incomplete. Since God's full revelation about a subject exceeds that which any passage gives, seek to understand what all the Bible teaches on that subject. A wrong understanding of a doctrine often rises from an exaggerated or a partial interpretation of a biblical truth. We should remember the principle of the self-consistency of the Scriptures, which says that there is in the Bible perfect agreement between the parts that comprise the whole revelation of a particular truth. Also, we should interpret obscure passages by what is clearly taught elsewhere in the Bible.

f. *Seek to discover what a passage is really saying.*

Try to be as objective as possible when interpreting the Scriptures. Distinguish between what a passage means and what it illustrates. It is easy to transport unconsciously New Testament illumination to an Old Testament passage and "see" more there than what it really says. On the other hand, when we are studying biblical prophecy, we know that its fulfillment (if given in the New Testament) clarifies certain ambigous features of it.

g. *Seek the enlightenment of the Holy Spirit.*

He is our teacher of divine truth (I Jn. 2:27; I Cor. 2:9-15). As you look to Him, He not only will direct your study but also will give you understanding of biblical truth.

h. *Use reliable reference tools.*

Use interpretation aids that are written by doctrinally sound people and that are faithful to the teachings of God's Word. These can be identified by the reputation of the writer and the publisher and by the content of the reference work. What does the book say about the Bible, God, the Lord Jesus, the Holy Spirit, and salvation? Does it agree with what the Bible teaches about these themes?

3. *HOW TO RELATE THE SCRIPTURES TO DAILY LIFE*

God has given us His Word for more than satisfying our academic curiosity. For the Word to do its sanctifying work in our life we must allow it to dwell in us richly (Col. 3:16), teaching us the divine will, revealing our inherent needs and infinite resources, alerting us to our spiritual enemies, and manifesting to us our imcomparable God. The following suggestions will help us to give it its proper place in our daily life.[14]

a. *Use the Bible in your fellowship with God.*

Regard the Scriptures as the means by which He will speak to you — enlightening, convicting, assuring, instructing, rebuking, restraining, warning, appealing, strengthening, encouraging, comforting, directing, and blessings (Ps. 19:7-11).

b. *Regard the Bible's treasures as being inexhaustible.*

You can expect God to use it daily to give you fresh insight and suitable provision for your spiritual needs. You need to be reminded of familiar truth as well as be taught new truth (Jn. 6:35).

c. *Look for truth that will relate to your needs.*

Whether your needs are due to problems, adversities, failures, duties, desires, weaknesses, or sins, the Sriptures are able to minister to these, for they are God's Word to you (II Cor. 2:16; 3:5; 12:9; Jn. 6:63).

d. *Be a doer of the Word and not a hearer only.*

Looking to God for enablement, strive to be responsive to the Scriptures (Jas. 1:21-25; cp. Lk. 8:18). If it is a warning, heed it; a failure or sin, confess it; a promise, claim it; an instruction, receive it; a command, obey it; a rebuke, accept it; or a blessing, give thanks for it.

e. *Seek to build up a systematic doctrinal belief.*

When you learn new truth, relate it to what you already know about the subject. In this way, you will accumulate a fund of knowledge about the various themes of which the Bible speaks. Aim to understand thoroughly what the Bible teaches about key doctrines, and share this with others.

f. *Prepare to give a Scriptural answer for your faith.*

From the Bible learn what Christians should believe and why they should believe it (I Pet. 3:15). Be able to appeal to the Scriptures for your assertions of spiritual truth when you are questioned by others (Acts 17:11).

g. *Seek to work out a practical ethical code.*

Only God's Word provides the absolute standard for the Christian behavior that is pleasing to Him. The Scriptures will show you what is right and wrong, good and evil, true and false. They give divine precepts and guiding principles, which you may relate to the moral decisions and situations that confront you and by which you may know God's will regarding these things (Ps. 119:105, 9-11).

h. *Recognize the need for returning daily to the Scriptures.*

Your need for all that the Bible offers never ends (Ps. 1:1-3). There is always more to learn, and there is always the need for walking in

---

[14]See Alan M. Stibbs, *Understanding God's Word* (London: The Inter-Varsity Fellowship, 1961), pp. 58-64.

obedience to God's will (II Tim. 2:15; 3:16-17; Eph. 5:17).

We thank God for this wonderful provision. However, it can benefit us only as we make use of it daily.

• The Holy Spirit

The heavenly Father has given to us who are saved the Holy Spirit to be our resident Helper (Jn. 14:16-17). As our Helper, He stands ready to enable us to do and to be all that God requires of our lives, such as expressing Christian character (Gal. 5:22-23; Eph. 5:9), waging victorious warfare against our spiritual enemies (Gal. 5:16), performing Christian service (Acts 1:8; I Cor. 15:10), and rendering acceptable worship (Phil. 3:3; Jn. 4:24). In fact, we can do the will of God only through the power of Christ Jesus which is communicated to us by the Holy Spirit (Phil. 4:13; Heb. 13:21; Jn. 15:5).

However, to receive help from the Holy Spirit, we must experience His filling (Eph. 5:18). This occurs when we adjust ourselves to His presence and cooperate with Him. We do this by dealing with known sins, by yielding ourself to His control, and by exercising faith that He assumes control (Eph. 4:30; I Thess. 5:19; Acts 6:5). This surrender to His control does not make us passive instruments in His hand. We must still exhibit right attitudes, attend to our duties, and fulfill our commitments. But in doing these things, we do them in union with Him, looking to Him to direct us and to enable us to do them in a manner that will glorify God. As long as we act in reliance upon and in obedience to Him, we allow Him to help us please our Lord. Whenever we fail to do this, we sin (Rom. 14:23; Gal. 5:16). Then, we must judge our sin, confess it to the Lord, and yield anew to our divine Helper.

Since the Holy Spirit is a person, we can talk to Him at any time about all that concerns us and can express our dependence upon Him for His help (II Cor. 13:14). This relationship becomes a precious fellowship with God as we share with Him all that makes up life for us.

• Prayer

Prayer is an amazing provision for the Christian life. It may be defined as our communicating with God by words, thoughts, or a glance (Mk. 6:41; 7:34). When we reflect upon the nature and works of God, the fact that we can talk to Him about everything (I Pet. 5:7; Phil. 4:6), at any time (I Thess. 5:17), provokes within us humility and awe. Yet, His many appeals encourage us to pray. He is pleased when we come often to Him with childlike simplicity and confidence.

1. THE FORMS OF PRAYER

Our prayers may assume any form of communication, as thanksgiving (II Cor. 2:14), praise (Acts 2:47), confession of sin (Ps. 51:1-4), petition (Rom. 1:9-10), intercession (Jn. 17:9), expression of reliance (II Chron. 14:11), holy argument (Ex. 32:11-13), questions (Ps. 10:1), complaint (Jonah 4:1-3), fellowship (Lk. 6:12; I Jn. 1:7), dedication (Isa. 6:8), and expression of salvational faith (Rom. 10:13). Actually, we can share with God all that is on our heart and all that concerns us, including our problems, desires, disappointments, duties, fears, pleasures, affections, weaknesses, and sins. We can be candid with Him, for He knows all about us (Ps. 139:1-6, 23-24; Mt. 6:8).

2. THE ADDRESSEES OF PRAYER

The believer may talk to each or any Member of the holy Trinity, as his desire or need may be. As a child he may address the Father; as a servant he may talk to the Lord Jesus, his master; and as one who needs assistance or direction he may speak to the Holy Spirit, his helper.

Misunderstanding Jesus' words in John 16:23-27, some feel that all prayers should be directed to God the Father (cp. Eph. 3:14). As I see it, the Lord seems to be saying to His disciples, who had not before looked to the Father for their needs, that they are now able to pray to the Father themselves in Jesus' name. His name represents His atoning work, by means of which believers can approach God (Eph. 1:6; 2:18; Heb. 10:19-22). Other passages indicate that we can pray to Jesus (Acts 7:59; I Cor. 1:2, 9; II Cor. 12:8; II Tim. 2:22; I Jn. 1:3) and to the Holy Spirit (II Cor. 13:14; Phil. 2:1) as well as to the Father (I Pet. 1:17).

3. SOME RULES OF PRAYER

There are no rules for posture, time, length, and place. These are determined by the direction of the Holy Spirit, custom, and circumstances. On the other hand, as in all spiritual exercises, we must depend upon the Holy Spirit to give us enablement and direction for our praying (Rom. 8:14; Jude 20); and we must be morally clean (Ps. 66:18; Prov. 15:29). Also, there are certain conditions we must meet if we are to receive answers to our petitions. As we consider these conditions, observe the promises that accompany them and that encourage our faith.

a. We must ask in Jesus' name (Jn. 14:13-14).

This is more than appending His name to our prayers. Representing His person and work, His name stands for what He is and does. To pray in His name is to pray according to His interests (Mt. 16:18), His will (I Jn. 5:14-15), and His objective to glorify the Father (Jn. 12:28; 17:4). The glory of God should be the supreme motivation for our asking Him for things. When we fail to do this and seek only the satisfaction of our own desires, we ask amiss (Jas. 4:3). God will never be our servant to minister to our whims, however worthy they may be. We are ever His servants, who exist for His glory (Eph. 1:12).

b. We must ask definite requests (Jas. 4:2).

But is this necessary since God knows everything (Mt. 6:8)? Our making definite petitions shows our recognition of need, our dependency upon God, and our faith in His ability and willingness to answer our petitions (cp. Eph. 3:20; Mk. 10:47-51).

c. *We must abide in Christ (Jn. 15:7).*

This concerns our daily relationship with Jesus. To abide in Him is to keep in touch with Him by self-surrender, obedience, faith and communication. As we do, we allow Him to abide in us in the fulness of His life. As we allow His Word to abide in us and direct us, we allow Him to influence us. Then we may ask what we desire with the confidence that God will grant our requests. He can do this without contradicting Himself or injuring us, for then our desires are surrendered to His will and are shaped by His indwelling Word (cp. Col. 3:16; I Jn. 3:22; Ps. 37:4).

d. *We must believe that God will answer as He promises (Mt. 21: 22; Mk. 11:22-24).*

God encourages us to pray by promising to answer our prayers. These promises give us something to believe. While we believe that He means what He says (Tit. 1:2) and is able to do what He promises (Eph. 3:20), do we have the faith to believe that He will do this for us? His promises assure us that He will. Also, He has no favorites, for He is no respecter of persons (Rom. 2:11). Let us not limit God to what we think is possible for Him. Since He is able to do exceedingly abundantly above all that we ask or think, let us ask Him for great things that will magnify His name (cp. Mt. 9:28-29).

e. *We must ask persistently (Lk. 11:5-10).*

Jesus' parable and the verbs He uses (present imperative) indicate the need for our continuing to pray about a matter until we receive our request or are shown that we are asking amiss. This kind of praying is similar to our placing an order with a catalog merchandising house and our daily looking for its arrival.

The condition of persistent praying is for our benefit. It expresses our confidence that God will answer; it prepares our heart for the answer and gives God time to work with others; it brings us the blessing of waiting on God in His fellowship; and it allows us to evaluate our requests and to make certain that they are in keeping with God's will and for His glory. Sometimes He requires us to present cause for His answering our requests (cp. Ex. 32:9-14).

Needless to say, petitions make up a large part of our praying. However, we must make certain that we meet God's conditions if we are to receive favorable answers to our requests. God is ready to do far more than what we ask of Him. Let us look to Him to do great things for the glory of His name.

4. SOME REASONS FOR UNANSWERED PRAYER

There are times when God does not answer or delays to answer our petitions. This may be due to one or more of the following reasons:

a. *Our failure to meet the conditions of His prayer promises.*

b. *Our not allowing Him to answer in His time and way.*

Regarding God's time we may not be ready for the answer, others for whom we are praying may not be ready, or perhaps the details that are involved in the answer have not yet been worked out. Regarding God's way of answering our petitions, it may be in a manner that we did not anticipate or do not recognize (cp. Rom. 15:30-32; Acts chs. 27-28; Phil. 1:12-13).

    c. Our faulty relations with God (Ps. 66:18) or with other people (I Jn. 3:16-23; I Pet. 3:1, 7; Prov. 21:13).

    d. Our having improper motivation for prayer (Jas. 4:3).

    "Lusts" refers to our own desires rather than to God's desires for us (cp. Eph. 5:10; I Jn. 5:14-15; Mt. 26:39). In everything we should be motivated to seek God's glory (I Cor. 10:31). This includes our prayers of petitions, as well.

    e. Our experiencing satanic hindrance (Dan. 10:12-13).

    f. Our asking for that which is not for our good (Mt. 7:11).

    God will only give us good things (things in keeping with His will for us, Rom. 12:2), that contribute to our spiritual well-being (Jas. 1:17; I Tim. 6:17).

We must never be contented with unanswered prayer. Our God would have us to examine our prayers, look for possible reasons for their not being answered, and make whatever adjustments that may be necessary. (When we speak of answers to prayer, we are not referring to "No" answers, but to God's granting our request.)

Since it is an essential ingredient of fellowship with God, prayer is very important to our life. A. J. Gordon once said, "You can do more than pray after you have prayed, but you can never do more than pray until you have prayed."

• Cleansing from Sin

Every believer is painfully aware that he still sins. This occurs when we give ourself over to the urges of the sin-principle, which is resident in the flesh of our body, and allow it to express itself through our members (Jas. 1:14-15; Rom. 7:15-23). However, God has graciously provided for our cleansing, which is so necessary for our fellowship and service with Him (I Jn. 1:5-7; II Tim. 2:21).

The means of cleansing is the blood of Christ (I Jn. 1:7), which speaks of our Lord's atoning work by His death and the shedding of His blood. His sacrifice is not only the ground of God's judicial forgiveness of our sins but also His parental forgiveness as well.

When we learn about our sins or knowingly commit them, we have the duty of dealing with them, or judging them (I Cor. 11:31) by repenting (changing our mind about them and repudiating them, Rev. 2:5; Prov. 28:13) and confessing them to God (I Jn. 1:9). We must also have a forgiving spirit toward them who have wronged us (Mt. 6:12, 14-15) when they have repented and fulfilled their obligation to us (Lk. 17:3). Also, we must seek the forgiveness of others whom we have wronged (Mt. 5:23-24). When we deal with our sins in this way, God immediately applies to us the value of Jesus' atoning work, releasing us from sin's guilt and cleansing us of sin's defilement (I Jn. 1:9).

It is urgent that we deal with our known sins promptly so that our fellowship with God is not interrupted and we do not incur His chastisement. Unjudged, known sins are the most common cause for the lack of the Holy Spirit's power and fruit in the lives of His people. While there is no sin which a Christian can commit that is not forgivable (I Jn. 1:7, 9), we must remember that they will enter the calculation of our reward, when our Christian life is appraised by the Lord (II Cor. 5:10; Col. 3:24-25).

- **The Ministry of Other Believers**

Fellow members of our local church as well as saved people among our acquaintenances can exert a great influence for good on our life. Some of the ways in which they can help us and we, in turn, can help others are these: by expressing Christian love (I Jn. 3:16-18; I Cor. 13:4-7), being an example (I Tim. 4:12), praying (II Cor. 1:11; Eph. 6:18-19), giving encouragement and reproof (I Thess. 5:14; Gal. 6:1), exercising spiritual gifts like teaching or showing mercy (I Cor. 14:26; Eph. 4:12-16), and giving material assistance (I Cor. 16:1; Gal. 6:10).

These divine provisions will help us only as we make use of them. Let us daily employ them and allow God to work through them to make us the kind of people that He wants us to be.

THE FRUITFULNESS OF THE CHRISTIAN LIFE

When we received the Lord as our Saviour, we were brought into a complete life-union with Him by means of the Holy Spirit's baptism and indwelling (Jn. 14:20). A result of this union is our bringing forth fruit unto God (Rom. 7:4). To this end we were chosen and appointed (Jn. 15:16). Other passages reveal that the fruit we are to bear consists of Christian character (Gal. 5:22-23), good works (Col. 1:10), knowledge of Christ (II Pet. 1:8), and service (Rom. 1:13) toward the lost (vss. 15-16) and the saved (vss. 11-12). This fruit represents the whole expression and productivity of Christ in the believer's spiritual life (cp. Gal. 4:19). The Lord's allegory in John 15:1-6 teaches that the production of this fruit is the cooperative work of the vine, the branch, and the vinedresser.

- **The Vine's Part**

The vine does everything in the production of the fruit as long as the branch keeps in living union with it. The vine bears the branch, nourishes it, and produces fruit in it.

In like manner the Lord Jesus produces in His people the fruit that the Father requires of their lives. As the source and dispenser of eternal life, He is the spiritual life of His people (Jn. 14:6; I Jn. 5:11-12). He is also the practical expression of this life in the daily experience of His people (Gal. 2:20; Phil.

1:21). In other words, a Christian is one who has Christ (I Jn. 5:12), and Christian living is Jesus' expressing Himself through His people (Phil. 1:21).

● **The Branch's Part**

The branch's part in fruitbearing is to keep in touch with the vine ("abide," Jn. 15:4-5). This allows the vine to produce its fruit in the branch.

Similarly, we believers must keep in practical touch with the Lord (vs. 4) if we are to be fruitful (vs. 5). This fruitbearing circuit was set up at salvation by the Holy Spirit's baptism and indwelling (cp. Jn. 14:20); however, we close this circuit practically by our abiding. This permits the Lord to abide in us in the full productivity of His life and power, as He promises (Jn. 15:4-5). We abide in the Lord when we surrender to His leadership, obey His direction, exercise faith in Him, and communicate with Him.

1. *Our Surrendering to Jesus' Leadership (Mt. 11:29)*

This is to acknowledge His claim upon us and to submit to His authority and leadership in our lives (II Cor. 5:15; Rom. 12:1). It is to take His yoke upon us and regard Him as the senior member of this two-person partnership. What claim does the Lord have to His people? The claim of creation (Jn. 1:3), possession (Jn. 17:9), and redemption (I Cor. 6:19-20). He has the sole right to manage our lives. We exist for the praise of His glory (Eph. 1:12; Jn. 17:10).

How do we yield ourself to Him? By a decision of our will and by prayer (cp. Isa. 6:8). It is urgent that we yield ourself to Him daily. When we fail to do so, we yield to the demands of the sin-principle within.

2. *Our Obeying Him (Mt. 11:29)*

Having given ourself to His management, it is then our duty to learn from Him his will and to do it in the Holy Spirit's power.[15] To obey Him is to please Him in all that we do (Eph. 5:10, 17).

The Lord encourages us to follow His direction by describing Himself as being "meek and lowly in heart" (Mt. 11:29). He knows what it is to live under a yoke (Jn. 6:38). He governs them who yield to Him by the constraint of love (II Cor. 5:14). He says that His yoke is easy (kindly to wear) and His burden is light (Mt. 11:30). Both "yoke" and "burden" represent His will for us. Being suited to our new life and renewed nature, His will is perfect for us (Rom. 12:2). It also is light, for He has given us a wonderful Helper (Jn. 14:16-17) and an inner desire to obey Him (Phil. 2:13). Contrary to Satan's lies, God's will is not burdensome or oppressive (I Jn. 5:3).

3. *Our Exercising Faith in Him (Gal. 2:20)*

This refers to practical faith, by means of which we share everything with Him (I Pet. 5:7) and depend upon Him in everything (Prov. 3:5-6). This kind of faith does not eliminate personal activity or responsibility, for God

---

[15] See Appendix F for suggestions about learning His will. In Matthew 11:29 "of Me" should read "from Me."

will not do for us what we can do for ourselves. We still must make preparation, attend to duty, wage battle, secure a livelihood, and bear adversity. But in all of these, we must look to the Lord for direction and help in order that we might please Him. To function independently of Him is to sin (Rom. 14:23; cp. Jn. 8:28).

The life of practical faith is one in which we share everything with the Lord — our work, problems, duties, recreation, aspirations, fears — and we depend upon Him to help us handle these things in a way which will please Him and will glorify the Father. Whatever need we may have, we can look to Him to satisfy this or to give us the grace to deal with it (Jn. 7:37-39; II Cor. 12:8-10).

4. *Our Communicating with Him (I Cor. 1:9)*

Since He is our senior Partner and Lord, He wants us to talk to Him about everything (I Thess. 5:17). This is necessary if we are to share everything with Him. He also wants us to read His Word and to heed what He says (Col. 3:16). This, too, is necessary if we are to know His will and the resources He provides.

When we abide in the Lord in this manner, we allow Him to abide in us in the full productivity of His life and power. On the other hand, apart from Him we are not able to do anything that pleases Him or that will count for eternity (Jn. 15:5). When He appraises our lives, He will be looking for that which we shared with Him. He will reward us favorably only for that in which He had a part (Eph. 6:8; Heb. 13:21).

- **The Vinedresser's Part**

The vinedresser's work is to cultivate the branches so that they bear more fruit. Here Jesus describes God the Father as the vinedresser who prunes the fruitful branches and removes the unfruitful ones (Jn. 15:2-3, 6).

1. *The Father prunes fruitful believers (vs. 2b).*

The purpose of this pruning is to remove from our life all that obstructs the production of spiritual fruit. He does this by His Word (vs. 3). When we expose our heart to the Scriptures and respond favorably to what God says, we allow Him to remove from us that which is undesirable in His sight and to sanctify us (cp. II Tim. 3:16-17; Ps. 119:9-11; Jn. 17:17).

The Father also prunes us by chastening us (Heb. 12:6, 11). When we fail to heed His Word, we incur His corrective discipline (Rev. 3:19). However, His chastening (child training) also has broader purpose in that it is instructive, maturative, and productive, as required. With infinite love and unerring wisdom our Father removes only what is hindering the bearing of spiritual fruit. Nothing essential to our spiritual well-being is lost. His dealings with us cast us upon the Vine and causes us to be more fruitful. Let us not faint from His discipline or ignore it, but endure it with the assurance of His great love for us and His thorough knowledge of what is best for us (Heb. 12:5-7).

2. *The Father removes unfruitful believers (vss. 2a, 6).*

Keep in mind that the Lord is not speaking about salvation. If one fails to meet the condition of fruitfulness and is unresponsive to God's chastisement, to the point of hating it, then he is prematurely removed from earth and is taken to Heaven (vs. 2), for such a person is a hindrance to the Lord's work on earth. To hate the Father's reproof or chastisement is to commit a sin that leads to certain physical death (I Jn. 5:16; Prov. 15:10; 29:1; Heb. 12:9).

With these truths in view, I understand that the branch's being cast forth is a reference to the insubordinate believer's physical death (Jn. 15:6), its drying up as his never bearing fruit on earth again, and its being burned as his works being consumed in the coming appraisal (I Cor. 3:15). It is our Lord's desire that our works survive this appraisal and that we receive a full reward (Jn. 15:16; II Jn. 8). Our Father is concerned about the amount of fruit we bear, for "much fruit" glorifies Him (Jn. 15:8). This reference to quantity suggests that He wants us to be spiritually fruitful throughout our Christian life. Observe that there are no degrees of quality since this fruit has only one degree that is acceptable to the Father — the life of Jesus (cp. vs. 5).

By this allegory the Lord Jesus describes the nature of Christian life and service. It is His living and working through His people who are on earth. We experience this as we abide in Him and submit to the Father's means of pruning us.

THE VICTORIES OF THE CHRISTIAN LIFE

Since we study these elsewhere, it is enough to say that we can now have occasions of victory over our spiritual enemies (Satan, the sin-principle, and the world) when we refuse to yield to their demands and we give ourself over to the Lord Jesus and His will for us. When we are attacked by these enemies, the formula for victory is our yielding ourself immediately to the Holy Spirit, resisting the enemy in His power, and believing that He will give us victory (Jas. 4:7; I Pet. 5:8-9). We must also do the Lord's will (Eph. 5:17), for victory includes our doing this as well as our not doing the enemy's will. Since no victory in this life is permanent, it seems best that we think of these triumphs as occasions of victory. The enemy attacks daily, so he must be defeated daily.

THE SEPARATION AND DEDICATION OF THE CHRISTIAN LIFE

Practical sanctification essentially concerns our doing God's will rather than sinning (Rom. 6:15-22; I Pet. 1:13-16; Mt. 5:48). While we cannot now live permanently without sin, we can experience periods of sinlessness in our daily life. In addition to our doing God's will in the power of the Holy Spirit, we initiate and experience holiness by separating ourself from that which is unlike God and by setting ourself apart unto Him for the doing His will and for His manifestation and use (II Cor. 6:17 – 7:1).

Incidentally, although their doctrinal views are similar, historic fundamentalism holds to personal and ecclesiastical separation while evangelicalism does not make this emphasis.

- **Our Separation**

We learn from the New Testament that we who are saved are to separate ourselves from sin, sinning believers, false religious teachers, and worldliness.

1. *We are to separate from personal sin (Col. 3:8; I Tim. 5:22; 6:11).*

This is achieved by our cleansing ourself from sin's defilement (II Cor. 7:1; cp. I Jn. 1:9) and by our refusing to submit to sin's demands (Rom. 6:11-13).

2. *We are to separate from unrepentant sinning believers (Mt. 18:15-17; II Thess. 3:14-15).*

We are to separate from believers who openly allow sin in their lives in violation of some clear, scriptural precept. As with church corrective discipline, we have the duty of praying for sinning believers (I Jn. 5:16) and counseling with them (Mt. 18:15; Gal. 6:1). If this fails to secure favorable results, then we should have no association with them (II Thess. 3:6, 14). Yet, we are not to count them as enemies but continue to seek their restoration (vs. 15). Needless to say, it is very important to receive them into our fellowship when they are repentant (II Cor. 2:5-11).

3. *We are to separate from false religious teachers (Rom. 16:17-18; I Tim. 6:3-5; II Tim. 3:1-5; Tit. 3:9-11; II Jn. 10-11).*

These false teachers are people who reject the primary doctrines of the Christian faith that one must believe to be a Christian, such as the divine inspiration of the Bible, the deity and humanity of the Lord Jesus, His atoning work, His physical resurrection, the deity of the Holy Spirit, and the doctrine of the holy Trinity. Like the Pharisees of old, these people lay aside, reject, and make void God's Word by their philosophy and vain deceit (Mk. 7:5-13; Col. 2:8).

a. *We are to mark them (Rom. 16:17).*

We can identify them by what they say (and sometimes by what they do not say) about the Bible, God, the Lord Jesus, the Holy Spirit, and salvation. We can also spot them by the character of their conduct and the results of their ministry (Mt. 7:15-20; Rom. 16:17b; Tit. 1:16). Jesus taught that the nature of a tree determines the kind of fruit it will bear. In spite of a veneer of piety and respectability, false religious teachers, like their leader Satan, live unholy lives (II Pet. 2:1-3, 10-22), use deceptive methods and masquerades (II Pet. 2:3; II Cor. 11:13-15), serve selfish interests (Phil. 3:19), and cause dissension and offences (lit. "snares") among the Lord's people (Rom. 16:17). Contrariwise, the marks of a true servant of Jesus are sound doctrine, a fruitful ministry, and a holy life (Mt. 7:17).

b. *We are to avoid them (Rom. 16:17c; I Tim. 6:5).*

When we recognize what these people are, we are to turn away from them (II Tim. 3:5). When they appear in our churches and start sowing their heretical seed, they must be rejected (Tit. 3:9-11). When they come to our homes, they are not to be welcomed (II Jn. 7-11). To befriend them and to encourage their ministry is to share in their evil deeds.

When these false teachers appear in a local church and have the majority support of its members, then the only option that spiritual, discerning members have is to sever their relationship with the church and unite with another where God's Word is honored and taught in its purity. However, if these false teachers have the support of only a minority within the church, then they and their confederates should be ejected by vote of the orthodox majority.

c. *We are to warn others against them (Acts 20:28-31).*

It is our duty to warn others of the doctrine and activity of false religious teachers, but we are not to search them out and destroy them (Mt. 13:24-30). The Lord will deal with these appropriately when He comes.

4. *We are to separate from worldliness (I Jn. 2:15).*

The word "world" (Gk. *kosmos*) has various meanings in the New Testament, determined by the context in which it occurs: the sum total of all that was created (Jn. 17:5); the earth (Jn. 9:5); mankind (Jn. 3:16; 12:19); and the world system embracing the total society, culture, and philosophy of lost mankind. At this point of our study we are concerned with this last meaning.

The world system is headed by Satan (Jn. 12:31; 14:30; 16:11); its works are evil (Jn. 7:7); it is condemned by God (Jn. 12:31; I Jn. 2:17); and it fails to meet man's spiritual need (I Cor. 1:21). Since we who are saved are no longer a part of this world system (Jn. 15:19; Col. 1:13), we are threatened by its hostility (Jn. 15:18) and influence (I Jn. 2:16). We cannot avert its hostility and remain loyal to Jesus (Jas. 4:4), but we can avoid its influence that would lead us into a state of worldliness. Let us look at this more closely.

a. *Our separation from the people of the world*

God does not direct us to isolate ourselves from the unsaved. For most of His people isolation would be an impossibility (I Cor. 5:9-11). Furthermore, it would block our ministry to the unsaved (Jn. 17:18; Mk. 16:15; Acts 1:8; II Cor. 5:18-20). On the contrary, our Lord freely mingled with the unsaved — entering their homes, eating at their tables, and listening to their problems (Lk. 7:36; 11:37; 14:1; cp. Mt. 9:9-10). Although He was known as their friend (Mt. 11:19), He did not participate in their sins or approve of their wrongdoing (Heb. 7:26; I Pet. 2:22). We, too, must make contact with the unsaved, be friendly toward them, and win their confidence if we are to gain their hearing and to share with them the gospel. Obviously, it is risky, but we are safe as long as we look to the Lord, remain yielded to Him, and follow His direction.

God does command us to avoid any association with the unsaved that would hinder our doing the Lord's will (II Cor. 6:14). Paul does not describe the problem at Corinth since this was known to his readers. Possibly, he is referring to their commitment to certain false teachers or, more likely, to pagan clubs or trade guilds, which required idolatrous practices of its members. Whatever the situation, the apostle states the principle that we who are saved are not to link ourselves with unbelievers in any association (like a business partnership or marriage) from which we cannot readily excuse ourselves and which would require us to violate God's will.

b. Our separation from the things of the world

As long as we are on earth we cannot isolate ourselves from the things of the world. We must use its products, attend its institutions, participate in its industries and arts, and be subject to its government. Many things of the world are not evil in themselves, but they may be used in a wrong way. Paul teaches that we are not to use the things of the world to the utmost extent (I Cor. 7:31, "as not abusing it"). He seems to say that we are not to extract all that we can from these things to the extent that we allow them to mean everything to us and we prize them above God (cp. Mt. 6:19-24). We are not to look at these things or live for them as unsaved people do (Mt. 6:32; Col. 3:1-3). To allow anything of this world to compete with our love for God, to weaken our spiritual life, or to hinder our doing God's will is to use it in an evil way. On the other hand, we should regard the amoral things of the world as commodities which God allows us to have and to use as He directs for His interests and glory and for our good. Anything that we cannot share with Him is prohibited.

We are to avoid worldliness. This is a state of life that results from an improper attitude toward the world and its things (I Jn. 2:15). The worldly believer is one who loves something of this world with the exclusive love that he owes to God (I Jn. 2:15, Gk. "love for the Father"; Mt. 6:24; 10:37). Jesus expressed this exclusive love by His obeying the Father (Jn. 14:31), delighting in Him, (4:34), trusting Him (Mt. 27:43), and honoring Him (Jn. 8:49). There are proper loves for country, spouse, parents, children, friends, Christians, and things. But we are to love God more than these and never to share with these that special affection that we owe to Him (I Jn. 2:15).

When we do share with others the love that we owe to God, we commit spiritual adultery (Jas. 4:4) and open our life to world conformity and domination (Rom. 12:2). The worldly believer's life is characterized by the fads, opinions, attitudes, and interests of the world. Contrariwise, the spiritual believer reckons himself to be dead toward the world and alive unto Christ and His interests (Col. 2:20-3:17; Mt. 6:33; Gal. 6:14). While he is still concerned about the needs of the unsaved and must live his life in the world, he is not dominated or polluted by it as the unsaved person and worldly believer are (cp. Col. 2:20-22; Jas. 1:27).

• Our Dedication

To be separate from unholy things is not enough. Separation alone forms a vacuum, which draws into one's life such unholy attitudes and actions as pride and faultfinding. With our separation there must also be commitment to God (Rom. 12:1-2). This involves our giving ourself to the Lord Jesus and our living unto Him (II Cor. 5:15). This in turn allows Him to express Himself in and through our lives (Gal. 2:20).

Having received the Lord Jesus as Saviour, every believer should dedicate himself entirely to the Lord and His interests (Mt. 11:28-30; Rom. 12:1; cp. Isa. 6:8). We do this by heart decision and prayer. Having initially dedicated ourselves to the Lord, we need to confirm this surrender each day. We also must yield anew to Him when we come under the domination of our spiritual enemies. Only the Lord Jesus has the absolute right to manage our life. This daily commitment allows God to bless us and use us to be a blessing.

THE DISCIPLESHIP OF THE CHRISTIAN LIFE

After He saves us, the Lord Jesus begins to show us the need for discipleship, which is necessary for Christian life and service (cp. Mk. 1:16-18). A disciple is a pupil or learner. True disciples are pupils who receive their teacher's instructions, apply them to their lives, and pass them on to others. Their supreme goal is to become like their teacher (Mt. 10:24-25). True disciples of Jesus not only receive His teachings and walk in His fellowship but also pass on His teachings to others and seek to forward His interests in the world. Discipleship is a spiritual discipline which is to continue throughout our lives.It is preparatory for the Lord's service and necessary during service. Let us consider the requirements, categories, and evidences of discipleship.

• Its Requirements (Lk. 14:25-35)

Because His ministry attracted many superficial followers, Jesus warned them of its cost by giving three parables and stating its requirements. By parables He pointed to the possibility of receiving ridicule for not completing the course (vss. 28-30), the folly of not counting its cost (vss. 31-32) and the results experienced by them who do not stay with it (vss. 34-35). What are the requirements of discipleship?

1. *OUR FORSAKING ALL FOR CHRIST (Lk. 14:33, 26)*

To forsake all is to set aside or leave behind everything which would keep us from giving Jesus first place in our life (cp. Mt. 6:24).

a. *It is to place Christ above our possessions (vs. 33).*

We must prize Him above all that we have (Lk. 12:34; Col. 3:2). Also, we must dispose of our possessions as He leads (Lk. 12:33), considering them as a trust from Him to be used as He directs and for God's glory.

b. *It is to place Christ above all other persons (vs. 26a).*

Jesus uses the word "hate" as a hyperbole (exaggeration). To hate others is contrary to the principle of Christian love (Mt. 5:44; Mk. 12:31; Jn. 15:12). We are not to love others less than what we do, but we are to love Jesus more with that exclusive love which we owe to God alone (Mt. 10:37). This means that when the claims of others conflict with those of Christ for us, we must always yield to His will (cp. Jn. 2:4; Acts 5:29; Lk. 1:38).

    c. *It is to place Christ above ourself (vs. 26b).*

    There is a proper self-love, which is concerned about one's value and well-being (Mt. 22:39; Rom. 12:3; Eph. 5:28-29). However, we are to love the Lord Jesus more than we love ourself to the extent that we are willing to give up anything to do His will, such as our personal comfort, plans, financial security, social status, pleasure—indeed, even life itself.

    2. *OUR TAKING UP THE CROSS (Lk. 14:27a)*

    Some understand cross-bearing to mean shouldering some heavy burden, such as a chronic ailment or some annoying adversity. But in the New Testament the cross is an instrument of humiliation and death. The only cross that concerns discipleship is that on which the Lord died and which stands today as a symbol of His humiliation and atoning work.

    a. *This cross-bearing is related to the denial of self (Lk. 9:23).*

    If "himself" is an accusative of reference and refers to the person, then the Lord appears to be speaking about our denying (with reference to ourself) the usurpation of our spiritual enemies over our life. As usual, He did not explain what He meant by this, but He left it to later New Testament revelation (Rom. ch. 6) to make this known. Neither sin, Satan, nor the world has any lawful claim to us who are saved since we are no longer under their authority (Rom. 6:14; Col. 1:13; Gal. 6:14).

    b. *This cross-bearing takes place when we act upon the truth*
       of Romans 6:1-13.

    To bear the cross is to reckon that we died to sin and are alive unto God. This means that discipleship requires us to refuse to yield to our former spiritual masters and to yield ourself to the Lord Jesus, our lawful master. We cannot serve Him and sin at the same time.

    3. *OUR FOLLOWING AFTER JESUS (Lk. 14:27b)*

    Having forsaken all and having taken up His cross in denying ourself the usurpation of sin, there remains our following His leadership. Following the Lord Jesus is essentially the same as abiding in Him (Jn. 15:4-5; cp. 8:12). To follow Him we must yield ourself to Him, obey Him, exercise practical faith in Him, and communicate with Him. This makes it possible for Him to disciple us and to use us in His work in this world.

- **Its Categories (Jn. 6:60-71)**

    Among the many people who followed Jesus, there were found three kinds of disciples—nominal, real, and false.

    1. *Nominal Disciples (vss. 60-66)*

These were disciples in name only. They represented the majority among Jesus' followers. Lacking proper motivation, they were attracted to Jesus by curiosity or by the possibility of receiving certain temporal benefits, such as a free meal. These were the ones whom Jesus challenged with the cost of discipleship (cp. Lk. 14:25-35; Jn. 6:48-58). Nominal disciples are not willing to pay the price of true discipleship (Jn. 6:60, 66).

2. *Real Disciples (vss. 67-69)*

These had proper motivation. Convinced that Jesus had the words of eternal life and was the Holy One of God, they realized that they could not live without Him. They determined to follow Him regardless of the personal cost.

3. *False Disciples (vss. 70-71)*

While nominal disciples fade away and quit following when the demands are too great, the false disciple remains and acts like a true one. Judas did not manifest any offense at Jesus' teaching. He continued with the twelve as an imposter, who was so influenced by Satan that he was called "a devil." The Lord knows who these are and will one day reject them (Mt. 7:21-23).

- **Its Evidences**

How can we identify true disciples of Jesus? The Lord declared that they are people who abide in His Word (Jn. 8:31). They give close attention to the Scriptures and carefully ponder them. Rather than going away and forgetting what they have read or heard, they seek to understand the truth and apply it to their lives.

Jesus also said that true disciples are people who bear His spiritual fruit in their lives (Jn. 15:8). As they keep in touch with Him, He abides in them in the fulness of His vitality (vss. 4-5) and produces in them the fruit of Christian character and conduct (Gal. 5:22-23; Col. 1:10). He who is the spiritual life of His people (Jn. 14:6) expresses this life in and through them who are truly His disciples (Gal. 2:20; 4:19; Phil. 1:21).

Finally, Jesus revealed that true disciples are people who exercise His love toward others (Jn. 13:34-35). Under the Mosaic Law God's people were to love one another as they loved themselves (Lev. 19:18; we are still to do this, Gal. 5:13-15), but this kind of love was limited to one's "neighbor" or friend. According to the new dispensation, it is our duty to love others with Christ's love—a love that is concerned about the well-being of our enemies as well as our friends (Mt. 5:44; cp. Jn. 3:16). It is noteworthy that this love does not require us to like people, as human love demands (God did not like us when we were sinners), but it does require us to be concerned about the well-being of others, spiritually and materially (I Jn. 3:16-20). We can exercise Christ's love only as we are filled with the Holy Spirit and as He produces this love in our hearts (Gal. 5:22; Rom. 5:5).

It is noteworthy that the Lord Jesus made the exercise of His love (Jn.

13:35), not orthodox belief, the badge of Christian discipleship. While orthodox belief is important to us who are saved, the world cannot distinguish between true and false doctrine. But it does readily recognize real Christian love because of its uniqueness and practical expressions. It is tragic that many churches that are orthodox in their doctrine have lost their testimony of being true disciples of Jesus, because of their lack of love.

The scarcity of teaching regarding discipleship may account for the little response of believers to appeals for Christian service. Not many are willing to serve when they have not been prepared by discipleship. It is noteworthy that our Lord called men to follow Him before He sent them out to special service (Mk. 1:16-17; 3:13-14; 6:7-13).

CHANGE IN THE CHRISTIAN LIFE

Earlier, we saw that the Christian life is capable of growth and, thus, of change. This change concerns our daily life-style — its words, thoughts, attitudes, motivations, and actions. We who are saved should seek to change our life-style from what it was before we came to know the Lord to what He wants it to be (Rom. 12:2). Increasingly, our life should express the moral and spiritual qualities of the Lord Jesus, our new life (Gal. 2:20; 4:19; Eph. 5:1-2; I Pet. 2:21). The New Testament reveals what this is, and the Holy Spirit is ready to bring this about in us by transforming us from glory to glory. However, to experience this we must take the initiative by accepting the responsibility of our conduct, by understanding the basis for this change, and by taking those steps which allow God to effect this in our life.

- **The Responsibility of Our Conduct**

That we are responsible to God for our words, thoughts, attitudes, motivations, and actions is indicated by His commands to us about these things (Eph. 4:29; II Cor. 10:5; Eph. 4:31-32; II Tim. 2:15; Jas. 4:17) and by our accounting for them in the coming appraisal (II Cor. 5:10).

- **The Basis of and the Motivation for this Change**

The basis of change in the believer's daily life is what took place at salvation. We were made new creatures in Christ by our re-creation and baptism into Him (Eph. 2:10; II Cor. 5:17). By this divine work we put off the old man with his deeds and put on the new man, which is being renewed in knowledge after the image of Him that created him (Col. 3:9-10).

1. *We did put off the old man (Col. 3:9; cp. Eph. 4:22).*

The "old man" is what we were in Adam, sharing his corrupt kind of human nature, being guilty of his initial sin, and practicing the sinful life-style that characterizes his unsaved posterity. But at salvation we put this off. Our relationship to Adam was severed, and the old, unholy spiritual realities that we had in him were removed from us (II Cor. 5:17-18; Rom. 5:15-19). Although our bodies are still unredeemed, they are properly the instruments of Christ and His righteousness (I Cor. 6:15; Rom. 6:13, 18-19).

2. We did put on the new man (Col. 3:10; cp. Eph. 4:24).

The "new man" is what we are now in Christ, where all things (spiritual realities) are new (II Cor. 5:17). In God's sight we now have Christ's kind of human nature and righteousness (I Cor. 1:30). Possessing His life (eternal life), we now have the capacity and the ability through the Holy Spirit to practice a new, holy life-style (II Pet. 1:3).

These absolute, positional realities provide us the motivation for changing our life-style in compliance with God's will. Having through salvation put off what we once were, it is no longer proper and suitable to live as we once did (Rom. 6:2; Eph. 4:17-20; Col. 3:8). Being new creatures in Jesus, it is fitting that we strive for Christlikeness in morals and spirituality, in disposition and character (Rom. 6:4; I Jn. 2:6; cp. Eph. 5:8-10). This points to the principle that underlies this basis of change: we should conduct ourself in such a way because we are something, not to become something; we should be Christlike because we are new creatures in Him, not for the purpose of becoming new creatures in Him.

• The Steps that Lead to This Change

Notice that God's commands are directed to our will, not to our emotions. (He doesn't say, "Do this if you feel like it.") Having the direction of the Scriptures and the assistance of the Holy Spirit, we possess the dynamics that are required for this change. Because of this, God appeals to us to walk worthy of our calling (Eph. 4:1) and to be imitators of Him (5:1). Accepting these truths, we can make changes in our life by the following:

1. Learn what we are to put off in our conduct. We are to put off those sins of which we are aware (Col. 3:5-9; Eph. 4:25-31).

2. Learn what we are to put on in sin's place. This is the biblical alternative to our sinning (Col. 3:12-17; Eph. 4:25-5:2). For instance, we are to put off malice (the desire to injure others) and to put on in its place kindness (Eph. 4:31-32).

3. Deal with those sins of which we are aware. We should not repress this awareness, but respond to it by acknowledging, renouncing, and confessing our sins to God (Rev. 2:5; Prov. 28:13; I Jn. 1:9).

4. Depending upon the Holy Spirit, practice the biblical alternative. We should ask the Holy Spirit to help us to do and to be what God desires for us. Sometimes it is necessary to restructure our life to make way for this change, such as our eliminating, avoiding, or rearranging that in our circumstances which makes it easier for us to sin.

By these steps we can break the unholy practices of the old life-style and develop holy ones in keeping with our position in Christ. Occasionally we fail, but gradually we establish a life-style that glorifies God. Obviously, this requires perseverance and time.

THE MINISTRY OF THE CHRISTIAN LIFE

Resting upon the principle of giving (Mt. 10:8), Christian service is the believer's response to all that God has given to him (Rom.12:2; II Cor. 5:14-15). This service assumes both vertical and horizontal dimensions. Vertically, it is his duty as a personal creature to worship God. Horizontally, it is his duty as a Christian to labor with the Lord Jesus in His ministry to unsaved and saved people. Let us examine these.

- ## The Ministry of Worshiping God

The English word *worship* comes from worthship. It refers to the act of paying honor or ascribing worth to one who deserves this. The essence of divine worship is giving—our giving to God what is due Him.

Worship is a spiritual exercise that involves our total being (Mk. 12:30) and that is expressed by our words (or thoughts) of praise, adoration, and thanksgiving (Ps. 138:1-2; Heb. 13:15), our attitude of reverence (Ps. 5:7, "fear"), our love (Mk. 12:30), our obedience (Mt. 4:10), and our spiritual sacrifices (Heb. 13:15; Rom. 12:1). Both Jesus and Paul indicated that worship involves service (Mt. 4:10; Rom. 12:1). Not all who serve worship whom they serve, but all who worship serve whom or what they worship. Moreover, worship includes the giving of honor (Jn. 5:23). This does not prohibit our honoring humans (I Pet. 2:17; Eph. 5:33; 6:2), but we are not to ascribe to them the honor that belongs to God alone (Isa. 42:8).

Jesus declared that we are to worship God "in spirit and in truth" (Jn. 4:23-24). To worship "in spirit" seems to mean that true worship is spiritual — in accord with the Holy Spirit in character and by means of Him in activity (cp. Jn. 6:63; Phil. 3:3). This is in contrast to the worship of the world, which is confined to certain places (Jn. 4:20-21), which consists of certain outward rituals, and which is demonic (I Cor. 10:20). Regardless of our circumstances, true worship involves our total being (Rom. 12:1; cp. Lk. 1:46-47) as we are energized by the Holy Spirit (Phil. 3:3). The outward accessories, such as architecture, music, and liturgy, should be regarded as aids to worship. They should never be substituted for worship.

"Truth" conveys the ideas of reality and accuracy. Unlike much of Judaism which was symbolic, true worship occurs in the sphere of spiritual reality. The Levitical ritual and sacrifices anticipated the priestly work of the Lord Jesus, but with the completion of His atonement these shadows are no longer useful today (Heb. 8:5-6; 9:9-11; 10:1-14). True worship now takes place in the sphere of spiritual reality wherein we have direct access to God through Christ (Eph. 2:18), we offer spiritual sacrifices (I Pet. 2:5; cp. Rom. 12:1; Heb. 13:15-16), and we live our whole life as a service of worship (Rom. 12:1; 14:6-9). The only symbols that remain are the ordinances of Water Baptism and the Lord's Supper. The cross was not regarded as a symbol by the Christian church until the 2nd century (Tertullian).

True worship also is characterized by accuracy. The Samaritans worshiped in ignorance (Jn. 4:22). Their worship was a mixture of paganism and the Mosaic Law (II Kings 17:24-41). True worship is in keeping with the new dispensation, given in the New Testament. There we learn of the wealth of God's grace and of the divine provisions for life and service. Motivated and directed by these, we can walk in the light with God and ascribe to Him appropriate honors by our words and actions (see Eph. 5:20; Phil. 4:4; I Cor. 10:31; I Jn. 1:7).

- **The Ministry of Working with God**

Paul states that we who are saved are laborers together with God (I Cor. 3:9). While mankind has been given the responsibility of ruling the earth and using its resources for the glory of God (Gen. 1:28; 9:1-2), let us give our attention to an additional duty that we believers have as the Lord's servants (slaves, cp. I Cor. 6:19-20; Jn. 15:20; Rom. 6:16-18; Gal. 1:10; Col. 3:24; I Pet. 2:16). Upon saving us, the Lord has left us here in order that we might be engaged with Him in His present work on earth.

1. THE NATURE OF THIS WORK

On the eve of His death Jesus declared that His disciples would do what He did and greater works than these (Jn. 14:12). Besides His atoning work, which was exclusively His to do, the Lord Jesus also presented Himself to Israel as the Messiah of Old Testament prophecy for their acceptance or rejection (cp. Isa. 49:1-6; Mt. 9:35; 15:24; Lk. 4:43-44). He did this, not by public proclamation but by fulfillment of what the Old Testament said that the Messiah would do (cp. Lk. 4:18-19). His miracles testified to His office and commission (Acts 10:38). These signs (miracles) also attended the ministry of His apostles as a confirmation of their commission (II Cor. 12:12; Heb. 2:4). We do not have to do these things today, for our commission is given in the New Testament (Mt. 28:19-20; Acts 1:8), and it is confirmed by the results of the ministry of the Word (Rom. 1:16).

The Lord also said that His disciples would do "greater works than these" because of His returning to the Father. These greater works (greater in kind than the physical miracles He wrought) refer to His present work of building His church. The giving of spiritual life and sight is greater than its physical counterpart. He predicted His building the church several months before He died (Mt. 16:18) and began this construction on the Day of Pentecost, ten days after His return to Heaven (Acts 2:41, 47). This is one of His Messianic works that He is doing as a man from the Father's side.

To accomplish this work He is using the Scriptures (II Tim. 3:15-17), the Holy Spirit (Jn. 3:6; I Cor. 12:13, 27), and us who are saved (I Cor. 3:5-10). Through these means He is building His church quantitatively by saving them who believe the gospel (Acts 2:47) and by joining them to His body (the church) through the baptism of the Holy Spirit (I Cor. 12:13, 27). Moreover, He is building the church qualitatively by developing the spiritual lives of His people (I Cor. 14:26; Eph. 4:14-16).

What, then, is Christian service? It is our cooperating with the Lord in such a way that will allow Him to use us in the building of His church both quantitatively and qualitatively (Acts 14:27; 15:4). This cooperation involves our abiding in Him (Jn. 15:4-5) and our exercising our spiritual gift(s) according to His will and power in the salvation and edification of others (Rom. 15:15-16; I Cor. 14:26).

2. THE MINISTRIES OF THIS WORK

The Lord has given to the church pastors and teachers for the purpose of equipping the saints for the work of service, which contributes to the building of the church (Eph. 4:11-12). This work of service seems to represent two kinds of ministries, by which the Lord is building His church through His people.

a. The Ministry of General Service

This ministry belongs to every believer alike. It includes such spiritual exercises as prayer (Jn. 14:13; Eph. 6:18; Rom. 10:1), living a consistent Christian life (I Pet. 1:15; II Tim. 2:21; II Cor. 3:2), beneficial speech (Eph. 4:29; Acts 1:8), giving[16] (Eph. 4:28; II Cor. 8:1-15), and earning a livelihood (cp. Eph. 6:5-8). Though the believer may be a child, he can be taught to do these things and to serve the Lord in these ways. This is a full-time ministry, which belongs alike to every saved person.

b. The Ministry of Special Service

Determined by one's native abilities and spiritual gifts, this is a special ministry which each believer has, yet which differs from that of many other people. God has created us in Christ Jesus for good works, which He prepared beforehand in order that we might walk in them (Eph. 2:10). Paul would have his Christian readers to reflect soberly about themselves according to the measure of faith and grace which God has bestowed on them in the form of spiritual gifts (Rom. 12:3-8). As the human body has many organs and each has its own function, so Christ's body, the church, consists of many people, each of whom has his own function in the building of the church. It is important that each of us knows what his function is and allows the Lord to use him in his special way.

Native abilities are powers with which we are born. These may include verbal comprehension, reasoning, manual dexterity as well as mathematical, musical, clerical, dramatic, persuasive, linguistic, engineering, and literary abilities. Often these abilities need training and development, and generally they are used in the pursuit of a career, livelihood, or avocation. It appears that when they are associated with the gift of helps or service, they may be used in various roles in the Lord's work, as that of musician, vocalist, treasurer, builder, caretaker, translator, secretary, and others.

---

[16] See Appendix N.

Spiritual gifts are measures of divine grace, or special manifestations of the Holy Spirit's power, that enable believers for special ministries in the building of the Church (see Rom. 12:3-8; I Cor. 12:4-11, 28; Eph. 4:7-11). These specific manifestations of the Lord's power operate concurrently with human activity and produce through this the divine purpose (I Cor. 15:10). Some of these, as pastoral care, teaching, evangelism, and exhortation, relate to the ministry of the Word. Others, as administration, helps, and showing mercy, are associated with practical forms of service. Still others such as tongues and miracles were for signs and proofs, which are no longer needed since we have the New Testament. While it is possible to go through the motions of the exercise of spiritual gifts, as teaching or administration, these will not be used of the Lord unless they are done in the Holy Spirit's power. Needless to say, it is important that we learn what our spiritual gifts are and exercise them in the Holy Spirit's power when we have opportunity. We can learn what our gifts are by asking God to show us, yielding ourselves to the Holy Spirit, trying services for which we are burdened or have an interest, and evaluating the results.

It is the work of the pastor and teacher to equip the Lord's people for their special service (Eph. 4:11-12). The text is God's Word (II Tim. 3:16-17), augmented by any special training which the work requires. Obviously, there are many applications of these gifts. In contrast to full-time general service, special service is a part-time work. Our Christian living should be our concern throughout our day, while the exercise of some spiritual gift may occur during only part of a day or week.

3. THE CALLS TO THIS WORK

While the Lord sometimes calls people in an unusual way to extraordinary service (cp. Ex. ch. 3; Acts 26:13-18), we should not expect this for ourselves. His calling us to the ministry of general service simply consists of His appeals through the Scriptures for our doing the things of which this service consists such as praying (Eph. 6:18-19), witnessing (Acts 1:8), and living a Christian life (Rom. ch. 12). His calling us to some special service seems to be His showing us what this ministry is.

Although the Lord's call to us for special service is unique for each of us, it appears to have the following ingredients by which we may recognize it: our becoming impressed with our serving the Lord, while reading the Scriptures; our having an inner desire (with right motives) for some service (I Tim. 3:1; Phil. 2:13; I Cor. 10:31); our learning what our spiritual gifts and native abilities are; our seeing the need for the ministry we desire and our having a growing burden for this work; our trying out the service of our interest and our evaluating the results; and our having a growing conviction that a certain work is what the Lord would have us to do. The Lord will show us what our special work is, as we look to Him and are willing to do His will (Prov. 3:5-6).

4. THE PLACE OF THIS WORK

Until the Lord leads us elsewhere, we should seek to do our special ministry where we are (cp. Paul, Acts 9:30; 11:22-26). If the Lord wants us to serve in another place, He will make this known to us. Wherever we are, we must be on the alert for opportunities to serve and not allow our gifts to lie dormant (Eph. 5:16; II Cor. 2:12; 6:1). Whatever ministry we undertake, we must remember that we cannot do anything apart from the Lord Jesus (Jn. 15:4-5; Phil. 4:13). Also, we should keep in mind the purpose for Christian service—the building of the Lord's church to the glory of God. There is no place in the Lord's work for pride and self-exaltation (II Cor. ch. 10).

LAW AND THE CHRISTIAN LIFE

In the Scriptures "law" has various meanings. Determined by their context, these are the Pentateuch (Lk. 24:44), the Old Testament (Jn. 12:34; 15:25), the Mosaic Law (Mt. 22:36), the Ten Commandments (Rom. 7:7), some divinely revealed moral law (Rom. 2:12-15), the Levitical ceremonial law (Heb. 8:4; 9:22), some principle or force (Rom. 7:23, 25; 8:2), law in general (Rom. 7:1-2), civil law (I Cor. 6:1, 6), principle of divine dealing with men (Rom. 3:27), principle of life experience (7:21), and the Law of Christ (Gal. 6:2). Because it is the duty of us who are saved to obey the higher law of God, what is our obligation to man's moral and civil laws?

• Our Obligation to Moral Law

Although God's revealed moral laws, as given in the different dispensations, are not identical in their statement, they are similar in their substance, for underlying them is His unchanging righteousness. For example, the Ten Commandments were given to the nation of Israel (Ex. 20:1-17), but with the exception of Sabbath observance, they are all restated in the teachings of grace in the present dispensation (Mt. 6:24; I Jn. 5:21; Jas. 5:12; Eph. 6:1-2; I Jn. 3:11-15; I Thess. 4:3-7; Eph. 4:28-29; Col. 3:5; Rom. 13:8-10). Paul considered himself to be under Law to Christ (I Cor. 9:21). We too are subject to Christ's law, which is given in the New Testament in the form of precepts and principles (Gal. 6:2; I Jn. 3:23). The completest expression of this law is the exercise of His love in our relations with others, whether saved or unsaved (Jn. 13:34-35; 15:12; Rom. 13:8-10; Col. 3:14; I Jn. 3:16-18; Mt. 5:44).

But what is our duty toward man's moral laws? Paul declared that we died to all law (Rom. 7:1-6), excepting Christ's Law, when we were saved. Sharing Jesus' death and resurrection, we were released from bondage to man's law and became obligated to observe Christ's Law as given in the New Testament (cp. I Cor. 9:19-23). Being neither legalistic nor antinomian, Paul respected man's laws and accommodated himself to them, whenever possible, so as to win others to Christ. But never for a moment did he forget that he was under Christ's Law, which had priority in his life.

- **Our Obligation to Civil Law**

Our heavenly citizenship does not lessen our duty to earthly government (Phil. 3:20; Rom. 13:1-7). The duties of both realms rest upon us simultaneously, with our duty to God having priority over our duty to man (cp. Acts 4:19-20; 5:29).

1. *Why are we responsible to civil government?*

First, because civil government has been instituted by God and serves His purpose in human affairs (Rom. 13:1-4). God uses government to prevent anarchy in this sinful world and to carry out His program for humanity. Government fulfills its function in two ways. It carries the sword (vs. 4), with the right to protect life, curb evil, and thwart injustice. Also, it promotes good (vss. 3, 4) by allowing people to live in a peaceable, orderly way. Paul speaks of civil authority as being "the ordinance of God" (vs. 2) and of the civil official as being "the minister of God" (vs. 4). Long ago, God spoke of Nebuchadnezzar as His servant (Jer. 25:9); the Assyrians, His rod (Isa. 10:5); and Cyrus, His shepherd and anointed one (Isa. 44:28; 45:1). This is not to say that God approves of everything that civil officials do, but they are as His agents, accountable to Him for their actions, and are used by Him to accomplish His purpose (cp. Dan. ch. 4).

A second answer to the question is that the rights and privileges which we derive from government require our supporting civil authority. Paul testified that he lived "as a citizen" in all good conscience before God (Acts 23:1 Gk.). At the same time, he was mindful of his civil rights when he appealed his case to Caesar's court (Acts 25:10-11). The government that provides services, protection, and regulation for an orderly community also requires its subjects to live as law-abiding citizens.

2. *Of what does this responsibility consist?*

a. *We are to honor government officials (I Pet. 2:17).*

To honor government officials is to evaluate correctly their offices and their discharges of duty and to give them appropriate respect. If we cannot respect the official as a man, we still must respect his office as God's agent.

b. *We are to obey government (Rom. 13:1).*

Since government is God's institution and agency, no one is exempted from obeying it in so far as this obedience does not conflict with God's will, which is clearly stated in the Scriptures (Acts 5:29; Dan. 3:1-18; 6:10). Scriptural motivations for our obeying government are penalties for violations of law (Rom. 13:2, 4, "wrath's sake"), conscience's sake (vs. 5), and the Lord's sake (I Pet. 2:13). Good citizenship contributes to our gospel witness.

c. *We are to support government by paying taxes (Rom. 13:6, 7; cp. Mt. 22:17-21).*

Taxes are the price we must pay for government services.

d. We are to serve government in the will of God (Tit. 3:1).

Believers often are called upon to serve their government in some civil or military capacity. This is proper as long as the service will support or promote one's basic human rights such as justice, self-preservation, and deliverance from oppression, as well as the honoring of worthy national alliances and commitments.

e. We are to pray for government officials (I Tim. 2:1-3).

We are to pray and give thanks for them, for they are God's servants, divinely used to carry out (in part) His purpose for mankind. Our prayers result in better government and a peaceable life.

Again, we must obey government intelligently, not blindly. When the will of the state clearly conflicts with God's will, as revealed in His Word, then the believer must obey God.

Although the Christian as a citizen may make full use of his rights under the law (Acts 16:37; 22:25), he must also be prepared to accept the denial of these rights, as did our Lord during His trials before Jewish and Roman courts. C. B. Eavey writes, "Opposition to one in lawful authority should not be made for the purpose of securing one's personal rights, but only in defence of the *right*. Often it may be the Christian's right to give up his rights. Never is a Christian justified in attacking the lawful right which belongs to a ruler or a government."[17] On the other hand, our Lord stood in defence of right when He questioned the motivation of His abusers (Jn. 18:22-23).

Dr. Eavey adds, "If and when a ruler becomes so corrupt as to be unable to adhere at all to the principle of true right and eternal justice, the Christian may find it necessary to resist his authority even to the extent of revolting against it and becoming a party to the establishment of another government. However, until it is clearly evident that a ruler or a government is unfaithful to its charge, it is the duty of the Christian to render allegiance to the existing authority, though it be guilty of much that is wrong."[18]

It is obvious that the Scriptures (especially the New Testament) have much to say about the Christian life and its divine provisions. It is urgent that we learn this truth and apply it to ourselves daily. We are grateful for that incomparable Helper, the Holy Spirit, who teaches us this truth and enables us to transfer it to our lives, as we trust Him to do so.

---

[17] C. B. Eavey, *Practical Christian Ethics* (Grand Rapids: Zondervan Publishing House, 1959), p. 200.
[18] Ibid.

A Review of Ecclesiology

1. What is the basic idea of the Greek work for "church"?
2. Define the universal church of Christ.
3. Where does the first direct reference to the universal church occur in the Scriptures?
4. In His prediction about the church (Mt. 16:18), what did Jesus say and what did He not say?
5. At what time did the universal church begin?
6. What two facts support this view?
7. In what two ways is the Lord constructing the church?
8. By what means is the Lord constructing the church?
9. Why is He using these means?
10. In addition to regeneration and sanctification, by what two ministries is the Holy Spirit doing His part in this construction?
11. Of all the redeemed of the ages, what saved people belong to the church?
12. Describe the two aspects of the baptism of, or with, the Holy Spirit.
13. What is the present function of the church?
14. What is its future function?
15. Give the time of the following events: the church's espousal (betrothal), preparation, wedding, and wedding feast.
16. Give several blessings that the church will enjoy as Christ's bride.
17. In what way will the church be Christ's fulness?
18. In what ways is the church to be distinguished from Israel?
19. In what ways is the church distinct from Christ's kingdom?
20. When and where was the first local Christian church established?
21. Define the local church in its content, organization, practice, mission, and hope.
22. What kind of people should make up the membership of a local church?
23. Who is the supreme head of a local church?
24. What N.T. offices should be found in a local church?
25. Describe the functions of these offices.
26. What church office is required by law today? Why?
27. Describe the kinds of church polity that exists today.
28. Give the two rites that Jesus has given to the local church.

29. Why is it better to call these rites "ordinances" rather than "sacraments"?

30. To what do these rites bear witness?

31. Of the several kinds of baptism mentioned in the New Testament, which two directly relate to the believer today?

32. According to the New Testament, who are the proper candidates for water baptism?

33. What should water baptism signify to these people?

34. What three modes of water baptism are practiced today?

35. Which of these is the biblical mode?

36. For what reasons do some denominations baptize infants?

37. In the light of these practices, why should infants not be baptized?

38. What is the relation of baptism to a person's salvation?

39. What is the symbolism of the Lord's Supper?

40. Give the three interpretations of the "bread" and "cup." Which is the biblical interpretation?

41. Describe the two prerequisites for the observance of the Lord's Supper.

42. On what three meanings should we meditate as we partake of this supper?

43. Why is the Lord displeased when we partake of His supper with known sin in our life? What should we do about this?

44. Describe the worthy observance of this supper.

45. What is the value of church discipline?

46. What procedure should be followed in administering this discipline?

47. What is the primary purpose of this procedure?

48. Give reasons for one's being a member of a local church.

49. What is the ecumenical movement? What is its purpose?

50. In what way is the Lord achieving the unity of His people today?

51. Define Christian experience.

52. What are some features of Christian experience?

53. By what means should we test the authenticity of our religious experiences?

54. What is Christian growth?

55. In what areas of our life does this growth take place?

56. What is the goal of Christian growth? Its means?

57. What has God given us for the maintenance of our Christian life?

58. In what ways is Bible reading and meditation profitable?

59. How can we read the Bible for personal profit?

60. Give five ways in which we can relate the Scriptures to daily life.

61. What is the primary role of the Holy Spirit in our daily life?

62. What must we do to allow Him to help us?

63. What is prayer? Give several kinds of prayer.

64. What rules must we follow in prayers of petition?

65. Why is it proper to talk to Jesus and to the Holy Spirit?

66. What reasons may be given for unanswered prayer?

67. What must we do to receive divine forgiveness and cleansing?

68. What fruit are we to bear in our lives?

69. Who actually produces this fruit?

70. What does it mean to abide in Jesus?

71. By what means does the Father cause us to be more fruitful?

72. What must we do to experience occasions of victory over our spiritual enemies?

73. What is practical holiness?

74. How is this initiated and experienced in one's daily life?

75. From what are we to separate ourself?

76. How can we separate ourself from sin?

77. How can we recognize false religious teachers?

78. What is worldliness?

79. What opens the door to moral world conformity?

80. Why is it necessary to practice dedication as well as separation?

81. How often should we dedicate ourself to God?

82. In addition to dedication what must we do?

83. What does it mean to be a disciple of Jesus?

84. What are the requirements of discipleship?

85. How can one know that he is truly His disciple?

86. What is the basis for change, or improvement, in one's Christian life?

87. What motivations has God given us for this change?

88. What steps will bring about this change in our life?

89. What is Christian service?

90. What is Christian service in its vertical and horizontal dimensions?

91. What is worship?

92. Of what qualities does true worship consist?

93. What is Jesus doing on earth during this age?

94. What means is He using in this work? Why?

95. Christian service involves two kind of ministries. What are these?

96. How can we know what our special ministry is?

97. Upon what does one's special ministry rest?

98. What is the Lord's call to general ministry?

99. What is His call to special ministry?

100. Where should we seek to do the special ministry that He has given us?

101. What is the believer's duty to moral law?

102. What is his duty to civil law?

103. Whose law has priority over all others?

104. Are you a growing, fruitful Christian?

105. Do you know what your special ministry is and are you involved in it?

106. Are you living a holy life?

Eschatology

ESCHATOLOGY
The Doctrine of Future Prophetic Events

In this section we shall consider those events of God's program that are still future and that are the themes of unfulfilled prophecy. The Bible is the only literature on earth that reveals with certainty the future of mankind (cp. Isa. 46:9-10). Hidden from the world's understanding (I Cor. 2:6-8), this revelation is given to God's people for the purpose of motivating their obedience (Jn. 15:14-15) and stimulating their hope (Deut. 29:29; Rom. 15:4).

INTRODUCTION

METHODS OF INTERPRETING PROPHECY[1]

One's understanding of prophecy will be determined by the method of interpretation that he follows. Here are two that are most widely used.

- **The Allegorical Method**

This method subjectively regards the words of prophecy to have other, hidden meaning than what they say. In my opinion, there are several faults with this method. Disregarding the common usage of words, it allows unlimited speculation. Also, the mind of the interpreter is the basic authority rather than the Scriptures. Finally, there is no way to test the conclusions of the interpreter. Because of these faults, I prefer the next method.

- **The Biblical Usage Method**

This method allows each word of prophecy the meaning it ordinarily has in biblical usage. As objectively as possible it seeks to interpret prophecy literally, even where figures of speech are used to convey literal truth. This method recognizes that the Bible is a single, coherent revelation. It bases interpretation on fact and allows the self-consistency of the Scriptures[2] to control it. Moreover, a precedent has been established for this method of interpreting prophecy by the literal fulfillment of many prophecies about Israel (e.g. Lev. 26:33; Deut. 28:64-67) and about the first advent of God the Son (e.g. Mt. 1:22-23). In the following studies I seek to follow this method of interpretation.

I heard Dr. John F. Walvoord, who has written extensively on prophecy, say that the study of unfulfilled prophecy is like putting a jigsaw picture together without first having seen the picture. The interpretation which fits

---

[1] See Paul Lee Tan, *The Interpretation of Prophecy* (Winona Lake: BMH Books, Inc., 1974).

J. Dwight Pentecost, *Things to Come* (Grand Rapids: Zondervan Publishing House, 1965), pp. 1-63. This is a comprehensive study of prophecy.

[2] This holds that there is in the Scriptures perfect agreement among the parts that comprise the whole revelation of divine truth. Because the whole biblical revelation of a specific teaching exceeds that which any single passage gives, we should seek to understand what all the Bible says about this doctrine.

the pieces together easily, with the least problems and in keeping with the general teaching of Scripture, is the one that should seriously be considered. This is likely to be the most accurate interpretation of the prophecy.

REASONS FOR STUDYING PROPHECY

As complex as the study of unfulfilled prophecy is, it is rewarding to all who strive to understand its meaning, for it is a part of the holy Scriptures (II Tim. 3:16-17). The biblical prophecies reveal truth that God wants His people to know and that He uses to incite them to holy living and service (Deut. 29:29; Rom. 13:11-12; Jas. 5:7-9; II Pet. 3:11; I Jn. 3:2-3). Reflection upon biblical prophecy has enlightened, challenged, and inspired hope in the hearts of God's people throughout history (cp. Gen. 3:15, 20; Jude 14; Gen. 15:5-6; Heb. 11:10; Dan. 9:2; Lk. 2:25; Rev. 22:20). Let us have an ear to hear what the Holy Spirit says to us through the prophecies of His Word. They speak of God's future program for mankind and of our place in it.

THE PROPHECY OF JESUS' RETURN FOR HIS CHURCH[3]

We have seen that during the present age the Lord is building His church. When He has completed this work, He will return to the earth's atmosphere and will receive His bride to Himself. This truth is taught in I Thessalonians 4:13-18 and II Thessalonians 2:1. It is implied in John 14:3; Acts 1:11; I Corinthians 1:7; 16:22 ("Maranatha" means "our Lord comes"); Philippians 3:20; I Thessalonians 1:10; 2:19; 3:13; II Timothy 4:1, 8; Titus 2:13; James 5:7-8; I Peter 1:7; 5:4; I John 2:28; 3:2; and Revelation 22:7, 12, 20. However, many, if not all, of these passages may also refer to Jesus' second advent to earth. They will fuel this anticipation in the hearts of believers who live on earth during the Tribulation Period.

ITS DETAILS

These are given in I Thessalonians 4:13-18.

- **Jesus' Descent from Heaven (vs. 16a)**

The Lord Jesus will come personally, descending to the earth's atmosphere (vs. 17) and bringing with Him the church saints who previously had died and had gone to be with Him (vs. 14; cp. Phil. 1:23; II Cor. 5:6, 8). These will return with Him in order that they might be reunited with their bodies (I Thess. 4:16).

- **His Command (vss. 16b-17a)**

The Lord's shout will be a word of command (Jn. 11:43; cp. Acts 8:38;

---

[3] I prefer to use the phrase, "the second coming," to refer to our Lord's second advent to earth, not to His coming for His church. By His second coming He will come to earth to remain as He did long ago by His first coming. I also prefer not to refer to the Lord's return for the church and His second coming to earth as two aspects of His second coming since these are separate events and this description applies to the post-tribulation rapture of the church.

25:23), which will raise the dead bodies of the saints (Jn. 5:28-29).[4] This shout will be with a commanding voice like that of an archangel — authoritative and loud (Jude 9; Rev. 10:1-3). The trumpet blasts will signal the change that will transform the bodies of His people — the dead from corruptibility to incorruptibility and the living from mortality to immortality (I Cor. 15:50-53).[5]

• His Reception of the Church (vs. 17b)

Upon changing the bodies of His people, Jesus will rapture them from the earth to meet Him in the air. Then He will escort them quickly and safely through Satan's domain to Heaven (cp. Eph. 2:2). All of this will take place at eye-twinkling speed (I Cor. 15:51-52).

ITS BLESSED ASSOCIATED EVENTS

The Lord's return for His church and the blessed events that are related to His coming comprise the believer's hope or expectation. This hope is described as being blessed (Tit. 2:13) and living (I Pet. 1:3), for Christ Himself is our hope (I Tim. 1:1). Being an expectation, this hope rests upon the certain Word of God, who cannot lie (Tit. 1:2). The various passages of the New Testament that speak of this hope have in view the Lord's return for His church and the blessed events that are associated with His coming. As we look at these events, we shall see that this expectation has no equal in the world (Eph. 2:12).

• The Transformation of Our Bodies (I Thess. 4:13, 16-17)

This transformation will complete the work of redemption in our lives (Rom. 8:23; 13:11; Phil. 3:20-21). Presently the bodies of the dead are in a state of corruptibility (the disorganization and decay of death), and the bodies of the living are in a state of mortality (destined to die and return to dust). They must be changed to incorruptibility and immortality (I Cor. 15:53).

While it is not difficult to understand the need which the bodies of the dead have for this change, we may not be as aware of the need which we who are alive have. Our bodies presently possess the sin-principle, inherent corruption, and certain limitations, determined by their constitution (Rom. 7:18-20; 8:10; Ps. 103:13-16). Moreover, the animating life-principle is the soul, which is associated with the blood (I Cor. 15:44, "natural" is "soulish"; Lev. 17:11, "life" is "soul"). While the body in its present form and state is suited to life on earth, it must be changed for the future that God has prepared for His people (I Cor. 15:50; I Thess. 4:17).

In I Corinthians 15:42-49, the apostle Paul contrasts the future changed

---

[4] Does the phrase, "the dead in Christ," also include the Old Testament saints who, I believe, are now in Christ (vs. 16, see Appendix D)? It may, but as I have pointed out elsewhere, they are not part of the church, Christ's body. It is more likely that they will be raised with the tribulation martyrs when the Lord sets up His earthly kingdom.

[5] According to Numbers 10:1-10, trumpets were used in Israel to signal the people for assembly (vss. 1-4), for travel (vss. 5-6), for alarm (vs. 9), and for the observance of religious events (vs. 10).

body with the present unredeemed one. First, he contrasts their outward qualities (vss. 42-43). The word "sown" probably refers to the whole course of our present physical life, including death. The unredeemed body is sown in corruption (the working of sin and death in our members that leads to physical death, disorganization, and decay) and will be raised in incorruption (a state freed from and unaffected by these). The unredeemed body is sown in dishonor (this has in view the lowly origin of the body, its physical functions, and the physical expressions of the sin-principle) and will be raised in glory (expressed in the body's future appearance, function, and dignity). The unredeemed body is sown in weakness (the narrow limits of physical strength and mental capacity, displayed in the helplessness of childhood, the frustrations of youth, the burdens of middle life, and the deterioration of advanced years) and will be raised in power (with new capacities and abilities). Being like Jesus' resurrected body, the resurrected bodies of all people, including those of infants and the aged, will be mature in development and size.

Paul also contrasts their inward constitutions (vs. 44). The unredeemed body is "natural" (lit. "soulish"), for the soul is its animating principle (Lev. 17:11). This means that the body is so constituted and animated that its present functions are suited to and concerned with only earthly existence (Jn. 3:6). Moreover, it is subject to the laws and conditions that govern earthly life. On the other hand, it will be raised a "spiritual" body. This means that its animating principle will be the Holy Spirit who will quicken the changed body (Rom. 8:11), which will be prepared for the new conditions and laws that will govern the future existence of God's people (cp. I Cor. 15:50; Lk. 24:36-39).

Finally, Paul contrasts the two models after which our body is fashioned (I Cor. 15:45-49). The unredeemed body is Adam's kind of body. The future changed body will be Christ's kind of body, reflecting His glorified likeness.

The changed bodies of the living will have the same qualities and constitution as the resurrected bodies of them who were dead. The bodies of both will be changed and will be made like the resurrected, glorified body of the Lord Jesus Christ (Lk. 24:36-43; Phil. 3:21; I Jn. 3:2).

• Our Seeing and Sharing in Christ's Glory (Rom. 5:2)

In an absolute sense, the glory of God is the visible radiance of all His perfections, fully and equally manifested by each Member of the Godhead (cp. Jn. 17:5). But we who are saved shall never have this divine glory, for we shall never essentially have God's nature which radiates this glory. On the other hand, it was our Lord's prayer that His people see and participate in His glory (Jn. 17:24, 22). This is the glory of His humanity. As the Last Adam, the glorified head and pattern of the new humanity, He will share His human glory with the members of the redeemed community (Heb. 2:9-13; cp. Jn. 17:22; Rom. 8:18-19, 29; Phil. 3:20-21; Col. 1:27; 3:4; I Thess. 2:12; II Thess.

2:14; II Tim. 2:10; I Pet. 5:10.

The glory that the Lord Jesus will share with His people appears to be the following: the glory of His changed body, which was transformed at His resurrection (Phil. 3:20-21); His moral glory (Jn. 1:14; Eph. 5:27); the glory of His exalted position, far above all creatures (Heb. 2:9; Eph. 1:20-21; 2:6); the glory of His Messianic works in which we were co-laborers, such as the building of the church (I Thess. 2:19-20; cp. I Cor. 3:9; 6:15); and possibly the visible radiant glory of light (Acts 9:3; cp. Col. 3:4; Eph. 5:8; Rom. 8:29).

- **Our Receiving Our Inheritance (I Pet. 1:3-5)**

In the Bible an inheritance is something that is given to another for his possession (cp. Lk. 15:12). God's people are His possession (Eph. 1:18), and their inheritance is the Lord Jesus (vs. 11). Let us consider the present and future aspects of this inheritance.

Today the Lord Jesus himself is our possession (cp. Eph. 1:11; I Jn. 5:12; Col. 1:27). Because of this, we have unlimited resources and blessings in Him (I Cor. 1:30; Eph. 1:3; II Cor. 12:9; Jn. 6:35).

As to the future, our inheritance will consist of those spiritual realities and blessings that He has prepared for us and that are reserved for us in Heaven (I Pet. 1:4; cp. Jn. 14:2; I Cor. 2:9). Peter describes these as being incorruptible (indestructible), undefiled (unstained by sin), unfading, and reserved for us. Also, we are being kept for them (I Pet. 1:5). Furthermore, we shall share in the Lord's earthly inheritance when He returns to reign (Heb. 1:2; Ps. 2:8-9; Mt. 11:27; Rom. 8:17).

The riches of this future inheritance are implied by the presence and ministries of the Holy Spirit in our lives, which are only the first installment of all that we shall experience at that time (Eph. 1:14). Having the Lord Jesus and all that He has prepared for us makes us rich indeed!

- **Our Seeing the Fruit of Our Earthly Life and Ministry (I Thess. 2:19)**

This anticipates the time when the Lord has completed His program of building the church and will appraise the lives of His people. Then all that the Lord was pleased to do through the lives of His people will be manifested (cp. Jn. 6:5-13). We who are saved should allow Him to do His work through us for our bringing glory to God (Jn. 15:4-5, 8) and our receiving a full reward (II Cor. 5:9-10; Jn. 15:16). We must remember that our labor is not in vain in Him (I Cor. 15:58).

- **Our Entering Eternal Life (Tit. 1:2; 3:7)**

The Scriptures teach that all who are trusting Christ for their salvation now have eternal life (Jn. 1:12; I Jn. 5:11-12). But because our bodies are still unredeemed, we cannot now experience all that this new life in Christ offers. When the Lord changes these bodies, He will translate us to Heaven, where we shall enter the full experience of all that eternal life means. With our changed bodies, we shall fully perceive all that God has for us and will completely express our new life in Christ without the eclipses of sin and the smudges of imperfection. With bodies like that of Jesus, we shall be like Him in will, emotion, and thought (Rom. 8:29; I Jn. 3:2; see Appendix V).

ITS TIME

The exact time of the Lord's return for His church has not been revealed. All who believe in Christ's literal thousand-year reign on earth hold that He will return to this world before His rule begins. Also, they hold that immediately before His millennial rule there will be a Tribulation Period on earth of some seven years. However, there are differences of opinion about the time of His return for His church as this relates to the Tribulation Period. Let us look at these.

• The Partial Rapture View

This holds that only spiritual believers who are watching and waiting for Christ's return will be raptured before the Tribulation Period begins. They who are not ready (carnal believers) will be left to pass through part or all of the tribulation with its "purifying fires." These will be raptured separately when they are ready or just before Christ returns to earth to set up His kingdom. This view is based on an interpretation of Matthew 24:13; Luke 21:36; Philippians 3:20; II Timothy 4:8; and Hebrews 9:28.

Objections to this view include these: It conditions the privilege of participating in the rapture, with the glorification of the body, on works, contrary to the whole scheme of salvation (cp. Eph. 2:8-9; Rom. 13:11). It ignores the sufficiency of Christ's atoning work to deliver the believer from judicial condemnation and to prepare him for eternity (cp. Rom. 8:30-34). It violates the concept of the unity of the church (Jn. 17:21-22). Finally, it overlooks the final sanctification of the saints when they shall be presented faultless before the presence of God's glory (Jude 24; Eph. 5:26-27). Indeed, I Thessalonians 4:13-17 does not suggest this theory. Matthew 24:13 and Luke 21:36 occur in contexts that speak about the Tribulation Period. The words "be counted worthy" literally read "be strong," "be able," or "prevail," without any idea of merit.

• The Posttribulational Rapture View

This holds that the Lord will return and will remove His church from the earth at the end of the Tribulation Period, just before or as part of His second advent. There are three views of this posttribulational event: one, that the Tribulation Period is now past and the rapture may occur at any time; two, that the church is now in the Tribulation Period and the rapture is still future; and three, that the Tribulation Period is still future, with the rapture at its close. Posttribulational rapturists base their view on an interpretation of Matthew 13:24-30; the use of "coming" (Gk. *parousia* meaning "kingly visit") in I Thessalonians 4:15 and Matthew 24:3; and the anticipation of tribulation (I Thess. 3:3-4; Acts 14:22).

Objections to this view include its ignoring the possibility of another interpretation of Matthew 13:24-30, which understands the wheat to represent postrapture saved people who will be on earth during tribulation days; its disregarding *parousia* as an ordinary word for "coming" (I Cor. 16:17; II Cor. 7:6) and "presence" (II Cor. 10:10); the failure of some to distinguish between the church's suffering from man's hostility and from God's wrath (Phil. 1:29; II Tim. 3:12 contra I Thess. 1:10; 5:9); and its overlooking the absence of a resurrection event in Revelation 19:11-21 like that in I Thessalonians 4:16. The Old Testament saints and Tribulation Period martyrs will be resurrected for the kingdom, but this appears to be later, before Revelation 20:4. If the rapture takes place at the end of the Tribulation Period, why does the Lord separate between the sheep and the goats in His judgment of Tribulation Period survivors (Mt. 25:31 ff.)? There would be no sheep left on earth to judge if the rapture had just recently occurred.

• The Midtribulational Rapture View

This holds that the church will be raptured in the middle of the Tribulation Period, before the final three and a half years. Believing that the church saints will not be exposed to God's wrath, this position holds that the church saints will be translated before the outpouring of the vials (bowls) of God's wrath (Rev. 16:1-12). For the time of the rapture, it identifies the "last trump" of I Corinthians 15:52 (cp. I Thess. 4:16) with the seventh trumpet blast of Revelation 11:15.

There are two objections to this view. One, it overlooks the word "filled" in Revelation 15:1 (meaning "completed" or "finished"), which indicates that all of the divine judgments of this period, including those introduced by the breaking of seals and the blowing of trumpets, are expressions of divine wrath. We read, "For by them (the Bowl Judgments) is completed the wrath of God." And two, this view disregards the fact that trumpets, as in the past, will signal various events in the future (cp. Mt. 24:31; Num. 10:1-10). The "last trump" (I Cor. 15:52) may represent the last of a series of trumpet blasts, which signal a series of events involved in the resurrection of dead bodies and the transformation of living ones.

• The Pretribulational Rapture View

This holds that the church in its entirety will be raptured before the revelation of Satan's human agent (the Beast; II Thess. 2:1-8) and the beginning of the "seventieth week" of Daniel, chapter nine. I prefer this view for the following reasons:

1. The church appears to be unrelated to the Tribulation Period.

If the church were on earth at this time, it seems that there would be some direct reference to it. None is found between Revelation 4:1 and 19:7. It is significant that the church is unrelated to the divine purpose, ministry, and people of this period.

a. The church is unrelated to the divine purpose for this period.

The divine purpose for the Tribulation Period is to prepare the world for Christ's second coming to earth. This preparation will include His worldwide evangelistic mission through the 144,000, His dealing with Israel so as to bring the elect remnant to repentance, and His pouring out three series of judgments upon wicked Gentiles. The church does not need any special preparation before its rapture.

b. The Church is unrelated to the ministry of this period.

The Tribulation Period is divided into two parts, politically: the first part, during which Satan's human agent will rise politically within a ten-nation confederacy in the Mediterranean area, and the second part, during which this agent (the Beast) will exercise satanic authority over the entire earth for three and a half years. Throughout the Tribulation Period God's servants will be active on earth.

During the first part of the Tribulation Period the 144,000 saved Hebrew evangelists will preach the gospel of the kingdom throughout the world with unprecedented results (Mt. 24:14; Rev. ch. 7). These will be killed at the beginning of the second part by the Beast (Rev. 12:17; 14:1-5).

During the second part, God's two witnesses will minister on earth (Rev. 11:3-14). Although he will prohibit any witness to God or proclamation of God's message, the Beast will not be able to silence these two men. Endowed with divine power, they will bear witness to the fact of God's existence in the midst of worldwide atheism. Also, being prophets, they will cry out against the unprecedented sin and blasphemy of the day and will declare that the world upheavals and distresses are visitations of divine wrath. At the end of this period, they will be killed, be resurrected, and ascend into Heaven.

If the church is on earth during this time, why does God use special forces to do what ordinarily has been entrusted to the church to do?

c. The church is unrelated to the believers of this period.

Several groups of saved people belong to this period: the 144,000 (Rev. 7:1-8; 14:1-5), the earlier martyrs killed during the forepart of the Tribulation Period (Rev. 6:9-11), the later martyrs killed during the latter part (Rev. 7:9-17; 13:7, 15; 15:2), the elect Jewish remnant (Rev. 12:13-14), and a few saved Gentiles who will survive the persecution of this period (Mt. 25:31-34). But nowhere is there any indication that the church will be on earth during this time.

2. An interval of time will be needed between the church's removal from earth and her return with Christ to earth.[6]

This time will be needed for the formation of a nucleus of saved people (only saved people will enter Christ's earthly kingdom) to repopulate the millennial earth (Mt. 25:34). Saved survivors of the Tribulation Period will

---

[6] See John F. Walvoord, *The Rapture Question* (Grand Rapids: Zondervan Publishing House, 1964), p. 92 ff.

enter the kingdom with unredeemed bodies, which will be capable of reproduction and of transmitting original sin. If the church were raptured just before Christ's second advent, these survivors also would be changed and raptured.

   3. *Christ's return for His church is imminent.*

   His return may occur at any time. This truth is indicated by the present tense of "look" (Phil. 3:20), "to wait" (I Thess. 1:10), and "looking" (Tit. 2:13). The present tense speaks of a continuous expectancy which we should have toward the Lord's coming. Also, if the church were to pass through part or all of the Tribulation Period, the church saints would know the approximate time of the Lord's return, because of the many details that have been revealed about this period. This knowledge would diminish the concept of imminency. On the other hand, those believers who will be living on earth during tribulation days will look forward to the Lord's coming to deal with their enemies and to establish His kingdom (Mt. 24:42, 44). The truth of His coming will encourage them to endure steadfastly in their loyalty unto death or unto His coming. However, they will not have a sense of imminency until the very end of the Tribulation Period.

   In view of the above evidence, I firmly believe that the Lord Jesus will come for His church before the Tribulation Period begins. There is no prophecy that must be fulfilled before this glorious event. Prophetic events, such as the rebuilding of the temple in Jerusalem, may come to pass, but these are not prerequisites to His coming. Many signs will attend His second coming to earth, but no sign, save the trumpet blast, will signal His return for His church. He may come today!

ITS PRACTICAL VALUE

   The truth of our Lord's imminent return for His church makes a great impact on the lives of all who receive it. It comforts the saved who are bereaved (I Thess. 4:18); it engenders patience in the face of trial (Jas. 5:7-11; Rom. 8:18); it deters us from sinning (I Jn. 3:2-3; cp. Mt. 24:48-49) and from spiritual lethargy (Rom. 13:11; I Thess. 5:6-7); and it incites diligence (Lk. 19:12-13), abiding in Christ (I Jn. 2:28), and love for Jesus and His coming (II Tim. 4:8).

   We can learn from the Lord's appeal to the tribulation saints to be watchful and ready (Mt. 24:42-44). To be watchful is to keep awake, be alert. God has wisely withheld the time of the Lord's return in order that we might continually be on the alert for Him and always be occupied with our spiritual duties (cp. vss. 48-50). To be ready is to be prepared for His return. Of what does this preparedness consist? The answer is suggested by what we would do if we knew that the Lord was coming one week from this hour. Some of our preparation might include making certain of our salvation, putting our spiritual life in order, spending more time in meditating on His Word and in prayer, witnessing to lost friends and relatives whom we have been neglecting, righting some wrongs, seeking the Lord's will for the remainder of time we are on earth, and taking inventory of our stewardship. Would you be prepared if He were to come today?

THE PROPHECY OF JESUS' APPRAISAL OF THE CHURCH SAINTS

We who are saved are subject to three divine judgments. As sinners we were judged at the cross in the Person of our beloved substitute, the Lord Jesus Christ (Rom. 5:8; I Pet. 2:24; II Cor. 5:21). Being justified, we shall never again be divinely condemned because of our sins (Jn. 5:24; Rom. 5:9-10; 8:1, 30-34). As God's children we are now subject to His corrective chastisement when we fail to deal with known sins in our lives (Heb. 12:5-11; I Cor. 11:28-32). Finally, as the Lord's servants (slaves), our Christian lives will be appraised by Christ (II Cor. 5:9-10; Col. 3:24-25; I Cor. 3:8-15; II Jn. 8). It is to this last judgment that we direct our attention. Observe that this judgment in no way relates to our salvation or destiny. These were settled when we received the Saviour (Jn. 3:36; 5:24). Also, salvation is God's gift to all who place their trust in Jesus as Saviour. It is not a wage that we earn or an item that we purchase (Eph. 2:8-9; Rom. 6:23).

Many saved people do not seem to be aware of their present responsibility and of their future accountability to the Lord Jesus. Having received Him as their Saviour, they suppose that they have fulfilled their spiritual duty and now await their removal to Heaven. This situation is aggravated by incomplete teaching about eternal security and by the erroneous view that equates divine forgiveness with divine forgetfulness (cp. Jer. 31:34, God does not remember sins in a judicial way by requiring offenders to pay their debt). These hold that they will go to Heaven, regardless of their present spiritual condition, and that they will not have to answer for their wrongdoing during the course of their lives as Christians. For these the coming appraisal will be a startling moment of truth.

ITS PURPOSES

- **That each believer may give an account of his life.**

This means that we shall be required to explain the reasons for our earthly behavior as Christians. This accounting rises from the fact that we who are saved are the Lord's servants (slaves), whom He has purchased with His blood (I Cor. 6:19-20; Rom. 6:16, 18). Since it is our duty to obey His will and to carry out His commission for our lives (II Cor. 5:15; Mt. 28:19), we are responsible for our conscious life, from the time we were saved (Rom. 14:12).

- **That each believer may receive his proper reward.**

By this appraisal the Lord will look for that in our life for which He can give us a suitable reward (I Cor. 3:8; II Cor. 5:10). This will require Him to appraise our good and bad works in order that a just calculation may be made (Col. 3:24-25).

ITS TIME AND PLACE

The appraisal of the church saints will take place after the translation of the church to Heaven, before she prepares herself for her marriage to the Lord Jesus (Rev. 22:12; 19:7). The saints' present work will end with the completion of the church. We should be anticipating what the Lord is doing with that part of our lives which we yield to Him (I Thess. 2:19-20).

The appraisal will take place in Heaven before "the judgment seat of Christ" (II Cor. 5:10). In the Scriptures this "judgment seat" is a judicial bench where court decisions are made (Mt. 27:19; Acts 18:16). However, this appraisal should not be regarded as a judicial examination, which will bring upon us divine condemnation for our sins. The atoning work of the Lord Jesus has adequately taken care of this for all who are trusting Him for their salvation (Rom. 8:1, 30-34). But we still have to answer for the total output of our lives during the time we were Christians on earth, for we are responsible for our actions.

ITS EXAMINER

Various references to this appraisal reveal that our master, the Lord Jesus Christ, will be our examiner (Rom. 14:7-12). The apostle John describes our Lord's judicial appearance in Revelation 1:13-16, with each symbol presenting some aspect of His judicial bearing. His clothing marks His dignity and honor. His white hair speaks of the wisdom and equity of His judgments. His fiery eyes, penetrating and searching out all things, show His assessing all things in the light of divine holiness. His glowing feet indicate His readiness to trample upon all that He does not approve. His roaring voice assures that His word will be final. His hand speaks of His sovereign control over His people. His mouth, projecting a sword, declares God's Word, the criterion of what is good and right. Finally, His dazzling face reflects the unveiled glory of God. Although John fainted at the sight, he was assured that he had nothing to fear (vss. 17-18). Elsewhere, John declares that they who abide in Christ will have boldness in His presence, but the rest will shrink from Him in shame (I Jn. 2:28).

In appraising the lives of His church saints, the Lord will adhere to those principles that He follows in all of His judgmental works (Rom. 2:1-16). His judgments are according to truth (vs. 2), that is, factual; they are according to people's deeds (vs. 6), that is, appropriate; and they are without respect for persons (vs. 11), that is, impartial. These principles guarantee that each person will be dealt with fairly and will receive his due reward (I Cor. 3:8).

ITS QUESTION

The Lord will examine and evaluate all our works (good and bad), done during the time we were Christians (II Cor. 5:10; Rev. 22:12). These works will represent the total output of our Christian life, including our actions, words, thoughts, attitudes, motives, and intentions.

Paul speaks of this appraisal in I Corinthians 3:8-15. Many teachers were busy in Corinth, so he warns them to take heed how they build on the foundation that he laid during his pioneer gospel work in that city. His words tell us three things about this appraisal. One, everyone's work will be made visible (vs. 13). Everything in our Christian life will be made manifest to us for the purpose of review and evaluation. Since this is a personal matter between the Lord and His people, I believe that this will be a private review, which occurs simultaneously for all who are involved (cp. Lk. 24:34).

Two, everyone's work will be tried by fire (I Cor. 3:13). Fueled by the holiness of God, our Lord's fiery gaze will examine and weigh these works for the purpose of approving that which meets His standards (Rev. 1:14; Heb. 4:12-13; 12:29). The phrase, "of what sort it is," indicates that the Lord will be concerned with quality rather than quantity. The works that He will approve are represented by materials that withstand fire (I Cor. 3:12). All else that He rejects will be consumed like such flammable materials as wood, hay, and stubble. What kind of works will He approve? Only that in which He had a part—that which was in keeping with His will and was done in His strength (Eph. 6:8; Heb. 13:21; Jn. 15:5; I Cor. 15:10; Phil. 1:11, 21; 4:13). All that was done independently of Him will be rejected, regardless of its appearance or results, for it represents nothing more than what unsaved people can do (Rom. 14:23; Heb. 11:6; Jn. 15:5).

Three, everyone's work will receive its proper reward (I Cor. 3:8, 14-15). The purpose of the appraisal is not to punish the saints for their sinful works but to reward them for their good works and to provide for their accounting of their Christian lives.

ITS RESULTS

The Lord's appraisal of our lives will bring us both gain and loss (II Cor. 5:10). What these are is illustrated by the parable of Matthew 25:14-30.

• The Gain (I Cor. 3:14; Mt. 25:20-23)

The works which survive the appraisal will bring wages of gain or reward. The Scriptures identify three kinds of reward.

1. *The Lord's Expressing Approval and Granting Honor*

In the parable the lord of the servants commended the faithful servants (Mt. 25:21, 23, "Well done"; cp. I Cor. 4:5; I Pet. 1:7). Several symbols are used in the Scriptures to express the Lord's approval of His servants.

a. *The Garland (I Cor. 9:24-25, "crown")*

When he portrays the Christian life as a race, Paul alludes to the Isthmian games, which were held every two years in a grove of spruce trees (sacred to Poseidon, the Greek god of the sea) near Corinth. Comparable to our Olympic gold medal, the prize was a wreath or garland of spruce. This represented the highest pinnacle of human achievement and happiness. It brought the winner the highest honors and the most coveted distinction a Greek could acquire.[7] Unlike that of the Greek athlete, the believer's garland will be an imperishable one (I Cor. 9:25). The garland that the Lord will give as a reward will represent His recognition and commendation of His people's good works (cp. I Thess. 2:19; I Pet. 5:4; II Tim. 4:8; Jas. 1:12; Rev. 2:10).

b. *The Engraved White Stone (Rev. 2:17)*

This also appears to be a symbol of recognition and honor. Similar to our trophy cup, this tablet of white stone, with the victor's name upon it, was a certificate of his victory. The believer's honor will be personalized with his receiving a new name and its being engraved upon some trophy.[8]

c. *The White Garment (Rev. 3:5)*

Sometimes the Greek winner was clad in a purple mantle. The overcoming believer will by his good works clad himself in a white garment, the fabric of which will consist of his righteous deeds (cp. Rev. 19:8, "righteousness" should be "righteousnesses" or "righteous deeds"). We are now weaving this fabric by allowing the Lord to do through us His works of righteousness (I Jn. 2:29; Phil. 1:11; Jn. 15:1-5). Careless believers who are not walking in fellowship with the Lord and who are not faithfully dealing with their sins will have defiled garments (Rev. 3:4; cp. 3:18; 16:15).

2. *The Lord's granting an administrative position in His kingdom.*

In the parable the lord of the servants increased the stewardship of the faithful ones (Mt. 25:21, 23, "I will make thee ruler over many things"). It is noteworthy that administrative positions in Christ's millennial kingdom will be filled by His people, regardless of the age in which they lived, as a reward (Rev. 2:26-27; II Tim. 2:12; Lk. 19:12-19; Rev. 20:4). The extent of one's authority will be determined by his works for which he is rewarded.

3. *The Lord's allowing intimate fellowship with Himself.*

In the parable the lord invited his faithful servants to participate in the celebration of his return (Mt. 25:21, 23, "enter thou into the joy of thy lord"). An intimate fellowship with the Lord as a reward is indicated by the promises to the overcomer that assure him of his receiving "the hidden

---

[7] Harry Thurston Peck, ed., *Harper's Dictionary of Classical Literature and Antiquities* (New York: American Book Company, 1896), p. 159.

[8] In Revelation chapters two and three the "overcomer" has in view the Greek athlete who carries off the victory. Contextually, the overcomer refers to the believer who hears and comprehends what the Lord says by the Holy Spirit (through the Scriptures) and who obediently responds to His message. By the Lord's strength the overcomer rises above the spiritual declension that is about him and keeps the Lord's works (does His will) unto the end (Rev. 2:26). The Lord's promises to the overcomer reveal much about the nature of rewards.

manna" (Rev. 2:17) and "the morning star" (vs. 28, both of which seem to refer to Jesus), of his being made a "pillar" in the temple of God (3:12), and of his being given a place at Christ's side (vs. 21). This is supported by the degrees of fellowship with the Lord that the disciples experienced — one (Jn. 21:20), three (Mt. 17:1), twelve (Mk. 3:14), seventy (Lk. 10:1), and many (Lk. 7:11). If during this lifetime we are developing a capacity for our future experience with Christ (cp. II Cor. 4:17), will not the believer who now often abides in Him have a greater spiritual capacity (not capacity of human nature) and desire for the Lord's fellowship in the future than he who seldom does? A person with a small capacity will not be able to appreciate fully or enjoy completely all that the Lord will offer. He will be like a person with little background in and understanding of art touring a gallery.

When we consider the nature of these rewards and the kind of works for which they will be given, we marvel at the grace of God. Although all the credit will belong to the Lord (cp. Lk. 17:7-10), He will still be pleased to reward us for allowing Him to express Himself through us while we were on earth. Even this act of will is of Him (Phil. 2:13).

- **The Loss (I Cor. 3:15; Mt. 25:24-30)**
  The loss which believers will sustain for those works that do not meet the Lord's approval appears to be the opposite of the gain he will receive for approved works. Again, the parable of Matthew 25:24-30 seems to illustrate what this loss will be, in addition to our experiencing shame and remorse (I Jn. 2:28; Heb. 13:17).

1. The Lord's Reprimand
In the parable the lord reproved his servant for being "wicked," "slothful," and "unprofitable" (Mt. 25:26, 30). In the appraisal the Lord will express His disapproval of our unacceptable works (cp. Rev. 2:4, 14, 20). This reprimand is not a judicial judgment, which measures out the penalty of sin, which is death. But it will not bring us joy.

2. The Lord's Deprivation of Stewardship
In the parable the lord took away the servant's stewardship, for the slave's conduct demonstrated that he was unworthy of responsibility (Mt. 25:29). In our case, our evil works will limit our stewardship (cp. Rev. 2:26-27).

3. The Lord's Denial of Intimate Fellowship
While the parable seems to say that the servant was disowned and banished, it does not necessarily mean this (Mt. 25:30). In a similar parable, the Lord Jesus will slay His enemies (Lk. 19:27). I prefer the view that the servant was not allowed to attend the festive celebration, honoring his master's return. This portrays the denial of intimate fellowship with Christ, which the more faithful will enjoy (cp. Rev. 3:20). Again, our evil works will limit our capacity for this fellowship (cp. Rev. 2:17; II Cor. 4:17; Jn. 12:26).

- ### The Calculation

Having done both good and evil works during the course of our Christian life, we shall receive commendation for the good and reproof for the evil. We shall receive a position of administrative responsibility in the millennial kingdom, yet not as great as though there had been no loss. We also shall enjoy, within the limits of our capacity, intimate fellowship with the Lord Jesus, yet not as much as though this capacity had been more developed by more abiding in Jesus during the present lifetime. We shall be joyful over that which the Lord will approve of our life; we shall feel sorrow and shame for that which He disapproves.

We shall not lose any rewards which we have gained. For instance, if our good works should bring us a reward, say, ten points, we shall receive the ten points. On the other hand, had we been more obedient and faithful, we would have gained more reward, say, fifteen points. It is our Lord's desire that we receive a full reward (II Jn. 8; some Gk. MSS give "you" for the first and third "we"), according to the measure of our God-given capacity and opportunities, but this will not be possible because of our sinning. However, we can earn reward by our dealing with our sins in obedience to God's Word.

Shall we be supremely happy because of the results of the appraisal? The Scriptures indicate that we shall experience all the happiness and blessing that our capacity will allow (Rev. 21:4-5). Still, it appears that our record of wrongdoing will remain as in the cases of Peter and Demas (Jn. 18:27; II Tim. 4:10; cp. I Pet. 1:23).

The fact of this coming appraisal clearly shows that our Lord regards our lives seriously and expects us to do the same. The grace of God in salvation does not cancel our personal responsibility but intensifies it, for this grace has provided us with everything that is necessary for our living full, productive lives (II Cor. 9:8; II Pet. 1:2-3). Other passages show that the Lord will also appraise the lives of His people who lived in other ages (Dan. 12:2-3, 13). He will do this when He establishes His earthly kingdom (Isa. 40:10; Rev. 22:12; cp. Mt. 25:14-19).

ITS CRITERIA

What measures will our Lord use in the appraisal of our works in order to determine what is acceptable to Him? I propose the following in the form of questions.

- ### Were the works done in conformity to God's will (Rom. 12:2)?

It is our duty to learn and to do that which is pleasing to God (Eph. 5:10, 17; II Cor. 5:9; I Thess. 5:21-22; II Tim. 2:15), with complete loyalty and reliability (I Cor. 4:1-2; cp. Lk. 16:1-13).

- ### Were the works done in association with Jesus (Jn. 15:4-5)?

Unless we act in union with Christ, our life, we cannot do anything that is spiritually productive (cp. Gal. 2:20; Phil. 1:21; 4:13; Heb. 13:21). All that we do independently of Him is sinful in God's sight (Rom. 14:23).

- **Were the works done heartily unto the Lord (Col. 3:23-24)?**

To do something heartily involves our total being, physically, mentally, volitionally, and emotionally (cp. Mt. 15:7-8). Since we are spiritually alive unto God (Rom. 6:11-13), our bent of life should be toward God and His will rather than toward sin and its demands or people and their desires (II Cor. 5:14-15). Our Lord not only disapproves of sin but also of slothfulness and dissipation as well (Rom. 12:11; Eccles. 9:10; cp. Mt. 25:24-30).

- **Were the works done to the glory of God (I Cor. 10:31)?**

To glorify the Father was Jesus' supreme motivation (Jn. 12:28; 14:13; 17:4). He will reject every work that does not manifest God and bring Him praise. We must seek to exalt God in everything that we do, however ordinary it may be (Mt. 5:16; II Cor. 3:5; Jer. 9:23-24).

Observe that the Lord Jesus himself met these criteria. This is seen in His doing the Father's will (Jn. 6:38; 8:29), acting in association with the Father (8:28; 14:10), and doing all things heartily unto the Father (4:34) and to His glory (12:28; 17:4).

One must use caution in making dogmatic statements about rewards. Enough has been revealed to indicate the fact of rewards and the need to take them seriously, but we cannot accurately calculate what ours will be. Only the Lord Himself is capable of making this appraisal (Rom. 14:1-13; I Cor. 4:1-5). Our part is to abide in Him and allow Him to abide in us in the full productivity of His life and power. As we do, we can expect a good measure of reward (II Tim. 4:7-8; Jn. 15:16). The apostle Paul was concerned about this, and so should we (II Cor. 5:9-10; II Tim. 2:15).

THE PROPHECY OF THE TRIBULATION PERIOD[9]

When the Lord has accomplished His present purpose of building His church and has removed this company to Heaven, He then will prepare earth dwellers for His second coming and the establishment of His millennial kingdom. The period of time between the Lord's return for His church and His second coming to earth is usually called "the Tribulation Period," or "the Tribulation Age," for the Scriptures describe it as a time of unprecedented trouble for the world (Jer. 30:7; Mt. 24:21-22, 29). As we shall see, the unsaved will suffer from intense divine judgments, Israel will be persecuted severely, and saved Gentiles will suffer martyrdom. The entire period of some seven years will be a time of unrest, strife, violence, wickedness, and anguish, especially during the closing three and a half years. This period seems to be

---

[9] See Appendix M for an outline of the Book of Revelation and Appendix L for an outline of the prophetic chapters of the Book of Daniel.

that part of the Day of the LORD when God will judge His enemies and will establish a new world order. The Day of the LORD extends from the rapture of the church until the great white throne judgment (for references to this day see I Thess. 5:1-9; II Thess. 2:1-3, Gk.; Joel 1:15; 2:1-11, 28-32; 3:14; Amos 5:18, 20; Obad. 15; Zeph. 1:7-2:3; Zech. 14:1-3; Isa. 13:6-16; II Pet. 3:10).

GOD'S PURPOSE FOR THIS PERIOD

This purpose is to prepare earth dwellers for Christ's second coming to earth and the establishment of His earthly kingdom. This preparation will include the following events, which will be examined in greater detail later.

• **The Worldwide Ministry of the Gospel of the Kingdom (Mt. 24:14)**

There will be an intensive ministry of evangelism during the first half of this period. This will give people everywhere the opportunity to be saved and to prepare for the Lord's earthly kingdom.

• **The Bringing of the Elect of Israel to Repentance (Hos. 5:14-6:3)**

This is necessary for Christ's return to earth (Joel 2:12-32) and the fulfillment of God's covenant promises to these people (Mic. 7:18-20). These promises include their salvation (Rom. chs. 9-11; Jer. 31:31-34), their restoration to Palestine (Deut. 30:1-10; Ezek. 36:16-38; 37:15-28), with David as their king (II Sam. 7:16; Ezek. 34:23-24) and his greater son, the Lord Jesus, as ruler over the earth (Lk. 1:31-33; Ps. 2:6-9; Isa. 11:1-9).

• **The Visitation of God's Wrath upon Wicked Gentiles (Isa. 26:21)**

In the past God used Gentiles to chasten disobedient Israel (II Kings 17:5-18; Isa. 10:5-18). But when these nations were satanically motivated with hatred and credited their victories to their pagan deities, they too incurred God's wrath and became subject to His judgments. God is going to use the hateful persecution of the Beast, Satan's human agent, to bring the elect of Israel to repentance. Then He will pour out the awful expression of His wrath upon the Gentiles for their abusive treatment of Israel and for their unprecedented wickedness (Isa. 13:11; Ezek. 38:16b-39:7; Zech. 12:9; Rev. 6:1-17; 8:7-13:18; 16:1-21; 19:11-20:3).

THE DURATION OF THIS PERIOD

According to the pretribulational rapture view, which this study holds, the Tribulation Period will extend from the rapture of the church to the Battle of Armageddon, which immediately follows Christ's second coming to earth. This period consists of both unknown and known quantities of time. An unknown quantity of time exists between the church's rapture and the Beast's confirmation of a pact with Israel. According to II Thessalonians 2:3, I understand the revelation of the Beast (Satan's human agent) to be the beginning of his biblical prophetic career. According to Daniel 7:23-24, he will begin to fulfill prophecy by gaining the leadership of a ten-nation federation.

It appears that when he has consolidated his position, he will be able to confirm an existing pact with Israel. How much time these events will take is not revealed. The known quantity of time is the seventieth "week" of Daniel 9:24-27, which, beginning with the confirmation of the pact, will span seven years.[10] Thus, the Tribulation Period will continue more than seven years.

THE MINISTRY OF THIS PERIOD

The ministry of this period is two-fold: the ministry up to the middle of the seventieth "week" and that during the remainder of the seventieth "week."

- **The Ministry During the First Part**

  1. *The Message*

  This will be the gospel of the kingdom (Mt. 24;14). This gospel will be the same message that is preached today (Acts 20:25; 28:31), with additional emphasis on Christ's soon return to establish His earthly kingdom and the need to prepare for this event (Mt. 24:42-44). Keep in mind that salvation is always by God's grace through faith in His salvational revelation (Eph. 2:8-9) and that entrance into God's kingdom is by the new birth (Jn. 3:3, 5). People will be saved in tribulation days as they are now.

  The Lord does not contradict the grace principle of salvation when He states the need for enduring to the end (Mt. 24:13). He seems to say that all who are truly saved will remain faithful to Him unto death or His second coming, when they will be delivered from their enemies. All who abandon their professed faith in Christ, so that they might avoid persecution and martyrdom, will manifest that they were never really saved. True believers persevere in their salvational faith, regardless of their circumstances (I Pet. 1:5; cp. Lk. 22:31-32).

  2. *The Messengers*

  This worldwide gospel ministry will be led by 144,000 saved Israelites (Rev. 7:4-8), who have the testimony of Jesus (Rev. 12:17). Regarding their spiritual state, they are described as being "redeemed" and "the firstfruits unto God," that is, the first to be saved in the Tribulation Period (Rev. 14:4; cp. Rom. 16:5; I Cor. 16:15). (If these were saved before, they would be raptured with the church.) They also are morally upright (Rev. 14:4, "virgins"), not defiled by the gross moral and religious impurity of that time (Rev. 9:20-21). Being God's slaves, they are sealed to indicate their divine ownership and to immunize them against the divine judgments of the period (Rev. 7:1-3; 14:1; cp. II Tim. 2:19; Mt. 27:66). But with the rise of Satan's human agent to world power in the middle of the seventieth "week," these will be the first to be martyred at his hand (Rev. 12:17; 13:7; 14:1-3). There will be no more need for evangelism, for all earth dwellers will be required to follow the Beast or die. They who choose the Beast will by this commit an unpardonable sin and

---

[10] See Appendix G for an analysis of Daniel 9:24-27.

place themselves beyond any hope of salvation (II Thess. 2:8-12; Rev. 14:9-11).

3. The Harvest

Although it is not explicitly stated, the fact that Revelation 7:9-17 so closely follows the description of the 144,000 (vss. 1-8) suggests that the passage is speaking about the people who will respond favorably to this ministry. They are described as being "a great multitude," who acclaim that salvation is by their God (vs. 10, "by" indicating instrumental agency is better than "to") and who are coming out of the great tribulation (vss. 13-14, Gk. pres. part.). Their wearing white robes indicates that they are overcomers (Rev. 3:5), apparently the later martyrs of the closing years of the Tribulation Period (Rev. 6:10-11; cp. 12:11; 13:7, 15; 15:2; 20:4). Very few saved people will escape the purge of the Beast, but they who do will enter the kingdom in their unredeemed bodies and will repopulate the earth during the millennial kingdom (Jer. 30:19-20; Ezek. 47:22). Meanwhile, the martyrs will enjoy unearthly blessings in God's presence (Rev. 7:15-17).

This gospel ministry during the first part of the Tribulation Period will bring divine judgment upon all who reject it (II Thess. 2:11-12). Many students of prophecy believe that Paul is speaking about people who hear and reject the gospel during the present Church Age and who are still alive to enter the Tribulation Period. Having rejected the gospel in the Church Age, it is believed that they will not be able to receive Christ as Saviour during the Tribulation Period. But this interpretation ignores the context. Paul is writing about the career of Satan's human agent, when with the devil's authority he rules over the earth (vss. 4-10). They who reject the gospel ministry of the 144,000 will come under God's judgment (vss. 11-12). They will believe "the lie" of the Beast, propagated by his lieutenant, the False Prophet (Rev. 13:11-17). To receive the Beast and his false doctrine will forfeit any further opportunity to be saved (II Thess. 2:12; Rev. 14:8-11).

• The Ministry During the Second Part

The Beast will not allow any gospel preaching or witnessing during the three and a half years of his worldwide rule (cp. Rev. 12:17; 13:5-6). But God will not be without a witness to Himself on earth. He will appoint two humans who, divinely sustained and gifted, will bear witness to Him during this time of unprecedented blasphemy and wickedness (Rev. 11:1-3).

1. The Identity of the Witnesses

The Scriptures symbolically represent these witnesses as "olive trees" and "lampstands" (Rev. 11:4). These symbols may emphasize that their ministry is of the Holy Spirit and conveys God's revelation in a dark place. Their standing before God points to their being His servants (cp. Zech. 4:14; I Kings 17:1). The fact that they die (Rev. 11:7) indicates that they are human, but what their names are is not certain or important.

2. The Ministry of the Witnesses

These men are witnesses and prophets (Rev. 11:3). As God's witnesses they will continually testify to His existence and to man's duty to Him. This will be especially appropriate at this time, for the Beast will try to remove every evidence of God's existence from the earth (Dan. 7:25; Rev. 13:5-6). As prophets these men will convey God's message to the world at a time when the Scriptures will be banned. Presumably, they will cry out against the gross blasphemies and wickedness of the day and will identify the frightful adversities suffered by earth dwellers as visitations of divine wrath. Perhaps they will warn the world of Christ's soon return.

These men will not preach the gospel, since everyone will have responded to the evangelistic ministry of the 144,000 and to Satan's lie (Rev. 13:15-17; II Thess. 2:11-12). They who embrace this lie (the Beast and his image) will by this commit an unforgivable sin and will forfeit all possibility of being saved (vss. 9-10; Rev. 14:9-11).

Energized with the Holy Spirit, these men will exercise superhuman power, which will be manifest in their self-preservation (Rev. 11:5), their working miracles (vs. 6), and their effectiveness (vs. 10). However, when their work is done, they will be slain (vs. 7). Then after three and a half days they will be resurrected and translated to Heaven (vss. 11-12). The ministry of these men will continue for three and a half years, throughout the time when Satan's human agent has world authority (Rev. 11:3; 13:5).

THE BELIEVERS OF THIS PERIOD

As we observed earlier, many people will respond favorably to the preaching of the 144,000 and will be saved (Rev. 7:9-14). I believe that these will be baptized into Christ (not into His body, the church) and will partake of His righteousness, sanctification, and redemption (cp. I Cor. 1:30; Mt. 25:37, "the righteous"; Rev. 13:7, "saints"; 5:9, "redeemed [men] to God by Thy blood"). I also believe that they will have the Holy Spirit, by whom they will be regenerated and by whose power they will remain loyal to Jesus unto death (Rev. 12:11). Moreover, they will have the Bible for their instruction and direction (cp. Rev. 12:17; Mt. ch. 24; there is no indication of any new revelation being given during this time). It appears that they will be living under the present Dispensation of Grace, which is given in the New Testament. The New Covenant will be in effect during this time (as it is today) since it is an everlasting covenant and it promises salvation through faith in Jesus, based on His atoning work (Heb. 13:20; 12:24). Their salvational faith will be manifest by their good works (Mt. 25:34-40; cp. Jas. 2:18, 26).

THE JUDGMENTS OF THIS PERIOD

In His dealing with earth dwellers during this time, the Lord will send upon the wicked unprecedented judgments for their gross sins, including the defiance of God and the persecution of Israel (Dan. 11:36; Rev. 13:5-6; see Mt. 24:21-22; cp. Isa. 13:11; 26:21; Rev. chs. 6, 8, 9, 11-13, 16). The passages in Revelation are prefaced by a vision of the judgment throne of God (ch. 4) and of the investiture of the Lamb, who is worthy to release these judgments upon the earth (ch. 5; cp. Jn. 5:22, 27).

There will be three series of divine judgments that will fall upon the wicked during the Tribulation Period. The first two series largely occur during the first part of the period; the third series takes place during the second part. How long these judgments continue is not always clear. Being expressions of God's wrath (Rev. 15:1), they will bring unique suffering to lost mankind (Mt. 24:21-22). Let us look at these briefly.

• The Seal Judgments (Rev. 6:1-17; 8:1)

These are released by the Lord's breaking the seals of a scroll. The first four judgments of this series (Rev. 6:1-8) appear to involve the rise of Satan's human agent, the Beast, out of the sea (Rev. 13:1-3), within a ten-nation federation (Dan. 7:7-8, 23-26), and the international conflict which follows. This will be accompanied by famine and death, dominating one-fourth of the earth (Mt. 24:6-8). It may be that this political struggle will upset the balance of power in the Middle East and will involve a confrontation between super powers like the United States and Russia, resulting in their mutual destruction.

The fifth judgment of this series (Rev. 6:9-11) is a vision of the first tribulation martyrs and their cry for vengeance. The sixth judgment (vss. 12-17) gives God's answer to their cry by describing events which take place immediately before Christ's second coming to earth (Mt. 24:29-30). He will avenge His people of their enemies (Isa. 61:2). The breaking of the seventh seal (Rev. 8:1) introduces a pause before the next series of judgments.

• The Trumpet Judgments (Rev. 8:2-9:21; 11:14-13:18)

This series is released by angels blowing trumpets. The first four judgments of this series affect a third of the earth, probably focusing on the Middle East (Rev. 8:7-12). I believe that these should be understood literally since similar events occurred when God dealt with Pharaoh to gain Israel's release from Egyptian bondage (Ex. 9:22-25; 7:17-21; 10:21-23). These judgments include hail, lightning, and a blood shower (Rev. 8:7), the sea becoming blood by volcanic or meteoric action (vss. 8-9), the poisoning of fresh water (vss. 10-11), and the curtailment of natural light (vs. 12).

These are followed by the remaining three Trumpet Judgments, which are described as woes (8:13). The first woe seems to be five months of awful demonic torment, which does not kill its victims (9:1-12). The second woe may also be demonic activity, which at a given hour destroys a third of the world population (vss. 13-21). It can hardly be said, as some do, that the first part of the Tribulation Period is peaceful when the fourth Seal Judgment and the sixth Trumpet Judgment bring death to half of the world's population. The third woe (11:14-13:18) begins with Satan's being cast unto the earth and consists of his working through his human agent (the Beast), persecuting Israel (12:13-17) and ruling the earth for forty-two months (ch. 13). Observe that the seventh Trumpet Judgment (the third woe) is released about the middle of the seventieth "week."

- ### The Bowl Judgments (Rev. 16:1-21)

  This series of judgments is described as bowls ("vials" KJV) of God's wrath, released by angels pouring their contents upon the earth. As we noted earlier, God's wrath is not confined to this series, but its expression during the Tribulation Period is completed by the Bowl Judgments (15:1). This series takes place during the second part of the Tribulation Period and is worldwide. It consists of such awful events as the affliction of humans with foul, painful ulcers that do not heal (16:2; cp. Ex. 9:8-11; the sea becoming like the blood of a dead man (Rev. 16:3); fresh water becoming blood (vss. 4-7; Ex. 7:17-21); increased solar radiation (Rev. 16:8-9); terrifying, supernatural darkness (vss. 10-11; cp. Ex. 10:21-23); the gathering of the nations to Armageddon (Rev. 16:12-16; cp. Zeph. 3:8; Zech. 12:2-3, 9; 14:1-3; Rev. 14:17-20; 19:17-21); a great earthquake and devastating hail, each hailstone weighing 110 pounds (Rev. 16:17-21), which splits Jerusalem (cp. 11:8, 13), levels the cities of the nations, initiates the destruction of Babylon (cp. 17:16-17; 18:8-10), and moves the islands and mountains of earth (cp. 6:14-16).

  The next prophetic event after these judgments will be Christ's second coming to earth (Lk. 21:20-28; Rev. 19:11 ff.). As destructive and painful as these judgments are, the wicked will not repent of their evil works (9:20-21). Their giving glory to God (11:13) does not necessarily indicate their repentance, but an acknowledgment that these events are of Him.

THE CAREER OF THE BEAST, SATAN'S HUMAN AGENT

As I see it, the most prominent person of the Tribulation Period will be Satan's human agent, "the Beast out of the sea" (Rev. 13:1-8),[11] whom some call the Antichrist (cp. I Jn. 2:18; 4:3), meaning the opponent and counterpart of Christ. Other biblical designations for the Beast are "the man of sin (lawlessness)," "the son of perdition (destruction)," "the wicked (lawless) one," "the lie" (II Thess. 2:3, 8, 11), "the little horn" (Dan. 7:8; 8:9), "the prince who shall come" (9:26), "the desolator (horror causer)" (9:27), "the king of the North" (11:21-45), "the abomination of desolation (detestable desolator)" (Mt. 24:15), and "Gog" (Ezek. 38:2-3; 39:1). He is depicted by the king of Babylon (Jer. 25:12; cp. chs. 50, 51) and by the Assyrians (Isa. 10:5).

Although this man is probably alive today, it is impossible to identify him,

---

[11] In Revelation 13:1; 17:3, "the beast" represents the political entity (the ten-nation federation) of which the Beast (Satan's human agent) becomes the leader at the beginning of his prophetic career (13:3-4) and which has worldwide authority during the second half of the seventieth "week" (Dan. 7:7, 23; Rev. 13:2, 5). Other references to this man are 13:12, 14, 15, 17, 18; 11:7; 14:9, 11; 15:2; 16:2, 10, 13; 17:8, 11-13, 17; 19:19-20; 20:4, 10.

for he does not begin his prophetic career (he does not become known by fulfilling prophetic Scripture about him) until after the rapture of the church (II Thess. 2:1-3). I interpret Paul's words "falling away" (vs. 3, also meaning "departure"), to refer to the rapture of the church (vs. 1) rather than to a general, indecisive departure from orthodox doctrine. The apostle seems to have in mind particular events which mark the beginning of the Day of the LORD and of the Tribulation Period. These events are the rapture of the church and the revelation of the Beast by his fulfilling prophecy.

- **During the First Part of the Tribulation Period[12]**

  In a time of political turmoil in the Mediterranean area, there will emerge a ten-nation federation (Dan. 7:7, 24), which during the last part of the Tribulation Period will be worldwide in its authority (vs. 23; Rev. 13:1-2; 17:3). Subduing three kings of the federation, the Beast will gain control and will serve as its head or president (Dan. 7:8, 24; 11:21-30a). He will be one of seven successive presidents who will lead the federation during the first part of the Tribulation Period (cp. Rev. 17:9-11). Daniel 8:9 reveals that he will rise out of one of the four areas into which the empire of Alexander the Great was divided. It will be the area of ancient Syria and Babylonia, the northern part of Alexandia's Kingdom which ultimately fell to Seleucus I (see Appendix I).

  When the Beast has consolidated his position as head of the ten-nation federation, he will confirm a seven-year pact with Israel (Dan. 9:27; 11:30b; cp. Isa. 28:14-29; Ezek. 38:8), which apparently will guarantee Israel's sovereign rights and safety. This confirmation will mark the beginning of the seventieth "week" of Daniel nine (see Appendix G).

  At some time during the first part of the Tribulation Period, the Beast will be killed "by a sword" (Rev. 13:14; cp. vss. 3, 12). The word "wounded" (vs. 3) means "slain" as in verse 8 and 5:6. Upon dying, the Beast will descend into the Abyss (Hades) to await his resurrection (Rev. 17:8, 10, 11). Another person will fill his place as president of the federation (cp. Rev. 17:10-11).

- **During the Last Part of the Tribulation Period**

  About the middle of the seventieth "week," Satan and his evil angels will be cast upon the earth (Rev. 12:7-12). Angry and aware that his time is short, the devil will try to exterminate the Jews and all who confess the name of Jesus and to erase God's name from the earth. Furthermore, he will secure for himself the open worship of mankind, lead the world into unprecedented blasphemy and wickedness, and make a last-ditch stand against the Lord Jesus. To attain these objectives, he will use a human agent, like Judas whom he used many years before (Jn. 13:27). This agent will be the Beast, whose career we have been following in the prophetic Scriptures.

---

[12] For a fascinating study of the Beast, see G. H. Lang, *The Histories and Prophecies of Daniel* (London: The Paternoster Press, 1950), chs. II, VII, VIII, IX, XI. Mr. Lang is a partial-rapturist.

The Scriptures show that the devil will use a man who previously had been a president of the ten-nation federation (Rev. 13:3, 12, 14; 11:7; 17:8, 10, 11). In spite of the theological problems it presents, it appears that Satan will raise the Beast from the dead, to the amazement of the world, to act as his agent during the second part of the seventieth "week" (II Thess. 2:9; Rev. 13:3-4, 14). This man's descent into and ascent from Hades show the reality of his previous death and resurrection. Moreover, he and the False Prophet will be cast alive into the Lake of Fire (Rev. 19:20).

Upon his resurrection the Beast will be restored to the head of the ten-nation federation as its eighth president (Rev. 11:7; 17:8, 10-11). With worldwide authority given by Satan, the Beast and his federation will rule over the earth for three and a half years (Rev. 13:2-7; Dan. 2:40-43; 7:7, 19-25; 8:24; 11:36-39; cp. Mt. 4:8-9). The rebuilt city of Babylon will be the seat of this world government (Rev. chs. 17-18; see Appendix I).

Although at the beginning of his career the Beast will be closely associated with false, organized religion (Rev. 17:1-3), this will not continue. When he receives his worldwide authority, he will abolish all religion and will proclaim Satan and himself as the lawful objects of worship (cp. II Thess. 2:4). By the deceitful proclamations and practices of the False Prophet,[13] the Beast will secure the worship of all the unsaved (Rev. 13:4, 8, 12-15; II Thess. 2:10-12). Moreover, he will speak great blasphemies against God and His institutions and will persecute the Lord's people (Rev. 13:5-7; Dan. 7:25; 11:36).

The Beast will have a commanding and fierce appearance (Dan. 7:8; 8:23), also satanic wisdom and power (Dan. 8:23-25; II Thess. 2:9). He will be deceitful (II Thess. 2:9-10), lawless (vss. 3, 8, "sin" and "wicked" mean "lawless"), cruel and blasphemous (Rev. 13:5-6), and a devil-worshiper (Dan. 11:36-39). He will intensely persecute the Jews (Rev. 12:13-17) and will seek to destroy all who refuse to receive his mark and worship his image (Rev. 13:7, 15; 15:2).

Near the end of these three and a half years, there will be a divinely inspired revolt against the authority of the Beast (Rev. 17:16-17; 18:8; Dan. 11:40-44). Babylon will be destroyed; there will be uprisings in the North and East; and the Beast (the king of the North) will be attacked by the king of the South. Insane with fury, the Beast will react by invading Palestine with the armies of the rebellious nations at his heels (Dan. 11:45). Meanwhile, the repentance of the elect of Israel will bring the Lord Jesus to earth to fight their

---

[13] The False Prophet ("the beast out of the earth," Rev. 13:11-17) will act as the Beast's minister of religion (vss. 11-15) and economics (vss. 16-18). Also endued with satanic power, he will carry out the wishes of the Beast. With miracles he will deceive the unsaved and will secure their allegiance for the Beast. He also will require everyone to receive the Beast's mark in order that they might buy and sell. It is not certain that he is human (some think that he will be Judas Iscariot, raised from the dead for this evil career; cp. Jn. 13:27; 17:12; 6:70), but he will suffer the same fate as the Beast (Rev. 19:20). Other references to the False Prophet are Revelation 16:13; 20:10.

enemies (Joel 2:12-20; Zech. 14:1-3). Upon the Lord's coming to earth, the military might of the earth will be led by Satan to unite against their common foe, the Lord Jesus (Rev. 16:14-16; Zech 12:1-3; 14:1-3). But this will be destroyed, and the Beast and the False Prophet will be cast into the Lake of Fire (Rev. 19:19-21). Thus, the King of kings will utterly defeat the Beast and his lieutenant, the False Prophet (Dan. 2:35, 44-45; 7:26-27; 8:25; 9:27; 11:45; II Thess. 2:8).

ISRAEL AND HER ELECT

Israel has a major place in the prophecies about the Tribulation Period.[14] This is not surprising since a divine purpose for this period is to bring the elect of Israel to repentance and fulfill to them the great covenant promises.

Little is said about Israel during the first part of this period. The Beast will confirm a seven-year pact with the nation (Dan. 9:27); the nation will dwell safely in peace (Ezek. 38:8); the temple will be rebuilt (Mt. 24:15); and orthodox Jewry will observe the Mosaic Law and its ritual (Dan. 8:11; Mt. 24:20). However, most of the prophecies about Israel relate to the second part of the Tribulation Period. Let us look at these in more detail.

- **The Beast's Program Against the Jews**

1. He will break the pact by a military assault against Jerusalem (Dan. 9:27; cp. vs. 26b; Lk. 21:20; Ezek. 38:8-16a).

2. He will invade the temple sanctuary and will proclaim himself to be the object of worship (Mt. 24:15; II Thess. 2:3-4).

3. Stopping the daily sacrifice, *he will erect an image of himself* and will require the Jews to worship him and his image (Dan. 8:11; 9:27; 11:31; cp. 12:11; Rev. 13:14-15).

4. He then will destroy the temple (Dan. 8:11-14) and will make Jerusalem desolate (Dan. 9:26b; Mt. 23:38-24:2), trampling it under foot for three and a half years (Lk. 21:20, 24; Rev. 11:2).

5. He will destroy many Jews and will lead others away captive (Dan. 11:31-34; Isa. 1:9; Jer. 30:7; Zech. 13:8; Mt. 24:21; Lk. 21:21-24).

6. Motivated by intense fury and hatred, *he will again come against Jerusalem,* followed by the military might of the nations (Dan. 11:44-45; Zech. 12:1-9; 14:1-3; Isa. 29:1-8; Ezek. 38:16b, 18; 39:2). This will result in the Battle of Armageddon (Ezek. 38:18-39:7; Rev. 19:11-21).

- **God's Preservation of the Elect Remnant of Israel**

God has chosen among the physical descendants of Jacob a remnant

---

[14] For a list of biblical prophecies about Israel, see Appendix K.

(part) which is the true Israel (Rom. 9:6-13, 27; 11:1-5). Today elect Jews who are saved are a part of the church. During the Tribulation Period the remnant of Israel appears to be made up of several groups of Jews, including some Palestinian Jews (Mt. 24:16-22), and some Jews who are dispersed throughout the world (Isa. 11:10-12; Jer. 23:3; 31:7-8). While the 144,000 evangelists will be martyred (Rev. 12:17; 14:1-3), the Jewish remnant will be divinely preserved from Satan's wrath and will be alive when Jesus comes (Rev. 12:13-16; Mt. 24:22, 31). The remnant will be only a small part of the total number of Jews who will be on earth during tribulation days (Isa. 1:9).

God's care of this remnant during this period is indicated by the following:

1. The Lord has given signs which will signal the Beast's breaking his pact with Israel and the time for the remnant's flight from Palestine. These signs are the Beast's attack against Jerusalem (Lk. 21:20-24) and his desecration of the temple (Mt. 24:15). Observe that two signs are given for positive identification (cp. Deut. 19:15).

2. The Lord has given instructions for the remnant to flee Judea (Mt. 24:16-22; Lk. 21:21-24) and to ignore any rumor of His return (Mt. 24:23-28).

3. The Scriptures indicate that the Lord will provide for the fleeing remnant with shelter and staples beyond the reach of their enemies (Rev. 12:14-16, 6; Isa. 26:20). The "flood" probably is a propaganda campaign to entice the remnant to leave their shelter (Mt. 24:23-26). Satan will use his prophets to spread false reports of Christ's return so as to lure the remnant from their hiding place. (On the other hand, a literal flood is not beyond possibility.)

4. Jesus declared that He will come in such a manner that announcements of any kind will not be necessary, for His coming will be known by all (Mt. 24:27; Rev. 1:7).

Although a judicial blindness rests upon Israel today because of their persistent disobedience and unbelief (Mt. 13:13-15; Jn. 12:37-41; Rom. 11:25; II Cor. 3:6-18), God will lift this blindness from the hearts of the elect and will save them (Rom. ch. 11; Isa. 1:9; 10:20-22; 11:11-16; Jer. 23:3-4). Their repentance and prayers will bring Christ to earth, who will deliver them from their enemies (Deut. 30:1-3; Joel 2:12-18; Hos. 5:14-6:3; Zech. 13:8-14:3). (Compare Daniel's prayer of confession, Dan. 9:1-19.)

THE PROPHECY OF JESUS' SECOND COMING TO EARTH

We must distinguish between our Lord's return for His church and His second coming to earth. His return for the church is not an advent to earth or a part of His second coming. Properly, His second coming to earth is His second advent, which is similar to His first advent almost 2,000 years ago.

CONTRASTS BETWEEN HIS RETURN FOR THE CHURCH AND HIS SECOND COMING TO EARTH

• His return for His church is called "the rapture," for the church will be caught away (I Thess. 4:17). His second coming is called "the revelation," for He will reveal Himself to the world (II Thess. 1:7).

• When He returns for His church, He will come to the earth's atmosphere (I Thess. 4:17). In His second coming He will come to the Mount of Olives, east of Jerusalem (Rev. 19:11-19; Zech. 14:4).

• He will return *for* His church (II Thess. 2:1). In His second coming He will *bring* His church (I Thess. 4:17b).

• His return for the church will occur quickly and secretly (I Cor. 15:51; Rev. 22:12). His second coming to earth will take place suddenly and openly (Mt. 24:27; Rev. 1:7).

• The rapture will lead to great blessing for the saved (Tit. 2:13) and grief for the world, unleashing the Tribulation Period (II Thess. 2:3). The second coming will be a time of grief for the world (Rev. 1:7) and blessing for the Lord's people who are looking for deliverance from their enemies (Lk. 21:28).

• The rapture will be signaled by trumpet blasts (I Thess. 4:16; I Cor. 15:52), while Christ's coming will be attended with visible signs (Mt. 24:29-30; Lk. 21:25-27).

SOME FACTS ABOUT JESUS' SECOND COMING

• **Its Time (Mt. 24:29-30)**
His second coming will occur at the close of the Tribulation Period. The Battle of Armageddon, which immediately follows His coming, will be the final event of this period.

• **Its Attending Phenomena (Mt. 24:29)**
The heavens and the earth will be shaken, and men's hearts will be seized with fear (Rev. 6:12-17; 16:20; Lk. 21:25-26). Celestial bodies will not give their light, meteorites will fall to the earth, and the sky will be swept away like a scroll.

• **Its Manner (Mt. 24:30)**
The Lord Jesus will come bodily (Rev. 19:15-16), personally (22:20), openly (Mt. 24:27; Rev. 1:7), powerfully (II Thess. 1:7; Rev. 19:14-15), and gloriously (Mk. 8:38; Rev. 19:16; II Thess. 1:10; Col. 3:4). The world has not seen Him since He hung upon the cross. His coming with power and glory will send shock waves throughout mankind (Rev. 1:7).
The Lord will be striking in appearance (Rev. 19:11-16). His fiery eyes of penetrating omniscience and holiness, His crowns of universal authority, His bloody garments of conquest (Isa. 63:1-6), His verbal sword of judicial

destructiveness (II Thess. 2:8; Heb. 4:12; Jn. 12:48), and His sign of dazzling glory (Mt. 24:30; cp. Ex. 40:34-38; Mk. 8:38) will combine to terrify His enemies and to overpower all opposition against Him (Rev. 6:16-17).

- **Its Company (Rev. 19:14)**
  There will come with Him his holy angels (II Thess. 1:7; Mt. 24:31), His bride, the church (Jn. 14:3; I Thess. 4:17b; Col. 3:4), and the disembodied precross saints and saved tribulation martyrs, who will be reunited with their bodies (cp. Lk. 13:28-29; Rev. 20:4).

THE PURPOSE OF JESUS' SECOND COMING

Upon His second coming to earth, the Lord Jesus will complete the Messianic work which He was commissioned by the Father to do (cp. Rev. 11:15-18). This work will include His dealing with them who oppose Him (Rev. 19:17-20:3; Mt. 25:41), His delivering His people from their enemies (Dan. 12:2-3; Zech. 14:3; Rom. 11:26) and blessing them (Ezek. 36:24-30; Mt. 25:34), His establishing the millennial kingdom of prophecy and ruling until every enemy is wholly subjugated (Rev. 19:15; I Cor. 15:25), His fulfilling the great covenant promises (II Cor. 1:20), and His judging the lost (Rev. 20:11-15). Finally, after His thousand-year rule Jesus' earthly kingdom will merge with the universal kingdom of the Father (I Cor. 15:28). All that He achieved during His first advent will be the basis of His work during His second advent (cp. Heb. 9:28; Col. 1:20).

THE EVENTS RELATED TO JESUS' SECOND COMING

Immediately upon our Lord's arrival, the following events will take place:

- **The Battle of Armageddon**
  The word "Armageddon" (Rev. 16:16) is from the Hebrew words *Har* (mount) and *Magedon*. The meaning of *Magedon* is uncertain, although some identify it with the site of Megiddo in Galilee. Upon Christ's return to earth, the military might of the Beast and the nations will unite against their common foe and will attack the Lord, who will be at Jerusalem (Zech. 14:4; 12:1-3; Dan. 8:25; Zeph. 3:8; cp. Rev. 16:13-16). But their effort will not succeed, for they will fall under the Lord's word and will be destroyed (II Thess. 2:8; Rev. 19:19-20; Zech. 14:12-15; 12:4; Ezek. 39:3-7; Isa. 34:1-8).

The carnage of this battle is described as being like a harvest of grapes, which are trodden in a winepress (Rev. 14:17-20). Blood will flow the length of Palestine (some 180 miles) to the depth of a horse's bridle (4 to 5 feet). It is also described as "the supper of the great God," to which the vultures are invited to devour the carrion (Rev. 19:17-18; Lk. 17:34-37; Isa. 34:2-3; Ezek. 39:17-20). This battle will end all resistance to the Lord's establishing His authority on earth. Not only will His human enemies be destroyed but also Satan and his demon confederates will be confined to the Abyss for a thousand years (Rev. 20:1-3; Isa. 24:21-22; 14:9-17).

Since the Lord will come to the Mount of Olives (east of Jerusalem) and will tread upon His enemies outside the city (Zech. 14:4; Rev. 14:20), it appears that this conflict will extend throughout Palestine, with Jerusalem as its focal point.

- **The Judgment of the Tribulation Period Survivors**

After the Battle of Armageddon with the destruction of the world's military power, the Lord will send forth His angels to bring to Him all who are alive on earth (Mt. 24:31; Jer. 16:16-17). This is to determine who among surviving earth dwellers are qualified to enter His millennial kingdom. Only they who are born again will qualify (Mt. 7:13-14, 21-23; Jn. 6:29; 3:1-7). To make this determination He will judge both surviving Jews and Gentiles.

1. *His Judgment of the Jews*

When He has gathered these people together (Isa. 11:11-12; 27:12-13), the Lord will pass judgment on them (Ezek. 20:33-38; Mal. 3:1-6, 17-18). They who are repentant and receive Christ as their Saviour (Hos. 5:15-6:3; Joel 2:12-18; Zech. 13:9; Ezek. 36:24-26) will receive the blessings of the New Covenant (Jer. 31:31-34) and will be restored to their promised land (Deut. 30:1-8; Isa. 10:20-23; 11:10-16; 43:1-13; Jer. 23:1-8; Ezek. 34:11-31; 36:16-38; 37:20-28; 39:23-29). The apostate Jews who embraced the Beast will be destroyed (Ezek. 11:21; 20:38; cp. Lk. 19:27).

2. *His Judgment of the Gentiles*

The Lord's judgment of the Gentile survivors will be personal and individual, not national (Mt. 25:31-46). Again, the purpose of this is to determine who are qualified to enter His earthly kingdom (vss. 32-33). The "sheep" represent "the righteous" who are qualified, while the "goats" represent "the cursed" who are not qualified (vss. 37, 41).

What is it that will qualify one for entrance to the kingdom? A casual reading of verses 35-40 might lead one to believe that entrance is based on good works, but this interpretation is contradictory to the salvational principle of grace (Eph. 2:8-9; Tit. 3:5). The works to which the Lord refers indicate the presence of salvational faith (Jas. 2:14-26; I Jn. 2:29). The salvation of these "sheep" will be manifested in tribulation days by their kind treatment of the Lord's "brothers," that is, people who belong to Him (Mt. 12:49-50). Only saved people will have the desire and the courage to give aid to them who suffer from their enemies for Christ's sake. The unsaved will not have this love (Mt. 24:12, 10).

The "sheep," for whom the kingdom is prepared, will be invited to enter (Mt. 25:34). On the other hand, the "goats" will be banished from the Lord's presence (vs. 41) and will die (cp. Rev. 19:21; Lk. 19:27), to await their resurrection and final judgment (Mt. 25:41, 46). Those earth dwellers who are saved will enter the kingdom in their unredeemed bodies in order that they might repopulate the earth. The children who are born to them during kingdom days will be corrupted by original sin and will need to be saved.

- ## The Resurrection of Precross and Tribulation Period Saints

  Since the precross saints and Tribulation Period martyrs are members of Christ's kingdom (cp. Lk. 13:28-29; Mt. 8:11; Rev. 20:4; cp. Ezek. 34:23-24), they must be raised from the dead to participate in His millennial kingdom (cp. Rev. 20:4-5; Dan. 12:2-3, 13; Isa. 26:19; Jn. 5:28-29).

- ## The Appraisal of These Believers

  The Lord will not only determine who is qualified to enter His earthly kingdom but will also appraise the works of His people in order to reward them. He will appraise and reward His people who survive the Tribulation Period (Mt. 16:27). Also, He will appraise and reward the precross saints and Tribulation Period martyrs, all of whom He will raise from the dead to enter His earthly kingdom (Rev. 22:12; Lk. 14:14; cp. Mt. 25:14-30).

- ## The Marriage Supper of the Lamb

  In Bible times the wedding ceremony was very simple, but the wedding feast which followed comprised several days of happy festivity. While the marriage of the Lord Jesus and His bride takes place in Heaven (Rev. 19:7-8), the festivities celebrating this occasion will be on earth when the Lord sets up His millennial kingdom (Rev. 19:9). Doubtlessly, the redeemed of other ages will be the invited guests (cp. Jn. 3:29). At this time all the redeemed of humanity will be on earth in their bodies, so they will be able to participate in this feast, which will include the consumption of food (Mt. 8:11; Lk. 22:16).

THE PROPHECY OF THE MESSIANIC, MILLENNIAL KINGDOM[15]

Any consideration of this kingdom must distinguish between God's universal kingdom and Christ's mediatorial kingdom, the topic of our study.[16] God's universal kingdom, which is everlasting (Ps. 10:16; 74:12; Jer. 10:10), embraces all the things that are determined by His decree (Ps. 103:19; I Chron. 29:11-12; Eph. 1:11). While being a part of the universal kingdom, Christ's mediatorial kingdom is His rule as the Father's servant over the earth to bring God's enemies into subjection to His authority and to accomplish other divine objectives, which we shall look at later.

This rule was briefly realized in Adam before his fall (Gen. 1:26) and was

---

[15] See Appendix R, the kingdom of God.

[16] See Alva J. McClain, The Greatness of the Kingdom (Grand Rapids: Zondervan Publishing House, 1959), chs. IV, V. Observe that McClain proposes that the mediatorial kingdom (the rule of God over the earth through a human agent) has existed since Adam. I prefer the view that the mediatorial kingdom has not existed since Adam's fall. The earth is now under Satan's rule. Being synonymous with Jesus' Messianic kingdom rule, the mediatorial kingdom will be established after His second coming to earth.

later foreshadowed in the regional reigns of Saul, David, and Solomon (I Sam. 9:16; 16:1, 12-13; II Sam. 7:8, 12-13; I Kings 1:13, 46-48; I Chron. 22:9-10). But God's revealed objectives for these reigns were not achieved because of the disobedience of these men and their subjects. Therefore, God spoke through His prophets about a time in the future when this kingdom would be established and governed by a perfect Ruler and His laws would be written on the hearts of His subjects (Ps. 2:6-9; ch. 72; Isa. 11:1-9; Jer. 31:33).

God the Son came to earth, assumed a human nature, and was anointed (as a man) to be the Father's Servant for the purpose of achieving the divine objectives for the mediatorial kingdom (Isa. 42:1-7; 49:1-9; 52:13-53:12; 61:1-2; Jn. 6:38; 8:28-29; Phil. 2:7-8). During His first advent the Lord Jesus Christ presented Himself to Israel for their acceptance or rejection, and by His death and resurrection He laid the foundation of his future Messianic work, which includes His mediatorial kingdom. Let us look more closely at this kingdom.

ITS ASPECTS

Presently, the Lord's kingdom in its visible, earthly form is represented by Christendom — all that represents Christ in this world including all professing Christians and their institutions (cp. Mt. ch. 13). In its real form the kingdom is spiritual, nongeographical, and nonpolitical, embracing all who are saved, whether living or dead (Col. 1:13).

In the future this kingdom in its real form will be political and earthly, embracing at that time the world's total population. Still, as we shall see, it will have spiritual qualities as well as physical features.

ITS DURATION

Upon His second coming to earth, our Lord's earthly kingdom will continue for a thousand years (Rev. 20:1-7). When it has ended, His millennial kingdom will merge with the Father's universal kingdom (I Cor. 15:24-28; Lk. 1:33), and the Father and the Lord Jesus will jointly rule forever. Still, Jesus as a man will continue to be the Father's servant and will remain in subjection to Him forever (I Cor. 15:28). This indicates that there will be other divine projects for the Lord Jesus to do in the ages to come (Eph. 2:7), which have not been revealed. His people will serve with Him in these projects.

ITS OBJECTIVES

Being the same as those belonging to His Messianic work, the following objectives of the mediatorial kingdom will be completed by our Lord's rule.

- **The Domination of the Earth and Its Creatures (Heb. 2:5-8)**
The Lord Jesus will accomplish what Adam and his posterity has failed to do (Gen. 1:26, 28; Ps. ch. 8). He will rule over the earth in a manner that will reflect God's wise, benevolent authority and that will glorify the Father

461

(cp. Jn. 12:28; 17:4).

- ### The Salvation of the Elect (Jn. 6:37; 14:6; cp. Isa. 45:5-25)

The final group of elect humans, born during kingdom days, will be saved (Isa. 49:6). Also, all the redeemed of mankind will experience the blessings of our Lord's rule.

- ### The Subjugation of All Rebels Against God (I Cor. 15:25; Phil. 3:21)

When He establishes His kingdom, the Lord Jesus will cast Satan and his demon allies into the Abyss (Rev. 20:1-3) and will judge earth dwellers to determine who are qualified to enter His kingdom (Mt. 25:31-46). Unsaved subjects who are born during the millennium will be dealt with at the end of His rule (Rev. 20:7-9). Finally, being related to the unredeemed body, death and sin will be abolished, with the physical change of saved earth dwellers to immortality and the resurrection of the unsaved dead (I Cor. 15:25-26; Jas. 1:15; Rev. 20:12-14).

- ### The Restoration of the Earth to Its Primeval State (Col. 1:20)

When the Lord establishes His earthly kingdom, He will lift the divine curse upon creation (Gen. 3:17-19; Rom. 8:19-23; Isa. 11:6-9), cleanse the earth of its pollution, and restore it to its original fertility and beauty (Isa. ch. 35).

- ### The Fulfillment of the Divine Covenant Promises (Num. 23:19)

Almost all of these promises were made to Israel (Rom. 9:4), including a land (Gen. 15:18; 17:8), their restoration to the land (Deut. 30:3-5), and their being governed by David's house (II Sam. 7:16; Lk. 1:31-33), never to be dispersed again (II Sam 7:10). Also the true Israel as well as saved Gentiles will enjoy the blessings of the New Covenant (Jer. 31:31-34; Heb. 12:24; 8:6).

It is noteworthy that the supreme goal of all that our Lord does in His Messianic works is to glorify the Father (Jn. 12:28; 14:13; 17:4; Phil. 2:8-11). This should be our goal as well (I Cor. 10:31).

ITS CITIZENS

When He sets up His earthly kingdom, the Lord Jesus will allow only saved people to enter, that is, to live in His earthly kingdom, which will embrace all the earth (cp. Mt. 7:21-23; 25:31-46; Jn. 3:5; Heb. 8:11). These will include the risen, glorified saints of other ages as well as saved earth dwellers who survive the Tribulation Period. These saved earth dwellers will enter the kingdom with unredeemed bodies and will repopulate the earth (Ezek. 36:10-11; 47:22; Jer. 30:18-20; Isa. 65:20-25). Because of their having original sin and their sinning, people who are born during kingdom days will need to be born again. The deceptive and rebellious character of sin is revealed by the fact that many will not receive Jesus for their salvation (Rev. 20:8-9).

ITS ADMINISTRATION

The Lord Jesus Christ will be the sovereign ruler of the kingdom (Rev. 19:15-16; Isa. 9:6-7). His authority will be worldwide (Ps. 72:8-11; Mt. 11:27; 28:18), with the seat of His government at Jerusalem (Isa. 24:23; 2:3; Zech. 14:16-17; Mt. 5:35). His administration will include David as king of Israel (Ezek. 34:23-24; 37:24-25; Jer. 30:9), the Twelve Apostles as rulers of the individual tribes of Israel (Mt. 19:28), possibly Paul as governor of the Gentiles nations (Rom. 15:15-16), and the faithful precross saints, church saints, and saved tribulation martyrs as holding other administrative positions as rewards (Rev. 2:26-27; 20:4; cp. Mt. 25:21). Apparently, angels will not have administrative positions over earth dwellers.

The character of our Lord's rule will be unique to human history (Isa. 11:1-5). Having divine wisdom and knowledge, Jesus will not need counselors and advisers. He will rule with fairness, faithfulness, and severity, for He will be endued with the Holy Spirit, who empowers Him for all His Messianic works (Isa. 61:1-2). Rebellion against the King will be dealt with directly and unsparingly (Isa. 65:20; cp. Mt. 5:29-30). With Satan and his demon agents bound, there will be no outward temptation or moral pollution (Rev. 20:1-3). Yet, having the sin-principle, earth dwellers with unredeemed bodies will sin. But there will be available to the lost salvation through faith in Jesus and His atoning work and to the saved cleansing from sin (cp. the sin-offering of Ezek. 43:19-27, which does not necessarily indicate a return to the Mosaic ritual but possibly a symbolic portrayal of our Lord's atoning work and the personal appropriation which is needed for cleansing from sin).

ITS BLESSINGS

Our sinful world has dreamed of an earthly utopia, but it has never been able to bring it off. However, the zeal of the LORD will achieve what sinful man cannot do (Isa. 9:6-7).

• Its Spiritual Blessings

All who enter the Lord's earthly kingdom will be saved people and will enjoy the blessings that accompany salvation (Jer. 31:31-34; Ezek. 36:26-28). The Holy Spirit will be poured out upon everyone (Joel 2:28-29), bringing them the blessings of his manifold ministry. Everyone (who is saved) will "know" the LORD with that knowledge that springs from a personal relationship with Him (Jer. 31:33-34).

• Its Ethical Blessings

With Satan and his demonic allies imprisoned (Rev. 20:1-3), there will be no external temptation or moral pollution. The Word of the LORD will go forth from Jerusalem (perhaps by prophecy) throughout all the earth (Isa. 2:3; cp. Joel 2:28). It will be the standard of all moral judgments and values. It will be taught to children as well as to adults (Isa. 54:13; 2:3). Saved people will be motivated and enabled to obey the Lord (Ezek. 36:27; Jer. 31:33). Also, they will have moral discernment (Isa. 32:4-5; Mal. 3:18).

• Its Social Blessings

All warfare will be permanently abolished (Ps. 46:9; Isa. 2:4; Mic. 4:3-4). Absolute social justice will prevail everywhere (Ps. 72:4, 12-13; Isa. 11:4). The helpless and the hopeless will be rejuvenated (Isa. 35:5-6), and all will be tenderly cared for (Isa. 40:11; 42:1-4; Zech. 8:1-8). With the curse of Babel removed, there will be one universal language (Zeph. 3:9).

• Its Political Blessings

Although Israel, the wife of the LORD (Yahweh), will be exalted above the nations (Ps. 47; Isa. ch. 60), the Gentiles will also be richly blessed (Rom. 11:11-12; Mic. 4:1-7). The King not only will make wise, impartial decisions, which will contribute to the good of all, but He also will be able to carry them through (Isa. 2:3-4; 11:2-5; Jer. 23:5-6). Nations will live together in perpetual peace, and they will enjoy unprecedented prosperity as long as they honor the King (Zech. 14:16-18).

• Its Physical Blessings

Everyone will enjoy health and long life, with saved people living throughout the millennium (Isa. 35:5-6; 33:24; 65:22). While earth dwellers will experience the natural events of procreation, birth, and development, they will not die unless they are incorrigible sinners, who refuse to submit to the King's authority (Isa. 11:4; 65:20; Jer. 31:30). All the unsaved who are still alive at the end of the millennium will die in the final revolt (Rev. 20:7-9). Apparently, the ordinary hazards of human existence will be eliminated (Ezek. 34:23-31; Ps. 91:10-12; Isa. 11:9; 65:23-25).

With the Edenic curse lifted, desolate areas will be reclaimed and inhabited (Isa. 61:4), animals will be at peace with each other and man (Isa. 11:6-8; Hos. 2:18; Ezek. 34:25), the land will be more productive (Isa. 32:13-15; 35:1-2; Ezek. 34:29; 36:4-11, 29-30; Amos 9:13). There will be more rainfall and new water supplies in desert areas (Joel 2:23; Isa. 35:6-7; 32:15). Natural light will also be increased (Isa. 30:26; 60:19-20). The topography of Palestine (and possibly the whole earth) will be changed, with the Dead Sea being fed by a river flowing from Jerusalem and made to support life (Zech. 14:10; Ezek. 47:1, 8-12; the "sea" of vs. 8 is the Dead Sea, the "sea" of vs. 10 is the Mediterranean).

ITS WORSHIP

People will worship the Lord everywhere (Mal. 1:11), but formal worship will be observed in Jerusalem, the city of the King (Zech. 6:12-13; 14:16-17; Jer. 33:15-18). Ezekiel chapters 40-48 seems to give details of the millennial temple (chs. 40-43), worship (chs. 44-46), and land (chs. 47-48). The worship services will include offerings and feasts similar to those of the Mosaic ritual

(Jer. 33:18; Ezek. 43:18-27; 45:21; 46:4). Like the Lord's Supper these offerings and feasts appear to have commemorative and symbolic significance, celebrating various aspects of our Lord's atoning work and appropriating its benefits to the worshiper. They will not replace the Lord's atoning work, but they will remind the worshiper of this work and of their responsibility to appropriate it to their needs (cp. I Cor. 11:24-26; II Cor. 7:1; I Jn. 1:9). There will be a priesthood, with Christ Jesus as the high priest (Heb. 5:5-6; Zech. 6:13). People who neglect worship will be visited with divine chastisement (Zech. 14:16-19).

ITS END

The Lord's kingdom will close with a revolt led by Satan (Rev. 20:7-10). As we have observed, people will be born during these thousand years who will not receive Jesus as their Saviour. At the close of this time God will release Satan and his demons from the Abyss and will use them to sift out these unbelievers who are still alive. Satan will lead them against Jerusalem where they will be slain with fire. Satan himself will be cast into the Lake of Fire.

The reference to "Gog and Magog" (Rev. 20:8) seems to be speaking of the unsaved earth dwellers who participate in this revolt. Although, in my opinion, these terms have no relation to the prophecy of Ezekiel Chapters 38 and 39, they are used to describe these rebels who will have the same character as the Beast and his confederates who invaded Palestine many years earlier.

This revolt will forever demonstrate the fact that unsaved people are incurably evil and incapable of correcting their spiritual state. In spite of perfect government and temptation-free environment, they still need to be born again. Their depravity is manifest in their revolting against the Lord. Without the new birth people remain sinners and outside God's spiritual kingdom. Their inherent disposition and character are the same as their spiritual father, the devil (Jn. 8:44).

Immediately following this revolt and its judgment, God will bring about the dissolution of the present universe (II Pet. 3:10-13; Mt. 24:35; Rev. 20:11; 21:1). That this is a dissolution rather than a purging is indicated by the words "shall pass away" (II Pet. 3:10) and "were passed away" (Rev. 21:1), "melt" (II Pet. 3:10) and "dissolved" (11-12), all meaning "loosed," or "broken up." Thus the present universe will revert to formless energy, with which God will make the new heaven and the new earth. Keep in mind that sin is not an inherent part of the present universe. It is presently confined to fallen angels and human earth dwellers.

THE PROPHECY OF THE RESURRECTION AND JUDGMENT OF THE LOST

The resurrection and judgment of unsaved humans will be the last part of our Lord's revealed Messianic work relating to the present universal order

(Rev. 20:11-15; cp. I Cor. 15:25-26; Jn. 5:28-29). Following His millennial rule, this will also include His judging fallen angels or demons (Jude 6; I Cor. 6:3; II Pet. 2:4). Let us look at this judgment more closely (Rev. 20:11-15).

ITS SCENE (Rev. 20:11)

With the heaven and earth gone (Mt. 24:35; II Pet. 3:10-13), we see a "great white throne," reflecting God's awesome majesty and consuming holiness. The occupant will be the Lord Jesus Christ, the judge of the universe (Jn. 5:22; Acts 10:42; 17:31).

ITS SUBJECTS (Rev. 20:12, 13)

They are called "the dead," though they have been resurrected (Jn. 5:28; Acts 10:42; Rev. 20:5a). These are the unsaved who, being in their sins and dead toward God, are spiritually dead (Eph. 2:1; 4:18). Their personhood and immaterial part of human nature have been ejected from Hades and reunited with their body, which has been given up by the sea or grave ("death," Rev. 20:13). Regardless of their station in earthly life, they stand alike before God, with no place to hide.

The nature of the resurrected body of the lost probably will be similar to that of the saved, so that it might exist forever (Mt. 25:46). It seems that it will be reorganized without the sin-principle and inherent corruption and that it will be animated by the Holy Spirit, for it will have, so it appears, the same life support system as ours. Probably Paul's description of the resurrection body in I Corinthians 15 applies to that of the unsaved as well as the saved, since the nature of resurrection appears to be the same, regardless of its subject. If this is so, then the truth of Colossians 1:20 might apply to the bodies of the lost so as to give them everlasting existence. Still, the unsaved must forever endure in Hell the punishment of their sins.

ITS INQUIRY (Rev. 20:12, 13)

It is not the purpose of this judgment to determine people's spiritual state and destination. These are settled during man's earthly life (Jn. 3:36). However, having self-determination and moral awareness, all unsaved people must answer for their works and receive their dues (Rom. 2:6).

The unsaved will be judged according to the contents of certain books (Rev. 20:12). These books seem to include those that have a full, accurate record of their works (their total output of life); the Scriptures, which reveal the absolute standard of right and wrong and which make known God's will for mankind (Jn. 5:45-46; 12:48; 17:17);[17] and "the book of life," which is a register of all who are saved (also vs. 15: Phil. 4:3; Rev. 3:5; 13:8; 17:8; 21:27; 22:19).

---

[17] In the case of those people who never had access to God's Word, it appears that they will be judged by the "law written in their hearts" (Rom. 2:14-15), which was an inherent part of their essential morality.

With the record of their works opened before them, the unsaved will answer for the total output of their accountable lives — their deeds (Rom. 2:6), words (Mt. 12:36-37), thoughts (I Chron. 28:9; Heb. 4:12), secrets (Rom. 2:16), motives (Heb. 4:12), omissions (Jas. 4:17), attitudes (Eph. 5:3-6), and response to God's revelation (Rom. 1:18), both general (vss. 19-20) and special (Jn. 3:18; 12:48). Memory will confirm all as being true.

ITS SENTENCE (Rev. 20:12-15)

Since the sentence will be according to people's works (vs. 12-13b), each person will receive what is due him. Although all will share the same doom (Mt. 25:41, 46), like people assigned to the same prison, yet there will be degrees of punishment according to the measures of guilt (Mt. 10:15; 11:21-24; Lk. 12:47-48; Rom. 2:5-6). This measure of guilt will be determined by the amount of light or knowledge a person has had of God's truth (II Pet. 2:21) and the wickedness of his sin (Mk. 14:21). While none will be guiltless (Rom. 1:18-20; 3:19), some will have sinned against greater light than others. Thoroughly knowing everyone and his life circumstances, the Judge will pronounce a just sentence upon each person (Jn. 2:25; Rev. 19:11; Gen. 18:25).

Each one whose name is not written in the book of life will be cast into the Lake of Fire, which is called "the second death" (Rev. 20:14-15). Man's first death ends his career on earth, with the separation of his immaterial nature from his body (Jas. 2:26). The second death will be the unsaved person's everlasting conscious separation from God (Mt. 7:23) in the sense of terrifying alienation and abandonment (25:46; cp. 27:46).

The statement that death and hell (Hades)[18] were cast into the Lake of Fire (Rev. 20:14) indicates that they are no longer needed. "Death" represents physical death and the grave, the receptacle of the dead body, while "Hades" represents the receptacle of unsaved people's personhood and immaterial nature upon their physical death. When the lost are resurrected, these receptacles will be discarded, and the last enemy, death, will have been for-

---

[18] It is unfortunate that the KJV translates the Greek word *Hades* "Hell" (Mt. 11:23; 16:18; Lk. 10:15; 16:23; Acts 2:27, 31; Rev. 1:18; 6:8; 20:13-14). Hades is the place where the unsaved go upon their physical death to await their resurrection, judgment, and final doom. The English word "Hell" should be exclusively used for the Lake of Fire, the final doom of the lost, as in the passages where it stands for the Greek word *Gehenna* (Mt. 5:22, 29-30; 10:28; 18:9; 23:15, 33; Mk. 9:43, 45, 47; Lk. 12:5; Jas. 3:6). *Gehenna*, a synonym for Hell, was the valley of Hinnom, south of Jerusalem, where refuse was burned. Jesus used this place-name as a reference to Hell, the Lake of Fire.

During the precross period all people went to *Sheol*, the O.T. counterpart of Hades. (*Sheol* is Hebrew for "grave" in Gen. 37:35; Job 7:9; Ps. 6:5; Isa. 14:11; and for "pit" in Num. 16:30, 33). Luke 16:19-31, the record of a historical event, reveals that Hades was divided into parts, including a place for the righteous ("Abraham's bosom") and a place for the wicked, separated by an impassable gulf (vs. 26). Upon His ascension, Jesus took the inhabitants of Abraham's bosom to Heaven (cp. Eph. 4:8). Today believers who die do not go to Hades but go directly to be with Christ (Phil. 1:23; II Cor. 5:8). This is probably what Jesus had in mind when He said that the gates of Hades would not prevail over the church (Mt. 16:18). Fallen angels are confined to another part of Hades, called "Tartaros" (Gk. for "hell" in II Pet. 2:4, KJV), to await their final judgment and doom.

The Scriptures indicate that Hades, or Sheol, is within the earth (Ezek. 26:20; 31:14-18; 32:18; cp. Isa. 14:9, 15; Phil. 2:10; Rev. 5:3, 13). After the resurrection of the unsaved and the dissolution of the universe, Hades will be abolished, for it will be no longer needed. The unsaved will be cast into the Lake of Fire (Rev. 20:13-14).

ever destroyed (I Cor. 15:25-26). Confined to the body (Rom. 7:17-18), sin ceases upon the body's death. Neither sin nor its fruit, physical death, will enter the eternal state.

THE PROPHECY OF MAN'S FINAL STATES

After the passing away of the present universe and the judgment of the lost, the Day of the LORD will end and will be followed by the Day of God. This day will continue forever (II Pet. 3:10, 12). The eternal state will begin with the creation of a new universe and its order (II Pet. 3:13; Rev. 21:1). Two aspects of the eternal state are the subjects of prophecy: the final state of the redeemed and that of the lost. Both of these states will continue forever (Mt. 25:46). Let us look at them more closely.

THE FINAL STATE OF THE REDEEMED

• Their Habitation

The redeemed will dwell with God forever on a sealess earth, which He will create (Rev. 21:1, 3). Their residence will be the New Jerusalem, which will descend from Heaven to earth (vss. 2, 9, 10). Throughout human history God's people have been anticipating this city, which will offer them a permanent, secure home (cp. Heb. 11:10, 13-16; 13:14; Rev. 3:12; Jn. 14:1-3).

John describes this city as being in the form of a cube (Rev. 21:16), with sides 1,380 miles long. It is made of pure gold (vs. 18), surrounded by a jasper wall 216 feet high (vs. 17). This wall rests upon twelve foundations, which are colorfully arrayed with precious stones (vss. 14, 19, 20) and which are pierced by twelve entrances, three on a side and each with a pearl gate (vss. 12, 13, 21). Each gate is attended by an angel and has written above it the name of a tribe of Israel (vs. 12). In the middle of the city there is a wide central square ("street") of pure gold (vs. 21), through which runs the river of the Water of Life (Rev. 22:1-2). This river flows from the throne of God to water the Tree of Life, which straddles it. Fed by the Water of Life, the Tree of Life will perpetuate forever the lives of all who eat of it (cp. Gen. 2:9; 3:22; Rev. 2:7). This city will have no temple building or external light, whether artificial or natural (Rev. 21:22-23; 22:5), for the Father and the Lord Jesus are its temple and light. The unholy will never be allowed to enter its open gates (21:25-27), and there will be no night or curse there (21:25; 22:3).

• Their Experience

If the presence of the Holy Spirit and the blessings of His ministry in our lives are a foretaste of future good (Eph. 1:14), then what wonderful things God has prepared for us (I Cor. 2:9; I Pet. 1:4)! The Scriptures reveal that the redeemed will have unrestricted fellowship with God (Rev. 21:3); that everything will be new (Rev. 21:4-5); and that there will be absolute security (Heb. 12:28), new knowledge (I Cor. 13:12), rest from present trials and

labors (Heb. 4:9; Rev. 21:4), endless pleasure (Ps. 16:11), loving companionship (Jn. 14:3; I Thess. 4:17), the satisfaction of every desire (Rev. 21:6), and
ceaseless worship (Rev. 5:11-14).

This does not mean that eternity is going to be like a long church service.
The phrase, "the ages to come" (Eph. 2:7), suggests that the Lord and His
people will be involved in new programs, or work projects, which have not
yet been revealed. Having Jesus' kind of body, his people will be wholly
concerned with His interests, will experience His emotions, will have His
understanding and skills, and will be in perfect agreement with His decisions
(see Appendix V). Also, the word "ages" indicates time. Being creatures, we
shall always experience time, which rises from the succession of events.

THE FINAL STATE OF THE LOST

• Their Habitation

After their judgment the lost will be cast into the Lake of Fire (Rev. 20:15)
or Hell (Mt. 10:28; 23:33), a place originally prepared for Satan and his angels
(Mt. 25:41). Hell is described as a place burning with fire (Mk. 9:43; Rev.
20:15), a place of darkness (II Pet. 2:17; Jude 13), worms (Mk. 9:48), and the
awareness of God's absence (Mt. 7:23; II Thess. 1:9; cp. Mt. 27:46). Like
Hades, its location may be in the heart of the earth. But this is not likely since
the Beast, the False Prophet, and Satan are cast into the Lake of Fire before
the dissolution of the present universe (Rev. 19:20; 20:10; II Pet. 3:10).

• Their Experience

The unsaved in Hell will experience various kinds of mental and sensual
torments, including unfulfilled desires, loneliness, hopelessness, and restless-
ness. There will be conscious suffering and torment (Rev. 14:10-11; Rom. 2:8-
9), crying and gnashing of teeth (Mt. 13:42), stark loneliness (II Thess. 1:9),
shame and contempt (Dan. 12:2), utter ruin (Mt. 10:28, "destroy"; Jn. 3:16,
"perish"; II Pet. 3:7, "perdition" but not annihilation, Mt. 25:46), and the terror
of endless darkness (Jude 13). There will be no social communication with
others in Hell. There will only be the terrible experience of God's perpetual
wrath (Rev. 14:10-11; Rom. 9:22) and abandonment (Mt. 7:23).

• Their Duration

Contrary to such false views as the annihilation of the wicked and their
eventual release and restoration to God, the Scriptures teach that the
unsaved will suffer for their sins forever (Mt. 25:46; Rev. 14:11). Because of
the nature of their reconstructed bodies, the unsaved will not burn up in the
Lake of Fire. Also, the wages of sin is death, not death for a certain period of
time. Experiencing the "second death," the unsaved will have no means by
which to make themselves "alive," to remove themselves from this awful
plight, or to be restored to God. Their destruction (II Thess. 1:9; Mt. 7:13) is
not a loss of essential existence but a loss of useful, meaningful existence, as

in the case of money (Acts 8:20) and ointment (Mt. 26:7-8, "waste"). Their spiritual ruin and guilt will be perpetuated forever (Jn. 3:16, 18).

APPROPRIATE QUESTIONS

One cannot reflect upon these final states without facing several questions. *How is the eternal destiny of the lost compatible with God's love?* God's attributes have their own areas of expression; therefore, His love cannot override His holiness and justice, which require the lost to pay the debt of their sins (cp. Lk. 19:41-44). God's love is expressed supremely in His giving Jesus for humanity's sins (Jn. 3:16). All who reject this love must face His wrath (vs. 36).

Will the lost eventually be annihilated? No, they will experience conscious suffering forever (Mt. 25:46; Rev. 14:11).

Will the lost eventually be saved? No (Mt. 25:46). When Paul speaks about the reconciliation of all things unto God (Col. 1:20), he does not refer to them who are now under the earth in Hades.

How can we who are saved be happy when we know that our unsaved relatives and friends are suffering in Hell? Since we shall be like Jesus (I Jn. 3:2), we shall regard these people as He does. Our natural ties with them will be severed (Rev. 21:4), and we shall understand the enormity of their sins and shall accept the justice of God in His punishing them as He does.

Will people who never heard about Jesus go to Hell? Yes, for having the continual witness of general revelation, they are without excuse (Rom. 1:18-20). Unsaved people are already condemned for their sins (Rom. 5:18; 3:9-19). If people who have never heard the gospel would respond favorably to God's general revelation and seek Him, in time they would be contacted with the gospel, as was Cornelius (Acts ch. 10). This is God's use of missions.

Do people go to Hell because of Adam's initial sin? No. While all people are condemned because of his sin (Rom. 5:18), they who die before having moral awareness and the ability to respond to the gospel have divinely applied to them at death the value of Jesus' atoning work (I Jn. 2:2) and are saved (cp. Mt. 18:14). People go to Hell because of their actual sins, one of which is rejecting God's self-revelation. Anyone who desires to be saved may receive the Saviour, for He died for all mankind (I Jn. 2:2).

Will people continue to sin in Hell? I believe not. While the penalty of their sins will continue forever (Mt. 25:46), sin itself, as a principle and act, seems to cease in humans with the death of the body, as the changed attitude and concern of the rich man in Hades indicate (Lk. 16:27-30). People in Hell will be wholly submissive to Jesus' authority (Phil. 2:11) and will accept the justice of their punishment (cp. Lk. 23:41). They will never again rebel against God. The description of the lost in Revelation 21:8, 27 seems to refer to their moral character during their earthly life, with which in God's sight they will be imprinted forever. This does not necessarily mean that they will continue to do these things forever. I do not see sin as an everlasting principle. It had a definite beginning, and it will have a decisive end.

Needless to say, nothing can now be known of the eternal state apart from that which God has revealed. He has given us all the information that we need to know at this time. The reality of these things so supercedes our present experience that more revelation would be of little value to us now. On the other hand, God has revealed enough to show the lost the need to receive the Saviour and to motivate us who are saved to walk in His fellowship until He calls us to glory (Deut. 29:29; Jn. 15:14-16).

If the reader should not be an authentic Christian, that is, one who has been born again by God, then it is urgent that you obey God's command to believe on the name of Jesus (I Jn. 3:23; Jn. 20:31). This belief is more than intellectual assent to facts about Jesus. It is to exercise salvational faith in Jesus' person and work, which I have described earlier (see Salvation: Man's Part in This Application).

Jesus himself declared the necessity of our being born again (Jn. 3:7). In the context of His words we find that there are two things that keep people out of Heaven — their inability to go there (vss. 3-6) and their liability to God for their sins (vss. 9-12). Our natural birth equips us for life on earth, but it does not prepare us for life in Heaven. We cannot physically leave the earth without some kind of earthly life support system. By the new birth God changes one's human nature (eventually the body) so that His people can live in Heaven with Him. Furthermore, in their natural state all humans are sinners and owe to God the debt (penalty) of their sins, which is death and Hell (Rom. 6:23). There is no way that anyone can discharge himself from this obligation and live (Mt. 25:46).

In His great love and grace God the Father sent His Son to earth to be our Saviour (Jn. 3:14-16). The Son took upon Himself a human nature, allowed Himself to be crucified, and while upon the cross bore our sins (I Pet. 2:24). Being made sin, He died for us and His blood was shed (II Cor. 5:21; Rom. 5:8). His effectiveness in dealing with our sins is manifest by His resurrection from the dead (Rom. 1:4; 4:25). On the basis of Jesus' atoning work, God is now able to save everyone who places his trust in Jesus and His atoning work for salvation.

Paul says that with the heart we believe unto righteousness and with the mouth confession is made unto salvation (Rom. 10:10). To believe with the heart involves a decision of our total being — volitionally, intellectually, and emotionally. With a change of attitude toward God and self, it is to decide to trust Jesus and His atoning work completely for salvation. This decision is then expressed to God in prayer, together with the admission of one's guilt as a sinner and the acknowledgment of Jesus' atoning work. When this kind of confession is made to God, He immediately applies to the believing sinner the value of Jesus' atoning work and saves him (vs. 13). In saving him, God delivers him from the debt, guilt, ruin, and power of sin and gives to him a new kind of life which rises from a personal relationship with Himself. If you have never made this decision and commitment, I urge you to do so now.

THE PROPHETIC FUTURE

New heaven and earth—	Lake of Fire (Hell)	ETERNAL STATE (forever)	
The judgment of the lost— The dissolution of the present universe— Satan's final revolt—		KINGDOM AGE (1000 years)	Dis. Kingdom
The restoration of Israel to their land— The judgment of surviving earth dwellers— The battle of Armageddon— Christ's second coming to earth——▶			
The Beast breaks pact with Israel— The resurrection of the Beast— Satan's ejection from Heaven unto earth——▶	The Abyss (Hades)	the seventieth "week" (3½ yrs.) ministry of the 144,000 — (3½ yrs.) ministry of 2 witnesses — TRIBULATION PERIOD (7 - years)	Dispensation of Grace
The Beast's death— The Beast's pact with Israel— The rapture of the church— Christ's return for His church		CHURCH AGE (1900 + years)	
The Day of Pentecost— Christ's ascension into Heaven ◀— Christ's death— Christ's first coming to earth——▶		the sixty-nine "weeks" (483 years) — POSTEXILIC JEWISH AGE (483 years)	Dispensation of Law
Artaxerxes' decree to rebuild Jerusalem, 445 B.C.—			

A Review of Eschatology

1. What are the two primary methods of interpreting prophecy?
2. Which method does the author prefer? Why?
3. What are some of the practical reasons for studying prophecy?
4. Why is it better to speak of Jesus' coming for the church as His return rather than as His second coming?
5. Where are most N.T. details given of His return for the church?
6. Where will the church meet the Lord upon His return?
7. What blessed events will the saved experience when the Lord returns for the church?
8. Describe the qualities and constitution of the believer's changed body.
9. What features of Christ's glory will saved people share?
10. What inheritance will they receive? What inheritance do they now have?
11. What does it mean to enter eternal life?
12. Briefly explain the various views regarding the time of the rapture with reference to the tribulation period.
13. Why does the author prefer the pretribulational rapture view?
14. What impact should the prospect of the Lord's imminent return have on us?
15. Why must believers appear before the judgment seat of Christ?
16. Where and when will this appraisal take place?
17. What will the Lord examine in our lives?
18. What criteria will He follow in this appraisal?
19. What do the gainful rewards appear to be?
20. What loss will we sustain for those things of which He disapproves?
21. Why does not this judgment exact retribution for our sinful works?
22. What is the overall purpose for the tribulation period?
23. By what three events will the Lord achieve this purpose?
24. When does the "seventieth week" of Daniel ch. 9 begin? When does it end?
25. When will the 144,000 Jewish evangelists minister? What will be their message?
26. When do God's two witnesses minister? What is the purpose of their ministry?
27. Why do not the two witnesses preach the gospel?
28. Give the three series of judgments that God will send upon the earth during the tribulation period.

29. Which of these is an expression of divine wrath?

30. When will Satan be confined to the earth?

31. What two humans will Satan use to carry out his activities on earth?

32. What appears to be unusual about these two men?

33. Which one will be Satan's political ruler? His director of religion?

34. Trace the career of the beast out of the sea as given in Daniel and Revelation.

35. When will the beast out of the sea confirm a peace treaty with Israel? When will he break this treaty?

36. What Jews will be the first that Satan will slay after his confinement to earth?

37. Why does not Satan succeed in destroying the remnant of Israel?

38. Why is the Holy Spirit still on earth during tribulation days?

39. What event will bring the Lord back to earth to deal with Israel's enemies and to set up his earthly kingdom?

40. To what place does Jesus come when He returns to earth the second time?

41. What people are involved in the Battle of Armageddon?

42. What will be unusual about this battle?

43. What judgment will Jesus hold after this battle?

45. What is the purpose of this judgment?

46. What will the Lord do with the remnant of Israel?

47. Distinguish between the Lord's kingdom in its present form and in its future millennial form.

48. Give five objectives for the Lord's earthly rule.

49. Give the administrative organization of the kingdom.

50. What kind of people will be the kingdom's citizens when it is established.

51. Describe the blessings of the kingdom.

52. Will people be saved during kingdom days?

53. Why will this be necessary in view of the fact that only saved people will enter at its beginning?

54. Why is Satan released at the close of the kingdom?

55. How will the reign of Jesus be extended forever?

56. When does God bring the present material universe to an end?

57. What is the purpose of the great white throne judgment?

58. What will be final habitation and experience of the saved?

59. What will be final habitation and experience of the unsaved?
60. Why does the author think that people will not sin in Hell?
61. How long will the state of existence of the saved and of the unsaved continue?
62. What will be the everlasting activities of the saved?
63. What is your everlasting destination?

Appendices

APPENDICES

Appendix A
The Gift of Tongues

The widespread practice of tongues speaking requires us to examine more closely what the Scriptures teach about this subject. I understand that the gift of tongues was a special, nonrational utterance, which was unique to each possessor. Also, I believe that the exercise of this gift is no longer needed, for we have the New Testament which replaces its functions. Tongues was not given for self- edification. Like all spiritual gifts, it served to edify the church.

THE NATURE OF TONGUES

What was the gift of tongues?

IN ITS EXPRESSION

Bible students are not agreed on what this utterance was. Some hold that it was a foreign language, unknown to the speaker but known to others. Others hold that it was an ecstatic utterance that had no grammatical character. Still others hold that it was a foreign language in Acts (chs. 2, 10, 19) and an ecstatic utterance in I Corinthians (chs. 12, 14). I prefer the view that in every New Testament instance tongues was an ecstatic utterance, unique to the one who had the gift. I believe that the following considerations support this view.

• A foreign language does not necessarily have a greater capacity for expressing one's thoughts or feelings than one's own language.

• The gift of tongues appears to have been a nonrational, ecstatic utterance of a divinely incited human spirit (I Cor. 14:2, 14, 15). It was not as important for the one speaking in tongues to know what he was saying as it was for him to express how he felt in his spirit. Thus, his speaking did not have to be rational. (Compare one's response to his being pricked with a pin. He does not reason how he will react to this, but he spontaneously expresses his feelings and he does so effectively.)

• The words "other" (Acts 2:4, Gk. *heterais*) and "new" (Mk. 16:17, Gk. *kainais*) indicate an utterance that is different from others and new in nature.

• The tongues spoken by the disciples on Pentecost (Acts 2:4) were addressed to God and to themselves before the crowd gathered.
• That each heard the disciples speak in his own dialect (Acts 2:6, 8, 11) may have been the result of a miracle of hearing, similar to the gift of

intepretation. The Scriptures do not say that the disciples actually spoke in these languages.

• The use of foreign languages to communicate with the people was unnecessary as Peter's following address shows (Acts 2:14 ff.). Greek was the universal language of the eastern Mediterranean area.

• The charge of intoxication indicates that the disciples used ecstatic utterance (Acts 2:13-15). Apparently, the mockers were not miraculously hearing the disciples' words in their own dialects (vss. 6-8).

• Being novel, ecstatic utterance would better serve as a sign to skeptical people (I Cor. 14:22).

• The plural number of the word "tongues" (Acts 2:4; 10:46; 19:6; I Cor. 12:28, 30; 14:5-6, 18, 22-23), indicates that the utterance was unique to each speaker and that no utterance was the same for all. This view is supported by the words "kind" and "diversities" (I Cor. 12:10, 28, Gk. *gene*), which indicate varied manifestations of this gift.

• That tongues required interpretation (I Cor. 12:30; 14:5, 13, 27, Gk. *diermneuo*) rather than translation (Gk. *methermneuo*) indicates an ecstatic utterance that has no grammatical construction. The primary emphasis of interpretation is making clear the meaning of something (Lk. 24:27, "expounded"; Jn. 1:38; cp. I Cor. 14:2, the use of tongues in explaining "mysteries," things unknown to unaided understanding), while the emphasis of translation is turning a literary work or statement from one language into another (Mt. 1:23; Mk. 5:41; 15:22, 34; Jn. 1:41-42; Acts 4:36; 13:8).

IN ITS CONTENT

Speaking in tongues was a form of ecstatic prayer (I Cor. 14:2, 14, 28), expressing praise (Acts 2:11; 10:46) and thanksgiving to God (I Cor. 14:16-17). Unlike prophecy, tongues did not communicate divine revelation (see I Cor. ch. 14). Paul exalted the gift of prophecy above tongues, for it better edified the church (I Cor. 14:4-5, 19) and had something meaningful to say to unbelieving persons (vss. 23-25).

THE PURPOSES FOR TONGUES

While tongues expressed praise to God, this gift served man in several ways: for a proof, a sign, and edification.

• **It served as a proof.**

Tongues bore witness to the fact of certain spiritual realities, namely, the truth of the believer's baptism and anointing with the Holy Spirit, which Jesus had predicted (Acts 1:5, 8). Since these spiritual realities are undetected by the senses, there had to be some way by which it would be indicated that they had occurred. Together with hearing the wind and seeing the fire, the disciples spoke in tongues on the Day of Pentecost as proof of these spiritual realities (2:1-4). Tongues speaking was also proof of these activities of the Holy Spirit to the people who were gathered in the home of Cornelius in Caesarea (10:44-46; 11:15-17) and to the disciples of John the Baptist in Ephesus (19:1-6). We no longer need this kind of proof today, for the New Testament teaches that the baptism and anointing with the Holy Spirit take place when one is saved (Gal. 3:26-28; I Cor. 12:13; II Cor. 1:21-22; I Jn. 2:20, 27).

- **It served as a sign.**

Speaking in tongues conveyed special meaning to skeptical people (I Cor. 14:22), especially to Jews (I Cor. 1:22; Mt. 12:38-39). It was a sign to unsaved Jews that Jesus was Lord and Messiah (Acts 2:4-6, 29-36). It also was a sign to saved Jews that believing Gentiles receive the blessings of salvation (10:23, 34-36, 45). Finally, it was a sign to precross saved Jews (the disciples of John the Baptist) that John's message and baptism had been replaced with the message of Christ's completed atonement and the personal witness of baptism in His name (19:1-7). Tongues speaking in the Corinthian church may have been a sign to the unsaved Jews, whose synagogue was next door (18:7), that God blesses all who receive Jesus as Messiah and Saviour (vss. 3-11; I Cor. 1:4-5). Because of the authoritative teaching of the New Testament and the effectiveness of the gospel in the lives of them who believe, skeptics no longer need tongues as a sign.

- **It served as a means of edification.**

Tongues edified the speaker and, when interpreted, the congregation (I Cor. 14:4-5). However, since tongues required interpretation and in content was praise rather than revelation (God's Word), it was not as effective as prophecy in edifying the church. Prophecy, which communicated God's Word in the language known to the congregation, could better meet their spiritual needs (I Cor. 14:1, 3, 4, 19, 31). Obviously, the giving of praise is an important part of worship, but our hearing God's Word is more important since it is God speaking to us and ministering to our spiritual needs. Also, we should keep in mind that spiritual gifts are given for the edification of others, not for self-edification (vss. 5, 12, 26; Eph. 3:2).

THE DURATION OF TONGUES

It is debated among believers whether or not the gift of tongues has ceased and, if it has ceased, when. Since the value and duration of spiritual gifts during this age are determined by their usefulness in the building of the church, I believe that both tongues and prophecy ceased with the completion and distribution of the New Testament. This portion of the Bible now fulfills the purposes for tongues (proof, sign, edification) by its teachings. Having the

New Testament which is more certain than sights and sounds (II Pet. 1:16-21), the church no longer needs the gifts of tongues, prophecy, the interpretation of tongues, the discernment of spirits, and apostleship, for this Scripture replaces the functions of these gifts. Moreover, praise in divine worship can be adequately expressed in one's own language.

Some appeal to I Corinthians 13:8 for proof that tongues have ceased. Paul does not clearly state here when this cessation will be. He seems to imply that all spiritual gifts, represented by tongues, prophecy, and knowledge, will cease when they are no longer needed. He underscores this point by contrasting our present experience, which is partial and which requires certain gifts, with our future experience, which will be full (vss. 9-10). He illustrates this contrast between the partial and the complete by referring to a child's speech and comprehension (vs. 11) and to one's reflection in a first century mirror, which was imperfect (vs. 12).

THE PRACTICE OF TONGUES

Although Paul valued prophecy more than tongues (I Cor. 14:1-5, 23-25), he did not prohibit the exercise of tongues (vs. 27), for as we have seen, it served God's purposes at that time. However, he did regulate its practice. Tongues were to be spoken only if an interpreter were present (vss. 13, 28). The one speaking in tongues could be his own interpreter (vs. 5). Only two or three were to speak in tongues, taking turns (vs. 27). Apparently, this allowed other gifts to be exercised during the service (vs. 26). Except for their prophesying and praying, women were to remain silent in the church (11:5; 14:34). All things were to be done "decently" (becomingly, properly) and "in order," with a view to edifying the Lord's people (14:40, 26).

SOME OBSERVATIONS

• While tongues could be spoken to one's self (I Cor. 14:28), like all spiritual gifts its use was for the edification of the church, not for self-edification (vss. 5, 26).

• Like all spiritual gifts speaking in tongues could be restrained if there was no need for this ministry (I Cor. 14:28, 32).

• We should never make any spiritual gift a test of spirituality, for no one spiritual gift is the common possession of all believers (I Cor. 12:8-10, 14-25; Rom. 12:4-6).

• No radical action that divides or confuses the Lord's people should be allowed in the church service (I Cor. 14:28-33). The peace, unity, and edification of the Lord's people are more important than the exercise of some spiritual gift that disrupts these (I Cor. 14:26, 33, 40; Eph. 4:3). If people feel constrained to exercise some gift that is not acceptable or needed by a congregation, then they should seek out the fellowship of others who will receive this, or in the case of an obsolete gift like tongues, they should stop seeking to exercise it.

• While rejecting the practice of tongues speaking in the church service, some believe that it is permissible to do this in an informal gathering or during one's private devotions. While one may do whatever he pleases during the course of his devotional exercises, any so-called tongues speaking should not be regarded as the exercise of the gift of tongues, which, to my mind, no longer exists. It should be regarded as a religious phenomenon like shaking, barking, rolling, and other unusual behavior that have occurred in times of religious fervor.

• Spiritual gifts are effective and beneficial only as they are exercised in the power of the Holy Spirit. They may be humanly exercised apart from Him, but this neither edifies others nor glorifies God. Such fraudulent activities are used by Satan to deceive and confuse the unalert and to inflate with pride the impostor.

• Paul exhorted his Christian readers to seek the gifts that most edify the congregation (I Cor. 12:31; 14:1-5, 39). The desirability of a gift should be determined by its usefulness rather than by its display.

• Believers must be wary of seeking spiritual satisfaction through some unusual experience, such as tongues speaking. We must always look to the Lord Jesus and His Word for the satisfaction of our spiritual needs and the progress of our spiritual life (Jn. 10:9; 6:35; 7:37-39). Satan can provide us with an experience that counterfeits what we seek (Mt. 7:21-23; 24:24; cp. II Cor. 11:13-15). Contrariwise, the Holy Spirit ministers to us in ways that exalt the Lord Jesus and that are in harmony with the teachings of the Scriptures (Jn. 16:12-14; II Tim. 3:16-17).

• The apostolic laying on of hands was a significant act by the official representatives of Christ whereby on some occasions the Holy Spirit was communicated to the recipients of the gospel (Acts 8:14-17; 19:6) and at other times spiritual gifts were imparted or ignited (II Tim. 1:6). However, this was not always done (Acts 10:44-48), nor is it necessary today since the New Testament teaches us of the Holy Spirit's ministry. Again, like tongues, this was a sensuous experience that indicated non-sensuous spiritual realities.

In Acts 13:3 and I Timothy 4:14, the laying on of hands was an act of identification by which the local church expressed their fellowship with these Christian workers in their ministry.

APPENDIX B
The Conscience

We human beings possess two faculties of moral awareness — the conscience and the mind. The conscience appears to be a part of our memory bank, with its input of moral values through moral teaching and training. It nonrationally, involuntarily, automatically judges the rightness of an action by its programed input (II Cor. 1:12; I Cor. 10:27-28)). On the other hand, the mind deliberately, voluntarily reflects upon the rightness of an action in the light of a moral standard and decides what course should be followed (Rom. 7:25; 12:2). Because of this, the mind can override the conscience and reprogram it. A part of our spiritual growth is the reprograming of the conscience as we learn true moral values and righteous behaviour from God's Word.

Some hold that the conscience itself determines what is right and what is wrong, but this leaves it without an objective ethical standard. Others hold that it is the voice of God, but the Bible does not teach this. While the Holy Spirit may speak to the conscience, this faculty seems to be an automatic, nonrational judge of and witness to moral action (I Jn. 3:20; Acts 23:1; Rom. 2:15). It appears to be programmed for its function by moral training and conditioning (I Cor. 8:7; cp. Rom. 14:14), and it plays this back in the form of involuntary moral evaluations and direction in everyday life. It is also sensitive to the unexpressed, innate moral law which is inherent in man's personhood (Rom. 2:14-15) and to God's Word (II Sam. 12:7-13; cp. Ps. 32:3-4; Acts 2:37; 5:33; 7:54).

THE CONSCIENCE OF UNSAVED PEOPLE

This may be conditioned by moral and ethical training, dictated by the moral philosophies of the world, by the precepts of the Scriptures, and by innate, moral awareness — the law written on the heart (Rom. 2:15). Because the mind transcends the conscience, the unsaved (also the saved) can rationally reject this conditioning and justify their wrong conduct (I Tim. 4:2; Rom. 2:15).

The Scriptures speak of the conscience of the unsaved as a witnessing one (Rom. 2:15), testifying to their moral discernment and accountability; an evil one (Heb. 10:22), being affected by false moral standards and sin; and in some cases a seared one (I Tim. 4:2), being rendered insensible to certain claims of right. Upon hearing of their sin, the unsaved may be pricked in their conscience (Acts 2:37; 5:33; 7:54).

THE CONSCIENCE OF SAVED PEOPLE

This, too, is conditioned by moral and ethical training and by the teachings of the Scriptures, before and after salvation. It is susceptible to the influence of the Holy Spirit (Isa. 30:21; Rom. 8:14; 9:1) and can be transcended by the mind (Rom. 14:5).

The conscience of the saved may be stained by sin (Tit. 1:15, "defiled"), especially when one acts contrary to its program input (I Cor. 8:7, 12); it may be a weak one because of some prejudice or lack of spiritual understanding (I Cor. 8:7); it may be pure, good, or uncondemning because one's actions conform to God's will (II Tim. 1:3; Acts 23:1; 24:16); and it may be a witnessing one, testifying to the integrity of one's conduct (Rom. 9:1; II Cor. 4:2).

In I Corinthians 8:7-13 Paul sets forth the principle that when one acts contrary to his conscience, he sins, whether the action is inherently sinful or not (cp. Rom. 14:14, 20, 23). To act contrary to the conscience is to sin, for it is to act independently without faith in God for His direction, help and blessing. Moreover, to influence another to act contrary to his conscience is to sin against him and Christ (I Cor. 8:12). On the other hand, the conscience of a "weak" believer may be enlightened and reprogrammed by the biblical teaching that shows him that the "wrong" action does not violate any precept or principle of Scripture which relates to the present dispensation. We should keep in mind that a mind given over to sin may so rationalize a wrong action that the conscience no longer protests against it. Nevertheless, the Holy Spirit and the Scriptures will continue to bear witness against it.

APPENDIX C
The Relation Between Personhood and the Soul

While the soul often represents human beings (Gen. 46:22-27) and one's own being (Ps. 42:5-6), it should not be equated with personhood (self, I) alone, as traditional theologians have done, for the Scriptures distinguish between these parts of our being (Job 7:11; Ps. 131:2; Isa. 26:9). The human soul is a part of human nature, which is wholly propagated by human parents. I suggest that personhood — that unique personal entity (self, I) which is God's image in man and which distinguishes him from lower forms of life — is at the moment of conception created by God and permanently united to the propagated human nature (Mal. 2:10; cp. Ps. 139:13-15). With this union one's human nature qualifies his personhood to make him a human being. In turn, his personhood gives to his human nature selfhood, morality, and perpetuity.

This distinction between personhood and nature is seen in the constitution of the divine Trinity, which consists of three distinct Persons, who possess the one divine nature. Each of these Persons has individual, unique personhood which is not to be equated with the divine nature. However, their possessing the divine nature makes them to be divine Persons. It is also shown by our Lord's incarnation. In this case an eternal divine Person assumed a complete human nature (body, soul, and spirit), divinely made of Mary's substance. In our case the concept of our personhood's being directly created by God accounts for our unique individuality and morality (moral awareness and accountability are not inherent in human nature), and its union with our propagated human nature accounts for our human personality, by which our personhood expresses the qualities and powers of our human nature.

This view, I believe, accounts for the various functions of the soul and spirit, as taught in the Scriptures, such as intelligence, emotions, and will. Our personality does not exist independently of these parts of human nature, but it is the result of their acting upon our personhood. Because of the union of our personhood with our human nature, we are human beings who express and experience all the features of personality, such as reasoning, feeling, emotions, and making choices.

Since one's propagated human nature is wholly affected by original sin, his sinful human nature adversely qualifies his created personhoods and makes him in his natural state a fallen, corrupted human being (Ps. 51:5). Adam's image in his posterity consists of the fallen, propagated human nature, with which everyone is born (Gen. 5:3; I Cor. 15:49). Salvation renews one's personhood and immaterial human nature to the extent that he is made a new creature in Christ (II Cor. 5:17), with a human nature that is being made in Christ's image (Eph. 4:24; Col. 3:10; II Cor. 3:18; Rom. 8:29).

This view which sees personhood and human nature as distinct, yet inseparable, entities, allows God to be the creator of unique personhoods, who at their creation are morally and qualitatively neutral (Ps. 139:14-15; Jer. 1:5; Mal. 2:10). The personhood receives its corruption from its propagated, inherently corrupted human nature. Since human nature is wholly propagated, this accounts for those hereditary characteristics that offspring receive from their parents and ancestors as well as the inherent corruption they receive from original sin. This explains why the soul and spirit are portrayed in the Scriptures as expressing the functions of human personality (Ps. 42:5-6; 139:14; Gen. 42:21; Job 7:11). When they contribute their human powers to our personhood, the soul and spirit give us the human ability to think, express verbal concepts, make decisions, feel and show emotion, and select motivations and direction.

Objectors to this view may say, "God has ceased His creative work (Gen. 2:2)." While this is true of material things, it does not apply to the immaterial realm (Eph. 2:10). God is now creating people anew in Christ (II Cor. 5:17).

"Christ's incarnation was a unique event, involving an eternal, divine Person." True, but it still demonstrates the distinction between personhood and human nature. God the Son assumed a human nature, which He did not have before His incarnation. "The descendants are said to be in the loins of their ancestors (Heb. 7:5, 9-10; I Cor. 15:22)." Since one's human nature qualifies his personhood to make him human, in effect, people are in the loins of their ancestors, for their human nature was involved in all that their ancestors were and did. The solidarity of the human race rests upon their having a commonly derived human nature, not upon their having a common personhood or their being the same person (Acts 17:26; I Cor. 15:45, 47, 49). Finally, "God would not unite a newly created personhood with a corrupted human nature." It should be remembered that God's procedure for creating man was established before man's fall. The newly created personhood has no features that are destroyed by its union with its fallen human nature, though it is affected by this nature. The features of selfhood — individuality, morality (moral capacity), and perpetuity — continue in fallen man. If it is God's procedure to create personhood and to unite this to one's propagated human nature, then any impropriety of this would be due to man's sin which corrupted his entire nature. It would not be due to the procedure that God established before man's fall.

It is wrong to equate personhood with the soul, as traditional theologians have done. This leads to confusion and irresolvable problems. To my mind, the view that I have presented better relates to the Scriptures, to the functions of soul and spirit, to the solidarity of the race, and to the doctrine of personal beings, whether God, angels or man. All are persons with a certain kind of nature that makes them to be what they are.

APPENDIX D
The Ones Who Are in Christ

Observing the distinction between the Holy Spirit's baptizing gospel believers into Christ (Gal. 3:27) and His baptizing them into the body of Christ, the universal church (I Cor. 12:13), it seems to be the teaching of Scripture that all the redeemed of human history are baptized into Christ. This conclusion is based on the following considerations.

1. Since salvation is only in and through Jesus (Acts 4:12; I Thess. 5:9; Heb. 5:9), it follows that all saved people must be baptized into Him to partake of the spiritual blessings that are in Him (I Cor. 1:30; Eph. 1:3) and to be made complete in Him (Col. 2:10). If there is any righteousness or redemption apart from Jesus that God accepts, then our Lord's atoning

work was not necessary. The Scriptures show that the method of salvation is the same in every age. It is always by God's grace through faith in the divine revelation about the atonement, whether promised (Gen. 3:15; 15:5-6; Heb. 11:4) or fulfilled (Jn. 3:16). To be accepted by God, one must partake of that which Jesus was morally and that which He accomplished efficaciously (Rom. 5:19; II Cor. 5:21).

2. It appears that all of the redeemed of every age must be in Jesus to be members of the new humanity of which He is the first and pattern (I Cor. 15:22, 45-49; Rom. 8:29). God sees each member of the human race as being in either Adam or Christ — the unsaved in Adam and the saved in Christ. In striking contrast to those who are in Adam, all the saved share Christ's kind of human nature, His obedience unto death (the ultimate manifestation of divinely acceptable human righteousness), and His life which is eternal (see Rom. 5:17-19). No third group of human beings is indicated by the Scriptures.

3. The regenerative aspect of salvation requires that one be in Christ, for this involves the deliverance of one's immaterial human nature from inherent corruption (I Pet. 1:22), its being created in righteousness and true holiness (Col. 3:10; Eph. 4:24), and its being infused with spiritual life (Rom. 8:10; Eph. 2:1). With Christ as our life (Col. 3:4), these realities spring from our being created in Him (Eph. 2:10) and our being new creatures in Him (II Cor. 5:17).

4. While precross believers received divinely imputed righteousness (Gen. 15:6) and enjoyed a personal relationship with God (17:1), they did not go to Heaven when they died (Gen. 25:8; cp. Lk. 16:22) or receive the promised inheritance (Heb. 11:13-16). These realities were not possible before our Lord's incarnation, atoning work, resurrection, and return to Heaven (Heb. 9:15). Only then could He bring His people into union with Himself and impart the blessings of the New Covenant. Probably the precross saints who had died were united to Him at the time of His return to Heaven when they were taken with Him (cp. Eph. 4:8). With this union He became their righteousness and redemption (I Cor. 1:30), fulfilling what previously had been extended to them, as it were, on credit (Rom. 3:25; Heb. 9:15-17).

5. One of God's objectives is to bring together for Himself all things in Christ (Eph. 1:10; cp. Col. 1:20). Whatever this means, it seems to include the redeemed of all the ages as well as the things that are involuntarily affected by sin (cp. Jn. 17:20-22).

6. Again, to be in Christ does not mean to be in His body, the church, for

these are distinct concepts and realities. The baptism into Christ (Gal. 3:27) is a distinct work from the baptism into His body (I Cor. 12:13, 27; Col. 1:18). While the church saints (those saved during this age) experience both aspects of the Holy Spirit's baptism, all other redeemed people of human history, I believe, are (in the case of precross saints), or will be (in the case of tribulation and millennial saints), baptized into Him and partake of the positional blessings that are in Him.

APPENDIX E
The Problem Sins

THE UNPARDONABLE SIN (Mt. 12:31-32)

This unforgivable sin is one that only unsaved people can commit. It appears from our Lord's words that this is not just any sin, nor is it a quality that any sin can assume. It is a sin that is against the Holy Spirit. It is to blaspheme the Holy Spirit, that is, to speak abusively against Him.

Some of the Jewish religious leaders of Jesus' day deliberately and hatefully attributed the power of Satan to Jesus' casting out demons (Mt. 9:32-34; 12:22-24; Lk. 11:15). Although this charge was directed to the Lord, it was an act of blasphemy against the Holy Spirit, in whose power Jesus did His work (Mt. 12:28; Lk. 4:1, 14; Acts 10:38). The reason for this sin's being so abhorrent to the Lord Jesus seems to be that He sought to honor and uphold the integrity of the Holy Spirit, in whose power He lived and served as a man.

A study of the character and attitudes of these blasphemers reveals that this sin cannot be committed ignorantly or mistakenly by a child of God. Knowing Jesus' divine commission, these religious leaders refused to accept Him and His ministry (cp. Jn. 3:1-2; 5:31-39; 7:28). Also, boasting of their cleverness not to be taken in by Him, they sought to do away with Him (Jn. 7:45-49; Mt. 12:14).

A saved person could not commit this sin without doing two impossible things. He must overthrow his salvational faith in Jesus, which is God's gift (Acts 3:16; II Pet. 1:1) and which is sustained by our Lord's prayers (Lk. 22:31-32). Furthermore, he must render ineffective the sovereign work of God in his heart (Phil. 2:13; 1:6).

Some believe that this sin cannot be committed today because our circumstances differ from those of Jesus' time, but this is not certain. Since our Lord is building His church today through the ministry of the Holy Spirit in His people (I Cor. 12:13; Acts 1:8), it may be that an unbeliever could commit this sin if he recognizes the true nature of our Lord's work and deliberately, maliciously assigns it to Satan. This sin will be committed in the

Tribulation Period when unsaved people choose to follow the Beast, Satan's human agent (Rev. 14:9-11; II Thess. 2:10-12).

THE SIN UNTO DEATH (I Jn. 5:16)

This sin which leads to premature death is one that saved people can commit. This sin appears to be hatred against God's reproof in His corrective chastening of His people (Prov. 15:10; 29:1; Heb. 12:5-7, 9). Our heavenly Father constantly deals with us in order that He might cultivate our spiritual life and fruitfulness. However, if we should refuse to respond favorably to this discipline and set our heart against it to the extent of hating it, then we would render ourself useless for bearing spiritual fruit. Consequently, He would prematurely remove us from earth and take us to Heaven (Jn. 15:2, 6).

This sin has no relation to the offender's salvation, but it does relate to his fulfilling God's revealed will for his life (I Cor. 5:5; 11:32). When we recognize that another believer has committed this sin, we are not to pray for his deliverance from God's disciplinary action, for our prayers for him will not be heard (I Jn. 5:16; cp. Jer. 7:13-16). On the other hand, we have an obligation toward them who commit other sins (Gal. 6:1). Obviously, we have to be cautious in our speculation of the reason for the death of God's people. Only when we are closely associated with a person can we know what his attitude toward God is.

APPENDIX F
The Ascertaining God's Will

Our obedience to the Lord is not only a fulfillment of duty but also an expression of love for Him (Jn. 14:15, 21, 23; Mt. 6:24). In spite of Satan's lies to the contrary, obedience to God is not grievous, but suitable to our renewed nature and necessary for our well-being (Prov. 3:13-18; Rom. 12:2; I Jn. 5:3). While we have an inner desire to obey the Lord (Phil. 2:13), we also experience inner resistance from the sin-principle (Rom. 7:15-18; 8:7) and outer temptation from Satan, who would have us to rebel against God (I Pet. 5:8). Our obedience to the Lord requires our learning His will about everything and doing it in His strength (Eph. 5:10, 17; Phil. 4:13). It is noteworthy that the Lord's commands and appeals to us are directed to our will, not to our feelings. He never relieves us of our duty because we do not feel like obeying Him.

How, then, can we know His will for us? Wherever His will for us is clearly stated in the Scriptures, especially in the New Testament which reveals our stewardship, we need not seek further guidance, for the Lord has spoken. On the other hand, because the Scriptures do not speak directly on everything that enters our life's experience, I offer the following suggestions for our ascertaining God's will in daily life, in moral matters, and in deciding between options.

HEART PREPARATION

Discovering the Lord's will is impossible if our relationship with Him is not right. Heart preparation requires the following:

OUR BEING WHOLLY YIELDED TO GOD (Rom. 12:1)
Self-dedication to God has no value unless we are motivated by some purpose. In this case, our purpose should be both learning His will and doing it.

OUR BEING WILLING TO DO HIS WILL (Rom. 12:2)
This requires our confidence in the fact that God's will, whatever it may be, is best for us, for it is good, suitable, and perfect.

OUR BEING PRAYERFUL ABOUT HIS WILL (Col. 1:9)
We can ask God to make known to us His will (cp. I Jn. 5:14-15).

OUR DEALING WITH KNOWN SINS IN OUR LIFE (Ps. 66:18)
We do this by a change of attitude toward them (repentance, Rev. 2:5) and by confessing them to God (I Jn. 1:9).

SPIRITUAL DISCERNMENT

Having prepared our heart and asked the Lord for direction, we then can depend upon the Holy Spirit to give us an understanding of His will for us (Rom. 12:2; 8:14). The following procedures may help you to gain this understanding.

GOD'S COMMITMENT WILL FOR DAILY LIFE
What is the Lord's will for you in the daily round of life?

- **Your fulfilling plain duty (cp. II Cor. 8:10-11; II Thess. 3:12)**
Unless the Lord definitely leads otherwise, you should fulfill your obligations and commitments, including the contracts and promises that relate to your livelihood and business ventures. Each of us has obligations from which he cannot excuse himself (cp. I Tim. 5:8).

- **Your following sanctified common sense (cp. Mt. 2:19-23)**
God has given you reasoning ability for your practical use. His will for you is often the reasonable course to follow in the light of your circumstances, such as Joseph's returning to his home town of Nazareth where he had been employed and was known. The Holy Spirit renews and illuminates the minds of His people when they give themselves to Him (Rom. 12:2). Although His complete course for you may presently be unknown, God's leading is not irrational or erratic.

- **Your responding to the Holy Spirit's impressions (cp. Acts 16:6-10)**

When direct guidance from the Scriptures is lacking, you will often be led by inner impulse or urge of the Holy Spirit. However, you must determine the source of this urge before acting upon it. Every urge must be tested by the Scriptures and prayer, for sin and Satan can also induce these. God will never lead His people contrary to His Word. If the impression is from God, it will become stronger with continued prayer.

- **Your adjusting to your circumstances (cp. Phil. 1:12; 4:10-14)**

This concerns those things in life over which we have no control. From the Scriptures we know that God, controlling all things, uses adverse circumstances to test our faith and to sanctify our lives (Jas. 1:2-4; Heb. 12:3-11). Because of this, you must be cautious in responding to your circumstances, for what may be apparent may not be real. For instance, a door of opportunity that is apparently closed may yield to the touch of faith, and one that is apparently open may close before you cross the threshold (cp. II Cor. 5:7; I Thess. 2:18; Acts 13:14 with Gal. 4:13-14).

GOD'S PRECEPTIVE WILL FOR MORAL BEHAVIOR

The Bible is the criterion of right and wrong, good and bad. It has precepts (commands or appeals which express explicitly God's will for us) and principles (spiritual guidelines) which we may apply to moral matters and by which we may determine what is right for us to do. When we consider biblical precepts, we should observe dispensational distinctions. While all the Bible is profitable for us (II Tim. 3:16), it is not all directed to us. The Dispensation of Grace, which expresses God's will for His people today, is given in the commands of the New Testament. On the other hand, the Bible does not give special precepts for every form of human conduct. God has left it to us to exercise our mental and moral faculties to discern between right and wrong. To guide us in these judgments, He has given us in His Word spiritual principles that can be applied to every moral matter and that can show us what is God's will for us. These principles, which follow in question form, are grouped according to the relation of the proposed action to God, to others, and to one's self.

- **Principles that relate our behavior to God**

a. *Will this action glorify God (I Cor. 10:31)?*

To glorify God is to bring Him praise by allowing Him to produce in us His character and to do through us His work (Phil. 1:11; I Pet. 4:11; Mt. 5:16).

b. *Can I do this by faith in God (Rom. 14:23)?*

Practical faith in God consists of our sharing our activities with the Lord and our looking to Him for strength and direction to do these. This allows Him to participate with us in these activities. On the other hand, to act independently of Him and His resources is to sin (Jn. 15:5; Heb. 11:6). Also, one cannot have doubt about the rightness of an action and act in faith at the same time (Rom. 14:23; cp. Mt. 21:21).

   c. *Can I do this in Christ's name (Col. 3:17)?*

   To act in His name is to perform in harmony with His will and interests. Our giving thanks is our recognition of His faithfulness to help us and to work through us to accomplish His purpose.

- **Principles that relate our behavior to others**

   These principles express Christ's love, which is to govern all our relations with other people, whether saved or unsaved (Jn. 13:34-35; Rom. 13:8-10; Gal. 5:13; I Jn. 3:23; Mt. 5:44). The expression of this love does not consist of our liking people but of our concern for their needs and our willingness to help them.

   a. *Will this action cause others to stumble (I Cor. 8:9, 13; 10:32)?*

   To cause another to stumble is to throw an obstacle in his way that will hinder him spiritually. The obstacle may be a wrong action that leads him to sin or a right action that is lawful in itself but that leads him to sin. When our actions influence others to act contrary to their conscience, we lead them to sin and we sin against them (I Cor. 8:10-12). We also have a testimony to maintain before the lost (I Pet. 2:12). In our association with others, we must be willing to respect their opinions and prejudices and to accommodate ourself to these in matters of moral indifference (I Cor. 9:19-23; 10:24-29). This does not mean that we should become the helpless victims of the opinions of others. We can teach them that believers have died to social customs and prejudices (Rom. 7:1-6) and are now obligated to follow Christ (I Cor. 9:21). Also, when we cannot agree with their notions, we should not try to hide our differences, but we should explain why we believe as we do. Still, when we are with them, we must accommodate ourself to their beliefs in matters of moral indifference, such as kinds of food and forms of modest dress. In matters of doctrinal convictions, we must remain loyal to our understanding of the Word, regardless of the cost.

   b. *Will this action promote the well-being of others (I Cor. 8:1; 14:26)?*

   When the Lord's love possesses our heart, it prompts us to seek the well-being and edification of others, even at personal cost (I Jn. 3:16-18; cp. I Cor. 13:4-7; 8:13; 9:19-23; 10:23-33; Rom. 13:10).

- **Principles that relate our behavior to ourself**

   a. *What effect will this action have on my body and mind?*

   We must avoid doing those things that will injure the body and mind. Although it is still unredeemed, the believer's body is holy, for it is Christ's member (I Cor. 6:15), the Holy Spirit's temple (vs. 19), our means of glorifying God in this world (vs. 20), and when used by God, an instrument of righteousness (Rom. 6:13). Therefore, we must respect our body's integrity and function by avoiding that which would harm it or violate its sanctity (cp. I Thess. 4:3-7; I Cor. 6:18).

We must also avoid that which would enslave the body or mind (I Cor. 6:12; Rom. 6:12). Since the Lord Jesus alone is our absolute master, He has the sole right to use our body and mind as He pleases. It is our duty to yield them to Him and His Word for His expression through us. It is wrong for us to yield them to any principle that would use them in ways that are contrary to His will for us (cp. Rom. 6:11-13; Gal. 6:8; Col. 3:5-8; Acts 5:3).

    b. *What effect will this action have on my spiritual life?*

In reply we may ask the following questions: Will this action lessen my love for God (I Jn. 2:15)? Will it disrupt my fellowship with Him (I Jn. 1:6-7)? Will it dull my appetite for reading His Word, prayer, worship, the fellowship of His people, and service (I Pet. 2:1-2)? Will it deaden my concern for the well-being of others (Gal. 5:13; I Pet. 2:12)? Does it conflict with my conscience (Rom. 14:5, 23)?

If we sincerely want to know whether or not a proposed action is right for us, we can readily learn this by applying these principles.

GOD'S SELECTIVE WILL FOR AMORAL OPTIONS

Often we must choose between amoral options (choices that do not have moral qualities), such as what career to follow, what person to marry, or what car to purchase. How can we discover the Lord's will regarding these matters? The following procedure will help you to consider one option at a time, starting with the one that appears most likely to be the Lord's will for you.

- **Consider the various options that are open to you.**

Carefully consider all the facts that you can obtain about these.

- **Select the option that seems most suited to you.**

Choose the option that is most suited to your needs, interests, personality, abilities, health, convictions, financial status, and circumstances. In the light of these personal qualities, tabulate the advantages and disadvantages of your options, and choose the one that seems best for you.

- **Examine the selected option in the light of the following indicators:**

    a. *Does your selection agree with the teachings of Scripture?*

    b. *Does your selection agree with inward impression?*

The Holy Spirit often leads by inner urge or impression. However, you must determine the source of this before acting. Every urge must be tested by the Scriptures and prayer. If the impression is of God, it will become stronger as you wait on Him in prayer.

    c. *Does your selection agree with circumstances?*

Since God controls all circumstances, it is possible to do His will in His time. Do your circumstances allow you to act upon this option at this time?

If your selection agrees with these indicators, then take the next step. If not, select another suitable option and examine this in the light of the indicators.

- **Pray about your selection.**

If with prayer and time your conviction deepens that your selection is right and you have inward peace, then decide that this is the Lord's will for you. If you do not have peace or if you see that your selection is not the best for you, select another one and examine this in the light of the indicators. Continue this procedure until you have peace and you believe that an option is the Lord's will for you.

- **Pursue this option.**

Do this with the confidence that the Lord has shown you His will. Give Him thanks for this and seek to glorify Him by it. You may confirm your decision by reexamining your selection by the foregoing procedure.

WILLING OBEDIENCE

When we learn the Lord's will for us, it is imperative that we do it (Jas. 4:17; Jn. 13:17; 14:21). It may be that God will not show us all of His will at once, but He will unfold this as we obey Him in what He has already shown us (cp. Acts 8:26-27). He has so designed the Christian life that His people must continually look to Him for direction (Prov. 3:5-6). This is a part of our walking in His fellowship (I Jn. 1:7). Since we cannot do the Lord's will in our own strength, we must continually depend upon the Holy Spirit to direct and help us (Jn. 14:16-17; Rom. 8:14; Gal. 5:25). Furthermore, we should seek to glorify God when we do His will (I Cor. 10:31). As we obey the Lord, we discover that His will for us is good (it contributes to our well-being), acceptable (it is suitable to our new creaturehood in Christ), and perfect (being complete, it is best for us; Rom. 12:2). As we follow the Lord, we must continually be on the alert for Satan's efforts to divert us from God's will (I Pet. 5:8; cp. Mt. 4:1-10).

Appendix G
An Analysis of Daniel 9:24-27

THE PEOPLE WHOM THE MESSAGE CONCERNS (vs. 24)

These are Daniel's people (like himself, elect Jews) and Jerusalem, his city.

THE THINGS THAT GOD WILL ACCOMPLISH (vs. 24)

These things will take place at the close of the seventy "weeks," not during this time.

GOD WILL DEAL WITH THE SINS OF THE ELECT REMNANT OF ISRAEL.

- "To finish the transgression and to make an end of sins."
  He will make an end of their sinful condition and practice.

- "To make reconciliation (atonement) for iniquity."
  He will apply to them Christ's atoning work and save them (Rom. 11:26-27; Ezek. 36:25-26).

GOD WILL "BRING IN EVERLASTING RIGHTEOUSNESS."

This probably refers to the character of Jesus' millennial rule (Jer. 33:14-16; Isa. 11:4-5).

GOD WILL "SEAL UP (COMPLETE) THE VISION AND PROPHECY."

All will be fulfilled in His appointed time (cp. Dan. 12:4).

GOD WILL "ANOINT THE MOST HOLY (HOLY OF HOLIES)."

This seems to refer to the sanctification of the millennial temple, which will mark the beginning of our Lord's priestly rule over the earth (cp. Ex. 40:9-11; Dan. 8:13-14; Zech. 6:12-13).

THE TIME SPAN OF THIS MESSAGE

"Seventy weeks" (a "week" means "seven") represent 490 units of time. From the context (vs. 2) these units appear to be years, with 490 years in view. These 490 years are divided by the prophecy into two parts, 483 years and 7 years, with an undisclosed interval between them.

THE FIRST PART: SIXTY-NINE "WEEKS" OR 483 YEARS

This began with the decree to rebuild Jerusalem (vs. 25), which was issued by the Persian King, Artaxerxes I, in 445 B.C. (Neh. 2:1-6), and continued unto Messiah the Prince (the Lord Jesus Christ). Why this part is divided into two periods (seven "weeks" and sixty-two "weeks") is not clear. Perhaps the restoration of the city took seven "weeks" (49 years).

According to the calculation of Sir Robert Anderson, this first part (483 years) was 173,880 days (a prophetic year being 360 days). It began on the first of Nisan (March 14), 445 B.C., and ended with the Lord's presenting Himself to Jerusalem on the tenth of Nisan (April 6), A.D. 32.[1] However, some chronologers regard this year to be later than that of our Lord's death, though not an impossibility. Robert C. Newman offers an attractive proposition, which bases the calculation on sabbatical or seven-year cycles, with the

---

[1] Sir Robert Anderson, *The Coming Prince* (London: Hodder and Stoughton, 1895), ch. X.

result that Jesus died during the sixty-ninth cycle (A.D. 27-34).[2] This view requires that the word "after"(vs. 26) be interpreted as a Jewish idiom meaning "during."

THE UNDISCLOSED INTERVAL BETWEEN THE TWO PARTS

In my opinion, there is an undisclosed interval between the phrases "but not for Himself" and "the people of the prince" (vs. 26), which represents the Church Age. (Remember that the present Church Age is nowhere revealed or mentioned in the Old Testament.) That this interval exists is implied by the separate part of one "week" (seven years) and by the words "the end" and "the consumation" (vss. 26-27), which often relate to events associated with Christ's return to earth (cp. Dan. 8:19; 11:27, 35, 40; 12:4, 9, 13; Mt. 24:3, 6, 13-14).

THE SECOND PART: ONE "WEEK" OR SEVEN YEARS

This part is described in verse 26 as follows: "And the city and the holy place shall the people of a coming prince (chief, leader) destroy; and it shall be with a flood, and unto the end there shall be war, determined desolations." Although most futuristic commentators believe that this refers to the destruction of Jerusalem by the Roman general Titus in A.D. 70, the context does not require this interpretation, which introduces a part of the Church Age into the prophecy. In my opinion, this prophecy is a reference to the future fall of Jerusalem to the Beast (Satan's human agent) when he breaks his pact with Israel (Lk. 21:20-24; Mt. 23:38-24:2, 15-21; Rev. 11:2; Dan. 8:11-14).

I believe that verse 27 is an explanation of events that will lead to the fall of Jerusalem in the middle of the seventieth "week," as described in verse 26b. If "and" is interpreted as an explanatory conjunction, then verse 27 may be translated this way: "That is, he shall make strong a covenant with many seven of one; and (at) the half of seven he will cause sacrifice and meal offering to cease, even upon a wing of abominations (detested things), desolating even unto complete destruction; and that which is determined shall pour forth upon the desolator."

This verse (27) gives us important details about the Beast and his relation to Israel. His confirmation of a pact with Israel will mark the beginning of the seventieth "week." He will break the pact in the middle of the "week" by stopping the daily sacrifice and by destroying the temple and the city. But in time (three and a half years later), that which has been divinely determined will be poured upon "the desolator" (the Beast cp. Rev. 19:19-20; Dan. 2:44; 7:26; 8:25; 11:45). Incidentally, we should not assume that the Beast is a Roman simply because the Romans took Jerusalem in A.D. 70.

---

[2] Robert C. Newman, "Daniel's Seventy Weeks and the Old Testament Sabbath-Year Cycle," *The Journal of the Evangelical Theological Society,* Vol. 16, No. 4 (1973), pp. 229-34.

APPENDIX H
An Analysis of Ezekiel 38 & 39

Many interpreters of these chapters expect Russia to invade Palestine in fulfillment of this prophecy. The view that these chapters speak of Russia is based on the similarity between the place-names "Meshech" and Moscow, "Tubal" and Tobolsk, and "Rosh" (Septuagint translation for "chief" in 38:2) and Russia. Moreover, this view is supported by Russia's chronic hostility toward Israel and by the invading army's coming from the north (38:15; 39:2).

While Russia, indeed, may invade Palestine to strike against Israel, this would not necessarily be in fulfillment of this prophecy. It is known from cuneiform texts that Meshech (ancient Mishku) and Tubal (ancient Tabal) were located in central and eastern Anatolia (modern Turkey).[1] It is noteworthy that the man whom Gog prophetically represents was the subject of several prophets earlier than Ezekiel (Ezek. 38:17; cp. Isa. 10:5-34; Jer. 25:12; Joel 1:1-2:11; Micah 5:3-15; Zeph. 1:1-2:3). This is not true of Russia or its leaders.

Without question these chapters look ahead to the time when God will deal with the nation of Israel by the hand of Gentiles (38:8, 16) and will restore them permanently to their land (39:23-29). The prophecy will be fulfilled at a time when Israel will dwell safely in their land (38:8, 11, 14), before their final restoration (39:22-29). Apparently, their safety will be the result of an international agreement, which "in the latter years" will be confirmed by the Beast, Satan's human agent (Dan. 9:27). He will confirm this treaty at the beginning of his prophetic political career when he secures the leadership of a ten-nation federation (Dan. 7:7-8, 19-27). Rather than speaking of Russia, which is not a common subject of prophecy (in fact, it is not found in prophecy at all), historical Magog, with its leader Gog, more likely represents the prophetic ten-nation federation and its leader, the Beast, whom Satan will use during the last half of the Tribulation Period to rule the earth (Dan. 7:7-8, 19-27; 8:9-12, 23-25; 11:21-45; Rev. 13:1-10; 17:8-11).

These chapters appear to enlarge upon Ezekiel 37:28 by describing the time and manner by which the LORD will make himself known to the nations as the One who sanctifies Israel and restores them permanently to their own land (vss. 20-27). Moreover, these chapters serve as a preface to the millennial scene of chapters 40 through 48 (cp. 43:7; 48:35).

---

[1] Edwin Yamauchi, "Meshech, Tubal, and Company: A Review," *The Journal of the Evangelical Theological Society,* Vol. 19, No. 3 (1976), p. 239.

My understanding of these chapters follows in outline form:

A. God's declaration of His dealings (38:1-7)

God declares His opposition to Gog and his land Magog and reveals what He will do with them. He will turn Gog and his confederates back and will bring them against Israel a second time (so implied in 38:4). Gog's confederates are probably members of the ten-nation federation which he leads (vss. 5-6). This federation will consist of nations belonging to the Mediterranean area (Dan. 7:2, with the federation described in vss. 7, 19; Rev. 13:1-2). In His sovereignty God will bring Gog and his confederates against Israel twice, and then on to Armageddon (Zeph. 3:8; Zech. 12:1-3, 14:1-2).

B. The details of God's dealing with Gog (38:8-39:20)

Representing the enemy of God's people (cp. Rev. 20:8), Gog in these chapters is the Gentile Beast, who as Satan's agent will rule the earth through the political structure of the ten-nation federation, with satanic authority, wickedness, and cruelty.

1. The Beast's invasion that breaks the treaty with Israel (38:8-16a)
See Daniel 9:27; Luke 21:20-24; Matthew 24:15-21.

    a. The time and target of the invasion (vs. 8)
    This takes place right after Satan's ejection to the earth in the middle of the Tribulation Period (Rev. 12:7-13).

    b. The Beast's assault against Israel (vss. 8-9, 14-16a)

    c. The Beast's motivation (vss. 10-12)

    d. International protest against this invasion (vs. 13)

Upon this violation of the treaty, Jerusalem will be trampled under Gentile foot for the remaining three and a half years of the Tribulation Period (Rev. 11:1-2). At this time, the temple will be razed, the city will be destroyed, and the people will be dispersed (Mt. 24:1-3, 15-26; Lk. 21:20-24).

2. The Beast's second invasion, leading to Armageddon (38:16b-39:20)
    Politically frustrated and supernaturally influenced, the Beast will attack Jerusalem again at the close of his world rule (Dan. 11:44b, 45; Rev. 16:13-16). This will lead to the remnant of Israel's repentance (Joel 2:1-20), Christ's second coming to earth (Zech. 14:1-3), and the Battle of Armageddon, wherein the Beast and his confederates will be utterly defeated (Rev. 19:17-21). The battle itself will extend throughout Palestine, with Jerusalem as its focal point (Rev. 14:20; Zech. 12:1-3).

    a. The Beast's second assault against Jerusalem (38:16b-17; 39:1-2)
    This will occur at the close of the Tribulation Period.

    b. God's judgment upon the Beast and his confederates (38:18-39:7)
    This judgment will include various expressions of divine wrath (38:18-19a; cp. Lk. 21:22; Rev. 14:14-20; 16:17-21; 19:15), such as a convul-

sion of the land (Ezek. 38:19b-20; cp. Rev. 6:12-17; 16:18), a battle in which the Beast's soldiers will irrationally fight one another and God will discharge lethal volleys of disease, rain, hail, and fire and brimstone (Ezek. 38:21-23; cp. Zech. 12:4; 14:12-15; Rev. 16:21). These weapons of divine wrath will devastate the enemy on the battlefield (Ezek. 39:1-5) and at home (vs. 6).

    c. The following cleanup (39:8-20)

The debris and carnage of battle will be so great that it will take seven years to burn the litter (vss. 9-10) and seven months to bury the remains of the dead (vss. 11-16), whose flesh was devoured by scavenger birds and animals (vss. 17-20; cp. Lk. 17:37; Rev. 19:17-18, 21).

C. The outcome of God's dealings with Gog (39:21-29)

    1. God will be glorified (vs. 21; 38:23).

He will be exalted in the eyes of surviving nations by His awful expressions of holy wrath (cp. Rom. 2:8-9; 9:22). He will also be known as the LORD, the Holy One in Israel (Ezek. 39:7).

    2. The elect remnant of Israel will be blessed (vss. 22-29).

    a. They will know the LORD (vss. 22, 28).

This means that they will be saved and will have a right relation to the LORD according to the promises of the New Covenant (Ezek. 36:24-29; Jer. 31:31-40; cp. Jn. 17:3).

    b. They will be restored permanently to their land (vss. 23-28).

See Genesis 17:8; Deuteronomy 30:1-5; Ezekiel 11:17-20; 20:33-44; 34:11-31; 36:6-38; 37:12-14, 21-28.

    c. They will be anointed with the Holy Spirit (vs. 29).

They will receive Him and the blessings of His manifold ministry (36:26-27).

APPENDIX I
Babylon

PROPHETIC BABYLON

While many commentators hold that prophetic Babylon (Rev. chs. 17-18) is Rome, I believe that it is better to regard it as the actual city of Babylon, which will be rebuilt on or near its ancient site. After the Noachic flood false religion seems to have been organized under the leadership of Nimrod, the builder of the first kingdom of Babylon (Gen. 10:8, 10).[1] With the people its

---

[1] See Alexander Hislop, *The Two Babylons* (London: Partridge, 1926), pp. 21-40.

doctrines were dispersed over the earth. Today they are perpetuated by all the religions of the world, including unbiblical forms of Christianity. In the future they will be united in the worship of the Beast (Rev. 13:8; 17:2; 18:3), with the result that Satan will be honored (13:4), the nations will be deceived (13:13-14; 18:23), and God will be blasphemed (13:5; 17:3; Dan. 7:25).

ITS IDENTITY

Though portrayed as a woman (Rev. 17:3-4, 9, 18), Babylon is identified as being a city (17:18; 18:10, 16, 18-19, 21). I believe that the city will be rebuilt, for the prophecies of its career and destruction must be fulfilled. For instance, its destruction will take place in the Day of the LORD (Isa. 13:1, 6, 9; cp. Jer. 51:6), suddenly and completely (Jer. 50:26; 51:8, 25, 37), making it a desolation forever (Jer. 50:13, 39, 40; 51:26, 62; Isa. 13:19-20) at a time when Israel returns to the LORD (Jer. 50:4-7).

Ancient Babylon never experienced these things. When Cyrus the Great took the city (539 B.C.), he restored it and made it the provincial capital of Babylonia. The city continued to flourish until 293 B.C. when the Greek general Seleucus built Seleucia, some forty miles north of Babylon. The rubble of Babylon was used for the construction of many buildings (cp. Jer. 51:26). In 275 B.C. Antiochus I ordered the remaining civilian population of Babylon to be removed to Seleucia. A hundred years later Antiochus IV placed a Greek colony in Babylon, which flourished for a time. Early in the second century B.C., the city was destroyed by the Parthians. In the first century A.D., merchants from Palmyra colonized the site. Emperor Trajan wintered there (116) during his campaign against the Parthians. Thus history shows that the area was not deserted forever. To this day men pitch their tents among its ruins (cp. Isa. 13:19-20).

ITS CAREER

According to prophecy Babylon will be the Beast's capital during the three and a half years of his world rule (Rev. 13:5). Supported by the Beast's political structure (Rev. 17:1-3; cp. 13:1-2), the city will be the administrative (Rev. 17:15; cp. Dan. 2:31-35), commercial (Rev. 18:3, 9-19), and religious (17:4-5; 13:11-17) center of earth.

ITS DESTRUCTION

It appears that this is brought about by the leaders of the federated nations that make up the Beast's political entity (Rev. 17:16-17). Impelled by God, they will destroy the city in "one hour" (Rev. 18:10, 17, 19), utterly burning it with fire and making it desolate (vss. 8, 18-19). This will fulfill the prophecies of the city's destruction (Isa. ch. 13; Jer. chs. 50-51).

AN ANALYSIS OF REVELATION 17 AND 18

THE CITY'S DESCRIPTION (17:1-6)

The "whore" is the city of Babylon (vs. 18). She is seen:

- **Politically** — supported by the Beast's political entity, the ten-nation federation (vss. 1-3).

- **Commercially** — arrayed in costly garments and jewels (vs. 4). See Revelation 18:12-14.

- **Religiously** — holding the cup of her doctrinal and ritualistic abominations and filthiness and labeled as the mother of these (vss. 4-5).

- **Morally** — drunk with the blood of the saints whom she slew (vs. 6). See Revelation 6:9; 12:17; 13:7, 15; 16:5-6.

THE CITY'S RELATION TO THE BEAST (17:7-15)

In verse 7 "the beast" is the political entity of Satan's human agent, the Beast of verses 8-11 (cp. "many waters," vss. 1, 15; "a scarlet colored beast," vs. 3; 13:1-2). "The seven heads" or "the seven mountains upon which the woman sits," (vs. 17:9) are the "seven kings" (vs. 10) or presidents of the ten-nation federation, which becomes the political entity of Satan's human agent. "The ten horns" (vss. 12, 16; Dan. 7:24) are the governors of the individual nations of the federation. "The waters" (Rev. 17:1, 15) are the people of earth over whom the Beast rules during the three and a half years of his world power (Rev. 17:18; 18:3; 13:7).

At the time of the vision these ten kings had not yet received their authority and kingdoms (Rev. 17:12), but they will have these when the Beast begins his predeath prophetic career (Dan. 7:7-8, 19-27). These kings will give their authority to the Beast when he is restored to life and will acclaim him as their leader (Rev. 17:13; cp. 13:3-7). Having been a president of the federation before his death (cp. 17:10; Dan. 7:24), the Beast upon his resurrection will become the eighth president of the federation (Rev. 17:11), which under Satan will become worldwide in its extent (Dan. 7:23; Rev. 13:2-5), with Babylon as its capital.

THE CITY'S DESTRUCTION (17:16-19:6)

• The Destruction Event (17:16-17)

Unwittingly motivated by God, the governors of the ten nations that comprise the federation will destroy Babylon. This will be an act of rebellion against the Beast, who at the time is in or near Palestine (Dan. 11:44-45; Rev. 18:8, 18-19).

• The Proclamation of the City's Fall (18:1-8)

This includes an announcement (vss. 1-3), an order for God's people to leave the city, perhaps in the middle of the seventieth "week" (vss. 4-5; cp. Mt. 24:15-21), and a command for its judgment (Rev. 18:6-8).

• The Universal Reactions (18:9-20; 19:1-6)

Of earth dwellers: rulers (vss. 18:9-10), merchants (vss. 11-16), and haulers (vss. 17-19). Of Heaven: (18:20; 19:1-6).

- **Its Permanence (18:21-24)**
  See Isaiah 13:19-20; Jeremiah 50:39; 51:62.

APPENDIX J
The Order of God's Decree

In their thinking about God's decree as it concerns man's creation, fall, election, and salvation, theologians have attempted to put these parts in an order which, to their minds, properly portrays their relation to one another. The names of these proposed orders are based on the word *lapsarian* (Latin, *lapsus*, fall), which relates the orders to man's fall. The two primary orders are *supralapsarianism* and *infralapsarianism*.

SUPRALAPSARIANISM (*supra* is Latin for "before")
Held by high Calvinists, this view follows this order:

a. To elect some people to salvation and to reprobate (foreordain) the remainder to perdition. This is called double predestination.[1]

b. To create the people who are elected and reprobated.

c. To permit their fall.

d. To justify the elect and to condemn the nonelect.

The main objection to this order is that election and reprobation concern nonentities since they precede the decree to create.

INFRALAPSARIANISM (*infra* is Latin for "after")
Held by moderate Calvinists, this view follows this order:

a. To create man.

b. To permit man's fall.

c. To elect some people to salvation. This is called single predestination for it does not hold that God reprobates the lost to perdition.

d. To leave the remainder (nonelect) to their sin and its punishment. This is called preterition.

This order is more in keeping with the Scriptures and logic.

L. S. Chafer distinguishes between *infralapsarianism* and *sublapsarianism*, which, as he sees it, differ in their location of the decree to provide salvation. In infralapsarianism he places this between Steps b and c; in

---

[1] Calvinists commonly regard the word "predestination" to include election and reprobation. See L. Berkhof, *Systematic Theology*, p. 113. I see predestination as following election and as the divine predetermination of what God would do with the people whom had chosen to save (Rom. 8:29; Eph. 1:5; 11-12).

sublapsarianism, after Step d.[2] Other Calvinists do not recognize this distinction.

The Arminian view is infralapsarian, with the distinction that God's election and preterition are based on divinely foreseen faith or unbelief, as the case may be. They consider these to be judicial (not sovereign) acts in the nature of reward and punishment.

W. G. T. Shedd observes that the decree of preterition (passing by the nonelect) does not necessitate, or bring about, perdition, though it makes it certain. It is a permissive act, not an efficient one, on the part of God. He decides to do nothing in the case of the nonelect sinner. Leaving him alone, God allows him his own self-determination and voluntary inclination. This permission is not causation. The nonelect sinner is not condemned and lost because God did not elect him, but because he sinned and came short of God's glory. While election is the efficient cause of salvation, preterition is not the efficient cause of perdition. It only makes perdition certain to them who have fitted themselves for destruction (Rom. 9:22).[3] By contrast, the decree of reprobation, as held by some Calvinists, is efficient, necessitating perdition. I believe that the concept of preterition is more biblical than that of reprobation.

APPENDIX K
Israel's Future in Prophecy

Genesis
Their land: 15:18; their future: ch. 49.

Leviticus
Their dispersion: 26:27-39; their restoration: 26:40-45.

Deuteronomy
Their dispersion: 28:15-68; their restoration: 30:1-10.

Psalms
Their restoration: 53:6; 69:35-36; kingdom blessings: chs. 67, 72.

Isaiah
Their restoration: 10:20-22; 11:11-16; 14:1-3; 26:1-19; 27:12-13; 29:17-24; 30:15-26; 32:15-20; 35:1-10; 41:14-20; 43:5-9; 49:5-26; 51:11; 52:8-12; 54:1-17; 59:20-21; 60:1-22; 62:1-12; 65:9-10, 19-25; 66:10-14; kingdom blessings: 2:1-22; 4:1-5; 11:1-9; 51:3; 65:17-25.

---

[2] L. S. Chafer, *Systematic Theology*, III, 180 ff.
[3] W. G. T. Shedd, *Dogmatic Theology*, I, 444 ff.

Jeremiah

Their restoration: 3:14-18; 16:14-21; 23:3-8; 24:6-7; 30:3-9, 17, 22; 31:8-16; 32:37-44; 46:27-28; 50:19-20; their return: 3:12-14, 22-4:9; the remnant: 15:11, 19-21.

Ezekiel

Their dispersion: 33:23-29; their judgment: 11:21; 20:37-38; 34:17-22; their restoration: 11:17-20; 16:60-63; 17:22-24; 20:33-44; 28:25-26; 34:11-31; 36:6-38; 37:12-14, 21-28; 39:25-29.

Daniel

The Jewish age: 9:24-27; their relation to the Beast: 8:11-14; 9:27; 11:31-35; 12:11.

Hosea

Their judgment: 1:4-6, 9; 9:11-12; 13:7-8, 15-16; their return to the LORD: 3:4-5; 5:14-6:3; 14:1-2; their restoration: 1:10-11; 2:14-23; 11:9-11; 13:9-10, 14; 14:4-8.

Joel

Their judgment: 1:4-20; 2:1-11; their restoration: 2:12-3:1, 17-21.

Amos

Their judgment 9:1-10; their restoration: 9:11-15.

Obadiah

Their blessings: 1:17-21.

Micah

Their restoration: 2:12-13; 5:3; 7:7-20; kingdom blessings: 4:1-8.

Zephaniah

Their restoration: 3:14-20; the remnant: 3:12-13.

Zechariah

Their restoration: 8:1-8, 11-14, 23; 10:1-12; 12:10-13:1, 8-9; kingdom blessings: 2:8-13; 14:9-11, 16-21.

Malachi

Their judgment: 3:1-5; the remnant: 3:16-18; 4:2-3.

Matthew

The remnant: 24:9-31 (cp. Mark 13:11-27; Luke 17:20-32; 21:12-28); their judgment: 25:14-30.

Romans

The remnant: 11:25-36.

Revelation

The remnant: ch. 12.

APPENDIX L
An Outline of the Prophetic Chapters of Daniel

CHAPTER TWO: Nebuchadnezzar's Dream

This seems to teach that the Beast's seat of government will be Babylon where the image stands.

1. The dream (vss. 31-35)
2. The interpretation (vss. 36-45)
   a. Of the image.
      (1) The head of gold: Babylon under Nebuchadnezzar (vss. 37-38).
      (2) The breast and arms of silver: Persia (vs. 39; 5:28).
      (3) The belly and thighs of brass: Greece (vs. 39; 8:21).
      (4) The legs and feet of iron with clay: the kingdom of the Beast (vss. 40-43). I do not see Rome in unfulfilled prophecy.
         (a) His empire will be strong (vs. 40; 7:7, 23; Rev. 13:7-8).
         (b) Its authority will be satanic (vss. 41-43), expressed by demon-possessed humans (cp. 7:7, 24-25; 8:23-24; Rev. 13:1-5).
         (c) Its seat will be the city of Babylon (Rev. chs. 17, 18).
   b. Of the Stone (vss. 44-45).
      The Lord Jesus will terminate the Beast's kingdom and will establish His own rule on the earth (Rev. 19:11-21).

CHAPTER SEVEN: The Vision of the Four Wild Beasts

This appears to represent the political environment in which the Beast will arise and the worldwide extent of his kingdom.

1. The vision (vss. 1-14)
2. The interpretation (vss. 15-27)
   a. Of the four kingdoms or federations of nations.
      These arise in the Mediterranean area (vss. 2-7, 17; cp. Ezek. 47:15, 19-20) at the same time (Dan. 7:3, 12; cp. Rev. 13:1-2).
   b. Of the fourth kingdom, the empire of the Beast (vss. 7, 19-25).
      (1) Its structure at the time of Beast's political rise.
         (a) It will be a ten-nation federation (vss. 7, 24; Rev. 13:1).
         (b) The Beast will subdue three of these nations (vss. 8, 24). This takes place at the beginning of his prophetic career.
      (2) Its character at the time of Beast's world supremacy.
         (a) It will be worldwide in extent (vss. 7, 23; Rev. 13:1-7).
         (b) It will continue for three and a half years (vs. 25; Rev. 13:5).
      (3) Its termination at Christ's coming (vss. 9-14).
         (a) The setting up of God's judgment throne (vss. 9-11; Rev. ch. 4).

(b) The investiture of the Son of God (vss. 13-14; Rev. ch. 5).

(c) The destruction of the Beast's kingdom and the establishment of Christ's kingdom (vss. 11, 14b, 26b, 27; cp. 2:44-45; Rev. 19:11-21).

CHAPTER EIGHT: The Vision of the Ram and He-goat

This seems to teach that the Beast will arise in the part of Alexander's empire which lay north and east of Palestine.

1. The vision (vss. 2-14)
2. The interpretation (vss. 15-25)
   a. Of the ram and the he-goat (vss. 3-8, 15-22).
      (1) The ram represents the kings of Media and Persia (vs. 20); the great horn represents Cyrus, who conquered Babylon and forged the great Persian empire.
      (2) The he-goat represents the king of Greece (vs. 21). This seems to refer to Alexander the Great who conquered Persia (vss. 5-7) and whose empire eventually fell to four of his generals —Egypt to Ptolemy, Macedonia and Greece to Antipater, Asia Minor to Antigonus, and Babylonia to Seleucus (vs. 22).
   b. Of the little horn, the Beast (vss. 9-12, 23-25).
      That this prophecy refers to our future is indicated by the time designations found in verses 17, 19, and 23, which point to the Tribulation Period and Christ's second coming (cp. Lk. 21:22).
      (1) The Beast's political achievements (Dan. 8:9, 23). This prophecy suggests that he will rise in the area of ancient Syria or Babylonia.
      (2) His anti-God exploits (vss. 10-12, 24).
      (3) His character (vss. 23-24).
      (4) His end (vs. 13-14, 25b; cp. 7:11; 2:35, 45; Rev. 19:19-20).

CHAPTER NINE: The Vision of the Seventy "Weeks" (vss. 24-27).

See Appendix G.

CHAPTERS TEN THROUGH TWELVE: The Vision of the Time of the End

This last vision concerns what shall befall Daniel's people in the last days of God's dealing with them (10:14). Again, this looks ahead to the seventieth "week" as the time designations of 11:6, 13, 27, 35, 40; 12:1, 4, 7, 9-13 indicate (cp. Mt. 24:3, 6, 13-14). The message begins with Daniel 11:2.

1. The activities of the Beast (11:2-45)
   As in chapters two and eight, this prophecy divides into two parts:
   a. That beyond Daniel's time (vss. 2-4)
      This concerns four kings of Persia (vs. 2) and Alexander (vss. 3-4).
   b. That beyond our time (vss. 5-45)

Commentators usually interpret verses five through thirty-five as referring to the conflict between Egypt and Syria after the division of Alexander's empire. In my opinion, this passage outlines the political events which lead to the rise of the Beast. This is supported by references to "the latter days" (10:14; cp. 11:6, 35).

(1) Conflict between the North and the South (vss. 5-20)
    During this period there are successively two kings of the North (vss. 6, 10) and two kings of the South (vss. 5, 7). With Palestine as the hub, the North seems to represent Syria or some other northern nation, and the South appears to be Egypt. This conflict will set the stage for the Beast's career as given in the prophetic Scriptures.

(2) The beginning of the Beast's career (vss. 21-30a)
    Rising from obscurity as the third king of the North, he becomes leader of the ten-nation federation (7:24) and collides with the (third?) king of the South (11:25-27).

(3) The Beast's dealings with the Jews (vss. 30b-35).

(4) The Beast's world supremacy (vss. 36-39)
    He receives his power from Satan ("the god of forces," "a strange god"), whom he honors (vss. 38-39; cp. Rev. 13:4-5).

(5) The closing events of the Beast's career (vss. 40-45)
    When subject nations revolt against him (vss. 40, 44; cp. Rev. 17:16-17; 16:13-16), the Beast will invade Palestine a second time (Dan. 11:41-45a; cp. Ezek. 38:16b-17; 39:1-2) and will come to his end (Dan. 11:45b; cp. 9:27; Rev. 19:19-20).

2. God's dealings with Israel (12:1-3, 5-12)

   a. He promises to deliver the remnant from the trials of the Tribulation Period (vs. 1).

   b. He promises them resurrection and glory (vss. 2-3).

   c. He declares the duration of these events (vss. 5-7, 11-12).
   The prophecy seems to speak of the Beast's world supremacy for three and a half years (cp. 7:25; Rev. 11:2; 13:5) or 1,260 days from his breaking his pact with Israel (Dan. 9:27; 8:11; 11:31). However, verse 11 speaks of 1,290 days (30 extra days), and verse 12 promises a blessing to them who come to 1,335 days (75 extra days). Perhaps these extra days are required for our Lord's judgments and the establishment of His kingdom, the beginning of which is marked by the anointing of the Holy of Holies (9:24). They who survive unto this event will be members of His kingdom (Mt. 25:34).

3. God's final words to Daniel (12:4, 13)

   a. He is to seal the book (vs. 4).
   The prophecy will not be understood until the time of the end. Verse 4b

probably refers to the study of the Scriptures and to their illumination which will be given at the time these things will be fulfilled.

b. He must go his way (unto death) until his resurrection and appraisal (vs. 13).

Appendix M
An Outline of the Book of Revelation

PASSAGE	OUTLINE	TIME[1]
1:1-8	1. Introduction	
1:9-20	2. "The things which thou hast seen" (Vision of Christ among the lampstands)	
2:1-3:22	3. "The things which are" (Christ's letters to the seven churches)	
4:1-22:5	4. "The things which shall be" (Visions of the future)	
4:1-19:10	a. Visions of Tribulation Period judgments	
4:1-8:1	(1) The Seal Judgments	
4:1-5:14	(a) Introduction	
4:1-11	1) Judgment throne of God	1
5:1-14	2) Investiture of the Lamb	1
6:1-8:1	(b) The judgments	
6:1-2	1) Rider on white horse (Rise and political conquests of the Beast)	1
6:3-4	2) Rider on red horse (International war rising from 1))	1
6:5-6	3) Rider on black horse	1
6:7-8	4) Rider on pale horse (Bringing death to one-fourth of world population)	1
6:9-11	5) Vision of first tribulation martyrs	1, 2
6:12-17	6) Vision of their vengeance	4
7:1-17	(c) The first interlude[2]	
7:1-8	1) Vision of the 144,000	1, 2
7:9-17	2) Vision of the great multitude	4
	(These people are the fruit of the 144,000's ministry.)	

---

[1] The time of these events is indicated by the following numbers: 1, before the seventieth "week"; 2, the first half of the seventieth "week"; 3, the middle of the seventieth "week"; 4, the second half of the seventieth "week"; and 5, after the seventieth "week."

[2] An interlude is a pause in the progress of the vision. It gives additional details about the vision.

APPENDIX N
Giving

Although the love of money is a root of all evil (I Tim. 6:10), money or other means of exchange hold a very important place in the Lord's work. Since almost every kind of Christian work requires money, giving is a major spiritual exercise in the believer's life, service, and worship. Let us consider what God says about this.

THE LORD'S ADVICE TO TREASURE SEEKERS (Lk. 12:13-37)

Our materialistic and affluent age ever tempts us to have an improper attitude toward material possessions (cp. I Tim. 6:8-10; I Jn. 2:15). Jesus gives timely warning and appeal in this passage.

- **He warns against our laying up treasures on earth (vss. 15-21).**

Other passages teach that we should provide for our dependents (II Cor. 12:14; I Tim. 5:8), the needy (Eph. 4:28; Gal. 6:10), the Lord's work (Phil. 4:14), and our personal needs (Acts 18:3; II Thess. 3:7-13). But there are several objections to our laying up for ourselves treasures on earth.

1. *It opens the door to covetousness (vs. 15a).*

Covetousness is a dissatisfaction with what we have and an eager, greedy desire for more. This is a form of idolatry (Col. 3:5).

2. *It does not constitute life (vs. 15b).*

Man is not only a physical being but also a spiritual one with a capacity for spiritual life and fellowship with God. Consequently, material things do not completely satisfy him, for they do not minister to his spiritual needs. Only the Lord Jesus can do this (Jn. 6:35).

3. It does not bestow eternal benefit (vss. 16-21).

This farmer was a shrewd, successful businessman, but God said that he was foolish. He lived for time and not eternity. He was not rich toward God, for he had left God out of his work and did not consider his possessions as a trust from Him. Thus, he did not seek divine guidance for the use and disposal of his property. Our Lord does not condemn thrift and the possession of earthly goods, but He does warn against our having a covetous attitude toward them, our giving them God's place in our life and our using them in a wrong way.

- **He exhorts us to lay up treasure in Heaven (vss. 22-37).**
  How can we do this?

  1. By trusting His loving care rather than uncertain riches (vss. 22-30).

  Since life does not consist of the abundance of one's material possessions, then we do not have to worry about these things. We must not make them the primary object of our trust or concern (vs. 22). This does not excuse us from the duty of providing for ourselves (II Thess. 3:10). Ordinarily, we must earn our own livelihood, manage our income, live within our means, and look to the Lord for direction and help in these things (Lk. 12:22-30).

  2. By seeking the things of God's kingdom (vs. 31a).

  Unlike the unsaved (vs. 30), we are to seek those things that concern God's kingdom and interests (vs. 31; Col. 3:1-2). He has not left us on earth to pursue selfish, materialistic ambitions; we are here to serve Him. Although much of our time is spent in securing a living, we can regard this as a service to Christ as well as an opportunity to minister unto others (Col. 3:22-24; Acts 1:8). As we place the Lord's interests first in our life, we can depend upon Him to help us to provide for our needs and those of our dependents.

  3. By disposing of our possessions as He directs (vss. 31b-33).

  Since we are God's stewards (I Pet. 4:10), all that we have is from Him and belongs to Him (I Cor. 4:7; Ps. 24:1). We should use our possessions as He directs and for His glory (I Cor. 10:31). We must not prize these things and live for them (Lk. 12:34). When we have right attitudes toward our possessions, we can trust the Lord to provide for us when we cannot provide for ourselves (vss. 31b-32). All who anticipate the Lord's imminent return sit lightly on their possessions (vss. 35-37) and look forward to the dividends which their heavenly investment will bring (vss. 42-43; cp. Mk. 8:34-37).

PRINCIPLES THAT SHOULD GOVERN OUR GIVING

The New Testament presents several principles that guide us to give in a manner which pleases God. They recognize the distinction between the stewardship of the Mosaic Law and that of grace, under which we live today. They are given in the answers to the following questions.

• **Who should give to the Lord and His work?**

Only saved people, for the admonitions and instructions about giving are addressed to His people. Giving in God's way is a spiritual exercise, for which unsaved people have neither desire nor ability. Contrariwise, the gifts of Cornelius, a Gentile with no sacrifice, were a memorial before God (Acts 10:2-4). His giving was in response to general revelation and a means of honoring God.

But why should saved people give to the Lord and His work? In addition to being motivated by gratitude and love, the promise of reward, and the urgency of need, the believer will also be impelled by his relationship to God, as in the following:

1. *Each believer is a steward of God (I Pet. 4:10).*

A steward was the chief servant of a household who had the responsibility of administering his master's possessions (Lk. 16:1). Being God's stewards (I Cor. 4:1), we have the duty of using the things that He has entrusted to us for His glory. These things include our life, body, energy, time, talents, and material possessions. We are to discharge this stewardship blamelessly — according to His will (Tit. 1:7), faithfully — with His purpose and interests in view (Lk. 12:42), wisely — according to His direction (vs. 42), and efficiently — by means of His strength and for His profit (vs. 43), until Jesus comes (19:13).

2. *Each believer is a priest unto God (I Pet. 2:5).*

Since there is no hierarchy within God's family, all believers have equal priestly rank and privilege. Through Jesus all have direct access to God (Heb. 10:19-22; Eph. 2:18). Moreover, our allegiance is to the Lord Jesus, our great High Priest (Heb. 4:14). In addition to worship and prayer, we have the priestly function of offering to God spiritual sacrifices. Although they do not contribute to our salvation, these sacrifices are an expression of worship and a means of glorifying God. They include our offering our body to God (Rom. 12:1), our giving Him praise (Heb. 13:15), our fruitful witness (Rom. 15:16), our offering our life in death (Phil. 2:17), and our sharing with others our possessions (Heb. 13:16; Phil. 4:18).

3. *Each believer is a partner with Christ in His work (I Cor. 1:9).*

In this fellowship of building the church, we share in His interests, possessions, and activities. As members of His body (I Cor. 12:13, 27), we are used by Him in the building of the church. This includes our giving.

• **By what means are we to give?**

All spiritual exercises, including giving, are by means of God's grace (II Cor. 8:1-7; cp. I Cor. 15:10). The Macedonian believers' giving was not prompted by sentimentality, generosity, or the nuisance of surplus wealth. It was by means of divine grace, which motivated and enabled them to give in spite of the obstacles of persecution (Phil. 1:28-30; I Thess. 1:6; 2:14) and poverty (II Cor. 8:2). In spite of these, they gave sacrificially (vs. 2) beyond their natural ability (vs. 3) and voluntarily without external pressure (vss. 3b, 4). Their submission and obedience to the Lord (vs. 5) allowed God's grace to operate in their giving (cp. vss. 1, 9).

- ## How much should we give?

  1. *The basis for this determination is not the Mosaic Law (Rom. 6:14; Gal. 5:18).*

  The law directed Israel to give certain tithes of their gross income and certain offerings to the LORD. One tithe of herds and crops was given annually to the Levites (Lev. 27:30-34; Num. 18:21); a second tithe of herds and crops was brought annually to the worship center (the temple) during the sacred festivals (Deut. 14:22-26); and a third tithe was given every three years for the support of the local Levites, strangers, widows, and orphans (Deut. 14:28-29; 26:12-14). In addition to these tithes, the law also required the people to offer various sacrifices throughout the year (Lev. chs. 1-7). Tithes were given to God before the Dispensation of the Mosaic Law, but these appear to be voluntary in nature, expressing to God both gratitude (Gen. 14:20) and devotion (28:22).

  2. *The basis for this determination is Christ's law (I Cor. 16:1-2; II Cor. chs. 8-9).*

  Since giving today is by the grace of God and the believer is God's steward, then we must look to God for the amount and the place we are to give. Under grace giving is not simply a mathematical calculation, the payment of a debt, or an impulsive response to an appeal. The Lord has so designed our giving that we must assess the possessions He has given us, seek His direction, learn His will, and look to Him for the needed grace to give as His responsible stewards. Under grace giving is a spiritual exercise that rises from fellowship with Christ. It is a source of rich spiritual blessing and a means of spiritual growth.

  Under grace no percentage is stipulated in giving. We must learn the amount directly from God as He makes known His will to us. Each believer must determine this for himself (II Cor. 9:7a) when he reviews God's material provisions and blessings in his life (II Cor. 8:11-12; I Cor. 16:2). Incidentally, Paul distinguishes between ordinary giving and sacrificial giving (II Cor. 8:11-15). Ordinary giving is from that which is in excess of what we need for ourselves; sacrificial giving is from that which we need for ourselves (cp. the Macedonians, vss. 1-5). God does not command us to give sacrificially (Paul speaks of a principle of equality in vss. 12-15), but He is pleased when we follow His leading to give in this way (Mk. 12:41-44).

- ## What is the recompense of giving?

  A universal spiritual law decrees that a person will reap as he sows (II Cor. 9:6). By this law God gives both inducement and warning. He promises the generous giver that he will reap bountifully now (cp. Phil. 4:10) and in the future (cp. Lk. 12:33). God will not be a debtor to anyone (cp. Prov. 3:9-10; 11:25). He warns that the miserly giver will reap sparingly (cp. Prov. 11:24b). He will suffer material lack as well as spiritual impoverishment.

- **To whom or to what should we give?**

1. The Law Method

Sometimes called "storehouse tithing," this requires people to bring all their tithes and offerings to their local church and the church to determine how these gifts are to be used or distributed. This method is based on God's appeal to Israel when the Jews were neglecting their duty (Mal. 3:7-12; cp. Deut. 14:22-26). While this appeal may offer us a spiritual lesson, it is not binding on us since we are not under the Mosaic Law.

2. The Grace Method

The order we should follow today is given in I Corinthians 16:2. Paul writes, "Upon the first day of the week, let every one of you lay at the side of himself, storing up whatever he may be prospered in, that there be no gatherings when I come." This verse provides several details about giving under grace.

a. The place in which we are to give.

We should keep in mind that the local church building does not have exactly the same function as did the temple in Jerusalem. The temple was the place where God dwelt among His people. There they brought their gifts and offered their sacrifices. God does not dwell in a church building today, for the bodies of His people are His temple (I Cor. 6:19). Moreover, He is present with His people wherever two or three are gathered in Jesus' name (Mt. 18:20).

Rather than depositing gifts in a church, Paul directs the believer to accumulate his gifts "at the side of himself" in a private fund at home. This is to be held in reserve for the Lord until some need arises and direction is given by the Holy Spirit for its use. At the appropriate time and occasion each household is to give from their fund whatever they believe the Lord would have them do. When the collection was being received for the Jerusalem believers (I Cor. 16:1, 3), the united action of believers in support of this program was a church action, yet it allowed each one with an income to give from his private fund as he was persuaded of the Lord.

b. The day on which we are to give.

This is the first day of the week (I Cor. 16:2). While there may have been some practical reason for this, the Lord's day is a fitting time to review His blessings, to worship Him with gratitude, and to lay by in store as He directs. It is also a time we have opportunity to give to needs of the local church and its program.

c. The people and causes to which we should give.

During the first century believers gave to the support of the local church (Gal. 6:6; I Tim. 5:17-18; I Cor. 9:7-14), missions (Phil. 1:3-5; 4:14-18), and needy people (Gal. 6:10; Eph. 4:28). In our giving to these or other needs, we must exercise caution by asking such questions as these: Is there really a need? Will the money be used wisely? Can we assist in a better way, than by giving money? Is the person or work truly Christian? Is the organization doctrinally and financially sound? Does it do what it was established to do? Does it publish regular accounts of its financial receipts and disbursements, or are its records open to public inspection? As we seek God's direction regarding what and where we are to give, we must base our decisions on facts rather than on impulses, feelings, or appeals.

• How should we give?

While man looks on the outward appearance, God looks on the heart. He evaluates people's actions by assessing their motivations. If our giving is to please God, we must be motivated by proper attitudes, such as the following:

1. *Love (II Cor. 8:24, 2)*

This prompts us to give obediently (Jn. 14:21) and sacrificially (I Jn. 3:16-18) as the need requires.

2. *Willingness and eagerness (II Cor. 8:8-12; 9:2)*

3. *Generosity (II Cor. 9:6; 8:2-5)*

4. *Resoluteness (II Cor. 9:7)*

This means that our giving is to be with personal conviction regarding the Lord's will in the matter.

5. *Cheerfulness (II Cor. 9:7)*

We should not mourn over that with which we must part, for God promises to give us something better (Lk. 12:32-33; Heb. 10:24). Also, we are not to give of necessity under the pressure of external coercion. Rather, we are to respond to God's inner restraint of love (II Cor. 8:8, 24). We are to give cheerfully with the joy of the Holy Spirit (II Cor. 8:2; Acts 20:35; Gal. 5:22).

6. *Confidence (II Cor. 9:8)*

This is faith in the sufficiency of God's grace to enable us to abound in every good work. Practical faith activates this grace in our life (Gal. 2:20).

THE PATTERN OF GIVING (II Cor. 8:9)

As the Lord Jesus Christ is our pattern for the Christian life (Jn. 14:6; Mt. 10:24, 25; Gal. 4:19; Eph. 5:1; I Pet. 2:21), so is He the pattern for our giving. When we submit ourself to the Holy Spirit and follow His direction, we allow the Lord to give through us in His characteristic way. What are the qualities of His giving?

• His giving is gracious.

The Lord Jesus was motivated by divine grace. We did not deserve the least benefits of His atoning work.

- **His giving is sacrificial.**

Giving Himself for us, the Lord Jesus gave His all (Mt. 20:28). Laying aside His visible glory, He came to earth, assumed a nature lower than His servants the angels, and became beggarly poor (Lk. 9:58). Furthermore, He gave His life in atonement for our sins.

- **His giving is beneficial.**

We who are saved possess every spiritual blessing in Him (Eph. 1:3). Indeed, we are rich (Rev. 2:9)! With the apostle Paul we say, "Thanks be unto God for His inexpressible Gift" (II Cor. 9:15).

In like manner if our giving is to please God, it too must have these qualities. This means that we must be willing to give to undeserving people, even at personal cost, with a view to benefit them. These qualities of giving manifest Christlikeness.

As stewards of God we should be looking forward to the Day of Christ when the Lord Jesus will escort His church to Heaven. Then we shall experience the redemption of our bodies (Phil. 1:6; Rom. 8:23), be presented faultless before God's presence (Jude 24; I Cor. 1:8), and see what He did with our lives in His program of building the church (Phil. 2:16; II Cor. 1:14). Until this day we should be living suitable lives that glorify God (Phil. 1:10, 11).

APPENDIX O
The Mysteries of the New Testament

These mysteries are "sacred secrets" or divine truths that had not been revealed in previous ages but that have been made known to the Lord's people by New Testament revelation (cp. Eph. 3:1-5, 9; Rom. 16:25). A list of these follows.

THE MYSTERIES OF THE KINGDOM (Mt. 13:11; Mk. 4:11; Lk. 8:10)

Given in parabolic form, these mysteries describe the present course of Jesus' kingdom in this world (Christendom) during His physical absence from earth. In Matthew 13:5-53 these include the kinds of responses to the gospel ("The Sower and the Soils"), the Lord's present policy regarding His enemies ("The Wheat and the Weeds"), the phenomenal growth of Christendom ("The Mustard Seed"), the false teaching, hypocrisy, and bad politics found in Christendom ("The Leaven"), the present status of the elect of Israel ("The Hidden Treasure"), the redemption of true believers ("The Valuable Pearl"), and Christ's judgment of earth dwellers when He sets up His millennial kingdom ("The Dragnet").

THE MYSTERY OF ISRAEL'S BLINDNESS (Rom. 11:25)

Although this judicial blindness or hardening to spiritual truth was a subject of prophecy (Isa. 6:9-10), the mystery concerns its extent ("in part") and its duration ("until the fulness of the Gentiles be come in"). During the present age the deliverance of elect Jews from this blindness by their salvation makes them an exception (Rom. 11:5-6). While "the fulness of the Gentiles" may refer to the opportunity Gentiles now have to receive the Saviour and become a part of the church (Acts 15:14; Rom. 15:8-24), to my mind, it more likely refers to their final opportunity to be saved through the ministry of the 144,000 evangelists during the first part of the Tribulation Period (Mt. 24:14; II Thess. 2:10-12; Rev. ch. 7). In the middle of the Tribulation Period, if not earlier, God will remove this blindness from the elect remnant of Israel and will eventually bring them to repentance and faith in Jesus by the intense persecution waged by the Beast (Rev. 12:3; 13:5-7; cp. Deut. 30:1-3; Joel ch. 2). At that time "all Israel shall be saved," that is, they will be delivered from their enemies as well as from their sins (Rom. 11:26; Zech. 14:3-9; Ezek. 36:25-29). "All Israel" is a figurative expression (synecdoche) for the elect remnant of Israel (Rom. 9:6-13).

THE MYSTERY OF THE GOSPEL (Rom. 16:25; Eph. 6:19; cp. Col. 4:3)

Hidden from times eternal, yet contained in the Old Testament revelation (Rom. 1:1-2; Acts 17:1-3; Lk. 24:25-27; Jn. 5:39), the gospel was not fully expressed or understood until Jesus' earthly ministry (II Tim. 1:8-10), the giving of the New Testament (Jn. 16:12-15; 20:30-31; Mk. 1:1; Lk. 1:1-4), and the teaching ministry of the Holy Spirit (Jn. 14:26; I Cor. 2:9-12; cp. Lk. 24:44-45). Only in the light of this additional revelation and illumination can people fully understand the events and message of the gospel which was anticipated in the Old Testament.

THE MYSTERY OF GOD'S WISDOM (I Cor. 2:7-8)

In this context wisdom is God's special revelation which He has given to His people in the form of the holy Scriptures. While the meaning of this revelation is hidden from the world, it is taught to the Lord's people by the Holy Spirit (I Cor. 2:9-14; I Jn. 2:27; cp. Deut. 29:29).

THE MYSTERY OF THE CHANGED BODY (I Cor. 15:51)

The resurrection of the body was a subject of prophecy (Job 19:23-27; Dan. 12:2). The mystery seems to concern the instantaneous change of the bodies of both dead and living people from corruptibility to incorruptibility, from mortality to immortality (I Cor. 15:52-53).

THE MYSTERY OF GOD'S WILL (Eph. 1:9)

Here God's will appears to be His plan (decree) that relates to the future, as explained in verse 10. This anticipates the reconciliation and union of all things in the heavens and on earth that have been involuntarily affected by sin. Based on the Lord's atoning work (Col. 1:20), this will be achieved during His millennial reign (Acts 3:20-21). In addition to His dealing with His enemies (I Cor. 15:25), this will be His climactic Messianic work with regard to the present universe (cp. Rom. 8:19-22).

THE MYSTERY OF GENTILES AND JEWS BEING MEMBERS OF THE SAME BODY (Eph. 3:3,9)

Speaking of Gentiles and Jews who are saved during this age, this mystery (Eph. 3:1-6) reveals their having equal status and blessing in Christ (Gal. 3:28; Eph. 1:3) as well as their being members of the same body, His church (Eph. 1:22-23). The Old Testament anticipated God's blessings for Gentiles (Gen. 12:3), but not equal status with Jews. Jesus also referred to this (Jn. 10:16). This "fellowship" (Eph. 3:9, meaning "arrangement") of saved Jews and Gentiles in Christ makes known to angelic beings the manifold wisdom of God (vs. 10).

THE MYSTERY OF THE UNION BETWEEN JESUS AND HIS PEOPLE (Col. 1:26-27)

This truth was stated by Jesus (Jn. 14:20; 17:21-23, 26) and was illustrated by Paul (Eph. 5:22-33). This spiritual truth consists of the Lord Jesus' being in His people through the indwelling Holy Spirit (Rom. 8:2, 9) and their being in Him through the Holy Spirit's baptism (Gal. 3:27; Acts 1:5). Because of this union, the bodies of the Lord's people who are on earth are His members through which He works to build His church (I Cor. 6:15; cp. Jn. 15:1-5). This union was not possible before our Lord's incarnation and exaltation.

THE MYSTERY OF GOD AND CHRIST (Col. 2:2-3)

This seems to refer to the relationship between the Father and the Son, especially with reference to Jesus' Messianic role as the Father's servant (lit. slave; Jn. 6:38; 14:9-11, 28). The Old Testament anticipated this role (Isa. 42:1-7; 49:1-7; 52:13-53:12; Ps. 110:1), but it was not understood until the Son's incarnation and the New Testament's revelation (cp. Mt. 22:41-46; Jn. 1:1-3, 14; Phil. 2:5-7). See Jesus' Messianic Work (pp. 190 ff.).

THE MYSTERY OF INIQUITY (II Thess. 2:7)

This speaks of the lawlessness that is widespread throughout the world. Its guiding mind is Satan (Eph. 2:2), and its source is the sin-principle that is active in every person on earth (Rom. 8:7-8). Lawlessness, especially against God, will reach its climax in the worldwide rule of the Beast, Satan's human agent, during the last half of the Tribulation Period (Rev. ch. 13; II Thess. 2:3-10).

THE MYSTERY OF THE FAITH (I Tim. 3:9)

If the phrase "the faith" refers to the body of truth which God has given through Christ by divine revelation (Jude 3), then this mystery refers to the New Testament (cp. Eph. 3:4). Deacons are to be loyal believers in this portion of the Bible and followers of its teachings.

THE MYSTERY OF GODLINESS (I Tim. 3:16)

This mystery seems to refer to that character of life which, though enigmatic to the world, effectively bears witness to the essential elements of Christ's first advent (cp. I Tim. 3:1-15). When filled with the Holy Spirit, the believer's life manifests the reality of the gospel and of all that is associated with it, including the person and work of the Lord Jesus (cp. Rom. 1:16; 13:12-14; II Cor. 2:14-16; Gal. 2:20; 4:19; Phil. 1:21).

THE MYSTERY OF THE SEVEN STARS AND LAMPSTANDS (Rev. 1:20)

This concerns the Lord's relation to the seven churches of the Roman province of Asia and their messengers ("angels"), to whom the messages are addressed. The context indicates that the Lord Jesus is present with His people (Mt. 18:20), appraising their actions, and that He supplies them suitable leaders and instructors (Eph. 4:11-16; I Pet. 5:1-4; Heb. 13:17). The Old Testament anticipated Christ's return to earth and rule (Deut. 30:3; Zech. 14:3-4; Isa. 40:10), but it did not foresee His being with His people now (Mt. 28:20) to minister and to lead them (Eph. 4:20-21), although as a man He is seated in Heaven at the Father's right hand (Heb. 1:3).

THE MYSTERY OF GOD (Rev. 10:7)

This seems to refer to the remainder of God's program for the last half of the Tribulation Period and the establishment of the millennial kingdom (Rev. chs. 12-19; cp. 11:15-18). Without further delay in the progress of these events (10:6), the seventh trumpet will introduce the third woe, which represents Satan's activities on earth during this period (11:15-13:18). This period will end with Christ's return to earth, His triumph over His enemies, and the establishment of His earthly rule (Rev. 19:11-20:6).

THE MYSTERY OF BABYLON (Rev. 17:5)

Under Satan ancient Babylon conceived and fostered false doctrine, idolatry, and abominable ritual (Gen. 11:1-9). I believe that the city will be rebuilt to be the world center of religion, administration, and commerce during the Beast's three and a half years of rule over the earth (Rev. chs. 17-18). The mystery appears to be the association and perpetuation of all false religion with this city until its final destruction.

We who are saved are stewards of these mysteries (I Cor. 4:1). It seems to be our duty to seek to understand them and to respond to them suitably (cp. Mt. 13:51-52).

APPENDIX P
Baptist Distinctives

While historically Baptists have been both Arminian (General) and Calvinistic (Particular) in their doctrinal persuasion, they have agreed on certain propositions which have made them distinctive from other denominations. Some of these are gleaned from Edward T. Hiscox, *The New Directory for Baptist Churches.*[1]

THE ABSOLUTE AUTHORITY OF THE BIBLE IN FAITH AND CONDUCT

"The Bible is a Divine Revelation given of God to men, and is a complete and infallible guide and standard of authority in all matters of religion and morals; what it teaches is to be believed; whatever it commands is to be obeyed; whatever it commends is to be accepted as both right and useful; whatever it condemns is to be avoided as both wrong and harmful; but what it neither commands nor teaches is not to be imposed on the conscience as of religious obligation."[2]

THE LOCAL CHURCH, CONSISTING OF SAVED, IMMERSED MEMBERS

"Baptists assert that the only proper subjects for baptism are regenerated persons; those who have exercised and professed a saving faith in Christ, and are living orderly Christian lives."[3]

"What class of persons should be admitted as members of the fellowship of Christian churches? Baptists say that godly persons, baptized on a profession of faith, are the only proper and suitable persons. That all others should be denied admission, and if already within the Church should be cast out. Consequently, to receive unconverted persons, whether infants or adults, destroys the spiritual character of the body, and forms an unholy alliance with the world, instead of maintaining a broad and distinctive separation between them."[4]

---

[1] Philadelphia: The Judson Press, 1944, ch. 1. Used by permission of Judson Press. This is now published by Kregel Publications under the title, *Principles and Practices of Baptist Churches.*
[2] Ibid. 11.
[3] Ibid. 16.
[4] Ibid. 17.

SEPARATION BETWEEN CHURCH AND STATE

"Civil governments, rulers, and magistrates are to be respected, and in all temporal matters, not contrary to conscience and the Word of God, to be obeyed; but they have no jurisdiction in spiritual concerns, and have no right of dictation to, of control over, or of interference with, matters of religion; but are bound to protect all good citizens in the peaceable enjoyment of their religious rights and privileges."[5]

"No organic union of Church or State should be tolerated, but entire separation maintained: the Church should neither ask for, nor accept of, support from civil authority, since to do so would imply the right of civil dictation and control. The support of religion belongs to those who profess it."[6]

THE AUTONOMY OF THE LOCAL CHURCH

"Baptists assert that each particular local Church is self- governing, and independent of all other churches, and of all persons and bodies of men whatever, as to the administration of its own affairs; that it is of right, and should be, free from any other human authority, whether civil or ecclesiastical, and that this is the New Testament idea of church government."[7]

THE LIBERTY OF CONSCIENCE (Soul Liberty)

"Every man by nature possesses the right of private judgment in the interpretation of the Scriptures, and in all religious concerns; it is his privilege to read and explain the Bible for himself, without direction from or dependence on, any one, being responsible to God alone for his use of the sacred truth."[8]

"Every man has the right to hold such religious opinions as he believes the Bible teaches, without harm or hindrance from any one on that account, so long as he does not intrude upon, or interfere with the rights of others by so doing."[9]

"All men have the right, not only to believe, but also to profess and openly declare, whatever religious opinions they may entertain, providing they be not contrary to common morality, and do no injustice to others."[10]

"All men possess the common right to worship God according to the teachings of the Scriptures, as they understand them, without hindrance or molestation, so long as they do not injure or interfere with the rights of others by so doing."[11]

Other distinctives that are often given are the two officers of the local church — pastors and deacons; the two ordinances — Water Baptism and the Lord's Supper; and the priesthood of all believers, which asserts the ability and right of all believers to worship God without the help of any inter-

---

[5] Ibid. 12.   [6] Ibid. 12 f.   [7] Ibid. 17 f.   [8] Ibid. 11 f.   [9] Ibid. 12.   [10] Ibid. 12.   [11] Ibid. 12.

Mediary, except the Lord Jesus Christ (I Tim. 2:5).[12]

APPENDIX Q
Passivity and Demon Possession

Using the word possession to means "a hold of evil spirits on a man in any shade of degree." Mrs. Penn-Lewis and Evan Roberts write:

"Christians are as open to possession by evil spirits as other men, and become possessed because they have in most cases, unwittingly fulfilled the conditions upon which evil spirits work, and, apart from the cause of willful sin, given ground to deceiving spirits, through (1) accepting their counterfeits of the Divine workings, and (2) cultivating passivity, and non-use of the faculties; and this through misconception of the spiritual laws which govern the Christian life.

"The primary cause of deception and possession in surrendered believers may be condensed in one word, *passivity*, that is, a cessation of the active exercise of the will in control over spirit, body, and soul, or either, as the case may be. It is, practically, a counterfeit of 'surrender to God.' The believer who 'surrenders' his 'members' — or faculties — to God, and ceases to use them himself, thereby falls into 'passivity' which enables evil spirits to deceive, and possess any part of his being which has become passive.

"The deception over passive surrender may be exampled thus: a believer surrenders his 'arm' to God. He permits it to hang passive, waiting for 'God to use it.' He is asked, 'Why do you not use your arm?' And he replies, 'I have surrendered it to God. I must not use it now; God must use it.' But will God lift the arm for man? Nay, a man himself must lift it (Mk. 3:5), and use it, seeking to understand intelligently God's mind in doing so.

"The word 'passivity' simply describes the opposite condition of activity; and in the experience of the believer it means, briefly, (1) loss of self-control — in the sense of the person himself controlling each, or all of the departments of his personal being; and (2) loss of free-will — in the sense of the person himself exercising his will as the guiding principle of personal control, in harmony with the will of God.

"All the danger of 'passivity' in the surrendered believer lies in the advantage taken of the passive condition by the powers of darkness...(Passivity is) in exact opposition to the condition which God requires from His children for His working in them. Granted the

---

[12] See Paul R. Jackson, *The Doctrine and Administration of the Local Church* (Des Plaines, Ill.: Regular Baptist Press, 1968), Ch. XVII.

surrender of the will to God, with active choice to do His will as it may be revealed to them, God requires cooperation with His Spirit, and the full use of every faculty of the whole man. In brief, the powers of darkness aim at obtaining a passive slave or captive to their will; whilst God desires a regenerated man, intelligently and actively willing, and choosing, and doing His will in liberation of spirit, soul, and body from slavery.

"The powers of darkness would make a man a machine, a tool, an automation; the God of holiness and love desires to make him a free, intelligent sovereign in his own sphere — a thinking, rational, renewed creation created after His own image (Eph. 4:24). Therefore, God never says to any faculty of man, 'Be thou idle.' "

*   *   *   *   *

"Passivity must not be confused with quietness, or 'the meek and quiet spirit,' which, in the sight of God, is of great price. Quietness of spirit, of heart, of mind, of manner of voice and expression, may be coexistent with the most effective activity in the will of God (I Thess. 4:11)."[1]

APPENDIX R
The Kingdom of God

Ordinarily, a kingdom must have a government, territory, and people who are subject to a king. In the Scriptures the concept of God's kingdom has various meanings, determined by its use in a passage and its context.

IN THE OLD TESTAMENT

1. *God's universal kingdom,* which embraces all persons and things (Ps. 103:19; cp. II Chron. 20:6)

2. The *predicted millennial kingdom* of the Lord Jesus Christ (Dan. 2:44; Ps. 2:6-9). This will be earthly, visible, geographical, and political.

IN THE NEW TESTAMENT

1. The *millennial, earthly kingdom of prophecy* (Mt. 3:2; Rev. 11:15)
   This is Jesus' worldwide, Messianic kingdom, over which He will rule a thousand years.

2. *Christendom* (Mt. ch. 13)
   This is that which represents Christ in the world today during His absence from earth. This includes both true and professing Christians.

---

[1] Mrs. Penn-Lewis and Evan Roberts, *War on the Saints* (Leicester: The "Overcomer" Book Room, Cartref, 1922), pp. 69 ff.

3. *Christ's true kingdom today (Col. 1:13)*

Being invisible, nonpolitical, this kingdom includes all people who are saved. This is entered by the new birth (Jn. 3:3-7; cp. Mk. 12:34).

4. *Christ's physical presence (Lk. 17:21)*

Jesus' words (vss. 20-21) may mean that the millennial kingdom of prophecy was not to come at that time, with the manifestations and in the manner that the unspiritual Jews expected. It was already among them in the presence and power of the King (cp. Lk. 10:9; 11:20). "Within" can also be read "among."

5. *Heaven (II Tim. 4:18; cp. Phil. 3:20)*

6. *The eternal state of the saved (I Cor. 15:50)*

Paul declares that our bodies, animated by the soul (with blood), cannot now enter the eternal state without being changed (vss. 51-53).

7. *The Jews of Jesus' day with their corrupted Judaism (Lk. 13:18-21)*

8. *God's future universal kingdom (I Cor. 15:24-28)*

When Jesus has achieved the objectives of His millennial rule, then His kingdom will merge with that of the Father, and they will jointly rule forever.

APPENDIX S
The Inerrancy and Infallibility of the Scriptures

While the adjectives *infallible* and *inerrant* are often used synonymously, there is a difference in their meanings. *Infallible* emphasizes the incapacity for making mistakes or errors, as in the revelation of spiritual truth or the definition of doctrine, while *inerrant* emphasizes the absence of errors. With reference to the Scriptures, *inerrancy* is that quality which describes them as being without error in their recording of facts. This asserts that the Bible is accurate, not only in the recording of facts but also in the inspired utterances and writings of God's agents — the holy prophets, the Lord Jesus, His apostles, and their associates. *Infallibility* is that quality which describes the Scriptures as being without error in their intrinsic teachings (that is, in what they teach, not in what we think they teach). This asserts that the teachings of the Bible are true and reliable for faith and conduct.

With these definitions in view, consider the following observations about their application to the Scriptures:

First, inerrancy can be asserted only of the original writings or autographs. It is recognized, as we shall see, that errors have entered the text in its transmission by reproduction and translation. However, in so far as the present editions of the Bible represent the original writings, they are the inspired Word of God and are infallible and authoritative in their teachings and commands.

Second, whereas inerrancy always relates to the Bible's recording of facts (utterances, events, people, etc.), it does not always relate to the things that are inerrantly recorded, like Satan's lie (Gen. 3:4) and the opinions of Job's friends (Job 22:5-11; 42:7). Satan's lie was errant, for it was deceptive, and the accusations of Job's friends were unfounded and untrue. Yet, God was pleased to have these errant statements inerrantly recorded in His Word, for the one has an important place in the history of man's fall and bears witness to the devil's character, and the other shows the fallibility of unaided human judgment. Because of the inerrancy of the recording of these errant statements, they convey to us profitable, infallible truth about Satan and man (cp. Rom. 15:4; I Cor. 10:11). On the other hand, both the recording and the content of the inspired utterances of God's agents are inerrant and infallible (cp. Jesus' teachings, Jn. 3:32-34; John's witness, 21:24; contra Nathan's uninspired remark, II Sam. 7:3).

Third, the infallibility of the Scriptures in their teachings rests upon the inerrancy of their record of utterances, events, and facts of sacred history. The accuracy of this record is paramount if the divine purpose of conveying truth to the reader is served. If the record were in error, then the teachings based on this errant record would be fallible.

Fourth, both inerrancy and infallibility are rooted in the divine inspiration of the Scriptures (II Tim. 3:16; II Pet. 1:21). This is that special work of God the Holy Spirit whereby He acted upon fallible men in such a way that He secured by them God's very Word in human language. He enabled these men to receive the divine revelation and to convey it orally or to record it verbally, without error or omission, as the very Word of God.

Still the question remains, Does the Bible teach its inerrancy? It does. If God, who cannot lie (Tit. 1:2) and is true (Jn. 7:28; 8:26), produced the Scriptures (II Tim. 3:16), then they must be true. Moreover, the Lord Jesus, who is the truth (Jn. 14:6), and is true (Rev. 19:11), bore witness to the truth (Jn. 3:32-34) and spoke the truth (8:40). He Himself appealed to the Scriptures (Mt. 4:1-11; Lk. 20:37-38; Jn. 5:45-47), submitted Himself to their authority (Lk. 4:18-19; 18:31; Mt. 5:17), and declared that they are truth (Jn. 17:17) and cannot be broken (10:35). Finally, the Holy Spirit, the divine agent who produced the Scriptures, is the Spirit of truth (Jn. 14:17) and is no lie (I Jn. 2:27). To assert that the Scriptures are not inerrant and infallible is to speak against God, who has declared His Word to be true (Ps. 119:160) and pure (Ps. 12:6; Prov. 30:5).

If inerrancy is a quality that belongs to the original writings, then what errors are found in present editions of the Scriptures? There are real and apparent errors. Among the real errors there are scribal errors, which entered the text, either mistakenly or intentionally, when it was copied. However, because of the vast manuscript witness to the New Testament, most of these errors are known. A hundred years ago Wescott and Hort declared that only a thousandth part of the New Testament was still in question (The New Testament in Greek, p. 565). The Dead Sea scrolls bear witness to the remarkable accuracy of the Hebrew Masoretic text of the Old Testament. Other real errors, found in present editions of the Bible, include translation errors (KJV, S. of Sol. 2:7; 3:5; 8:4, "he" for "she"), interpretation errors (KJV, Acts 2:38, "for" for "because of," cp. Mt. 12:41), printers' errors (KJV, Mt. 23:24, "at" for "out"), and recited errors, which God incorporated in His Word for our learning (Gen. 3:4; II Kings 5:22).

Apparent errors are not real errors, but difficulties which rise from our lack of knowledge. Scholars who hold the inerrancy of the Scriptures have adequately resolved these difficulties and have shown that they are not actual contradictions or mistakes. These difficulties occur in the areas of chronology, numbers, historical statements, grammar and style, parallel passages, Old Testament quotations found in the New Testament, and conflicts with current scientific opinion. The fact remains that these difficulties are not proven errors.

Generations of believers have unhesitatingly accepted reliable editions of the Scriptures to be God's Word and have experienced the benefits of this acceptance without any knowledge of textual criticism. Our faith does not rest upon the proof of the inerrancy of the Scriptures. Rather, the doctrine of inerrancy rests upon one's faith in the Bible's claim to its divine inspiration and to its being the very Word of God. "Let God be true, but every man a liar" (Rom. 3:4)!

APPENDIX T
Classes of Books Relating to the Biblical Period

The following lists are classifications of both canonical and noncanonical literature relating to the Old and New Testament periods.

OLD TESTAMENT PERIOD

THE CANONICAL BOOKS

- **The Undisputed Canonical Books (homologoumena)**

These are the Old Testament books which not only were received as being canonical without dispute from the first but their place in the canon was never later challenged by the Jews or the church. This group consists of all the books of the Old Testament Canon save those of the next group, which immediately follows.

- **The Disputed Canonical Books (antilegomena)**

At first these books were recognized as being canonical, but later they were challenged by certain rabbis at Jamnia (c. A.D. 90). The outcome of their debates was their firm acknowledgment of the canonicity of these books. These disputed canonical books follow:

1. *Esther*, which does not have the name of God. The book shows God's providential care and sovereignty.

2. *Ecclesiastes*, which seems to oppose orthodox teaching (3:19-20). But the context shows that Solomon is speaking about death and the return of the bodies of humans and animals to dust. He does distinguish between the directions which the spirit of man and that of animals take upon death (vs. 21).

3. *Proverbs*, which has an apparent contradiction (26:4-5). Ordinarily, it is better to ignore a fool, but occasionally he needs a suitable reply to remind him that he is a fool.

4. *The Song of Solomon*, for its erotic passages (chs. 4 and 7). This song of human married love portrays the spiritual relationship which the Lord has with His people.

5. *Ezekiel*, which seems to differ from the ritualistic laws of the Pentateuch (chs. 40-48). These chapters appear to describe the temple and its ritual that will exist during our Lord's millennial rule.

THE NONCANONICAL BOOKS

These were religious compositions, written between 300 B.C. and A.D. 100, which generally were circulated under false titles or unsubstantiated claims of authorship. Never recognized as being divinely inspired or authoritative, this literature was apparently written by pious Jews (all of whom but one are unknown) about persons and events relating to the Old Testament and intertestament periods. Their objectives appear to be filling in the gaps of Jewish history, strengthening the Jewish mind against the influence of paganism, and extolling the dignity and glory of Israel. The value of this literature follows: Historically it provides information about the intertestament period. Religiously, it sheds light on the spiritual, philosophical, and intellectual life of Judaism during this period, especially with reference to the person and work of the Messiah, life beyond death, and the reality and activity of angels and demons.

• The Apocrypha ("hidden")

Early Christians included fifteen noncanonical books in their Greek and Latin translations of the Old Testament. At the Council of Trent (1546), the Roman Catholic Church declared these writings to be canonical, excepting I Esdras (III Esdras in the Latin Vulgate), II Esdras (IV Esdras in the Latin Vulgate), and the Prayer of Manasseh. These fifteen books are I Esdras, II Esdras, Tobit, Judith, The Additions to the Book of Esther, The Wisdom of Solomon, Ecclesiasticus (The Wisdom of Jesus the Son of Sirach), Baruch, The Letter of Jeremiah, The Prayer of Azariah and the Song of the Three Young Men, Susanna, Bel and the Dragon, the Prayer of Manasseh, I Maccabees, and II Maccabees.

- **The False Writings (pseudepigrapha)**
  This group consists of the rest of the noncanonical literature of this period that was circulated under false titles. It includes *The Book of Jubilees, The Letter of Aristeas, The Book of Adam and Eve, The Martyrdom of Isaiah, The Book of Enoch, The Testaments of the Twelve Patriarchs, The Sibylline Oracles, The Assumption of Moses, The Book of the Secrets of Enoch, Baruch, Ezra, The Psalms of Solomon, IV Maccabees, Pirke Aboth,* and *The Story of Ahikar.*

NEW TESTAMENT PERIOD

THE CANONICAL BOOKS

- **The Undisputed Canonical Books (homologoumena)**
  These are the New Testament books which were universally received as being canonical from the first. These include the Four Gospels, Acts, Paul's Epistles, I Peter, and I John.

- **The Disputed Canonical Books (antilegomena)**
  These were not at first universally received as being canonical.

  1. *Hebrews,* questioned in the West on the point of authorship.

  2. *James,* considered to be in conflict with Paul on the doctrine of justification (2:14-26; cp. Gal. 2:16; Eph. 2:8-9). James does not deny justification by faith, but he emphasizes that true faith is manifest by good works.

  3. *II Peter,* questioned because of difference in vocabulary and style from I Peter. Peter may have used a different secretary (cp. I Pet. 5:12) or wrote himself. Also, II Peter contains different subject matter.

  4. *II and III John,* questioned on the ground of authorship.

  5. *Jude,* questioned because of the possibility of his referring to the pseudepigraphical *Book of Enoch* (1:9; 5:4) in Jude 14-15. Even if true, Jude does not endorse the book any more than Paul does the writings of Epimenides (Tit. 1:12) and Menander (I Cor. 15:33).

  6. *Revelation,* questioned on the point of authorship.

  In the West the canonicity of the twenty-seven books of the New Testament was recognized by the Synods of Hippo (393) and of Carthage (397). The canon was recognized in the East by the close of the fifth century.

THE NONCANONICAL BOOKS

- **The Writings of the Apostolic Fathers**
  These were noncanonical writings, produced by Christian men who were the immediate successors of the apostles. Their writings did not have false

titles and content like the New Testament Apocrypha, but they lacked apostolic authority, for they were not divinely inspired. Written during A.D. 80-180, these books were intended for the edification of other believers. For a time some churches regarded some of these to be canonical, but later they changed their view.

These writings include Clement (Bishop of Rome), *The Epistle to the Corinthians;* Ignatius (Bishop of Antioch), *The Epistle to the Ephesians, The Epistle to the Magnesians, The Epistle to the Trallians, The Epistle to the Romans, The Epistle to the Philadelphians, The Epistle to the Smyrnaeans;* Polycarp (Bishop of Smyrna), *The Epistle to the Philippians; The Teaching of the Apostles* (author unknown); Barnabas (of Alexandria?), *The Epistle of Barnabas;* and Hermas, *The Shepherd.*

- **The False Writings (pseudepigrapha)**

Sometimes called the New Testament Apocrypha, these were fictitious writings, circulated under false titles of New Testament persons. Taking the canonical books as their models, they are absurd and impious. Writing during A.D. 100-800, their authors, presumably Christians, are unknown.

Some of these writings are *The Protevangelism of James, The Gospel of Thomas, The Gospel of Peter, The Gospel of Philip, The Acts of John, The Acts of Peter, The Acts of Paul, The Acts of Andrew, The Acts of Thomas, The Epistle to the Laodiceans, The Epistle of the Apostles, The Apocalypse of Peter, The Apocalypse of Paul,* and *The Apocalypse of Thomas.*

The value of these noncanonical books is that they reflect the belief of their authors and the tastes of their readers. They also set forth certain ideals of the Christian life and concepts of the Christian faith which were widespread during the second century and thereafter.

Appendix U
Our Inward Desires

The Scriptures indicate that there are at least two kinds of desires (often "lusts" in KJV) that we who are saved inwardly experience. These are demand desires and need desires.

THE DEMAND DESIRES

These are desires that are expressed by those resident principles that would dominate our life. These principles are God and evil.

- **The Desires of God for Us (Jas. 4:5)**

If "spirit" here refers to the indwelling Holy Spirit, then He desires to the point of envy. Other passages indicate that God desires to dominate our life and use us as an instrument of righteousness (cp. Rom. 6:11-22). He also desires to suppress the sin-principle within us and give us victory over its demands (Gal. 5:16-17). His desires for us are outwardly expressed by His revealed will, given in the Scriptures (cp. Rom. ch. 12). Inwardly, they are impressed upon our heart by the Holy Spirit (Phil. 2:13).

- **The Desires of Evil for Us**

  Our spiritual enemies desire to dominate us and use us for their evil expressions. These enemies are the sin-principle (Rom. 6:12; Gal. 5:16-21; Jas. 1:14-15), Satan (I Thess. 3:5), and the world (I Jn. 2:16-17). See Romans 7:8; 13:14; Galatians 5:24; Ephesians 2:3; 4:27; Titus 2:12; II Peter 2:18-19.

  Observe that "flesh" in these passages means the sin-principle dominating us and our human nature. Unsaved people are completely dominated by the sin-principle (Eph. 2:3; 4:22; Tit. 3:3; II Pet. 3:3; Rom. 1:24). In principle the believer has been delivered from this bondage that he might give himself over to God's command (Rom. 6:2, 6-7, 11-19; I Pet. 2:11, 21).

  Also observe that I John 2:16 speaks about "all that is in the world" — that system consisting of the total society, culture, and philosophy of unsaved mankind, which is headed by Satan (Jn. 16:11) and the works of which are evil (7:7)—as being "the lust of the flesh, and the lust of the eyes, and the pride of life." This may mean that the world solicits us to satisfy our physical and aesthetic desires in unholy ways. "The pride of life" ("life" means "goods," 3:17) may be the world's soliciting us to acquire and regard material possessions and personal achievements as it does and to exalt their importance and value above God (cp. Lk. 12:15, 34).

THE NEED DESIRES

These are desires that arise from the needs of our human nature and spiritual life. For believers these desires are not sinful, for our inner human nature has been renewed (Col. 3:9-10; Tit. 3:5; I Pet. 1:22; Acts 15:9) and our body, though mortal, is no longer the proper tool of sin (Rom. 6:6-7). However, to avoid sinning, we must seek to satisfy these need desires in God's time and way (cp. Mt. 4:1-10). Because unsaved people are wholly affected by sin, their need desires are corrupted and are inclined toward sin (cp. Mk. 7:21-23).

- **The Need Desires of Our Human Nature**

  These desires relate to the needs of our body, soul, and spirit. Eve's desires for food, aesthetic satisfaction, and wisdom were not sinful (Gen. 3:6). Rising from her unfallen human nature, they were wholesome and natural. In addition to these, we also experience the need for self-preservation, companionship, love, sexual satisfaction, self-determination, and self-expression displayed in communication and the exercise of our abilities. Contrary to unbiblical, pagan concepts, these desires of our saved human nature are not in themselves sinful. However, we are not always able to satisfy these desires in the will of God. When this is so, we can compensate for these needs by drawing upon His sufficient grace (II Cor. 12:7-10).

- **The Need Desires of Our Spiritual Life**
  These desires include longings for spiritual knowledge, righteousness, fellowship with God and with His people, the exercise of spiritual gifts, victory over our spiritual enemies, obedience to God, and the salvation of the lost (Mt. 5:6; Rom. 1:11; 10:1; Phil. 1:23; 2:13; I Thess. 2:17). We can daily satisfy these desires by looking to Jesus, meditating on the Scriptures, and by faith allowing the Holy Spirit to minister to these needs (Jn. 7:37-39; 6:35, 63; Ps. 1:1-3; 37:4). Whatever our needs may be, we can learn to be content in every experience of life through the Lord Jesus (Phil. 4:10-13).

Appendix V
The Human Body-Grid

Our makeup as human beings consists of personhood (self) plus our human nature (body, soul, and spirit; cp. Job 7:11). Our personhood brings to our human nature self-awareness, individuality, morality, and perpetuity. Without personhood we would be only human animals rather than human persons. On the other hand, our human nature makes us to be human beings and provides for us the capacity and mechanism for personal expression and impression, or perception.

In addition to presently animating the body, the soul and spirit give us the inner capacity for intellect (with its rational thinking, understanding, and memory), emotion, and will (with its ability to make decisions and choices). The soul and spirit of saved people appear to be the same in quantity and quality for everyone. These parts of our human nature are saved, that is, delivered from original sin and renewed for spiritual functions (I Pet. 1:22; Rom. 8:10; II Tim. 2:22). Because of this, we can express holy emotions, think right thoughts, understand spiritual truth, make right moral decisions, and submit ourselves to God and His will.

Personality differences are caused by the body, which provides the mechanism that allows these inner soul/spirit capacities to function in human experience. This mechanism itself is affected by certain internal and external factors, which restrict or enhance the body's ability to express the functions of the soul and spirit in human experience. Some of the factors that alter the body-grid appear to be the body's genetic code, environmental conditions and external input, physical development, and physical disabilities, all of which differ with each person. For instance, if one is mentally retarded or his brain is damaged, then this may restrict his ability to understand or to make decisions. By contrast, medication may help the body to function better. Thus I see the body as a grid that directly acts upon and affects the functions of the soul/spirit in human expression and impression. The body affects the functions of soul/spirit adversely when it is ill. It can also affect the functions of soul/spirit by relaying to it partial or distorted information.

Because he has a human nature, a person has the potential of experiencing human actions, thoughts, emotions, feelings, attitudes, understanding, decisions, evaluation, and the like. The quantitative and qualitative extents of these human experiences are determined by the body-grid. Furthermore, the moral character of these activities is determined by the principle-input, whether God or sin, that energizes these activities for good or bad (Rom. ch. 6). If he acts in the energy of God, the believer does holy human things. If he acts in the energy of sin, he does sinful human things. It is impossible to act consciously apart from one of these forces. Believers act in sin's energy whenever they give themselves to it or fail to yield themselves to the Holy Spirit and to act in His power.

Thus the body provides the mechanism that allows a person to exercise his soul/spirit capacities of emotion, intellect, and will in expressing himself and in receiving communication. For example, when a person sings a song, it is his personhood that does it. He sings with his soul and spirit. These provide the capacity for him to sing with emotion, understanding, and will. He sings by means of the mechanism of his body and in the manner which it allows. His body determines the quality of his voice, indeed, whether he can sing at all. His yielding to God or sin will determine the moral character of his singing, whether it will glorify God or it will be sinful.

The reverse of this process takes place in human impression, or perception. When a person hears a sermon, for instance, his body-grid which provides the mechanism of perception in hearing, sight, and understanding will effect the reception of the message. His soul and spirit which provide the capacity for intellectual, emotional, and volitional responses will deal with the data that is relayed by the body-grid. This data, imbued with understanding and emotion, in turn, will be relayed to and impressed upon his personhood. If he is yielded to God and his body is functioning normally, he will understand the truth that God has for him in the message and will make a favorable response in obedience and praise. If he is yielded to sin, then his response will be negative. If his body-grid is defective in its sensory organs or mentality, then the communicated data will be distorted and his perception will be faulty. If the body-mechanism is seriously affected, he may not comprehend the message at all.

With this in view, it can be seen that the body-grid directly affects one's transmitted expressions and received impressions. Because of this, no two people understand things entirely alike. This accounts for the variety of human personalities and opinions that we have in this world.

But what about the next world? Upon death the believer's personhood, together with his soul and spirit, leaves his body and goes to Heaven (II Cor. 5:8; Phil. 1:23). Because he requires soul/spirit for the capacity of intellect, emotion, and will, his personhood perpetuates these immaterial parts of human nature and uses them after death. Moreover, because he needs a body-mechanism that will allow him to receive impressions and to transmit expressions, a person upon death is "plugged" into an intermediate body until the resurrection of his own body (see Lk. 16:22-30; Rev. 6:9-11, "souls" is a synecdoche for people; 14:1-5). Without a body, people would have no means of receiving external stimuli or communication and of transmitting their thoughts, emotions, and decisions.

Upon the resurrection of their own bodies, believers will be permanently "plugged" into their renewed body-grid (I Cor. 15:35-53), which will be animated by the Holy Spirit (Rom. 8:11). The resurrection bodies of saved people will be like Christ's glorified body (Phil. 3:20-21; I Jn. 3:2; I Cor. 13:12; 15:49). This will give them the Lord's body-grid, which will enable them to experience forever unimpeded expressions and impressions of Christlikeness in their thinking, emotions, and will.

With Jesus' kind of body-grid, all the redeemed will be the same in their thinking, feelings, and decisions. While this sameness would be intolerable in our present world, it will be perfect for the eternal state. Having the one divine nature and representing the quintessence of perfection, the Members of the Godhead have been the same in their will, emotions, thoughts, qualities, and powers from all eternity. Thus there will be perfect harmony among the Lord's people forever as there is among the Members of the divine Trinity. With the renewal of our bodies and our having Jesus' kind of body-grid, we shall then fully experience all that eternal life is (Tit. 1:2). This experience will be like hearing the Philadelphia orchestra live in the Academy of Music rather than from a recording through a three-inch speaker. (See chart on next page.)

HUMAN EXPRESSION

(direction: from within to without, with reference to the believer)

Personhood→	Soul & Spirit→	Body-Grid→	Potential Human Expressions qualified by grid.	Principle	Personality Expressions
giving to human nature…	(same in all people)	(differing with each person)		influence or energy, consisting of…	
1. Self-awareness	**giving capacity for…**	consisting of…	1. Actions	1. Holy Spirit→	Righteous human expressions
2. Individuality	1. Emotion	1. Genetic code	2. Thoughts	2. Sin-force→	Sinful human expressions
3. Perpetuity	2. Will	2. Development	3. Reasoning		
4. Morality for evaluation decision conscience	3. Intellect: understanding memory conscience	3. Disabilities	4. Emotions	This acts upon personhood and human nature.	
	giving…	4. Results of external stimuli and conditioning.	5. Attitudes		
	4. Physical life		6. Communication		
			7. Understanding		
			8. Evaluation		
			9. Decisions		

HUMAN IMPRESSION

(direction: from without to within, with reference to the believer)

Outside Stimuli→	Body-Grid→	Soul & Spirit→	Principle→	Personhood
			influence or energy	
1. Environment	1. Senses	1. Emotion	1. Holy Spirit→	Holy human impression
2. People	2. Genetic code	2. Will	2. Sin-force→	Evil human impression
3. Pictures	3. Development	3. Intellect: understanding memory conscience		
4. Literature	4. Disabilities			
5. Odors	5. Conditioning			
6. Physical needs				
7. Experiences				
8. Evil influences				
9. Holy influences				

NOTE

Man's makeup consists of Personhood (I, me) plus Human Nature (body, soul, and spirit). We transmit expressions and receive impressions with the capacity provided by soul and spirit and by means of the mechanism of the body. While the capacity of soul and spirit is the same in all people, the body-grid causes the personality variations which we now experience. When the Lord Jesus makes our body-grid like His, then we shall be like Him, experiencing complete Christlikeness.

ADDENDA

Common Grace
This is that general influence of the Holy Spirit on the world which allows the unsaved, in spite of their depravity, to experience the features of their personhood in daily life, such as morality, virtue, and religious interest as well as to seek civil order. However, this grace does not affect or issue in their salvation. Apparently, this grace as well as the Holy Spirit's restraint upon evil will be removed from the lost during the latter part of the Tribulation Period (Mt. 24:12; II Thess. 2:7; Rev. 9:20, 21).

The Times of the Gentiles
This appears to refer to that time, perhaps from the days of Nebuchadnezzar (Dan. ch. 2), when the Gentiles have the preeminent place in God's program. This will reach its climax in the world rule of the Beast during tribulation days when he tramples Jerusalem under foot for three and a half years (Rev. 11:2). After this, God will restore repentant Israel to her proper place as the head of the nations (Acts 15:14-17; see Appendix K).

Jesus' Commission to Israel
During His first advent this commission was His presenting Himself to Israel for their acceptance — that He might restore them to a right relation with God — or for their rejection — that He might be crucified (Isa. 49:5, 7; 50:5, 6; 52:13-53:12; 61:1, 2a). He fulfilled this commission, not by proclamation, which would be a witness to Himself (Jn. 5:31), but by words and works which were the Father's witness to Him (vs. 32, 36, 39) and that were predicted in the Old Testament as credentials of His Messiahship. This presentation attracted those people who knew the Scriptures to exercise faith in Him (cp. Jn. 5:36, 39; 10:23-28; see Mt. 1:21; Lk. 1:76, 77; 2:25-32; Jn. 1:29-31; Acts 2:22-32; 3:25, 26; 4:25-28; 13:26-41; 26:22, 23). During the present age and the first half of the Tribulation Period, He is a light unto the Gentiles through gospel preaching (Isa. 49:6; Lk. 2:25-32; Mt. 24:14; Jn. 8:12; 10:16).

Christian Forgiveness
In the Bible we find two kinds of forgiveness, divine forgiveness and Christian forgiveness. These kinds of forgiveness have a feature which is unalike and one which is alike. The unalike feature is the nature of these two forgivenesses. Divine forgiveness, whether judicial or parental, consists in the cancellation of the debt, or penalty, of sin (Col. 2:13; I Jn. 1:9; cp. Mt. 18:27, 32). The gospel believer is not required to pay to God the debt of his sins. In Christian forgiveness the offended one is not to release the offender from his obligation, that is, he is not to regard the matter to be settled before the offender has fulfilled his duty for his offense (see below). This fulfillment of duty is the condition of Christian forgiveness (Lk. 17:3). The alike feature of divine forgiveness and Christian forgiveness is that both require the fulfillment of certain conditions if one is to receive them. It is to this second

feature that we address ourselves.

How is the believer to respond to offenses that are committed against him? In the same manner God does (Eph. 4:32). But keep in mind that God does not ignore the offenses (sins) of His accountable personal creatures. Sin incurs a penalty that must be paid. God's forgiveness of sinners rests upon two conditions: one, the payment of sin's debt by Jesus' atoning work (I Cor. 15:3; I Jn. 4:10); and two, the sinner's exercise of repentance and faith in Jesus and His atoning work (Acts 20:21). Also the believer must exercise repentance and confession to receive God's parental forgiveness (Rev. 2:5; I Jn. 1:9). If the sinning person does not meet the conditions for divine forgiveness, he is not forgiven. God does not ignore the sins of people who fail to deal with them. Their sins block His relationship with them.

In like manner, we cannot forgive others of their offenses against us until they have fulfilled the conditions of forgiveness. These "offenses" may be defined as violations of one's conviction of what is right or wrong or violations of his person, property, or privilege. If they are not dealt with immediately, these violations will adversely affect the relationship between the offended one and the offender. While Jesus identified offenses as sins (Lk. 17:3), we must distinguish between moral offenses and amoral annoyances. An amoral annoyance may be irritating, but it does not have moral implication unless it is done with the intention of provocation. For instance, one would be offended if another was telling lies about him. But he should not be offended if one was singing off pitch.

In the case where an offense has been committed, the duty of the offender is to repent of his wrong-doing (Lk. 17:3), go to the offended one, and make right his wrong (Mt. 5:23-24). This involves his confessing his wrong-doing (cp. Lk. 15:21) and his making restitution if there was property damage or loss (cp. Lk. 19:8).

The duty of the offended one is, after he has prepared his heart for this encounter, to go to the offender (if the offender has not come to him) and show him his wrong-doing (Mt. 18:15; Lk. 17:3; cp. Gal. 6:1). Moreover, he must forgive the offender when the wrong-doer has fulfilled the conditions of forgiveness, as given in the preceding paragraph (Lk. 17:3). When he sees that the offender has fulfilled his obligation, then the offended one must forgive him by acknowledging that he has done his duty and by accepting the matter as being forever settled. Besides, the offended one must be willing to forgive the offender innumerable times as long as he fills the conditions of forgiveness (Lk. 17:4). If the offended one is unwilling to forgive, then he will not receive divine parental forgiveness (Mt. 6:14-15).

On the other hand, if the offender does not meet his obligation for wrong-doing, then he is not to be forgiven by the offended one (Lk. 17:3, note the conditional conjunction "if"). This does not mean that the offended one is to retaliate against the offender (Rom. 12:19-21), feel bitter toward him (Mt. 5:44), or hold a grudge against him (I Cor. 13:5), but he is not to act as though no offense has taken place. If both parties are members of the same church, then the procedure given in Matthew 18:15-19 and II Thessalonians 3:14-15 must be followed. It is an act of love for the offended one to confront the offender with his wrong-doing in the spirit of Galatians 6:1 and seek his restoration. To ignore the situation is to condone the offender's sin and to perpetuate disharmony between believers.

Someone may ask, "Are we not to turn the cheek?" (Mt. 5:39). In context the Lord was speaking about retaliation, not forgiveness (vs. 38). It is never right for a believer to retaliate, for only God can even scores in a just way (Rom. 12:19-20).

Another may ask, "Did not Jesus forgive his enemies?" (Lk. 23:34). It appears that He was praying for the soldiers who crucified Him. These men were unaware of the identity of their victim. On the other hand, the people who called for Jesus' crucifixion and who delivered Him to this execution remain guilty before God for their hatred and injustice (Mt. 27:18, 24; cp. Acts 3:14-15; 4:27). Our Lord's action of forgiveness illustrates the principle that we should ignore the offenses of people who commit them ignorantly and not require them to fulfill their obligation to us. If these offenses continue, then it is an act of Christian love to make the offender aware of what he is doing and to help him put them away.

Regarding the offenses he receives from unsaved people, the believer must consider these to be part of the world's hostility against God's people and absorb them (Jn. 15:18-21; Mt. 5:44). If some illegality is involved, then we can take unsaved people to law.

Synecdoche

Several times the figure of speech called "synecdoche" occurs in this book (e.g. pp 183, 285, 334). Since examples of this figure of speech occur in the Bible, it is important to understand what this means, especially in doctrinal passages. When one interprets a synecdoche, he must keep in mind that it can express one of two ideas as it best fits the context.

One, occurring rarely in biblical usage, this figure is a word that is the whole of something and that represents only a part of the entity of which it is the whole. For example, if I said that I ate an apple, I could mean that I ate only the fleshy part, not the core and skin. In this case, "apple" is a synecdoche for the part that was eaten. In like manner, "bread" can be a synecdoche for the seed-grain, which was sown, germinated, matured, was harvested, and was ground into flour, from which the bread was made (Eccles. 11:1). When he wrote that all Israel shall be saved (Rom. 11:26), it appears that Paul used "all Israel" as a synecdoche to stand for the elect, true Israel, not all the descendants of Jacob.

Two, a synecdoche can be a word that is a part of something and that represents the whole entity of which it is a part. For example, if someone said that he bought a new set of wheels, he could mean that he bought a new car. In this case, "wheels" is a synecdoche for the car. When he recorded that there were 276 "souls" on board the ship that was carrying Paul to Rome (Acts 27:37), Luke used "souls" as a synecdoche for people.

With this latter aspect in mind, it is better to say that the "blood of Jesus" is a synecdoche of the atonement rather than a symbol of His atoning death, for the atonement process involved our Lord's death and the offering of His blood. Since a symbol like a wedding band may represent the marriage of its wearer to another, the ring itself will not be as important or valuable as the marriage that it represents. (In this case, "ring," as a figure of speech, is a metonymy.) Thus to speak of the "blood of Christ" as a symbol of the atonement is to diminish grammatically its importance.

Metonymy

This is a word that stands in a close relation to something, but unlike a synecdoche it is not a part of what it represents. For instance, a policeman's badge represents the authority of the municipality for which the officer works, but it is not a part of this authority. The word "cross" sometimes is used as a metonymy for the atonement (I Cor. 1:17-18). The cross, together with crucifixion, had no part in the atonement process, but it was closely related to this process and came to represent it. Likewise, in many passages Jesus' "name" is a metonymy for (1) His person and atoning work (Jn. 1:12; 3:18; Acts 2:38), (2) His interests and will (Jn. 14:13-14; 15:16), (3) His authority (I Cor. 1:10; 5:4), (4) His person (I Cor. 1:2), or (5) all that He has done and is doing for our approach unto God (Jn. 16:23, 24, 26).

Good Works

In the Scriptures "good works" means more than doing things that are good by human standards. Good works represent our doing God's will in Christ's strength for God's glory (Heb. 13:21; I Cor. 10:31). This is how we should understand James 4:17 and Romans 3:12. [See the criteria by which the Lord will appraise our works (pp. 445 f.)]. All other works are evil in His sight (Rom. 14:23).

Carnal Christians

"Carnal" means "fleshly," that is, to act in the energy of sin (I Cor. 3:1). This is in contrast to "spiritual," which means to act in the energy of the Holy Spirit (2:15; cp. Gal. 5:16). We believers are either carnal or spiritual according to the force which is energizing us at the time. Needless to say, God wants us to walk in the energy of the Holy Spirit rather than in that of sin (Gal. 5:16, 25; Rom. 8:1-13). Unsaved people are continually carnal, for they are living under the complete domination of sin (Eph. 2:3).

Amillennialism, Postmillennialism

Based on an allegorical or spiritualizing interpretation of Revelation 20:1-6, conservative amillennialists hold two views of Christ's thousand-year reign. Some see it as fulfilled during the present age in the church either on earth (Augustine) or in Heaven (B.B. Warfield). Others see it as referring to Jesus' rule over His people in the eternal state, immediately following His second coming to earth (O.T. Allis, L. Berkhof, F.E. Hamilton).

Postmillennialism is the view that the present age will see the whole world Christianized and the prophecies of the millennial age fulfilled before Christ's return. Outstanding theologians (L. Boettner, C. Hodge, W.G.T. Shedd, and A.H. Strong) held this view. Like amillennialism, postmillennialism is growing in popularity.

SUBJECT INDEX

Entries are defined or explained on the pages whose numbers are in brackets or stand alone. Related entries are indicated by an asterisk [*].

A

Abel, **104 f., 365**
Abiding in Christ, **403, (406 f.)**
Abilities, native, **(219), 220, 223, 419**
Abraham
    bosom, **177, 467**
    children, **(119), 379**
    dispensation, **108 f.**
    faith, obedience: **108, 119, 122 f.,**
        (365), 379
    *Seed, **119, 379**
Abrahamic Covenant, **111, (121 ff.),**
    132 f., 462
Abyss (*Hades), **238, 241, 278, 453,**
458, 462
Accountable age, **305, 368**
Accountability (*Saved people,
*Unsaved people), **83, 134, 261**
Acquittal (*Justification), **(307), 352**
Actual sins (*Sin, sins), **303**
    *Cleansing, **307 f., 404 f.**
    decision, **289**
    diversity, **304**
    expressions, **287 f.**
    *Jesus, sinlessness, **162**
    mechanics, **303**
    saved people, **217, 286, (312 ff.),**
        395, 409
    sources, **303 f.**
    unsaved people, **286, 298**
Adam, generic, **273**
Adam and Christ, **296 f., 434**
Adam and Eve (*Eve)
    creation, **253 f.**
    covenant, **120**
    disobedience, **102, 291 f.**
    duties **101, 103 f.**
    historicity, **101**
    judgment, divine, **102, 134, (293 f.),**
        296 f.
    salvation, **102 f., 120, 365**
    test, **101 f.**
Adam's image in lost people, **486**
Adam's sin (*Original sin), **292, 297 ff.**

Adaptation, organic, **92, 274**
Adoption **331, (350 f.), 363**
Adultery, spiritual, **411**
Advocacy (*Jesus), **342**
After its kind, **87**
Age, **(97), 353**
Age of universe, **91, 255**
Ages to come, **193, 469**
Agnosticism, **44**
Amillennialism, **540**
Angel of the LORD, **77**
Angels, **235 ff.**
    character, **235 f.**
    classification, **236 f.**
    creation, **87, 235**
    condemnation, **178**
    constitution, **235**
    evil (*Demons), **238**
    fall, sin, **238 f., 290**
    future, **239 f.**
    instruction, **236**
    *Judgment, Messianic, **239 f., 408 f.**
    millennial kingdom, **458, 463**
    organization, **236 f.**
    *Personhood, (image of God), **235**
    antediluvians, **105, 238**
    Satan, **240 ff.**
    *Sons of God, **235, 238**
    works, **237 f.**
Anger (*Wrath, divine)
Anglicanism, **18**
Animals
    constitution, **87**
    covenant, divine, **120**
    creation, **85, 87**
    *Curse, divine, **103 f., 294, 464**
    death, **90, 103 f., 261, 277 f.**
    domestication, **101**
    fearing man, **106**
    human consumption, **101, 106**
    millennial kingdom, **464**
    perpetuity, **261**
    *Sacrifice, **102, 104**
    sin, **290**
    soul, spirit, **87**

D

Daniel, prophecies, **495 ff., 505, 506 ff.**
Davidic Covenant, **(128 ff.), 160, 462 f.**
Day, days
  Christ, **517**
  creation of earth, **87, 90 f.**
  God, **468**
  LORD, **447**
  Pentecost, **211, 374, 376, 380**
Deacon, deaconness, **223, (383 f.)**
Dead
  in Christ, **433**
  in sin, **347**
  to sin (*Saved people,
  dead to sin), **310 f.**
Death, **306**
  Adam and Eve, **102, 293, 296**
  *Animals
  *authority, **278**
  Christ (*Atonement), **173 f., 268**
  millennial kingdom, **464**
  physical, **277 ff.**
  punishment, **293, 306**
  saved people, **278, 374, 533 f.**
  second, everlasting, **467, 469**
  spiritual, **297, 314**
  unsaved people, **278, 467**
  with Christ, **311 f.**
Death of sin to saved people, **312**
Debt (*Penalty), **305**
Decree, divine, **58 f., (78 ff.), 503, 519**
  efficient, **80**
  permissive, **81, 83, 289**
Dedication (*Surrender), **412**
Deism, **45**
Deity
  Father, **141 f.**
  Holy Spirit, **202**
  never angels, **235**
  never humans, **144, 211, 256**
  Son (Jesus), **153 ff.**
Deliverance (*Salvation), **325**
Demons (fallen angels)
  activity, **238**
  character, **238**
  judgment, **239 f., 466**
  human possession, **246, 317**
Depravity, human nature, **297 f.**
Designations (*Names)
Desires, lusts

divine (*Duties, *Will, divine), **81, 530 f.**
human
  evil, **531**
  holy, **347, 532**
  natural, **531 f.**
  selfish, **404**
  sin, **303**
Devotions (*Fellowship), **397 f.**
Dichotomy, human nature, **271**
Discernment
  gift, spiritual, **226**
  God's will, **491 f.**
  truth and error, **215, 226**
Disciple, discipleship, **412 ff.**
Discipline
  divine (*Chastisement)
  local church, **391 f.**
Disease (*Sickness)
Dispensations, divine, **96 ff. (96)**
  age, **97**
  application, **98 f., 492**
  Bible interpretation, **97 f., 399**
  current, **112 f.**
  descriptions
    Christ's Earthly Rule
      (*Kingdom, millennial), **114 f.**
    Created Man, **101 ff.**
    Fallen Man, **103 ff.**
    Governed Man, **105 ff.**
    Grace, **112 f.**
    *Mosaic Law, **109 ff.**
    Patriarchs, **108 f.**
  relation to covenant, **99 f., 115**
  Tribulation Period, **97, 113**
Dispensationalism, **97**
Dispensationalists, **97, 118 f.**
Divine nature (*Nature, divine; *Deity), **50 f.**
Divisions (schisms), **409, 482 f.**
Dualism, philosophical, **45, 289**
Duties
  saved people, **112 f., 144, 310**
    discipleship, **412 ff.**
    forgiveness, **537 ff.**
    fruitfulness, **405 ff.**
    growth, **395 ff.**
    highest, **82**
    knowing God's will, **490 ff.**
    life maintenance, **397 ff.**
    obeying law, **319, 421 ff.**
    salvational, **362 ff.**
    service, **471 ff.**

G

God
>Word (*Bible), **23 ff.**
>*Works, **72 f., 84 ff.**
>*Wrath, **356**
>zoomorphisms, **67**

Godly life (*Christian life)

Gog, Magog, **465, 498 ff.**

Good works of saved people, **317, 337, 340, 353, 364, 405, 445 f., (540)**

Good works of unsaved people, **298, 341**

Gospel
>belief, **333 f.**
>content, **169 f., 328**
>ministry (*Evangelism)
>pre-Mosaic traditions, **107, 366**

Gospel of Kingdom, **366, (448)**

Government, divine (*Attributes, sovereignty; *God, authority), **94 ff.**

Government, human, **106, 422 f.**

Grace, divine, **64**
>*Common grace, **537**
>Covenant of Grace, Works, **118**
>covenants, gracious, **117 f.**
>*Dispensation, **112 f.**
>enabling, **64, 104, 107, 110, 113, (339)**
>election, **329**
>falling from grace, **111**
>gifts, spiritual, **219**
>giving, gracious, **515 f.**
>irresistible, efficacious, **209**
>prevenient, **209, 301, 338**
>principle of God's dealing, **117, 338 f.**
>sacramental, **384 f.**
>salvation, **131, 333, (338 f.), 365**

Greece, **506 f.**

Growth, spiritual (*Christian life, Christlikeness; *Sanctification, practical), **313 f., (395 ff.), 415 f.**

Guidance
>Bible, **397 f., 399 f., 492**
>circumstances, **494**
>God's will (*Will, divine), **319, 421, (490 ff.)**
>*Holy Spirit, **215 f., 492**

Guilt, **305**
>Adam and Eve, **293**
>God's enemies, **177 ff.**
>saved people, **307, 309, 352**
>unsaved people, **299, 305, 351**

Guilt, imputed (*Original sin),

Guilty feelings, **305, 307**

H

Habits, **317, 416**

Hades, Sheol, (*Abyss), **467**
>church, universal, **374, 467**
>fallen angels, **238**
>God, **58, 86**
>Jesus, **179, 185**
>precross saints, **177, 366, 467**
>*Under the earth
>unsaved people, **278, 306, 467**

Hatred, hostility
>divine (*Attributes, *Wrath), **63 f., 305 f.**
>human, **63, 356**
>*Satan, hostility
>*World, hostility

Headship
>Adam, old humanity, **(296 f.), 299 f.,**
>church, **382**
>human social order, **101, 103, (259), 294**
>Jesus, new humanity, **211, 257, (296 f.), 331, 345, 488**

Healing, physical, **184, 224 f.**

Healing, gift, **224 f.**

Health, physical, **264, 464**

Heart, **268**

Heartily, **334, 446**

Heaven, **349 f.**
>Father, **145 f.**
>its final state, **468 f.**
>Jesus, **188 f.**
>precross saints, **176 f., 488**
>saved people, **278, 433, 533 f.**

Heirs of God, **349, 435**

Hell, Lake of Fire (*Death, second death), **58, 173, 299, 306, 354, 455, 467, (469 f.)**

Hereditary corruption (*Depravity),

Holiness, divine (*Attributes), **60 f.**

Holiness, holy (*Sanctification), **360 ff.**

I

Illumination (*Holy Spirit, teaching), **26**
Image of Adam, **486**
Image of Christ, **257**, **(331)**, **345**, **362**, **396**, **486**, **534**
Image of God (*Personhood), **106**, **254**, **(256 f.)**, **259 ff.**
Immanence, divine, **57**, **86**
Immortality (*Body, saved people: redemption)
Imputation, **353**
    Imputed righteousness, **352 f.**, **487 f.**
    Imputed sin (*Original sin), **299**, **309**
    Imputed sins to Jesus, **169 f.**, **173**, **415**
In Adam, **267**, **(296)**, **415**
In Christ, **211 f.**, **267**, **(296)**, **359 f.**, **361**, **416**, **487 ff.**
Inability, human (*Depravity), **298**
Individuality, **260 f.**
Inerrancy, infallibility (*Bible), **28 f.**, **(525)**, **525 ff.**
Infants
    baptism, **123**, **325**, **386**, **389**
    glorified state, **434**
    guilt, **305**
    salvation, **367 f.**
Infralapsarian, **503 f.**
Inheritance, heir, **(349)**, **353**, **378**, **435**
Inner man, inward man, **267**
Inspiration, divine (*Bible), **26 ff.**
Intercession (*Prayer) of
    Holy Spirit, **215**
    Jesus, **189**, **192 f.**, **342**
    saved people, **368**, **401**, **423**
Intermediate body, **534**
Interpretation, Bible, **97 f.**, **(398 f.)**, **431**
Interpretation of tongues, gift, **225 f.**
Iraq (Babylonia), **453**, **507**
Irresistible call, divine, **332 f.**
Irresistible grace (*Grace), **209**
Israel, elect remnant, **455 f.**
    Abrahamic Covenant, **121 f.**
    *Beast (Antichrist), **455 f.**
    church, universal, **378f.**
    God, **143**, **358**, **379**
    Holy Spirit, **229**
    identity, **455 f.**
    Jesus, **128**, **537**
    judgment, **459**
    millennial kingdom, **379**, **462**
    ministry, **(24)**, **68**, **124**, **126 f.**, **130 f.**, **448**

Mosaic law, **111**, **126**
New Covenant, **130**, **358**
Palestinian Covenant, **127 f.**, **462**
preservation, **455 f.**
prophetic future, **504 f.**
*Repentance, **128**, **456**, **518**
restoration to land, **98**, **122**, **124**, **128 f.**, **500**, **504 f.**
salvation, **126**, **130**
title to land, **12 f.**
Tribulation Period, **453 f.**
wife of Yahweh, **98**, **379**, **464**
Israel, nation
    blindness, **456**, **518**
    covenants, divine, **132**, **358**, **462**
    deliverance from Egypt, **35**, **109**, **122**
    dispersion, **110 f.**, **127**
    distinct from church, **98**, **118 f.**, **(378 f.)**
    future, **504 f.**
    Jesus, **151**, **175**, **459**, **(537)**
    judgment, **110 f.**, **125**, **127**, **455**, **459**, **504 f.**
    Mosaic law, **109 ff.**, **124 ff.**
    Palestine, **121 f.**, **124**, **127**
    persecution, **295**, **455**
    purpose, (*Israel, elect remnant, ministry), **111**, **124**, **376**
    relation to God, **124**, **358 f.**
    restoration (*Israel, elect remnant)
    salvation (*Israel, elect remnant),
    sojourn in Egypt, **35**, **109**, **122**
Israel of God (*Abraham, seed), **379**

J

Jerusalem
    kingdom, **463 f.**
    new, **468**
    present, **380**, **452**, **455 f.**, **459**, **497**, **499**
Jesus,
    Abrahamic Covenant, **122**
    advocacy, **342**
    *Anointing, **191**, **206**
    ascension, **188 f.**
    assertions, divine, **157**
    *Atonement, **169 ff.**
    attributes, divine, **155**
    *Authority, Messianic, **159**, **188 f.**

(Jesus)
from evil men and angels, **171,
174 f.**
from God the Father, **170, 174,
268**
teaching, **192**
temptations, **163 f.**
throne of David, **129, 160**
victories, **164, 177 ff., 241 f., 278,
458, 462**
Vine, **405 f.**
Word, **154**
works
divine, **73, 155 f.**
human (Messianic), **166,
(192 f.), 374 ff.,461 f.**
Jewish remnant (*Israel, elect remnant)
Jews (*Israel, nation)
Judaism, N.T., **110**
Judicial forgiveness, divine, **307, 352**
Judgment, divine (*Chastisement), **306**
Judgment, divine (*Wrath), **133 f., 305 f.**
at the cross, **170, 177 f.**
in the future (*Judgment, Messianic)
principles, criteria, **134, 445 f.**
reason, **63, 305 f.**
Judgment, O.T. divine, **134**
*Adam and Eve, **102, 293 f.**
angels, **239 f.**
curse on creation (*Curse), **294**
humans, **104 f., 107, 109, 134**
*Israel, **110 f., 125, 459**
Satan, **295**
serpent, **294 f.**
Judgment, Messianic, **134, 156, 193**
angels, **465**
Battle of Armageddon, **458 f.**
Beast, False Prophet, **455**
precross saints, **460**
Satan, **241**
*Saved people, **440 ff.**
Tribulation Period
judgment series, **450 ff.**
martyrs, **460**
survivors, **459 ff.**
*Unsaved people, **465 ff.**
Judgment, self, **217, 390**
Judgment seat of Christ, **441**
Justification, **307, 333, (351 f.), 363**

K

Killing people, **106**
Kinds of creatures, **92**
King, Messianic, **193**
Kingdom (*Authority),
Beast, **452 ff., 506 f.**
Father, **143**
God, **349, 524**
Jesus (*Kingdom, Messianic,
millennial), **461**
Satan, **187, 239, 278, 293**
Kingdom, Messianic, aspects, **461**
Kingdom, millennial, **460 ff.**
administration, **129, 463**
*Animals, **464**
blessings, **463 f.**
church universal, **380**
citizens, **349 f., 367, 380, (462)**
curse, divine, **179, 462, 464**
dispensation, **114 f.**
duration, **114 f., 461**
entrance, **459 f.**
Holy Spirit, **229**
Jesus, **193**
laws, **114 f.**
mediatorial, **460**
merger with Father's kingdom, **458,
525**
objectives (goals), **461 f.**
reward, **443**
salvation, **367**
Satan, **458**
sin, **463**
throne rights, **160**
worship, sacrifices, **464 f.**
Kingdom, mysteries, **517 ff.**
Kinosis (Jesus' self-emptying), **158 f.**
Kinsman redeemer, **354**
Knowledge
God's, **58 f.**
saved people's, **13**

L

Lake of Fire (*Hell), **467, 469**
Languages, **274, 464**
Law, meanings, **421**
Law, moral and civil, **421 f.**
Law, principle of God's dealings, **117, 339**
Law and saved people, **318 f., 421 f.**
Law and sin, **318**
Law of
Christ, **112, 319**

Metaphysical (supernatural), **53, 58, 143**
Metonymy, **540**
Mind (*Human nature, *Reasoning),
   266, 270
Ministry (*Gifts, *Service)
Miracles, **225**
   apostles, **156, 225, 228, 418**
   gift, **225**
   Jesus, **156, 418**
   satanic, **454**
Missions (*Evangelism), **381**
Monergistic salvation, **338**
Monotheism, **53 f.**
Moral character, **533**
Morality, ethics, **60, 400, 492 ff.**
Mosaic Covenant, **124 ff.**
   duration, **125**
   legal character, **117, 125**
   promises, **124**
   recipients, **124**
   signs, **126**
   use, **126**
   weakness, **125**
Mosaic Dispensation (*Law of Moses),
   109 ff.
   bondage, **353**
   duration, **111**
   laws, **109**
   misuse, **110**
   observance, **110 f.**
   recipients, **109**
   salvation, **110**
   use, **111 f.**
   weakness, **110**
Mutation, **43, 92, 274**
Mysteries, N.T., **517 ff.**

N

Names, titles, designations,
   angels, holy, **236 f.**
   *Beast (Antichrist), **452**
   demons, **238**
   Father, God, **146**
   God, **73 ff.**
   Holy Spirit, God, **203**
   Jesus, God-man, **193 ff.**
   Satan, **240**
   saved people
      children, **143, 348**
      citizens, **349**
      saints, **361**
      sons, **144, 350**
   Son, God, **153 ff.**
Natural
   body (soulish), **439**
   law, **89, 93**
   man (unsaved), **296**
   selection, **43, 92, 274**
   theology, **14**
Nature (*Universe)
Nature, essence, substance, **162, 285**
   angelic, **235**
   animal, **87**
   divine, **50 f.**
   *Human, **261 ff., 532**
      corrupted, fallen, **297 f.**
      saved, **309 f., 375 f.**
   *Jesus, **162 ff.**
   not sin (*Sin-principle), **285**
Nearness to God (*Sanctification),
   (358 ff.), 364
Need, spiritual
   of saved people, **532**
   of unsaved people, **326 f.**
New birth (*Regeneration), **209 ff.,
   346 ff.**
New Covenant, **25, (130 ff.), 179, 183,
192, 343, 389, 462**
New creature (*New man), **210, 296,
(345), 347, 488**
New humanity, **296, 331, (345), 488**
New Jerusalem (*Jerusalem)
New man, **267, 310, (416)**
New Testament, **25 f.**
   arrangement, **25**
   authority, **26, 112 ff., 382**
   *Canon, **33 f., 529**
   *Dispensation of Grace, **112 ff.**
   given through Jesus, **31, 192, 229**
   Holy Spirit, **229**
   *Inspiration, **31, 229**
   *Law of Christ, **319**
   *Mysteries, **517 ff.**
   *New Covenant, **25**
   relation to O.T., **24, 26**
   replacing some spiritual gifts, **221,
      223, 225**
   *Revelation, special, **48**
   value, **26**
New universe, **93 f., 465, 468**
Noachian Covenant, **120 f.**
Noah, **105 f., 120, 365**
Noncanonical books, **34 f., 529 f.**

R

T

SCRIPTURE TEXT INDEX